HUMAN RESOURCES MANAGEMENT

HUMAN RESOURCES MANAGEMENT

Wendell L. French
UNIVERSITY OF WASHINGTON

Houghton Mifflin Company   BOSTON
DALLAS   GENEVA, ILLINOIS
LAWRENCEVILLE, NEW JERSEY   PALO ALTO

**To Marjorie, Andy, Tom, and Amy,
and future adventures together**

Cover Photography: Martin Paul

Cover and Interior Design: Anna Post

Printed in the U.S.A.

Library of Congress Catalog Card Number: 85-80966

ISBN: 0-395-35662-8

ABCDEFGHIJ-VB-898765

Contents

PART 3 JOB DESIGN AND STAFFING *169*

7 Job Design and Analysis *170*

8 Work Rules and Schedules *204*

PART 6 EMPLOYEE PROTECTION AND REPRESENTATION 495

17 Labor Organizations 496

18 Negotiating the Labor Agreement 524

PART 7 THE FUTURE OF HUMAN RESOURCES MANAGEMENT *617*

21 Participative Strategies for Organization Improvement *618*

22 Looking Ahead in Human Resources Management *651*

Preface

Human resources management, or personnel management, is an exciting subject to study because it deals with the basic human issues facing all people who work. Every working life has been touched, at some point or another, by concerns about selection or rejection, promotion or demotion, retention or termination, rewards or penalties, fairness or unfairness, safety or injury, teamwork or conflict. Studying the ways in which human resources management deals with these issues will certainly help students to prepare for the complex and evolving world of work.

This book is written for students enrolled in the basic, overview course in human resources management. I personally believe this course to be one of the most important that students will ever take because human resources policies and practices will affect every day of their working lives. Further, students taking this course now are the future supervisors, managers, professionals, and executives who will help create the kind of work environment that will exist in tomorrow's organizations. For students who are currently employed, the course—and this text—will have immediate relevance.

I use the plural "human resources management" in contrast to "human resource management" to emphasize that everyone in the organization is important and that people bring an unlimited array of talents to a given organization. As will be explained in Chapter 1, the terms *human resources management* and *human resources director* (or *human resources manager*) are used interchangeably with the still very respectable and much used terms *personnel management* and *personnel director* (or *personnel manager*).

Organization

The text is organized so that students will be able to move from one subject to another easily and smoothly. Part 1 is an introductory section covering a general description of the field of human resources management, the history and evolution of the field, and contemporary issues facing all human resources managers. Part 2 considers the organizational factors that affect human resources management. Factors such as an organization's financial, technological, and physical resources are discussed along with management philosophy, leadership style, and organizational culture and climate. Discussions on motivation and performance focus on the ways in which individuals and groups can naturally contribute to organizational effectiveness. The complex and vital nature of human resources planning is also examined as an integral part of human resources management.

Part 3 focuses on job design and staffing, covering topics such as job design and analysis, work rules and schedules, recruitment and selection, and orientation and career transitions. Part 4 deals with employee development and appraisal with chapters on skill training, management and career development, and performance appraisal and review. The important topic of compensation is discussed in Part 5, with chapters on wage and salary administration, incentive plans, and employee benefits. Part 6 focuses on employee protection and representation by discussing the role of labor organizations and the dynamics of negotiating and managing the labor agreement; the issues of employee rights, responsibilities, and justice; and health and safety management. Finally, Part 7 discusses the future of human resources management, focusing on the importance of employee participation in organization improvement, the directions the field appears to be taking, and its current status today.

Features

The text presents an overview of current procedures and practices that are in general favor in the field. I have strived to present a balanced treatment of the dilemmas and pros and cons surrounding the application of these various techniques and programs. For example, the concept of flexible working hours—flextime—is appropriate to some situations, but not all; even under the best of circumstances new problems can be created.

My view is that human resources management is at the center of organizational life, interacting with such important factors as leadership philosophy and style, organizational culture and climate, group and intergroup behavior, technology, and strategic planning. For example, the compensation system can affect the level of cooperation and teamwork within and between small work groups, departments, and divisions. Top management philosophy about how people should be treated has tremendous influence on the human resources policies and practices of the total organization.

Much attention is paid both to the origins of modern human resources management and to the directions in which it seems to be heading. There have been numerous incremental changes and some dramatic occurrences in the past that have helped shape contemporary human resources management, and we can anticipate many changes in the future.

It should be noted that the book displays a point of view about a number of matters. Themes that run throughout the text include the following: (1) Effective management of human resources is central and vital to organizational effectiveness; (2) All supervisors and managers, including human resources specialists, must work cooperatively in the management of human resources if the organization is to be optimally successful; and (3) The modern organization, to be highly effective over the long run, must involve all organizational members in improving the way the organization functions, including improvements in the way that people work together.

Obviously, attention to these human matters must occur at the same time as careful attention is paid to other extremely important matters like technology, financial resources, markets, inventories, and government regulations, to name only a few. Effective human resources management makes dealing with these matters all the more effective.

Pedagogical Aids

Several elements of the text are designed to aid in the learning process:

- Each chapter begins with a set of chapter objectives and a chapter outline to help orient the student to the material to be presented.
- Each chapter closes with a summary of key points.
- Discussion questions at the end of each chapter are designed to reinforce the student's understanding of the subject matter.
- Numerous in-text examples show how human resources management is practiced in real-life organizations.
- Cases at the start of each chapter ease the student into the text content by presenting situations that face human resources managers in many organizations. These cases present realistic characters and problems that students will immediately understand. Opening cases are referred to within the chapter text to highlight a certain point or illustrate a certain concept. At the end of each chapter, discussion questions relate the opening case situations to the chapter content.
- Boxed extracts, called Perspectives, from relevant and contemporary articles, present real-life applications of human resources practices and policies, provide up-to-date information on personnel topics, and highlight different points of view on human resources issues.
- Cases at the end of each chapter deal with real-life applications of personnel concepts. Many of these cases focus on well-known organizations and the ways in which personnel policies and practices have affected their overall operation and effectiveness.
- A comprehensive study guide/activities manual, entitled *Experiencing Human Resources Management,* by Robert Lussier, is also available to students.

Acknowledgments

There are a number of people who have contributed to the book and supplementary materials in important ways. I want to thank Karlyn Tierney for her work with the test bank, and Jane Karns for her assistance with case notes. Thanks are also due my wife Marjorie, for her editorial suggestions and constant support.

The following contributed extensively to the writing of certain chapters: Bob Hollmann, University of Montana, the chapter on appraisal; Dudley Buffa, Oregon State University, the chapters on labor organizations and collective bargaining; and Gary Smith and Danny Arnold, Mississippi State University, the chapters on training and development. Jack Drexler of Oregon State University made an important contribution by reviewing and making suggestions during each stage of production. A special note of appreciation is also extended to the following colleagues who helped make this project possible:

Barbara Hastings
University of South Carolina

Irving Mason
Herkimer County Community College

Jeff Mello
Bay State Junior College

William B. Pierce
Morehead State University

R. P. Beaulieu
Central Michigan University

William A. Recker
Northern Kentucky University

Herbert S. Parker
Kean College of New Jersey

Steven Winter
Orange County Community College

Thomas Patten, Jr.
California State Polytechnic University

Joseph F. Byrnes
Bentley College

Sylvia Poster Keyes
Bridgewater State College

Daniel S. Cochran
Mississippi State University

Durward Hofler
Northeastern Illinois University

Finally, I want to thank Tom Patten, Jr., of California State Polytechnic University, and his wife Julie, for their hospitality and discussions on the island of Molokai, Hawaii, which helped launch the project.

To all of these people, and to others who worked behind the scenes, I am most grateful.

Wendell L. French

part 1

An Overview of Human Resources Management

This section provides an overview of human resources management, traces its historical development, and explores the changing environment in which the profession is currently practiced. Chapter 1 defines human resources management from a process-systems perspective and describes its vital role in modern organizations. Chapter 2 describes the evolution of human resources management from its earliest beginnings to its present role as a major force affecting organizational success. Chapter 3 examines the impact of current social, economic, and legal forces on contemporary human resources management.

The Field of Human Resources Management

LEARNING OBJECTIVES

- **Define human resources management and explain how it differs from the traditional view of personnel management.**
- **Identify the basic processes in human resources management.**
- **Describe the relationship between the human resources department and other managers within the organization.**
- **Explain the vital role of human resources management in modern organizations.**

CASE 1.1 MARTHA BURKE

Martha Burke, president and majority stockholder of Metro Publications, wrote "human resources director" on the agenda for the next department head meeting. Metro, formed three years before with only Martha and one assistant on staff, now employed almost 150 people — and things were getting complicated.

In the beginning, Martha herself had done all the recruiting and hiring, established the salaries, and reviewed the performance of all employees. As the company grew, however, she found it necessary to turn over some of these activities to department heads and supervisors. And that wasn't working as well as she had hoped.

In Martha's view, Metro Publications faced a number of serious problems. In the first place, some of the department heads were less careful than others. Some people were hired with insufficient experience or training, and it showed in their performance. Salaries varied widely from department to department. It seemed to Martha that certain department heads were overly generous, whereas others were downright stingy. It was also obvious that morale was high in some units and low in others. A minority employee who felt he had unfairly been passed over for promotion had threatened to bring a discrimination suit. Some employees seemed to be learning quickly; others were getting very little personal attention or training. There seemed to be no rhyme or reason to the pattern for employee time off. (Martha had recently issued instructions that no one could have more than a half-day off with pay in any one month, for whatever reason, but she knew that policy was too arbitrary.) Some very capable employees seemed to have too many menial tasks, and occasionally one would resign before Martha could nudge the department head into broadening that employee's job. On the other hand, some key people appeared to be overworked and under a good deal of stress. A few supervisors would let very capable people transfer to more responsible jobs; others would try to transfer only those people they didn't want. Sometimes it seemed that people with potential were let go; other times it seemed as though supervisors were protecting people who really weren't contributing much to the success of the organization.

These and other problems, all related to the management of people, had convinced Martha that Metro Publications needed a specialist in this area. As she wrote "human resources director" on the agenda, her thoughts ran along these lines: "I wonder how department heads will react to our bringing in a personnel director? I wonder what the person's exact responsibilities should be? Clearly, all of the department heads and supervisors have 'people' responsibilities. How do we make sure that this person's responsibilities are distinct from those of the other managers? How will we know if things are getting any better if we do hire a human resources director? I wonder whether this person should report to me or to the operations manager. Well, it's time we started sorting this out."

CASE 1.2   MORE THAN PIZZA

Perroni's, a small Italian restaurant near the university, was doing very well. The tables were typically full at both lunch and dinner, and there was usually a line of people waiting to get in on weekend evenings. Perroni's was popular with the college students and faculty members but drew customers from the broader community as well. Most people raved about the food, especially the pizza. But it seemed to Professor Jill Anderson that there must be other things going on behind the scenes, along with the good cooking, that contributed to the restaurant's success. She had some hunches, because her son Don, a sophomore at the university, worked at Perroni's as a busboy, or "busperson," as he put it. He appeared to like his job and the other employees. The hours he worked seemed to be ideal and the tips were good, although not as high as the waiters received. Jill teased him from time to time about being "the world's most overqualified busperson."

One evening, just before closing time, Jill came into Perroni's for some dessert. Don and two other employees, Manuel and Kim, joined her for a cup of tea. "What makes this such a good restaurant?" Jill asked. "I'm sure there's more to it than great pizza."

Manuel answered first. "It's the people that work here. Everyone's on the ball and we know we have to work together to make this place run right. We help each other out, too. We all work together to make the salads if the kitchen people are jammed up. We spend a lot of time training new people so that everyone's working procedures are consistent. We even work it out among ourselves what days and hours each of us will work during the upcoming week."

Don added, "That's all a big part of it, but there's more. The food-service help and the chefs really get along. Everyone agrees that pleasing the customer is the most important thing. Our chefs are the best around, but if a customer complains, we'll take the food right back to the kitchen. The chefs never get upset — they just get busy and do it over right. Happy customers mean bigger tips, and all the waiters give an equal share of their tips to the buspeople and the chefs. All of us make pretty good money here."

"Don't forget that the owner of this place is also a great boss," said Kim. "He pretty much leaves us alone during the shift, but he gets us together every now and then for a free dinner and asks us how the place might be run better. Once we figured out that the restaurant was losing money on several entrees, so we got him to raise the prices on those items, and no one complained. We saved his shirt! He even lets us take care of most of the hiring — we bring in friends we think will work well here. The boss really respects our judgment and no one seems to take advantage of that."

Jill thanked Don and his coworkers for their comments. "Very enlightening," she said. Their remarks confirmed some of her hunches about why the restaurant was doing so well, although she realized she needed to talk with more people, including the owner and the chefs, to get the whole picture. "Some of this informality, such as their hiring practices, might not work in a large organization," she thought. "On the other hand, some of it is super. One thing is clear — these people like each other. At least the ones I've seen and talked to act as if they do."

The issues Martha Burke faces at Metro Publications are basic concerns of all business and service organizations. From the smallest to the largest enterprise, fundamental activities pertaining to all employees, or **human resources,** of an organization must be managed — and managed effectively. If human resources are neglected or mismanaged, the organization is unlikely to do well and, in fact, may fail.

From a positive standpoint, it is people — human resources — that create organizations and make them survive and prosper. It is their efforts, talents, and skills in using other resources, such as knowledge, materials, and energy, that result in the creation of useful products and services.

In Case 1.2, it is clear that the employees were a critical factor in making Perroni's restaurant successful. In fact, the restaurant workers were Perroni's greatest resource. Management probably appreciated this, although we aren't given enough detail to know much about the role management played in this situation. If the owner doesn't know exactly why Perroni's is so successful, however, the restaurant could easily drift into practices that would cause it to fail. For Perroni's to be successful in the long run, the owner must continue to pay careful attention to the management of its human resources. Further, the owner must be skillful in integrating human resources with other important resources, including finances and technology — in this case, the technology involved in creating first-class manicotti and pizza.

WHAT IS HUMAN RESOURCES MANAGEMENT?

Both opening cases deal with issues that pertain to human resources management. In Case 1.1, Martha Burke was aware all along that many "people activities" required attention in the day-to-day operations of Metro Publications: attracting talented people to the organization; choosing the most qualified candidates from among the applicants; orienting and training new employees; retraining experienced employees; motivating all employees and evaluating their performance; rewarding and compensating everyone on the staff; and sometimes disciplining, discharging, transferring, or promoting someone. These are all aspects of human resources management.

Martha also realized eventually that more thought and planning were needed for these activities. The lack of a clearly formulated management philosophy and the absence of carefully planned human resources policies and procedures were causing her considerable concern. These deficiencies were also costly to Metro Publications in efficiency and overall performance.

In Case 1.2, a number of human resources activities were going well at Perroni's, either by accident or by design. Capable people were being recruited and trained; standards of performance and expectations about people helping each other were high; work scheduling seemed to be satisfactory to everyone; the compensation system seemed to be working well; and management was listening and responding to employee suggestions. These are all key concerns of human resources management.

Human resources management is the term increasingly used to refer to the philosophy, policies, procedures, and practices related to the management of people within an organization. The term *personnel management* — or perhaps *modern personnel management* — means the same thing.*

---

*The term *human resource management* is also used frequently. Sometimes the terms *personnel and industrial relations, personnel and labor relations,* and *employee relations* are used to designate the same concept.

Honeywell

Effective management creates an atmosphere in which employee motivation and morale are high—often leading, in turn, to high productivity and quality.

Changing Perspectives on the Field

Although *human resources management* is used within this book, and although terms like *human resources department* and *director of human resources* are being used more and more, the more traditional terms are still widely used. For example, in thousands of contemporary organizations, the terms *personnel department, personnel director,* or *vice president, personnel* are extensively used and respected. In fact, the top human resources person is most likely to have the title *director, personnel.*[1]

Changes in terminology reflect the increased significance associated with the management of people in organizations as well as the broader perspective from which the field is currently viewed. In the past, personnel management had a strong functional focus. That is, personnel specialists were primarily concerned with the administration of specific employee-related functions such as hiring, training, wage-setting, and disciplinary action. A more modern view is that all personnel functions are interrelated; that is, each function affects the others. Moreover, how well these functions are managed has a tremendous effect on an organization's ability to meet its overall objectives. As these ideas have become more and more accepted, especially within the last twenty or thirty years, the view of "people management" has changed accordingly. It is now generally accepted that human resources management encompasses a dynamic, organization-wide perspective that is action-oriented and based on theory and research from many disciplines, including the study of human behavior.

This broad-based view of human resources management has great practical value. With such a perspective, it is possible to understand the interrelationship of all human resources management activities and to appreciate how they contribute to the overall success of an organization. Within the organization, such an awareness increases the effectiveness with which human resources are used to achieve desired outcomes — outcomes that benefit employees and the organizations in which they work.

A Process-Systems View

A useful way to describe human resources management as it is practiced today is in *process-systems* terminology. The significance of the process-systems view is that it (1) takes into account the interdependence of all aspects of human resources management and (2) recognizes the relationship between human resources activities and organizational goals.

A **process** is an identifiable flow of interrelated events moving toward some goal, consequence, or end. An example in human resources management is the staffing process, a flow of events that results in the continuous filling of positions within the organization. These events will normally include such activities as recruiting applicants, making hiring decisions, and managing career transitions such as transfers and promotions.

A **system,** on the other hand, is a particular set of procedures or devices designed to control a process in a predictable way. The staffing system of a given organization, for example, might include such devices and procedures as application blanks, interviews, reference checks, a six-month probationary period, a procedure for posting job openings within the organization, and procedures for applying for transfer. Thus, the term *process* refers to a combi-

---

PERSPECTIVE 1.1 Starting Over

Two years ago, when the bottom fell out of the oil-field equipment business, Ray Gorcyca was confronted with both a challenge and a rare opportunity. As manufacturing vice president of the Houston-based McEvoy Div. of Smith International Inc., he knew that business as usual would be the wrong response — on both counts. . . .

In the face of the drastic contraction in the marketplace, the challenge was to keep McEvoy economically viable. The flip side was that the business lull made it possible to institute sweeping changes without seriously disrupting ongoing operations.

It was a chance, in other words, to start over. And Ray Gorcyca and George Helland [president of the division] seized it. . . .

Over a period of two years Mr. Gorcyca, other manufacturing managers, and Thomas Eastland, personnel director, developed — and began to implement — a combination human-relations and manufacturing plant overhaul. It included moving machines from the closed Houston plant to Tyler

Source: Excerpted from Thomas M. Rohan, "Starting Over: Business Slump Spurs a Rejuvenation," *Industry Week,* February 4, 1985, pp. 29–30.

and relocating all 60 major tools at Tyler to fit the manufacturing-cell approach. (Instead of a lathe department, drill department, and milling department, the machines are arranged in family-of-product clusters which can produce related parts. The body-manufacturing cell, for example, includes all the tools needed to produce valve bodies.)

McEvoy calls it "enterprise manufacturing." And enterprising workers have a chance to increase their earnings by learning to operate several machines; they receive a 7% increase for each new machine they master. The pay differential extends through four grades to "master machinist" — a worker who can operate any machine in the shop. All workers are now on salary and occasionally sit in on management staff meetings.

In addition to restructuring jobs in the shop, the management organization was flattened out so that no one has more than ten people reporting to him. New purchasing practices were installed — ordering in smaller quantities (though at a higher unit price) to keep inventory levels down. A version of quality circles — called "McEvoy Action Teams" — was adopted. And, to reinforce the new corporate culture, status symbols were eliminated, including reserved parking spaces for managers.

---

nation of events that leads to some end result, while the term *system* identifies specific procedures and devices used to control those events.

According to the process-systems view, *human resources management is the systematic control of a network of interrelated processes affecting and involving all members of an organization. These processes include human resources planning, job and work design, staffing, training and development, performance appraisal and review, compensation and reward, employee protection and representation, and organization improvement.* To control and improve these processes, human resources systems are planned, developed, and implemented through the combined efforts of all managers and human resources specialists in an organization. Overall, the systems are intended to achieve organization-wide goals and contribute to organizational effectiveness and productivity.

KEY PROCESSES AND SYSTEMS
IN HUMAN RESOURCES MANAGEMENT

The fundamental processes in human resources management are shown in Figure 1.1. All the processes are linked in the diagram to depict the idea that they interact and are interdependent. What happens in one process tends to influence events in one or more of the others. For example, offering an unusually high salary in recruiting and hiring efforts (part of the staffing process) may cause serious problems in the management of the compensation and reward process. People already on the payroll may complain bitterly about what they are paid and press for a readjustment.

The quality of the design and management of the systems used to control and direct human resources processes is directly related to an organization's overall effectiveness. In some organizations the human resources systems may be very primitive or haphazardly designed. In others, the systems used in human resources management can be so cumbersome that the organization is strangled by its own bureaucracy. Assume, for example, that you are a supervisor, you have a budgeted position for a typist, and you desperately need help; but you are required to write and rewrite a job description three times before your personnel requisition will be accepted for processing. Then you must wait until the job is advertised within your company for one month, and only after that can you accept outside applications. In this situation, you are certainly going to feel that something is wrong with the system. Systems in human resources management must be designed to further, not impede, the attainment of organizational goals.

A brief description of the fundamental processes in human resources management will help familiarize you with the scope and challenges of this field. The various chapters of the book will describe these processes in more detail and, in particular, will focus on systems that are used in their management.

Human Resources Planning

Human resources planning is the process of assessing the organization's human resources needs in light of organizational goals and making plans to ensure that a competent, stable work force is employed. The planning process includes an analysis of skill levels among employees and in the external labor market, of current and expected job openings, and of plans for expanding or reducing staff throughout the organization. The planning process, then, is closely

FIGURE 1.1   Major processes in human resources management

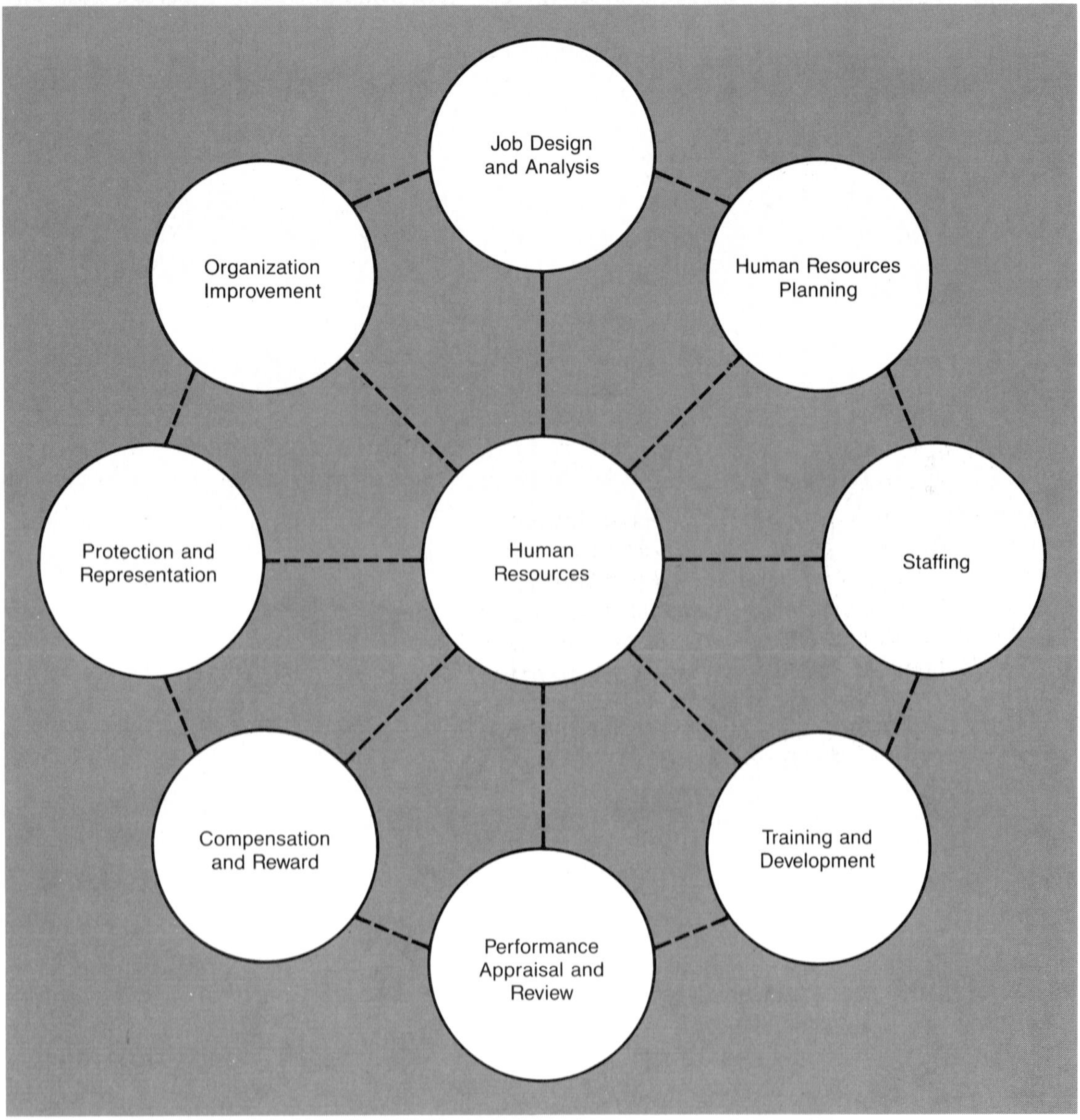

related to the staffing process and depends also on the overall strategic plans of the organization.

The systems designed to control and direct the human resources planning process include such devices as computerized records of employees' skills and qualifications; forecasts of the numbers of employees with certain skills, who are likely to leave over the next year; analysis of the extent to which affirmative action goals have been met; and confidential organization charts showing possible candidates for promotion to various executive positions. Human resources planning is the subject of Chapter 6.

Job Design and Analysis

Job and work design specifies the tasks to be performed by individuals and groups within the organization, and establishes the rules, schedules, and working conditions under which people perform those tasks. Through careful design, or circumstance, or both, events converge to create jobs to which people are assigned and the conditions surrounding those jobs. Some of the systems used to help manage the process of job design include techniques such as time-and-motion study and work simplification, which aim to make jobs easy to learn and workers more efficient. Other job-design systems, such as job enrichment, involve techniques to restructure jobs to make them more interesting and challenging.

Job analysis is the process of investigating the tasks and behaviors associated with a particular job. Various systems used in job analysis include observations of workers as they perform their jobs, interviews, and questionnaires. Typically the information obtained from job analysis is used to write job descriptions and to establish what is required of the person who will perform each job. In turn, job descriptions are useful in the staffing process, especially in recruiting, hiring, and training new employees. Job design and analysis is discussed in Chapter 7.

Staffing

Staffing is the process that results in the continuous assignment of workers to all positions in the organization. This broad process includes the following activities: attracting qualified people to the organization; selecting from among candidates; bringing new people aboard and assigning and orienting them to their jobs; reassigning employees through transfer, promotion, or demotion; and ultimately managing employee separation through resignation, discharge, or retirement.

Some examples of systems used to manage the staffing process include school and college recruiting, advertising of job openings in newspapers and professional journals, skill tests, oral group interviews, and policies on transfers and promotions. This broad process and the systems frequently used in its management are discussed in Chapters 9 and 10.

Ford/Reproduced by permission of *Punch*

Training and Development

The **training and development** process is a complex mixture of activities intended to improve the performance of individuals and groups within the organization. Some organizations, especially those that carry out complex and specialized operations and are confronted with rapid changes in technology, are heavily committed to training and development. Others view the process as a way to foster the career development of their employees at all levels. But almost all employees in any organization need some initial training, or orientation, when they start new jobs.

The systems that are used frequently in this process include skill development programs, coaching by a supervisor, general management courses, and training seminars. Training and development are covered in Chapters 11 and 12.

Performance Appraisal and Review

The **performance appraisal and review** process is the ongoing evaluation of individuals' and groups' contributions to the orga-

PERSPECTIVE 1.2 An Ounce of Prevention

Bob Harris had fought for Sandra Coughlin's latest promotion and was committed to helping her succeed once she became a credit manager at All Service Inc. For two years he encouraged her, but also made it plain that he was unhappy with her progress. When he realized last winter that she couldn't adapt to her expanding responsibilities, he fired her.

Convinced that the California company had no basis for its action, Coughlin filed a suit charging Harris with sexual harassment and the company with discrimination. She also alleged that Harris told her that she would be replaced by a man.

It is still uncertain whether the case will go to trial. . . . But the personnel manager worries that written documentation on Sandra Coughlin's performance won't suffice to justify her firing. Much of Harris's criticism and counseling over the two years was done informally and never recorded.

Discrimination charges in the past decade have become the whiplash of the workplace. As federal and state laws and judicial rulings tend increasingly to protect workers' rights, employees are more inclined to sue their bosses. . . . When employees win, the target companies are rudely reminded of

Source: Excerpted from Ellen Kolton, "An Ounce of Prevention," *Inc.*, October 1984, p. 153. Reprinted with permission. Copyright © 1984 by Inc. Publishing Company, 38 Commercial Wharf, Boston, MA 02110

the futility of closing the barn door after the horse escapes. The door is closed anyway, against the rest of the stable. Businesses are now beginning to adopt strategies designed to keep them out of court in the first place, taking recent trends in labor law as a primer for rewriting their policies on hiring, promoting, and firing.

Ironically, All Service had been part of this so-called proactive (as opposed to reactive) trend, although the Sandra Coughlin case clearly showed it still had work to do. The company began revising its personnel policies three years ago. But since the charges were leveled, All Service has significantly altered its termination procedures, and now requires extensive documentation and a three-tier internal review before dismissing an employee.

The process of formalizing personnel policies isn't fun. In many small companies — All Service included — managers are initially put off by anything resembling the corporate bureaucracy they fled when they started their own businesses. . . .

But at some point in the growth of a company, the cherished informality becomes a liability. "You can't show me an entrepreneur who has built a fast-growth business who is concerned with formal policies. He wants to sell product," says the owner of a highly successful service firm in Texas. After settling an overtime-wage dispute with a former employee, however, he stepped up his business's attention to personnel policies.

nization and communication of those evaluations to the persons involved. Such evaluations are made for a variety of purposes: to determine the need for training, to make decisions about pay increases, to select people for promotion, or to make judgments about the need for discipline.

The communication of appraisals (review) is part of this process, because how the appraisal is communicated will affect the extent to which it becomes a learning experience. Appraisals may be highly subjective or they may be highly systematic and based on carefully developed criteria and specific behavior. Some performance systems in current use are discussed in Chapter 13.

Compensation and Reward

The **compensation and reward** process is the flow of events that determines what wages, salaries, and incentives are paid and what supplemental benefits and nonfinancial rewards are provided. The presence or absence of rewards and recognition is important to employee morale and performance. Nonfinancial rewards, such as recognition and privileges, are particularly important in organizations staffed by unpaid volunteers.

Some of the systems involved in the management of this process include job evaluations, plant-wide productivity plans, suggestion plans, and wage and benefit surveys. Compensation and other rewards are discussed in Chapters 14 through 16.

Protection and Representation

Most organizations have formal or informal ways to protect employees — to some extent, at least — from arbitrary and impulsive

The human resources director plays a key role in designing and monitoring the systems used to manage personnel processes.

Aronson/Stock, Boston

treatment and from physical danger and health hazards. In addition, individuals or groups may represent the interests of others, again either informally or in an organized, formal fashion. This broad process of **protection and representation** can be divided into three important subprocesses: the *accommodation process,* the *collective bargaining process* (found in unionized organizations), and the *health and safety management process.*

Accommodation.   The *accommodation process* refers to the extent to which management listens and responds to — or accommodates — the needs, wants, and complaints (or grievances) of organization members. People working in organizations expect to be treated fairly; moreover, they feel they have the right to be heard and to be respected as individuals. Morale is severely affected when there is a sense of unfair treatment or when workers perceive that management does not care about their feelings, complaints, and suggestions. Because these human tendencies pervade all organizations, it is only natural that management devote some time and energy to determining what is just and fair treatment and to "tuning in" to employees' attitudes and perceptions. Systems for managing the accommodation process include questionnaires, suggestion boxes, an "open-door" philosophy, and formal grievance procedures. The effectiveness with which the accommodation process is managed varies within organizations and depends on a number of factors, such as prevailing leadership style and management philosophy. This topic is addressed throughout Part 2 and again in Chapter 19.

Collective Bargaining.   The *collective bargaining process* refers to those events that establish a formal agreement between workers and management regarding such matters as wages and employee benefits, hours, working conditions, and grievance procedures. The process includes both the negotiation and the administration of the labor-management contract. The collective bargaining process and the systems used to manage labor-management relations are discussed in Chapters 17 and 18.

Health and Safety Management.   The *health and safety management process* attempts to protect organization members from illness and physical dangers in the workplace. The process also includes the protection of the surrounding community from pollution and toxic substances. For many organizations, protecting the health and safety of human resources is a prime social responsibility that is reinforced by the increased awareness among workers and the general public of health and safety issues. Systems used in health and safety management are numerous and varied. Some examples are safety guards on machines, meetings with employees about safety, the availability of first-aid stations or dispensaries, the use of special equipment by technicians to monitor air purity, and stress management programs. Health and safety management is discussed in Chapter 20.

Organization Improvement

The **organization improvement** process is the flow of events that determines the strategies by which organizations attempt to improve their effectiveness, increase employee satisfaction, or otherwise enhance the organizational environment. Such strategies vary in kind and effectiveness, as do the specific systems for managing this process. In general, the goal of these strategies and systems is to increase the level of trust, cooperation, teamwork, and performance throughout the organization. The organization improvement process is discussed in Chapter 21.

WHO MANAGES HUMAN RESOURCES?

All managers in most organizations, including first-line supervisors, are heavily involved in human resources management, above and beyond their day-to-day supervision of people. That is, they participate in human resources processes such as staffing, performance appraisal, and compensation. For example, managers are likely to interview all or a selected group of candidates applying for any position that reports to them. They typically review the performance of subordinates, perhaps using an organization-wide merit rating form. Or, they may make recommendations on pay increases, using some formula agreed upon within the top management group.

Nonsupervisory employees may also contribute to the management of the various human resources processes. For example, engineers in the design department of an aircraft manufacturing company might interview college graduates who are candidates for entry-level engineering jobs. Production workers who are members of self-managed work teams might participate in the selection and training of new team members. Shop stewards (officers of a union who are also employees of the company) are likely to be involved in processing grievances and in grievance hearings.

FIGURE 1.2
Structure of the human resources department in a small company (top) and in a large corporation (bottom)

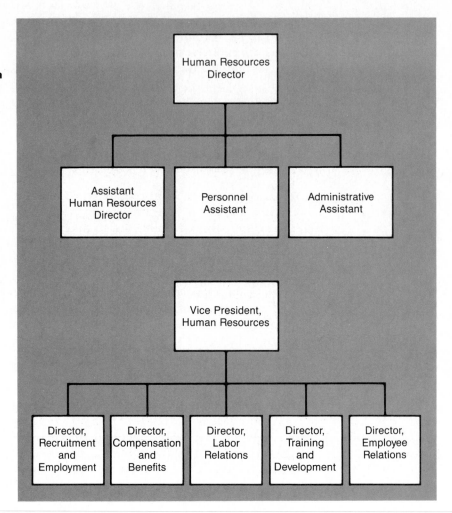

Structure of the Human Resources Department

In organizations large enough to have a human resources or personnel department, the personnel director and his or her staff will play a key role in the design and monitoring of human resources systems. (Even in very small organizations, some person or persons — perhaps the president or owner or that person's assistant — will coordinate human resources activities for the entire enterprise.) Regardless of organization size, the fundamental human resources processes must be managed. The larger the organization, however, the more likely it employs persons with specialized expertise to help design and implement human resources systems.

Figure 1.2 compares the typical human resources department in a small company employing approximately three hundred persons with the structure of that department in a corporation of several thousand employees. Responsibilities assigned to various human resources positions may be quite different in large and small companies. Table 1.1 lists activities that would most likely be allocated to the human resources department in a small company and in a large corporation. The activities are comparable, but in the smaller organization each personnel staff member is likely to have a wider variety of responsibilities. In larger corporations, more **specialization**, or expertise in a particular area, is permitted in each personnel job. As can be seen in Figure 1.3, the corporate personnel department at Hewlett-Parkard (an electronics firm with 56,000 employees in the United States) is structured according to specialization areas. Further, in the large corporation, there may be several levels in the department structure. For example, the director of compensation and benefits might have a manager of employee benefits and a manager of compensation administration reporting to him or her, and both these managers would have their own staffs.

Relationship with Other Managers

What the organizational charts in Figure 1.2 do not show is that responsibility for employee activities is usually shared with other managers. For example, human resources departments typically do not make the final hiring decisions for accounting or manufacturing departments. Rather, controllers or manufacturing directors, respectively, have the final say. But human resources departments typically do have major responsibility for designing and overseeing major components of the hiring system, including initial screening and referral.

Similarly, human resources departments are likely to do much of the human resources planning, most of the advertising and recruiting, and much of the interviewing. But these activities are usually performed in cooperation with other managers throughout the organization. The human resources staff typically does not have final decision-making authority over pay increases but is active in designing pay systems, administering those systems, and monitoring decisions made about pay to ensure that those decisions are based on uniform guidelines and are in agreement with organizational goals. In short, human resources departments are typically responsible for the effective management of the various personnel systems, and their activities are usually conducted in

TABLE 1.1 **Responsibilities of the human resources department in a small company and a large corporation**

SMALL COMPANY		LARGE CORPORATION	
Position	*Responsibilities*	*Position*	*Responsibilities*
HUMAN RESOURCES DIRECTOR	Human resources planning Managerial/professional compensation Recruiting Labor relations Grievances	*VICE PRESIDENT, HUMAN RESOURCES*	Executive committee Organization planning Human resources planning Policy Organization development
ASSISTANT HUMAN RESOURCES DIRECTOR	Wage and salary administration Recruiting Interviewing Orientation Training Reassignments Terminations Safety and health Special programs	*DIRECTOR, RECRUITMENT AND EMPLOYMENT*	Recruiting Interviewing Testing Placement Terminations
		DIRECTOR, COMPENSATION AND BENEFITS	Job analyses and evaluation Surveys Performance appraisal Compensation administration Bonus, profit-sharing plans Employee benefits
PERSONNEL ASSISTANT	Testing Interviewing Job descriptions Job evaluation Training Employee benefits Employee services Suggestion plan	*DIRECTOR, LABOR RELATIONS*	Negotiations Contract administration Grievance procedure Arbitration Health and safety
ADMINISTRATIVE ASSISTANT	Secretary to staff Word processing Records Interviewing	*DIRECTOR, TRAINING AND DEVELOPMENT*	Medical plans Cafeteria Orientation Training Management development Career planning and development Quality circles Exit interviews
		DIRECTOR, EMPLOYEE RELATIONS	EEO relations Contract compliance Staff assistance programs Employee counseling Outplacement

FIGURE 1.3 Structure of the corporate personnel department at Hewlett-Packard

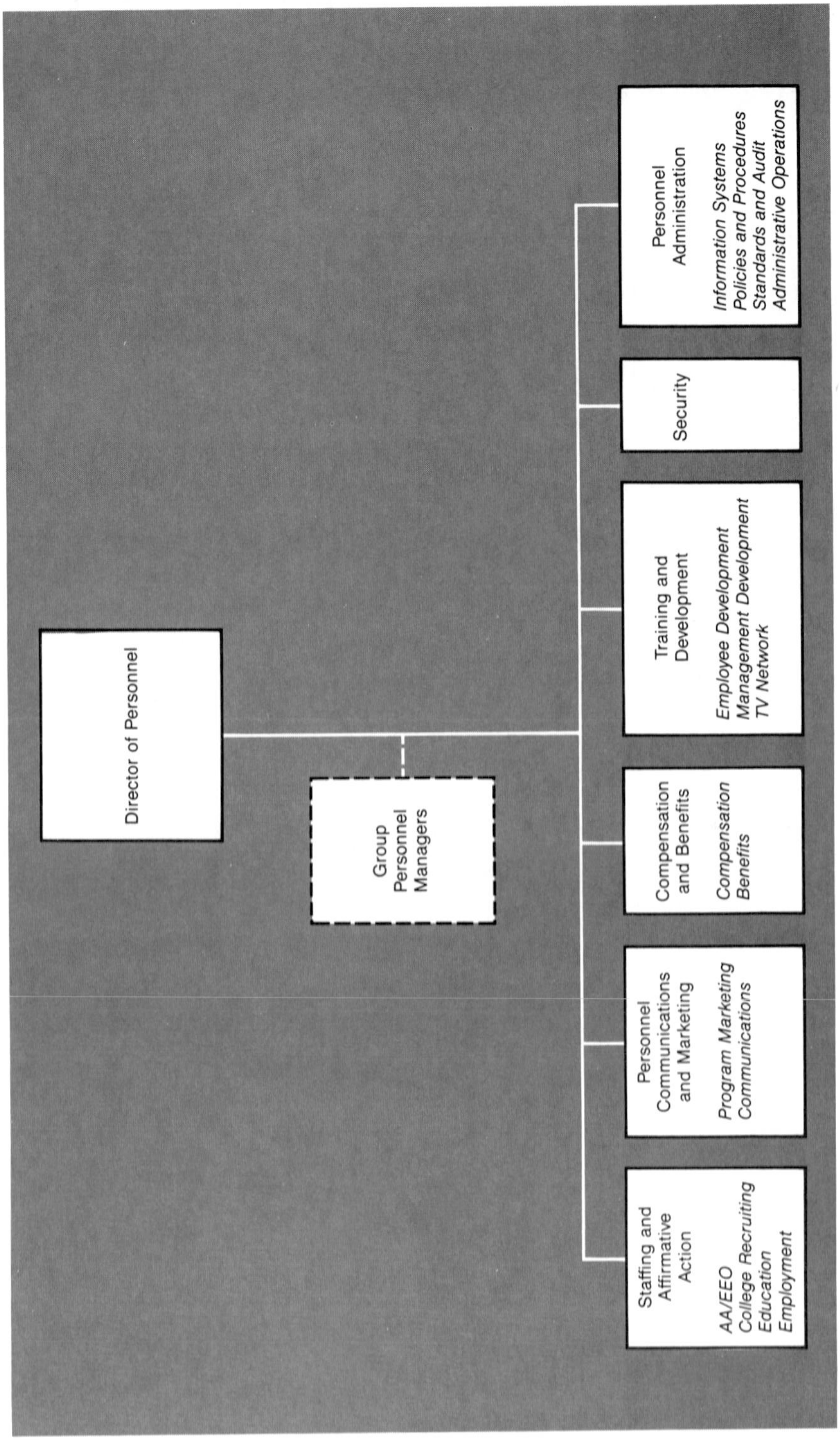

Director of Personnel

Group Personnel Managers

Staffing and Affirmative Action
- AA/EEO
- College Recruiting
- Education
- Employment

Personnel Communications and Marketing
- Program Marketing
- Communications

Compensation and Benefits
- Compensation
- Benefits

Training and Development
- Employee Development
- Management Development
- TV Network

Security

Personnel Administration
- Information Systems
- Policies and Procedures
- Standards and Audit
- Administrative Operations

Source: Hewlett-Packard.

FIGURE 1.4   **Reporting relationship of the human resources director to top management in a large manufacturing firm**

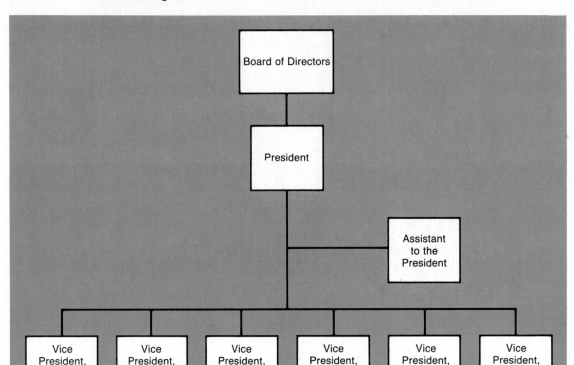

cooperation with the management group. Most of the key human resources policy decisions are made jointly by the human resources director and the other top managers.

This sharing of decision making — particularly where the various managers make decisions relating to one phase of a system and the human resources director makes decisions relating to another — can strain relationships. For example, to enforce agreed-upon policy, the personnel director might inform a department head that he or she cannot increase a subordinate's pay beyond the top of the range unless there has been an appropriate increase in responsibilities. The department head may not like that. Also, a personnel director might become too zealous in monitoring policy and be perceived as setting policies that do not have broad managerial support.

If there has been broad management participation in establishing human resources policies, these kinds of tensions are not likely to be very serious or very lasting. Nevertheless, because some managers may not appreciate the organization-wide implications of human resources decisions, the human resources director may need to conduct an ongoing educational effort about the unique role of the department.

Rising Prominence of Human Resources Management

The vital nature of human resources management and its overall impact in modern organizations are increasing the influence of human resources directors within those organizations. As will be seen in the next two chapters, both historical and environmental forces have created an urgent need for high-quality human resources management in contemporary organizations.

The typical reporting relationship between the human resources director and other members of top management, shown in Figure 1.4, indicates the responsibility and competence required of the human resources director today. Although he or she may report to a vice president or executive vice president, a clear trend in the last two decades has been for a higher and higher percentage of human resources or personnel directors to report to the chief executive officer (CEO). Two-thirds to three-fourths of human resources or personnel directors now report to the CEO.[2]

In most organizations, decisions about overall strategic planning and organizational change are the responsibility of the chief executive and immediate subordinates. These decisions have a direct impact on the way human resources will be used in achieving company-wide goals. Including the expertise of human resources specialists throughout the planning process, therefore, can help minimize undesirable aspects of organizational change and maximize the achievement of organizational goals.

SUMMARY

People — human resources — create organizations and make them survive and prosper. If human resources are neglected or mismanaged, the organization is unlikely to do well.

Human resources management is a broad concept referring to the philosophy, policies, procedures, and practices used in managing people throughout the organization. Using the concepts of processes and systems, human resources management is the systematic control of a network of fundamental organizational processes affecting and involving all organization members; these processes include human resources planning, job and work design, staffing, training and development, performance appraisal and review, compensation and reward, employee protection and representation, and organization improvement. To control and refine these processes, systems are planned, developed, and implemented by top management.

All managers are heavily involved in human resources management. In small organizations, a central figure, such as the owner or president, coordinates the organization-wide aspects of human resources management. In organizations large enough to have human resources (personnel) departments, that department plays a major role in the planning, development, and implementation of personnel systems.

Typically, key policy decisions in human resources management are made jointly by the human resources director and other top managers. Further, the human resources department typically makes decisions relating to certain steps in personnel procedures (such as initial screening and referral), whereas other managers make decisions relating to other steps in those procedures (making a final selection from among several qualified candidates). Although this joint decision making can lead to strains in relationships, broad management participation in the development of human resources policies will tend to minimize these tensions.

The organization-wide impact of human resources management, coupled with the vital nature of the organizational processes involved, gives the human resources director a great deal of influence in today's organizations. A clear trend in the last twenty years has been for a higher and higher proportion of human resources directors to report to the chief executive officers of organizations.

KEY TERMS

human resources
human resources
  management
process
system
human resources planning

job and work design
job analysis
staffing
training and development
performance appraisal and
  review

compensation and reward
protection and representation
organization improvement
specialization

REVIEW QUESTIONS

1. Define "human resources management," using process-systems terminology. How does this concept differ from the meanings sometimes associated with the more traditional term "personnel management"?
2. Identify and briefly describe the basic processes in human resources management.
3. Describe the respective roles in human resources management carried out
   by (a) the human resources department and (b) other managers.
4. Why is human resources management considered a vital aspect of the
   total management process?

OPENING CASE QUESTIONS

Case 1.1   Martha Burke

1. What were the problems facing Metro Publications that caused Martha
   Burke to consider hiring a human resources director?
2. What steps will Martha need to take to assure a smooth transition after
   hiring a human resources director

Case 1.2   More than Pizza

1. What are Don and his coworkers really saying about the success of Perroni's?
2. What are the advantages and disadvantages of the lack of a hiring system
   at Perroni's?

CASE 1.3   CONTRASTS IN HUMAN RESOURCES MANAGEMENT

If the human resources manager's role is viewed as a continuum, the endpoints are clearly placement and separation — hiring and letting go. Although these functions define only a small portion of the human resources function, they may be the most "visible" of human resources activities and may potentially have the greatest impact on employees and the firm. This is not to say that the human resources manager makes placement and separation decisions in isolation; of course that is not the case. But in the areas of implementation and procedures, the human resources function takes on great importance.

Charles Bischoff, Jr. has had ample experience at both ends of the continuum. Mr. Bischoff, a human resources specialist for thirty-one years, is director of managment resources at the Allied Corporation, which produces fibers, plastics, and energy; is the Fortune 500's fifty-fifth largest member; and employs 55,000 people. At one end of the continuum, Bischoff has had extensive experience with finding the right executives to meet Allied's needs. The hiring process begins within Allied itself, and the files of potential candidates are reviewed. If the right person fails to emerge from this review, Allied refers the position to an outside executive employment agency. But in the end, it is the people at Allied who make the final decision, based on their own judgment. For Bischoff, this is one of the high points of human resources management: "I get great satisfaction every time I match up the right candidate with the right job. When I'm able to assist a person in his individual career, I get something out of that."*

At the other end of the continuum, though, Bischoff finds his role difficult. In 1979, Allied had a new chief executive officer who made the painful decision that the firm's payroll was simply too big and endangered profitability. Layoff notices were delivered to 842 employees in order to save $30 million.

However, under Bischoff's direction, Allied tried to take as much of the trauma out of the termination process as possible. One conjures the image of employees being told of termination and finding that their personal effects have already been packed in preparation for their departure. At Allied the situation was quite the contrary. The firm made genuine efforts to help place separated employees. Thirty offices were set up for separated workers to prepare resumes and use phones. Each worker got company-paid postage for two hundred letters. And Bischoff, who believes that even in the case of a performance-related separation an employee should be treated "with max-

Case Sources: N. R. Kleinfield, "A Human Resource at Allied Corp.," *New York Times,* June 6, 1982, sec. 3, p. 4; and "Handing Out Pink Slips," *New York Times,* June 6, 1982, sec. 3, p. 15.

*Quoted in N. R. Kleinfeld, "A Human Resource at Allied Corp., *New York Times,* June 6, 1982, sec. 3, p. 4.

imum dignity," wrote personal letters to one hundred companies on behalf of the separated workers.

The results of the effort were positive; Allied believes that most of the laid-off workers were able to find positions elsewhere. Still, the process engendered ill feelings among some; and even three years later, Bischoff viewed it as a deeply troubling experience.

Discussion Questions

1. In this chapter, part of the definition given for human resources planning was "making plans to ensure that a competent, stable work force is employed." Do you think that Allied's efforts on behalf of the laid-off workers contributed to this goal? Why or why not?
2. Although most of Allied's separated employees found jobs, some of them could only find positions that didn't pay as well as their old jobs. If you were in the latter group, would you feel bitter toward Allied's current management?

A History of Human Resources Management

LEARNING OBJECTIVES

- **Identify the major movements affecting the development of human resources management.**
- **Cite key legislation affecting labor-management relations.**
- **Identify the personnel specialists who were the forerunners of the modern human resources department.**
- **Describe the contributions of the behavioral sciences and systems theory to contemporary human resources management.**

CASE 2.1　　FACTORY WORK, 1815*

In the manufacturing districts it is common for parents to send their children of both sexes at seven or eight years of age, in winter as well as summer, at six o'clock in the morning, sometimes of course in the dark, and occasionally amidst frost and snow, to enter the manufactories, which are often heated to a high temperature, and contain an atmosphere far from being the most favorable to human life, and in which all those employed in them very frequently continue until twelve o'clock at noon, when an hour is allowed for dinner, after which they return to remain, in a majority of cases, till eight o'clock at night.

The children now find they must labour incessantly for their bare subsistence; they have not been used to innocent, healthy, and rational amusements; they are not permitted the requisite time, if they had been previously accustomed to enjoy them. They know not what relaxation means, except by the actual cessation from labour.

The Industrial Revolution, which began in the mid-eighteenth century in England, was characterized by the development of machinery, the linking of power to machines, and the establishment of factories employing many workers. Extensive specialization of labor — that is, individual workers' performing very narrow tasks, such as replacing bobbins on a sewing machine — was a key feature of the design of work in these factories. Case

* Reprinted from Robert Owen, *Observations on the Effect of the Manufacturing System*, published in England *circa* 1815, p. 258.

Photographed by Lewis Hine. Library of Congress

Children laboring in the coal mines, like these breaker boys who removed slag and sorted coal, were often exhausted by their long hours in the dark, dust-filled mines.

2.1 is a partial description of the terrible conditions under which children often worked during this era.

But a consequence of the grouping of workers into shops and factories, and of the specialization of labor, was a gradual emergence of more systematic attention to the design of jobs, to the choice of workers for those jobs (selection), to the provision of pay and benefits (compensation), and to the welfare of employees both on and off the job. In the late 1800s, when unions were battling for recognition and violent strikes became a significant concern, these developments in management practices accelerated. By the early 1900s, as this chapter will demonstrate, many of the components of modern human resources management were falling into place.

THE SCIENTIFIC MANAGEMENT MOVEMENT

The **scientific management** movement of the late 1800s and early 1900s concentrated particularly on job design, selection, and compensation. The name most closely associated with this movement is Frederick W. Taylor. Working in the steel industry in the late 1870s, Taylor believed the same techniques used by scientists in the laboratory — experimentation, forming and testing hypotheses, and proposing theories based on research and testing — could be used by management to increase efficiency in the workplace.[1]

For Taylor, the science of management included systematic job design that began with observation, recording, and classification of job activities as they were typically carried out. Tasks could then be simplified and jobs made more efficient. Scientific selection involved choosing workers with the skills and capacities needed to carry out the now efficiently organized jobs. Scientific training and development meant training workers for particular tasks and was intended to replace the centuries-old practice of permitting workers to choose their own work methods and train themselves as best they could. By applying these principles, Taylor was able to raise

Frederick W. Taylor (above) and Frank and Lillian Gilbreth (right)

the average worker's productivity at the Bethlehem Steel Corp. by over 300 percent.

Frank and Lillian Gilbreth were among the contemporaries of Taylor who extended his ideas. Frank Gilbreth analyzed workers' body movements by studying motion pictures of tasks being performed, and from these studies he formulated laws of efficient motion. This analytical approach to efficiency in industry, called time-and-motion study, was a forerunner of industrial engineering and the development of more effective automatic machinery.[2] Lillian Gilbreth is credited with one of the early books relating the principles of scientific management to psychology.[3] In general, the scientific management movement emphasized the importance of management planning down to the smallest details of factory operations.

THE INDUSTRIAL WELFARE MOVEMENT

In addition to directing attention to "scientific management" around the turn of the century, many firms were beginning to be involved in what has been called the **industrial welfare movement**. Industrial welfare work consisted of "voluntary efforts on the part of employers to improve, with the existing industrial system, the conditions of employment in their own factories."[4] Actually, the movement extended beyond the workplace to some aspects of the workers' lives off the job: " . . . management made available various facilities such as libraries and other recreational premises, offered financial assistance for education, home purchase and improvement, provided medical care and instituted hygienic measures."[5]

As an outgrowth of this movement, many business firms began to employ staff members called **social secretaries** or **welfare secretaries.** These people were employed to help with employee finances, housing, health, recreation, education, and other matters.[6]

EARLY INDUSTRIAL PSYCHOLOGY

Applications of psychology to business and industry, or **industrial psychology,** began to emerge in the 1890s and early 1900s as psychologists studied selling techniques and ways of testing job candidates. The most notable industrial psychologist was Hugo Münsterberg, whose major contributions were (1) the analysis of jobs in terms of their physical, mental, and emotional requirements and (2) the development of testing devices for selecting workers. In his

---

PERSPECTIVE 2.1   A 1920 Commentary — How Long Shall We Work?

In Massachusetts in 1881, a textile manufacturer told his experience in the Bureau of Statistics of that year. He began, he said, with the thirteen hour day. He began also to watch his men and women at their work. He soon saw that "something was wrong with the hours and more so with the arguments popular among employers.

"Soon after I took charge, I persuaded the rest of the directors to allow me to reduce the hours to eleven. Before this, the weekly product of the mills had been 90,000 yards of print cloths. After it, with the same machinery, the weekly product rose to 120,000 yards.

"Now granting that a part of that increase was due to improved management, yet it is clear that

Source: Excerpted from John Graham Brooks, *Labor's Challenge to the Social Order* (New York: MacMillan Company, 1920), p. 245.

this improvement could not have been made nearly so effective without the improved physical conditions which so great a reduction of hours afforded."

A few years later Frederick Hazzard went to Europe to study the effect of the prevailing eleven hour day. He became convinced that even eleven hours was a business blunder. At the end of long a varied tests, he concluded that in spite of high wages per unit of time, "the result in cost is less than it was before the eight hour change was made." Since then experiments in great numbers have shown at least this: that *with high class management*, the case for the shorter day is among the practical possibilities for almost every kind of business. The United States Bureau of Labor shows the lopping off of hours from 1907 to 1914, in eighty-nine trades, with results that show this to be a reform as practicable as that of properly guarded machinery.

---

book *Psychology and Industrial Efficiency,* published in 1913, Münsterberg described his experiments for selecting streetcar operators at the Boston Elevated Railway Company. He wanted to test motormen candidates for their ability to discriminate between figures representing obstacles that were likely to move onto the streetcar track (people, horses, automobiles) and those that were likely to remain parallel to or off the track. The device he developed used a series of twelve cards that the subject moved by turning a crank. When the tests were completed, Münsterberg reported a strong correspondence between test performance and actual job performance.[7] Münsterberg also performed experiments in the telephone industry, successfully enough to claim that his tests helped to select better telephone operators.[8]

In addition to developing tests for measuring differences in aptitude, industrial psychologists were developing the concept of statistical validity. Both Münsterberg and Edison D. Woods recognized the importance of comparing test scores with criteria for success to determine **predictive validity,** the extent to which a test accurately predicts job success or lack of it.[9] Before World War I, other personnel techniques were being developed, including reference checks, the use of rating sheets by interviewers, and comparison of applicants' ratings with ratings of successful workers.

THE HUMAN RELATIONS MOVEMENT

What came to be called the **human relations movement** has been a major influence on modern human resources management. This movement is characterized by its focus on group behavior and workers' feelings as they relate to productivity and morale. Some of its beginnings were with a group of researchers in an industrial plant near Chicago.

The Hawthorne Studies

In 1924 researchers at the Western Electric Company's Hawthorne Plant near Chicago began some experiments to determine how lighting affected workers and their output. In one experiment production increased when the lighting was improved, but in another it also increased when the lighting was severely reduced. After three years of experimentation with such "illogical" results, the researchers concluded that, in experiments involving people, it was impossible to change one variable (lighting) without affecting other

Experiments at Western Electric's Hawthorne Plant found that human interaction affected morale and motivation and, in turn, productivity.

Courtesy of Western Electric Corporation

variables such as worker interaction or worker-supervisor interaction. It became clear that it was human interaction that was affecting morale and motivation, which, in turn, were affecting production.[10]

The Organization as a Social System

Further inquiry and experimentation led researchers to conclude that productivity depended at least in part on the extent to which the employees became a team and cooperated wholeheartedly and spontaneously. Worker cooperation and enthusiasm seemed to be related to the interest in the work group shown by the supervisor and experimenters, the lack of coercion or force, and the extent to which workers participated in making decisions and changes that would affect them.[11] In short, the researchers came to view the industrial organization as a social system. Therefore, for several decades a great deal of research focused on group behavior and employee attitudes.

THE LABOR MOVEMENT

In a democratic society, it was probably inevitable that associations of wage earners, or **labor unions,** would arise to protect workers against some of the abuses of the Industrial Revolution and to improve their lot in life. Joint action by groups of workers began taking place as trade or labor unions spread from factory to factory and shop to shop. Eventually, labor unions won their greatest victory: the right to bargain collectively. **Collective bargaining** is the process in which union leaders, as representatives of workers, negotiate with employers over working conditions such as hours of work and compensation.

Even before the Industrial Revolution, collective **protests** and **strikes** — workers, as a group, refusing to work — were not unheard of. For example, in 1636 a group of fishermen in Maine protested against their wages being withheld.[12] In general, employers reacted to such collective action with outrage and attempts to thwart further organizing. In 1799 the Philadelphia Journeymen Cordwainers (shoemakers) attempted to bargain collectively with their employers, which resulted first in the employers' locking their shops to keep out the workers — called a **lockout** — and then in a negotiated settlement between the union and the employers. Nevertheless, the union was taken to court, and in 1806 the Philadelphia Cordwainers were found guilty of "criminal conspiracy" to raise wages.

It was not until 1842 that the Massachusetts Supreme Court overturned the conspiracy doctrine. In *Commonwealth* v. *Hunt,* the court ruled that unions were not criminal per se and that labor organizations could have honorable as well as destructive objectives.[13]

The Growth of Unions

The *Commonwealth* v. *Hunt* decision allowed unions to grow and prosper. One of the most important early unions was the Knights of Labor, formed as a national organization in 1869. From the beginning, this group emphasized the brotherhood of labor and sought to include all workers, both skilled and unskilled. Its early constitution included goals pertaining to workers' cooperatives, the eight-hour work day, the prohibition of child labor, and equal pay for women and men. **Boycotts** — refusing to buy from certain companies — were supported, but strikes were considered necessary only when other negotiating measures failed.

Partly as a result of widespread unemployment and wage cuts in the 1880s, the Knights of Labor became more and more involved in strike action. At first, most of the strikes were successful. Soon, however, the union grew too large to control its membership, unauthorized strikes involving sabotage occurred, and many business leaders used **strikebreakers** — nonunion workers who were willing to replace striking employees. By the 1890s the Knights of Labor were in decline.[14]

Meanwhile, the American Federation of Labor (AFL) had been organized in 1886 as an association of national craft unions. From the beginning, the AFL was pragmatic in seeking immediate improvements in wages and working conditions for the craft workers. Its officers were determined to avoid direct participation in politics and to reward its friends and punish its enemies regardless of political affiliation. These strategies served the union well, and it experienced slow but relatively steady growth, surviving the depressions of the 1890s and 1930s.[15]

By 1935, however, controversy had arisen within the AFL between leaders who favored craft unions and those who wanted to organize unskilled workers into industrial unions. This conflict resulted in the formation of the Committee for Industrial Organization. Originally the Committee intended to work within the AFL, but in 1937 the AFL expelled ten unions that were CIO affiliates. In 1938, the break was formalized when the Committee reorganized as the Congress of Industrial Organizations (CIO).

In 1955, power struggles and philosophical differences were put aside and the CIO merged with the AFL to form the AFL-CIO. In addition to using collective bargaining to secure an improved standard of living for workers, the AFL-CIO increasingly turned to political action. Now an international organization, the AFL-CIO continues to lead the labor movement today. The current status of the labor movement is discussed in Chapter 17.

Violence in Labor Relations

Violence characterized many of the strikes of the second half of the nineteenth century. In the 1860s and 1870s, the Molly Maguires, a secret society of miners of Irish descent, carried out terrorist activities, including beatings and murders of employers, in the coal fields of Pennsylvania. In 1886, a further example of the violence of this period occurred when police killed four people during a strike for an eight-hour work day at the McCormick Reaper Works in Chicago. At a resulting protest meeting in Haymarket Square in Chicago, a bomb was thrown into the ranks of police. Seven police officers and four workers were killed in the clash that followed.[16]

The turn of the twentieth century did not end this kind of violence. In 1913 open warfare broke out in the mine fields of the Colorado Fuel and Iron Corporation. The fighting reached a terrible climax when the Colorado state militia attacked a group of strikers at Ludlow. After firing machine guns at the tents in which workers' families were living, the militia doused the tents with oil and set them afire. Eleven children, two women, and six miners were killed. This incident has been called the Ludlow Massacre by historians.[17]

Violence continued to appear from time to time in American labor relations through the late 1930s. Early in 1937, U.S. Steel executives agreed to unionization, but the smaller steel companies refused to go along with U.S. Steel's lead, and violent strikes broke out. On May 30, ten people were killed and eighty wounded when police in South Chicago attacked marchers at a Republic Steel Company plant. The strike gradually dissipated, and the smaller steel firms were not organized until 1941.[18]

Government and Labor: 1914–1959

The federal government's attitude toward the labor movement gradually moved from opposition to neutrality and finally to support of the concept of collective bargaining, including the right to strike. (Table 2.1 shows the sequence of significant laws and other

TABLE 2.1 **Significant laws and other government influences on labor relations 1806–1959**

DATE	LAWS, COURT DECISIONS, OR EVENTS	EFFECT ON LABOR RELATIONS
1806	Philadelphia Journeymen Cordwainers tried for conspiracy	Philadelphia shoemakers are found guilty of criminal conspiracy to raise wages and are fined.
1842	In *Commonwealth* v. *Hunt,* Massachusetts Supreme Court rules on conspiracy doctrine	Massachusetts Supreme Court holds that unions are legal organizations and overturns the conspiracy doctrine.
1914	Clayton Act	Act limits the use of injunctions against unions during labor disputes and legalizes picketing.
1918	National War Labor Board created	Federal government creates National War Labor Board which establishes "work councils" in factories during World War I.
1926	Railway Labor Act	Act establishes collective bargaining, outlaws company unions, and provides for grievance and arbitration procedures in the railroad industry.
1932	Norris-LaGuardia Act	Act essentially prohibits injunctions in labor disputes and makes the "yellow-dog" contract illegal.
1933	National Industrial Recovery Act	Act gives most workers the right to organize and bargain collectively. Act is later declared unconstitutional, but its labor provisions are written into the Wagner Act.
1935	Social Security Act	Act establishes an unemployment compensation system, an old-age pension system, and various services for the blind and disabled.

government influences on labor relations starting with the Philadelphia Cordwainers of 1806.)

One of the most important laws was the Clayton Act, passed in 1914. This act limited the use of court orders, or **injunctions,** against workers and unions during labor disputes and legalized **picketing** (a line of workers carrying placards) and certain other union activities. The courts, however, tended to ignore or downplay the provisions of the Clayton Act until the passage of the Norris-LaGuardia Act in 1932, which essentially prohibited the use of

TABLE 2.1 *(Continued)*

DATE	LAWS, COURT DECISIONS, OR EVENTS	EFFECT ON LABOR RELATIONS
1935	Wagner Act	Act allows union employees to choose representatives who exercise exclusive bargaining rights for all employees in the unions. Act further specifies the following as unfair labor practices: coercion or restraint by employers of employees in the exercise of their rights, dominating or interfering with a labor organization, or refusing to bargain.
1938	Fair Labor Standards Act	Act establishes minimum wages and a maximum work week beyond which overtime must be paid. Act outlaws employment of children under age sixteen in industries in interstate commerce.
1947	Taft-Hartley Act	Act makes certain union practices illegal, such as refusal to bargain, sympathy strikes, and closed shops. States are allowed to pass right-to-work laws. Make-work and featherbedding provisions in labor contracts are made illegal. Act further establishes the Federal Mediation and Conciliation Service.
1959	Landrum-Griffin Act	Act includes provisions for secret-ballot election of union officers, gives union members protection from embezzlement by union officers, and outlaws picketing to extort money.

injunctions in labor disputes. That act also made the **yellow-dog contract** illegal. A yellow-dog contract is an agreement between management and a worker under which the worker agrees not to join a union in exchange for continued employment.

The Wagner Act of 1935, also called the National Labor Relations Act, focused on labor's right to organize. The act allowed union employees to choose representatives who exercise exclusive bargaining rights for all employees in that union. It became an unfair labor practice for an employer to coerce or restrain employees in the exercise of their rights, to dominate or interfere with a labor organization, or to refuse to bargain collectively with a legal representative of the employees. The administration of the Wagner Act was given to a newly constituted National Labor Relations Board (NLRB).

But with the Taft-Hartley Act (Labor Management Relations Act) of 1947 Congress began to restrict union power. Certain union practices, such as sympathy strikes, refusals to bargain, and **closed shops** (situations in which the employer may hire only union members), were declared illegal. States were allowed to pass **right-to-work laws,** which permitted any state to outlaw **union shop provisions** in contracts as well. (In a union shop situation, all workers in a bargaining unit are required to become union members after a certain period of employment.)

Make-work (creating jobs with no substance or purpose) or **featherbedding provisions** (requiring the employer to hire unnecessary employees) in labor contracts were also deemed illegal. The act allowed the president of the United States to take action to postpone strikes or lockouts for eighty days when national health or safety was imperiled. The act also established the Federal Mediation and Conciliation Service, an independent department in the federal government with responsibility for helping unions and management reach agreements and avoid work stoppages.

In 1959, the Landrum-Griffin Act (Labor-Management Reporting and Disclosure Act) was passed to further protect employees and employers against arbitrary union power. This law included provisions for secret-ballot election of union officers, gave protection against embezzlement of union funds by union officials, and outlawed picketing to extort money from employers.

DEVELOPMENT OF HUMAN RESOURCES MANAGEMENT AS A PROFESSION

Besides the growth of unions, the late nineteenth and early twentieth centuries witnessed the emergence of human resources management as a profession. The earliest developments came in the federal civil service.

The Federal Civil Service

The Civil Service Commission, established by the Pendleton Act of 1883, has had a major influence on the development of human resources management in the United States. Drawing many of its

1914...Thomas J. Watson Sr., 40, joins Computing-Tabulating-Recording Co. (C-T-R) as general manager...One hundred shares of C-T-R stock worth less than $3,000...Company has 770 stockholders.

Endicott, N.Y., plant produces time-recording equipment; Dayton, Ohio, plant makes scales; Washington, D.C., plant produces punched cards.

Accounting product line includes mechanical key punch, hand-operated gang punch, vertical sorter and tabulator...Customers include railroads, chemical companies, utilities and life insurance companies...By year-end, company grows to 1,340 employees and gross income from sales, service and rentals in U.S. to $4 million.

1915...Thomas J. Watson Sr. becomes president and general manager of C-T-R...First sales convention, forerunner of Hundred Percent Club conventions, is held.

1917...C-T-R enters Canadian market under name of International Business Machines Co., Ltd...Company grows to more than 3,000 employees...Office in Brazil opened.

Computing-Tabulating-Recording Co. logo.

1919...C-T-R enters European market...Electric synchronized time clock system introduced.
1920...Printing tabulator introduced...Gross income triples since 1914.
1923...Other sales offices opened in Latin America and Far East...Electric key punch is introduced.
1924...C-T-R adopts name of International Business Machines Corporation...Quarter Century Club organized...Carroll rotary card press developed to produce cards at high speed...IBM introduces self-regulating time system...First issue of employee publication "Business Machines" appears.
1925...IBM opens office in Philippines...Introduces horizontal sorting machine...Introduces accounting machines in Japan...Company pays first stock dividend to shareholders at rate of 20%.
1926...IBM stock splits three-for-one...Company wins grand prizes for products at Sesquicentennial Exposition in

Sales training class at Endicott, N.Y., 1930.

IBM logo and slogan, circa 1937.

Philadelphia...IBM has 3,953 employees.
1928...Punched cards now hold 80 columns, almost double previous capacity...Subtracting-accounting machine introduced...Customer engineering training course starts...Suggestion Plan for employees established...Stock dividend of 5% paid.
1929...Stock market crashes...IBM declares 5% stock dividend...Gross income exceeds $18 million.
1930...Despite depression, IBM adds employees, trains more salesmen, increases engineering efforts...Stock dividend of 5% paid.
1931...New products include the 400 series alphabetical

accounting machines and 600 series calculating machines...First permanent installation of the Filene-Finlay Translator is set up at League of Nations in Geneva...Stock dividend of 5% paid.
1933...New education building and engineering laboratory built at Endicott...Development of Carroll Carriage improves alphabetical accounting machines by automatic handling of special forms and variable line spacing...IBM acquires Electromatic Typewriters, Inc., of Rochester, N.Y.
1934...Company sells Dayton Scale Division to Hobart Manufacturing Co....The 405 Alphabetical Accounting Machine introduced...Group Life Insurance plan for employees initiated...Piecework discontinued.
1935...First commercially successful electric typewriter placed on market by IBM...First issue of "Think," employee and customer magazine, appears...Proof machine to

First class of women systems service professionals, 1935.

IBM typewriter introduced in 1935.

clear bank checks introduced...Survivor benefits added to Group Life Insurance for employees...Stock dividend of 2% paid.
1937...IBM, among first companies to announce policy of paying employees for holidays annually, includes six holidays in plan...Begins paid vacations...The 077 collator and a test-scoring machine are introduced
...IBM now has more than 10,000 employees...Gross income passes $30 million...Stock dividend of 5% paid.
1938-40...Stock dividends of 5% paid each year.

1941-45...IBM offers all facilities to government for World War II effort...Sets nominal 1% profit on war products, such as naval and aircraft fire control instruments, Browning automatic rifles, 30-caliber carbines, director and prediction units for 90 mm anti-aircraft guns and bombsights.

Washington, D.C., card plant makes paper forms for war bonds. Thousands of IBM accounting machines handle wartime paperwork; accounting machines in mobile units follow U.S. troops in battle.

IBM builds plant at Poughkeepsie, N.Y., in 1942 and expands Endicott plant. Both plants win Army-Navy "E" awards.

In 1944, IBM presents its first large-scale calculator, the ASCC (Automatic Sequence Controlled Calculator), to Harvard University...Watson Scientific Computing Laboratory is founded at Columbia University in 1945.

Sickness and accident and retirement plans announced...Special programs begun for handicapped employees...IBM is first company to give grants to United Negro College Fund...Stock dividend of 5% paid each year.
1946...The IBM 603 Multiplier, first small commercial electronic calculator, announced...Hospitalization Plan announced...IBM manufactures pocket-sized Braille writing devices...Family Dinners initiated to give recognition to employees and spouses...Thomas J. Watson Jr. elected to Board of Directors...Employees total 22,492...Stock splits five-for-four.
1947...Total and Permanent Disability Income Plan to

nounced...Vested rights pension added to IBM retirement plan.
1948...Announcements include the SSEC (Selective Sequence Electronic Calculator); 604 Calculating Punch; IBM Model A Typewriter...Gross income reaches $156.4 million...Stock splits seven-for-four.
1949...Thomas J. Watson Sr. elected chairman of IBM board...World Trade Corporation is formed as an independently

New building for customer and employee education, 1933.

Courtesy of International Business Machines Corporation

Highlights in human resources management at IBM, 1914–1984.

ideas from the British civil service system, the Pendleton Act established the use of competitive examinations for admission into public service; provided job security for public employees, including those who refused to engage in politics; prohibited political activity by the civil service; and encouraged a nonpartisan approach to employee selection. A commissioner was appointed to administer the act.[19]

The major effect of the Pendleton Act was to foster employees' appointment and career development in federal service on the basis of performance. Over the years this law has stimulated progressive personnel policies in private organizations as well. For example, around 1890 the Civil Service Commission was developing the forerunners of general intelligence tests and trade tests that became popular in private industry.

Personnel Specialists in Industry

Between 1900 and 1920, concurrently with developments in scientific management, industrial psychology, and the federal civil service, some companies began hiring specialists to assist with such matters as employment, safety, and training.

This trend was influenced by a number of management books published between 1899 and 1912 in Great Britain and the United States. Moreover, the first comprehensive text in the field appeared in 1920 — Tead's and Metcalf's *Personnel Administration*.[20] Such publications stimulated interest in the field and encouraged the use of personnel specialists.

Several kinds of personnel specialists, in addition to the social or welfare secretary discussed earlier, were particularly evident shortly after the turn of the century. Companies such as B. F. Goodrich hired **employment agents** to centralize the recruiting and screening processes.[21] Some firms established departments of labor, as did the National Cash Register Company (now NCR Corporation) in 1901; the **labor department specialists** would respond to complaints from union employees and monitor working conditions and wage policies.[22] Some companies employed **wage** or **rate clerks** to set wage rates based on time-and-motion studies and analysis of job tasks.[23] Similarly, **pension administrators** were hired to manage the pension (retirement) and insurance plans that were proliferating in many railway and labor organizations.[24] A number of companies established training programs, staffed by **training specialists,** to teach employees new skills, particularly sales techniques.

In 1902 Maryland became the first state to pass a **workmen's compensation** (now **workers' compensation**) law, requiring employers to pay workers for lost time and injuries resulting from occupational accidents. The law was subsequently declared unconstitutional. But in 1911, the United States Supreme Court upheld the workers' compensation laws of several other states, and from then on **safety specialists** became very common in industry. Industrial firms wanted to reduce claims against themselves, and they depended on the safety specialist to help ensure safer working conditions in their plants. As a parallel development, physicians were employed by some companies to ensure that employees would be assigned jobs suited to their physical qualifications.[25]

The Emergence of the Personnel Department

As early as the 1880s, in some companies, a few specialized personnel activities were grouped into larger departments. But not until the second decade of the twentieth century did the modern personnel department emerge. In 1911, U.S. Steel created a Bureau of Safety, Sanitation, and Welfare. By 1918, International Har-

FIGURE 2.1 Time line: The development of human resources management

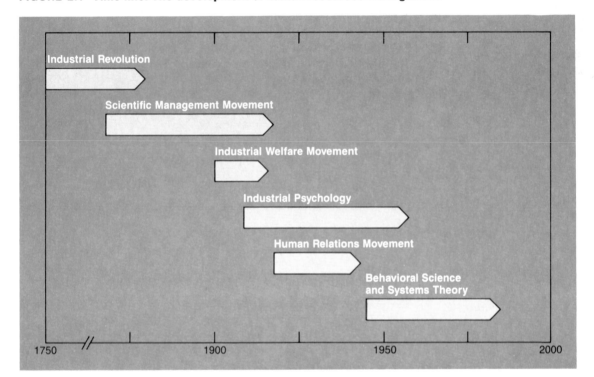

vester had established a Department of Industrial Relations, and Ford Motor Company had created a Sociological Department that combined medical, welfare, safety, and legal aspects of employee relations. By the same year, B. Kuppenheimer and Company had a Department of Industrial Relations that included subdivisions such as health, employment, grievances and discipline, and wage and rate setting.[26]

In 1917 Standard Oil of New Jersey approved a plan that provided for regular conferences between labor and management. At the same time the company established a retirement income plan, substantial insurance benefits, a safety program, and a medical division. To coordinate many of the new programs, Standard Oil created a personnel and training department.[27] In such ways were modern personnel departments born.

The Behavioral Sciences and Systems Theory

Since the late 1940s, and especially during the 1970s and 1980s, human resources practitioners have drawn on the emerging knowledge from the **behavioral sciences** and **systems theory**.

Systems theory, by emphasizing the relationships among the parts of a totality, helps personnel managers understand how a change in one component of an organization can have repercussions throughout the firm. For example, if a corporation hires people with greater skills and more education than those it has hired previously, it may also need to upgrade its training program and pay more attention to opportunities for advancement. The process-systems view of human resources management described in the previous chapter is partially an outgrowth of systems theory.

The behavioral sciences — the social and biological sciences pertaining to human behavior — have provided especially important insights into such issues as motivation, group behavior, and leadership. As will be evident throughout this book, behavioral science theory and research can be useful in job design, employee selection, orientation, promotion, and many other areas of human resources management.

SUMMARY

Modern human resources management has emerged from six interrelated sources: (1) the scientific management movement, (2) the industrial welfare movement, (3) early industrial psychology, (4) the human relations movement, (5) the labor movement and the emergence of free collective bargaining, and (6) the development of human resources management as a profession. (See Figure 2.1)

Scientific management and early industrial psychology emphasized the proper design of tasks, selection and training of employees, and individual incentives. The human relations movement was mainly concerned with the feelings, interactions, and attitudes of employees and with the organization as a social system. The industrial welfare movement grew out of concerns about working conditions in factories and mills and other places of employment; it also grew out of concerns about the off-job lives of employees.

The establishment of workers' rights to organize and bargain collectively was a slow process, punctuated by violence. Nevertheless, strong unions and associations of unions emerged — most notably the AFL-CIO — and a series of federal laws established both the rights of unions and the rules under which unions must operate.

The emergence of human resources management as a profession began with developments in the civil service and the rise of personnel specialists in private industry. Eventually the specialized personnel functions coalesced into a single personnel department. Since the 1940s, the profession has been strongly influenced by research in the behavioral sciences and systems theory — research that has affected ideas about job design, employee selection, leadership, and many other areas of human resources management.

KEY TERMS

scientific management	lockout	featherbedding provisions
industrial welfare movement	boycott	employment agent
social or welfare secretary	strikebreakers	labor department specialist
industrial psychology	injunction	wage or rate clerk
predictive validity	picketing	pension administrator
human relations movement	yellow-dog contract	training specialist
labor union	closed shop	workers' compensation
collective bargaining	right-to-work laws	safety specialist
protest	union shop provisions	behavioral sciences
strike	make-work provisions	systems theory

REVIEW QUESTIONS

1. What were the major movements since the late 1800s that have influenced the evolution of human resources management? Briefly describe each.
2. Explain why it is useful to go beyond viewing the organization as a technical system and also view it as a social system.
3. What were the key laws passed in the United States up through 1959 that had significant influence on labor-management relations? What was the impact of each law?
4. Identify the personnel specialists who were the forerunners of the modern human resources department.
5. In general terms, what have been the contributions of the behavioral sciences and systems theory to contemporary human resources management?

OPENING CASE QUESTIONS

Case 2.1   Factory Work, 1815

1. What were some of the changes in the management of human resources brought about by the Industrial Revolution?
2. Briefly discuss some of the differences between general working conditions today and those prevalent in the early days of the Industrial Revolution.

CASE 2.2   HUMAN RESOURCES: THE VIEW AT IBM

International Business Machines is an industrial giant by any standard. It is by far the nation's largest computer manufacturer, and its domestic success is echoed by foreign success — even in Japan. Yet IBM has never laid off a worker. Nor has there ever been so much as a vote on unionizing any of the company's domestic operations.

The watchword in IBM's human resources policy, and one of the keys to the company's continued success, is loyalty. Today, IBM offers employees not only security, but also a system of career development that is expected to extend throughout their working lives; IBM wants its employees to stay and to grow along with the company. In addition, most people in the industry feel that IBM is the leader in compensation and fringe benefits as well as sales. In return, the company expects employees to work hard and THINK (a company motto of sorts) and to behave, while working, in keeping with the IBM image. That image was developed under Thomas Watson, Sr., who ran the company from 1914 until 1956. Watson's techniques for instilling loyalty ranged from creating a company songbook to rigidly prescribing employees' behavior (even off the job in some respects). His strict dress code created an image familiar to many Americans. IBM was long associated with the dark suits, ties, and white shirts of its almost exclusively male representatives.

IBM's codes of behavior have been relaxed somewhat in the twenty years since Thomas Watson, Sr. died, although there are still clear rules and expectations. However, better than those codes, the company's attitude toward layoffs may give insight into its human resources philosophy. For example, in the 1970s, the company's vice president in charge of personnel developed an innovative vacation policy aimed specifically at avoiding the need to cut employees during business downturns. To keep from having to hire extra workers during years when business was good, the company encouraged employees to put off vacation time during those years for use later. Then, when business was down, employees were expected to use their saved-up vacation time. In practice, the absence of extra workers that would have been required during big years balanced out the need to pay the vacationers during the recessionary year of 1975. Despite economic difficulties, IBM made no layoffs. According to IBM's chairman at the time, Frank Cary, "You can't put a dollar sign on this sort of thing. The real benefit is in terms of morale. Our people know our policies are designed to keep them on the payroll."*

Case Sources: "The Colossus That Works," *Time,* July 11, 1983, pp. 44–54; and Herbert E. Meyer, "Personnel Directors Are the New Corporate Heroes," *Fortune,* Feb. 1976, pp. 84–88.

* Quoted in Herbert E. Meyer, "Personnel Directors Are the New Corporate Heroes," *Fortune,* Feb. 1976, p. 87.

Discussion Questions

1. What parallels do you see between IBM's attitude toward its human resources and the industrial welfare movement?
2. Why do you think none of IBM's U.S. facilities has tried to unionize?

chapter 3

Contemporary Challenges in Human Resources Management

LEARNING OBJECTIVES

- **Identify changes in the lifestyles and attitudes of the work force that affect human resources management today.**
- **List eight criteria for analyzing the quality of work life in an organization.**
- **Describe the impact of economic conditions and international competition on the American work environment.**
- **Identify recent government acts and court decisions related to fair employment practices and worker protection and explain how they affect contemporary human resources management.**

CASE 3.1   MEETING AT THE COUNTRY INN

Doug McLennan, president of Southwest Telecommunications Equipment, had called a two-day meeting involving the top management group and its immediate subordinates, some forty people in all. The announced agenda was "cost-cutting" and "quality improvement." The meeting was held at a country inn featuring comfortable accommodations, excellent food, a swimming pool, and extensive trails for jogging or walking. The dress was casual.

The meeting started at 9:00 a.m. Coffee, tea, fruit juice, and sweet rolls were available, and before people settled down in their comfortable chairs there was much good-natured greeting and repartee. There was an undercurrent of tension, however. For example, one department head was overheard saying to another, "Well, I guess Doug is going to turn on the heat." Another comment was, "We're going to have to work a lot smarter."

Doug started the meeting with a few words of welcome, and then talked about the purposes of the gathering. "I hope," he said, "that we can have a good exchange of ideas and points of view in the areas of quality control and cost reduction. I hope by the time we leave tomorrow we'll have formed some task forces to investigate and put into effect some of the more promising ideas." He then started talking about what he called "the realities."

"The reality is," Doug began, "that the Japanese and West Germans are capturing a larger and larger share of our markets. Some of our East Coast competitors are moving up fast, too. Our products are very good, but theirs are almost as good and steadily getting better. I wouldn't admit that outside this room, but it's true. To compound the problem, the Japanese, in particular, are producing comparable items at substantially less cost. They've also developed a new transistor that's giving them an edge, and we can't find comparable ones on the market yet. We've got to find ways both to improve our products and to manufacture them at less cost. Let me show you some figures." He then displayed a series of charts portraying sales and cost trends, share of the market, and so on.

After a brief period of questions and discussion, Doug called on Beverly Shaw, vice president of human resources, to discuss the schedule for the rest of the meeting. Beverly explained that a series of small-group sessions was on the agenda for the rest of the day. Each group would discuss general topics of concern to the entire firm, such as "potential approaches to reducing costs" and "suggestions for improving productivity in manufacturing." Groups were encouraged to brainstorm freely and to suggest where they felt task forces could explore and implement proposed solutions to specific concerns. In some sessions, people were assigned to groups according to their area of specialty in the firm; in other sessions, group membership cut across departmental lines. In every instance, the small groups reported the results of their deliberations to the total group for further discussion.

Among the task forces appointed before the end of the second day was one on training and development and another on recruitment and selection. Beverly Shaw was appointed to chair both. Although she felt a little defensive that there had been suggestions for improvement in "her" areas, she was also encouraged by the interest other managers had expressed in both training and selection — areas where she had been attempting to secure their support. She had been trying to interest the manufacturing people in helping develop better specifications for hiring new people, for example, and here was a chance to work jointly with them on that matter and others, since the manufacturing vice president was on both task forces. Beverly was also pleased that her assistant, Don Wills, was appointed to the task force on cutting costs in the offices because both she and Don had been concerned about inefficiencies in office procedures.

People were tired at the end of the two-day meeting, but generally pleased with the results. Doug had expressed his concerns, but he had not really "turned on the heat." No person or department had been scolded, and it was clear that Doug wanted to maintain a congenial, problem-solving approach to addressing issues. There had been some time for exercise and socializing, which was appreciated, and people were particularly pleased with the approaches to cost-cutting and quality improvement. In closing, Doug thanked the members of the group for their participation and told them, "I want to get us all back together for a one-day meeting six weeks from now to report on progress."

CASE 3.2 STUDENT OR AIRLINE PILOT?

Larry Randle was enrolled in Professor Talcott's course in human resources management. At the beginning of the course he approached the professor and said, "I'm a pilot with TransContinental Airlines, and working on my degree on and off. The pilots are on strike, and the company has filed for reorganization under the bankruptcy laws, so I thought this would be a good quarter to go back to school full time. I don't know what will happen, but I assume I can finish the course. I thought I should let you know." Professor Talcott thanked Larry for informing him and added, "I hope everything works out all right for you." Talcott had read in the newspapers that TransContinental, partly as a consequence of the deregulation of U.S. airlines, was in financial trouble. He had further read that the president of the airline had pressed the unions, including the pilots' union, to take wage cuts of up to 40 percent. The airline president had also insisted that the pilots and other crew members fly longer hours per day to cut costs further. There was speculation in some quarters that the airline was trying to "break the union," but also general agreement that the airline was in deep trouble.

Larry was in class for the next two sessions. Meanwhile, Professor Talcott had read that the airline had, indeed, filed for reorganization in federal bankruptcy court and had immediately put the reduced wage scales and increased flying hours into effect. After the union had called the strike, which was supported by the flight attendants' union, the president of the airline had announced that all crew members who wished to stay on could do so, but that TransContinental was going to hire replacements for any strikers who did not return to work within two weeks.

Before the fourth session of the class, Larry came by the professor's office and said, "I'm afraid I'll have to withdraw from class. I've decided to go back to work, strike or no strike. I really like flying, and I want to build up my hours and seniority. Sorry to have to drop out." "I'm sorry, too," the professor said, "but I wish you good luck, Larry, and I'm sure the other members of the class do, too."

These two cases suggest that forces outside the organization can have a major impact on human resources management. In Case 3.1, intense national and international competition was forcing the management group at Southwest Telecommunications Equipment to take a hard look at its management practices. Included in the practices to be examined were employee training and development and the way the company was recruiting and selecting new employees.

In Case 3.2, the impact of external forces was even more dramatic. In this situation, government deregulation of the airlines and heightened competition had precipitated a financial crisis at TransContinental. As a result, top management had taken action that drastically changed the compensation plan and work rules and, in effect, set aside contracts with the unions. The pilots' union, in turn, called a strike against the company. The human resources aspects of the company, then, were being severely influenced by outside events.

Many environmental, organizational, and cultural influences affect human resources management today. Changing social and political trends and recent economic developments around the world help account for the growing importance of the human resources department to the organization. These trends and developments also intensify the importance of all managers' roles in selecting and managing human talent.

These influences, many of which represent ongoing challenges in contemporary human resources management, can be grouped into three major categories: (1) the nature of today's work force, (2) influences of the external environment, and (3) regulatory measures — federal and state laws, court decisions, and administrative rulings — that govern human resources management.

THE NATURE OF TODAY'S WORK FORCE

The American work force as a whole is different from what it was ten, or even five, years ago. Many of the changes have been occurring gradually over the years; some are very recent or still in process. For example, the number of workers in the prime working ages (25–54) is growing dramatically and will continue to grow throughout the 1980s (see Figure 3.1). Certainly, the challenge for

FIGURE 3.1

Age of the U.S. work force 1970–1990: The prime age group (25–54) is growing dramatically

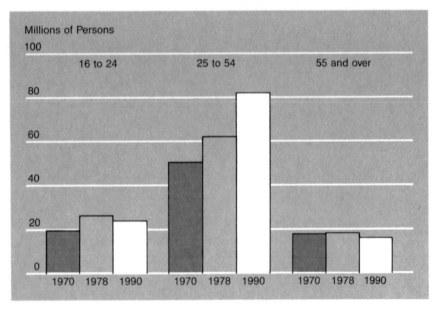

Source: Bureau of Labor Statistics, *Occupational Outlook Handbook, 1980–81 Edition,* pp. 17–18.

human resources managers is to keep abreast of all the trends and forces shaping today's work force.

Social Conditions and Expectations

Among the most challenging problems in the management of human resources are current social conditions as they are reflected in workers' attitudes, values, and expectations:

Increasingly, people are better educated. As recently as 1970, only 1 in 7 adult workers had a college degree. Now, as shown in Figure 3.2, nearly 1 in 4 adult workers has completed college.[1] One implication is that organizations need to look continuously to see whether talents are being used, whether jobs are sufficiently challenging, and whether there are avenues for advancement.

It is in the organization's interest to realize the optimal return from its human resources as well as to make the organization an attractive place to work. In addition, the higher a person's education, the higher his or her expectations about challenging and interesting work. A survey in a large manufacturing organization found, for example, that employees with bachelors', masters', and doctorates ranked "challenging and interesting work" first in a group of thirteen factors. Employees with associate degrees ranked this item third, those with high school diplomas ranked it fourth,

FIGURE 3.2
Years of school completed by labor force in 1984

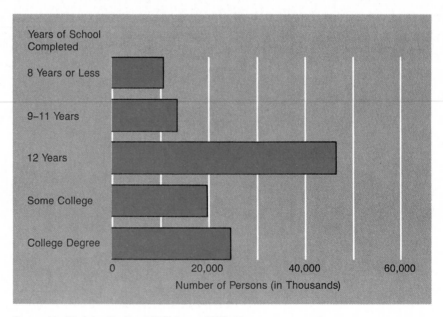

Source: Monthly Labor Review, 108 (February 1985): 43.

and those who had not completed high school ranked it thirteenth, the bottom of the scale.[2] Strategies for designing jobs to challenge and motivate workers are described in Chapter 7.

People have higher expectations about participation. **Participation,** or employee involvement in organizational problem solving and decision making, is a key aspect of contemporary human resources management. More and more, employees want to participate in decisions about their work lives. For example, they want to be consulted before a major change is made in work schedules or in work assignments. People also want more freedom to question supervisory and management practices. They are less and less inclined to assume that "management knows best." Participation is introduced in Chapter 4 and discussed in various contexts throughout the text.

There is a growing trend toward acceptance of collective action, such as unionization, among segments of the work force where collective action historically has not been widely used. Unionization and strike action have been increasing, for example, among nurses, government employees, teachers, professional athletes, and even physicians. As a result of these trends, human resources directors and other managers, as well as union leaders, have been paying more attention to human resources practices that might make organizations vulnerable to unionization. Why workers join and form unions is discussed in Chapter 17.

Expectations about "due process" in the work situation are greater. Partly as an outgrowth of the trends just discussed, members of the work force at all levels have higher expectations about **due process,** that is, fair and orderly procedures for the airing of problems and complaints without fear of recrimination, and fair and orderly procedures for making decisions affecting the lives of employees (see Chapter 19). These expectations are being reflected in a growing acceptance of "progressive discipline," which relies on responsive, corrective action rather than severe penalties, and the use of grievance procedures in an increasing number of organizations.

Lifestyles and life circumstances are changing. More and more people express concern about the appropriate balance of work with leisure and other aspects of their lives. Thus, they may be less willing to accept overtime assignments or to work long hours or weekends. Further, there are growing numbers of single-parent families and families in which both spouses work. A record 6 out of 10 mothers with children under 18 years old were in the labor force in 1984, compared with only 4 out of 10 in 1970.[3] These trends create pressures on organizations to be flexible enough in working hours so that children can be picked up from school or

---

PERSPECTIVE 3.1   Stride Rite Pioneers Child Care Partnership

Stride Rite's day care program, which has existed since 1971, is considered a model for industry-community day care. It provides quality day care to both employees of Stride Rite and residents of Roxbury and Cambridge. The community recipients' fees are subsidized by the Department of Social Services; the employees' sliding scale fees are parent-paid. Around 70% of the food costs are reimbursed under a contract with the Massachusetts School Lunch and Nutrition Bureau. Stride Rite pays for those costs not met by parent fees, DSS fees, and lunch program reimbursements. . . .

According to Miriam Kertzman, the center's founding director, the employees' children range from working class to managerial or professional. The fee for full-time day care is 10% of the employee's salary if he or she earns up to $250 a week, 15% if he or she earns over $250 a week. . . .

Family involvement in the day care center is central to the program's success. Parents and staff attend regular supper meetings to discuss program development and curriculum planning. Lunchtime makes industry-sponsored day care special; employees are encouraged to spend their lunch break at the day care center, and the family atmosphere

Source: Excerpted from Sarah Cliffe, "Stride Rite Pioneers Child Care Partnership," *MASC Journal* (June 1984): 7–8.

this creates is "largely responsible for making the center such a positive experience." . . .

Staff turnover has been unusually low for a day care center. This may be because employees are integrally involved in decision-making concerning curriculum, center policies, and additional staffing. Staff is also able to get further professional training through university vouchers and federal title training monies. Low staff turnover has been integral to both the quality and stability of the program and the degree of parent and community confidence in the center. . . . Personnel costs are lower than they might be because Stride Rite encourages high school volunteers and teacher trainees from local universities to become involved in the centers' activities.

According to Kertzman, the center can accommodate nearly all the employees who wish to enroll children. She adds that the day care program is an important factor in attracting and keeping desirable employees. Although the startup money was substantial ($40,000), the company considers the program "a valuable investment." Arnold Hiatt, Stride Rite's president, is deservedly proud that the program is being used nationally as a model for industry-community day care programs. . . . The Stride Rite experience proves that, given sufficient commitment and planning, industry-community day care works.

---

taken to the doctor or dentist. There are also more pressures on organizations and communities to provide day-care centers. Lifestyle considerations also influence the organization's ability to recruit or transfer people. *Where* people are willing to live and work is becoming a serious issue for a significant number of workers.

The proportion of women in the work force has increased dramatically. Two-thirds of the jobs created in the past decade have been filled by women.[4] Because women have traditionally carried the major burden of child rearing, the pressures mentioned above for flexible work scheduling, time off, and day-care centers are intensified. This also means that the "equal pay for comparable work" issue is going to be debated more frequently, and a larger number of people will be pressing for higher pay for women. Statistics show that for over 30 years women have consistently earned about 60 cents for each dollar earned by men (see Figure 3.3). This complex issue — comparable worth — is discussed in Chapter 14.

Experience with job loss or the threat of job loss in recent years has undoubtedly had a great impact on many people at all levels in the work force. The experience of having lost a job, or of having survived a "reduction in force," has probably influenced the attitudes of many workers and managers in various ways. For example, some who have lost one job and then found another may feel fortunate to be employed and are likely to work harder and better than ever before. Others, especially those who feel their employers could have avoided layoffs or were less than humane in the way they reduced staff, may be mistrustful and resentful even though they themselves stayed on the payroll.

Some executives may come to realize that people were let go too quickly, that the options they considered in a crisis were too limited, and that the organization's human resources have been seriously depleted. By contrast, other managers will find they have weathered a crisis, treated their employees humanely, and retained both efficiency and good will. Still others will wish they had faced up to the necessity of reducing the payroll more quickly. The important thing is that human resources directors and other execu-

FIGURE 3.3
The relative earnings of male and female workers

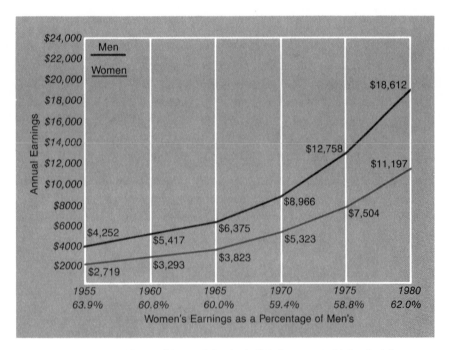

Source: Perspectives on Working Women: A Databook, U.S. Department of Labor Statistics, October, 1980, p. 52.

tives recognize the importance of looking at numerous options when confronted with budget cutbacks. We will look at some of those options in Chapter 10.

People are more aware of the fragility of the natural environment and of the interdependence of humans with their surroundings. Consequently, there are more pressures on organizations to follow environmentally sound practices, including more attention to health and safety, to the control and disposal of pollutants and toxic materials, and to transportation control so as to minimize traffic congestion and air pollution. Developing safe and healthful working conditions is the topic of Chapter 20.

The Quality of Work Life

More and more employees and managers are interested in and concerned about the **quality of work life,** a concept that encompasses the entire range of organizational life—particularly as it is reflected in human resources management. Richard E. Walton provides us with eight criteria for analyzing the quality of work life in an organization:[5]

1. *Adequate and fair compensation.* One criterion is the extent to which "the income from full-time work meet[s] socially determined standards of sufficiency . . ."[6] and the extent to which compensation is perceived as fair by the employee.

2. *Safe and healthy working conditions.* This criterion includes the extent to which working conditions minimize health and injury risks.

3. *Opportunity to use and develop human capacities.* To Walton, this criterion is the extent to which the job involves a whole task rather than fragments of tasks. In addition, it includes the extent to which the job involves planning activities as well as implementation activities, allows "substantial autonomy and self-control," and provides opportunity to use a wide range of skills.[7]

4. *Opportunity for continued growth and security.* This criterion includes the extent to which the employee's capabilities are encouraged to develop rather than allowed to become obsolete, the extent to which there are opportunities for advancement, and the extent to which there is reasonable job security.

5. *Social integration in the work organization.* This criterion includes the extent to which there is freedom from prejudice and the opportunity for upward mobility in the organization. It also includes the extent to which organization members experience group

Merck & Co., Inc.

Quality of working life includes the opportunity to use and develop human capacities.

support and a "sense of community" that extends beyond the immediate work group.

6. *Constitutionalism.* This criterion includes the extent to which the organization adheres to the concept of "due process" mentioned earlier and honors people's rights to privacy — e.g., the right to withhold information about off-the-job behavior and family matters.

7. *Balanced role of work.* This refers to the extent to which the organization avoids interfering in an appropriate balance between work and other spheres of employees' lives, such as family life.

8. *Socially beneficial and responsible work.* This reflects the extent to which the employee sees the organization as being socially responsible in its products, its disposal of wastes, its employment practices, its dealings with underdeveloped countries, and so on.

Increasingly, people at all levels in the work force have higher expectations about these eight characteristics. In turn, these expectations influence how contemporary organizations are managed, particularly how human resources are managed.

INFLUENCES OF THE EXTERNAL ENVIRONMENT

Many other forces, largely external to the organization, are having a major impact on human resources management. Like the trends we have already described, they tend to be interrelated.

Economic Conditions

Economic conditions, both at home and abroad, have a strong influence on human resources management. In a strong, highly productive economy, organizations have greater financial resources for attracting workers with higher pay, for implementing training and development programs, and for funding other personnel programs. In contrast, a struggling economy plagued by high inflation and lower productivity intensifies the need for more cost-effective management of human resources. Current economic forces include the following factors

Inflation and Energy Costs.   Inflation periodically plagues the U.S. economy and is rampant in some countries. Rising costs and prices create a wide range of problems in human resources management, including chronic difficulties with compensation decisions, starting salaries, and pension plans. In addition, control of oil prices by the Organization of Petroleum Exporting Countries (OPEC) and declining sources of energy have resulted in high energy costs and intensified pressures for conservation and production efficiency. Working conditions, such as office and plant heat in the winter and air conditioning in the summer, have been affected. Other forms of adaptation to high energy costs are prevalent, such as companies' encouraging employees to form car or van pools. In some cases, companies subsidize van pools.

Increased Competition.   International competition among organizations is becoming more intense for many reasons. For example, increased management capability in many countries, heavy competition for energy and raw materials, and government subsidies in some nations all intensify competition. The jet plane and satellite communications have increased the tempo of business trade and the sharing and dispersal of information enormously. As only one example, commerce between Europe and the southern United States requires only a few hours' travel between London and the Atlanta and Dallas airports.[8] Further, there has been wide sharing of technology, some voluntary and some based on spying or smuggling of high-technology items. The smuggling of helicopters into North Korea from California via a West German exporter and Rotterdam is an example.[9]

Some of the U.S. industries most troubled by international competition are automobiles, steel, mining, textiles, and shoe manufacturing.[10] The reasons are complex, but one is surely the rapid dissemination of information and technology. Cheap labor and extensive reserves of raw materials in some countries are other important factors. The United States mining industry, for example, is in serious difficulty for these reasons.[11]

Overall, increased national and international competition intensifies the pressure on executives, supervisors, and all employees to become more innovative, more efficient, more cost-conscious, and more quality-conscious. In turn, organization members, such as those at Southwest Telecommunications Equipment in Case 3.1, expect human resources management to become increasingly effective in helping with these matters.

Government Deregulation.   In the last few years, federal legislation and decisions by the Supreme Court and federal agencies have drastically decreased or eliminated government regulation and control of a number of industries, including telecommunications, the airlines, banking and financial services, and the trucking and railroad industries.[12] This **deregulation** has had many consequences, including increased competition among firms, and management pressures on unions for wage cuts and less restrictive work rules. While many new firms have sprung up, many others have gone bankrupt or been purchased and absorbed by other companies, leading to extensive layoffs. In many instances, employees with twenty or more years of experience have lost their jobs. Events such as these, of course, create major problems for human resources management. On the one hand, they pose a challenge to find ways to avoid or minimize the adverse consequences to people. On the other hand, they constitute a challenge to find creative and productive ways to help organizations and people make the necessary transitions.

Concern for Productivity.   Finally, how to increase productivity and product quality are matters of deep concern to management, government, labor, and the public. While there has been a resurgence in **productivity** (the total amount of worker output) from the slow rates of growth in the 1970–1982 period,[13] awareness of the importance of sustaining and improving upon productivity and quality is greater than ever before. These concerns get translated into challenges for all areas of human resources management, including more effective work and job design, and the selection, use, training, development, and motivation of employees.

Innovations in Management and Technology

Successful management practices in other areas of the world, such as Japan and Europe, are affecting the use of human resources in the United States. For example, the successful adaptation by Japanese firms of the American-invented "quality circle" idea, in which groups of workers meet to discuss ways to improve products and work methods, has influenced many U.S. firms to experiment with this form of worker participation for the first time. (Quality circles are discussed in Chapter 21.) As another example, many American firms have adopted the Japanese practice of maintaining low inventories of parts and requiring suppliers to maintain very high quality standards. One implication is that the suppliers now expect higher quality work from their employees. Another example is flextime, an innovation that came out of West Germany. Originally called *Gleitzeit,* meaning "gliding time," the concept permits employees to set their own starting and stopping times within broad boundaries.[14] (Flextime is discussed in Chapter 8.)

Technological change and improvements are also creating rapid change, particularly in certain industries. The transistor, the laser beam, the microcomputer (the personal computer for home or office or the more sophisticated versions for small businesses or engineering), and the robot are examples of innovations that have changed and are changing the nature of products and jobs. Computers and robots will help build the new Saturn cars at General Motors, for example, contributing to a restructuring of the traditional assembly line, making possible more flexible working assignments, and giving workers substantial responsibility for quality control.[15]

REGULATORY MEASURES

Since attention will be paid throughout this book to the influence of federal legislation, court decisions, presidential executive orders, and administrative rulings, we will mention them only briefly

---

PERSPECTIVE 3.2 Wowing the Yanks in Toyota City

"Tape it together, wire it together, just get it out the door." At GM, Ford, Chrysler, and Mack Trucks, says Curtis M. Spears, that was the foreman's job — pushing as many vehicles as possible along a filthy assembly line, bucking a hostile union rank and file all the way. Spears, 40, is a tall, black veteran supervisor who has been around the U.S. industry for 11 years without, he says, finding a company or plant prepared to put quality before output. So the factories in the giant Toyota City complex came as a surprise to him, as they did to the rest of the 25 group and team leaders for the Toyota-GM joint venture sent to Japan in early June for training — the first wave of the 150 or so who will be trained there before production begins in December.

At the Takaoka plant, where Americans worked alongside Japanese on jobs the Yanks would be directing at Fremont, non-slip green carpeting is laid down on either side of a spotlessly clean assembly line; every part and tool is within easy reach. Huge overhead air-conditioning tubes keep work areas cool. In place of a boxlike foreman's cage against the nearest wall, with a locked filing cabinet full of absentee and disciplinary records, the group

leader's office is an open space right on the line with a small table, a couple of chairs, a teapot, and a tiny vase of chrysanthemums. Upstream from final assembly, automation has been pushed to the limits: body-welding lines are manned mostly by robots, and in the newest shop at the super-modern Shimoyama engine plant, 200 workers turn out 40,000 engines a month.

"If I had not seen it, I wouldn't have believed it," says Darlene Dobrolenski, 31, who will be supervising the installation of Shimoyama's engines at Fremont. At the now shuttered Mack Trucks plant near Fremont where she worked along with Spears, she injured her back manhandling one-ton truck engines on casters across the 40 feet of rough concrete floor between the engine line and chassis line — a massive bottleneck where backed-up engines created an obstacle course for workers.

Veteran UAW members in the group speak no less enthusiastically than the foremen. George W.J. Nelson, 51, a paint shop team leader, is a longtime political activist who retains a cheery tendency to burst forth with choruses from old union organizing songs. But he too is excited by what he's seen. Becoming front-line efficiency and quality-control experts, he says, is something the guys will go for back in Fremont.

---

here. Table 3.1 lists a number of recent laws, court decisions, and executive orders that have had, and continue to have, a profound effect on human resources management. Essentially, these apply to all categories of employees, including supervisors, professionals, and executives, who work for employers with fifteen or more employees. Similar state laws and regulations may affect even smaller organizations.

In particular, the Equal Pay Act, the Civil Rights Act, the Age Discrimination in Employment Act, the Equal Employment Opportunity Act, and the Vocational Rehabilitation Act have given women, minorities, the older worker, and the handicapped worker greater protection against **discrimination,** or employment decisions based on prejudice in human resources practices. A 1965 executive order required that firms having federal contracts estab-

TABLE 3.1 **Recent laws, Supreme Court decisions, and executive orders affecting human resources management**

DATE	LAW, COURT DECISION, OR EXECUTIVE ORDER	EFFECT ON HUMAN RESOURCES MANAGEMENT
1963	Equal Pay Act	Prohibited discrimination on the basis of sex in wage payments for jobs that require equal skill, effort, and responsibilities under similar working conditions in the same establishment.
1964	Civil Rights Act	Title VII prohibited employment or membership discrimination by employers, employment agencies, and unions, based on race, color, religion, sex, or national origin. Act created the Equal Employment Opportunity Commission (EEOC).
1965	Executive Order 11246	As amended by Executive Order 11375, prohibited discrimination based on race, color, religion, sex, or national origin on government contracts. Also required federal contractors to develop affirmative action plans to raise the level of minority and female employment in their firms.
1967	Age Discrimination in Employment Act	Prohibited discrimination against persons aged forty to sixty-five in such matters as hiring, job retention, compensation and other terms, conditions, and privileges of employment.
1970	Occupational Safety and Health Act (OSHA)	Authorized the secretary of labor to establish mandatory safety and health standards.
1971	*Griggs* v. *Duke Power Company*	U.S. Supreme Court ruled that the employer unlawfully discriminated against blacks by requiring a high school education or successful completion of an intelligence test as a condition of employment in certain jobs.
1972	Equal Employment Opportunity Act	Permitted the EEOC to bring enforcement actions in the federal courts.
1973	Vocational Rehabilitation Act	Required federal contractors to take affirmative action to employ and promote qualified handicapped persons.
1974	Employee Retirement Income Security Act (ERISA)	Prescribed eligibility rules, vesting standards, and an insurance program for private pension plans.

lish **affirmative action** programs to raise their levels of minority and female employment. The Occupational Safety and Health Act (OSHA) helped establish mandatory safety and health standards for work organizations, and the Employee Retirement Income Se-

TABLE 3.1 *(Continued)*

DATE	LAW, COURT DECISION, OR EXECUTIVE ORDER	EFFECT ON HUMAN RESOURCES MANAGEMENT
1978	Amendments to Age Discrimination in Employment Act	Extended protection until age seventy for most workers and without upper limit in federal employment.
1979	*Kaiser Aluminum Chemical Corp.* v. *Weber*	Supreme Court endorsed right of employers and unions to jointly adopt quotas to eliminate racial imbalance in a work force through affirmative action.
1981	*Washington County* v. *Gunther*	In case involving female guards alleging sex discrimination in pay, the U.S. Supreme Court held that such suits were not barred under Title VII of the Civil Rights Act merely because the plaintiffs were performing work similar to but not identical with that performed by male guards.
1983	*Newport News Shipbuilding and Dry Dock Co.* v. *EEOC*	Supreme Court ruled that employers must treat male and female employees equally in providing health insurance for their spouses.
1983	*Arizona* v. *Norris*	Supreme Court ruled that employer-sponsored retirement plans may no longer pay women smaller benefits than men, despite studies showing different life expectancies for the sexes.
1984	*NLRB* v. *Bildisco & Bildisco*	Supreme Court ruled that employers filing for reorganization in federal bankruptcy court may temporarily terminate or alter collective bargaining agreements even before the judge has heard the case.
1984	*Firefighters Local Union No. 1784* v. *Stotts et al.*	Supreme Court ruled that courts may not interfere with seniority systems to protect newly hired black employees from layoffs.
1984	Retirement Equity Act	Broadened conditions under which spouses receive retirement benefits, and further amended ERISA through such provisions as allowing pension plan members to take maternity or paternity leave of up to one year without loss of service credit for the period.

curity Act (ERISA) was designed to protect employees covered by private pension plans.

A 1984 Supreme Court decision (*NLRB* v. *Bildisco & Bildisco*) gave companies filing for reorganization under the bankruptcy

laws the freedom to alter or terminate a labor agreement temporarily, even before a federal judge hears the case, providing
the employer has made a "reasonable" effort to negotiate a more
favorable contract with the union.[16] This was part of the tense
labor relations situation described in Case 3.2, "Student or Airline
Pilot?"

A Supreme Court decision in 1971 (*Griggs* v. *Duke*) was aimed
at reducing discrimination against minorities caused by educational requirements or testing practices. The Court found that the
employer unlawfully discriminated against blacks by requiring a
high school education or successful completion of an intelligence
test as a condition for employment into certain jobs. A 1979 decision (*Steelworkers* v. *Weber*) provided additional support of affirmative action programs by permitting companies and unions to adopt
quotas jointly to eliminate racial imbalance in the work force. A
1984 decision modified this support, however, by saying that courts
may not interfere with seniority systems to protect newly hired
minorities against layoffs. (*Firefighters Local Union No. 1784* v.
Stotts et al.)[17]

As shown in Table 3.1, significant Supreme Court decisions in
1983 focused on personnel practices relating to the pay and benefits
of female employees. One decision (*Newport News Shipbuilding
and Dry Dock Co.* v *EEOC*) held that employers must treat male
and female employees equally in providing health insurance for
spouses. In *Arizona* v. *Norris,* the court ruled that employer-sponsored retirement plans could no longer pay women smaller benefits
than men, despite actuarial studies showing different life expectancies for the sexes. A 1984 amendment to ERISA broadened the
conditions under which spouses, whether male or female, receive
retirement benefits and provided that participants in a retirement
plan could take maternity or paternity leave for up to one year
without loss of service credit under the pension plan. During the
remainder of this decade and into the 1990s, there will undoubtedly
be more legislation and court decisions mandating greater equality
in the treatment of male and female employees, as well as court
decisions pertaining to minorities, the older worker, and the handicapped.

Thus, most aspects of human resources management, including
recruitment, selection, promotion, separation, training and development, performance appraisal, compensation, labor relations, and
health and safety management, are affected by federal legislation,
regulations, and rulings. Almost all aspects of human resources
management — including the questions that can be asked in an
employment interview — are now potential areas for litigation. We
will go into more detail in subsequent chapters.

SUMMARY

Many environmental, organizational, and cultural influences affect human resources management. We have grouped these forces into three major categories: the nature of today's work force, influences of the external environment, and regulatory measures.

Members of today's work force are better educated, have higher aspirations about participation, and have more expectations about due process in the work situation. Some segments of the work force are more likely to find collective action such as unionization acceptable than in the past. Because lifestyles and life circumstances are changing, there is more concern about the balance between work and leisure. The major increase in the number of women in the work force, including mothers with children under 18 years of age, has given rise to expectations and pressures about work schedules and day-care centers and has intensified concerns about male-female pay differentials. There are also more pressures on organizations to avoid layoffs, to follow environmentally sound practices, and to be concerned about the quality of working life.

Influences on human resources management from the external environment, in addition to those already mentioned, are many. Some of the more salient, which tend to be interrelated, are: the high cost of energy, inflation, intense national and international competition among organizations, successful management practices in other countries, government deregulation of several industries, technological innovations, and deep public and private concerns about productivity and product quality.

Federal legislation and presidential executive orders have had, and continue to have, a profound effect on human resources management. In particular, the Equal Pay Act, the Civil Rights Act, the Age Discrimination in Employment Act, the Equal Employment Opportunity Act, and the Vocational Rehabilitation Act have given women, minorities, the older worker, and the handicapped worker greater protection against discrimination in human resources practices. An executive order requires affirmative action programs in firms having federal contracts. The Occupational Safety and Health Act helped establish mandatory safety and health standards for work organizations, and the Employee Retirement Income Security Act (ERISA) was designed to protect employees covered by private pension plans.

In recent years, Supreme Court decisions have also had a major influence on human resources management. Many decisions have been aimed at reducing discrimination and eliminating racial imbalance in the work force. Many others have dealt with the disparate treatment of men and women in pay and benefits.

KEY TERMS

participation   deregulation   discrimination
due process   productivity   affirmative action
quality of work life

REVIEW QUESTIONS

1. What are some of the major changes in the lifestyles and attitudes of the work force that affect human resources management today?
2. List, and briefly explain, eight criteria for analyzing the quality of work life in an organization.
3. Describe the impact of economic conditions and international competition on the internal environment of American organizations.
4. Identify the major federal laws and executive orders related to fair employment practices and worker protection that have been issued since 1960. How has each affected human resources management?
5. Identify significant Supreme Court decisions related to fair employment and worker protection issued since 1960. How has each affected human resources management?

OPENING CASE QUESTIONS

Case 3.1   Meeting at the Country Inn

1. Why do you think Doug McLennan chose to hold the planning session at the county inn? What made it more conducive to his purpose than holding the meeting in Southwest Telecommunications Equipment boardroom?
2. What impact could such a meeting have on the managers' perceptions of their quality of work life?
3. From a human resources perspective, how can Southwest Telecommunications Equipment compete in the national and international markets and still be sensitive to cost reduction?

Case 3.2   Student or Airline Pilot?

1. What are some of the environmental factors affecting Larry's decision to drop the course?
2. How important are the limits placed on human resources by outside factors (such as unions, government, etc.)?

CASE 3.3   COMMITMENT THROUGH PARTICIPATION

Traditionally in U.S. industry, hourly-wage earners have been managed based on a strategy of control. Jobs have been clearly defined, and standards limmited and rigid, often constrained by adversarial collective bargaining. In this system, employee initiative has seldom had a lot of room to maneuver.

Today, foreign competition and increased employee consciousness of working conditions are undermining the primacy of the control strategy in U.S. industry. Companies in the forefront of efforts to improve productivity are now experimenting with a strategy of trying to instill in workers a commitment to productivity, improved product quality, and the overall economic success of the company. Underpinning this strategy in many cases are organizational efforts to increase employee participation in traditionally management activities.

One attempt to improve productivity through increased worker commitment was undertaken at ALCOA's Tennessee Operations (AT). In 1979, because of its history of poor performance and labor difficulties, AT was threatened by ALCOA's corporate headquarters with disinvestment and possible termination of some operations. In its effort to save the facility, which would require improvements in both productivity and quality, AT's management tackled quality of work life as one of its starting points.

Together, AT's management and labor union representatives implemented a Trust and Cooperation (T&C) Program to bring forth joint worker-management proposals for improving quality of work life and productivity. The program directed individual departments to form T&C committees made up of both managers and union rank-and-filers. The committees were required to address specific issues, such as management-worker communication, for instance, and to present their findings and suggestions to a Union-Management Committee for action. Within about a year and a half, the Union-Management Committee had handled over ninety such issues. By the end of the program's second year, progress had become obvious. Grievances and discipline had declined radically, and extremely significant improvements had occurred in productivity and quality, as well as in cost savings. In consequence, AT regained the confidence of ALCOA's corporate headquarters, which soon approved a plan for upgrading the operation.

However, perhaps the best-known recent effort at increasing worker participation has been Ford Motor Company's Employee Involvement (EI) program. The main flaw that EI was intended to attack was erratic product quality — a traditional pitfall in the auto assembly line environment, where the rapidly

Case Sources: Russell L. Ackoff and William B. Deane, "The Revitalization of ALCOA'S Tennessee Operations," *National Productivity Review,* (Summer 1984): 239–245; "The Old Foreman Is on the Way Out, and the New One Will Be More Important," *Business Week,* April 25, 1983, p. 73; and Richard E. Walton, "From Control to Commitment in the Workplace," *Harvard Business Review,* (March-April 1985): 77–84.

moving line can mezmerize a worker who has barely a minute to perform his or her repetitive task. According to independent research, EI has indeed improved Ford's quality in relation to other U.S. automakers. It has also changed the way line workers and supervisors interact with their jobs and with each other. Smiles have replaced scowls on the assembly line, and the workers, quite simply, feel better about what they are doing.

Under EI, workers and supervisors hold regular meetings to discuss shortcomings on the production floor and try to find remedies. But more to the point, EI continues in day-to-day operations. Formerly, if a worker failed to perform a task correctly, the foreman's reaction was usually hostile and disciplinary. The need to keep the assembly line moving at all costs was the controlling factor. Now the foreman not only collaborates with workers in trying to solve problems on the line but also supports the workers in their use of new stop buttons that halt the line while a defect is corrected. When an employee encounters a problem and pushes the stop button, the foreman quickly goes to that work station, and together, worker and supervisor figure out what adjustments are needed. The whole process usually lasts less than a minute.

Pundits of business believe that programs like those at ALCOA's Tennessee Operations and Ford may be a necessary response if U.S. industy is to remain competitive with foreign producers. But even without that incentive, the evolving expectations of the work force will make worker participation in mangement a major issue in the 1980s.

Discussion Questions

1. How do you think employee participation programs like those at Ford and AT can improve quality of work life?
2. Why would increased participitation increase in worker's commitment to the organization?
3. How can worker participation be a valid concept for assembly line workers when many of them will soon be working alongside robots? Discuss.

part 2

Organizational Considerations in Human Resources Management

This section discusses various factors affecting organizational effectiveness and explores the important role of human resources management with regard to these factors. Chapter 4 presents a model of organizational performance and explains how organizational culture, climate, and leadership are intertwined with personnel activities and the overall success of the organization. Chapter 5 discusses motivation and performance, their relationship to job satisfaction, and the role of human resources management in enhancing the contributions of individuals and groups to desired organizational outcomes. Chapter 6 examines the human resources planning process, emphasizing that human resources needs must be assessed in light of an organization's goals, its overall strategic plan, and the realities of the external environment.

Factors in Organizational Performance

LEARNING OBJECTIVES

- **Identify factors in the external and internal environment of an organization that influence organizational outcomes.**
- **Describe the outcomes that can be used to measure organizational performance.**
- **Explain how the structure of an organization channels behavior.**
- **Explain the significance of management philosophy for human resources management.**
- **Define the catalyst role of the human resources director.**
- **Characterize effective leadership.**
- **Define organizational culture and its components and indicate how it can be assessed.**
- **Define organizational climate and explain the role of human resources management in measuring it.**

CASE 4.1   GLACIER VALLEY BANK

Mary Sue had never worked so hard in her life, but she was enjoying her job as a loan officer at Glacier Valley Bank. It was clear that the president of the bank and Mary Sue's supervisor expected all employees to be particularly sensitive to customer needs. The slogan "the customer comes first" was not a cliché but a reality in the organization, although there were few rules or official guidelines about how to comply with the slogan. The bank officers and supervisors went out of their way to compliment employees when a particularly difficult customer problem was solved well or to pass along customers' expressions of appreciation. Good customer service was also frequently recognized in performance reviews. Further, the open layout of the bank and its decor contributed to the pleasant atmosphere and to the ease with which employees could help customers and each other.

There was a story told from time to time among employees about how the president had opened the bank during a severe blizzard that closed most of the businesses in town so an elderly lady could get an important document out of her safe deposit box. The president, so the story went, had picked up the woman in his four-wheel-drive Jeep, taken her to the bank, allowed her to get the document, and driven her home again. The story was told with some awe, and usually in the context of reminding new employees of the importance of going out of their way to help customers. This didn't mean the bank was easy on loans, but it did mean it would go to great lengths to help a customer solve a problem.

Mary Sue felt she was quite free to use her own initiative and judgment to solve customer problems, and she liked this freedom. Another thing she liked about working at the bank was that when problems needed to be solved or changes in procedure were necessary, everyone involved was consulted, and solutions and decisions were usually based on opinions and recommendations agreed to by the group. Even job candidates were interviewed by members of the group in which they might be employed. The president believed strongly in employee participation because, as he said from time to time in branch meetings, "Involved people are committed people."

CASE 4.2   GEORGE'S STYLE

George was tough in meetings. He was the head buyer at Sheldon-Saxon, a large department store in a resort city in Florida. At his regular Thursday morning supervisors' meeting, he always questioned individual supervisors relentlessly. Anyone expected to give a report had better be ready and fully informed or George would be quick to respond with caustic interrogation and sarcastic remarks. Two or three such episodes in a row would almost guarantee such treatment indefinitely, no matter how hard the supervisor tried to reverse the trend. Usually, the person would eventually be eased out of the department, through either transfer or discharge. George was even tougher on the supervisors and even more sarcastic at meetings now that the company was experiencing a severe cash-flow problem.

On several occasions, subordinates had complained about George's behavior to the vice president who was his superior. When they did so, they were rebuffed with comments like, "We back up our managers here," or, "If you can't stand the heat, you should get out of the kitchen." As a result, department members stopped going to George's boss with complaints. Most people were aware through the company grapevine that, under this particular vice president, leadership style varied a great deal from unit to unit. A common problem, however, seemed to be that managers at George's level were unskilled in running meetings. It was generally known that a few departments were much happier places. For example, a buyer who had transferred to the Advertising and Public Relations Department, which reported to a different vice president, commented that her new department seemed like a "happy family" compared with the "chain gang" atmosphere in George's unit.

Tomorrow would be Thursday, and Al, one of the more senior supervisors, was due to give a report. He wasn't ready, but it wasn't his fault. On Monday, George had given him a rush project that had simply eaten up most of his time. Now, with just a few hours to go, Al did not have all the figures he needed to prepare the thorough, sensible progress report he was expected to give. "I could talk to George now and tell him what's happened," Al thought, "but he's likely to give me a lecture on time management and tell me that the world won't wait for the slow folks."

Al stewed about the matter for a while, and then telephoned another supervisor. "Sharon, the Dictator has me caught between a rock and a hard place. Maybe I'm going to have the flu tomorrow. At any rate, can you meet me in the cafeteria? I need some advice."

These two situations give some idea of the factors people consider when evaluating how they feel about their jobs and indicate how these factors are tied to perceptions of the environment within a particular organization. Mary Sue enjoys her job and can identify several reasons why: the supportive approach of management toward employees and customers, the spontaneous rewards for effective customer service, and the involvement of all employees in making changes and decisions. Al feels intimidated by George's leadership tactics, in spite of the fact that he does his best to perform promptly the tasks George assigns him. When assignments conflict, George's tendency to be unsupportive and sarcastic makes it difficult for Al to discuss the conflict with him. Instead, he ponders the idea of calling in sick to avoid George's criticism, and rather than finishing his progress report, he schedules a break with a friend to elicit some support.

This chapter and the next explain how the factors that contribute to an individual's job satisfaction are intertwined with human resources management activities and influence the overall success of an organization. This chapter describes how human resources management affects and is affected by key features of the organization's environment. Chapter 5 discusses individual and group motivation and performance and suggests how human resources management can strengthen both. The discussion begins with an overview of factors related to organizational performance — factors that must be well managed if an organization is to be successful.

A MODEL OF ORGANIZATIONAL PERFORMANCE

Figure 4.1 is a model of the factors to which management must pay attention if the organization is to survive and prosper. The model groups these factors into three categories: from left to right, the external environment, the internal (or organizational) environment, and outcomes. These categories are linked by large arrows to indicate that extensive influences flow from the factors on the left to the center and then to the right side of the diagram.

There are reciprocal, or return, influences as well, which are suggested by the arrows at the bottom of the diagram. For example, the executives of an organization (part of the internal environment) may influence regulatory measures (a factor in the external environment) through lobbying of government officials or may support educational and training programs in the community in order to have a steady source of qualified people to employ. The organization's effectiveness (an outcome) in producing goods and services of the quality and price desired in the marketplace influences consumers and creates a level of demand (market response) in the external environment.

A brief description of the three groups of factors shown in the model will clarify what is involved in efforts to improve organizational performance.

The External Environment

The factors shown in the left-hand side of the model are realities of the external environment that influence activities within the organization. Management may have only limited control over these factors, but as Chapter 3 showed, the external environment has a strong impact on organizational life and on human resources policies and procedures in particular. Understanding and coping with the external environment is an important part of any effort to improve organizational performance, and human resources specialists must constantly adapt their activities to these factors.

Among the many human-cultural factors that affect organizational performance are technical and managerial skills and abilities. Knowledge about the Japanese and German management practices mentioned in Chapter 3 would be an example. Values people hold about the treatment of others and about the products of a given organization are other human-cultural factors. Still others are attitudes about work and leisure, attitudes about collective action (such as whether one is willing to help form a union), and attitudes about participation in decision making and problem solving.

Another external factor is the technology available in the society. This includes not only equipment, such as the microcomputer or the robot, but also techniques for using the equipment, and the theoretical and applied knowledge behind it.

The cost and availability of natural resources is another impor-

FIGURE 4.1 A model of organizational performance

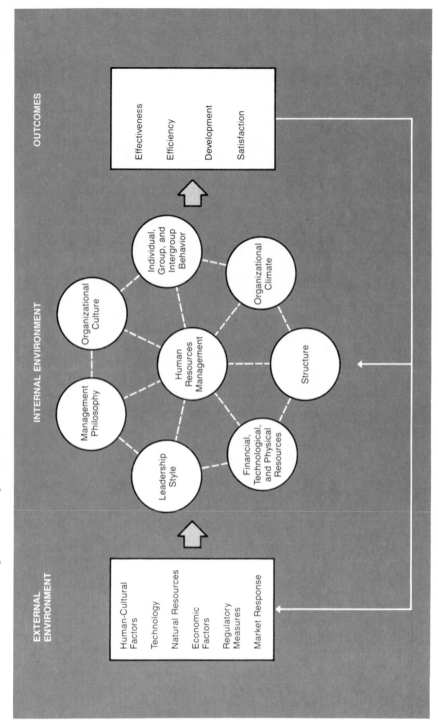

tant external factor affecting what the organization does and how well it performs. Economic factors of importance include markets (the number of people wanting a certain product), the purchasing power that people have, the level of employment and unemployment, and the competition that exists for markets and resources. Regulatory measures — laws, court decisions, and administrative regulations — also influence how organizations function and have particularly strong implications for human resources management. (The previous chapter listed numerous laws and other regulatory measures that have a direct influence on practices in human resources management.)

Finally, the response of the marketplace to whatever the organization is producing will affect the firm's profitability and long-term survival. In successful organizations, determining market needs and user reactions are high-priority activities that serve as a basis for establishing goals and making adaptations to suit market preferences.

The Internal Environment

The factors shown in the center of the model are aspects of the organization's internal environment over which management and employees together have a great deal of control. In particular, management has extensive control over the organization's human resources policies and practices; the financial, technological, and physical resources it uses; its structure; management philosophy; and leadership style. Factors that are managed less directly include organizational culture, organizational climate, and motivated behavior and teamwork.

"Human resources management" appears at the center of the model because the effective use of human resources is of primary importance to the organization's survival and long-term success. People form the organization, and people manage the processes that create the product or service for which the organization is in business. In fact, how well these human resources are managed is probably the most critical factor in an organization's overall performance.

The internal factors are connected by dotted lines to symbolize that they all tend to affect or interact with each other; these interactions are discussed in detail later in this chapter. For now, it is enough to say that for an organization to be highly successful, *all* these internal factors must be intelligently and harmoniously managed.

Outcomes

The factors shown in the right-hand side of Figure 4.1 are **organizational outcomes,** or consequences. These outcomes represent four measures of performance that are useful in evaluating the success of an organization:

Effectiveness, perhaps the most important outcome, can be defined as the extent to which organizational goals are achieved. An example of effectiveness in a successful organization is the production and sale of high-quality bicycles that meet the profit and market goals established by top management. In evaluating effectiveness, it is important to assess the extent to which the goals of individual workers and of groups of workers are in line with overall organizational goals. Thus, individual effectiveness is the extent to which an individual contributes to the attainment of organizational goals, and group effectiveness is the extent to which group goals are achieved in the context of reaching the organization's goals.

Efficiency involves weighing a desired outcome against the resources used to achieve that outcome. It is the ratio of outputs to inputs, or benefits to costs. An organization can be effective in meeting major goals and, at the same time, terribly inefficient (that is, very wasteful). Or an organization can be efficient in doing something other than achieving its goals, in which case it is ineffective.[1] In 1982 and 1983, when U.S. Steel was losing $1.5 billion in its steel operations, numerous managers were resisting cost-cutting measures, including the termination of unnecessary employees at all levels. This prompted the manager of the company's Fairfield Works to say, "Fairfield is a profit center, not an employment center."[2] To exaggerate, the plant had become efficient at hiring and retraining unnecessary people rather than in reaching its goals, which included making a profit.

Development is the extent to which individual employees, groups of workers, and the total organization are developing in their capacity to meet future opportunities and challenges. This outcome is very important to the long-term survival of the organization. It is quite possible to reach short-term goals, such as attaining a certain level of profits, but so seriously deplete human resources that the organization falters and ultimately goes bankrupt. This can happen if insufficient attention is paid to such matters as hiring, training, and giving people the opportunity to assume broader responsibilities.

Participant satisfaction refers to employees' emotional responses to aspects of work or to work itself. The satisfaction of individuals is important, but so is the collective satisfaction of individuals in groups and in the organization as a whole. High performance is not likely to result from focusing solely on employee satisfaction, but ignoring this factor is to risk some highly negative consequences, such as inability to retain valuable employees or to recruit desired talent.

To contribute effectively to overall organizational success, top executives, all managers and supervisors, and, ideally, all employees need to maintain an awareness of *all* the factors identified in Figure 4.1. Human resources management, as a field of study and as a professional area of practice, must be especially concerned with these factors and their interrelationships. Factors in the external environment must be accommodated, perhaps even influenced; the internal factors must be intelligently and harmoniously managed; and the outcomes must be evaluated continuously to determine the extent to which the organization is successful. Of particular significance is the way factors in the internal environment influence the design and implementation of human resources systems. It is therefore worthwhile to examine these internal factors one at a time.

HUMAN RESOURCES MANAGEMENT

The knowledge and skills of managers and all employees in an organization — and the extent to which these are used — will have a major influence on the organization's effectiveness. Further, the way in which this knowledge and these skills are melded into high motivation and teamwork in the pursuit of organizational goals is particularly important.

Thus, in human resources management we need to think not only about individual performance, but about the performance of people in twos — such as the interaction of a supervisor and a subordinate, or an employee and a customer — in groups — such as work groups, task forces, and project teams — and between groups or units, such as the interactions between manufacturing and marketing personnel. Further, we need to think not only about the quality of those relationships, but about how they are influenced by human resources management. For example, at the Glacier Valley Bank described in Case 4.1, good customer relationships were recognized and rewarded through the performance appraisal system, thus reinforcing effective employee-customer interactions. The Sheldon-Saxon department store desperately needed some kind of an appeal procedure supported by top management — or at least an agreed-upon leadership style — that would permit subordinates to raise and resolve serious concerns. Human resources management in that organization was deficient to that extent, and the organization was that much less effective.

MOTIVATED BEHAVIOR AND TEAMWORK

Motivated behavior represents the extent to which individuals will put their abilities to use on the job, whereas teamwork refers to people's willingness and ability to work together to achieve organizational goals. Group and intergroup behavior (relationships among various groups) are significant aspects of teamwork.

Motivated behavior is an important component of the model be-

Perseverance, patience lead to Post-it Notes

When 3Mers hear about 3P, they typically think about the Company's widely acclaimed Pollution Prevention Pays program.

But 3M product development also is often characterized by a kind of 3P: perseverance, patience and, hopefully, eventual payoff.

Such was the case with the invention of 3M's Post-it Note pads.

The product has its genesis in the Company's Central Research Laboratories. In 1970, Dr. Spencer Silver was working to develop an adhesive with greater holding power than anything then available from 3M. Instead of a more aggressive adhesive, Silver's efforts resulted in an adhesive with just the opposite effect: it would stick to objects, but could be easily lifted off and then be repositioned.

While the adhesive wasn't what he was looking for, Silver recognized it offered unique properties and sent samples to researchers in other laboratories to help find possible applications.

For several years, no major uses were discovered. Who needed an adhesive that didn't stick very well? Art Fry, a 3M scientist in the Company's Commercial Tape

Dr. Spencer F. Silver   Arthur L. Fry

Division, helped answer that question. A member of a church choir, Fry was accustomed to using pieces of ordinary scratch paper to find his place in hymnals. Unfortunately, the markers kept falling out, making it difficult to keep his place.

Familiar with Silver's work, Fry coated pieces of paper with a thin layer of the new adhesive. The result: the adhesive-backed markers would hold securely in place, yet lift off without damaging pages of the hymnal.

What followed was the idea of producing pads of adhesive-backed note paper that would do away with the need for paper clips and staples. After successful market testing, the product was introduced nationally in 1980, 10 years after Silver's discovery, and overseas a year later.

In this case, perseverance by 3M researchers, combined with an organizational system attuned to keeping alive new product ideas, contributed to a product that today is one of the hottest-selling office items in the world.

3M

cause the desire and willingness of employees to expend effort to reach higher and higher levels of performance is a critical factor in organizational success. The nature of motivation, what motivates individuals and groups, and what organizations can do to enhance individual and group motivation are complex issues that are dealt with in detail in the next chapter. For now, be aware that motivated behavior and teamwork are complex phenomena that result from the interplay of many forces, including all other features of the internal environment shown in Figure 4.1.

FINANCIAL, TECHNOLOGICAL, AND PHYSICAL RESOURCES

In addition to people, there are other resources organizations use to achieve their goals that affect overall performance. For example, the technology an organization uses will influence its effectiveness and efficiency. If a construction company can use computers to process bidding contracts ten times faster and more accurately than most of its competitors, that company may have a strong competitive edge. If an automobile manufacturer can reduce the costs of welding body frames by ten percent over a two-year period by using robots, such a step may help the company stay in business. (But how the company handles the displacement of those employees who previously did the welding — a human resources matter — may also have both short- and long-term consequences for profitability and survival.) Finally, financial resources are important to organizational success. If the owner or managers of a company cannot raise the money they need to buy necessary equipment and supplies or to employ skilled workers, the organization will be ineffective and may not survive.

STRUCTURE

Structure is another major internal factor that is crucial to organizational performance. **Structure** refers to all the arrangements in an organization through which the activities and behavior of its employees are directed toward desired goals. In most organizations, mechanisms for channeling activities and controlling behavior will include these kinds of formal arrangements:

- *Job design:* the grouping of tasks into particular jobs to establish the way work is to be carried out and the specific requirements of the jobs to be performed.

FIGURE 4.2 **Organizational chart showing hierarchical structure and some of the communication patterns that exist**

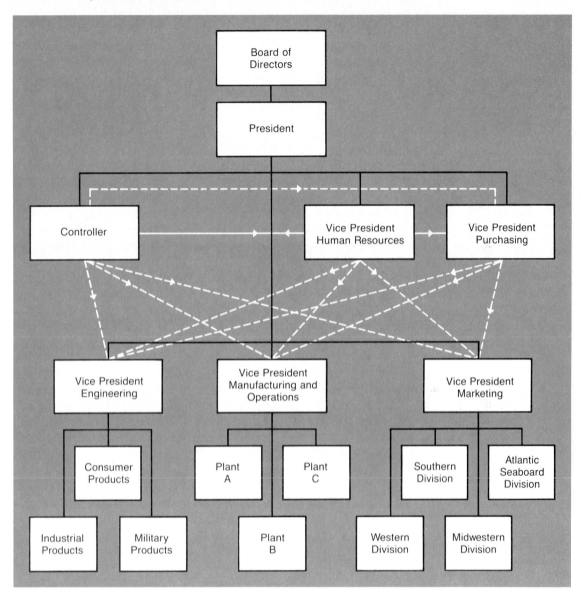

- *Organizational hierarchy:* the grouping of workers into units (such as departments and divisions) and levels that determines who is held accountable to whom. (See Figure 4.2 for an example of an organizational chart showing hierarchical structure and, to some extent, the communication patterns that exist.)

- *Layout and physical arrangements:* the design of the workplace itself, the technology and equipment made available for completing tasks, and other characteristics of the organization's physical environment.
- *Work rules and regulations:* the standardized procedures for controlling, rewarding, and punishing employees' behavior.

All these mechanisms for organizing the workplace affect the interaction among employees and the level of cooperation or conflict among individuals and groups in the organization.

Further, structure strongly affects the overall environment of the organization, which can be a positive or negative influence on desired organizational outcomes. Technology and physical arrangements influence structure in the sense that plant equipment and layout put people in close proximity to some workers while preventing interaction with others. It is difficult to interact face to face with someone who is stationed on the other side of a loud metal-cutting saw or enclosed high up on a mobile crane. A dangerous, excessively noisy, or unpleasant physical environment can have negative effects on efficiency and employee satisfaction. At Glacier Valley Bank in Case 4.1, the open layout of the bank made it easy for employees and customers to interact, a condition favorable to the bank's business.

Some kinds of organization activities require more structure than others. For example, an automobile assembly plant requires more structure than the advertising department of the same company. But not all manufacturing plants need to be structured according to traditional assembly-line technology, in which a worker performs one or a very small number of tasks over and over again. Alternatives in job design, such as job rotation or the formation of self-managed work teams responsible for planning and directing their own work, can minimize structure with positive effects on organizational outcomes.

The degree of structure in an organization is in part a consequence of management philosophy. If a plant manager holds a pessimistic set of assumptions about people, he or she is likely to impose more rules and regulations than if an optimistic set of assumptions is held. (See the discussion of Theory X and Theory Y that follows.) Further, many human resources policies and practices (such as standards for performance evaluation and procedures for handling employee complaints and grievances) channel behavior and so become part of the organization's structure. These policies and practices may be a reflection of a well-thought-out management philosophy, or they may partly shape the structure of the organization without any deliberate planning.

PERSPECTIVE 4.1   Iverson: Smashing the Corporate Pyramid

When F. Kenneth Iverson, chairman and chief executive of Nucor Corp., goes on vacation, he packs survival gear, rents a single-engine plane, and heads for the Alaskan woods or the Australian outback with an old buddy. The solitude, the danger, and the challenge of living far from civilization are an elixir for the 6-ft., 59-year-old Iverson.

Being a loner and doing things his own way are Iverson's major strengths. When he couldn't find a cheap enough domestic supplier 17 years ago, Iverson decided to make steel himself. Using scrap and modern technology, he pioneered the minimill steel industry and challenged giant U.S. Steel Corp. Starting from scratch, Iverson has built an internationally competitive steel company with annual sales of $542 million from within the rot of decaying smokestack America. "I had a real advantage," Iverson says. "I built it the way it should be built." Blubber. He put together his corporate bureaucracy the same way — based on individual achievement. He decentralized decision-making and cut layers out of management blubber. His entire corporate staff consists of 15 people.

There are only three bureaucratic tiers between the chairman and the workers who pour the metal. "Everyone who works lives in some kind of cage," Iverson says. "You can't have anarchy, so I want to set the bars of the cage as far out as possible so every manager has the opportunity to rattle around in his own style."

Iverson epitomizes the egalitarian thrust of the new corporate elite. Every Nucor employee — from the newest production worker to Iverson himself — has the same number of vacation days. Every employee in the plant wears the same color hard hat, a stark contrast to the multicolored hats in big steel factories that correspond to different levels of bureaucracy. "We're trying to eliminate the hierarchy of management," Iverson says.

At the heart of Iverson's drive toward meritocracy is Nucor's incentive pay policy. All employees receive a base pay equivalent to only 50% of what their counterparts make at big integrated steel producers — about $15,000 annually for a steel worker. But production bonuses raise the figure considerably. Last year many hourly workers at all of Nucor's plants earned more than $30,000. All employees also share the pain. In 1983, Iverson earned no incentive pay, and his total compensation fell from $279,360 in 1982 to $106,716.

Yet the "loner" trait in Iverson, which has allowed him to play ministeel's David to Big Steel's Goliath, could return to haunt him. Protectionism for Big Steel can only work against the more efficient minimills. Yet Iverson has no intention of going to Washington to battle against current policy. He prefers building a company, taking wilderness trips, and sitting on a deck watching Chinese geese glide through a lake behind his house.

Source: Scott Seredon, "Iverson: Smashing the Corporate Pyramid," reprinted from the January 21, 1985 issue of *Business Week* by special permission, © 1985 by McGraw-Hill, Inc.

Structure, then, constrains or channels behavior. The design of personnel policies and procedures should take into account the existing structure of the organization, and all managers should be concerned with whether the structure imposed on the workplace enhances or inhibits organizational performance.

MANAGEMENT PHILOSOPHY

A key feature of the environment in any organization is **management philosophy,** the set of ideas and beliefs held by the executives about how people should be managed. Examples of different management philosophies can be seen in Cases 4.1 and 4.2 at the beginning of this chapter. At Glacier Valley Bank, the president's statement that "involved people are committed people" was a strong message to managers and supervisors throughout the organization. It conveyed the president's underlying belief that employee participation in important matters was critical to the organization's success. At Sheldon-Saxon, the vice president's repeated statements that "we back up our managers here" (which also means "we are not going to act on any subordinate's complaints") and "if you can't stand the heat, get out of the kitchen" (which probably means something like "we expect you to accept and adapt to whatever higher management does") were expressions of powerful philosophical attitudes that governed much of his subordinates' behavior.

The philosophy of top management is particularly important because managers and supervisors down through the organization react and adapt to the signals higher management gives off about acceptable supervisory behaviors. For example, if top management believes strongly that employees are to be told exactly what to do with no questions asked, this belief will tend to be acted out down through the organization. If, in contrast, top management believes strongly that employees should have considerable voice in matters concerning their jobs and working conditions, middle and first-line managers will tend to act on this philosophy. Certainly, different management philosophies have very different consequences, particularly for morale and employee development.

Theory X and Theory Y

Douglas McGregor dramatized the impact of management philosophy by analyzing the assumptions managers make about people in organizations. He described two sets of assumptions, Theory X and Theory Y, that are qualitatively different and that lead to distinct leadership behaviors and human resources policies and practices.

A Theory X set of assumptions essentially holds that the average person dislikes work and responsibility, has little ambition, and primarily wants security. Managers who subscribe to Theory X believe that most people need to be directed, controlled, coerced, and threatened with punishment to get them to work toward organizational goals. A Theory Y set of assumptions involves a more positive view of human nature. Theory Y contends that work is as natural as play or rest, that people will exercise self-direction in working toward goals to which they are committed, and that commitment stems from the rewards associated with attaining those goals. In addition, Theory Y asserts that people can learn to accept

"I think it's time we established new guidelines for corporate behavior."

Drawing by Stevenson; © 1981 The New Yorker Magazine, Inc.

and seek responsibility and that most people have more creativity and ingenuity than is usually recognized.[3]

McGregor also described how each of these management philosophies leads to different human resources practices. For example, under Theory X, performance appraisal is very much a top-down process, in which the superior communicates a judgment of the subordinate's performance based on standards established by management. Under Theory Y, performance appraisal can involve more employee participation, with real give-and-take in the review process. Such an approach is far more likely to help both the superior and the subordinate develop their capacities. Compensation practices also reflect different managerial assumptions. Traditional wage plans are consistent with Theory X, while participative incentive systems, in which employees share the benefits of increased profits or savings, reflect Theory Y assumptions.

According to McGregor, Theory X underlies traditional "principles of management" that have tended to dominate managerial literature as well as much of the managerial strategy in business and industry. Theory Y, on the other hand, is consistent with recent research in behavioral science and shows promise of stimulating much more individual growth and development than has been possible under Theory X.[4]

Corporate Philosophy Statements

In most organizations, management philosophy must be inferred from what managers say and do. In some organizations, however, philosophy statements have been developed and published, and these serve as guides to managerial behavior throughout the organization.

For example, at Hewlett Packard the statement of corporate objectives includes the following remarks about "Our People":

> The company has been built around the individual, the personal dignity of each, and the recognition of personal achievements . . . the opportunity to share in the success of the company is evidenced by our above-average wage and salary level, our profit sharing and stock purchase plans. . . . The objective of job security is illustrated by our policy of avoiding large ups and downs in our production schedules . . .[5]

While formal statements of management philosophy do not guarantee that managers will behave accordingly, experience suggests there is often strong consistency among management philosophy statements, personnel practices, and leadership style. In any event, whether it is written down or must be inferred, management philosophy does seem to have considerable influence on human resources policies and practices.

For example, when the two partners who acquired North American Tool & Die (NATD) developed their management philosophy, they had three objectives in mind. Explicit in their philosophy statement are specific goals, values, and the importance of trust:

> First, we planned to steadily expand our company and raise profits. Our second goal was to share whatever wealth was created. Third, we wanted everyone to feel satisfaction and even have fun on the job. The only way to achieve these goals, we decided, was to create an atmosphere of complete trust between us, the owners, and all our employees.[6]

The compensation practices and leadership behaviors at NATD show clear links to this management philosophy. Each year NATD *gives* shares of stock to each employee under an employee stock ownership plan. In addition, the company provides cash bonuses to employees who offer innovative and worthwhile suggestions. Top management works hard to build and maintain trust by carrying out its commitments, keeping everyone informed through plant-wide meetings held on company time and involving all employees, and walking through the plant at least two or three times a week to chat informally with employees.[7]

North American Tool & Die has been highly successful. According to the partners, in three years the company increased sales from $1.8 to $6 million, increased pretax earnings 600 percent, doubled productivity, reduced the customer reject rate from 5 percent to 0.3 percent, reduced employee turnover from 27 percent to 6 percent, and, in the words of the president, "We've all had a good time." The partners attribute these successes to their belief that "a company's most important asset is its employees" and that management should act accordingly.[8]

Implications for the Human Resources Director

Management philosophy is a powerful influence in the organizational environment and can dramatically affect the design of human resources systems. But if the top management group is unaware of its own philosophy, management practices at all levels may be unguided or whimsical and will certainly be less than optimally effective. This suggests a special responsibility for the human resources director: that is, he or she may serve as a *catalyst,* one who initiates a discussion within the executive group to reach agreement about management philosophy. It is the human resources director who can raise questions such as the following:

- What is our philosophy of management and what assumptions about people underlie it?
- If we disagree on philosophy, how can we reconcile these differences?
- If our philosophy is inadequate or incorrect, what should it be?
- How can we translate our philosophical attitudes into concrete organizational objectives?
- Do our present human resources policies and supervisory procedures reflect this philosophy?
- How can we communicate our management philosophy effectively?

Dealing directly with such issues can help unify management efforts within an organization. Open discussions can raise the awareness of all who share responsibility for effective use of the organization's human resources. But what if the human resources director's philosophy is substantially different from the philosophy of other top managers? Then he or she is in the difficult position of having to persuade others to change their thinking or trying to change his or her own. If either approach fails, the person needs to find an organization where his or her views will be more compatible. Practically, however, in most situations the human resources director has been selected partly because top managers believe the person has a philosophy that is congruent with theirs or that will constructively balance many of the prevailing beliefs and attitudes.

LEADERSHIP STYLE

A constructive leadership style that furthers cooperation and productive group effort is critical to effective organizational performance. **Leadership** is the process of influencing the behavior of others in the direction of a goal or set of goals. Effective leadership in organizations is the process of influencing individual and group behavior toward the attainment of organizational goals.

The Nature of Effective Leadership

Although the nature of effective leadership has been debated extensively over the years — and is still being debated — there is substantial agreement about most of the following conclusions.

Traits and Behaviors. It was once believed that certain personal traits, such as intelligence, physical attractiveness, and self-confidence, differentiated leaders from nonleaders. A massive amount of research was conducted in an attempt to identify special leadership traits. However, as researchers found they were not successful in identifying consistently useful leadership traits, they began to turn their attention to the actual behaviors and actions of leaders. The goal became one of gaining insight into the different factors affecting successful and less successful leadership.[9]

It is now generally believed that *effective leadership requires a mixture of traits and behaviors.* Effective leadership requires intelligence, alertness, and insight regarding the tasks to be performed as well as into the feelings of the persons performing the tasks. Effective leadership requires behaviors such as giving instructions, suggesting new procedures, supplying information, and providing encouragement and support. Another way of saying this is that effective leadership requires an appropriate blend of **production-centered behavior,** such as assigning tasks, establishing deadlines, and reviewing deficient work, and **employee-centered behavior,** such as being friendly and approachable, listening to subordinates, and involving them in planning or decision making.[10]

Situational Forces. A second conclusion about leadership is that *the appropriate blend of leadership behaviors depends on various conditions or forces present in the situation.* Among these might be the nature of the tasks to be performed or the technology being used. For example, some kinds of manufacturing require more structure and less participation than do research laboratories.[11]

One analysis of leadership, now considered a classic, advances the idea that effective leadership requires assessing the forces in the situation before choosing an appropriate leadership style. Leadership behavior is seen on a continuum from maximum use of authority by the manager — for example, the manager simply makes a decision and announces it — to considerable freedom for subordinates (see Figure 4.3).[12]

Forces that a manager should consider in deciding how to lead are seen as falling into three categories: forces in the manager, forces in the subordinates, and forces in the situation (see Table 4.1). The manager should consider his or her personal qualities: his or her feelings, values, and leadership strengths. Does he or she feel sufficient trust in subordinates? How well does he or she accept uncertainties? The manager should also consider the forces influencing subordinates. How knowledgeable are they about the situation or the problem? Are they interested in solving problems and are they able and willing to take on responsibility? Other important considerations include their need for independence, their understanding of and identification with the goals of the organization, and their expectancies about sharing in decision making. Once all of these factors have been identified and analyzed, the manager must consider forces in the situation itself. What are the skills needed to address the situation and what are the time constraints, if any? How well do the subordinates work together as a group? Another important factor is the organization itself. How do the values and traditions of the organization impact on the situation? Careful analysis of all of these forces is important in determining the most appropriate leadership approach.[13]

Interaction and Participation. A third conclusion, widely shared, and implied by the discussion thus far, is that *effective leadership is an interactive process.* Leadership does not occur in isolation but in interaction with others. Thus, it is important to understand and improve on those interactions. An important aspect of this interactive process is participation.

A fourth conclusion about leadership that can be drawn from research and theory is that *participation by subordinates in attempts to remove barriers to productivity, quality, and cooperation tends to have beneficial results in terms of organizational out-*

FIGURE 4.3   Continuum of manager-nonmanager behavior

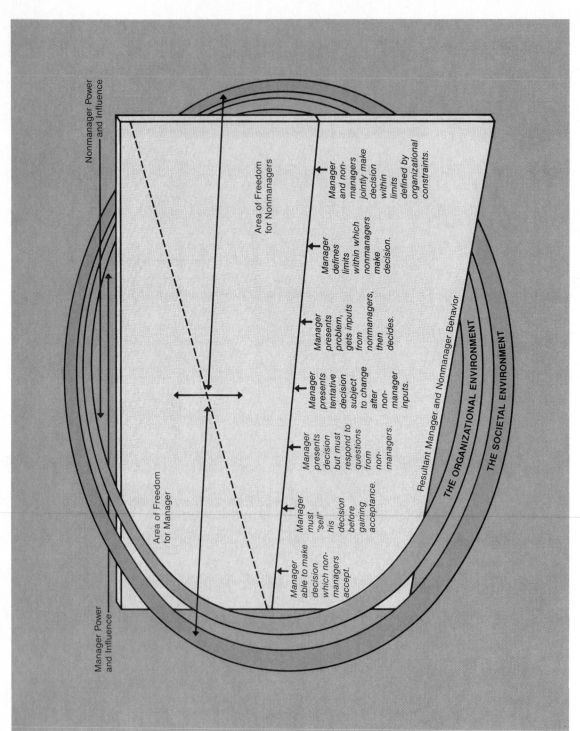

Source: Reprinted by permission of the Harvard Business Review. An exhibit from "How to Choose a Leadership Pattern," by Robert Tannenbaum and Warren Schmidt (May/June 1973). Copyright 1973 by the President and Fellows of Harvard College; all rights

TABLE 4.1 Forces influencing leadership style

FORCES IN THE MANAGER	FORCES IN THE SUBORDINATE	FORCES IN THE SITUATION
Own value system	Need for independence	Values and traditions of the organization
Confidence in subordinates	Readiness to assume responsibility	How effectively the subordinates work together
Own leadership inclinations	Tolerance of uncertainty	The nature of the problem
Tolerance of uncertainty	Degree of interest in the problem	Time pressure
	Understanding and identification with the goals of the organization	
	Knowledge and experience	
	Expectations about participation	

Source: Reprinted by permission of the Harvard Business Review. Adapted from pp. 95–101 of "How to Choose a Leadership Pattern," by Robert Tannenbaum and Warren Schmidt (May/June 1973). Copyright © 1973 by the President and Fellows of Harvard College; all rights reserved.

comes. These outcomes include productivity and satisfying human needs for autonomy, a sense of accomplishment, and interaction with others in accomplishing tasks.[14] Some research studies reach less optimistic conclusions about participation,[15] but there is an explanation for this. Participation is of different kinds and quality. Therefore, studies that do not define and describe the exact nature of that participation are bound to produce mixed results.[16] A major review of the research on participation concludes with these summary remarks:

> Decades of research show conclusively that given half a chance — with competent implementation under appropriate circumstances — participative management can assuredly benefit organizations in terms of hard criteria of performance and productivity. . . . Participative management also has important benefits for workers, in terms of satisfying the. . . primary human work needs of autonomy, . . . the opportunity to derive feelings of accomplishment from the completion of meaningful work, and interaction with others in the context of accomplishing a task.[17]

Team Versus One-on-One Leadership. A fifth conclusion about leadership — a point that is not widely recognized in the literature — is that *it is important to make a distinction between a team leadership style and a one-on-one form of leadership.* Much of the research and theory on leadership and participation does not make this distinction. Some managers meet frequently with their sub-

FIGURE 4.4   **One-on-one (left) and team (right) leadership patterns**

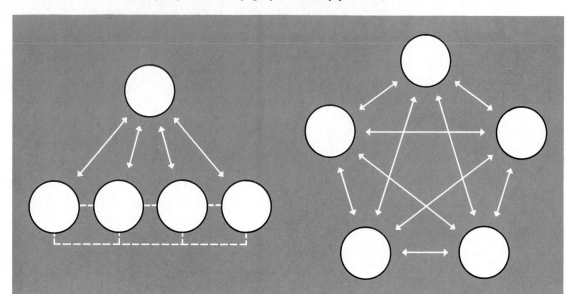

ordinates as a group; others seldom, if ever, do so. Some managers think of their subordinates as an interdependent team; others think of them as a collection of individuals who report to a common superior. Figure 4.4 diagrams these two forms of leadership.

The dynamics of these two styles of leadership are quite different. To illustrate, a group of people whose jobs are interdependent and who never get together to discuss mutual problems must rely on their supervisor to be the link between them. Or, they must rely on informal communications among peers. In both circumstances, the people who might well contribute to the solution of some problem are probably not all present. Never meeting together might make some sense if there were so much conflict between two or more subordinates that they had to be kept apart; yet this absence of group discussion occurs in some organizations even when there is no such conflict. Of course, both approaches are used in most organizations, but in widely varying proportions.

Shared Leadership.   A sixth conclusion about leadership comes out of the group dynamics field: *effective group or team leadership requires a sharing of responsibility between the formal leader and all of the members of the group in carrying out effective task behaviors and those behaviors that relate to the emotional life of the group.* (The formal leader is the person who has been assigned or elected to the leader or supervisory role.) In short, effective team leadership is a shared process. For example, providing information and encouragement cannot be assumed to be the sole responsibility of the formal leader.

Implications for Human Resources Management

These conclusions about leadership have implications for several areas of human resources management:

Staffing. Selection and promotion practices need to take into account the traits and behaviors required for successful leadership in the particular setting. For example, in selecting supervisors, fewer participatory skills may be required if the job is supervising workers on an assembly line rather than self-managed work teams. Someone supervising untrained workers is likely to need greater skills in assigning tasks, training, and reviewing deficient work than someone supervising highly skilled subordinates.

Training and Development. Programs in training and development need to help supervisors and managers acquire a range of leadership skills that can be used under changing circumstances. Participatory leadership skills, in particular, are important in today's organizations. In addition, to the extent that organizational performance depends on effective team leadership and interaction, all team members should be trained in effective team behaviors. Many contemporary organizations have recognized this. For example, factories in which self-managed teams are used tend to involve all team members in team skills training, including group decision making. Organizations that use quality circles tend to give quality circle groups some training in group dynamics and team decision making.

General Design of Personnel Systems. Some personnel systems can be designed in such a way that they reinforce a team leadership approach, or they may be designed to support a participative or directive, controlling approach. For example, an individual incentive system may get in the way of a team leadership approach by encouraging competition among employees. A plant-wide productivity plan that makes extensive use of task forces, by contrast, may emphasize participation and cooperation. Or, a performance appraisal procedure may be so directive that it creates resentment among subordinates and becomes an obstacle to effective participation at other times.

PERSPECTIVE 4.2 Fitting Employees into the Company Culture

What corporate strategy was in the 1970s, corporate culture is becoming in the 1980s. Companies worry about whether theirs is right for them, consultants hawk advice on the subject, executives wonder if there's anything in it that can help them manage better. A strong culture — a set of shared values, norms, and beliefs that get everybody heading in the same direction — is common to all the companies held up as paragons in the best-seller *In Search of Excellence.*

There is, however, one aspect of culture that nobody seems to want to talk about. This is the process by which newly hired employees are made part of a company's culture. It may be called learning the ropes, being taught "the way we do things here at XYZ Corp.," or simply training. Almost no one calls it by its precise social-science name — socialization. . . .

The crux of the dilemma is this: We are opposed to the manipulation of individuals for organizational purposes. At the same time we increasingly realize that a degree of social uniformity enables organizations to work better. One need not look to Japan to see the benefits of it. Many of the great American companies that thrive from one gener-

Source: Excerpted from Richard Pascale, "Fitting New Employees into the Company Culture," *Fortune,* May 28, 1984, pp. 28–41. © 1984 Time Inc. All rights reserved.

ation to the next — IBM, Procter & Gamble, Morgan Guaranty Trust — are organizations that have perfected their processes of socialization. Virtually none talk explicitly about socialization; they may not even be conscious of precisely what they are doing. Moreover, when one examines any particular aspect of their policy toward people — how they recruit or train or compensate — little stands out as unusual. But when the pieces are assembled, what emerges is an awesome internal consistency that powerfully shapes behavior.

It's time to take socialization out of the closet. If some degree of it is necessary for organizations to be effective, then the challenge for managers is to reconcile this necessity with traditional American independence.

Probably the best guide available on how to socialize people properly is what the IBMs and the P&Gs actually do. . . .

The New York investment banking house of Morgan Stanley encourages people it is thinking of hiring to discuss the demands of the job with their spouses, girlfriends, or boyfriends — new recruits sometimes work 100 hours a week. The firm's managing directors and their wives take promising candidates and their spouses or companions out to dinner to bring home to them what they will face.

Interaction with Other Managers.   Finally, the human resources director and his or her professional staff need to exercise effective leadership in planning, developing, and managing the various human resources systems in the organization. Because authority in human resources matters is shared with others, effective interaction with top managers and supervisors at all levels is essential.

ORGANIZATIONAL CULTURE

Another factor in the internal environment that is crucial in organizational performance is **organizational culture.** This concept is widely discussed in business and industry today, but frequently it is not well defined.

The point is to get a person who will not be happy within Morgan's culture because of the way his family feels to eliminate himself from consideration for a job there. . . .

Someone going to work for Delta Air Lines will be told again and again about the "Delta family feeling." Everything that's said makes the point that Delta's values sometimes require sacrifices — management takes pay cuts during lean times, senior flight attendants and pilots voluntarily work fewer hours per week so the company won't have to lay off more-junior employees. Candidates who accept employment with Delta tend to buy into this quid pro quo, agreeing in effect that keeping the Delta family healthy justifies the sacrifices that the family exacts.

All companies have their stories, but at corporations that socialize well the morals of these stories all tend to point in the same direction. In the old Bell System, story after story extolled Bell employees who made heroic sacrifices to keep the phones working. The Bell folklore was so powerful that when natural disaster struck, all elements of a one-million-member organization were able to pull together, cut corners, violate normal procedures, even do things that would not look good when measured by usual job performance criteria — all in the interest of restoring phone service. Folklore, when well understood, can legitimize special channels for moving an organization in a hurry. . . .

What about the cost of conformity? A senior vice president of IBM asserts: "Conformity among IBM employees has often been described as stultifying in terms of dress, behavior, and lifestyle. There is, in fact, strong pressure to adhere to certain norms of superficial behavior, and much more intensely to the three tenets of the company philosophy — respect for the dignity of the individual, first-rate customer service, and excellence. These are the benchmarks. Between them there is wide latitude for divergence in opinions and behavior."

A P&G executive echoes this thought: "There is a great deal of consistency around here in how certain things are done, and these are rather critical to our sustained success. Beyond that, there are very few hard and fast rules. People on the outside might portray our culture as imposing lock-step uniformity. It doesn't feel rigid when you're inside. It feels like it accommodates you. And best of all, you know the game you're in — you know whether you're playing soccer or football; you can find out very clearly what it takes to succeed and you can bank your career on that."

Organizational culture consists of those values, beliefs, assumptions, myths, norms, and goals that are widely shared in the organization. A *value* is something that is prized or esteemed. An example is IBM's adherence to "respecting the decency of the individual."[18] All members of the organization are expected to share and uphold this value.

A *belief* is a conviction that something is true. To illustrate, Edward M. Carson, then president of the First Interstate Bank of Arizona and subsequently president of First Interstate Bankcorp, articulated the belief that "people are a bank's most valuable assets, and if you treat them right, you'll be successful."[19] Although this belief is part of management philosophy, it becomes a facet of organizational culture when all employees come to hold this belief and act accordingly. An *assumption* is something that is taken for granted and is similar to a belief, although it is less likely to be stated with such certainty. It may not be stated at all, but simply held in people's heads. An example was the assumption held by the executives and employees of Continental Illinois National Bank just prior to its near collapse in 1984 that "we're too big and important to go under."[20] A *myth* is a legendary or traditional story that may be true, half-true, or fictional and keeps recurring. An example was the commonly repeated story within Allied armies before World War II that the Maginot Line — a line of concrete fortifications across the border between France and Germany — was impregnable. A *norm* is an unwritten rule or standard about how people should behave. For example, well-rehearsed stand-up presentations using flip-chart displays appear to be the norm at IBM for presenting proposals or analyses of problems.[21] A *goal* is a stated purpose or desired result toward which people aspire. In sum, the cluster of values, beliefs, assumptions, myths, norms, and goals that are widely shared in an organization make up that organization's culture.

Overlap with Management Philosophy

The concept of organizational culture, although broader than the concept of management philosophy, overlaps it in two ways. First, organizational culture includes management philosophy — the latter consisting largely of management's assumptions and beliefs. Second, management philosophy has a profound effect on the culture of the organization, largely because subordinates tend to be strongly influenced by the way management thinks. In reviewing the policy statements of the Dana Corporation, for example, one can assume that the company has a strong culture reflecting its management philosophy (see Figure 4.5).

Variability

Organizations, and sometimes subdivisions within them, can differ markedly in their cultures. We can infer, for example, that the culture of Glacier Valley Bank (Case 4.1) was distinctly different from the culture at Sheldon-Saxon (Case 4.2). The culture at Glacier Valley Bank was pervasive throughout the organization. Attention to customer and employee needs was reflected in all the bank's practices and even its atmosphere. At Sheldon-Saxon there was apparently no consistent culture. Depending on the department

FIGURE 4.5 **Dana Corporation's policy statements reflect management philosophy**

 **POLICIES**

EARNINGS

The purpose of the Dana Corporation is to earn money for its shareholders and to increase the value of their investment. We believe the best way to do this is to earn an acceptable return by properly utilizing our assets and controlling our cash.

GROWTH

We believe in steady growth to protect our assets against inflation. We will grow in our selected markets by implementing our market strategies.

PEOPLE

We are dedicated to the belief that our people are our most important asset. Wherever possible, we encourage all Dana people within the entire world organization to become shareholders, or by some other means, own a part of their company.

We believe people respond to recognition, freedom to participate, and the opportunity to develop.

We believe that people should be involved in setting their own goals and judging their own performance. The people who know best how the job should be done are the ones doing it.

We endorse productivity plans which allow people to share in the rewards of productivity gains.

We believe in stability of employment. We believe that all Dana people should identify with the company. This identity should carry on after they have left active employment.

We believe that wages and benefits are the concern and responsibility of managers. The Management Resource Program is a worldwide matter — it is a privilege of all career Dana people. We endorse and encourage income protection, health programs, and education.

We believe that on-the-job training is an effective method of learning. A Dana manager must prove proficiency in at least one line of our company's work — marketing, engineering, manufacturing, financial services, etc. Additionally, these people must prove their ability as supervisors and be able to get work done through other people. We recognize the importance of gaining experience both internationally and domestically.

We believe our people should move across product, discipline, and organizational lines. These moves should not conflict with operating efficiency.

We believe in promoting from within. Career people interested in other positions are encouraged to discuss job opportunities with their supervisor.

Managers are responsible for the selection, education and training of all people.

All Dana career people should have their job performance reviewed at least once a year by their supervisors.

We believe in providing programs to support the Dana Style. We encourage professional and personal development of all Dana people.

PLANNING

We believe in planning at all levels.

The Policy Committee is responsible for developing the corporate strategic plan.

Each operating unit within its regional organization is responsible for a detailed five-year business plan. These business plans must support the corporate strategic plan and market strategies. These plans are reviewed annually with the Policy Committee.

Commitment is a key element of the Dana Management Style. This commitment and performance will be reviewed on a monthly basis by the appropriate regional operating committee and on a semi-annual basis during Mid-Year Reviews.

ORGANIZATION

We discourage conformity, uniformity and centralization.

We believe in a minimum number of management levels. Responsibility should be pushed as far into the organization as possible.

Organizational structure must not conflict with doing what is best for all of Dana.

We believe in small, highly effective, support groups to service specialized needs of the Policy Committee and the world organization at large as requested. We believe in task forces rather than permanent staff functions.

We do not believe in company-wide procedures. If an organization requires procedures, it is the responsibility of the manager to create them.

This organizational environment stimulates initiative and innovation. It develops the entrepreneurial expertise that is the cornerstone of our success.

CUSTOMERS

Dana is a market-oriented company. We supply products and services to fulfill the needs of our selected markets.

We are dedicated to the belief that we have a responsibility to be leaders in our selected markets.

We believe it is absolutely necessary to anticipate our customers' needs for products and services of the highest quality. Once a commitment is made to a customer, every effort must be made to fulfill that obligation.

It is highly desirable to maintain a balance between in-house activity and outsourcing. This balance protects the stability of employment for our people. It also protects our assets and assures performance to our customers.

The Policy Committee is responsible to know our customers and their needs.

COMMUNICATION

We will communicate regularly with shareholders, customers, Dana people, general public, and financial communities.

It is the job of all managers to keep Dana people informed. Each manager must decide on the best method of communication. We believe direct communication with all of our people eliminates the need for a third party involvement. All managers shall periodically inform their people about the performance and plans of their operation.

CITIZENSHIP

The Dana Corporation will be a good citizen worldwide. We will do business in a professional and ethical manner.

Laws and regulations have become increasingly complex. The laws of propriety always govern. The General Counsel and each General Manager can give guidance when in doubt about appropriate conduct. It is expected that no one would willfully violate the law and subject themselves to disciplinary action.

We encourage active participation of all of our people in community action.

We will contribute to worthwhile community causes consistent with their importance to the good of the community.

The Policy Committee
Dana Corporation

Approved by The Board of Directors
Dana Corporation

10/28/69   Rev. 9/20/83

Source: Dana Corporation Toledo, Ohio.

and its manager, the culture could be open and employee-centered or oppressive and authority-centered.

Organizational culture is somewhat difficult to pin down or measure, but can often be inferred from immersion in it and observation of what people say, write, and, in particular, do. At Glacier Valley Bank, the high priority given customer needs was not only spoken about and acted on, it was also reinforced by the reward system. From time to time the president articulated his belief that "involved people are committed people," and we can infer that this belief was widely shared in the organization. An underlying assumption undoubtedly was that employee commitment is related to organizational success. Another aspect of the bank's culture could be sensed in the story about the president's opening the bank for the elderly woman during a blizzard. Whether true or not, the story conveyed the high value bank employees placed on service to customers.

Need for Analysis

Whether a particular cultural aspect of an organization is beneficial or harmful depends on the extent to which that aspect is useful throughout the organization. In Case 4.2, the beliefs or assumptions about people that caused George to belittle and humiliate his staff may have satisfied George's power needs, but they were very harmful to departmental morale and productivity.

It is important for the people in an organization — the top managers and the human resources people, in particular — to be analytical and concerned about the culture of their organization. Specifically, it is important to keep in mind questions like these:

- How is the basic culture of the organization — the shared values, beliefs, assumptions, myths, norms, goals — affecting the organization's performance?
- In what way is the culture being reflected in human resources policies and practices?
- Are personnel policies and practices creating a certain kind of culture?
- Are personnel policies and practices congruent with — or inconsistent with — the desired broader culture of the organization?
- Which aspects of that culture are useful and beneficial, and which hinder organizational success?

The reason it is important for human resources directors — and all managers — to be concerned and analytical about organizational culture is that people and organizations can become victims of organizational culture rather than masters of it. Unless organization members understand and actively shape the culture, highly dysfunctional aspects can emerge. For example, an organization can gradually drift into a situation in which there is very little recognition or support, very little training and opportunity for development, an absence of trust, distorted communications, and so on. Some of these conditions had emerged at the Sheldon-Saxon department store. If such conditions were to become pervasive in that organization, it is very likely that profits and other success measures would decline.

We will now turn to a practical means of measuring some aspects of organizational culture. Culture can be examined through in-depth interviews, discussions, and observations that reveal values, beliefs, assumptions, and so on, but some aspects can also be measured through the use of "organizational climate" questionnaires.

ORGANIZATIONAL CLIMATE

Organizational climate, another major factor in organizational performance, is heavily influenced by, and interacts with, the human resources practices in organizations. **Organizational climate** can be defined as the measurable, collective perceptions of organization members about those aspects of their working life that affect their motivation and behavior — in particular, the culture of the organization, the prevailing leadership style, the degree of structure, and the personnel policies and practices.[22]

Climate surveys are questionnaires used to measure individual perceptions of the prevailing climate in the organization. Although climate is usually measured for the entire organization or a major division, scores are typically calculated by departments as well so that management can assess the climate in different units. The human resources department ordinarily coordinates the entire procedure, from obtaining or designing the questionnaire, to administering the questionnaire and tabulating the results, to helping managers and groups use the results in constructive ways.

Although climate surveys vary in content, a typical one would ask employees to indicate their perceptions or feelings about these kinds of categories:

1. *Structure:* the feeling that employees have about the constraints on the group, how many rules, regulations, procedures there are; is there an emphasis on "red tape" and going through channels, or is there a loose and informal atmosphere?

2. *Responsibility:* the feeling of being your own boss; not having to double-check all your decisions; when you have a job to do, knowing that it is *your* job.
3. *Reward:* the feeling of being rewarded for a job well done; emphasizing positive rewards rather than punishments; the perceived fairness of the pay and promotion policies.
4. *Risk:* the sense of riskiness and challenge in the job and in the organization; is there an emphasis on taking calculated risks, or is playing it safe the best way to operate?
5. *Warmth:* the feeling of general good fellowship that prevails in the work group atmosphere . . . the prevalence of friendly and informal social groups.
6. *Support:* the perceived helpfulness of the managers and other employees in the group; emphasis on mutual support from above and below.
7. *Standards:* the perceived importance of implicit and explicit goals and performance standards; the emphasis on doing a good job; the challenge represented in personal and group goals.
8. *Conflict:* the feeling that managers and other workers *want* to hear different opinions; the emphasis placed on getting problems out in the open, rather than smoothing them over or ignoring them.
9. *Identity:* the feeling that you belong to a company and you are a valuable member of a working team; the importance placed on this kind of spirit.[23]

A good deal of research suggests that how people perceive the organization on such climate dimensions is related to organizational productivity, profitability, and labor relations. For example, a study of two General Motors plants, Doraville and Lakewood, found that unfavorable climate measures at Lakewood were associated with low productivity and quality, high costs, and poor labor relations. In contrast, favorable climate measures at Doraville were associated with high productivity and quality, low costs, and excellent labor relations.

When the plant manager of Doraville was transferred to Lakewood, he undertook to improve the climate through such means as supervisory training in communications and team building; keeping employees informed about plant operations, costs, and future plans; more direct contact between supervisors and employees; and employee participation in planning changes in work flow, physical arrangements, and job design. Over a three-year period, substantial improvements occurred in organizational climate, productivity, costs, and profits.[24]

If climate surveys were used in the organizations described in the cases at the beginning of this chapter, they would probably reveal wide differences. Employees of Glacier Valley Bank would probably indicate that there was an emphasis on rewards rather than punishment; that there was considerable warmth and support; that standards of performance were high, at least with respect to customer relations; and that employees had strong feelings of identification with the bank. In Case 4.2, on the other hand, George's subordinates would probably indicate on a climate questionnaire that there was too much structure, that they did not feel as if they were their own bosses, that punishment was emphasized more than positive rewards, that playing it safe was the best way to operate, that support was lacking, and that conflict was suppressed.

The consequences of unfavorable climate characteristics include using job time to confer with peers in order to cope, high stress, looking for another job, considering reporting in sick, reduced communications with superiors, and considerable job dissatisfaction. We can infer that the likely consequences of the favorable climate characteristics in Case 4.1 were open problem solving, loyalty, cooperation among peers and across groups, enhanced motivation and satisfaction, and high-quality customer service. We can also infer that top management, with the assistance — or perhaps the leadership — of the human resources department, had formulated a conscious strategy to create and maintain the favorable climate that existed in the bank.

SUMMARY

This chapter has presented a model of the factors that are considered crucial in organizational performance. These factors fall into three categories: external, internal, and outcomes. All are interrelated, and influence or are influenced by human resources management.

The external factors are human-cultural factors, technology, natural resources, economic factors, regulatory measures, and market response. The internal factors are human resources management; financial, technological, and physical resources; structure; organizational climate; motivated behavior and teamwork; organizational culture; management philosophy; and leadership style. The extent to which the organization attains success on measures of organizational performance (outcomes) — effectiveness, efficiency, development, and participant satisfaction — depends heavily on how well the internal factors are managed and how well the organization accommodates to and uses such external factors as available human skills and capabilities, available technology and natural resources, and regulatory measures.

The various kinds of structure — job structure, organizational hierarchy, layout and physical arrangements, and work rules and regulations — constrain and channel behavior. Structure affects interactions among employees and, in turn, efficiency and employee satisfaction. It is important to be alert to the degree to which various structuring mechanisms — including those in human resources management — strengthen or inhibit individual and organizational performance.

Management philosophy about how people should be managed has a powerful effect throughout the organization. The human resources director can serve as a catalyst to discussion within the top management group of the consequences of different philosophies leading to agreement about what philosophy is desirable for the organization.

Effective leadership, the process of influencing individual and group behavior toward the attainment of organizational goals, requires a mix of traits and behaviors appropriate to the conditions or forces present in the situation. Leadership is an interactive process; it can be thought of as a one-on-one process or as a team matter or both. Participation by subordinates tends to have beneficial results, providing the appropriate conditions are present; the leader and subordinates must share responsibility for carrying out task behaviors and behaviors relating to the emotional life of the group. These assertions have a number of implications for human resources management in the areas of staffing, training and development, and the design of personnel techniques and programs generally.

Organizational culture is another internal factor crucial to organizational performance, and one that interacts with human resources management. Human resources directors — and all managers — should be concerned about organizational culture because people and organizations need to be masters of that culture rather than victims of it.

Organizational climate is the measurable, collective perceptions of employees about the culture, leadership style, structure, and personnel policies and practices of an organization. The human resources department usually assists the organization in the use of climate surveys. Research indicates that how people perceive the organization is related to organizational performance.

KEY TERMS

organizational outcomes	structure	employee-centered behavior
effectiveness	management philosophy	organizational culture
efficiency	leadership	organizational climate
development	production-centered behavior	climate survey
participant satisfaction		

REVIEW QUESTIONS

1. Identify factors in the internal environment of an organization that influence organizational outcomes.
2. List, and briefly explain, the outcomes that can be used to measure organizational performance.
3. How does structure channel behavior in an organization? Give examples.
4. Discuss the impact of management philosophy on human resources management.
5. Describe the catalyst role of the human resources director.
6. Describe some of the behaviors that characterize effective leadership.
7. Define organizational culture and its components. How can organizational culture be assessed?
8. Define organizational climate. How can it be measured?

OPENING CASE QUESTIONS

Case 4.1   Glacier Valley Bank

1. What is the basic management philosophy of Glacier Valley Bank?
2. Is the president of the bank a Theory X or Theory Y manager? Explain your answer.
3. What are the implications of the bank's philosophy for the human resources department?
4. What is the organizational climate of the bank?

Case 4.2   George's Style

1. What style of leadership does George demonstrate?
2. What might happen to George's division if he continues in his leadership style?
3. What impact does George's leadership style have on Al?

CASE 4.3   INFLUENCING CORPORATE CULTURE

Companies of all kinds try to create and manipulate corporate culture. An organization's culture can, after all, significantly influence employees and the firm's identity in the marketplace.

One exceptionally successful executive, Jack Kilmartin, who runs Mervyn's stores (a branch of Dayton Hudson's network), believes that he has brought success to his company mainly through the corporate culture he's introduced. With a culture that emphasizes teamwork and employee initiative, Kilmartin feels, Mervyn's has been prepared for growth that doubled its sales revenues in six years and resulted in a projected 16.5-percent yearly expansion into new stores. In addition, Mervyn's stores have established an identity that attracts customers so successfully that many other stores are copying it.

At another firm, Thorneburg Hosiery Company of Statesville, North Carolina, the owner decided to autocratically dictate corporate culture—albeit for decidedly humanistic reasons. Thorneburg Hosiery experienced an eightfold growth in its sales between 1980 and 1985. Yet in 1982, when it was becoming clear how well the company was doing, its head, Jim Thorneburg, was offering $500 "exit bonuses" to any employees who had misgivings about the future shapes of their jobs. Why? Because Thorneburg had decided that if his company was to survive its rapid growth and still be a place where people wanted to work, its organizational culture would have to change. In the new climate that Jim Thorneburg wanted to create, supervisors were to become instructors and counselors. Instead of making subordinates do their jobs, they were to help them do their jobs. For their part, employees were expected to take new responsibility for what they did and for the final product. No longer would supervisors make the decisions about how work was performed; that would now be up to the workers. Thorneburg wanted satisfied employees, and he even hoped to bring them in to share ownership sometime in the future. But he told employees that if the company failed to make his new vision work within two years, he would sell it.

Other, more light-hearted ways of influencing corporate culture have been tried. At Honda's U.S. manufacturing plant in Marysville, Ohio, each new employee plants a pine tree with his or her name on it. The growth in the number of pine trees symbolizes the growth in the number of employees and, thus, the company's growth. Mary Kay, founder of Mary Kay cosmetics, gives leading salespeople pink cadillacs—certainly a showy symbol of her company's cultural style. The *Reader's Digest* Association, in a more practical vein, allows employees to rent space for gardens on company grounds. Such

Case Sources: Holly Klokis, "Kilmartin: Mervyn's Man with the Midas Touch," *Chain Store Age Executive*, April 1985, pp. 19, 20, 25: Sharon Nelton, "Socking It to the Old Style," *Nation's Business*, May 1985, p. 63; Michael Cieply, "Meanwhile, Back in Marysville," *Forbes*, March 12, 1985, p. 127; and Susan Narod, "Off-Beat Company Customs," *Dun's Business Month*, November 1984, pp. 65–66.

practices, although they may not seem crucially related to organizational performance, nonetheless give insight into how a company approaches its employees and its business.

Discussion Questions

1. Why do you think Jack Kilmartin gives so much credit to the corporate culture at Mervyn's stores?
2. Do you see any contradiction in the leadership style that Jim Thorneburg exhibited in implementing his new system?
3. Formulate a statement of management philosophy for Jim Thorneburg.
4. Think about a company where you have worked or that you are familiar with and describe some of the characteristics that help give a sense of its corporate culture.

chapter 5

Motivation and Performance of Individuals and Groups

LEARNING OBJECTIVES

- **Summarize the key theories of motivation and their implications for human resources management.**
- **Describe the relationship among motivation, performance, and satisfaction.**
- **Give several reasons why human resources management should be concerned with employee dissatisfaction.**
- **Explain the importance of work groups in the modern organization.**
- **Identify the role of human resources management in the development of effective work groups.**
- **Explain the consequences of excessive intergroup conflict and competition in the organization, and discuss the implications for human resources management.**

CASE 5.1   THE MERGER

Tom Nelson was a young, college-trained, and ambitious purchasing agent at Lakeview General Hospital in upstate New York. Until recently he had been sure his superiors considered him an excellent employee. His pay increases had been substantially above average, and his boss frequently complimented him on his work. He had been highly motivated and displayed the same enthusiasm for his job that he showed in his competitive handball and volleyball games. Tom liked the area and hoped to stay, having aspirations to move up the ladder to the top administrator's job.

Lately, however, Tom sensed that all was not well. The hospital had been purchased by a private, profit-oriented organization, and there were frequent directives from corporate headquarters that things should be done differently. Some were reasonable, but others seemed to Tom to decrease efficiency and were very irritating. The corporate vice president in charge of purchasing had visited only once, and that brief visit had left the impression that the corporation was going to do most of the talking and very little listening. Tom's boss seemed subdued and preoccupied, and now seldom commented on Tom's work. There had been some speculation that the purchasing function might be consolidated with the purchasing department of another hospital owned by the same corporation. This possibility was not unreasonable, because the other hospital was only 15 miles away. Tom wondered whether he would soon be out of a job.

Tom's coping with the situation took several forms. For one thing, he stopped making proposals that would increase efficiency. Further, he triple-checked his work to make sure there were no mistakes. He had a reputation for being accurate, but now accuracy was becoming almost an obsession. He also stopped volunteering for task forces that the hospital had traditionally used to tackle procedural problems involving several departments.

Tom was aware of the reasons for his changed attitudes and behavior: "If I make a mistake, they'll build up a file to use against me so they can lay me off; if I don't, somebody in headquarters will get the credit anyway; I'm not going to give headquarters any excuse to criticize my work," Tom thought. "And I'm not going to waste my time improving the efficiency of this place when those fools at corporate systematically make things worse. I'm going to lie low for a while and concentrate on my handball game."

CASE 5.2   SOLVING CUSTOMER PROBLEMS AT HYDRAULIC SYSTEMS CORPORATION

Jack Korman, manufacturing director at Hydraulic Systems Corporation, had a problem. Sharon Yee, marketing director, had just phoned with reports from three field representatives. Several newly installed hydraulic activators were malfunctioning, customers were complaining, and the company might lose some important business if the problems weren't corrected immediately.

"How soon can you get the field reps plus some of our customers' engineers together with two or three of my manufacturing people?" Jack asked Sharon.

"That would depend upon where they meet. Denver is central, and one of the customer problems is there. I'll call the customer to see if we can set up a meeting at their Denver plant tomorrow, and we'll fly the others in," responded Sharon.

"Let me know," said Jack. "If you'll give me the names of the reps, I'll have my people get on the phone with them to do some preliminary work before they leave for Denver, and I'll ask my assistant, Joe Stevens, to arrange an agenda with your staff."

After they had hung up, Jack thought to himself, "I'm glad we've got a company-wide bonus plan. It doesn't create cooperation between the marketing staff and my people, but it sure helps."

The meeting with the customers was held in Denver the next day. Three hours beforehand, the marketing and the manufacturing departments met together to share information on the nature of the problem and to plan how to make the meeting with the customers as productive as possible. Joe Stevens presided at both meetings.

At the preliminary meeting, Joe first presented a tentative sequence of items for discussion and then rearranged it, on the basis of suggestions from both the marketing reps and the manufacturing people. The first agenda item was "Field reps' information about the problem." During this part of the meeting, the manufacturing people mostly listened to the field reps' reports and asked questions for clarification. There was no effort to find out who was at fault, no blaming of one department by the other, and no sarcasm. As the meeting went on, it was clear that each department was using the other as a resource to solve a shared problem. The mood seemed to be, "We've got a problem that needs to be solved together, and everyone in both groups has a contribution to make."

This mood carried over into the meeting in Denver with the customers. By early evening there was agreement that the manufacturing department knew how to correct the products already sold and eliminate the problem in future production runs. Everyone at the meeting was satisfied with the outcome. Before adjourning, the Denver customer said, "I know a good steak house. You can't leave until morning anyhow, so please be our guests."

"Oh, no," replied Joe. "We created the problem and you helped us solve it. The steaks are on us, but we'll let you pick the place."

After the group had arrived at the restaurant and ordered, Joe telephoned Jack long distance to tell him the results of the meeting. Jack was pleased and said he would call Sharon first thing in the morning. He also commented, "When you get back tomorrow, we'll want to send a short note thanking the people who met with you. Once again, Joe, you've done a first-rate job in running a problem-solving session, and it's really appreciated. Have a good trip back."

These situations suggest that individual motivation and job satisfaction are influenced by many of the organizational factors shown in Figure 4.1 in the preceding chapter. In turn, motivation and satisfaction have a direct influence on organizational performance.

At Lakeview General Hospital, in Case 5.1, Tom Nelson's motivation and performance were influenced by organizational climate factors such as increased "red tape"; by changes in leadership style that included less support, less recognition, and less listening; and by a perception that management's concern with financial resources might cost him his job. Although his way of coping may not have been constructive for himself and for the hospital, it was certainly understandable, given the circumstances.

At Hydraulic Systems Corporation, Case 5.2, a high level of cooperation existed between the sales and manufacturing departments. Problems were addressed by everyone in both departments for the benefit of customers and employees alike. Human resources systems — specifically the company-wide bonus plan — and supportive leadership behavior reinforced employee participation and effective problem-solving behavior within and among separate groups. The strong group skills displayed by Joe Stevens suggest that Hydraulic Systems had supported group dynamics or leadership training, or that people like Jack Korman or other top managers were excellent role models, or both.

The motivation and performance of individuals and groups within an organization are the major topics of this chapter. First, the complex process of individual motivation and the relationships among motivation, performance, and job satisfaction are explored. Next, how dissatisfaction affects the worker and the workplace is investigated. Finally, the chapter discusses group behavior, which also has a strong effect on individual motivation and organizational outcomes. Throughout, the role of human resources management in enhancing motivation, performance, and satisfaction in the organization is emphasized.

INDIVIDUAL MOTIVATION

What motivates people? How do we motivate our employees? How can we get people to do a better job? Why did she quit? Why is he so upset? Questions like these, and the answers arrived at by management, underlie many of the personnel policies and practices in a given organization. But the reality is that asking these questions is far easier than answering them.

Motivation may be defined as the desire and willingness of a person to expend effort to reach a particular goal or outcome. Individual motivation is a consequence of many forces operating simultaneously in the person and in the person's environment. Motivated behavior in the organizational setting is just as complex. As we saw in the last chapter (Figure 4.1), motivated behavior results from the interplay of many factors, including organizational culture, leadership style, structure, and human resources policies and practices. Individual personality traits, skills, and attitudes that a person brings to the job also play a large part in motivation.

There is no single, generally accepted theory of what motivates people in the workplace, but reviewing several contemporary theories is helpful in understanding the concept. These theories also have important applications for human resources specialists and managers for a significant reason: *enhancing motivation can lead to improved performance and greater organizational success.*

Need Theories of Motivation

It is fairly widely accepted that a good deal of motivation has its origins in certain basic needs. Need theories of motivation are based on the assumption that basic wants or requirements govern much of people's behavior. Abraham Maslow, in particular, has been identified with the development of a need theory of motivation. Other researchers, such as Clayton Alderfer, have revised and extended Maslow's ideas. Another theorist, David McClelland, has focused largely on three needs: achievement, power, and affiliation. A brief review of the major need theories will help you understand the complex process of motivation.

Need Hierarchy Theory.   According to Maslow, individuals are motivated by the desire to fulfill particular needs that are shared by all people:

1. *Physiological needs* include the basic requirements for food, water, and sleep.
2. *Security or safety needs* include shelter, clothing, and ways of defending oneself.
3. *Belonging and affection needs* include the desire to relate to other people and to give and accept love, care, and cooperation.
4. *Esteem needs* include the desire for self-worth, independence, and achievement, and for recognition and respect from others.
5. *Self-actualization needs* include the desire for growth, development, and self-fulfillment and the urge to realize one's potential.[1]

Maslow's theory states that for each individual these needs emerge in a particular order, and that needs at one level must be satisfied before a person is motivated to satisfy needs at the next higher level. That is, a person's physiological and security needs must be satisfied before the "higher" needs for esteem and self-actualization can predominate. Maslow's priority ordering, or *hierarchy*, of needs is shown in Figure 5.1.

In essence, Maslow believed that a strongly felt need for accomplishment and growth can emerge only with the satisfaction of the more basic needs. (This could partly explain why Tom Nelson in Case 5.1 had temporarily abandoned working up to his potential — he was preoccupied by unmet security needs.) Maslow acknowledged, however, that there can be reversals in this hierarchy. A notable example is the martyr who is willing to give up everything in the service of a particular ideal or value.

The major implication of Maslow's theory for human resources management is that policies and practices in the organization, in-

FIGURE 5.1
Maslow's need hierarchy.
Maslow believed these needs are interrelated in that the emergence of higher-level needs depends on the satisfaction of the preceding lower-level needs.

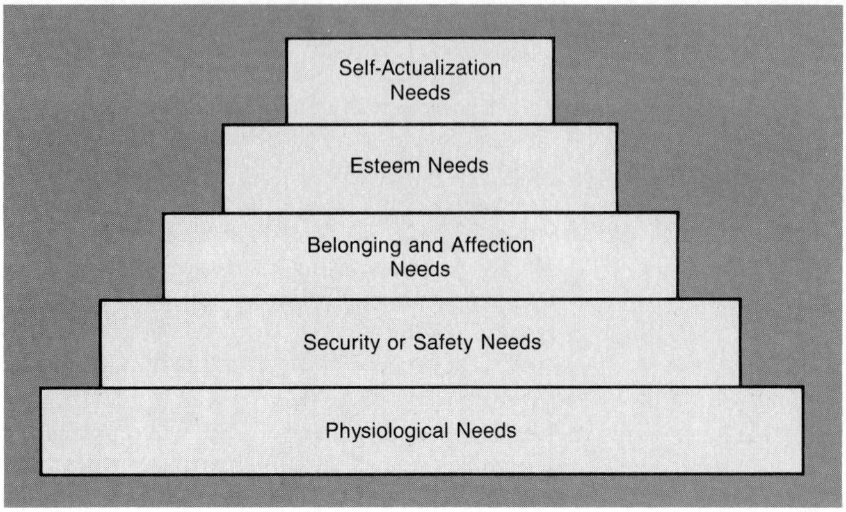

cluding leadership style, must pay attention to all of these needs if the organization hopes to have people working up to their full potential. For example, making supervisors and managers work such long hours that they do not get enough sleep probably reduces their desires for achievement and creativity. Being arbitrary and capricious about employees' job security interferes with cooperation, initiative, and other desirable behaviors. On the other hand, paying exclusive attention to the more basic physiological and security needs and ignoring the needs for achievement and self-esteem would defeat organizational purposes. Thus, the human resources director and all managers would be wise to examine periodically the extent to which organizational practices further or impede fulfillment of human needs and the extent to which there is an appropriate balance in need fulfillment.

ERG Theory. Alderfer, a researcher interested in further testing and explaining Maslow's ideas, identified three categories of needs: existence, relatedness, and growth (ERG).

1. *Existence needs* relate to material desires and include the essential requirements for food, clothing, and shelter.
2. *Relatedness needs* are the desires for human relationships that are satisfied through interaction with families, coworkers, work groups, superiors, subordinates, friends, and friendship groups.
3. *Growth needs* are the needs to be creative and productive and to be most fully what one can be.

While these categories parallel the needs in Maslow's hierarchy, ERG theory states that two or more needs can operate simultaneously as motivating forces and that the emergence of relatedness and growth needs does not require satisfaction of the existence needs. Further, inability to meet relatedness or growth needs can increase the motivation to satisfy existence needs. For example, failure to earn a promotion and thereby meet growth needs could result in greater concern about working conditions, pay, and benefits. In addition, ERG theory suggests that relatedness and growth needs may become more intense in an organization where there is ample opportunity to meet them.[2]

An implication of ERG theory is that in designing and managing human resources policies and practices one must assume that all employees have the potential for continued growth and development. This in turn suggests, for example, the desirability of ongoing opportunities for training, for transfer or promotion, and for developing interaction skills.

Need for Achievement, Affiliation, and Power.　The work of McClelland and his colleagues focuses on the need for achievement, affiliation, and power.

1. *The need for achievement* is the need to excel and to strive for accomplishment and success.
2. *The need for affiliation* is the need for social contact, for approval, for mutual support.
3. *The need for power* is the need to influence others and situations, to be dominant, to control.[3]

Basically, McClelland concluded that while the need for achievement is the main motivator for those who wish to start and develop their own small businesses, the need for power is the crucial motivator of top executives in larger, more complex organizations. Further, to be successful in a large organization, a manager should have a greater need for power than for affiliation. These conclusions were tempered by the observations that the most successful managers exercise their power in a controlled and disciplined way on behalf of others and the organization, not themselves, and that they create a strong sense of team spirit among their subordinates.[4]

One implication for human resources management is that training for supervisors and managers with strong achievement or power needs should include training in effective interpersonal and group skills to help ensure that their leadership behaviors and peer relationships will contribute to effective teamwork.

Motivation-Hygiene Theory

Frederick Herzberg developed a theory of motivation based on factors that produce job satisfaction and dissatisfaction. Although controversial, the *motivation-hygiene theory* has stimulated a great deal of research focusing on ways of improving performance through a clearer understanding of motivation and satisfaction.

Herzberg tested this theory in a study of engineers and accountants in several firms. He found that the key factors in motivation and satisfaction are achievement, recognition, work itself, responsibility, and advancement. These factors are called *motivators*: their presence increases job satisfaction and motivation, but their absence does not lead to dissatisfaction. A second group of factors, called the *hygiene factors*, includes company policy and administration, supervision, salary, interpersonal relations with the supervisor, and working conditions. Herzberg claimed that if these factors are negative or absent, dissatisfaction results. The presence of positive hygiene factors by themselves, however, does not lead to satisfaction and motivation.[5] (See Table 5.1.)

The motivation-hygiene theory is an intriguing one because it takes into account a great variety of factors affecting motivation and satisfaction. But logic and the researcher's own work suggest that, in reality, these factors do not operate separately from one another in a given person. For example, the desires for advancement and for recognition — considered motivators — are probably both connected to feelings and attitudes about salary — a hygiene factor. In addition, the research indicates that some factors, such

---

TABLE 5.1

Motivators and hygiene factors*

MOTIVATORS	HYGIENE FACTORS
Achievement	Company policy and administration
Recognition for achievement	Supervision
Work itself	Salary
Responsibility	Interpersonal relations
Advancement	Working conditions

*According to Herzberg, the presence of motivators in the work environment increases job satisfaction and motivation, while the presence of positive hygiene factors prevents job dissatisfaction. Both groups of factors meet employee needs, but only the motivators lead to superior effort and performance.

Source: Based on Frederick Herzberg, *Work and The Nature of Man* (Cleveland: The World Publishing Company, 1966).

PERSPECTIVE 5.1   Is Money a Motivator?

At General Motors, traditional cost-of-living adjustments for 15,000 white-collar staffers gave way in January to a new system in which amounts equivalent to the COLA payment now go instead into a fund for raises based on merit. If the program proves effective, it could be expanded to cover all of the auto maker's 125,000 white-collar work force.

A still sharper break with the past is being taken at Bell Atlantic, where a new pay-for-performance plan goes into effect in April. Under the new system, money will be deducted from the annual pay of 23,000 management-level employes and set aside in a fund from which lump-sum, year-end payments are to be made to employes.

Managers who perform above the norm stand to receive more than was deducted, while poor performers or those with less-than-satisfactory grades could wind up getting back less than was deducted.

Pay Reductions. Underachievers in the Bell At-

lantic management, as a result, may find themselves receiving lower total compensation one year than they had earned the year before. "In the previous system, none of your pay was at risk," says a spokesman. "Now, it will be. It creates a strong incentive to achieve."

Ironically, employees themselves may turn out to be the biggest supporters of the switch away from automatic pay hikes. A study by the Public Agenda Foundation, a nonpartisan research-and-education organization based in New York, found that —

• Although a majority of jobholders want to do good work for its own sake, they feel the workplace does not reward people who put in extra effort.

• Only 1 worker in 5 feels there is a direct relationship between how hard one works and how much one is paid.

• Close to two thirds want a closer link between performance and pay.

• Nearly three quarters believe that the absence of such a link is one of the primary reasons why work effort has deteriorated.

Source: Excerpted from Carey W. English, "Pay for Performance — Good News or Bad?" *U.S. News & World Report,* March 11, 1985. Copyright, 1985, U.S. News & World Report, Inc.

---

as salary, appear to be associated with *both* satisfaction and dissatisfaction. Finally, research has shown that both categories of factors serve to motivate. In one study of managerial and professional workers, the hygiene factors were as frequently associated with self-reports of high performance as were the motivators.[6]

In spite of this controversy, Herzberg's theory has great value for managers and human resources professionals because it identifies a wide range of factors involved in motivation and satisfaction. Consideration of all these factors is useful in any attempt to enhance motivation and to diminish demotivating factors in an organization. The theory has also had a major influence on job design in many organizations, because it has made managers more aware of the importance of such matters as job challenge and responsibility in motivation. Some of these job redesign projects, in which employees are given significantly more responsibility for planning and control, are described in Chapter 7.

Reinforcement Theory

This theory, based largely on the work of B. F. Skinner, focuses on influencing behavior through rewards and punishments, or **reinforcement.** The process of shaping behavior through reinforcement is called **behavior modification** or *operant conditioning*. This approach to motivation has both common sense and controversial aspects.

Basically, the theory says that if a desired behavior is followed immediately by some reward, the person will be motivated to repeat that behavior. But if the consequence of the behavior is displeasing to the person, he or she is less likely to repeat that behavior. According to the theory, the shorter the time between the behavior and the reinforcement, the more likely it is that the behavior will be influenced. In addition, varying, intermittent patterns of reinforcement are more motivating than continuous reinforcement (a predictable reward after each desired behavior) and more motivating than reinforcement at regular intervals. Finally, punishment can be useful in eliminating undesired behavior; but it can also cause negative side effects such as aggression, which makes it less effective than positive reinforcement.[7]

A major implication of this theory for human resources management, as well as for the direct supervision of people, is that an emphasis on rewards will tend to be more effective than an emphasis on punishments. Further, this theory has led managers in many organizations to pay more attention to recognizing and praising good work.

Chapter 15, "Incentive Plans," describes particular positive reinforcement programs that some companies have used. A controversial aspect of some of these programs is whether praise per se is adequate or whether, in addition, adjustments need to be made in the compensation plan.

Equity Theory

The word **equity** refers to the quality of being just or fair. Determining what is fair or unfair treatment is an ongoing challenge for all managers and human resources specialists. Equity theory provides some insight into how people perceive fairness and unfairness and the consequences of these perceptions. A basic assumption of equity theory is that people want to be treated fairly and that individuals within an organization tend to compare their own contributions and rewards with the contributions and rewards of others.

To feel fairly treated on the job, one must perceive that what one puts in (for example, education, age, seniority, skill, effort, job performance, and loyalty) corresponds with personal outcomes (such as pay, privileges, job satisfaction, recognition, and opportunity). (See Figure 5.2 for an illustration of equity theory.) The person must also feel that his or her contributions and outcomes are in line with the contributions and outcomes of others. If a person believes that he or she produces far more than another but that they both are paid the same, a case of inequity exists and the person may try to do something to correct it. This might take a number of forms, including complaining, slowing down, being absent frequently, or quitting. The theory also suggests that if one perceives that personal outcomes are too high relative to what one puts in and, in turn, too high in comparison with what others contribute and receive, that person will feel motivated to bring the situation

FIGURE 5.2
Equity theory: A fair balance between contributions and outcomes

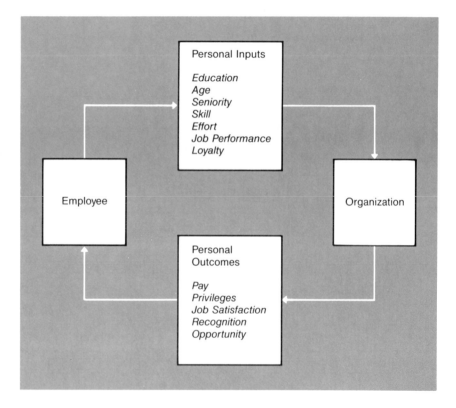

into psychological balance by such mechanisms as rationalization, more productivity, or higher-quality work.[8] The theory can also be extended to perceived fairness or unfairness of punishment.

A number of studies give some support to these assertions. Experiments have found that people will alter their performance in predictable ways if they feel underpaid or overpaid. If they feel underpaid, they tend to reduce quality or quantity of production or to be "tight-fisted" with subordinates. If they feel overpaid, they tend to increase quality or output, depending on the pay system. If one feels overpaid, however, it is easier to convince oneself that the pay is justified than if one feels underpaid.[9]

A major problem in applying equity theory is that different people and different groups have differing perceptions about what is just or fair. Because perceptions can differ about which contributions have the most merit, which performance behaviors are worth the most, and which rewards have the most value, there can be considerable disagreement over the proper allocation of rewards and penalties. Many of the problems in wage and salary administration stem from this problem of differing perceptions.

Expectancy Theory

In recent years, a number of authors and researchers have developed a theory of motivation called *expectancy theory*. According to this theory, motivation is a function of an individual's "expectancy" that a certain amount of effort will lead to a certain level of performance that, in turn, will lead to desired outcomes or rewards. Each potential outcome has a **valence,** which is its degree of attractiveness or value to a specific individual. These valences vary for different people because of individual needs and perceptions. To be highly motivated, a person must want the rewards that are available, must believe that these rewards are linked to performance, and must believe that his or her own effort can result in the necessary performance.[10]

Consider the case of Anita Green, an employee of a typical organization. If Anita believes that doing very good work will result in higher pay, and she very much wants higher pay to buy a new car, she is likely to be motivated to do high-quality work. For Anita, higher pay has a positive valence, or high attractiveness. But to be highly motivated Anita must also believe that her hard work will result in high performance. Therefore, Anita's motivation is a function of her expectancy that her effort will lead to performance that will result in desired outcomes.

JOB SATISFACTION

Job satisfaction can be defined as a person's emotional response to aspects of work (such as pay, supervision, and benefits) or to the work itself. The word *morale* is often used interchangeably with satisfaction, but morale frequently has more of a group or organizational connotation.

Like motivation, job satisfaction is a complex notion that manifests itself in different ways in different people. Whether job satisfaction is high or low depends on a number of factors, including how well a person's needs and wants are met through work, working conditions themselves, the extent to which an individual defines himself or herself through work, and individual personality traits.[11]

Job satisfaction has been an important part of human resources management ever since the Hawthorne studies (see Chapter 2), when it was thought that a firm correlation existed between satisfaction and performance. At that time, high satisfaction was thought to be a *cause* of high performance. It was assumed that management could improve performance simply by satisfying workers through pleasant working conditions, adequate rewards, and the like. Now, however, it is generally accepted that this cause-and-effect relationship is an incorrect view of the connection between satisfaction and performance.

Modern theory and research suggest that focusing solely on satisfying workers will not result in high performance and productivity. The relationship may be the other way around: high performance may cause high job satisfaction, which is reinforced by the rewards that accompany performance. In other words, performance leads to rewards that in turn produce satisfaction.

The Motivation-Performance-Satisfaction Relationship

Figure 5.3 depicts the relationship among motivation, performance, and satisfaction as suggested by recent research about job satisfaction and by theories of individual motivation. Note that the diagram includes some factors in organizational performance that were discussed in the last chapter and illustrated by Figure 4.1.[12]

From left to right, individual needs and goals (box 1) are fundamental driving forces in motivation. The extent and direction of an individual's motivation (box 2) is influenced by factors in the organizational environment such as leadership style, group norms and support, intergroup behavior, and human resources policies and practices (box 3). Individual motivation is further influenced by the desirability of the rewards (valence) and by the expectancy that effort will lead to the performance that will produce the desired outcomes (box 4). The effort that is expended (box 5), coupled with the individual's skills and abilities (box 6), results in performance (box 8). However, the technology that is in use, the support services that are provided (such as the proper raw materials or parts supplied at the right time), and the training given the person (box 7) are also factors in the level of performance. Performance leads to rewards of both an intrinsic and an extrinsic nature (box 9). **Intrinsic rewards** are internal reinforcements such as feelings of accomplishment and self-worth; **extrinsic rewards** are external reinforcements such as pay, recognition, or promotion.[13]

Job satisfaction (box 11) stems from performance and the accompanying rewards but is influenced by the extent to which the individual perceives the rewards as equitable (box 10). An arrow is drawn from box 11 back to boxes 1 and 2 because job satisfaction or dissatisfaction affects need fulfillment, future goals, and ongoing motivation.

Consequences of Dissatisfaction

Job satisfaction does not necessarily lead to better job performance. But what is the link, if any, between high dissatisfaction and performance? It seems reasonable to assume that a person who is highly dissatisfied on the job is less likely to perform at peak levels. Equity theory suggests that workers who are frustrated in attempts to attain some desired outcome will either aim for alternative goals (for example, giving up on the idea of being promoted to supervisor and aiming to become elected union steward) or exercise some kind of defensive behavior in an attempt to reduce the tension (for example, complain to coworkers).

Defensive Behavior.   Research and experience confirm the link between high dissatisfaction and certain behavioral reactions. For example, in a study of eighty-two employees at various levels in several organizations, it was found that frustration can have extremely negative consequences for organizational goals. Such self-reported behaviors as interpersonal arguments, complaining about the supervisor or organization to people outside, ignoring the supervisor, considering quitting, purposely damaging or defacing equipment, doing work incorrectly, taking undeserved breaks, or using drugs appeared with considerable frequency.[14]

FIGURE 5.3 The motivation-performance-satisfaction relationship

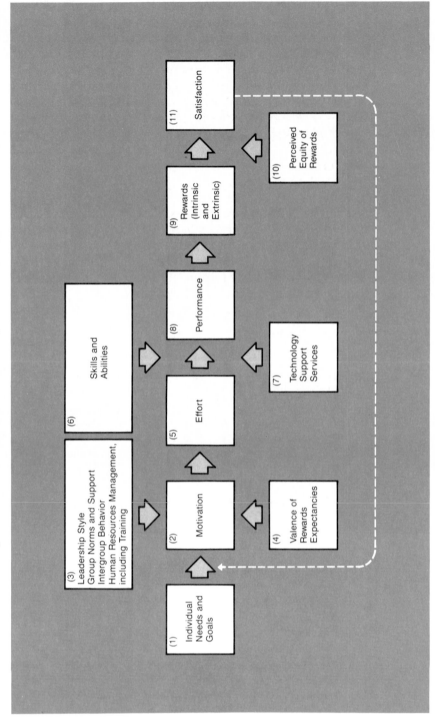

Source: Adapted from David A. Nadler and Edward E. Lawler III, "Motivation: A Diagnostic Approach," pp. 26–38; and Edward E. Lawler III, "Satisfaction and Behavior," pp. 39–50, in J. Richard Hackman, Edward E. Lawler III, and Lyman W. Porter, *Perspectives on Behavior in Organizations* (New York: McGraw-Hill Book Company, 1977).

Sabotage. The deliberate damaging of equipment or products — **sabotage** — by employees represents one of the more costly possible consequences of organizational frustrations. For example, deliberate damage to automobiles by employees in automobile assembly plants and sabotage of navy helicopters and jet airplanes have been documented.[15] It may be, however, that high job dissatisfaction is only one of several factors leading to sabotage. Other factors, such as an individual's psychological tendency toward extreme behaviors, may also be operating. Nonetheless, satisfying workers must be part of an effort to reduce sabotage in an organization.

Absenteeism. Failure to report to work — **absenteeism** — also appears to be associated with job dissatisfaction. A review of the literature on factors associated with job attendance concluded that job satisfaction was one of the major influences on attendance, although only one of many factors. Another major influence, for example, was ability to attend, i.e., the extent to which illness or accidents, family responsibilities, and transportation problems did not interfere with coming to work.[16]

Turnover. An Australian study of **turnover** — frequently calculated as the ratio of the number of employee separations during a month to the number of employees on the payroll at the middle of the month — found that one factor was dissatisfaction. This study found that high turnover was part of a broader set of problems, including lowered production and quality, higher costs, low satisfaction with superiors, work anxiety, absenteeism, and accidents. The researchers concluded that long-term solutions to turnover are to be found in "identifying and remedying specific issues producing dissatisfaction as well as more substantive programs of organization development or other forms of planned change."[17]

Implications for Managers and Human Resources Specialists

Although the connections between satisfaction and attendance and satisfaction and turnover are rather complicated, the costs of absenteeism and turnover provide ample reason for managers and human resources specialists to be concerned with job satisfaction. Although not all turnover or absenteeism can or should be prevented, it is obvious that high levels of both can be extremely costly to an organization. Further, high dissatisfaction tends to be costly in many other ways. When workers perform below their full potential, the organization suffers from reduced effectiveness and efficiency.

Data from national surveys of job satisfaction suggest that high levels of dissatisfaction are associated with certain groups of employees. These include younger workers, blacks, and other minorities; workers without a high school education; and laborers. Further, the relatively high proportion of workers who feel underutilized (36 percent) may represent a loss of great magnitude to organizations and the society.[18] These survey data may not apply to every given organization, of course, but top managers would be wise to assess satisfaction levels in their own organizations — by unit, by level, and by job category. One way to do this is to use climate or satisfaction surveys at intervals and then to take appropriate remedial action. IBM, for example, takes regular climate surveys and "the Personnel Department moves quickly when any downward changes are noted. . . ."[19]

GROUP INFLUENCES ON PERFORMANCE

The discussion until now has considered motivation and performance on an individual basis. But in the organizational setting, most individuals are members of work groups. A **work group** is a number of persons, usually reporting to a common superior and having some face-to-face interaction, who have some degree of interdependence in carrying out tasks for the purpose of achieving organizational goals.[20]

The development of effective work groups is an important part of human resources management. Groups affect individual behavior, motivation, and performance just as individuals can affect the way groups function. Moreover, group behavior is partly a function of organizational culture, climate, leadership style, and other aspects of the organization's environment. Finally, the extent to which group goals are consistent with organizational goals is a key factor in the overall success of an organization.

Formal Versus Informal Groups

Formal groups are groups established by management, such as the work group, special committees, and task forces. But there are numerous other group configurations in organizations that have not been established by management. These are usually called **informal groups** and form spontaneously as a result of proximity or similarity of work, mutual interests, mutual need fulfillment, or combinations of these reasons. For example, four people who work on the same floor of the building but in different departments may eat lunch together regularly. Six people, all from different work groups, may ride to work together and develop strong friendships. Informal groups are sometimes called "shadow groups" because they tend to be invisible to management, yet they can influence the organization powerfully by, for example, transmitting information or affecting attitudes.

Meeting Individual Needs and Organizational Goals

Work groups and informal groups tend to meet a number of human needs, such as the needs for affiliation, cooperation, and esteem. Groups are a source of identity, support, and friendship for individual workers who might otherwise feel lost in a large organization. Work groups, then, play an important role in meeting the emotional needs of individuals.

Peter Menzel/Stock, Boston

The development of effective work groups is an important part of human resources management.

In addition, work groups and other formal groups fill several important functions in helping the organization meet its task objectives. Because most jobs are interdependent, groups help get the work done. Further, they help orient new members to specific job procedures and to the organization's environment and help to train them. In addition, probably a high proportion of work groups in today's organizations participate to some extent in decision making and goal setting that affect organizational outcomes. How well work groups perform such functions, however, depends to a great extent on factors in the internal environment, including leadership style, human resources practices such as orientation and training, and organizational climate.

Group Control over Production

A number of studies over the years have shown that work groups have considerable control over productivity. Many studies have demonstrated that groups of workers can defend themselves against what they consider unreasonable or unfair performance standards.

For example, the Hawthorne studies described in Chapter 2 found that workers in the bank wiring observation room had a standard for output considerably below that set officially by management, and that this norm was enforced by pressure from the group. One of the ways pressure was exerted was through a game called "binging" in which one worker would strike another on the upper arm if verbal persuasion was not sufficient to get that person to reduce production.[21]

Another study showed that, in general, the higher the standards of performance established informally by work groups, the higher the production of those groups. Members of these work groups were absent or late for work less often and were less likely to leave the job early in comparison with groups that held lower standards of performance.[22]

Research also indicates that the members of a very unified and cooperative, or cohesive, group will conform closely to the standards set by the group, whether the standards are high or low. Groups that lack cohesiveness, however, tend to show considerable variation in productivity among members. A high degree of cohesiveness seems to lead to high productivity when the attitude of the group toward the company is favorable. If there are good relationships among management, union, and employees, the cohesive group sets high standards of performance. If not, a cohesive group tends to show lower-than-average productivity.[23]

Work banking is another illustration of how workers and work groups can control production. **Work banking**, which has been frequently documented, is the hiding of present production in order to demonstrate productivity up to some standard or quota at some future time. Motives for work banking might include having finished items to pull out when one is feeling ill and needing to slow down, wishing to take it easy at intervals, or protecting oneself against conditions affecting production over which one has no control. Robert Schrank, author of *Ten Thousand Working Days*, gives an example of work banking in a machine shop where propeller shafts for Liberty ships were being manufactured:

> We walked to the back end of the plant, out onto the loading platform. There I could not believe my eyes. I saw two guys burying a thirty-foot propeller shaft in the backyard. I burst out with, "What the hell are you guys doing?" They said, "Hey fellows, you watch us be heroes at the end of the month when the boss gives us that we-need-to-break-quota b.s."[24]

Characteristics of Effective Groups

Group dynamics theory and research have important things to say about the characteristics of groups that are highly effective in attaining their goals. The degree to which group goals are consistent with broader organizational goals will of course be a function of a number of factors, including management philosophy and leadership style, organizational climate, and the reward system. For example, if management does not talk about the importance of departments cooperating with each other, does not exert leadership in this direction, and does not reward cooperation, groups are more likely to pursue their own narrower objectives at the expense of total organizational performance.

Some of the conclusions from group dynamics theory and research about the characteristics of highly effective groups follow. (See Figure 5.4 for a summary of these conclusions.) There are important implications for human resources policies and practices.

1. Group members, including the formal leader, are skilled both in *task behaviors* — behaviors bearing directly on getting the task done, such as suggesting procedures or paraphrasing to make sure there is understanding — and in *group-maintenance behaviors* — behaviors that pertain to the emotional life of the group, such as expressing encouragement or making sure each member feels included in group discussions. This has particular implications for training and management development in organizations: training

FIGURE 5.4
Characteristics of effective groups

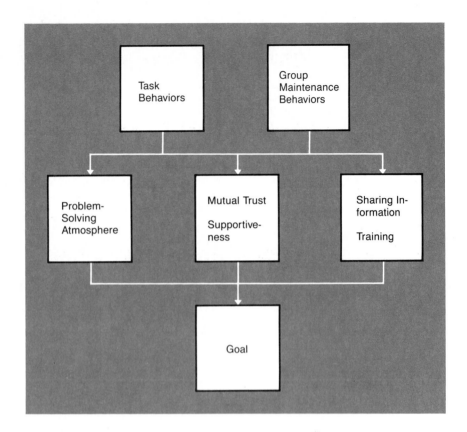

in group skills needs to be supported and encouraged. Further, this has implications for supervisory selection and leadership style: supervisors and managers need to run meetings in such a way that these behaviors can be used. To illustrate, group members cannot use their group skills if the formal leader dominates the discussion.

2. Group members and the leader trust each other and have high confidence that each can carry his or her share of the load. This has implications for personnel selection: additions or replacements should have the skills and attitudes (or the potential) needed to help the group carry out its mission. Conversely, if the human resources department, through inattention to transfer practices, permits a group to become a "dumping ground" for unqualified people, the group and the organization are likely to pay a high price in terms of group performance.

3. Meetings have a problem-solving, supportive atmosphere. When there are differing points of view, issues are worked through to everyone's satisfaction in contrast to forcing methods of decision

making, such as lining up support behind the scenes and then taking a formal vote. This has implications for leadership style and training in group problem-solving approaches.

4. The leader is influential in setting the supportive, problem-solving tone of the work group by his or her own behaviors. Again, this has implications for supervisory selection and training.

5. Group members and the leader actively help each other develop skills of a technical, interpersonal, and group nature. At the group level this means sharing information and suggestions, and mutual training. At the level of human resources systems, it means making training programs available for upgrading technological and human relations skills and rewarding people for being effective trainers, both within their groups and in formal programs.[25]

What is known about effective groups, the influence of groups on individual motivation and job performance, and the influence of

---

PERSPECTIVE 5.2   Building Effective Groups: "The Wilderness Experience"

Far from the conference center and on the cutting fringe of the off-site phenomenon is "the wilderness experience." More and more companies these days, including Wang Laboratories, Polaroid, and Standard Oil of Indiana, are sending their people into the woods in the hope of changing not just managerial minds but hearts as well. The vehicle is typically a variant of Outward Bound, a program originally developed to instill self-confidence in adolescents by teaching them to survive in the wilds. In the corporate version, denizens of the office are dispatched — with guides, of course — to pilot rubber rafts through whitewater rapids, or ride horses all day and sleep on the ground.

Anton Lahnston, a professor of organizational behavior at Boston University and the director of that school's booming Executive Challenge wilderness sojourns, explains why managers are taking to the woods: "The outdoor medium as a classroom offers the intersection of three learning experiences — cognitive learning; an emotional component generally lacking in traditional educa-

tional settings, involving such issues as fear, trust, and commitment; and the engagement of people's physical selves."

All the jargon comes alive in the experience of a group of Federal Express executives. The vice president of the company's western region took a dozen of his subordinates, not all of them exactly enthusiastic about the prospect, to a coastal town in Maine. When they got off the bus from the airport, they were put aboard an open 30-foot boat and told to sail it to an island on the horizon. As described by Roy Yamahiro, Federal Express's vice president of human resources development: "Twelve people couldn't sail this boat, they couldn't even get together enough to row to the island. They became angry, cursed each other and the situation, damn near threw two of the instructors overboard, and spent the night in the boat on the water. In the morning they finally figured out how to sail it." And what did the crew get out of their experience as galley slaves? "They came away a more cohesive unit," Yamahiro says. "They still get together socially, even though they live all over the West, and they all work much more effectively with the V.P."

management practices on group behavior makes it clear that human resources management must be concerned about groups. By extension, intergroup theory and research can also shed light on how relations between groups affect organizational performance.

INTERGROUP BEHAVIOR

Relationships among groups in an organization can contribute extensively to organizational performance or can inhibit or even destroy it. High-quality communications and cooperation, in particular, can enhance organizational outcomes, whereas conflict that is not managed or that escalates can have a severe dampening effect. Excessive competition among groups is similar to unmanaged conflict in its consequences.

Conflict and Competition

Conflict in the organization consists of opposing behaviors between two or more people or groups who have incompatible goals. A certain level of conflict can be healthy from time to time if it serves to raise issues, thus leading to problem solving, a restructuring of goals, or a redefinition of purpose. An example of conflict might be two department heads each trying to get the other person fired by withholding and distorting information. Unless a dialogue takes place — probably with the help of a neutral third party — the costs to the organization in efficiency and effectiveness are likely to be considerable.

Competition, on the other hand, may involve common goals and a good deal of common interest, along with limited opposing behaviors. An example might be two groups set up by management to develop a prototype of some instrument, with the winning group given the go-ahead to manufacture and market the winning design. IBM uses this kind of internal competition, with winners selected at performance "shootouts" where actual performance is demonstrated and measured.[26] While the groups may be competing for people and materials for the project, underlying the competition is substantial job security, as well as rewards for everyone when the organization is successful.

When competition and conflict within an organization are mismanaged or excessive, there are predictable negative consequences. Some of these, as indicated by research on conflict and competition between groups, are as follows:

1. Although both groups take pride in their accomplishments, each makes favorable evaluations of "our" group and negative evaluations of the other.

2. Each group has distorted perceptions and judgments about the other group. The performance of the other group is frequently underestimated; the performance of one's own group tends to be overestimated.

3. Each group sees the other as the "enemy," people make disparaging remarks within their own group about the other group, and contact with the other group is frowned on. Considerable energy is used to outwit the "enemy."

4. If one of the groups has grossly inadequate resources, members may become discouraged and demotivated. There is likely to be considerable friction within the group, and members may have difficulty dividing the tasks.

5. Information is used to erode the position of the other group and to enhance one's relative position rather than to clarify matters or solve problems. For example, in talking with superiors who have control over resources needed by both groups, one group may be quick to pass on negative information about the other group but fail to mention compliments or favorable information they have heard.[27]

Managing Conflict and Developing Cooperation

What we know about competition and conflict between groups strongly suggests that management philosophy and practices, including human resources policies and procedures, should contribute to cooperation, effective communication, and problem solving across groups. This assertion can be stated negatively: management must be careful that it does not consciously or unconsciously create policies and practices that produce unnecessary competition and conflict and their negative consequences.

There are some specific implications for various human resources managers who wish to maximize cooperation and minimize the negative consequences of conflict and competition:

1. Recruitment and selection — attract and employ people who are oriented toward collaborative relationships and already have well-developed group and intergroup skills or who have strong potential in these areas.

2. Promotion — use effective group and intergroup skills as one criterion for promotion.

3. Training and management development — provide training for all supervisors and team members in group and intergroup skills and the underlying theory.

4. Performance appraisal and review — make group and intergroup skills an area for review and coaching. Hold supervisors and managers accountable for cooperation across the organization.

5. Compensation and rewards — recognize effective group and intergroup behaviors and include these areas in pay-increase decisions. Design compensation systems so that there are no rewards for withholding cooperation and so that cooperation is rewarded.

6. Organization improvement strategies — use conflict-management techniques such as intergroup problem-solving workshops.

Developing cooperation in the organization, of course, must be the example set by top management. The actual style and behavior of top management will largely set the tone for the entire organization.

SUMMARY

Individual motivation — the desire and willingness of a person to expend effort to reach a particular outcome — is a consequence of a complex interplay of factors. These factors include intraorganizational factors, such as those discussed in Chapter 4, and intrapersonal factors, such as needs and expectations.

Among the various need theories of motivation are Maslow's need hierarchy theory; Alderfer's ERG theory; and McClelland's achievement, affiliation, and power theory. Maslow and Alderfer both assert that motivation springs from basic needs of all humans, but they have different views on the extent to which the more basic needs must be satisfied before the self-actualization or growth needs emerge. McClelland sees the need for achievement as the main motivator of entrepreneurs, while the need for power is crucial for top executives of large, complex organizations.

Herzberg's motivation-hygiene theory holds that some factors in the work environment serve as motivators and some serve as hygiene factors that prevent dissatisfaction. Reinforcement theory holds that if a desired behavior is followed immediately by some reward, a person will be motivated to repeat that behavior. Equity theory focuses on the consequences of perceived fairness or unfairness. Expectancy theory holds that motivation is a function of an individual's expectation that a certain amount of effort will lead to a certain level of performance that, in turn, will lead to desired outcomes or rewards.

Satisfaction may be usefully thought of as an outcome rather than a cause of performance. Job satisfaction, according to contemporary theory, stems from performance and accompanying rewards. Attempting to improve performance by simply improving pay, benefits, or working conditions may not work.

Work groups, both formal and informal, are important to understand in human resources management because they are important in meeting individual needs and organizational goals. Work groups have a great deal of control over productivity through such means as restriction of production and work banking. Members of a cohesive group will conform to standards set by the group, whether high or low. If the attitudes in a cohesive group are favorable to management, the group tends to set high standards of performance.

Effective groups tend to have members and leaders who are skilled both in production-centered behaviors — behaviors that bear directly on the task to be done — and in employee-centered behaviors — those behaviors associated with managing the emotional life of the group. Effective groups tend to have members who trust each other; their meetings tend to have a problem-solving, supportive atmosphere, and group members actively help each other in developing skills of a technical, interpersonal, and group nature. Further, these conditions are actively influenced and supported by the leader.

Relationships between units in an organization can contribute to, or seriously detract from, organizational effectiveness. Conflict or excessive competition between two groups (or two people) that is not brought out in the open and managed properly will have negative consequences. Management practices, particularly in the areas of management philosophy, leadership style, and human resources policies and procedures, can contribute much toward managing conflict in constructive ways.

KEY TERMS

motivation	intrinsic reward	formal group
reinforcement	extrinsic reward	informal group
behavior modification	sabotage	work banking
equity	absenteeism	conflict
valence	turnover	competition
job satisfaction	work group	

REVIEW QUESTIONS

1. List and briefly explain the key theories of motivation. What are their implications for human resources management?
2. Describe the relationship among motivation, performance, and satisfaction.
3. Why should human resources management be concerned with employee dissatisfaction? Provide several reasons.
4. Explain the importance of work groups in organizations. In what ways are they related to organizational outcomes?
5. Identify the characteristics of effective work groups.
6. Discuss the role of human resources management in the development of effective work groups.
7. Explain the consequences of excessive intergroup conflict and competition in the organization. What are some of the implications for human resources management?

OPENING CASE QUESTIONS

Case 5.1   The Merger

1. Discuss the motivation-performance-satisfaction relationship in Tom's situation.
2. What could the human resources department have done to assure continued good performance on the part of employees?
3. What can the human resources department do now?

Case 5.2   Solving Customer Problems at Hydraulic Systems Corporation

1. What human resources practices led to the successful problem-solving session between the marketing and manufacturing people at Hydraulic?
2. Discuss what might have happened if the marketing and manufacturing employees came into the meeting blaming each other and feeling very competitive.

CASE 5.3   AN APPROACH TO MOTIVATING EMPLOYEES

High-technology companies require high-tech people. The success of such companies can be greatly influenced, even altogether determined, by their ability to attract and retain employees with necessary skills. In addition to employee retention, employee motivation is a pivotal issue in an industry where creativity and perseverance are essential foundations to building marketable product lines. And these two people issues seem to go hand in hand. As complex as the issue of motivation is, one thing seems clear—motivated employees are more likely to stay where they are.

One of the most unusual examples of successful employee motivation may be that of Tandem Computers, Inc., a silicon valley company that experienced growth of as much as 100 percent per year during the early 1980s. Tandem is run by James G. Treybig, Jimmy T. to his coworkers. Treybig's approach to human resources management manifests itself in a variety of forms, from two-day orientation sessions on company philosophy to regular Friday afternoon beer parties for all employees. To some, Treybig's might seem to be a seat-of-the-pants philosophy, but it is actually based on his systematic view of people and the art of managing them.

Treybig feels that an important ingredient in motivation is awareness on the part of all employees of how their jobs affect all other jobs in the organization and, ultimately, of how their jobs affect the company's end products and performance. His orientation book on the company's philosophy, which is given out to all new employees, includes a giant chart that shows how activities at one point in the organization influence other points. Treybig prepared the chart himself, which consumed a great deal of time. But when it comes to time, he feels that human resources projects take high priority.

To help employees feel involved in the company, Tandem offers generous stock options to everyone who works there. Also in place are organizational practices that encourage communication. On the informal side, the beer parties are an example; but the company also pursues an open-door management policy. Any employee can walk into a manager's office to express ideas, discuss problems, or even complain. In one extreme incident, a group of assembly workers approached Treybig himself because they were unhappy with their supervisor. (The supervisor didn't remain at the company much longer, which sent a clear message to his peers.)

Tandem's systematic respect for employees doesn't stop with a loose management philosophy and beer parties. In developing managers, the company

Case Sources: Myron Magnet, "Managing by Mystique at Tandem Computers," *Fortune,* June 28, 1982, pp. 84–91; Henry Eason, "Keeping Good People," *Nation's Business,* July 1984, pp. 37–39; "What Makes Tandem Run," *Business Week,* July 14, 1980, pp. 73–74; and Robert Levering, Milton Moskowitz, and Michael Katz, *The 100 Best Companies to Work for in America,* rev. ed. (New York: New American Library, 1985), pp. 353–355.

concentrates heavily on promoting from within. It also provides a swimming pool, a volleyball court, and a jogging trail; employees working overtime on weekends can sometimes take a break for a company-provided barbecue; and employees are required to take a six-week "sabbatical" every four years. Such perquisites aren't revolutionary, and research has shown that they increase productivity. But coupled with Tandem's corporate culture, they can reasonably be viewed as part of an overall system of motivation aimed at creating an employee-centered environment. Such a system might not work for a more complex organization, but it seems to work for Tandem. The company's management has claimed a turnover rate that is far less than half of the industry average; and Tandem's success speaks for itself.

Discussion Questions

1. When Tandem offers someone a job, salary is never discussed until the candidate accepts the job offer. What reasons can you think of for this policy?
2. Discuss Treybig's management style in terms of equity theory.
3. Referring to McClelland's work, do you think that someone with a high need for power would fit in at Tandem?

Human Resources Planning

CHAPTER OUTLINE

LEARNING OBJECTIVES

- **Define human resources planning and describe the two major steps in the planning process.**
- **Explain how human resources planning is related to the overall strategic plan of the organization.**
- **Explain the relationship of human resources planning to the staffing process.**
- **Indicate why an understanding of the external labor market is so important in human resources planning.**
- **Outline the impact on human resources planning of federal legislation and regulations.**
- **Define affirmative action and explain its essential role in the planning process.**
- **Explain why the human resources department plays a major role in human resources planning.**

CASE 6.1   A CAN OF WORMS

Quality Chemicals, a medium-sized manufacturer of varied chemical products, had closed the year with impressive sales. But Alan Corelli, personnel director, was worried about the future prospects of the firm. He knew that several top executives would retire within the next two or three years, which meant that a number of key positions would need to be filled soon. But where would the replacements come from? Some talented employees reported to these older executives, but most were relatively young and inexperienced. In fact, Alan's impression was that very few departments had any employees who could be promoted immediately to upper-level management positions. He figured that executives would have to be recruited from outside the organization, as he himself had been a year ago.

Alan also knew that the company's strategic plans for the next five years included more aggressive research, manufacturing, and marketing of pharmaceuticals and reagent-grade chemicals. He was aware, however, that the company's present strengths were in manufacturing, and that it probably had too few employees with technical research skills.

Alan had recently mentioned his concerns about future staffing to the president of the company, who had said, "I'm beginning to be worried, too. It seems we need some concrete plans for making sure we're employing the right people in the right jobs at the right time. You're our people specialist. How about coming up with some recommendations on how to proceed?" "I will," said Alan. "I'll try to get back to you in a few days."

The first thing Alan did was to sketch out an overall organizational chart. He then prepared a detailed chart for each division, with names of all employees down through the first level of supervision. Beside each name he tried to make some notations about whether the person was immediately promotable, potentially promotable, or not likely to be promotable. But he soon realized he didn't know the work of some people well enough to make an accurate classification and he would need to involve top and middle management in this evaluation process. He was also convinced that training and development opportunities were important in promotability and that there should be some kind of plan to expose potentially promotable employees to those opportunities.

"An effective training program is going to take some bucks," Alan thought. "I wonder if there's any money in the budget for a management development program. And what about the pros and cons of promoting from within versus hiring from the outside? I wonder if there is a consensus among top management on that."

When he began to make notes on employees in the research labs, he became painfully aware that he had little insight as to what talent currently existed among the research staff and what additional skills were needed in the chemical engineering side of the business. The more he thought about the matter of human resources planning, the more complicated it became. "This is a can of worms," he said to himself. "I'll need lots more information before I can make any intelligent recommendations."

The "few days" grew to six weeks before Alan met with the president again about staffing concerns. By this time Alan had talked with at least fifty people at all levels of the organization and had developed a lengthy report containing a dozen categories of recommendations. One of the recommendations was that human resources planning committees be appointed in research and development, manufacturing, marketing, and administration. Alan also proposed that he serve as an adviser to each committee. The main job of these committees would be to make a preliminary assessment of the potential management and technical talent in each unit and to develop broad recommendations on training and development needs. Alan also recommended that a small corporate committee be appointed to develop the overall philosophy and strategy.

CASE 6.2   NOT VERY CLEAR AT KLEER

Ed Kleer, president of Kleer Optics, was annoyed, to put it mildly. He had just received a letter from the Department of Labor instructing his company to develop an affirmative action plan to raise the proportion of women and minority employees in the firm, including at the supervisory and management levels. Ed was irritated because he and everyone in the firm were scrambling to fill government orders for military optical equipment, and this new task came at an inconvenient time. "Well," he thought, "I'd better talk to our human resources director."

Ed walked down the hall to Sam Kagi's office. "Well, Mr. H.R. Director," he said to Sam, as he dropped the Labor Department letter on his desk, "we've got our work cut out for us." Sam quickly skimmed the letter and sighed. "I could see this one coming," he said. "Remember, you and I talked about women and minorities a while back. My people have been keeping their eyes open, but we get almost no minority applicants. The women who apply are usually not technically trained, and practically none of them have supervisory experience."

"Yes, and the last two black engineers we hired left within a year for about double the salaries we were paying them," added Ed. "I can just see us getting into an expensive recruiting and training program, with the bigger companies picking up the winnings."

Sam nodded in agreement. "It would be a gamble all right," he said. "Maybe we ought to look at all of our personnel policies and practices and see if there's anything we can do to keep good people, *if* we can hire the people we want in the first place."

"That's a good idea, Sam," Ed responded. "I suppose there's no point in our moaning and groaning about affirmative action if we're going to protect our government contracts. We need to develop some kind of overall, long-range plan. Maybe you ought to get several of our department heads involved in that. We'd better get them aboard if any program is going to succeed. Meanwhile, I'll leave this letter with you to draft a reply."

"O.K., Ed," Sam replied. "But I've got a suggestion. I would appreciate it if you would bring up the matter of the letter at Tuesday's department head meeting and tell people we will be calling on them for help in planning an affirmative action program. I'm not entirely clear on how to proceed beyond that, but I'm sure you're right about involving the department heads. If people realize you're behind this, things will go a lot better."

A s Alan Corelli found out in Case 6.1, human resources planning is a complex process. Once one digs into the matter, it quickly becomes clear that all personnel processes are related to human resources planning. The promotability of managers to higher positions, for example, is tied in with the effectiveness of the recruitment and selection procedures used when these people were originally hired, their training and development opportunities, the kind of leadership and performance reviews they have experienced, the opportunities for mobility in the organization, and management philosophy about such matters as whether the organization should make every effort to promote from within.

As Alan became aware, human resources planning must be tied to the strategic plans of the organization.

Human resources planning must also be attuned to the realities of the external environment. Laws, court decisions, and administrative rulings enforcing equal employment opportunity have a major influence on human resources planning in most organizations today. Ed and Sam, in Case 6.2, for example, were beginning to face up to the necessity of implementing an affirmative action program if Kleer Optics was to be in compliance with federal regulations. Other influential factors in the environment are economic, social, and political conditions; changing skill levels in the labor force; market conditions and competition; and technology.

This chapter presents the broad scope of human resources planning and the basic considerations involved in any planning effort. The first part of the chapter reviews key aspects of human resources planning and explains how this process relates to overall organizational planning and to the staffing process in particular. The second part of the chapter describes forces in the external environment that affect human resources planning and staffing. This discussion focuses on the external labor market and the legal background against which all planning decisions must be made.

WHAT IS HUMAN RESOURCES PLANNING?

In Chapter 1, **human resources planning** was defined as the process of assessing the organization's human resources needs in the light of organizational goals and making plans to ensure that a competent, stable work force is employed. Some examples of human resources needs are to recruit employees with certain abilities and knowledge, to create training programs for developing particular skills or ensuring management succession, and to ensure compliance with government legislation regarding equal employment opportunity and affirmative action.

The starting point of effective human resources planning is the organization's overall **strategic plan**, or plan for conducting its business as profitably and successfully as possible, which establishes specific **organizational goals**. (The term "goal" will be used to refer to long-term, broad purposes or ends, and the term **"organizational objective"** to refer to short-term purposes or ends.) Translating goals into specific human resources policies and systems is the primary aim of human resources planning. The interdependence of human resources planning and organizational planning stems from the shared purpose of improving organizational performance and the overriding need to make the most effective use of human resources.

Human resources planning is closely linked to the staffing process, which results in the assignment of workers to all positions in the organization. To function smoothly and efficiently, organizations must be able to anticipate and cope with staff vacancies due to retirement, promotion, resignation, and so on. Plans must be made to manage these internal shifts or losses in human resources as well as the deliberate expansion or reduction of particular departments. But the planning process is not strictly confined to staffing changes within the organization. Human resources planning must also be responsive to rapidly changing forces in the external environment, such as market demand, changes in the labor market, technological innovations, and regulatory measures.

Aspects of the Planning Process

Figure 6.1 depicts this broad-based view of human resources planning. The figure isolates two major steps in the process: needs forecasting and program planning. **Needs forecasting** is the process of determining an organization's future demand for human resources. This forecast, or prediction, of needs is derived from a broad information base that includes, among other things, a careful analysis of external conditions; present and potential skill levels within the organization; organizational considerations such as job design, management philosophy, and budget; and staff reductions and transfers (reallocations) throughout the organization.[1]

Program planning is done once the forecast of human resources needs is completed. According to James Walker, program planning takes place in two areas: performance management and career management. Performance management includes the planning of broad organizational matters (such as performance standards and quality of work life) and of specific human resources management processes, including performance appraisal and compensation. Career management includes the planning of staffing policies and systems, including recruitment, selection, and training, and management succession. (Figure 6.2 is a form used in succession planning. **Succession planning** is the process of anticipating future managerial staffing needs and making plans for the development of managers to meet those needs.)[2]

Relationship to Strategic Planning

According to James Walker, effective human resources planning is "a process of analyzing an organization's human resource needs under changing conditions and developing the activities necessary to satisfy those needs."[3] These changing conditions include changes

FIGURE 6.1   The human resources planning process

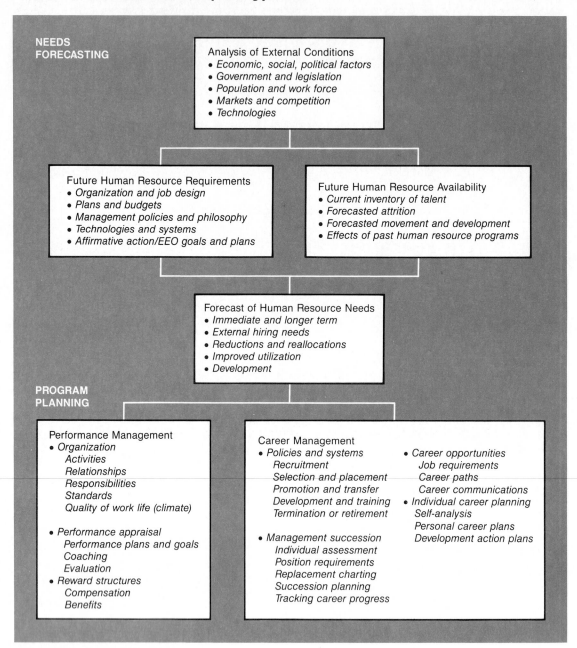

NEEDS FORECASTING

Analysis of External Conditions
- *Economic, social, political factors*
- *Government and legislation*
- *Population and work force*
- *Markets and competition*
- *Technologies*

Future Human Resource Requirements
- *Organization and job design*
- *Plans and budgets*
- *Management policies and philosophy*
- *Technologies and systems*
- *Affirmative action/EEO goals and plans*

Future Human Resource Availability
- *Current inventory of talent*
- *Forecasted attrition*
- *Forecasted movement and development*
- *Effects of past human resource programs*

Forecast of Human Resource Needs
- *Immediate and longer term*
- *External hiring needs*
- *Reductions and reallocations*
- *Improved utilization*
- *Development*

PROGRAM PLANNING

Performance Management
- *Organization*
    Activities
    Relationships
    Responsibilities
    Standards
    Quality of work life (climate)

- *Performance appraisal*
    Performance plans and goals
    Coaching
    Evaluation
- *Reward structures*
    Compensation
    Benefits

Career Management
- *Policies and systems*
    Recruitment
    Selection and placement
    Promotion and transfer
    Development and training
    Termination or retirement

- *Management succession*
    Individual assessment
    Position requirements
    Replacement charting
    Succession planning
    Tracking career progress

- *Career opportunities*
    Job requirements
    Career paths
    Career communications
- *Individual career planning*
    Self-analysis
    Personal career plans
    Development action plans

Source: Human Resource Planning, by James W. Walker. Copyright © 1980 by McGraw-Hill, Inc. Used with the permission of McGraw-Hill Book Company.

FIGURE 6.2 **Management succession plan form**

MANAGEMENT SUCCESSION PLAN

Organization _____   Date _____

Probability of Vacancy:

Within 1 Year .... A
1 to 3 Years .... B
Beyond 3 Years C

Position Incumbent		(A) Ready Now	(B) Ready 1–3 Years	(C) Ready Beyond 3 Years	Contingency Plan

in the strategic plans of the organization that result in specific organizational goals. "Strategy," according to the chairman of General Electric, "is trying to understand where you sit today in today's world. Not where you wish you were and where you hoped you'd be, but where you are. And it's trying to understand where you want to be in 1990. It's assessing with everything in your head the competitive changes, the market changes that you can capitalize on or ward off to go from here to there. It's assessing the realistic chances of getting from here to there."[4]

Strategic plans are as unique as the organizations that develop them, but underlying most organizational strategies is the determination of some unfulfilled need for products or services that the organization can satisfy. Supplying these products or services then becomes part of the organization's goals.

The process of identifying organizational goals is usually based on careful research into market need, existing competition, and cost and profit estimates. Most manufacturing organizations, for example, are constantly seeking to improve their products or to develop new ones. Progress in research and development can make an organization's current products obsolete almost overnight. This means that strategic plans and organizational goals must be periodically reassessed and adjusted.

To a great extent, organizational goals influence the nature of all managerial processes and of human resources management in particular. This means that the structure of the organization, the specific jobs to be performed, the financial and technological resources needed, and the qualifications and numbers of people employed will consistently reflect organizational goals. In fact, without clearly defined goals, activities become confused and erratic, and the management of one process may interfere with the management of another. Without goals, there are no standards against which to evaluate the performance of individuals or that of the total organization. But the development of organizational goals that are clearly defined in response to current conditions means that all managerial processes—including human resources planning—can be conducted from the point of view of what is best for the organization as a whole.

To be effective, human resources planning must also be conducted in the light of the desired organizational culture and cli-

---

PERSPECTIVE 6.1   Human Resources Planning at IBM

Employment Security

In nearly 40 years, no person employed on a regular basis by IBM has lost as much as one hour of working time because of a layoff.

When recessions come or there is a major product shift, some companies handle the work-force imbalances that result by letting people go. IBM hasn't done that, hopes never to have to. People are a treasured resource. They are treated like one.

What does IBM do? It retrains, reassigns, and even relocates employees when necessary. The object? To provide them with both meaningful jobs and jobs in which they have a real chance for success and satisfaction. Of course, this requires employees to be flexible—willing to change, work overtime, and adapt to new situations quickly.

It's hardly a surprise that one of the main reasons people like to work for IBM is the company's all-out effort to maintain full employment.

Source: IBM publication. Courtesy of IBM.

mate. More and more top executive groups are describing the culture and climate they want in their organizations. As was pointed out in Chapter 4, management philosophy and organizational culture and climate dramatically affect the design of human resources programs.

Human resources planning, then, is the ongoing planning of the organization's human resources philosophy, policies, and programs in the context of the overall strategic plans and the changing conditions within and outside of the organization. Clearly it is a much more complex and broader process than a personnel director's sitting at a desk drawing an organization chart and making notes, as Alan Corelli started out doing in Case 6.1. That was a good start, but as Alan found out, it was only a start.

Relationship to the Staffing Process

The role of human resources planning in the staffing process is critical (see Figure 6.3). In all but the smallest organizations, human resources planning must be systematic and ongoing to ensure continuous and adequate staffing. In large organizations, planning should be continual for all units and for the entire organization, with a central planning group analyzing information obtained from a variety of sources. However, organizations sometimes pay too little attention to human resources planning until there is some emergency, such as when needed skills are in short supply. Then planning may be too late. It may not be possible to solve the problem on an immediate or short-term basis.

Consequences of Inadequate Planning. One example of inadequate planning is the case of an organization caught in a severe budget crisis for which management sees only one solution—to lay off large numbers of employees. Careful planning for such a crisis during better times might have resulted in a series of alternatives making layoffs unnecessary. The first step might be to curtail hiring and allow retirements and resignations to reduce the payroll. In some cases, the effect might be great enough to permit the organization to survive the crisis without further action. If a hiring freeze is not adequate, the organization might induce voluntary retirements by offering financial incentives to those people within a few years of retirement. (The organization would need to analyze the probable consequences for various units, however, before offering the early retirement possibility. In Case 6.1 at the beginning of the chapter, an early retirement offer might seriously deplete the management ranks.) The merits of nontraditional staffing methods (such

FIGURE 6.3   Human resource planning: The first step in the staffing process

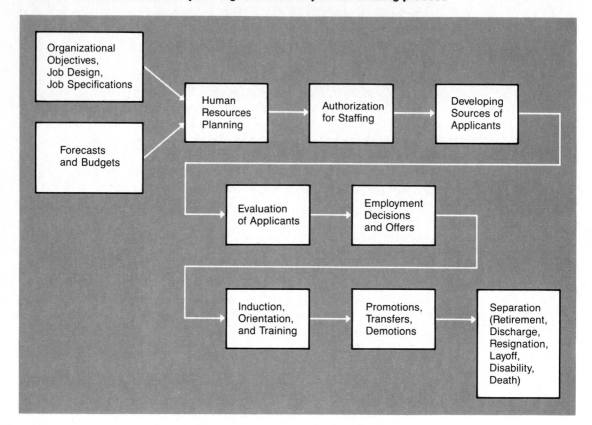

as permanent part-time work and job-sharing) and other approaches to reducing the work force can also be evaluated as part of the human resources planning process.

Many other problems can occur if human resources planning is haphazard or neglected. For example, planning should take into account staff reductions in all parts of the organization and should be tied into any system for transferring employees. Staff reductions might be contemplated by top management because of declining sales or increased automation, including the use of computers or robots. However, it would be obvious mismanagement to lay off people in one part of the organization if their critical skills are needed in another area.

In addition, effective human resources planning requires careful monitoring of attrition rates in various units. **Attrition** is the voluntary separation of employees from the organization through resignation and retirement. Such data not only provide information

---

PERSPECTIVE 6.2 Du Pont's Early Retirement Plan Backfires

Wilmington, Del.—Du Pont Co. has been caught off-guard by the popularity of a voluntary early-retirement plan it offered its employees in January.

About 12,000 employees, or twice as many as Du Pont expected, have agreed to retire early by April 30, including many in important technical and supervisory jobs whom the company had expected to keep, according to company sources. The early retirements amount to 8% of Du Pont's work force. . . .

John R. Malloy, Du Pont's vice president for external affairs, described the program as a "huge success," though he conceded that the company will lose some people it wanted to keep. "The impact of the program is that we will be leaner faster than we anticipated," he said. "We knew we would get someplace soon and we are there sooner." . . .

Several Du Pont employees said the retirements would deplete the work force in a number of areas throughout the company, notably among hourly workers at certain plants and researchers in textiles, chemicals and pigments. The sources also said some valued employees who planned to retire early were induced to stay through raises and bonuses.

Under the plan, as many as five years of credit were added to an employee's age and length of service in calculating pension benefits. With the credit, the pension of a 53-year-old retiree with a salary of $25,000 and 22 years of service would be $675 a month, compared with $275 a month without the incentive.

"Because the program hits at the 50- to 60-year-old age group, it has taken some key people who are very creative," said a retiring agricultural chemical researcher in his mid-50s. He described the plan as "manna from heaven."

The early-retirement plan is expected to hinder operations at some Du Pont plants, particularly as longtime workers are replaced by less-experienced ones. At a textile plant in Martinsville, Va., 500 members of a 2,200-worker bargaining unit are leaving, union officials estimated. At Chambers Works in Deepwater, N.J., Du Pont's largest plant for non-military products, plant manager Robert Shinn estimated that 440 of the 4,000 employees are leaving.

"The bottom has dropped out," said one Chambers Works employee. "Du Pont never expected so many people would bail out." The employee said that some workers were asked to delay their departure until the fall to give the company time to regroup.

Source: Alix M. Freedman, "Du Pont Surprised as 12,000 Employees Accept Company Early-Retirement Offer," *Wall Street Journal,* April 9, 1985, p. 6. Reprinted by permission of *The Wall Street Journal,* © Dow Jones & Company, Inc. 1985. All rights reserved.

---

for planning recruiting and hiring but can provide some clues about morale as well. If the resignation rate in a given department is high, the human resources staff can make discreet inquiries about why. Once the causes are understood, corrective action can be taken.

Budgetary Considerations. Human resources planning should also take into account budgetary allocations for staffing; in addition, staffing budgets must be based on a realistic appraisal of human resources requirements. Obviously, hiring should not occur at a faster rate than the overall budget permits. There may be times when the organization cannot afford to employ workers with certain skills because of limited financial resources. Planned expenditures for wages and salaries must be balanced against plans for adding machinery and increasing inventories. It is important that the human resources department work closely with the accounting and finance departments during the planning process and that this collaborative planning be based on realistic marketing, income, and cost projections.

The Labor Agreement.   An organization's labor agreement is also a major consideration in staffing decisions. Typically, the labor contract contains provisions regulating transfers, demotions, discharges, bidding on job openings, and layoff procedures. For example, many labor contracts require that seniority be a factor in layoff procedures and that recall of laid-off employees be based on reverse order of layoff. In addition, rules in the labor contract concerning transfers and promotion will affect which jobs are filled from the outside. If the contract requires the posting of a job in order to give union members an opportunity to apply for it, the net effect may be that higher-level jobs are filled from within and that new employees are hired into lower job classifications. Strikes, of course, are emergency situations requiring planning for such matters as the proper shutdown of equipment, protection of plant equipment and property, and whether to continue operations with nonstriking employees.

Data Collection and Monitoring.   If continual and high-quality planning is to take place, data on individuals such as skill level, job title, pay grade, date of birth, and department must be systematically collected, processed, and interpreted. Computer programs can be particularly helpful in large and medium-sized organizations to manage data involving hundreds, if not thousands, of employees under several pay plans and in numerous skill classifications and pay grades. Charts and tables can be helpful in visualizing trends in the external labor market. The low cost of a personal computer with a printer and the availability of useful programs can enable even the smallest organizations to have an important human resources planning and record-keeping tool.[5]

THE EXTERNAL LABOR MARKET

Understanding the external labor market is extremely important in human resources planning. Because of the need for continuous and adequate staffing, every enterprise depends on the quality and quantity of human resources external to it. Thus the quality of training and education in the broader society is of great consequence to each organization.

Innovations in technology and science, in particular, tend to have a dramatic and often immediate impact on skill and talent needs. Obsolete products, equipment, or work methods can create surpluses of skills in a relatively short time. For example, projections indicate that the need for keypunch operators, stenographers, and airline reservations and ticket agents will decline in the late 1980s as a result of improved technology.[6] On the other hand, the new technology—in this case small computers and related equipment—will increase the demand for workers who are skilled in using this equipment. Shortages of certain skills in the external labor market may suggest the need to develop specialized internal training programs, to redesign certain jobs, or to encourage educational institutions to expand programs in certain skills. Skill surpluses may suggest reductions in these programs.

Figure 6.4 suggests that the demand for workers through 1990 will vary widely among different categories of employment. Em-

FIGURE 6.4   Projected changes in employment by occupational groups through the 1980s

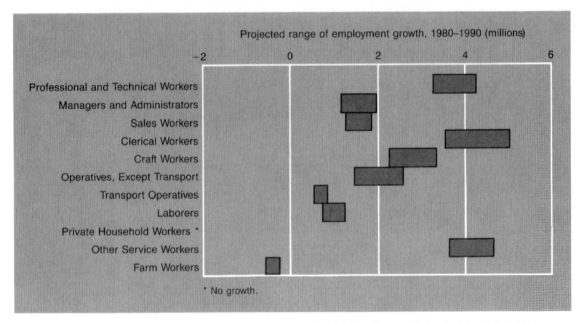

Source: U.S. Department of Labor, *Occupational Outlook Handbook, 1982-83 Edition,* Bureau of Labor Statistics, Bulletin 2200, April 1982, p. 17.

ployment of clerical workers is projected to grow by 3.5 to 5 million workers between 1980 and 1990. Employment of professional and technical workers will grow by 3.3 to 4.3 million. Employment of sales workers, on the other hand, will grow by only 1.3 to about 2 million.[7] Note that these statistics reflect national trends, and that regional and local trends may be very different. Human resources specialists need to track trends at all three levels to forecast skills available in the external labor market accurately.

IMPACT OF FEDERAL LEGISLATION AND REGULATIONS

Over the years, attitudes of both managers and employees in many organizations have tended to suppress the employment of minorities in certain jobs, particularly supervisory and white-collar positions. Members of minority groups have commonly been employed as unskilled laborers or relegated to production and maintenance jobs. Similarly, women have traditionally been underemployed in a wide range of occupational categories. While these situations are gradually being corrected, much remains to be accomplished. For example, although blacks and Hispanics have increased their share of white-collar and skilled jobs in the last two decades, they are still poorly represented in some job categories, particularly in professional, technical, managerial, and sales occupations.

Today all organizations share the need to eliminate from the workplace **discrimination**, or employment decisions based on racial or sexual prejudice. In the past twenty years, legislation protecting employees and job applicants from discrimination has made **equal employment opportunity**, or equal consideration regardless of such personal characteristics as sex and race, the single most important requirement of all human resources planning efforts. These efforts must, at the very least, ensure compliance with existing legislation; in addition, human resources planners must stay informed of current litigation and new court decisions that provide organizations with guidelines for improving their equal opportunity programs.

This section describes in some detail the antidiscrimination laws, major court cases, and changing social attitudes affecting all planning and staffing decisions in human resources management today. The underlying theme of this discussion is that a firm commitment to equal employment opportunity is advantageous to any organization because (1) discrimination suits are costly to the organization in terms of court-enforced financial settlements and poor public image and (2) discriminatory hiring practices have systematically excluded much-needed skills and talents from the workplace. In an organization committed to thorough, high-quality human resources planning, much can be done actively to improve job opportunities for women and minorities. In turn, such planning efforts can have positive effects on overall organizational performance.

The Civil Rights Act and the Equal Pay Act

Title VII of the Civil Rights Act of 1964, as amended by the Equal Employment Opportunity Act of 1972, prohibits discrimination in employment on the basis of race, color, religion, sex, or national origin. Title VII applies to private employers of fifteen or more persons, state and local government, educational institutions, employment agencies, and labor unions. There are certain exemptions, such as the U.S. government (covered under executive orders) and Indian tribes. The most significant aspects of the law are shown in Table 6.1.

Occasionally, exceptions to the law may be made where religion, sex, or national origin (but not race or color), is a **bona fide occupational qualification** (BFOQ). An example of a BFOQ might be a French restaurant's hiring a French cook.[8] Such exceptions, however, are very rare. In most cases, it is difficult if not impossible to justify any personnel decision solely on the basis of sex, religion, or national origin.

The Equal Employment Opportunity Commission (EEOC), an independent federal agency composed of five members, was created by the Civil Rights Act of 1964 to investigate charges of discrimination and to resolve problems "by informal methods of conference, conciliation, and persuasion." Originally, court action beyond this step had to be undertaken by the party charging discrimination if these informal methods did not solve the problem. Amendments made to the law in March 1972 now permit the EEOC itself to bring lawsuits against employers in the federal courts. This means the EEOC is free to seek court orders to enforce its decisions. In addition, the EEOC prepares written guidelines that translate Title VII requirements into legal employment practices. Although these are guidelines, not binding laws, they can be used as standards for evaluating the extent to which an organization is complying with Title VII. (See Chapter 9 for a discussion of the "Uniform Guidelines on Employee Selection Procedures" issued jointly by the EEOC and other federal agencies.)

In many parts of the country, appropriate local agencies are given a period of time in which to process discrimination charges

TABLE 6.1   Excerpts from Title VII, Civil Rights Act of 1964 (as amended by the Equal Employment Opportunity Act of 1972)

Sec. 703:

(a) It shall be an unlawful employment practice for an employer—

(1) to fail or refuse to hire or to discharge any individual, or otherwise to discriminate against any individual with respect to his compensation, terms, conditions, or privileges of employment, because of such individual's race, color, religion, sex, or national origin; or

(2) to limit, segregate, or classify his employees or applicants for employment in any way which would deprive or tend to deprive any individual of employment opportunities or otherwise adversely affect his status as an employee, because of such individual's race, color, religion, sex, or national origin.

(b) It shall be an unlawful employment practice for an employment agency to fail or refuse to refer for employment, or otherwise to discriminate against, any individual because of his race, color, religion, sex or national origin, or to classify or refer for employment any individual on the basis of his race, color, religion, sex, or national origin.

(c) It shall be an unlawful employment practice for a labor organization—

(1) to exclude or to expel from its membership, or otherwise to discriminate against, any individual because of his race, color, religion, sex, or national origin;

(2) to limit, segregate, or classify its membership or applicants for membership or to classify or fail or refuse to refer for employment any individual in any way which would deprive or tend to deprive any individual of employment opportunities, or would limit such employment opportunities or otherwise adversely affect his status as an employee or as an applicant for employment, because of such individual's race, color, religion, sex, or national origin; or

(3) to cause or attempt to cause an employer to discriminate against an individual in violation of this section.

(d) It shall be an unlawful employment practice for any employer, labor organization, or joint labor-management committee controlling apprenticeship or other training or retraining, including on-the-job training programs, to discriminate against any individual because of his race, color, religion, sex, or national origin in admission to, or employment in, any program established to provide apprenticeship or other training.

before the EEOC steps in for further action. Most states have fair employment practice laws and enforcement agencies to which the commission defers for initial action.[9]

Title VII specifies certain penalties for organizations found guilty of discrimination. These include the court's ordering the organization to stop engaging in the unlawful practice, the reinstatement or hiring of employees with or without back pay, and the payment of reasonable attorney's fees.[10]

The Equal Pay Act of 1963 prohibits discrimination on the basis of sex in wage payments for jobs that require equal skills, effort, and responsibility under similar working conditions in the same establishment. This act, along with the Civil Rights Act, has extensive effects on human resources planning and decision making in thousands of organizations today. The impact of the Civil Rights

Act and the Equal Pay Act can readily be seen in court awards and in out-of-court settlements:

- In an early case, AT&T agreed to pay $12 million in back wages and $40 million in pay adjustments to women and minority employees.[11]

- Merrill, Lynch, Pierce, Fenner & Smith agreed to a consent settlement including $1.9 million in back pay to women and minority employees; $1.3 million to recruit Spanish-Americans, blacks, and women into broker positions; and the promotion of one hundred women sales assistants to account executives.[12]

- General Motors agreed to spend $42.5 million to hire, train, and promote more women and minorities to resolve an EEOC administrative complaint.

- The Burlington Northern Railroad and the EEOC agreed to a $50 million settlement to resolve charges of racial bias in hiring, initial assignment, transfer, testing and training, discipline, and promotion. The award included $10 million in back pay, and the organization was required to give priority consideration in hiring to black applicants who had previously been rejected.[13]

- The Ponderosa steak-house chain agreed to pay over $1 million to 221 women who charged that the firm had discriminated against them in pay and managerial promotions.[14]

- In a decision that could cost the state of Washington nearly $1 billion, a federal district judge ordered that the state to raise the salaries of some 15,000 employees in predominantly female categories. (The decision was overturned on an initial appeal.)[15]

Overcoming Sex Discrimination

At first, the ban on discrimination on the basis of sex was referred to as a "sleeper" in the Civil Rights Act. Most of the congressional debate surrounding the act centered on racial discrimination, and the provision about sex was introduced by opponents in an attempt to defeat the bill. Alleged discrimination on the basis of sex, however, now constitutes a high percentage of the cases filed with the EEOC. Many of the recent cases culminating in consent settlements involved charges of discrimination against women in hiring, pay, and promotion. In response to these court-ordered settlements and to pressure from organized women's groups, many traditional employment practices are being altered dramatically.

Among these changing practices is the growing use of nonsexist terminology in job labels to avoid implications of discrimination in recruiting and hiring. For example, the *Dictionary of Occupational Titles* (DOT), published by the U.S. Department of Labor, has changed many of the job titles listed there.[16] To illustrate, *airplane stewardess* has been changed to *airplane flight attendant, surveying axman* to *surveying brush clearer, brewmaster* to *brewing director, bus boy* to *dining room attendant, fisherman* to *fisher, foreman* to *supervisor, governess* to *child mentor, new car salesman* to *new car associate,* and *salesman* to *salesperson.*

Some discrimination complaints are being filed by men seeking jobs traditionally held by women. Not long ago, for example, the Supreme Court declined to reverse a circuit court of appeals ruling that an airline's refusal to hire a male flight attendant was in violation of the Civil Rights Act.[17] Since that decision, an increasing number of men have been employed as flight attendants. More recently, Pacific Southwest Airlines agreed to pay $275,000 in back wages and offer flight attendant jobs to males and to blacks and Hispanics of both sexes.[18] As a result of the settlement with AT&T cited earlier, males are being hired as telephone operators with increasing frequency.[19]

The most dramatic change in employment practices, however, is the placement of women in jobs traditionally filled by men. Today, women are employed as police officers, blacksmiths, coal miners, boilermakers, truck drivers, army paratroopers, locomotive engineers, surveyors, hog buyers, firefighters, fire chiefs, baseball umpires, zoo keepers, commercial airline pilots, U.S. Navy and Coast Guard officers, and astronauts.

Overall, participation by women in the work force has increased dramatically during the last few decades. As shown in Figure 6.5, the proportion of women in the labor force increased 17 percent, from 33.9 percent of all women in 1950 to 51.2 percent in 1980. During the same period, the proportion of men employed dropped from 86.4 percent to 77.2 percent, a decline of more than 9 percent.

But in spite of the growing number of women in the overall work force and the increase in female employees in traditionally male jobs, statistics from the U.S. Department of Labor indicate that women are still substantially underrepresented in certain occupations. These include engineer, lawyer, physician, sales representative, carpenter, and mechanic.[20] Analysis of the data in Table 6.2 (on p. 159) shows that 15.2 percent of employed men are in executive, administrative, and managerial jobs, while 8.6 percent of women are employed in that category. Further, 20.7 percent of men are employed in precision production, craft, and repair work, while 2.3 percent of women are employed in these kinds of jobs.

The entry of women into the work force is associated with certain changes in stereotyped attitudes and mythical assumptions about

FIGURE 6.5
Percentage of men and women in work force, 1950-1980.

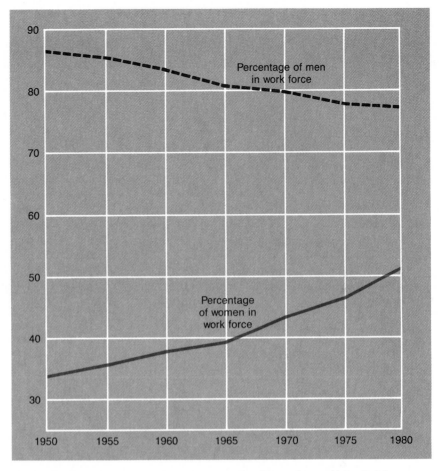

Source: U.S. Department of Labor, *Perspectives on Working Women,* Bureau of Labor Statistics, October 1980, p. 3.

working women. For example, the notion that most women are working "just for pin money" has been refuted by a University of Michigan study, which revealed that one-third of working women surveyed were the sole wage earners in their households. The same study found that most women were just as concerned about opportunities for self-actualization and promotion as were men.[21]

Findings like these have clear implications for the planning and design of all human resources management programs. Organizations must be concerned with satisfying the particular needs of female workers to reduce dissatisfaction and turnover and to enhance their contributions to organizational performance. Skill training and career development programs for female workers are

Courtesy of International Business Machines Corporation

Work force participation by women has increased dramatically in the last decade.

one way of reaching this goal. Organizations must also make some accommodation to the fact that women still carry much of the responsibility for child care in our society. Flexible work schedules and the provision of day-care services by some organizations are indications that this accommodation is beginning to take place.

The Age Discrimination in Employment Act

Certain stereotypes and distorted attitudes about older workers also exist. One is that the older worker is less productive. A research study by Schwab and Heneman, which involved a random sample of semiskilled assemblers in a factory, found this to be untrue. In the sample, productivity increased with age.[22] Other myths hold that the older worker costs the firm more in absenteeism, illness, insurance, pensions, workmen's compensation, and so on. None of these assumptions may be true in a given firm, and

TABLE 6.2 Employed civilians 25 to 64 years old by sex, selected occupation, and years of school completed, March 1984

| | | | PERCENT DISTRIBUTION | | | |
| | | | Years of school completed | | | |
SEX AND OCCUPATION	TOTAL EMPLOYED (THOUSANDS)	Total	Less than 4 years of high school	4 years of high school only	1 to 3 years of college	4 years of college or more
MEN						
Total, 25 to 64 years	45,412	100.0	17.3	36.2	18.3	28.2
Managerial and professional specialty	13,123	100.0	3.5	15.1	15.7	65.7
Executive, administrative, and managerial	6,899	100.0	5.8	22.6	19.5	52.1
Professional specialty	6,225	100.0	.9	6.8	11.5	80.7
Technical, sales, and administrative support	9,015	100.0	7.6	34.6	27.5	30.3
Technicians and related support	1,358	100.0	3.3	28.8	33.9	33.9
Sales occupations	5,199	100.0	7.7	32.5	26.2	33.6
Administrative support, including clerical	2,459	100.0	9.6	42.2	26.6	21.6
Service occupations	3,410	100.0	25.6	41.8	21.6	11.1
Private household	28	100.0	(1)	(1)	(1)	(1)
Protective service	1,131	100.0	10.3	43.6	31.8	14.3
Food service	645	100.0	30.2	38.1	20.6	10.9
Health service	132	100.0	25.8	38.6	18.2	16.7
Cleaning and building service	1,201	100.0	39.0	43.0	12.2	5.9
Personal service	273	100.0	17.6	38.5	24.5	19.0
Precision production, craft, and repair	9,386	100.0	23.2	52.5	18.4	5.9
Operators, fabricators, and laborers	8,629	100.0	34.7	49.7	12.1	3.6
Farming, forestry, and fishing	1,849	100.0	37.2	38.6	14.1	10.2
WOMEN						
Total, 25 to 64 years	34,953	100.0	13.6	44.8	19.1	22.5
Managerial and professional specialty	9,435	100.0	2.3	19.2	19.2	58.7
Executive, administrative, and managerial	3,442	100.0	3.7	36.2	24.8	35.2
Professional specialty	5,992	100.0	1.4	9.5	16.6	72.4
Technical, sales, and administrative support	15,085	100.0	6.6	56.1	24.7	12.5
Technicians and related support	1,269	100.0	3.1	36.6	33.8	26.5
Sales occupations	3,684	100.0	12.2	54.3	19.0	14.4
Administrative support, including clerical	10,132	100.0	5.0	59.2	25.7	10.1
Service occupations	5,632	100.0	31.3	52.0	12.1	4.6
Private household	549	100.0	51.4	38.3	9.8	.5
Protective service	128	100.0	14.8	53.9	20.3	10.9
Food service	1,823	100.0	32.4	54.6	10.1	3.0
Health service	1,135	100.0	23.6	55.4	15.9	5.0
Cleaning and building service	817	100.0	48.6	42.8	6.2	2.2
Personal service	1,178	100.0	17.5	57.4	15.8	9.3
Precision production, craft, and repair	835	100.0	26.9	53.8	12.3	6.9
Operators, fabricators, and laborers	3,632	100.0	40.0	50.6	7.3	2.2
Farming, forestry, and fishing	335	100.0	31.9	44.2	14.3	9.6

[1]Percent not shown where base is less than 75,000.

Source: Monthly Labor Review, 108 (February 1985): 45.

only a careful analysis of personnel policies in the individual company will reveal the true costs of employing older versus younger workers. Many employers have found the older worker to have greater experience and better retention rates, and to be more satisfied with the job and the organization.

The Age Discrimination in Employment Act of 1967 (ADEA) was designed to protect older workers against age discrimination in hiring, retention, promotion, compensation, and other conditions of employment. Essentially, the act makes it illegal to base salary decisions on age, to pass over older employees for promotions, and to discharge or impose retirement on older workers in order to replace them with younger workers or to lower costs of pension benefits. This act applies to any employer subject to Title VII and is enforced by the secretary of labor. Amendments to the ADEA in 1978 banned involuntary or **mandatory retirement** before age seventy by private employers of twenty or more people and at any age for most occupations in the federal government.

There are a few exceptions to the provisions of the ADEA. For example, mandatory retirement at age sixty-five is permitted for those executive or policy making employees who have held their positions for at least two years and whose annual retirement benefits total at least $27,000.[23] Occasionally, age is considered a bona fide occupational qualification, although this exemption is interpreted narrowly by the secretary of labor. An example of a BFOQ given by the government is a young actor required for a youthful role. In addition, employers may override age criteria when applying the terms of bona fide (nondiscriminatory) seniority systems and the legal provisions of company benefit plans. For example, the age provisions of a retirement plan are no excuse to refrain from hiring an individual, but an employer is not required to place the individual under the plan if his or her age bracket has been excluded. Finally, nothing in the act prevents an employer from disciplining or discharging an older worker as long as these activities are taken for valid job-related reasons.

Lawsuits involving charges of age discrimination are on the increase. In one court case, the Department of Labor charged that the Friendly Ice Cream Corporation had discriminated against older applicants for its management trainee program. In the resulting settlement, which affected 380 restaurants in eleven states, the firm agreed to establish an affirmative hiring program for older workers and to pay back wages to passed-over applicants.[24] Marshall Field & Company agreed to pay up to $2.5 million to one hundred current and former employees who charged the company with illegal demotions, discharge, or early retirement of older employees.[25] The U.S. Supreme Court held that TWA violated federal law when it forced some of its pilots to retire at age sixty by not permitting them to transfer to the job of flight engineer.[26] The Equitable Life Assurance Society agreed to a $12.5 million settlement in a case involving 363 former employees. All were over forty years of age and had been fired, according to the company, as part of a cost-cutting plan.[27]

Many other firms have been sued by managers who have been fired, forced into early retirement, or passed over for promotion. Some of the firms that have either lost age discrimination suits or settled out of court include Sandia National Laboratories, Eastern Air Lines, Atlantic Container Line, Textron, Connecticut General Life Insurance, ITT Corporation, Pan American World Airways, and Standard Oil Company of California.[28]

Clearly, human resources planning needs to accommodate to the ADEA to avoid charges of discrimination based on age. Beyond that, however, it is important that the organization develop personnel policies and practices that will enhance and maintain the motivation and morale of employees of all ages, including those over forty.

The Rehabilitation Act

It has been estimated that roughly 18 percent of the country's noninstitutional population aged eighteen to sixty-four is handicapped in some way. This percentage represents a larger group of workers than any one racial minority.[29] Out of this huge group, only about 15 percent of the employable disabled are working.[30]

Employer attitudes are a major factor in the underemployment of the handicapped. One study showed employer's attitudes to be less favorable toward the disabled than toward any other minority, including ex-convicts.[31] In addition to prejudice, there are other barriers to employment of the handicapped, such as overly strict job requirements, inappropriately designed jobs, and improper physical facilities.

Concern for the employable disabled led to the passage of a federal law prohibiting discrimination against the physically handicapped. The Rehabilitation Act of 1973, Section 503, requires employers with government contracts over $2,500 to take positive steps to enhance employment and promotion opportunities for qualified handicapped individuals. Section 504 requires every institution in the country getting federal assistance, such as colleges and hospitals, to take steps to assure that handicapped individuals are not discriminated against in employment.[32]

The hiring of the handicapped requires very careful planning by individual organizations. Disabled and handicapped workers have special needs, and advance planning is needed to place such workers in appropriate jobs and to make necessary adjustments in the physical plant (for example, building ramps and special restroom facilities and providing Braille lettering on elevator buttons).[33] Jobs may need to be redesigned so that handicapped employees can perform them effectively, and special training programs may also be necessary. Meeting these challenges should be an integral part of the overall human resources planning process.

Affirmative Action

A crucial element in the human resources planning process is the need for **affirmative action**. Affirmative action has been defined as "a remedial concept that requests employers and labor unions to take positive steps voluntarily to improve the work opportunities of women, racial and ethnic minorities, handicapped workers, and Vietnam veterans who have been deprived of job opportunities.[34] Affirmative action plans are legal requirements of most federal contractors and subcontractors under Executive Order 11246. This order is enforced by the Office of Federal Contract Compliance Programs (OFCCP), Department of Labor.[35] Affirmative action plans are also required under the Rehabilitation Act of 1973, under the Vietnam Era Veterans Readjustment Assistance Act of 1974 (which protects the employment rights of all disabled veterans), and under Executive Order 11478 (which calls for affirmative action in all federal agencies).

Under these executive orders and legislation, contractors are required to develop and administer affirmative action plans with specific goals and timetables for raising the level of minority and female employment in their firms. Typically, the long-term goal is to raise minority and female employment to a level comparable to the percentage of minority and female workers in the local work force. Voluntary affirmative action programs, however, may include higher interim goals or targets. Such interim goals can upgrade overall employment prospects for minority and female workers more quickly.[36]

Once these goals and timetables have been established, employers develop and administer specific programs to meet them. As part of this process, employers are advised to review *all* existing employment practices. In this way they can identify and remove barriers to equal employment opportunity and make changes that will increase employment and advancement opportunities for minorities and females. Thus the goals established in affirmative action plans will directly affect recruitment, hiring, training, and all other aspects of human resources management.

An example of the impact of affirmative action regulations is the

1980 consent agreement between Uniroyal and the Department of Labor in which the company agreed to establish special hiring goals for minorities and women and to pay $5.2 million in back pay to 750 women workers.[37] In the same year, Firestone was barred from doing business with the federal government until the company could demonstrate that it was complying with affirmative action regulations.[38]

The legality of affirmative action was upheld by the U.S. Supreme Court in 1979. In *Kaiser Aluminum and Chemical Corp.* v. *Weber*, the court ruled that affirmative action programs implemented voluntarily by employers and unions to enhance employment opportunities for minorities are legal. In this case, Brian Weber, an employee of Kaiser Aluminum & Chemical Corporation, had been passed over for a training program in favor of black employees with less seniority. The company had made its trainee selections under a union-management agreement establishing a 50 percent quota for black trainees until the proportion of black employees corresponded to the proportion of blacks in the local labor force. One implication of this ruling is that employers can establish "race-conscious" affirmative action programs unilaterally or in cooperation with unions in order to correct imbalances in a work force.[39]

The Weber decision did not guarantee that all affirmative action programs would be approved. Five years later, the Supreme Court ruled in *Fire Fighters Local 1784* v. *Stotts* that a bona fide seniority system cannot be overridden in a layoff situation to protect an affirmative action program. In that case, nonminority City of Memphis employees with more seniority than minority employees had been laid off or demoted. The union and the city went to court on behalf of the nonminority employees and ultimately prevailed. In writing for the majority, Justice White cited a 1964 memorandum issued by congressional sponsors of Title VII that said, "Title VII does not permit the ordering of racial quotas in business or unions."[40]

The dissenting opinions of several Supreme Court members suggest that the whole issue of quota systems has not been finally resolved. Human resources planners, as well as managers in general, will need to be alert to ongoing court decisions and administrative rulings affecting affirmative action efforts.

ROLE OF THE HUMAN RESOURCES DEPARTMENT

Typically, the human resources department has a major role in human resources planning. One study of 631 firms found that the personnel department was responsible for all or some of the human resources planning in 86 percent of them and was assigned all or some responsibility for EEOC compliance and affirmative action in

98 percent.[41] Another study of a variety of industries found labor-force forecasting to be a function assigned to the personnel department in 74 percent of the firms surveyed. The same study found that 95 percent of the firms had assigned management of EEOC activities to the personnel department.[42]

These assignments are appropriate because the personnel department is typically at the center of an information network on labor-market conditions, skill levels in various departments, mobility patterns within the organization, departmental wage and salary structures, and federal and state legislation and court rulings. To make its maximum contribution to organizational effectiveness, the personnel department must take the initiative in becoming actively and responsively involved in matters of human resources planning.

Teamwork among the total executive group in human resources planning, however, is extremely important. One study compared firms that were leaders in productivity with a random sample of other large firms. The study found that the human resources department of a leading firm was *three times* more likely to be working with line managers in such matters as succession and compensation-system planning. Further, when human resources executives were queried about the role their department played in the corporation, many more executives in the leading firms reported that their departments participated in business decisions and contributed to their company's achievement of its strategic goals.[43] Clearly, effective human resources planning is a collaborative effort that is closely related to the strategic planning of the organization.

SUMMARY

Human resources planning requires ongoing analysis of the organization's human resources needs in the light of the external environment, the organization's strategic goals, and the desired organizational culture and climate. The planning of specific human resources programs — such as recruitment, training, promotion, and compensation — to meet those needs can then follow.

Effective human resources planning should take into account the present and anticipated financial condition of the organization as well as the changing human resources needs within its various departments. It is an important coordinating function that ensures that the valuable human resources of the organization are carefully nurtured and developed. Systematic data collection and interpretation are essential to this process.

Federal legislation, Equal Employment Opportunity Commission rulings, and court decisions have a major impact on both human resources planning and specific program design. The Civil Rights Act, Equal Pay Act, Age Discrimination in Employment Act, Equal Employment Opportunity Act, Rehabilitation Act, and Vietnam Era Veterans Readjustment Assistance Act, in particular, have had a profound influence on recruitment, hiring, promotion, training, discipline, compensation, and separation practices.

Affirmative action requires employers and labor unions to take positive steps to improve the work opportunities of minorities, women, the handicapped, and Vietnam War veterans. The goals established in affirmative action plans will directly affect recruitment, hiring, training, and all other aspects of human resources management. Specific methods for implementing affirmative action mean that the human resources specialists must keep informed of changing government policy and legal actions in this area.

The human resources department has a major role in human resources planning. Ideally, effective human resources planning is a collaborative effort involving all managers in the organization. Further, human resources planning must be closely related to the overall strategic planning of the organization.

KEY TERMS

human resources planning	succession planning	bonafide occupational
strategic plan	attrition	qualification
organizational goal	discrimination	mandatory retirement
organizational objective	equal employment	affirmative action
needs forecasting	opportunity	

REVIEW QUESTIONS

1. Define human resources planning and describe two major steps in the planning process.
2. Explain how human resources planning is related to the overall strategic plan of the organization.
3. How are human resources planning and the staffing process related?
4. Why is an understanding of the external labor market important in human resources planning?
5. What federal laws and regulations have had the most impact on human resources planning and in what way?
6. What is affirmative action? How does affirmative action affect human resources planning?

OPENING CASE QUESTIONS

Case 6.1 A Can of Worms

1. Now that Alan Corelli has set up committees to assess the promotability of the company's present employees, what other steps in human resources planning should he take?
2. What options are available to Quality Chemicals to prepare current employees for the key positions Alan may soon need to fill?

Case 6.2 Not Very Clear at Kleer

1. Why was Sam Kagi concerned about all of Kleer Optics personnel policies when the focus was on affirmative action?
2. Whose reponsibility is it to make sure a company is meeting government standards with regard to EEOC?

CASE 6.3   FILLING THE TOP SPOTS AT GENERAL MOTORS*

General Motors (GM) is significantly reshaping itself to compete more effectively in the future. Inconsistent profitability is its prime motivating force for change. For example, GM tallied a $763 million loss in 1980, the company's first losing year since 1921. Just three years later, in 1983, GM recorded its most profitable year ever. One factor that will help GM reorganize for more stable profitability is the high quality of its executive personnel.

GM's top management is proud of its close-knit executive group, its record of hiring fewer executives from outside than other major U.S. companies do, and its low executive turnover. Two-thirds of the auto giant's executives reportedly have worked only for GM. It has been estimated, on the basis of executive turnover during 1980, that less than 1 percent of GM's 6000 highest executives will ever leave the company. GM admirers claim that the firm has a stable corporate culture and a Japanese-like organization in which loyalty is highly valued and rewarded. Critics have called GM a corporate hive of organization people in which innovation and risk taking are often in short supply.

No "Instant Executives" at GM

Most GM managers come from small towns and cities in the Upper Midwest where the traditional work ethic, respect for authority, and institutional loyalty have long been entrenched values. Managers who patiently work their way up through the ranks at GM usually develop strong loyalty based on the assumption that if they do a good job they will be appropriately rewarded. And in fact, GM is large and diverse enough to reward loyalty with job security.

Yet observers claim that outsiders are needed to bring vision and innovative leadership to GM. According to *Fortune* magazine, GM "probably would not have too much trouble in attracting a capable visionary to be, say, its president. But such an appointment from outside would have a devastating psychological effect and perhaps cripple the entire management system."*

Case Sources: Reprinted from Robert Kreitner, *Management,* 3rd ed. (Boston: Houghton Mifflin Company), pp. 338–339. For additional information on General Motors, see John K. Teahen, Jr., "GM Reorganizes for Greater Efficiency," *Automotive News* 59 (January 16, 1984): 1, 57; "Can GM Solve Its Identity Crisis?" *Business Week* No. 2825 (January 23, 1984): 32–33; David C. Smith, GM's Reorganization Is 'Off the Wall,' " *Ward's Auto World* 20 (February 1984): 50, 61; John McElroy, "GM's Reorganization: Streamlining For the Future," *Automotive Industries* 164 (February 1984): 21–22; Anne B. Fisher, "GM's Unlikely Revolutionist," *Fortune* 109 (March 19, 1984): 106–112; Neal Goff, "The Case for General Motors," *Financial World* 149 (August 1, 1980): 18–22; Allan Sloan and Christine Miles, "GM's Chance of a Lifetime?" *Forbes* 126 (September 1, 1980): 110–112; "A Tried and True Model for GM," *Fortune* 102 (October 6, 1980): 15–16; and Charles G. Burck, "How GM Stays Ahead," *Fortune* 103 (March 9, 1981): 48–56.
*Burck, "How GM Stays Ahead," p. 54.

GM's promote-from-within policy is not ironclad. Through the years, several vice presidents have been hired from outside to take charge of changing areas, such as personnel, in which new ideas were needed.

An Inventory of Executive Talent

GM's present staffing philosophy can be traced back to Alfred Sloan, the man originally responsible for GM's climb to dominance. Sloan believed that his most important job was finding the right people for the right jobs. Relying on what GM management calls its executive-personnel inventory, the executive committee and group vice presidents hold week-long progression and succession meetings twice a year. GM's executive-personnel inventory details the strengths and weaknesses, along with other relevant notations about promotability, of about 10,000 GM managers. Steps are taken to ensure that an individual manager's inventory entry contains the comments of more than just an immediate superior, that observations from other managers and peers are included as well. Ideally, these precautions help management avoid the problem of promoting or holding back an individual solely on the word of one person.

Discussion Questions

1. How would you characterize GM's human resources plan for the executive level?
2. How do you think a policy like GM's would influence needs forecasting?
3. In what way is GM's policy an example of program planning?

part 3

Job Design and Staffing

This section examines two key aspects of human resources management: determining the tasks to be performed and deciding who will perform them. Chapter 7 focuses on job design and analysis and shows how the content of one's job and the ability to influence job content affect motivation, performance, and satisfaction. Chapter 8 discusses the design and administration of work rules and schedules, which are needed to coordinate day-to-day operations in the organization. Recruitment and selection—critical aspects of the staffing process—are the topics of Chapter 9. Finally, Chapter 10 discusses the effective management of internal staffing changes and career transitions, which are of major consequence to the individuals involved and to the organization as a whole.

Job Design and Analysis

LEARNING OBJECTIVES

- **Define job design and describe the major considerations involved in establishing job content.**
- **Identify the goal of job enrichment and describe some of the positive and negative results associated with this approach to job design.**
- **List the purposes of job analysis and describe the common methods for obtaining information about job content.**
- **Indicate the importance of accurate job descriptions and of appropriate job specifications.**
- **Define performance standards and explain how they are developed.**
- **Describe the responsibilities of the human resources department with respect to job design and job analysis.**

CASE 7.1　　HIGH SEAS AUTOPILOTS

High Seas Autopilots was different from any place Vivian had ever worked. Mostly it was better. She liked the people. She liked the job. And she liked herself.

Before Vivian was hired, she had been interviewed by her present work group and had spent two hours watching the group at work. Now that she was aboard, she was working with the team assembling autopilots from start to finish. She had learned three of the jobs and was looking forward to learning the others, particularly those involving electrical connections. Her pay was increasing as she learned new tasks, which she liked, but she also liked the variety of jobs, and she liked working as part of a team. Her group planned its own production and ordered the necessary parts. The team also established its own production goals and quality standards every three months after meeting with the supervisor and the production manager.

It seemed to Vivian that her supervisor was more a consultant and trouble-shooter than a boss. He worked with several other groups in the same way but was usually available when Vivian's group needed him.

The group members got along very well with each other. It didn't take long before Vivian was being invited to the homes of the others on social occasions.

Vivian had some contact with the people in the front office in addition to the production manager. For example, on two occasions the employment manager dropped by. Once she chatted privately with Vivian to ask her how the orientation to the job had been and whether the training was going all right. The other time she dropped by to ask whether Vivian's pay increases were coming through properly. Somehow this helped make Vivian feel she was important to the company.

CASE 7.2   WHY DID WE WRITE THOSE JOB DESCRIPTIONS?

One of the first things Mary Neale accomplished after being hired as director of human resources for Superior Insurance Company was to write job descriptions — statements of the basic tasks and responsibilities of a job — for all the jobs in the organization. The process took six months and involved the help of all department heads and supervisors, as well as many employees. There was some grumbling behind the scenes about how much time and work the process was taking, but department heads, at least, seemed to concur that job descriptions were probably necessary.

A year after Mary joined the organization, the following conversation took place in the cafeteria between Ruth Altman, controller, and Mark Spence, claims manager. Ruth: "You know, Mary got us to put all that work into writing those dumb job descriptions, and I can't see that anybody has used them for anything. Ours have been filed away — I haven't referred to them once."

Mark: "We haven't used them either. It was mostly a lot of useless paperwork. We did get some things clarified, however. One of my supervisors and a claims adjuster found out they had quite different versions of what the job was about, and talking about that and rewriting the job description got them a little closer to agreement. But mostly the job descriptions just sit there in the files. I guess we need them, but . . ."

These cases describe several issues related to job design, an important concern of human resources management. **Job design** is the process of determining the specific tasks and responsibilities to be carried out by each member of the organization.

Effective job design is a complex process that must be viewed from several standpoints. Meshing jobs with organizational goals, maximizing employee motivation, achieving performance standards, and matching a worker's skills and abilities with job requirements are all key considerations in job design. Ignoring any of them can reduce organizational effectiveness, efficiency, or worker satisfaction.

Case 7.1, "High Seas Autopilots," describes an interesting situation. Vivian was part of a self-managed work group whose members learned a variety of tasks and took turns performing all jobs related to the assembly of autopilots. In this case, broadening the tasks assigned to individual workers and allowing the work group to participate in planning and managing its own operation had positive effects on worker motivation and satisfaction.

In Case 7.2, the new personnel director had seen to it that job descriptions were written for every position in the company. The process had taken six months and required cooperation from supervisors and employees throughout the organization. But as far as some managers were concerned, the effort had been a waste of time. It wasn't clear what purpose the written descriptions served or to what use the information was being put.

Together these cases suggest that organizations need to have a broad and well-thought-out strategy for job design and for analyzing, recording, and using information about particular jobs. Strategies in job design and the purposes of job analysis are the main topics of this chapter. The chapter begins with an overview of the basic considerations in job design and then goes on to describe a contemporary approach to job design known as job enrichment. Some approaches to job design focus on individual jobs, whereas others focus on the total work performed by a team. The need for careful job analysis, accurate job descriptions, and appropriate job requirements (or specifications) — all of which are a direct reflection of job design — are explored next. Throughout this chapter, it will be evident that job design and analysis are closely related to most, if not all, of the major processes in human resources management. Although human resources departments typically do not play a direct role in job design and redesign or in setting performance standards, they can make an important contribution in these areas. Their activities relating to job analysis, job descriptions, and job specifications, however, are much more direct and immediate.

CONSIDERATIONS IN JOB DESIGN

Job design is a fundamental organizational process with many implications for human resources management. As stated earlier, job design is the complex flow of events that establishes the responsibilities assigned to each member of the organization and the physical circumstances in which each employee carries out those responsibilities.

There are two major components of the responsibilities established through job design. One component is **job content.** Job content is the set of activities to be performed on the job, including duties, tasks, and job responsibilities to be carried out; the equipment, machines, and tools to be used; and the required interactions with others.

The other major component of the responsibilities established through job design is the set of **organizational responsibilities** attached to the job, that is, the responsibilities that each employee is expected to carry out, such as complying with rules and work schedules. Examples are filling out time sheets, following safety procedures, and adhering to the established schedule of the workday.

Another aspect of job design is the set of physical working conditions surrounding the job. Examples of working conditions are the extent to which there is comfortable temperature versus extremes of hot or cold, or excellent lighting versus poor lighting, or safe conditions versus hazardous conditions. Such working conditions are part of the design of the job.

Job Content

Establishing the content of a job is the central thrust of job design and is closely related to other human resources management processes. To illustrate, job content determines the skills and abilities the organization must seek in its recruitment and selection efforts. If the job of production supervisor requires several years of on-the-job welding experience with various kinds of metals, a firm is unlikely to recruit applicants from a vocational school. In turn, job content is a major factor in the training that is conducted. Welders who work with aluminum will require different training from welders who work with steel, and the training for both kinds of welding will be different from that needed by aircraft electrical assemblers. Performance appraisal will focus largely on how well the person is carrying out the content of the job. What the person is paid is likely to reflect several factors in the job's content, such as its complexity and the level of responsibility involved. And job content will frequently be a major bargaining issue in negotiations between management and labor unions. For example, the union may insist that a pipefitter should not do any kind of electrical work.

There are various ways to examine job content. For example, Ernest J. McCormick and others have designed a questionnaire that includes some 190 *job elements* that, in turn, can be used to analyze jobs. (These are discussed in the "Job Analysis" section of this chapter.) J. Richard Hackman and Greg R. Oldham, on the other hand, suggest that job content can be viewed in terms of five *core job characteristics:*

- *Skill variety:* The degree to which a job requires a variety of different activities in carrying out the work, involving the use of a number of different skills and talents of the person. . . .

- *Task identity:* The degree to which a job requires completion of a "whole" and identifiable piece of work, that is, doing a job from beginning to end with a visible outcome. . . .
- *Task significance:* The degree to which the job has a substantial impact on the lives of other people. . . .
- *Autonomy:* The degree to which the job provides substantial freedom, independence, and discretion to the individual in scheduling the work and in determining the procedures to be used. . . .
- *Job feedback:* The degree to which carrying out the work activities required by the job provides the individual with direct and clear information about the effectiveness of his or her performance. . .[1]

These core job characteristics can occur in different mixes in different jobs. For example, a mechanic may be employed to tear down and rebuild automobile engines (high task identity), but he or she may be subject to extensive direction from a supervisor and prevented from using efficient methods by the outmoded tools available in the shop (low autonomy). Another job may be high on autonomy but inadequate in skill variety and task identity. In turn, these job characteristics are related to certain individual and organizational outcomes.

Individual and Organizational Outcomes

Recently there has been a good deal of theorizing and research about the consequences for employees of job design and, in particular, job content. The argument is that people have become better educated and their expectations about job satisfaction have increased, but pressures for efficiency have resulted in jobs that are too specialized and narrow and thus less challenging and less meaningful. While most experts would agree that there are, indeed, job design problems in today's organizations, there is substantial disagreement about the extent of the problem. Some observers see worker dissatisfaction in American organizations as a major crisis; others recommend careful diagnosis of morale and productivity on an organization-by-organization basis.[2]

Hackman and Oldham suggest the latter approach and believe the important question is this: "How can we achieve a 'fit' between persons and their jobs that fosters *both* high work productivity and a high-quality organizational experience for the people who do the work?"[3] They propose that organizations analyze jobs using the five core job characteristics described earlier and then redesign jobs to maximize worker motivation.

According to Hackman and Oldham, these core job characteristics are associated with certain psychological states in the worker. As shown in Figure 7.1, skill variety, task identity, and task significance are related to "experienced meaningfulness of the work." Job autonomy is related to "experienced responsibility for outcomes of the work." Feedback from the job is related to the psychological state of "knowledge of the actual results of the work activities." In turn, these psychological states are associated with high work motivation, high satisfaction with the job and with one's growth on the job, and high work effectiveness. Thus, the five job characteristics are important dimensions to consider in designing new jobs or in redesigning existing jobs to increase motivation and improve performance.

As shown at the bottom of Figure 7.1, some factors can moderate or minimize some of these outcomes. One is knowledge and skill. A significant deficiency in either can lead to less than desirable performance and a sense of failure. Another factor that can moderate these outcomes is the strength of the person's need for growth.

FIGURE 7.1 The complete job characteristics model

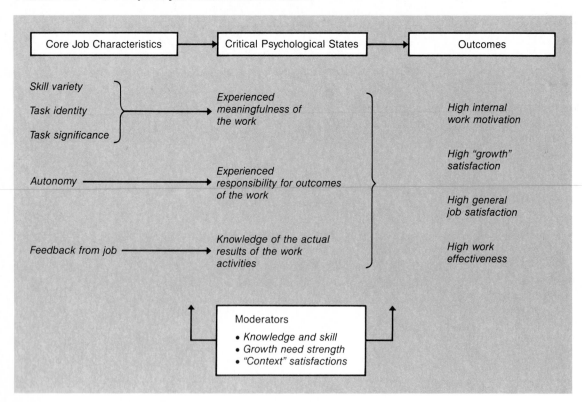

That is, if a person has a low need to learn and develop, the presence of the core job characteristics is less likely to lead to high motivation and high job satisfaction. On the other hand, if a person has a high need to learn and develop, the presence of the core job characteristics is more likely to lead to high motivation and high job satisfaction. In addition, dissatisfaction with the "context" of the job, such as with pay, job security, coworkers, or supervision, is likely to minimize the favorable consequences of designing more complex and challenging jobs.[4]

The five core job characteristics shown in Figure 7.1 can be measured by the Job Diagnostic Survey (JDS), a well-researched instrument that has been used in a wide variety of job redesign projects. The survey is used to determine whether there is a need to redesign work and whether doing so is feasible, given the existing structure of the jobs and existing conditions in the organization. Some of the conditions that need to be considered are provisions of the labor-management contract; how constraining the present technology is and how committed the organization is to it (if the company has invested millions of dollars in assembly-line equipment, it is not likely that there will be much enthusiasm for a job redesign project); and to what extent budgeting, auditing, inventory and other control systems would constrain job modification.[5]

JOB ENRICHMENT

A planned program for enhancing job characteristics is typically called **job enrichment.** We can define job enrichment as the process of enhancing the five core job characteristics for the purpose of increasing worker motivation, productivity, and satisfaction. This concept is different from **job enlargement,** which is the addition of more and different tasks to the job. (Job enlargement is called **horizontal restructuring** when it involves broadening the scope of the job to include tasks that previously preceded or followed in the flow of the work.)

Job enrichment, to use Hackman and Oldham's categories, involves increasing skill variety, task identity, task significance, autonomy, and feedback from the job. This process is sometimes referred to as **vertical restructuring** because it usually includes the addition of some activities previously performed by the supervisory level above, including some of the planning. Thus, job enrichment usually involves adding tasks from the level above, while job enlargement adds tasks from the same level.

Contemporary job enrichment programs have their historical

PERSPECTIVE 7.1   Unionized Companies Move Toward Job Redesign

A new, major objective is emerging for companies seeking to cut costs: Getting more-flexible work rules in union plants.

In industries as diverse as airlines, steel, aerospace, auto manufacturing, communications, and construction, restrictions on the deployment of manpower are being overturned in contract after contract.

By freeing workers to do more than one assigned task and ending an array of work practices employers consider inefficient, they are hoping to gain the kind of workplace flexibility long enjoyed by their nonunion competition.

That, experts say, is leading to increased productivity and ultimately to substantial savings for business. . . .

At its Lynn, Mass., aircraft-engine-parts complex, General Electric is building a highly automated machining center where members of the International Union of Electronic Workers will be employed in only three broad job classifications, compared with as many as 20 elsewhere. Says a company spokesman: "We're saying that one classification is going to be doing essentially a half-dozen different ones." This way, a worker could sweep a floor as well as operate a forklift without violating work rules.

Source: Excerpted from Carey W. English, "Now It's Bosses Who Are Giving the Orders Again," *U.S. News & World Report,* February 11, 1985. Copyright, 1985, U.S. News & World Report, Inc.

Joint venture

In the auto industry, much of the pressure for change is coming from overseas. To improve against Japanese competition, GM is building a new subcompact car with Toyota at a reopened GM plant in Fremont, Calif., using the Japanese firm's production techniques and manning system. Those same techniques are likely to be applied when GM builds a plant for its 5-billion-dollar Saturn small-car project.

Instead of retaining the 84 job classifications in place before the factory closed in 1982, Fremont has just four — three for skilled trades and the other for general production, covering about 80 percent of the work force. Employees will work in teams of six to 10, each able to perform the other jobs within the group.

The Toyota system "requires great flexibility," says Joel Smith, United Auto Workers international representative at Fremont. "As production needs change, we'll be able to move a person around from one place to another without going through the usual structural and administrative exercises."

Employers are also obtaining work-rule changes beyond job classifications. In Houston, leading construction contractors say there are virtually no barriers to using a job-site work force in ways they feel will be most productive.

As recently as two years ago, some Houston contracts required that a single foreman supervise a crew of five. Today, it is common for one supervisor to handle a crew of 10 to 20.

base in Abraham Maslow's need hierarchy theory and Frederick Herzberg's motivation-hygiene theory. These theories suggest that factors pertaining to the job itself, such as job challenge, independence, and responsibility, are powerful motivators. Some forms of job enrichment stem from notions that worker participation in production planning and quality control has positive effects on productivity and satisfaction. Some approaches focus on the jobs of individual workers, whereas others focus on the tasks and responsibilities of work groups, with considerable emphasis on the interactions among group members.

Individual Approaches

The job enrichment efforts of Robert Ford at AT&T and of Frederick Herzberg and colleagues in various places exemplify the focus on the individual job. At AT&T, some jobs were restructured both horizontally and vertically. That is, both the number of tasks and the degree of responsibility associated with a job were increased. In addition, more routine or monotonous tasks were automated or added to lower job classifications. Overall, the aim was to create more meaningful jobs for individual workers (see Figure 7.2).

FIGURE 7.2 **Steps in improving a job**

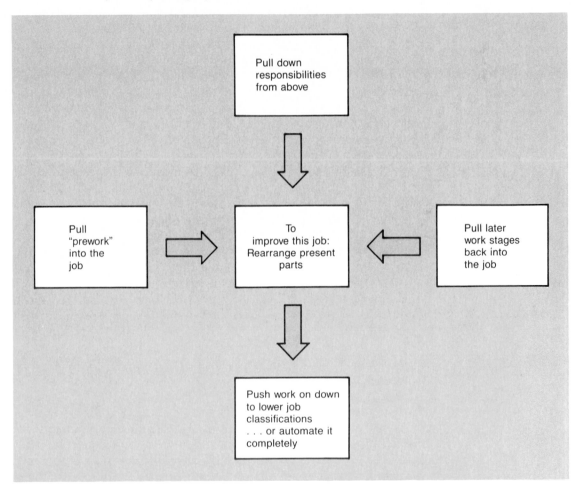

For example, at the Indianapolis office of the Indiana Bell Telephone Co., where all the directories for the state were compiled, the production of each directory required twenty-one separate steps, including manuscript verification, keypunch, and keypunch verification. Each employee performed very few tasks for each directory. Through a job enrichment effort, each employee became responsible for one or more directories, performing all of the twenty-one production steps.[6] In general, these kinds of job enrichment efforts have had positive results, including higher production, lower absenteeism, and a reduction in the number of employees needed.[7]

Any reduction in the number of employees through such programs needs to be handled through normal attrition (normal retirements and resignations) or transfer, as opposed to layoffs. The policy needs to be understood ahead of time or employees will resist job enrichment. The human resources department can play an important role in helping top management develop and communicate information about such policies and in making certain that the spirit of the policies is being carried out.

Herzberg and colleagues have taken a similar approach to enriching individual jobs. For example, in a British firm the jobs of laboratory technicians were modified to increase workers' involvement in planning and control. Specifically, the technicians were authorized to make their own materials, equipment, and maintenance requests and were encouraged to write the final reports on each of their experiments. In another of Herzberg's job enrichment projects, the position of sales representative was redesigned. Some people were given freedom to plan the frequency of their sales calls and were provided with technical assistance from the service department "on demand." They were also authorized to settle customer complaints up to a certain amount of money on the spot and were given suggested ranges within which prices could be quoted.[8] Thus in both projects employees were provided with broader, more complete jobs that included greater responsibility for planning and control.

Team Approaches

The team approach to job enrichment is a way of giving more responsibility and control to work groups in an effort to improve productivity, satisfaction, or performance. As described by M. Scott Myers, job enrichment can take the form of *more planning, more controlling,* and *more team participation.* (See Figure 7.3.) Myers describes how, at Texas Instruments, the jobs of electronic assemblers, which involved "intricate assembling, bonding, soldering,

FIGURE 7.3
Impact of job enrichment on job design

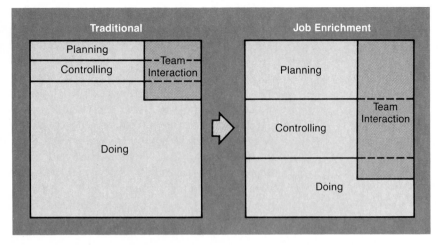

and welding operations," were enriched. First, the assemblers were given training in how to improve working methods and procedures and were encouraged to suggest improvements in the manufacturing procedures in their department. Second, work groups consisting of five to twenty-five assemblers were formed, and each elected a team captain to a six-month term. Each week the team captain solicited work improvement ideas from team members, recorded suggestions on a standard form, crediting each contributor, and presented recommendations to the supervisor and superintendent. After these weekly meetings with management, the team captain gave team members feedback on the extent to which their ideas would be adopted.[9] In other writings, Myers describes problem-solving and goal-setting meetings of these natural work groups, which he sees as a part of a broad job enrichment process.[10]

The team approach to job enrichment has had some impact on a number of industries; it has led, for example, to modification of the traditional assembly line in the European automobile industry. Two of the largest automakers in Sweden, Volvo and Saab-Scania, have experimented with team production methods in which a **self-managed team** — a work group that essentially manages itself with minimal supervision — is responsible for assembling some major component such as an engine. Under this system, the average supervisor oversees two groups of twenty subordinates and works with two team leaders who are responsible for production scheduling and material handling. The supervisor serves more as a consultant and a teacher than in the past, and the teams are given considerable freedom to organize their own work.[11]

The forerunners of the Swedish automobile industry experiments were studies by the Tavistock Institute in England. These experiments are often referred to as **sociotechnical programs** because they represent efforts to link social aspects of the factory and mine with the technology. One of the earliest experiments, in British coal mining, involved broadening the scope of jobs and building a team approach to coal production, supplemented by pay incentives.[12] Another Tavistock project, in a weaving mill in India, took the same thrust in terms of broadening tasks and creating self-managed work groups.[13]

Other team job enrichment projects outside the auto industry include the programs at a General Foods pet-food plant in Topeka, at a Corning Glass plant producing laboratory hot plates, at the Scandia Insurance Company in Sweden, and at a Sherwin-Williams paint factory in Richmond, Kentucky. The common elements have been the creation of work teams responsible for the production of an entire item or "whole" task, including the allocation of work, quality control, and product improvements. Typically, team members are paid according to the number of tasks they can perform or the number of skills mastered — called **skills-based pay** — and help screen applicants for vacancies. Case 7.1 at the beginning of the chapter, "High Seas Autopilots," gives an example of this kind of self-managed team.

Team leader positions are sometimes created in these self-managed work group projects and sometimes not. At the General Foods Topeka plant a team leader position was established but eliminated several years later, when work groups had learned to manage themselves without a formal leader.[14]

Benefits and Limitations of Job Enrichment

Generally, although not always, individual approaches to job enrichment have had positive results. For example, in the Herzberg project in a British firm described earlier, the technicians involved in the project improved the quality of their technical reports in comparison with those of the control groups. The sales representatives increased sales 19 percent over the previous year, while the sales of the control group declined 5 percent.[15] Results at AT&T included such outcomes as a reduction in the number of employees needed (from 120 to 74 in the Illinois Bell directory-compilation unit) and higher production and lower absenteeism at the Chesapeake and Potomac Telephone Company.[16]

Courtesy of Babcock & Wilcox

A team leader position is unnecessary when a work group has learned to manage themselves.

Similarly, team approaches to job enrichment usually have had mixed-to-positive results. At Texas Instruments, management reported reduced turnover and more cooperation.[17] At the Volvo plant, turnover declined dramatically and work quality went up; at the Saab-Scania plant, turnover and absenteeism decreased, while productivity and quality remained high and worker satisfaction increased.[18] In the British coal-mining project, productivity, safety, and morale all improved significantly, and results in the Indian project were favorable.[19] At the General Foods pet-food plant, quality rejects, turnover, accidents, and absenteeism were significantly below the norms of other plants. There was some erosion of these gains in later years, however, and the company had difficulty extending the program to other plants, partly because of lack of top management understanding and support.[20]

At the Corning Glass plant, reject rates and absenteeism dropped sharply while productivity increased.[21] At the Scandia Insurance Company, results were mixed. Productivity did not change significantly, but measures of organizational climate improved, and satisfaction went up slightly. However, absenteeism increased somewhat, and considerable resistance to the project emerged from middle management.[22]

At the Sherwin-Williams plant, the results have been generally positive. Twenty-five percent fewer people were needed to staff the plant than originally estimated, absenteeism is 63 percent below the company average, productivity is 30 percent higher than at sister plants, and costs per gallon of paint are 45 percent lower than in other plants making the same products.[23]

Not all of these gains can be attributed to job enrichment. Job enrichment — particularly of the self-managed team variety — typically involves changes in plant layout, technology, selection, training, compensation, and the role of the supervisor. Thus, most of the crucial factors in organizational performance shown in Figure 4.1 tend to be altered.

Supervisor and middle-management resistance is common in job enrichment efforts when the process does not take into account the interests of people at this level. Realistically, managers can see the possibility that their responsibilities might be reduced, or that a layer of supervision might be eliminated entirely. Thus, top management, including the human resources director, must take a broad view of the possible impact of job enrichment and develop procedures for these people that will enhance cooperation. Examples would be training supervisors for additional responsibilities and handling any resulting overstaffing at middle-management levels through normal attrition or transfer to other company operations.

ROLE OF THE HUMAN RESOURCES DEPARTMENT IN JOB DESIGN

Although job design affects almost every aspect of human resources management, the role of the human resources department in the actual design and redesign of jobs is usually indirect. Unless the human resources department has on its staff job design specialists who act as consultants to managers, that department will play largely supporting roles.

One important role it can play is in diagnosing organizational problems. This diagnosis might occur through informal contacts, interviews with supervisors and employees, discussions with supervisors and managers during training sessions, or questionnaires. If a need for job redesign in some units becomes evident, human resources specialists can provide preliminary design information and bring together the right people to discuss the feasibility of job redesign.

A second role is in training and management development, where both internal and external specialists can be recruited to provide information on job redesign methods.

A third role, and an extremely important one for the human resources director and his or her staff, is to assist in the planning and implementation of job redesign programs to ensure that sound human resources policies and practices are developed and followed. For example, what happens to any organizational members whose jobs are eliminated through a job redesign project will need to be thought through. This includes people at supervisory and middle-management levels. Implications for the wage and salary structure will need to be assessed. For example, if some unit, such as manufacturing, moves in the direction of self-managed teams, the organization will need to develop policies and practices related to skills-based pay.

Finally, the human resources department will need to be prepared to modify job descriptions, job specifications (the qualifications needed to perform a job), and recruitment practices, and perhaps to adjust pay scales. Job analysis plays an important role in all of these activities.

JOB ANALYSIS

Job analysis is the systematic investigation of job content, the physical circumstances in which the job is carried out, and the qualifications needed to carry out job responsibilities. The categories of information usually obtained in job analysis include what activities are performed, and how, when, and why; the machines, tools, or equipment used; what interactions with others are required; the physical and social working conditions; and the training, skills, and abilities required on the job.[24] While the terminology and specifics may vary from one job analysis approach to another, by and large most include comparable categories. This information can be used to develop written job descriptions and to establish what is required of the person who will perform the job.

Job analysis is becoming an increasingly important part of human resources management. Equal Employment Opportunity Commission (EEOC) requirements and recent court decisions require that all selection, promotion, and compensation decisions be based on job-related criteria, not on vague or subjective standards. This means organizations must be able to verify the job-relatedness of all personnel devices and techniques such as job requirements, application blanks, interviews, tests, and performance appraisals. Careful job analysis serves as the foundation for developing devices and techniques that will stand this scrutiny. Further, careful job analysis is good management in itself if the results are used to improve the effectiveness and efficiency of staffing, appraisal, reward, and other practices.

The person doing the job analysis, often called a job analyst, may be a member of the human resources department staff, a member of the unit where jobs are being analyzed, a member of an industrial engineering group, or an outside specialist hired on a project basis. Figure 7.4 is a job description for a job analyst and for a personnel recruiter. Various techniques are used in job analysis, including observation, interviews, questionnaires, and **critical incidents,** which are records that describe either very good or very poor employee performance.

One of the most popular devices used in job analysis is the *Position Analysis Questionnaire* (PAQ). This questionnaire requires the analyst to rate the job against approximately 190 job elements, usually on a 0 to 5 point scale.[25] Table 7.1 shows the major categories and subcategories measured by the instrument.

FIGURE 7.4
Job descriptions for a job analyst and a personnel recruiter

166.267-018 JOB ANALYST (profess. & kin.) personnel analyst.
Collects, analyzes, and prepares occupational information to facilitate personnel, administration, and management functions of organization: Consults with management to determine type, scope, and purpose of study. Studies current organizational occupational data and compiles distribution reports, organization and flow charts, and other background information required for study. Observes jobs and interviews workers and supervisory personnel to determine job and worker requirements. Analyzes occupational data, such as physical, mental, and training requirements of jobs and workers and develops written summaries, such as job descriptions, job specifications, and lines of career movement. Utilizes developed occupational data to evaluate or improve methods and techniques for recruiting, selecting, promoting, evaluating, and training workers, and administration of related personnel programs. May specialize in classifying positions according to regulated guidelines to meet job classification requirements of civil service system and be known as POSITION CLASSIFIER (gov. ser.).

166.267-038 PERSONNEL RECRUITER (profess. & kin.)
Seeks out, interviews, screens, and recruits job applicants to fill existing company job openings: Discusses personnel needs with department supervisors to prepare and implement recruitment program. Contacts colleges to set up on-campus interviews. Provides information on company facilities and job opportunities to potential applicants. Interviews college applicants to obtain work history, education, training, job skills, and salary requirements. Screens and refers qualified applicants to company hiring personnel for followup interview. Arranges travel and lodging for selected applicants at company expense. Performs reference and background checks on applicants. Corresponds with job applicants to notify them of employment consideration. Files and maintains employment records for future references. Projects yearly recruitment expenditures for budgetary control.

Source: U.S. Department of Labor, Employment and Training Administration, *Dictionary of Occupational Titles,* 4th ed. Supplement, 1982.

TABLE 7.1
Categories measured by the Position Analysis Questionnaire (PAQ)*

INFORMATION INPUT
Sources of job information: Use of written materials
Discrimination and perceptual activities: Estimating speed of moving objects

MEDIATION PROCESSES
Decision making and reasoning: Reasoning in problem solving
Information processing: Encoding/decoding
Use of stored information: Using mathematics

WORK OUTPUT
Use of physical devices: Use of keyboard devices
Integrative manual activities: Handling objects/materials
General body activities: Climbing
Manipulation/coordination activities: Hand-arm manipulation

INTERPERSONAL ACTIVITIES
Communications: Instructing
Interpersonal relationships: Serving/catering
Personal contact: Personal contact with public customers
Supervision and coordination: Level of supervision received

WORK SITUATION AND JOB CONTEXT
Physical working conditions: Low temperature
Psychological and sociological aspects: Civic obligations

MISCELLANEOUS ASPECTS
Work schedule, method of pay, and apparel: Irregular hours
Job demands: Specified (controlled) work pace
Responsibility: Responsibility for safety of others

*The Position Analysis Questionnaire (PAQ) is copyrighted by the Purdue Research Foundation, West Lafayette, Indiana.

Source: Ernest J. McCormick, Paul R. Jeanneret, and Robert C. Mecham, Position Analysis Questionnaire, © 1969 by Purdue Research Foundation, West Lafayette, Indiana 47907. Reprinted by permission.

Although the PAQ has been thoroughly researched and allows statistical comparisons among jobs, it is very lengthy and requires college-graduate reading ability. Thus some people find it difficult or frustrating to use.[26] But it can be a helpful tool in determining salary ranges for particular jobs. Because the total PAQ points for jobs tend to correlate highly with actual salaries paid, the questionnaire is often used to determine the relative worth of various jobs.[27]

JOB DESCRIPTIONS AND JOB SPECIFICATIONS

Job descriptions, sometimes called position descriptions, are written summaries, usually one or two pages long, of the basic tasks associated with a particular job. Job descriptions usually have a

FIGURE 7.5   Job description from a large bank

JOB DESCRIPTION

Job Title	RESEARCH ASSISTANT	Branch	
Job Number	3135-I	Division	ECONOMIC RESEARCH
Salary Grade	9	Department	
Date		Section	

JOB DUTIES

Compiles industrial and economic data by: obtaining current and comparative statistics relative to trends in production, commerce, employment, etc., from newspapers, periodicals, publications of government agencies, trade associations, and other standard sources; maintaining a set of statistical records for the department concerning industries and areas of the region; selecting and classifying for the department library pertinent articles from the above-mentioned sources; digesting suitable material on national and regional economic developments; plotting acquired statistics and developing informative graphs, tables, and charts; preparing special statistical and other reports.

Also computes department's own seasonally adjusted employment data series. Furnishes various industrial and economic data to bank and other officials.

Prepares the Weekly Business Briefs by gathering and assembling data and writing original copy to provide a digest of regional and national business news for the Bank's staff, officers, and customers. Uses own judgment in selecting articles of significance. Submits material for final approval.

Also researches and prepares section for the Summary of Regional Industries. Researches and prepares local business section for the Metropolitan Real Estate Research Report. Prepares statistical data for charts and tables in the quarterly and annual issues of the Summary. Prepares statistical data and writes a section on local home price trends for the Metropolitan Real Estate Research Report. Prepares special reports on various subjects as requested.

Assists in maintaining research library; assists Economist in developing new statistical series and ideas for charts; assists other staff members with miscellaneous functions.

The Research Assistant, under general supervision, is engaged primarily in the acquiring of pertinent, factual data relative to varied industries, their trends and any other significant details. In large part this material provides the basis for analysis, opinions, and recommendations by the Economist, although some of the analysis is included in the duties of the Research Assistant.

JOB REQUIREMENTS

Education A broad knowledge of a technical workfield applicable to duties such as economics and business theory, and an understanding of statistical methods and the application and analysis thereof. Equivalent to college degree in Economics or Business Administration.

Experience Job requires practical experience in statistical methods and analysis and a period to acquire a knowledge of various information sources. Time — six months to a year.

Resourcefulness Job requires judgment and initiative in determining sources of information and judgment in selection of significant data and application of statistical formulas to develop informative results. Under general supervision.

Responsibility Considerable care is required since most errors are difficult to locate. Reports and publications are distributed beyond the bank and relied upon as being correct and indicative of trends. Work must be prepared promptly, and deadlines met.

Contacts Routine staff contacts plus frequent public contacts by telephone and occasionally in person requesting or furnishing information. Courtesy and tact are required.

Supervision Does not supervise.

Mental Effort Requires considerable care and attention due to the concentration required for the selection, development, and analysis of economic information.

Physical Effort Medium office position. Job requires frequent use of calculator and adding machine. Also requires frequent referral to department library and occasional trips to public library and other outside offices for information.

Job Conditions Average office conditions.

label, called a "job title," and they frequently include a section describing the qualifications needed to perform the job. These qualifications are called **job specifications**. (See Figure 7.5 for an example of a job description that includes job specifications.)

Purposes of Job Descriptions and Specifications

Job descriptions and specifications can be very useful for a number of purposes, as shown in Figure 7.6. But if they are written and filed away, as might be happening in Case 7.2 at the beginning of the chapter, they are a waste of time. (It might have been that the human resources department was using them for a number of purposes, but that Mary Neale was not adequately communicating these uses to other managers.)

First, job descriptions are useful throughout the recruiting and selection process. They can be used in writing advertisements for job openings and in writing letters to people or organizations who are in a position to refer candidates. They provide the recruiter, the selection interviewer, and the interviewee with a basic outline of the job for which candidates are being considered.

Job descriptions are also useful in orienting and training new employees. They can provide an overview of the activities that need to be carried out, which can be explained to the employee in more detail by the supervisor and training people. The job description is not likely to list *all* the duties of a job, however, and both the supervisor and the new employee will need a clear understanding of the responsibilities not covered.

Job descriptions are also used in the development of performance standards. **Performance standards** expand the job description and establish, in measurable terms, how well the job is to be performed. Job descriptions are also relevant to the development of performance appraisal (or merit rating) forms, which are frequently designed to include some of the major categories covered in the job description.

Job descriptions and specifications can also provide basic information needed for job evaluation. **Job evaluation** is the process of determining the relative worth of jobs within an organization to establish wages and salaries.

In addition, job descriptions can contribute to a dialogue between supervisor and subordinate or a group discussion when it is necessary to clarify mutual expectations. This process can result in a renegotiation of responsibilities and a better understanding of what can and should be expected of workers holding particular jobs.

Finally, job descriptions can be used to think through and de-

FIGURE 7.6
**Potential uses of job
analyses and job de-
scriptions**

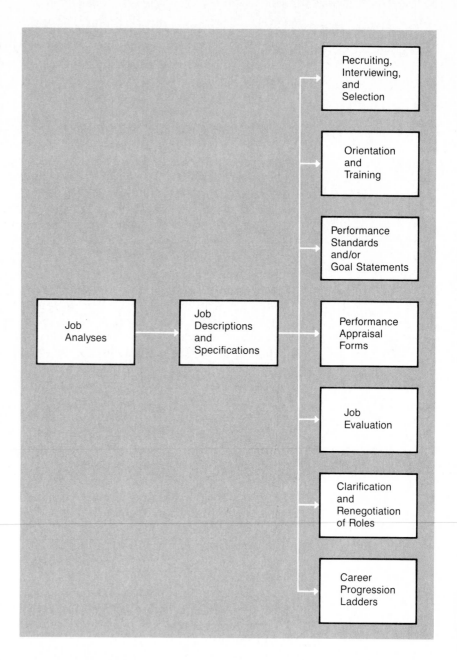

velop the avenues for transfer and promotion that lead to advancement in the organization. This process can culminate in the development of **career progression ladders**, which depict possible
career paths and advancement opportunities for individual employees.

Some organizations have two descriptions for each job. A lengthy, detailed version may be used in training and in job evaluation, while a shorter version may be used in human resources planning and in recruiting and interviewing.

The Importance of Accurate Job Descriptions

The need for job descriptions that accurately reflect actual job content is clear when we consider the weight given to job descriptions by applicants and recruiters. Potential applicants may make themselves available for interviews or screen themselves out of consideration according to how the job is described in an advertisement or bulletin board posting. Recruiters, particularly in large firms, may not have a detailed knowledge of the actual job other than

---

PERSPECTIVE 7.2   Accurate and Comprehensive Job Descriptions Are Important

A recent study conducted at Auburn University and a recent decision of the United States Court of Appeals for the District of Columbia Circuit emphasize the importance of accurate and comprehensive job descriptions.

In *Guinn* v. *Bolger*, 36 FEP Cases 506 (D.D.C. 1984), the court held that the job description of an employee, not the employee's actual tasks, should be used to determine whether the employee is a "qualified handicapped individual" under the Rehabilitation Act of 1973.

In *Guinn,* the employee was capable of performing all of the tasks set forth in the written job description for the position she held; however, she was unable to perform certain additional duties not contained in her job description.

The employer, the United States Postal Service, had a practice of sending employees on light duty home on days when the volume of work was reduced.

Pursuant to that policy, the Postal Service sent the employee home because she was unable to perform certain tasks that were unrelated to her job description.

The court prevented the Postal Service from showing additional job duties not formally set out in support of its contention that job descriptions are only a rough estimate of the "essential functions" of a job.

The court rebuffed the employer, observing that, had the employee been required to do only those tasks for which she was hired, as set forth in the job description, she would never have been placed on light duty status, and would not have been sent home. . . .

The *Guinn* decision makes clear that employers place themselves at risk when they use incomplete or inaccurate job descriptions, especially if personnel decisions will be based on the job descriptions.

Moreover, it is not enough to simply have such job descriptions in place. Employers should judge job performance against the criteria contained in the job descriptions and must apply the subsequent evaluation system in a uniform and consistent manner.

Source: "Manager's Newsfront," by Betty Southard Murphy, Wayne E. Barlow, and D. Diane Hatch, copyright March 1985. Reprinted with the permission of *Personnel Journal*, Costa Mesa, California; all rights reserved.

what is written in the job description; and they may make inappropriate judgments or provide misleading information if the job description is not accurate.

Further, inaccurate job descriptions can reduce the effectiveness of training or can result in the development of unrealistic performance standards. For example, if some of the more significant parts of the job are not included in the job description, any training designed using that job description may neglect those important aspects. Or performance standards may be developed for the less important aspects, while no clear standards are developed for the more significant parts of the job. These problems demonstrate the importance of gathering information systematically, writing job descriptions carefully, and checking the accuracy of the job description with both the job incumbent and the supervisor. And, because jobs tend to change over time — sometimes rapidly — it is important that job descriptions and specifications be updated periodically. Further, procedures need to be established to ensure a reanalysis of a job when it appears that job responsibilities have changed significantly.

The Importance of Valid Job Specifications

Government regulations state that job specifications should be related to actual job requirements. One Supreme Court case in particular has had a broad impact on job specifications. Drawing on the Civil Rights Act and rulings by the Equal Employment Opportunity Commission, the U.S. Supreme Court ruled in the *Griggs* v. *Duke Power Company* case that an employer had unlawfully discriminated against blacks by requiring a high school education or passage of an intelligence test as conditions of employment or advancement in certain jobs. The thrust of the court's argument was that these specifications were not significantly related to job performance. The Court went on to say:

> The facts of this case demonstrate the inadequacy of broad and general testing devices as well as the infirmity of using diplomas or degrees as fixed measures of capability. History is filled with examples of men and women who rendered highly effective performances without the conventional badges of accomplishment in terms of certificates, diplomas, or degrees. Diplomas and tests are useful servants, but Congress has mandated the common-sense proposition that they are not to become the masters of reality.[28]

This decision makes it imperative that job specifications be consistent with the activities described in the job description and with the actual duties of the job. Careful review and discussion of job descriptions will sometimes reveal that certain job specifications are unnecessary. For example, not all jobs require a high school diploma, and many do not require a college degree. In all cases, careful job analysis is the most reliable method for ensuring the validity of job specifications.

There are circumstances in which job specifications are realistic but management wishes to reduce the qualifications required for a particular job. If an organization wishes to expand its employment of disadvantaged minorities, if there is a shortage of certain skills in the labor market, or if labor costs have risen dramatically, it may be necessary to reduce the proportion of employees with certain degrees or certificates. In such cases there is often a conscious plan to restructure jobs — usually several simultaneously — to permit the hiring of people with lower skills. For example, the high cost of physician care might prompt the creation of a nurse practitioner or a physician's assistant position to absorb the more routine aspects of medical care. The creation of new skilled positions, however, often requires the development of special training programs, the cooperation of one or more unions, and, as in the case of health-care institutions, compliance with licensing regulations.

Thus, several questions should be asked periodically about job specifications. Are they too high? Too low? Are people being hired who are underqualified or overqualified, or who have the wrong skills? Do these factors result in job dissatisfaction or substandard performance? Are present job specifications unnecessarily screening out disadvantaged people? Is the quality of the work force too low? Are job specifications screening out too many people who would make good candidates for promotion? Job specifications, then, need to be evaluated in terms of whether they accurately reflect job content.

PERFORMANCE STANDARDS

While job descriptions are statements of *what* activities are to be performed, *performance standards* make explicit *the quantity and/or quality of performance expected in the basic tasks set forth in the job description.* Usually performance standards are statements of what is considered acceptable and attainable performance on a particular job. Thus they follow from job design and content and are logical extensions of job descriptions. Some organizations are very systematic in developing written performance standards for each job; others may rely on informal communications or occasional memoranda between subordinates and superiors.

Performance standards for production jobs have been fairly common since the development of scientific management and time-and-motion studies around the turn of the century. Most often these standards are written in terms of the number of units to be produced in a certain period. Typically, these standards are used in connection with incentive systems under which bonuses are paid for production above and beyond the standard rate.

The use of performance standards for managerial and professional positions is of more recent origin and, to a large extent, has been upstaged by interest in management by objectives (MBO), which will be discussed in Chapter 13. While performance standards tend to establish acceptable performance by the average incumbent of a particular job, management by objectives tends to be more future-oriented in that it involves setting goals or objectives leading to higher levels of performance. In practice, the two may be hard to distinguish because they can blend together easily.

Table 7.2 is a partial list of performance standards for a managerial position. The full document included nine major categories subdivided into forty-one more specific standards. (If this document were closer to an MBO format, we would see more statements of objectives and target dates by which they are to be achieved.)

Purposes of Performance Standards

One purpose of developing performance standards is to establish guidelines against which actual performance can be measured. This has benefits for both the person holding the job and the one or more superiors who evaluate that person's performance. The more the employee understands what is expected, the more likely it is that he or she will be able to carry out the responsibilities of the position successfully. In turn, the superiors' performance appraisal can be much more objective and relevant if based on statements of what is expected.

The advantage of writing performance standards is that the organization is more likely to be thorough and comprehensive about their development. Further, having things in writing is a convenient way to share and retrieve information. Most, if not all, organizations, however, will have some performance standards that are not written down. For example, if the president of a company has indicated that he or she wants and expects the sales department to gross $8 million in sales in the coming year, that statement really becomes a performance standard for the sales manager, whether or not it is put in writing. Similarly, targets that have been communicated with respect to safety, reduction in scrap, increases in new accounts, and so on are implicit — if not explicit —

TABLE 7.2
Performance standards for medical director

Compliance with performance standards is adequate when:

1. Medical treatment for occupational injuries or disease, first aid treatment for certain non-occupational conditions, and other care as necessary for the industrial health program is provided.

(a) There is no increase in Workers' Compensation claims due to inadequate medical care within the Division.

(b) The medical reviews of employee Workers' Compensation claims are completed within seven days.

(c) The number of dispensaries is adequate to handle the treatment of the plant population considering the geographic location of the area the dispensary will serve, the number of employees that can adequately be handled per shift by a nurse (50 calls), and the hazards of the area.

2. We have recommended and developed industrial health policies.

(a) Incidence of occupational disease as noted by Workers' Compensation claims and our frequency rates is 1 per 400 employees per month or less.

(b) Evidence that health programs are being adequately engaged in as indicated by current procedures and current physicians' program manuals.

(c) There are no reported employee terminations due to environmental factors that the Medical Section has failed to correct by preventive medical plans.

(d) The Corporate Director of Health and Safety approves and supports our program.

Used with permission.

performance standards for the jobs involved. Unless each person has specific standards relating to his or her part in reaching that target, however, there may be a tendency to "let the other person do it."

Another purpose in developing performance standards can be to enhance motivation and commitment. If the supervisor and the employee genuinely work together to write performance standards, the employee's participation can contribute to the fulfillment of needs for affiliation, recognition, and autonomy. In addition, the outcome is likely to be commitment to the standards established and increased motivation to reach them.

Developing Performance Standards

Procedures for developing performance standards vary widely. In a highly directive approach, the superior may simply write the standards and inform the employee. In a participative approach, there will be much more interaction between the supervisor and the employee. A participative procedure might be something like the following:

1. The supervisor solicits the cooperation of subordinates in developing performance standards and the procedure to be followed in writing them.
2. Each subordinate writes tentative standards for each aspect of his or her job and provides the supervisor with a preliminary draft.
3. Each subordinate meets with the supervisor to discuss the tentative standards and reach agreement on the final document.
4. The standards are used by the employee to track how well he or she is doing and by the supervisor and employee to appraise the employee's performance. In work groups where jobs are interrelated and interdependent, it can be productive to involve the entire group in a team approach to developing standards.

Performance standards are written in quantitative terms whenever possible, but in practice some job aspects are difficult to quantify, and qualitative statements must be used. An example of a qualitative statement is "uses tact in dealing with customers," although one could argue that the quantitative version "receives no complaints about lack of tact during the year" might be a more useful statement. Obviously, it is easier to develop performance standards for jobs that have a readily measured result than for jobs that have a high interpersonal component.

Ideally, the development of standards should be based on overall goals and objectives and should be an interactive process down through the organization. The process begins with the chief executive officer (CEO) working out her or his goals or standards (or a combination of both) with the board of directors. Those who report directly to the CEO then work out their goals and standards in interaction with the CEO and each other, and so the process continues down through the organization.

Problems with Performance Standards

One of the pitfalls in developing performance standards, or goal statements in an MBO program, is that management may not pay enough attention to the *process* of developing the standards or goals. If standards are imposed on members of the organization in

If subordinates understand the overall goals to be met and participate in setting their own performance standards, they are likely to set standards high and to be committed to achieving them.

an autocratic and dictatorial manner, the whole process is likely to be resisted. On the other hand, if subordinates understand the overall goals to be achieved and participate in setting their own standards, they are likely to set them reasonably high and be committed to meeting them.

In a unionized situation, a potential problem can be union-management relationships. In some situations, unions have cooperated with management in establishing standards based on approaches such as time-and-motion study. In other situations, unions have resisted the development of standards. In particular, in the absence of an incentive pay system of some kind, unions have tended to resist managerial attempts to increase performance beyond what is considered "a fair day's work." However, as was shown in Perspective 7.1, intense foreign competition and periods of high unemployment in some industries have prompted some unions to be more flexible in working with management to raise standards for productivity and quality.

One of the most serious problems with performance standards

is related to one of the five core job characteristics described previously — autonomy. If the standards are seen as overly restrictive and oppressive, motivation and morale are likely to be low. These conditions are likely to be accompanied by such costly outcomes as considerable job stress and high absenteeism and turnover. For example, many organizations with large data-processing requirements, such as insurance firms, banks, and credit-card companies, have developed computer programs to monitor the extent to which employees working at video display terminals meet production standards. In one company, while management might believe the system to be efficient, a claims processor has a different view: "The girls at work call it a sweatshop. Most of them figure they won't last more than two years."[29]

In some instances, management has restored some autonomy to employees with good results. For example, at a Ford Motor Company plant, a button was installed that allows an employee to shut down the entire assembly line at any time. Shutdowns by employees occur on average twenty times a day for ten seconds each, for a total of a little over three minutes. With this approach, defects dropped from seventeen to less than one per car in ten months.[30]

ROLE OF THE HUMAN RESOURCES DEPARTMENT IN JOB ANALYSIS, DESCRIPTIONS, AND PERFORMANCE STANDARDS

The human resources department must be concerned about job analysis, job descriptions and specifications, and performance standards because of their major impact on almost all aspects of human resources management. That department will typically have a major role in the planning and coordination of the systems used. That is, the department will be involved in determining what job analysis procedures are used, making sure that the information obtained through job analysis is used to write appropriate job descriptions and specifications, and then using job descriptions and specifications for the various purposes shown in Figure 7.6. These purposes include uses in recruitment, orientation and training, performance appraisal, performance standards, and job evaluation.

In some instances, the human resources department employs job analysts to analyze jobs and write job descriptions; in other instances, analysts are employed by an industrial engineering group and work cooperatively with the human resources staff. (Industrial engineers typically help the organization in such matters as the selection of the tools, machines, and equipment; plant layout; and development of performance measures and standards.) Frequently, the human resources department trains selected members from various units to write job descriptions and then coordinates and monitors the overall effort.

The human resources department is ordinarily *not* involved in writing performance standards for jobs outside its own department. That department may train supervisors and other employees in how to develop standards, but the actual development and writing of the standards is a matter between the various supervisors and managers and their subordinates.

The human resources department can play a major role in encouraging discussions between superiors and subordinates at all levels about the optimal level of autonomy versus control. In view of what is known about job design — and about characteristics associated with high motivation and performance, in particular — it is clear that performance standards can be used in ways that demotivate rather than motivate. Part of the solution lies in increasing the employee's participation in developing the standards and in using them to monitor his or her own performance. In particular, if the supervisor tries to control behavior through punishment, the consequences are likely to be negative.

Because job analysis, job descriptions, job specifications, and performance standards are used for so many purposes, and because how they are used has a major impact on employee motivation, morale, and performance, the human resources department has a great deal of interest in their development, accuracy, and relevance.

SUMMARY

Job design is the process of determining the specific tasks and responsibilities to be carried out by each member of the organization. It has many implications for human resources management. Both the content of one's job *and the ability to influence content and level of performance* affect a person's motivation and job satisfaction. Further, job content has a direct relationship to the qualifications needed on the job (job specifications), to the recruitment and training needed, to the development of performance standards, to what is reviewed in performance appraisal, and to compensation.

There are various ways to examine job content. Hackman and Oldham have provided a useful method based on five core job characteristics: skill variety, task identity, task significance, autonomy, and job feedback. Job enrichment, using Hackman and Oldham's terminology, is the enhancement of the five job characteristics.

There has been considerable experimentation in recent years with team approaches to job enrichment, including the concept of self-managed teams. Job enrichment efforts, particularly team approaches, frequently involve many organizational changes, including changes in technology, plant layout, selection, training, and compensation. Most, or all, of the crucial factors in organizational performance tend to be altered.

The human resources department's role in job design is usually indirect, although job design influences almost every aspect of human resources management. That department may diagnose organizational problems that suggest job redesign, incorporate information on job design in training and management development programs, and help plan job redesign programs to ensure that sound human resources policies and practices are developed. Further, the department will need to be prepared to modify job descriptions and job specifications and to modify recruitment, selection, training, compensation, and other practices to be consistent with any job redesign program.

Job analysis is the systematic investigation of a job's content. Careful job analysis is necessary for the development of accurate job descriptions and appropriate job specifications. In turn, these documents are important in recruitment, orientation and training, in the development of performance standards, in performance appraisal, in determining relative job worth (job evaluation), and in developing promotion ladders. The development of job descriptions can promote a useful dialogue between a supervisor and a subordinate — or a team of subordinates — about their respective roles and help in restructuring those roles as needed.

Government regulations, supported by the *Griggs* v. *Duke Power Company* case, require that job specifications be job related to guard against discrimination against minorities, women, and other protected groups. Management should periodically examine job specifications to see if they are furthering organizational goals and whether they are appropriate in light of legal requirements.

Performance standards can be considered an extension of job descriptions. Usually, performance standards are statements of what is considered acceptable, and they are frequently written in quantitative terms. The purposes of performance standards include communicating expected levels of performance and establishing guidelines against which performance can be measured. Written standards are useful for communicating and retrieving this information.

The human resources department typically plays a major role in helping plan the systems to be used in job analysis and in developing job descriptions, job specifications, and performance standards. Specialists in that department may be assigned to conduct job analyses and write job descriptions in cooperation with managers, supervisors, and employees. The human resources department is not involved in the actual writing of performance standards but helps play a diagnostic, training, and monitoring role.

KEY TERMS

job design	vertical restructuring	job description
job content	self-managed team	job specifications
organizational responsibilities	sociotechnical program	performance standards
job enrichment	skills-based pay	job evaluation
job enlargement	job analysis	career progression ladder
horizontal restructuring	critical incidents	

REVIEW QUESTIONS

1. Define job design.
2. What is job content?
3. What are the core job characteristics as described by Hackman and Oldham and with what psychological states are these characteristics associated?
4. What is job enrichment?
5. Give an example of an individual approach to job enrichment and a team approach to job enrichment. What are some benefits and limitations of each approach?
6. What is job analysis and what are its purposes?
7. Discuss the importance of accurate job descriptions and appropriate job specifications.
8. What are performance standards? How are they developed?
9. Discuss the responsibilities of the human resources department with respect to job design and analysis.

OPENING CASE QUESTIONS

Case 7.1   High Seas Autopilots

1. What effects do job design and the team approach have on Vivian's need fulfillment?
2. What are the benefits of allowing the team to establish its own production goals and quality standards?

Case 7.2   Why Did We Write Those Job Descriptions?

1. Why did Mary Neale spend six months writing all those job descriptions?
2. Do you think that EEOC requirements had any bearing on Mary's decision to write the job descriptions? Why or why not?
3. Will Ruth and Mark receive any benefits from their job descriptions?

CASE 7.3   BOREDOM AT WORK

Boredom in the work place can have any number of disruptive manifestations. It can contribute to turnover, undermine productivity, and make for inattentiveness that engenders mistakes. Even managers get bored, and their boredom has been known to negatively influence major business decisions and to drive them to meddle disruptively in their subordinates' activities.

Some of the solutions that have been tried to alleviate boredom seem rather simple. General Motors, for example, has successfully tried job rotation. It allows workers to perform different tasks on an assembly line, and they are also rotated off the line at times to perform other tasks. GM coupled the job rotation with self-management; workers, as a team, supervise themselves, adding further variety to the tasks they perform.

In contrast with such a job enrichment effort, however, are some efforts at job redesign for greater efficiency—something that often arises from advances in technology. Some persons involved in job redesign sometimes fail to consider adequately how boredom may play a part. One such case involved a biscuit-making company in Glasgow, Scotland. In the biscuit-making process, skilled workers called "doughmen" supervised a group of workers in combining ingredients in mixing machines. The job required know-how and the ability to make on-the-spot alterations to complete the mixing properly. But then the company introduced a computer-assisted system that automatically controlled the input of ingredients. The doughmen, while still necessary, were reduced to tasks like giving the go-ahead to start the machine and removing the dough from the mixer. The actual operation and monitoring of the mixing system were handled in a separate control room by other workers.

Although the computerized system actually improved the company's product quality, the doughmen understandably became dissatisfied with their jobs. They were bored. Their tasks were monotonous, they were no longer in a position of control, and they had only limited interaction with other employees in the process. Management, too, was dissatisfied, because the doughmen began to perform sloppily and didn't seem to care about their work.

Discussion Questions

1. In designing the doughmen's new role, what do you think could have been done to avoid the problems encountered?
2. Discuss the concept of job rotation and self-management at GM in light of Hackman and Oldham's core job characteristics.

Case Sources: "You have to Bend and Stretch a Little to Keep Your Job," *Business Week*, August 29, 1983, p. 56; Walter Kiechel, III, "Chairmen of the Bored," *Fortune*, March 5, 1984, pp. 175–176; and "New Technology with a Human Face," *Personnel Management* (April 1985): 28–31.

Work Rules and Schedules

LEARNING OBJECTIVES

- Identify the factors that affect the level of control in an organization.
- Explain why work rules are necessary in an organization.
- Specify the consequences of restrictive work rules for employee morale and organizational effectiveness.
- Discuss the considerations involved in administering work rules.
- Cite the usual steps in progressive discipline.
- List the advantages and disadvantages associated with each of the following work schedules: regular work schedule, overtime work, shift work, compressed workweek, flextime, permanent part-time work, job sharing, and telecommuting.
- Describe the role of the human resources department in managing work rules and schedules.

CASE 8.1   SALLY GRAY, VP OF SALES

Sally Gray, vice president of sales at Cosmopolitan Cosmetics in Philadelphia, had called a meeting of her department heads for the next morning. One of the agenda items was the question of giving sales employees at headquarters more freedom in starting and ending their workdays. The accounting department, in cooperation with the personnel department, was experimenting with a "flextime" work schedule, under which employees could arrive earlier or later than the traditional 8:00 a.m. and leave earlier or later than 5:00 p.m., providing they put in a full forty hours each week. Everyone was required to be on company premises between 10:00 a.m. and 3:00 p.m. each day, however. It was too early to tell precisely how well the procedure was working in accounting, but the personnel director had told Sally it seemed to be a success. Employees were saying they liked the new system, and the accounting supervisors were reporting that people were getting just as much done as before, and maybe more. Besides, there were no longer any tardiness problems.

Sally was concerned about adopting flextime in the sales department. For one thing, the flextime suggestion had come from a group of clerical employees in international sales, and Sally was afraid the company might be letting nonsupervisory employees influence policy too much. Besides, she had always worked an 8:00 to 5:00 schedule in the days before she had become a supervisor, and once she had started moving up the managerial ranks, she had typically worked much longer than an eight-hour day. Now she usually arrived about a half-hour later than her subordinates but stayed an hour or so longer at the end of the day and frequently had dinner meetings with customers after that.

Another thing bothering her was that West Coast customers frequently called as late as 2:00 Pacific Time, which was 5:00 p.m. at headquarters. Flextime might mean that employees would miss many of these calls, causing the company to lose business. Besides, it hadn't been many years since the company had agreed to let office employees fill out time sheets and dispense with the time clocks that seemed to be an annoyance to everyone. With flextime, people might have to start punching time clocks again.

"Well," Sally thought, "I'll see what my department heads have to say. Maybe they know more about it than I do."

CASE 8.2   JUST A BUNDLE OF LAUGHS

You had to admit that Charlie Shearson was funny a lot of the time. Charlie, an estimator in the purchasing department at Jones Manufacturing, was an accomplished storyteller and usually had a new joke to tell when you ran into him in the cafeteria or in the hallways. He was also a great practical joker — he had smuggled a dried fish into a coworker's desk during the holidays, causing a great deal of laughter and commotion, and had poured orange dye into the water cooler on Halloween, much to the consternation of some people who didn't know whether the water was fit to drink.

Bill James, Charlie's supervisor, had cautioned him about both incidents, telling him that not everyone thought his pranks were funny and that they were interfering with work.

This time Bill was furious. It was St. Patrick's Day, and Charlie had obtained three or four green plastic derbies and was sailing them across the work area. One of them went out a window — directly above the president's office — and another hit Bill right in the chest. There was laughter from coworkers when the first hat went out the window, but dead silence when the other hat hit Bill. Everyone looked at Bill uneasily. Bill didn't need any encouragement. He had had it up to the eyeballs with Charlie.

"You're fired," he shouted. "That's the last time you'll horse around here. Go pick up your paycheck." Charlie looked shocked, shrugged his shoulders, picked up a few things from his desk, and walked out.

The next day, the personnel and labor relations director telephoned Bill to tell him Charlie had filed a grievance, or formal complaint, through the union, protesting the discharge, and asked Bill to drop by his office. "I'll be there in a few minutes," Bill said. He leaned back in his chair and pondered the situation. "I'll bet I'll have to take that clown back," he thought. "I haven't got any warnings in the file, and I gave him a pay raise last time around. The union will claim it was a trivial matter, and that he's too good a worker to fire over such an incident."

These cases concern work rules and schedules — matters of considerable importance to how people feel about their jobs, how they feel about management, and how they get the work done. In Case 8.1, Sally Gray was considering giving her sales employees much more freedom to set their own work schedules. The accounting department experiment with flexible work schedules was being well received and seemed to have increased productivity. But she was worried about whether adopting such a plan would interfere with dealing with customers.

In Case 8.2, Charlie Shearson's pranks may have been more of a liability than an asset to the company, but an absence of rules about horseplay, or Bill James's failure to document previous warnings, may now result in Charlie's being reinstated. Maybe Charlie *should* be reinstated. At any rate, the company is now faced with a series of meetings with the union as the matter goes through grievance proceedings. If Charlie's grievance ultimately goes to an arbitrator, the arbitrator may order him reinstated with back pay.

From what is known about such matters as motivation, equity, employee control over productivity, and the necessity for the coordination of work, it is clear that these incidents are anything but trivial. The effective management of work rules and schedules is an important factor in job performance and satisfaction. This chapter is about work rules and what organizations do when rules are violated. The chapter also discusses various ways of scheduling the workday and workweek, and the role played by the human resources department in these matters.

CONTROL VERSUS FREEDOM

A broad question about work rules and schedules is whether organizations should control employees' behavior tightly — whether they should have **restrictive work rules** — or whether they should provide maximum freedom in the workplace. The answer depends on many factors, including the size and complexity of the organization; management philosophy; work-group norms (unwritten rules or standards of behavior); the technology, equipment, and materials used by the organization; and social or cultural norms and attitudes.

The organization's size and complexity are factors in the design of work rules and schedules. For example, a retail organization of eight people, all working in one large room in a small building, is not likely to need an elaborate set of rules governing work. Requirements about such matters as working hours and overtime and how much tardiness can be tolerated are set by the owner and communicated directly to workers. By and large, problems are handled informally. Everybody knows who is there and who is not, and who is working hard and who is taking it easy. Rare cases of discipline are handled by the owner. By contrast, a large aerospace manufacturer with thousands of employees at several locations — some of them in different states — requires a fairly elaborate set of rules and regulations. One of the reasons is that, with thousands of employees, all kinds of problems and dilemmas occur, and no one person can keep track of all the incidents and precedents. A company of this size and complexity has had thousands of such incidents, leading to a gradual codification of rules and regulations. This codification, in general, makes everyone's life easier. For example, the small firm may never have experienced a **garnishment,** a legal proceeding in which a creditor of some employee gets a court order requiring the company to turn over some fraction of that employee's wages to that creditor. The large company, on the other hand, may have experienced this nuisance many times and will have established rules, consistent with federal and state law, about what discipline, if any, is to be meted out to the employee if a garnishment occurs.

Management philosophy will have a major influence on work rules. A Theory X management philosophy, for example, will probably contribute to trying to solve problems by issuing edicts and

"Now I suppose you're gonna sulk because I wouldn't give you the afternoon off!"

restrictive work rules. A Theory Y philosophy will probably influence a manager to be less prone to handling problems by issuing edicts and more willing to discuss problems thoroughly with subordinates before taking any action.

Work-group norms influence work rules in two ways. First, the norms help determine the necessity for rules. For example, if group norms across the organization are that no one takes a break longer than fifteen minutes, there may be no need for a formal rule about this. On the other hand, if employees are casual about returning from breaks, with some people chronically staying a half-hour or so, and discussions and warnings have not corrected the problem, supervisors and managers are likely to want to start imposing rules.

In addition to influencing the need for rules, group norms are themselves informal rules governing behavior. Work groups develop their own attitudes and standards and put considerable pressure on members to conform. These standards may be consistent with or contradict those of management. Obviously, if group norms are in opposition to formal work rules, there will be an uneasy tug-of-war going on between management and employees, with employees attempting to circumvent rules and supervisors trying to enforce them.

Technology, equipment, and materials also affect work rules and schedules. A huge machine that stamps out automobile bodies will require the presence of a full crew, and because of its noise and potential danger, will require rules about wearing protective devices, how close one can get to the machine, and who can operate it. Some equipment and materials require swift and strict enforcement of safety regulations. Obviously, smoking must be prohibited in an area where liquid hydrogen or aviation gasoline is piped from one tank to another. Under such circumstances, smoking, or the use of welding torches, or any grinding that would produce sparks, cannot be tolerated for an instant.

Social or cultural norms and attitudes also influence work rules and schedules. For example, giving employees more flexibility in starting and stopping work has become much more acceptable as executives have come to realize that such programs may be partial solutions to traffic congestion in metropolitan areas and in and around plant parking lots. As another example, growing concern about the adverse effects on health of smoking has led an increasing number of organizations to develop rules that permit smoking in designated areas only. Attitudes in society about this particular issue are resulting in local and state laws requiring organizations to establish rules about smoking. In 1984, for example, San Francisco put into effect an ordinance that requires employers to "accommodate, insofar as possible, the preferences of nonsmokers and smokers and, if satisfactory accommodation cannot be reached, to prohibit smoking in the office work place."[1] Such laws have legal foundation in the *Shimp* v. *New Jersey Bell* case, in which a New Jersey court ruled that the New Jersey Bell Telephone Company's refusal to restrict smoking denied a nonsmoking, allergic employee the common-law right to work in a safe environment. A similar decision was handed down by the Missouri Court of Appeals in *Smith* v. *Western Electric Company.*[2]

The Purpose of Work Rules

Organizations typically have rules pertaining to such matters as starting and stopping work, total hours to be worked, rest periods, fighting and intoxication on the job, refusal to carry out instructions from a superior **(insubordination),** smoking in hazardous areas, and recording time worked. One purpose is to ensure reasonable predictability of employee behavior beyond that provided by group norms so that the organization can function without undue disturbance. Another purpose is to protect employees from hazardous conditions.

It is easy to visualize the consequences to an organization if unpredictable work schedules, unsafe practices, rough horseplay, intoxication, stealing, and falsification of records were condoned. Unless minimum standards of conduct are enforced, work will be seriously disrupted. Work rules are a necessity in organizational life.

Reasonable work rules help fulfill human needs for security, order, predictability, and avoidance of physical harm. Since most people understand that these needs will not be satisfied in a chaotic environment, they are willing to accept a minimum number of rules. In Case 8.2 above, Charlie Shearson's practical jokes, while humorous to some people, were probably a serious irritation to others. Certainly, they interfered with work. Most employees would probably agree with rules that give supervisors authority to discipline employees whose behavior gets too far out of line. As another example, people in military organizations will accept a high degree of control when it is related to survival in combat and to unit security. Mine workers understand the importance of strict rules about the firing of explosives. People in a manufacturing plant will ordinarily understand the interdependence of their jobs and will accept fairly rigorous rules pertaining to stopping and starting work.

Restrictive Work Rules

If work rules are too restrictive or confining, they can frustrate the fulfillment of human needs and interfere with organizational effectiveness. Rules limiting socializing on the job can frustrate needs for affiliation and cooperation. Rules that limit job scope, whether management- or union-imposed, can frustrate needs for autonomy and self-actualization. Rules that are seen as arbitrary and punitive tend to result in defensive — and sometimes aggressive — employee behavior.

In a unionized situation, work rules agreed upon by management and the union can sometimes handicap the organization severely in its ability to compete. Although originally negotiated to protect workers from arbitrary assignments out of their crafts and to protect jobs, many such rules have become impediments to job

---

PERSPECTIVE 8.1   Employee Fired for Violating Privacy Policy Wins Damages

A recent decision by the California Court of Appeal emphasizes the need for employers to adhere to established company policies.

In *Rulon-Miller* v. *IBM*, No. AO 16455 (1st Dist. 1984), the employee was awarded $300,000 in damages against her former employer when she was discharged for dating an employee of a competitor.

The plaintiff, a female employee of IBM, began dating a co-employee while they were both assigned to San Francisco. One year later, the male co-employee left IBM to join a competitor and was transferred to Philadelphia.

When he returned to San Francisco following a one-year absence, the plaintiff and he resumed their relationship. The fact that the two were seeing each other was widely known.

Not until one year later was the fact that the plaintiff was dating an employee of a competitor questioned. Because of the "conflict of interest," she was given a choice to stop seeing her former co-employee or to be terminated, and was given between two days and one week to make her decision.

The next day she was terminated. Of major significance in the case was a memorandum signed by a former chairman of IBM to all managers emphasizing the need to respect the right of privacy of IBM employees, and discouraging in no uncertain terms employment decisions based on private activities that have no impact on job performance and that are "not rightfully the company's concern."

Impact: This case emphasized three things of which employers must be aware. First, in drafting personnel policies and procedures some care must be taken not to insert gratuitous, overly broad policies that are not necessary to the efficient operation of the company.

Second, all managers with authority to make employment decisions must be aware of any policy affecting the manner in which such decisions are made, and must be cautioned to act at all times with such policies in mind.

Third, any decision with regard to employment, compensation, discipline, or termination should be based on verifiable job-related criteria.

Source: "Manager's Newsfront," by Betty Southard Murphy, Wayne E. Barlow, and D. Diane Hatch, copyright February 1985. Reprinted with the permission of *Personnel Journal*, Costa Mesa, California; all rights reserved.

security. For example, at the B.F. Goodrich plant in Akron, Ohio, union members who worked in one area could not be required to work in another, no matter how badly they were needed. The company and the United Rubber Workers agreed to eliminate the rule. At a Kaiser Aluminum plant in West Virginia, workers were divided into eighteen crafts, such as carpenters and electricians, and were prohibited by the union contract from doing the work of any craft but their own. This held true even if workers in a particular craft had run out of work and other crafts were short-handed. The company and the union agreed to reduce the eighteen categories to twelve, thus expanding the kinds of work to which employees could be assigned.[3] (See also Perspective 7.1.)

ADMINISTERING WORK RULES

When enterprises are small, the chief executive has the major responsibility for the development of work rules and schedules. As organizations become larger and more complex and the human resources department is created, the personnel director is usually expected — in cooperation with other managers — to suggest revisions in work rules and schedules to top management. Supervisors are then responsible for enforcing the rules. The more work rules are supported by group attitudes and norms, the more enforcement becomes a responsibility shared by all employees.

If management can engage supervisors and employees in problem solving rather than issue directives, it is more likely that work rules will be developed that are practical and have broad support. Some rules, of course, are so fundamental to organizational survival — such as rules against theft and rules prohibiting smoking near flammable materials — that most employees expect management to have established them long ago.

Just as the organization requires rules to operate, the employee needs information about those rules and an understanding of the consequences of violating them. Work rules are typically listed and described in employee handbooks (see Figure 8.1), and information is provided during orientation sessions at the time of employment. Organizations sometimes post work rules on bulletin boards and will almost always post warning signs in hazardous areas.

Violation of Work Rules

Work rules serve as control devices in that they represent standards of behavior that ensure a reasonable level of conformity

FIGURE 8.1
Sample page from an employee handbook

Time cards

Time cards are a record of an employee's regular working time, overtime, absences, and special situations. In order to make sure that non-exempt employees are fully and fairly compensated, those who are paid weekly are asked to submit a time card, signed by the supervisor and the employee, to the Payroll Office by noon on Friday. Non-exempt employees who are paid monthly should submit a signed time card to the Payroll Office by noon of the last working day of the month. When you are hired, you will be told when you will be paid and how to fill out your time card. Exempt employees are not required to submit time cards.

Payday

If you are paid weekly, you will receive your paycheck every Thursday. If you are on a monthly pay schedule, you will be paid on the 12th day of each month. If the 12th falls on a Saturday or a Sunday, you will be paid on the Friday before.

If you are absent from work on payday, your check will be held in the Payroll Office for you to pick up on your return. If you know that you will be on vacation and want to receive your paycheck in advance, you must make arrangements through the Payroll Office at least two weeks beforehand.

You may elect to have your pay deposited directly in your bank account. If you arrange for direct deposit, you will receive a statement of your earnings and deductions on payday.

Payroll deductions

When you are hired, we ask you to fill out federal and state withholding forms and certain benefit forms. The Payroll Office makes standard deductions for state and federal taxes and for F.I.C.A. (social security). Other deductions which may affect your paycheck are based on your requests, deductions for life or accident insurance, long term disability insurance, credit union, United Way, MBTA passes, and the like. If you suspect that a deduction is incorrect or if you wish to change a deduction, you should contact the Personnel or Payroll Departments.

Source: Houghton Mifflin Company

throughout the organization. An employee's failure to conform to the rules can lead to disciplinary action. **Disciplinary action** is the penalty or punishment associated with violation of a rule. A few organizations give positive rewards for above-average compliance in such matters as attendance or on-time arrival, but this practice is not widespread.

The following list illustrates some offenses that can lead to disciplinary action in business and industrial firms:

- Dishonesty, deception, or fraud, including computer fraud
- Unexcused absence
- Repeated tardiness
- Excessive absence
- Intoxication or possession of liquor or narcotics
- Willful damage to material or property
- Fighting
- Horseplay
- Gambling
- Theft of property, including trade secrets
- Sleeping on the job
- Failure to report injuries
- Failure to meet work standards
- Safety-rule violations
- Use of abusive or threatening language
- Insubordination
- Carrying concealed weapons
- Sexual harassment
- Working for a competitor

Some of these offenses require further definition in specific organizations. For example, what is meant by "excessive absence" and "repeated tardiness" needs to be defined so that employees and supervisors both know what standard is being applied. (In one study, about two-thirds of the manufacturing firms surveyed defined what was meant by those terms in their particular companies. Tardiness up to 10 times per year was within the acceptable range for about half the firms.[4])

A number of offenses may not be considered serious enough for **discharge** — permanent dismissal from the organization — the first time, but repeated offenses are more likely to involve discharge. Rule violations frequently considered serious enough to warrant immediate discharge are theft, falsifying the employment application or work records, possession of narcotics or weapons, or deliberate damage to material or property.[5]

Lighter penalties for violations of less serious infractions include oral or written **warnings**, **demotion**, or **disciplinary layoff**. A warning informs an employee that a more severe penalty (frequently specified) will be applied at the next infraction of the rules. A demotion is a reduction in job responsibilities, usually accompanied by a reduction in hourly pay or salary. In a disciplinary layoff, the employee is temporarily separated from the organization and the payroll, typically for a few days or weeks. **Docking** of pay — simply not paying for the time missed — for absenteeism or tardiness is a frequent practice. At least one organization — General Motors — reduces supplemental benefits for excessive absenteeism. Absenteeism by a few workers at the company had become so expensive that GM and the United Auto Workers agreed to cutting a violator's benefits — profit-sharing, health insurance, and bereavement pay — by 20 percent or more if the person's unexcused absences exceeded 20 percent for a six-month period. This was in addition to lost wages for the employee during the unexcused periods.[6]

Automatic application of penalties for offenses varies widely. There is growing sentiment that the circumstances of each case, including any organizational factors that may have contributed to the offense, should be considered in meting out discipline. On the other hand, to ensure it is consistent in the handling of disciplinary cases, the human resources department would be wise to keep records of serious incidents and the surrounding circumstances, and what action was taken, in order to advise supervisors and managers about how to handle future cases and to recommend any needed policy changes.

Progressive Discipline

The principle of **progressive discipline** is widely accepted in the administration of work rules. In essence, progressive discipline means that management responds to a first offense with some minimal action, such as an oral warning, but to subsequent offenses with more serious penalties, such as disciplinary layoff or discharge. A sequence of disciplinary actions might be as follows:

1. Oral warning
2. Written warning stating consequences of future offenses
3. Disciplinary layoff or demotion
4. Discharge

The overall goal of progressive discipline is to correct problems early and avoid the last-resort step of discharge. The seriousness of discharge is reflected in the label often given to discharge by union members and officials: "capital punishment." The wide acceptance of the progressive discipline principle probably stems in part from arbitrators' decisions made under grievance and arbitration provisions of union-management contracts. Arbitrators have typically examined both the correctability of a situation and the seriousness of an offense in comparison to the penalty imposed and have generally advocated progressive discipline procedures.

While Bill James, in Case 8.2, had cautioned Charlie Shearson about his practical jokes, he probably should have given Charlie a written warning after the water cooler incident. Although it is true that Charlie had engaged in intolerable horseplay, the union might take his grievance all the way to arbitration, and an arbitrator might hold that a written warning, or perhaps a disciplinary layoff, should have been administered before the company resorted to discharge.

Responsibility for Discipline

The supervisor is usually considered to be responsible for discipline in his or her unit. Many business firms, however, require each discharge case to be reviewed by higher authority before the discharge is made final. For example, a supervisor may be required to bring a recommendation for termination to the department head for review. The human resources department is usually involved in this review of the substance of the case and also usually monitors the procedures followed to make sure they are in accord with company policy. Federal civil service regulations, as well as most state and local civil service regulations, require all dismissals to be reviewed.[7]

Legal Ramifications

Although the principle of the right to discharge has been well established in the United States, increasingly discharges of employees are being affected by the Civil Rights Act, the Age Discrimination in Employment Act, EEOC rulings, and court decisions. For example, in one case, 160 older management and nonmanagement employees of Standard Oil of California were terminated during a reduction in force; they complained that they were being separated to make way for younger replacements. The U.S. Department of Labor sued on their behalf, and the outcome was an agreement that Standard Oil of California would reinstate the workers and pay them $2 million.[8]

THE WORKDAY AND WORKWEEK

Work schedules, like work rules, are a major condition surrounding jobs. "Work schedules" refers to matters such as starting and stopping times, the number and length of work breaks, how work beyond the regularly scheduled day or week is administered, whether the work is done on company premises or at home, and whether the employee is full-time or part-time. Like work rules, work schedules have a significant influence on the satisfaction, and frequently the performance, of employees, and how they are administered and changed is important. From the standpoint of management, work schedules are necessary to coordinate and control work. Further, a certain amount of uniformity is required to meet employee expectations of equitable treatment. Work schedules can be more flexible, however, than has been traditionally assumed in many organizations.

Traditional Work Schedules

The typical business and industrial workday and workweek have changed a great deal over the years. For example, in 1835, the workday in the Philadelphia Navy Yard was sunrise to sunset, with time off for breakfast and other meals. During the summer this meant an extremely long and exhausting day, while for a short period in December and early January working hours dropped to slightly fewer than eight. In late June 1835, employees actually worked eleven hours and fifty-four minutes, *not including time off for meals.* In 1836 the workday was reduced to ten hours the year around, largely through pressures from shipyard mechanics of the National Trades' Union who had already obtained this concession from private shipyards in the Philadelphia area.[9] Presumably employees worked these long hours six days per week, since the average number of hours worked in 1840 has been estimated at seventy-eight.[10]

About 150 years later, the typical workday in American business and industry is roughly 8 hours per day for a 5-day work week (see Figure 8.2). In November 1984, the average weekly hours worked by production or nonsupervisory employees in the private sector was 35.2, down from about 40 hours per week in 1950. There were some differences among industries, however. For example, the average of the weekly hours for workers in wholesale trade was 38.6, in retail trade 29.9, and in manufacturing 40.5 hours.[11] The low figure in retail trade partly reflects the widespread use of part-time workers in that industry.

Various forces have probably contributed to this decline in working hours. One clear factor is pressure from labor unions. Another is that, with rising real wages, it has become possible to have both a higher living standard and additional leisure.[12]

Overtime Work. **Overtime work** is work performed beyond the regularly scheduled workday or workweek as defined by the organization or by law. Since the Public Contracts (Walsh-Healey)

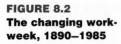

FIGURE 8.2
The changing work-week, 1890–1985

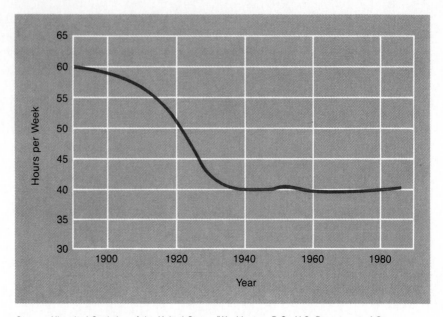

Source: Historical Statistics of the United States (Washington, D.C.: U.S. Department of Commerce, Bureau of the Census, 1975), pp.168, 169–170; *Monthly Labor Review* (January 1985), p.76.

Act was passed in 1936, employers having contracts with the federal government have been required to pay one and one-half times the regular rate of pay for work done beyond eight hours in one day or forty hours in one week. Since the Fair Labor Standards Act was passed in 1938, most employers in interstate commerce have been required to pay time and one-half for hours worked beyond forty in one week. The employees to whom these payments must be made are called **nonexempt employees** — i.e., employees who are protected by the laws. Executive, administrative, and professional employees, including outside sales personnel, need not be paid overtime and thus are called **exempt employees**.[13]

One effect of these laws, of course, has been to discourage management from scheduling workweeks longer than forty hours and, in the case of federal contractors, from scheduling workdays beyond eight hours. Another effect has been to spread jobs across the population. The laws were originally passed during a period of high unemployment and were intended to spread the available work.

Shift Work. **Shift work** is usually considered to be regular employment that occurs some time between 7 p.m. and 7 a.m. There has been a significant increase in shift work in the world over the past thirty years, in part because continuous-process operations, in which machines or procedures are run continuously, have been widely adopted in industries such as steel and petrochemicals where starting and stopping on a daily basis is prohibitively expensive. Other factors in the growth of shift work include the economic necessity to maximize the use of capital equipment (machinery, vehicles, buildings, and so forth) and the growth of "round-the-clock" service industries such as transportation and medical care.[14]

There are many variations of shift work, depending on whether the organization is operating twenty-four hours a day and seven days a week, and on the circumstances and history of the particular enterprise. For example, the day shift might be 8:00 a.m. to 4:30 p.m., with a half-hour unpaid lunch period; the afternoon shift from 4:15 p.m. to 12:15 a.m. (sometimes called the "swing shift"); and the night shift from midnight to 8:15 a.m. (sometimes called the "graveyard shift"). In some circumstances, organizations employ part-time workers on a four-hour shift (sometimes called the "twilight shift") at the end of a regular eight-hour day. "Split shifts" are sometimes used when there are peak workloads at widely different times of the day. In these circumstances, an employee may be scheduled to work two different partial shifts with a several-hour interval between the two periods.

On any one day in the United States, nearly one worker in six is working hours other than a regular day schedule. About half of these shift workers are employed on afternoon shifts, and the others work on night shifts.[15] Although schedules vary widely in the United Kingdom, typical practice is to rotate employees across shifts. A worker might be on the day shift for a week, the afternoon shift for a week, and then on the night shift for a week before rotating back to the day shift.[16] In many organizations, however, the workers on a given shift stay on that shift unless they apply and are selected for another schedule.

Research has found that certain conclusions can be drawn about the effects of shift work on employees, although the data are contradictory. Generally speaking, people experience both advantages and disadvantages with shift work.

Some of the benefits of shift work are that it permits some workers to find employment they might not otherwise find, to hold down two jobs, or to attend school. Other benefits that appeal to some people are the relaxed work pace and greater freedom from supervision sometimes found on shift work. Further, night work seems to fit the biological rhythms of some people better than day work. In addition, shift work usually pays more than day work. Shift premiums average 10 cents an hour for the evening shift and 13 cents an hour for night shift work.[17]

Some of the drawbacks of shift work, according to a review of the research, are the negative consequences frequently experienced

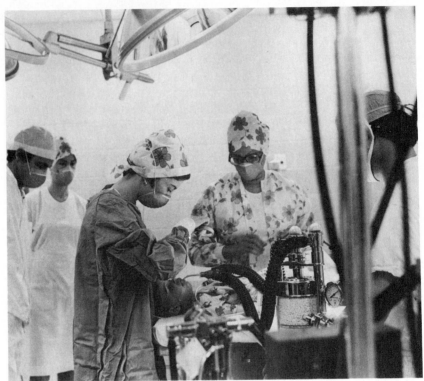

Shift work is necessary in round-the-clock service industries.

in terms of health, relationships with other people, leisure activities, and safety.[18] Shift workers may experience difficulties in
sleeping or digestion and appetite problems. They may regret that
they have less time to spend with children, spouses, and friends
because of their varying schedules. Research shows that shift
workers have problems in meshing their schedules with family
members and friends.[19] There is contradictory evidence as to whether
shift workers have more accidents than day workers, but there is
enough laboratory and other data to suggest that shift work, for
some people, may be a contributor to accidents. Laboratory studies
show that disturbances in the twenty-four-hour body cycles tend
to be associated with an increase in reaction time and errors.[20]

   In addition to being alert to the health, family, social, recreational, and safety consequences of shift work, management needs
to pay attention to the integration of afternoon and night shift
workers with the people and activities on a day schedule. This
integration is important both to the morale of shift workers and

for effective coordination and cooperation between shifts. Without attention to this integration, misunderstanding and conflict can arise between workers and supervisors on one shift and workers and supervisors on another. Examples of typical problems between shifts are complaints that the people on the previous shift do not clean up properly, do not maintain the equipment properly, misplace tools, and so on. One way cooperation and integration between shifts can be furthered is for daytime managers to meet periodically with shift employees. Another device is for shifts to overlap so there can be sufficient communication and coordination between the supervisors and employees of the adjoining shifts. The human resources staff can do much to assist in this integration by helping establish such mechanisms and, in cooperation with the appropriate managers, systematically assessing how employees see the level of cooperation and help between shifts.

New Patterns in Work Scheduling

Recent years have seen a great deal of experimentation with different kinds of work schedules, such as the compressed workweek, flextime, permanent part-time work, peak-time work, job sharing, and telecommuting, all of which are discussed below. The reasons for this experimentation include changing lifestyles and desires for more leisure time, attempts to mimimize traffic problems, the development of the personal computer, and attempts by management to increase both morale and productivity. Some, if not all, are based partly on pragmatic attempts by managers to reduce costs.

Compressed Workweek. The **compressed workweek** is a work schedule in which the employee works the same number of hours per week as previously but completes them in fewer days. The workweek declined by nearly twenty hours between 1901 and shortly after World War II and then leveled off at about forty hours.[21]

The typical pattern then became a five-day, forty-hour workweek. This five-day week is gradually being modified by the appearance of the four-day, forty-hour workweek in which the employee works for ten hours each day, four days per week. This concept is being tried or considered by a number of firms in the United States and elsewhere. A report of a few years ago stated that approximately 3,000 firms in the United States were under a four-day week for at least part of the work year or for part of the work force.[22] The federal government has encouraged experimentation in federal agencies with the compressed workweek and other forms of work schedules through the Federal Employees Flexible and Compressed Work Schedule Act of 1978.[23]

A four-day workweek does not mean necessarily that the plant or company operates only four days a week. Rather, it means that the individual employee's work commitment is for only four days, and typically for ten hours per day. Under different programs, however, the total hours worked per employee varies from as low as thirty-two to as high as forty-eight. In addition, not all employees in such organizations are on a four-day schedule. Frequent starting points for such programs are in units such as data-processing departments that may already be using afternoon or night shifts or hospital nursing staffs where round-the-clock shift work is necessary.[24]

Companies using the four-day week generally report desirable consequences, including increased morale, reduced absenteeism, enhanced recruiting, improvements in traffic flow, and increased productivity. Reported difficulties include resistance of working mothers to ten-hour shifts, complaints from parents that they are not spending enough time with children, less effective service to customers, scheduling and coordination problems, and worker fatigue.[25]

A major difficulty in adopting the four-day week for companies with government contracts is the Walsh-Healey Act requirement for overtime payment beyond eight hours in one day. Further, unions generally adhere to the idea that work beyond eight hours should be paid at overtime rates. Various state laws may also be obstacles to ten-hour days, although some states have modified their laws to encourage compressed workweek schedules.

Flextime.   Increasingly, **flextime** (sometimes called flexitime, flexible hours workweek, variable working hours, or *gleitzeit* — glid-

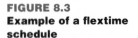

FIGURE 8.3
Example of a flextime schedule

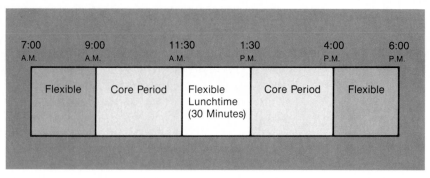

7:00 A.M.	9:00 A.M.	11:30 A.M.	1:30 P.M.	4:00 P.M.	6:00 P.M.
Flexible	Core Period	Flexible Lunchtime (30 Minutes)	Core Period	Flexible	

ing time) is being adopted by organizations around the world. Flextime is a schedule under which employees may choose when to arrive at work and when to depart and which includes a *core time* when everyone must be on the job. For example, employees may be free to arrive any time between 7:00 and 10:00 a.m. and leave between 3:00 and 6:00 p.m., but all must be on company premises between 10:00 and 3:00 (see Figure 8.3). Further, there are usually rules about the total number of hours that must be worked during one week (e.g., forty) or during two weeks (e.g., eighty). Typically under flextime, all employees fill out time sheets or punch the time clock.

In 1980, almost 12 percent of all nonfarm workers in the United States were on flexible schedules.[26] U.S. firms that have adopted the concept are Hewlett-Packard, Digital Equipment, Corning Glass Works, TRW, Conoco, Metropolitan Life, and Control Data.[27] Thousands of firms in Europe have also adopted some version of flextime, and in England, Parliament has authorized its use for Britain's half-million civil servants. Very few programs appear to have been terminated.[28]

Flextime is a substantial departure from traditional management practices. As shown in Case 8.1, "Sally Gray, VP of Sales," at the beginning of the chapter, flextime may require a change in management's attitudes about the control of worker behavior. Successful application also requires solving problems that are unique to each situation, such as accommodating Sally's West Coast customers.

Some of the advantages to flextime appear to be as follows:

- Employees can adjust their schedules to spend more time with their families.
- Employees and work units can manage their own schedules within limits to adjust to their own particular lifestyles.
- Stress over concern about tardiness beyond one's control (e.g., traffic jams) is reduced.
- Peak traffic times can be avoided, and less time is spent commuting.
- Personal matters such as dentist or doctor appointments can be attended to more easily.
- Tardiness almost disappears.
- Deceptive use of sick leave diminishes.

Some of the disadvantages of flextime appear to be:

- Compliance with wage and hour laws and laws pertaining to lunch and rest breaks restricts flexibility. For example, the Walsh-

Healey Act requires federal contractors to pay overtime to nonexempt workers who work more than eight hours in one day.

- There can be a lack of availability of employees during the flexible work periods at the beginning and end of the workday. This can adversely affect customers, suppliers, and fellow employees.
- There is an increased need to coordinate within and between units as to time availability and to ensure coverage of vital functions such as staffing switchboards.
- Time reporting becomes more burdensome because employees may vary their hours and carry over hours.[29]
- There can be abuses, such as some employees taking extended lunches, which occurred in some federal agencies. (As a result, Congress gave agency heads the authority to restrict or end flextime if continuation does not appear to be in the public interest.)[30]

Generally favorable results from flextime have been reported by both European and American organizations. The research studies that have been conducted report generally increased job satisfaction and either no change or an improvement in job performance.[31]

Permanent Part-Time Work. Increasingly, organizations are revising their work rules and employment practices to use **permanent part-time** employees. Such employees are frequently used to solve some operating problem such as the need for adequate coverage during peak hours. *Part-time* can mean some reduced proportion of the regular day or fewer days per week, or both, or fewer weeks or months per year. The word *permanent* can mean certain employees working part-time for an extended number of years or can connote the organization's ongoing allocation of a proportion of its payroll budget to part-time positions.

An example of widespread use of permanent part-time workers is the use of *peak-time employees* in banks and savings and loan institutions. For example, The Provident Bank in Cincinnati and the Western Savings & Loan Association in Phoenix supplement their staffs with part-time tellers at peak periods such as noon hours and Friday afternoons. Typically, such employees are paid a significantly higher hourly wage than regular employees, but they receive no supplemental benefits except those required by law if they work more than 1,000 hours per year.[32]

There are many variations in part-time work. For example, the Shawmut Bank of Boston has employed about a dozen people for a nine-month work year with summers off, a program that attracts women who want to spend substantial time with their children in

David Witbeck/The Picture Cube

Peak-time employees in banks are frequently permanent part-time workers.

the summers. They are replaced by college students during their three-month break.[33] Western Airlines uses many part-time ticket agents and baggage handlers to cover maximum staffing needs early and late in the day.[34]

Estimates range from half to three-fourths of business firms using permanent, part-time employees, although the proportion of the work force is usually only from two to seven percent.[35] This trend was further stimulated by federal legislation enacted in 1978 and by laws or policies in thirty-five states encouraging public agencies to employ permanent part-time workers, who are entitled to certain benefits and advancement opportunities ordinarily reserved for full-time people.[36]

Many of the regular part-time workers in the work force are women — and sometimes men — who need to be employed less than full time in order to take care of children or to pursue other responsibilities or interests. In particular, women returning from maternity leave tend to be interested in part-time work arrangements for several months or even several years. A frequently found work schedule is 9:30 a.m. to 2:30 p.m. Others who are employed part time in relatively large numbers are students.

Some firms report low turnover, ease in recruitment, and high productivity as advantages in using part-time employees. Further, part-time workers usually receive fewer employee benefits than full-time employees, and thus their use reduces labor costs. Disadvantages include increased complexity of supervision and increased administrative costs.[37] While part-time workers' job satisfaction has been found to be high in many instances, a study of fifty-five stores in a Midwest retail chain found part-time workers' job satisfaction to be lower than that of full-time workers.[38]

Job Sharing.   One version of the use of part-time employees is the concept of **job sharing,** in which a job is split into two four-hour segments and shared, for example, by two homemakers. Another version involves one person working full days for part of a week and the other person working the other days. Job sharing obviously requires coordination and compatibility between the two people to ensure continuity and effective performance from day to day.[39] Organizations frequently find that the total performance from the two half-time employees exceeds what ordinarily would be expected from one full-time employee.[40] (The concept of job sharing should not be confused with the concept of work sharing, which is a reduction in hours or days worked by a large group of employees, usually in order to spread the work and avoid layoffs with a budget cutback. For example, an entire plant may work thirty hours per week as opposed to the usual forty hours.)

An example of job sharing occurred at United Airlines during a period of financial difficulty in 1980. Rather than simply lay off junior flight attendants, the company approached the Association of Flight Attendants for recommendations about how to reduce the payroll. The union proposed, and the company accepted, a temporary job-sharing program under which two flight attendants could agree to share a job for a four-month period. Volunteers, in pairs, worked out their own schedules, and pay was allocated between the two in proportion to the amount of time flown.[41]

Some of the advantages of job sharing, in addition to the extra performance, according to both employers and employees who have participated, include the energy and enthusiasm the employees bring to the job, and employer accessibility to a wider range of applicants. For example, the pool of applicants can include retirees, students, people whose family responsibilities prohibit full-time work, and people who simply want more free time.

Job sharing has two main disadvantages. First, if the two people who are involved do not communicate and cooperate well, the costs in inefficiency could be considerable. This has usually not been a problem. The other disadvantage is the potentially increased costs of supplemental benefits. For example, state unemployment insurance and social security taxes may cost more for the two people than if only one person were employed.[42]

Telecommuting. It is predicted that **telecommuting,** or working at home for an organization through the use of computer and word processor equipment linked by telephone to the home office, will involve as many as 15 million workers in the United States by the mid-1990s. Organizations like Aetna Life & Casualty, Investors Diversified Services, Chase Manhattan Bank, and Blue Cross and Blue Shield have experimented with the idea with small numbers of employees and plan to expand their programs.[43] In 1981 Control Data employed some 100 employees at home or in satellite offices, and Digital Equipment employed several hundred at home.[44] Some 450 U.S. firms were experimenting with telecommuting by 1985.[45]

Typically, the telecommuter is in a nonmanagerial role, but some managers have found they can increase their productivity by working part-time at home using a computer linked to the home office. It appears that full-time telecommuters are paid differently from regular employees: they are often paid by the project — frequently grossing more than their colleagues back at the office — but sometimes are ineligible for supplemental benefits. Examples of these jobs are computer programming, financial analysis, processing insurance claims or catalogue orders, and word processing.[46]

The advantages of telecommuting are several:

- Parents with small children or persons who are handicapped can work at home.
- People who dislike commuting can avoid the traffic and time spent commuting.
- Employees save what it would ordinarily cost to commute to work.
- Employees can schedule their own hours.
- Employees can work some days at home and some days at the office, depending on the nature of the tasks to be done.
- Substantial increases in employee productivity have been reported.
- Telecommuters may earn more gross pay.
- Employers have a larger pool of potential employees from which to recruit.

But there are disadvantages:

- Telecommuting diminishes the ties between employee and supervisor and coworkers.
- The company of others helps meet some basic human needs;

PERSPECTIVE 8.2　When Employees Work from Home

"Telecommuting increases productivity, but if we let our employees do it, they'd finish their jobs by noon on Wednesday — and then what would they do?"

Loss of control of their employees' time is just one of the fears Marcia Kelly hears managers express about using home-based workers. As president of Electronic Services Unlimited, a Manhattan-based research and consulting firm, Kelly helps companies address this and other concerns as they implement computerized work-at-home, or telecommuting, programs. . . .

● **What kinds of jobs can be done remotely?** Ideal tasks are those that require little face-to-face contact, such as programming, financial analysis, sales projections, accounting, legal work, reports and correspondence, and word processing and forms and applications processing. Also suitable are projects with long-term deadlines that can be done during off hours, such as evenings and weekends, allowing employees to choose work times.

● **How should telecommuting jobs be structured?** Flexibility is paramount in any telecommuting program, and many companies allow managers to tailor jobs to specific needs and individuals. Most telecommuters are full-time, salaried employees. Some work at home one or two days a week, or occasionally for extended periods; others, especially disabled persons, work at home full-time. Some telecommuters, says Kelly, rotate in and out of the office every few months or so.

Some companies ask telecommuters to be available for consultation during certain hours of the day, but otherwise let them work whenever they choose. Others only ask telecommuters to check in periodically. . . .

● **How should telecommuters be supervised?** Supervision depends on the individuals, and managers should adapt to different work styles and habits. Some employees want to be left alone for long periods of time, while others want regular contact with the home base. Overall, most telecommuters like autonomy but still want to feel part of the corporate family.

"Managers of telecommuters must pay particular attention to career growth and development," says Ralph McCrae, manager of the Homework program for Control Data Corporation, in Bloomington, Minnesota, which employs about 100 telecommuters, three-quarters of them full-time. "Formal procedures need to be set up to prevent someone's being overlooked for promotion because they are 'out of sight, out of mind.' ". . .

Since managers of remote employees miss the advantages of eye contact and body language, they must learn to be very specific in verbal communication. Being a good listener is vital. Like a psychiatrist, a manager must be able to pick up signals of loneliness or difficulty with work that an employee might be reluctant to mention.

Managers also must develop a high degree of trust for their telecommuters and must be thoroughly familiar with their tasks and the amount of time required to complete them. And, says one telecommuter, "managers must have the skill to provide honest and timely feedback." With this kind of thoughtful supervision and planning, managers will be able to give employees the flexibility to work at home without jeopardizing their department's workflow.

Source: Excerpted from Rosemary Guiley, "When Your Employees Work from Home," *Working Women,* March 1985, pp. 27–28, 30. Reprinted by permission.

telecommuting decreases face-to-face interaction. (Some telecommuters have reduced the sense of isolation by meeting colleagues for lunch periodically; some firms have telecommuters work in the office one or two days per week.)

● Telecommuting requires changes in management style: supervisors must rely on the honor system or piecework compensation systems and plan to stay in touch with the employee because there is no longer the informal office contact.

- Telecommuters usually do not receive health and pension benefits.
- There is concern among some telecommuters and employees who are potential telecommuters that they may "stagnate" at home, losing touch with the company information and influence network and missing out on promotions.
- Some unions believe there is the potential for exploitation in the case of individually negotiated piecework arrangements, leading to wide disparities in compensation for telecommuters, similar to the problems that led to the outlawing of home work in the garment industries in the early 1940s. This is not considered a major problem.
- Weight gains because of easy access to the refrigerator are reported by some telecommuters.[47]

In general, it appears that telecommuting will increase. Its application is limited largely to information-manipulating or information-creating jobs such as writing, financial analysis, typing letters and statistical tables, computer programming, and data processing.

ROLE OF THE HUMAN RESOURCES DEPARTMENT

The human resources department has important and ongoing roles relative to work rules, disciplinary procedures, and work schedules. One role is to diagnose continuously the effects on employee morale and performance. This can be done through extensive and frequent informal contacts with employees, supervisors, and managers, and through more systematic procedures such as climate surveys that are tailored to include questions about these areas.

A related role for the human resources department is to suggest modifications in, or alternatives to, existing rules, procedures, and schedules. Acceptance and the workability of suggestions will depend partly on the thoroughness with which the human resources professionals have diagnosed present problems and worked cooperatively with other managers in those diagnoses. In addition, the usefulness of their proposals will depend in part on how accurately they have tuned into the norms and attitudes of individuals and groups in the organization.

Another important role — frequently overlooked by human resources departments and by managers in general — is anticipating and understanding the impact that a change in a rule or practice will have on other parts of the system. For example, when four

University of Tennessee employees became telecommuters for several months, they and their supervisors felt their work was as good as or better than before, but the employees left back at the office felt they were put under more pressure to answer phones and help out with rush jobs.[48] Ideally, the human resources department works with managers to anticipate such side effects of changes and helps alleviate these problems if they occur.

Similarly, the human resources department needs to be sensitive to problems or potential problems among groups of employees that relate to work rules and schedules. Potential problems between shifts have already been mentioned. As another example, chronic tardiness in one department will be noticed and resented by members of an adjoining department where expectations about being on time are much higher. The human resources director and his or her staff can play an important part in diplomatically pointing out such problems to the supervisors or managers involved and assisting in their resolution.

Finally, human resources specialists, and all managers, must treat all employees — day-shift employees, afternoon- and evening-shift workers, part-time people, and telecommuters — as valuable resources. High morale and motivation in these groups and strong organizational performance require this.

SUMMARY

Factors that influence the design of work rules and schedules are management philosophy; work-group norms; the technology, equipment, and materials used by the organization; and social and cultural norms and attitudes. Work rules and schedules are necessary in organizational life to ensure coordination and reasonable predictability of employee behavior. Work rules are also necessary to protect employees from hazardous conditions and inequities in treatment.

Work rules that are too strict or confining will impede the fulfillment of such human needs as those for affiliation, cooperation, autonomy, and self-actualization and may lead to subterfuge and resentment. Rules that are too lax may lead to inefficiencies as well as morale problems. Work rules that tend to protect jobs, such as lines of demarcation between crafts, may provide job security in the short run but if too restrictive may have serious consequences for organizational effectiveness and survival in the long run.

Management needs to be clear about the consequences of rule violations. The principle of progressive discipline is advocated as good practice in most discipline cases. Supervisors ordinarily have responsibility for discipline in their units. Most organizations require review by higher authority, however, before a discharge can be made final. Increasingly, the right to discharge is being affected by federal law, EEOC rulings, and court decisions.

The typical workday in the United States is slightly less than eight hours; the workweek is typically five days. Overtime payments of time-and-one-half for hours worked beyond forty in one week are required under the Fair Labor Standards Act. Under the Walsh-Healey Act, time-and-one-half payments are required for work beyond eight hours in any one day for firms having federal government contracts.

Nearly one worker in six is working on a shift other than a regular day schedule. While shift work has advantages for some people, negative consequences are also frequently experienced. Management needs to pay special attention to the problems of shift workers and make sure that they and their work activities are integrated with the work and the people on day schedules.

There has been substantial interest in and experimentation with different kinds of work schedules in recent years, including the compressed workweek, flextime, permanent part-time work, job sharing, and telecommuting. All of these practices have advantages and disadvantages, and their applicability depends on specific circumstances of the organization and the job.

The human resources department plays important roles with respect to work rules, discipline, and work schedules. Two of these roles are to diagnose continuously the effects of current rules, procedures, and schedules on employee morale and performance and to make suggestions for changes. Cooperation with other managers and sensitivity to employee needs and problems are important to the success of the human resources department in these matters. Other important roles for the human resources department are anticipating and understanding the impact that changes in rules and practices will have on other parts of the system and being sensitive to the problems that can occur among different groups of employees.

KEY TERMS

restrictive work rules
garnishment
insubordination
disciplinary action
discharge
warning
demotion

disciplinary layoff
docking
progressive discipline
overtime work
nonexempt employees
exempt employees

shift work
compressed workweek
flextime
permanent part-time work
job sharing
telecommuting

REVIEW QUESTIONS

1. Discuss several organizational factors that influence the extent of control over the behavior of employees.
2. Explain why work rules are necessary in organizations.
3. Discuss the consequences of overly restrictive work rules.
4. What is progressive discipline? Cite the usual steps in progressive discipline.
5. Who should have responsibility for discipline in organizations? Discuss.
6. Discuss the advantages and disadvantages of shift work, the compressed workweek, flextime, permanent part-time work, job-sharing, and telecommuting.
7. Discuss the role of the human resources department in managing work rules and schedules.

OPENING QUESTIONS

Case 8.1 Sally Gray, VP of Sales

1. What can Sally do to ensure that there are salespeople in the office to accept calls from West Coast customers?
2. What are some of the major advantages of flextime?
3. What are some of the disadvantages?

Case 8.2 Just a Bundle of Laughs

1. Does Bill have any grounds for firing Charlie since he has no warnings on file? Explain.
2. If you had been Charlie's coworker and were asked to testify at the grievance proceedings, how would you handle the situation?

CASE 8.3   FLEXTIME

In the United States and in other countries, industries of all kinds are experimenting with options in work scheduling. So far, of the available options, it appears that flextime is among the most popular. There are, of course, a number of reasons why flextime appeals to employees, but studies also indicate that it may very well improve performance and organizational efficiency.

One study that concentrated on the utilities industry found that for the majority of firms investigated, flextime had, at worst, no negative effects on performance. Certain factors, however, showed clear improvement under flextime. In general, employees were not late as often, and all of the firms studied reported that job satisfaction increased among employees working flexible hours. Overall, more than three-quarters of the firms studied were pleased with flextime.

Another study focused on clerical workers in three industries—banking, insurance, and utilities. The findings were somewhat similar to those of the first study, but in banking and insurance, several firms reported improvements in the quantity and quality of employees' work. Tardiness again fell in all three industries, and many firms also reported reduced absenteeism. Job satisfaction, too, again improved.

For some firms, though, flextime can be complicated to implement. Bendix Field Engineering Corp. put a great deal of effort into a computerized system that would allow employees to work on flextime at its main facility, in Columbia, Maryland. Bendix, a division of Allied Corporation, is involved in data processing systems services, and it is responsible for most of NASA's spaceflight and data tracking installations.

The system at Bendix is able to supply management each day with a summary of the hours each employee in the program has worked. Employees use a special card to enter their start and stop times on the computer. They are allowed to choose their hours each day, with clearance from management.

There were some objections to the program at first. For one thing, many of Bendix's employees are professionals who weren't used to having their hours monitored. For another, supervisors worried that flexible hours would undermine their authority. After fifteen months, however, questionnaires showed that the flextime program was a success with supervisors and nonsupervisors alike. All the employees had cooperated in ironing out problems, and 73 percent of those in the program who filled out surveys felt that flextime was helping the company.

Case Sources: "Flexible Word Schedules Benefit Aerospace Firm," *The Office* (May 1985): 114, 116; "Flextime in the Utilities Industry," *Personnel* (March-April 1984): 42–44; Edward Wakin, "Jobs a la Carte," *Today's Office* (September 1984): 43–46, 48; and J. Carroll Swart, "Clerical Workers on Flextime: A Survey of Three Industries," *Personnel* (April 1985): 41–43.

Discussion Questions

1. The findings of the two studies described agree with the advantages of flextime listed in the text. What reasons can you think of for why these advantages exist?

2. Suppose you are a human resources manager at a company that has recently experienced serious labor difficulties, including work stoppages, because of a union/management contract dispute. The dispute has been settled now, although the settlement came through a compromise that neither labor nor management is completely happy with. The company's upper management has asked for your recommendations on flextime as an option for the company. What would you recommend?

Recruitment and Selection

SOURCES OF INFORMATION ABOUT APPLICANTS
 Application Forms / Reference
 Checks / Physical Examinations
SELECTION TESTS
 Types of Tests / Legal and Ethical Challenges
THE SELECTION INTERVIEW
 Interview Scenarios / Interview
 Techniques / Problems in
 Interviewing / Effective Interviewing
THE SELECTION DECISION

LEARNING OBJECTIVES

- **Define the recruitment process and describe the organizational and environmental factors that affect it.**
- **Identify the basic methods of recruitment and the roles played by different types of managers.**
- **Explain how and why organizations attempt to recruit specific groups such as women, minorities, and the handicapped.**
- **Define the selection process and identify the roles of the human resources staff and other managers.**
- **Explain the concepts of reliability, validity, and job relatedness and their relation to selection standards.**
- **Describe the main sources of information about job applicants.**
- **Identify the advantages and difficulties of testing procedures.**
- **Explain the different types of interviews, the problems that an interviewer must confront, and the characteristics of an effective interview.**

CASE 9.1   NEW COMPONENTS IN THE ELECTRONICS BUSINESS

Electrotech, Inc. was a small electronics firm founded by two young and ambitious engineers. For the five years of its existence, the company had specialized in the design of circuits for complex industrial and scientific applications. Now, though, Electrotech was changing almost overnight. Jim Odrobina,

one of the founders, had patented a small component, known as the QT-48, that had proved extremely useful in the circuits the company designed. As word of the device spread, other firms began to order QT-48s for their own uses. Lately the orders had rolled in much faster than the company could fill them. Then last week had come the clincher: Jim had returned from a trip to Washington with the news that the Defense Department wanted 80,000 of the components and would probably order hundreds of thousands in the next year!

The implications were obvious. To meet such demand, the company would have to add an entire manufacturing department, different from all of the firm's other departments. Moreover, as a government contractor, Electrotech would be subject to many new rules and regulations. Beth Ann McNulty, human resources director, was especially concerned about government rules regarding equal employment opportunity (EEO) for such groups as women, minorities, and the handicapped. And in general, she felt that the question of finding *people* for the new jobs was being somewhat overlooked in all the excitement about machinery and robot arms and huge contracts. Today, after clearing her desk, Beth poured herself a fresh cup of coffee and began to list the major personnel problems:

- To begin with, where would the new manufacturing workers come from? Electrotech was located in a suburban town with little manufacturing industry. Would employment agencies in nearby cities be much help? For the less skilled positions, could Beth use the placement offices of regional vocational-technical schools? Where should she advertise?
- The surrounding suburban towns were almost all white, but the region as a whole contained sizable black and Hispanic communities. Would the federal or state government require the firm to recruit in these communities? If so, how could it best be done?
- According to the basic plan being developed, the supervisors for the manufacturing department would be chosen from among the current managerial-level employees — people who could be trusted, in Jim Odrobina's view. But would engineers make good managers of a manufacturing line? Wouldn't it be better to recruit from outside?
- Could some of the new jobs be designed to suit the handicapped? Wouldn't this be necessary, in fact, to establish equal employment opportunity?
- And, finally, a subject close to Beth's heart: What about women employees? Currently all but two of the engineers were men. All but three of the secretaries and clerks were women. Beth had excused this situation on the grounds that women engineers were hard to find, but now she believed, for both ethical and legal reasons, that the proportion of female employees — especially in high-level positions — would have to be increased as the company expanded.

In the heady atmosphere of the company's tremendous boom, Beth didn't want to be a lonely critic. Yet she felt that the personnel problems had to be confronted squarely or the results could be disastrous. She was glad she had convinced Jim Odrobina to convene a meeting of department heads so they could all discuss the hiring program. Beth drank another cup of coffee as she prepared her notes for the meeting. She was going to acquaint these engineers with the basic facts of EEO; she would recommend that a firm of outside consultants be hired to develop an affirmative action program; and she would offer her own plan for recruiting supervisors. Most of all, she hoped to convince everyone that recruiting and selecting the right people would require cooperation and commitment from every manager in the organization.

T he staffing process — putting the right people in the right positions at the right times — is one of the most critical tasks any organization faces. The quality of the work performed can be only as high as the capabilities of the people performing it. This chapter examines the two initial stages in staffing an organization. **Recruitment** is the process of finding qualified people and encouraging them to apply for work with the firm. **Selection** is the process of choosing among those who do apply. Together, these two facets of human resources management supply the life-blood of the organization.

THE RECRUITMENT PROCESS

Ideally, the recruitment process should ensure that, for every position available in the firm, there is a sufficient number of qualified applicants. As Beth Ann McNulty realized in Case 9.1, these applicants should include members of both sexes and various social groups such as minorities and handicapped workers. Especially for larger organizations, recruitment is a complex and continuing process that demands extensive planning and effort.

Organizational Factors

Many factors within the organization can affect the success of the recruitment program. The company projects a certain image to the community at large, and this will influence its ability to attract workers. In most cases, good advertising and successful public relations efforts can increase community knowledge of the company, raise public appreciation, and thus make a dramatic impact on recruitment.

Relations with labor unions can be critical to public perceptions of the firm, as can the company's reputation for offering high or low wages. Subtle elements in the organizational culture and climate are also important. Since many people hear about job possibilities from friends or relatives already working at the firm,[1] attitudes about the company are passed along through this informal network. For instance, if current employees are confused by the leadership style or annoyed by what they perceive as lack of recognition for their efforts, their casual comments may discourage their friends from applying.

Environmental Factors

In addition to factors within an organization, the external environment influences recruitment success in a variety of ways. Most obviously, the condition of the labor market affects the supply of qualified applicants. If a firm cannot find enough skilled applicants in the immediate area, it may need a regional or national search program. Competition from other companies can reduce the pool of qualified workers or raise salary expectations beyond what the firm is willing to pay.

Economic trends can influence both the number of people pursuing certain occupations and the demand for their services. While computer scientists are in demand, steel and textile workers may face layoffs. In this century, the rapid pace of technological change has accelerated these trends. Not only do products become obsolete from one decade to the next, but manufacturing processes and the skills needed to carry them out can undergo similar change. Since the labor market may not keep pace with these developments, special training programs may be necessary. Organizations can encourage colleges and vocational schools to offer courses in new specialties. At times, however, a firm may need to restructure some of its jobs to adapt them to the people available.

Social attitudes about particular types of employment will also affect the supply of workers. If a job is considered uninteresting, oppressive, or low in status, applicants will shun it unless the wages are extremely attractive. Some analysts have argued that the number of undocumented aliens in the United States has increased because of the need to fill such undesirable positions.[2]

In some industries unions may control the supply of applicants. In the garment and construction trades, for example, potential employees are often referred by the union hiring hall. Although discrimination against nonunion members is illegal, the union can evaluate applicants in terms of work experience and acquired skills, and under these conditions the applicants who are referred will usually be union members.

Finally, federal and state regulations concerning equal employ-

Courtesy Chrysler Corporation

The rapid pace of technological change has led to the development of special training programs for the people available to work in a company.

ment opportunity and affirmative action set the framework within which a recruitment program must function. Later sections of this chapter will discuss responses to the legal environment.

Managerial Roles

Responsibility for the overall recruitment process normally is assigned to human resources managers. They are responsible for designing and implementing a recruitment program that will meet the company's personnel needs while complying with all legal requirements. This responsibility includes finding sources of applicants; writing and placing advertisements; contacting schools, agencies, and labor unions; establishing procedures to guarantee equal employment opportunity; and administering the funds the firm has budgeted for recruitment.

FIGURE 9.1
**Example of a person-
nel requisition**

ERIE
INSURANCE
GROUP
An Equal Opportunity Employer

REQUEST FOR PERSONNEL

POSITION DATA

POSITION	☐ DIVISION
	☐ BRANCH OFFICE
IMMEDIATE SUPERVISOR	☐ DISTRICT CLAIMS OFFICE
	☐ DISTRICT SALES OFFICE

DEPARTMENT

☐ FULL TIME	
☐ PART TIME	SECTION
☐ TEMPORARY	
☐ CONTRACT LABORER (SEE BELOW)*	UNIT

☐ ADDITION   ☐ REPLACEMENT   WHO WILL APPLICANT BE REPLACING?

WHY? ☐ PROMOTION   ☐ TERMINATION
      ☐ DEMOTION   ☐ SPECIAL PROJECT
      ☐ TRANSFER   ☐ NEW POSITION (ATTACH POSITION DESCRIPTION)
      ☐ OTHER (PLEASE EXPLAIN)

LIST SPECIAL EDUCATION, QUALIFICATIONS OR SKILLS.

*FOR CONTRACT LABORERS ONLY	NUMBER NEEDED	HOURS NEEDED	DATES NEEDED

REQUEST/APPROVAL

REQUESTED BY	DATE
APPROVED BY (DIVISION OFFICER/BRANCH MANAGER)	DATE
WHO WILL INTERVIEW (NOT APPLICABLE FOR CONTRACT LABORERS)	EXTENSION
WHEN ARE CONVENIENT DATES AND TIMES?	

HUMAN RESOURCES USE

DATE RECEIVED	ASSIGNED TO		
ADVERTISEMENTS PLACED	FEE PAID	RECRUITERS/AGENCIES CONTACTED	FEE PAID

HUMAN RESOURCES USE

APPLICANT'S NAME	HR INTERVIEW DATE	SUPERVISORY INTERVIEW DATE	OTHER INTERVIEW DATE	STARTING DATE

Source: Designed by M. P. Eisert, Erie Insurance Group.

But these goals probably would not be attained without the co-operation of other managers, who are in the best position to predict the needs of their own departments. They are responsible for deciding how tasks should be accomplished and what kinds of people are needed to fill each type of position. They can often anticipate retirements, resignations, and other kinds of vacancies and can determine whether any of their current staff members are ready for promotion. Typically, when a vacancy occurs, the appropriate supervisor or manager completes a personnel requisition form, which usually requires higher management approval. (See the Erie Group's request-for-personnel form, Figure 9.1 on p. 241.)

RECRUITING WITHIN THE ORGANIZATION

For positions above the entry level, the best source of applicants may be the organization itself. Recognizing this, most firms follow a deliberate practice of recruiting from within.

Internal Recruiting Methods

Finding qualified applicants within the organization is the main goal of the internal recruiting effort. There are several methods for locating these applicants. Among the most common are job posting, referrals, and skills inventories.

Job Posting. Perhaps the most common method, **job posting** involves announcing job openings to all current employees. Bulletin board notices or printed bulletins can be used for this purpose. In some companies the personnel or human resources office publishes a monthly newsletter that lists the positions available. The announcements carry information about the nature of the position and the qualifications needed, and any employee who is interested may **bid** on the job — that is, enter the competition for it. Job posting can help ensure that minority workers and other disadvantaged groups become aware of opportunities to move up in the organization. For this reason, courts and federal agencies have begun to require job posting and bidding as part of the settlement of discrimination cases.[3]

Employee Referrals. Another way to find applicants within the organization is through **employee referrals** by other departments.

Informal communications among managers can lead to the discovery that the best candidate for a job is already working in a different section of the firm. In some cases, referrals are made through "support networks" established by certain groups of employees; in recent years women's groups have had a noticeable influence in this area.

Skills Inventories.   Many firms have developed computerized **skills inventories** of their employees. Information on every employee's skills, educational background, work history, and other important factors is stored in a data base, which can then be used to identify employees with the attributes needed for a particular job.

Advantages and Disadvantages of Internal Recruiting

The chief advantage of recruitment from within the organization is that the employee is already known. His or her performance in the job will usually be more predictable than that of an outsider. In addition, less general training and orientation will be required, and less time will be needed for the person to adapt to the work environment. Especially for higher-level positions, external recruitment searches can be costly and difficult, and for this reason recruiting from within is often the more cost-effective option. Internal recruitment also serves to raise employee morale and improve the organizational climate.

In some cases, however, it may be impossible for a firm to fill a position with a member of its own staff. In other cases, especially in smaller companies, internal recruitment may be possible but inadvisable. If filling a gap in one department means creating an equally critical gap in another, the best course may be to recruit immediately from the outside. Moreover, if opportunities for advancement are few, promoting an individual who is not clearly the most qualified, nor the group's choice, may cause resentment. Obviously the use of internal recruitment should be tied closely to long-range planning for career development.

Even for large organizations, an overreliance on internal recruitment can be harmful. Without occasional new blood from the outside, management may become stagnant, out of touch with the competition and the marketplace. Some firms may deliberately "raid" their competitors' staffs to bring in fresh ideas and to find out what competitors are doing. A major task in establishing an effective recruitment program is to decide the proper balance between internal and external recruiting.

RECRUITING OUTSIDE THE ORGANIZATION

Finding qualified applicants from outside the organization is the most difficult part of recruitment. The success of an expanding company or one with many positions demanding specialized skills often depends on the effectiveness of the organization's recruitment program. Typically, the external recruitment process makes use of a variety of methods.

As in internal recruiting, employee referrals can be an important source of applicants. To encourage referrals, many firms offer incentive programs that may include cash bonuses. In addition, labor unions can be a key source for applicants skilled in a particular craft. Under some contracts the company may be required to give the union first notice of job openings; even when this is not required, it may help the company maintain good labor-management relations.

Often, however, a firm must take a more active recruitment role, mounting advertising campaigns, contacting a variety of placement agencies, or sending recruiters into the field to search out qualified candidates.

Advertising

Advertising may range from the simplest "Help Wanted" ad to a nationwide, multimedia campaign. Whatever form it takes, it has the advantage of reaching relatively large numbers of potential applicants. An organization whose job openings are not rigidly defined may want to advertise widely in order to attract responses from people of many backgrounds. Normally, however, the most useful advertisement is one that specifies the exact nature of the job, the qualifications required, and the salary range. In all instances, the advertising medium should be selected carefully with the target audience in mind.

Placement Agencies

Educational institutions, ranging from high schools to universities, generally have placement offices to assist their graduates in finding work. Some universities and technical programs have their own newsletters to alert students and graduates to work opportunities, and an enterprising recruiter will take full advantage of this resource.

State placement agencies are another source of referrals. According to one study, 72 percent of the companies surveyed made use of the state employment service.[4] In most states the agency responsible for job placement is known as the **Job Service,** though the department to which it belongs may have any variety of titles, such as Department of Human Resources, Department of Employment, or Department of Labor and Industry. These agencies are partially funded by the United States Employment Service (USES) under the Wagner-Peyser Act of 1933.

Both educational institutions and state Job Services provide referrals without charge either to the applicant or to the prospective employer. In contrast, private employment agencies, which are in business to earn a profit, charge a commission that is payable if and when an applicant is hired. Usually the new employee is responsible for paying the fee, which can range as high as 20 percent of a year's wages. Sometimes a company will offer to pay the applicant's agency fee in order to make the position more attractive, and on occasion a firm may itself sign a contract with an agency.

A particular type of private agency, known as the **executive search firm,** has come into prominence recently. These agencies specialize in searching out top-level executives to fill critical corporate positions. Their clients are employers, not job seekers, and their sizable fees are generally payable whether or not any suitable candidates are found. Because they may lure the right executive away from another company, these firms have been derisively referred to as "headhunters"; yet many large corporations have come to rely on them. A substantial number of chief executive officers are now being recruited in this way.[5]

Campus and Field Recruiting

Companies interested in recruiting new college graduates will generally do more than simply contact school placement offices. They will send recruiters to the campus itself to tell students what the company can offer and screen potential applicants. The recruiting trip is coordinated with the placement office, which will arrange facilities, help to publicize the visit, and perhaps do an initial screening of the students. The company may also run notices in the student newspaper and other local publications that students are likely to read.

For positions above the entry level, firms often engage in a different type of field recruiting. An engineering firm in the Midwest, for example, might send recruiters to a West Coast city where engineers have recently been laid off. An ad in the local paper would invite prospective applicants to meet the company's representatives

---

PERSPECTIVE 9.1   First in the Race for the Best Teachers

The Chesapeake, Va., school district isn't waiting around for qualified teachers to show up on its doorsteps. It's going all out to find, woo and hire them — before the teacher candidates even finish college.

With the help of Virginia Tech U. and Norfolk State College, the 25,000-student district last fall selected the institutions' top education seniors and invited them to Chesapeake. They were dined, entertained and introduced to what the city and the school district has to offer. At the same time, they were interviewed extensively by the school board, subject specialists and other staff members. . . .

The plan is much more complex than just asking the universities for the names of their best students, however. Among other things, the district is using its staff development model to train the new teachers during their first year, supervised by both university and school district officials, said

Source: "First in the Race for Best Teachers," *Education U.S.A.*, February 25, 1985, p. 206. Reprinted by permission from *Education U.S.A.*, Copyright 1985 National School Public Relations Association.

Winston Whitehurst, assistant superintendent for personnel.

Long-range plans include a study to compare teachers recruited this way and through more usual means over the next five years. . . .

With 90 applications for every teaching position, Chesapeake isn't just trying to fill vacancies, Whitehurst noted. It wants to come up with a system that will allow the district to get the best teachers it can, Whitehurst said. Students must have at least a 3.0 average and be recommended by their professor before the district will consider them. . . .

The program's essence, he said, "is to promote excellence and provide security to teacher candidates so they are not dissuaded by thinking there are no jobs or upward mobility." To make sure the teachers stay around, the district is studying what it needs to offer in the way of benefits and quality of life.

As for the universities, the program is good for them, too, he said. "If a university provides great teachers, then students will know more about that university. The publicity helps them recruit students."

---

at a certain hotel on a certain date. Often the best locations for field recruiting are meetings of professional associations, where members of particular professions gather to conduct seminars and present research papers. The associations themselves may maintain lists of members seeking work. (An example of an evaluation form that may be used in screening recruits in the field is shown in Figure 9.2.)

Unsolicited Applicants

Recruitment is an active and often aggressive process. To find the best candidates for employment, organizations get out and search for them. From time to time, however, excellent applicants turn up unexpectedly. In fact, a Department of Labor study found that, from the employee's point of view, direct application to the employer was the most likely means of obtaining a job.[6] Another study suggested that the unsolicited applicant might become a better

FIGURE 9.2
Evaluation form useful for screening field recruits

INTERVIEWER'S REPORT

APPLICANT: _____ DATE: _____

INTERVIEWER: _____ POSITION: _____

At the conclusion of your interview, please take a few minutes to fill out this evaluation form, keeping in mind the requirements for the position and/or successful SCJ incumbents in similar positions. When completed, return it to U.S. Personnel M.S. 033. Your input is needed if a decision is to be made on this candidate during the next few days.

Dimensions	Low	1	2	3	4	5	High

IMPACT:

Neat & Professional Appearance

Comments _____

PROBLEM ANALYSIS:

Quick to Comprehend Discussion Points
Asked Pertinent Questions, Probes

Comments: _____

INITIATIVE:

High Degree of Work Effort
Demonstrates Tenacity & Makes Things Happen

Comments: _____

COMMUNICATIONS SKILLS:

Oral Presentation: Communicates Ideas
well, Easily Understood

Listening Skill:

Interpersonal Skill: Ability to Interface
Effectively With Others

Comments: _____

EDUCATION:

Appropriate to Position and for Career
Development and Growth

Comments: _____

CAREER ASPIRATIONS:

Knowledge of Field
In Line with Ability and Background

Comments: _____

WORK EXPERIENCE:

Are Previous Work Experiences Appropriate
Do They Predict Future Success

Comments: _____

Source: Courtesy of S.C. Johnson & Son, Inc.

employee than one recruited through advertising or a college placement office.[7]

Most of the time an unsolicited applicant will have to be told that no appropriate positions are currently available. By the time a position does become open, the applicant may have accepted work elsewhere. Nevertheless, carelessness in handling unsolicited applications can cost a firm some valuable employees, and a cold or haughty attitude in the personnel department can have a chilling effect on public attitudes toward the organization.

RECRUITING SPECIFIC GROUPS

A network of laws and regulations helps to prevent discrimination in employment on the basis of race, color, religion, sex, national origin, age, or physical handicap. Not all firms are covered by these government restrictions, but in most large and medium-sized organizations compliance with the law is a major concern in recruitment. An ad for a "salesman" would constitute sex discrimination in recruiting; a campaign to recruit only "recent" college graduates might leave the company open to charges of age discrimination. To comply with affirmative action guidelines, a firm is required to seek *actively* to develop sources of applicants in the legally protected groups.

Recruiting Women

In recent decades the proportion of women in the workplace has grown steadily, and by the mid-1980s women accounted for well over 40 percent of the civilian labor force in the United States.[8] Yet women are still underrepresented in many occupations and professions that have been traditionally held by men. Engineering is one example, as Case 9.1 showed; others are mechanics, industrial sales, and many types of administrative or managerial jobs. A major part of many recruitment programs is an effort to draw women into positions such as these.

For women advancing to managerial positions the organizational obstacles have been especially severe. Assumptions that women are too "emotional" to make rational decisions under pressure or that they will leave the company if they decide to have children are stereotypes that have prevented fair consideration of personal qualifications.

Some companies have found that career-planning and assertiveness-training programs can help to develop female managerial candidates while benefiting many male candidates as well.[9] Women's support networks have grown up within organizations and throughout major cities; these can nurture and encourage women managers and also provide useful referrals.

Recruiting Men for Jobs Traditionally Held by Women

As a counterpoint to hiring women in roles once reserved for men, many firms have begun to hire men for jobs traditionally performed by women. The legal actions cited in Chapter 6 opened the position of flight attendant (originally "stewardess") to males; in addition, a significant number of men are now being hired as telephone operators, nurses, and secretaries.

Recruiting Minorities

In recruiting minorities the most useful sources, according to one study, are community agencies, referrals from current minority employees, employment agencies, advertising, and campus recruiting, in that order.[10] When the recruitment campaign involves advertising, the ads may be most effective if they appear in minority media — a local newspaper for the black or Hispanic community, for example. Campus recruiting may take on an extra dimension as companies work with educational institutions to develop courses that will help minority students learn marketable skills. Some firms sponsor scholarships for minority undergraduates. Summer job programs can also help; a company that hires minority students for summer work will gain some word-of-mouth advertising in the community and a head start in screening and developing potential full-time employees.

Among minority groups, the hard-core unemployed are a particularly difficult segment to reach. Alienated from the majority culture, they may pay little attention to advertising campaigns, avoid private employment agencies that will charge them a fee, and perhaps even ignore the state Job Service. They may be convinced from the outset that they are essentially unemployable, and they may treat any recruitment initiatives with suspicion. Under these circumstances, referrals from current minority employees may be a company's best entry into the community. The firm can also work through community agencies, neighborhood groups, churches — any local organizations that are available.

Recruiting Older Workers and the Handicapped

In Chapter 6 the role of the Age Discrimination in Employment Act (ADEA) in limiting employment discrimination based on age was discussed. The principal beneficiaries have been employees and applicants between the ages of forty and seventy.

To guarantee equal opportunity for older workers, organizations must be careful to word job advertisements so as not to discourage older workers from applying. Organizations should also guard against the promotion of stereotypes that older workers are less energetic or are "set in their ways." Companies may also find a neglected source of talent in older workers already on the staff.

Publicity for handicapped workers has increased in recent years, as shown by the motto "Hire the Handicapped — It's Good Business." Yet the handicapped may face more discrimination than any other group, and their problems are compounded by the physical obstacles they must overcome in the buildings where they work.

Companies committed to hiring the handicapped need to establish careful plans for developing the right corporate attitudes. The physical needs of handicapped people should also be considered in advance. Jobs and equipment can be redesigned with the handicapped worker in mind. The term **reasonable accommodation** has been used to describe the efforts a company should make to adjust its physical facilities and job specifications.

THE SELECTION PROCESS

Once an effective recruitment program has supplied enough job applicants, the organization faces the task of choosing the best ones for specific jobs. The selection process involves judging candidates on a variety of dimensions, ranging from the concrete and measurable (for example, years of experience) to the abstract and personal (for example, leadership potential). To do this, organizations rely on a number of selection devices, including application forms, reference checks, tests, physical examinations, and interviews. All of these devices must satisfy strict requirements of relevance and legality, and their effects on the individual applicant and the organization as a whole must be considered carefully.

In almost all organizations, the human resources department is responsible for designing the selection system and managing its everyday operation. Human resources planners, in cooperation with other managers, largely set the overall strategy; they are very influencial in deciding, for example, whether the department should focus on choosing people who are best qualified for current vacancies or those who have the greatest long-term potential. The personnel managers also decide how the guidelines for equal employment opportunity should be met, and whether the company needs outside legal assistance in formulating its affirmative action plan.

Typically, **screening** of particular applicants to determine who will then be sent to department heads or other managers for final evaluation is performed by the human resources department. The

"Now then, Mr. Lawson, are you honest? Sincere? Highly self-motivated? Assertive? Can you put up with a lot of nonsense? Are you willing to play ball our way and handle petty office jealousies and be overlooked for pay raises and promotions. . . ."

© 1983 Henry R. Martin

eventual hiring decision usually comes from the supervisor or manager in whose department there is an opening. But in most organizations, the final steps of the selection process are coordinated with the human resources staff, which controls such matters as salary scales and benefits.

DETERMINING SELECTION STANDARDS

The particular standards to be used in selection — the criteria against which an applicant will be evaluated — need to be chosen with care. To allow an accurate prediction of a candidate's success on the job, they must satisfy several requirements: they must be reliable and valid and they must be job related.

Reliability and Validity

The **reliability** of a test or other selection device refers to the consistency of the results it produces. If the same person can score high on a test one week and low the next week, the test is not reliable. A device's **validity,** on the other hand, is the degree to which the scores or rankings it provides relate to success on the job. Obviously, reliability and validity are closely connected. If a selection device is not highly reliable — if an individual's score can vary significantly — then it cannot have a high degree of validity.

Although these two concepts apply to all selection devices, their meaning is clearest in relation to tests. This section focuses on how they relate to testing procedures, but their importance for other selection devices should be kept in mind.

Reliability is usually measured in one of three ways:

- The *repeat,* or *test-retest,* approach, in which the procedure is administered to the same individual a second time
- The *alternate-form* method, in which two forms of the same test are given
- The *split-half* procedure, in which a test is divided into two parts

With each method, the device will be considered reliable if a high correlation is found between the two sets of scores.

The means of determining validity are not so clear-cut. There are three general methods, but they tend to overlap, and in a particular situation they may all be appropriate.

Criterion-related validity refers to the correlation between scores on the selection device and ratings on a particular criterion of job performance. As an example, for the position of millwright, employees' scores on a test designed to measure mechanical skill could be correlated with performance in repairing machines in the mill. If the correlation were high, the test would be said to have a high degree of validity, and its use as a selection device would be considered appropriate. Because the validity of job criteria themselves can be called into question, however, validation studies must be designed very carefully.[11]

Criterion-related validity is normally expressed as a correlation coefficient. A coefficient of 1.0 represents perfect correlation between the test results and the job criterion; a coefficient of zero indicates the total absence of a correlation. In practice, validity coefficients for single tests rarely exceed .50.

Another kind of validity is **content validity,** which refers to the correspondence between the behaviors measured by the test and the behaviors involved in the job. For a secretarial position, a typing test would have high content validity if the secretary had to produce many letters a day. But for a job as administrative assistant involving minimal typing, the same test would have little content validity. This is the simplest kind of validity to determine, but it cannot apply to tests that measure learning ability or general problem-solving skills.

The third kind of validity, **construct validity,** pertains to tests that measure abstract traits in the applicant's makeup. For a position as a teller or management trainee, a bank might wish to test its applicants for "numerical aptitude." An aptitude is not a specific criterion or feature of behavior; rather, it is a concept created to explain a large group of behaviors. To prove that the numerical test had construct validity, the bank would need to show (1) that the test did indeed measure the desired trait and (2) that this trait corresponded to success on the job.

In evaluating a particular test, any combination of the three types of validity may be useful. Careful validation studies can not only help a firm comply with the law but can also improve business efficiency. One study estimated that widespread use of more valid selection devices for a single occupation, computer programming, could increase productivity by hundreds of millions of dollars.[12]

Job Relatedness and Uniform Guidelines

For selection standards to be job related, they must be relevant to actual performance on the job. If, for example, a secretarial position requires extensive typing, a test of typing speed would be job related, and it would be reasonable to set a minimum standard in terms of words per minute. The law does not discourage the use of testing and measuring procedures if they are relevant to the job and if they are reliable and valid.

To help employers develop legally acceptable selection standards, the Equal Employment Opportunity Commission (EEOC) cooperated with three other federal agencies to develop the **Uniform Guidelines on Employee Selection Procedures.** Issued in 1978, these guidelines may themselves be reinterpreted and revised over the years, but they provide a useful reference for all organizations to consult.

The guidelines give detailed explanations of job relatedness and validity, and they describe the technical requirements for each of the three methods of validation. A fundamental principle underlying the guidelines is the concept of **adverse impact,** a term used by the Supreme Court in the 1971 case of *Griggs* v. *Duke Power Company* (see Chapter 7). Briefly, the concept can be understood as follows: if a hiring practice has an adverse impact on any legally protected group, this is prima-facie evidence (if uncontested, establishes a fact) of discrimination; therefore the practice is illegal unless it can be justified by "business necessity." However, if a procedure has no adverse impact, it is generally assumed to be legal.

The guidelines provide that adverse impact will usually be determined with a rule of thumb known as the "four-fifths" or "80 percent" rule:

> A selection rate for any race, sex, or ethnic group which is less than four-fifths (4/5) (or eighty percent) of the rate for the group with the highest [selection] rate will generally be regarded by the Federal enforcement agencies as evidence of adverse impact, while a greater than four-fifths rate will generally not be regarded by Federal enforcement agencies as evidence of adverse impact.[13]

Two important points should be noted here. First, the firm's *intention* has nothing to do with the question of whether it did or did not discriminate. That is, willingness to hire members of protected groups is not enough to satisfy the law. Second, the burden of proof that adverse impact exists falls on the agency or person filing the complaint; but once adverse impact is shown, the company must demonstrate the business necessity of its selection procedure. To do this it will have to establish the procedure's validity.

The guidelines do include a **bottom-line principle,** according to which the judgment of adverse impact will be made on the basis of a firm's entire selection process. As long as the overall selection process does not produce an adverse impact, federal agencies will generally not challenge particular components of it. For example, a specific test that has an adverse impact on minorities may be ignored if the company selects a high enough percentage of minorities by other means.

SOURCES OF INFORMATION ABOUT APPLICANTS

Depending on the recruiting method, an organization may have several informal sources of information about an applicant: casual remarks from colleagues at other firms, for instance, or referrals from current employees ("Joe thinks this person is really good"). But the major sources of information about applicants are usually standard ones: application forms, reference checks, physical examinations, tests that the organization administers, and interviews. Later sections of this chapter will discuss the problems and techniques of testing and interviewing; this section considers the other three standard sources of information.

Application Forms

The application form is a sheet or small booklet with blanks to be filled in by the applicant. Its purpose is to supply the organization with basic information about the candidate's background: education, work experience, previous salary, and so forth. A sample is shown in Figure 9.3. The applicant's résumé may cover much of the same ground, but the application form has the advantage of a standardized format, which allows managers throughout the organization to glean the relevant information at a glance.

Studies have shown that background data such as educational level and work experience are generally good predictors of job performance. By correlating specific items on the form with measures of success on the job, researchers have assessed the validity of application forms in fields ranging from sales work to health care to military careers. The **weighted application form,** in which some items judged important are given more predictive weight than others, has proved especially useful.[14] Few organizations, however, have conducted validation studies for their own application forms.

The questions asked on an application form should be clearly job related. As the EEOC points out, if the firm inquires into matters pertaining to age, sex, race, or other such factors, it runs a risk of "encouraging unlawful discrimination" by its employees. "Even when the employer does not use the information," the EEOC continues, "the questions may have the unlawful effect of tending to discourage women or minorities from even applying for jobs."[15] (See the affirmative action section of the Hewlett-Packard application form, Figure 9.3.)

Reference Checks

Reference checks involve communicating with previous employers and others who can provide information about the applicant. The checks serve two purposes: they verify (or contradict) what the applicant has told the organization, and they produce supplemental information that can be very useful in a hiring decision. Reference checks are commonly conducted over the telephone; less often they are accomplished through an exchange of letters, and in rare cases they involve a personal visit.

Although applicants sometimes list the names of friends and relatives as references, these are the least reliable sources of information. More reliable are former teachers and professors, who may be able to describe a candidate's suitability for a certain field of work. Most reference checks focus on the applicant's previous employers, who should have the most pertinent knowledge (see Figure 9.4 on p. 258).

Another common source of information is the credit bureau or commercial credit-rating agency. These firms collect data not only

FIGURE 9.3
A sample application form

APPLICATION FOR EMPLOYMENT

Please read and fill out the attached application carefully and completely.

Typewritten or neatly printed applications will be greatly appreciated.

Please feel free to attach your resume.

Thank you for applying at Hewlett-Packard Company.

(hp) HEWLETT PACKARD

AFFIRMATIVE ACTION

To aid Hewlett-Packard in its commitment to Affirmative Action, applicants are asked to voluntarily provide the following information. This information will remain confidential and will be separated from your application. The success of our program depends on your assistance and we thank you in advance for your cooperation.

☐ M **MALE**   ☐ F **FEMALE**

☐ 3 **CAUCASIAN**

☐ 4 **BLACK**
   NOT OF HISPANIC ORIGIN – PERSONS HAVING ORIGINS IN ANY OF THE BLACK RACIAL GROUPS OF AFRICA.

☐ 5 **ASIAN OR PACIFIC ISLANDER**
   PERSONS WITH ORIGINS IN ANY OF THE ORIGINAL PEOPLES OF THE FAR EAST, SOUTHEAST ASIA, THE INDIAN SUBCONTINENT, OR THE PACIFIC ISLANDS.

☐ 6 **AMERICAN INDIAN OR ALASKAN NATIVE**
   PERSONS WITH ORIGINS IN ANY OF THE ORIGINAL PEOPLES OF NORTH AMERICA AND WHO MAINTAIN CULTURAL IDENTIFICATION THROUGH TRIBAL AFFILIATION OR COMMUNITY RECOGNITION.

☐ 7 **HISPANIC**
   OF MEXICAN, PUERTO RICAN, CUBAN, CENTRAL OR SOUTH AMERICAN OR OTHER SPANISH CULTURE OR ORIGIN, REGARDLESS OF RACE.

☐ 8 **OTHER**

Please check all that apply.

☐ 11 **DISABLED**   ☐ 12 **DISABLED VETERAN**   ☐ 13 **VIETNAM ERA VETERAN**

EMPLOYMENT DECISIONS WILL NOT BE BASED UPON WHETHER OR NOT YOU PROVIDE THIS INFORMATION.

(hp) HEWLETT PACKARD

FOR OFFICE USE ONLY
JOB GROUP NO.
ROUTE NO.	SUPERVISOR
RESPONSE LETTER NO.
PERSONNEL REPRESENTATIVE

APPLICATION FOR EMPLOYMENT

PERSONAL INFORMATION

NAME Last	First	Middle	SOCIAL SECURITY NO.	TELEPHONE NO. ( )
ADDRESS No. & Street	City	State/Zip Code	MESSAGE PHONE NO. ( )

GENERAL INFORMATION

HAVE YOU EVER INTERVIEWED AT HP BEFORE? If yes, give location(s) and dates
YES   NO | HOW WERE YOU REFERRED TO HP?

HAVE YOU EVER BEEN EMPLOYED BY HP? If yes, give location(s) and dates.
YES   NO | ARE YOU 18 YEARS OF AGE OR OVER? YES   NO

DO YOU HAVE ANY PHYSICAL CONDITION WHICH MAY LIMIT YOUR ABILITY TO PERFORM THE JOB FOR WHICH YOU ARE APPLYING (such as lifting, restrictions, etc.?)
YES   NO

DO YOU HAVE A RELATIVE EMPLOYED AT HP? If yes, provide the name, relationship and location at HP.

HAVE YOU EVER BEEN CONVICTED OF A FELONY? If yes, briefly describe the circumstances of your conviction, indicating the date, place and offense. Previous convictions do not exclude an applicant from consideration for employment.

IF NOT A U.S. CITIZEN, PLEASE NAME THE TYPE OF VISA.

ARE YOU LAWFULLLY ENTITLED TO WORK IN THE UNITED STATES?

CHECK APPROPRIATE BOX(ES) FOR TYPE OF EMPLOYMENT DESIRED.

REGULAR	FULL-TIME	DAY
TEMPORARY	PART-TIME	SWING
		GRAVEYARD

Source: Courtesy of Hewlett-Packard Company.

FIGURE 9.3
A sample application form (continued)

EDUCATION/TRAINING

CIRCLE LAST GRADE COMPLETED:

GRADE 1 2 3 4 5 6 7 8; HIGH 9 10 11 12; COLLEGE 1 2 3 4 5 6 7

SCHOOL	NAME AND LOCATION	DATES FROM MO./YR.	DATES TO MO./YR.	MAJOR SUBJECTS	GRADUATE MO./YR.	DEGREE/GPA
HIGH						
COLLEGE						
TRADE, BUSINESS CORRES-PONDENCE OR MILITARY						

WORK EXPERIENCE

LIST ALL YOUR WORK EXPERIENCE INCLUDING MILITARY **BEGINNING WITH YOUR PRESENT OR LAST** POSITION (ATTACH ADDITIONAL SHEET IF NECESSARY).

HAVE YOU EVER WORKED UNDER A DIFFERENT NAME? ☐ YES ☐ NO If yes, please give name

MAY WE CONTACT YOUR PRESENT EMPLOYER AS A REFERENCE? ☐ YES ☐ NO

	A) COMPANY NAME B) ADDRESS	SUPERVISOR A) NAME & TITLE B) PHONE NUMBER	DATES EMPLOYED FROM MO./YR.	DATES EMPLOYED TO MO./YR.	SALARY A) STARTING B) ENDING
1	A)	A)			A)
	B)	B)			B)
	POSITION TITLE & DUTIES		REASON FOR LEAVING		
2	A)	A)			A)
	B)	B)			B)
	POSITION TITLE & DUTIES		REASON FOR LEAVING		
3	A)	A)			A)
	B)	B)			B)
	POSITION TITLE & DUTIES		REASON FOR LEAVING		
4	A)	A)			A)
	B)	B)			B)
	POSITION TITLE & DUTIES		REASON FOR LEAVING		

IS THERE ANYTHING ELSE YOU WOULD LIKE US TO KNOW ABOUT YOU?

SIGNATURE

THIS APPLICATION IS NOT COMPLETE UNTIL THE FOLLOWING STATEMENT HAS BEEN READ AND SIGNED

I certify that the information on this form is true, current, and complete. I agree that any material misrepresentation or omission will be sufficient grounds for refusal or termination of employment. I authorize HP to investigate my previous employments, educational credentials, and other employment-related matters, and I authorize release to HP of such information as may be requested by HP in that regard. I hereby release HP and third parties supplying information to HP, their respective officers and employees, from any liability arising out of the furnishing or use of such information.

SIGNATURE | DATE

on a person's reliability as a bill payer but also on more general aspects of life and character. For a fee, they will submit a report that may cover such areas as home ownership, reputation in the community, and the use of alcohol or drugs. Reports of this nature, however, raise the issue of personal privacy. The Fair Credit Reporting Act requires that the applicant be notified in writing that a credit report has been requested. He or she is also entitled to a full disclosure of the agency's file.[16]

FIGURE 9.4
Telephone reference check form

TELEPHONE REFERENCE CHECK

Name of Applicant _____

Former Employer _____ Phone No. _____

Former Supervisor _____

Hello. I am _____ , _____ at Moog in East Aurora, New York.
                              (Name)   *(Title)*

_____ is being considered for employment as a _____ with our Company.
(Applicant's Full Name)   *(Job Classification)*

Do you remember him/her? ☐ Yes   ☐ No
(If No, could you refer me to the Personnel Office or someone who may have a recollection?)

_____ has authorized us to verify his/her former employment
              (Applicant's First Name)
and has given us your name as his/her former supervisor. We hope you can help us in our decision-making process by
answering a few questions about him/her. Our conversation will be held in confidence, of course.

1. _____ states he worked for you from _____ to _____ .
       (Applicant's First Name)
   Is that correct? ☐ Yes   ☐ No
   (If not, correct information on dates of employment _____ .)

2. He/she states he/she was earning $_____ per _____ when he/she left.
   Is that right? ☐ Yes   ☐ No
   (If not, correct wage information: _____ .)

3. What was he/she doing when he/she started working for you? _____
   When he/she stopped working for you? _____

4. What did you think of him/her as an employee? _____
   _____

5. Did he/she require close supervision or did he/she work well on his/her own? _____
   _____

6. How well did he/she accept responsibility? ☐ Excellent   ☐ Good   ☐ Average   ☐ Poor
   Comments: _____

7. How productive was he/she? _____

8. How good was the quality of his/her work? _____

9. How well did he/she get along with others? _____

10. How was his/her attendance record? ☐ Excellent   ☐ Good   ☐ Average   ☐ Poor
    If poor, why? _____

11. Did he/she have any disciplinary or other problems? _____

12. What was reason for his/her termination? _____

13. Would you rehire him/her? ☐ Yes   ☐ No
    Comments: _____

Thank you for your time today. We appreciate your cooperation, and if you ever have a need to contact us under similar
circumstances, we'll be happy to reciprocate.

_____   _____
Person Conducting Reference   *Date*

Source: Moog Inc., East Aurora, New York 14052.

The EEOC has established strict standards for the job related-ness of information obtained during a reference check. To prevent misunderstandings, some organizations now obtain a written re-lease from the applicant before beginning the checking procedure. Indeed, some employers will not release information about former employees unless such signed authorization is provided.[17]

Physical Examinations

As one of the final steps before the hiring decision, a physical examination may be conducted by a physician or nurse appointed by the organization. In some firms the candidate fills out a health questionnaire, and only those with apparent health problems are referred to a physician.

Physical exams serve several purposes. They help an organiza-tion place its employees in suitable jobs; someone with a back ail-ment, for instance, would not be assigned to push a wheelbarrow. The exams also permit firms to screen out applicants whose health problems may result in a high rate of absenteeism. Further, by establishing a record of the employee's health at the time of hiring, physical exams forestall possible claims for workers' compensation for pre-existing conditions. In most states, the firm's liability is reduced if a new injury is shown to be related to a pre-existing one.[18]

As part of the examination, a company may have the doctor measure various dimensions of the applicant's strength, reflexes, coordination, or other physical skills. These attributes can then be used to judge the individual's qualifications for a job involving physical effort. For example, for a job that involved walking along a narrow catwalk, measures of balance might be useful. The legal and ethical requirements that apply to other phases of the selection process apply to physical exams as well. Questionnaire items and physical standards may be challenged if they are not clearly job related.

SELECTION TESTS

Tests are generally administered and evaluated before the final stage of interviewing. Managers can then use the test results as guidelines in asking the candidate about his or her abilities, ex-perience, and interests. The testing of applicants offers two ap-parent advantages: test results seem to be objective, free from per-sonal bias; and they are usually expressed numerically, so that they lend themselves to statistical analysis and thus can be validated. Nevertheless, testing has been the most controversial part of the selection process. As a result of court cases and government challenges, the use of tests seemed to decline in the 1970s;[19] recently, however, testing shows signs of becoming more popular again as firms adjust to the legal restrictions.[20]

The employment of professionals to interpret and administer tests, the training of human resources staff in test use, and the provision of space and time for testing can involve considerable expense. Given these costs, human resources managers should restrict the use of tests to areas where they will do the most good. Above all, tests should be only one factor in the hiring decision. In the past, some managers — impressed by the statistical success and the scientific aura of tests — have given the results too much weight. Small differences in test scores are unlikely to indicate significant differences in the candidates.

Types of Tests

The tests used in the selection process generally fall into one of six broad categories:

- *Measures of proficiency, achievement, or knowledge.* A wide range of skills and information can be measured. In a test of manual dexterity, for example, an applicant might be asked to place small pegs into tight holes using a pair of tweezers. A test of clerical skills might involve spelling, reading comprehension, and arithmetic.
- *Measures of aptitude or potential ability.* These differ from proficiency tests in that they assess the candidate's ability to learn new skills rather than the amount he or she has already learned. Common types of aptitude tests include measures of short-term memory, spatial perception, number discrimination, and motor abilities. The U.S. Employment Service has developed a General Aptitude Test Battery (GATB) that can be administered, at a firm's request, by the state Job Service. Specific Aptitude Test Batteries (SATBs) are also available.
- *Measures of mental ability or intelligence.* These could be seen as a subcategory of aptitude tests. Generally they concentrate on a person's abilities with words, numbers, logical reasoning, and spatial relationships.
- *Measures of personality.* Personality inventories attempt to construct a profile of a person's attitudes, behavior, and habits. "Friendliness," "confidence," "conventionality," and "dominance" are examples of what such a test might measure.

- *Measures of physical ability.* As the preceding section noted, during the physical exam a doctor may test for strength, balance, reaction time, or other bodily traits considered necessary for the job.
- *Measures of interest.* Tests in this category attempt to discover a person's likes and dislikes. They may ask such seemingly irrelevant questions as whether the candidate enjoys golf, likes babies, or prefers math to history. The responses are built into an interest profile that may help predict a person's satisfaction in a particular job.

Legal and Ethical Challenges

Of all selection devices, tests have probably faced the most intense legal and ethical challenges. Validity is more difficult to establish for interviews than for tests, yet tests have been subjected to greater criticism and legal scrutiny.

In an early court case challenging testing procedures, *Myart* v. *Motorola* (1964), compensation was awarded to a black applicant who had been rejected on the basis of a brief intelligence test.[21] In *Griggs* v. *Duke Power Company* (1971), an intelligence test was again found discriminatory because the firm could not establish "a demonstrable relationship to successful performance."[22] More recently, in a case before a U.S. district court, Albermarle Paper Company agreed to pay back wages to a group of black employees who had been refused promotion because of scores on job qualification tests.[23] Many other court cases and EEOC rulings have prohibited tests that were not fully validated.

Although the early legal cases focused on intelligence tests, personality testing has received even more criticism. Some critics believe it is morally wrong to administer any such test; others feel measures of personality characteristics are sometimes used as a basis for rash decisions. There is also a question of privacy. According to one line of argument, applicants who think a test is improper can simply refuse to take it. But an applicant may presume that not taking the test means not getting the job; hence there may be no true choice.[24] A firm can perhaps reduce the applicant's fear of a personality test by explaining its nature and purpose beforehand, and by guaranteeing the results will be kept confidential.

Every firm should assess the full implications of its testing program and reassess the program periodically. Tests can be very helpful devices if used carefully, selectively, and with due consideration for the person being tested. Useful guidelines for evaluating selection tests are shown in Table 9.1.

PERSPECTIVE 9.2 School Days at Prudential High

During the past six years, about 8,000 members of minority groups were turned down for jobs at Prudential Insurance, in part because they could not meet minimal standards for reading or math. Though most were high school graduates, scores of 3 or lower were common on math-competency tests, where the scale runs to 9. Last week Prudential revealed that it was going into the business of remedial education. In a precedent-setting agreement with the U.S. Department of Labor, the company promised to spend an estimated $3 million to offer 260 classroom hours of training to the same people it had rejected for jobs. At least 600 graduates will be offered full-time employment.

Newark-based Prudential's endeavor, which could have a wide-ranging impact on affirmative-action programs in many industries, followed a five-year Labor Department investigation of the company's hiring practices. Prudential, wary of a potential Government suit and mindful of its $50 million worth of business with federal agencies and their employees, agreed to the compromise settlement. . . .

Prudential already has sent out 3,000 letters to rejected applicants in the New York–New Jersey area whose names are still in the company's files. The rest, for whom current addresses are not available, will be traced through Internal Revenue Service records. The company will help cover the Government's costs by paying the IRS up to 80¢ for every name the agency tracks successfully.

The agreement is the first requiring a company to upgrade a rejected applicant's skills. Stressed will be English, math, reading and keyboard training, all with the goal of raising competency to at least the ninth-grade level. Participants will be paid the minimum wage of $3.35 an hour while learning, and some of the classes will be at night so that trainees now working elsewhere can attend. At the same time, those employment tests that gave the applicants such a hard time will be reviewed with an eye to making them more job related. . . .

Source: Excerpted from "School Days at Prudential High," *Time,* September 3, 1984, p. 60. Copyright 1984 Time Inc. All rights reserved. Reprinted by permission from *Time.*

THE SELECTION INTERVIEW

Interviews can be used at several stages of the selection process. Screening interviews take place early in the process. Often short — perhaps ten to fifteen minutes — they focus on the applicant's basic qualifications for the job, with the goal of screening out candidates who are not qualified. Sometimes the final stage in the process is a job-offer interview, at which the best candidate is offered the position. In between these two stages fall one or more detailed selection interviews, which may be conducted by human resources staff, the supervisor, and the department head.

Although interviews can be the least objective part of the process, they are generally considered the most valuable. In one study 64 percent of the organizations rated interviewing as the most important selection device.[25] Interviews are also likely to have the greatest impact on the applicant, contributing more than any other element to his or her view of the firm and attitude toward the job.

TABLE 9.1
Evaluating selection tests: A checklist

1. Compare the tests and the jobs for which they are designed. Are the tests specifically related to the appropriate qualifications for the job?
2. Who designed the tests — a professional test-publishing company or someone in-house at the organization?
3. If designed in-house, were the tests validated by a professional on the basis of specific job-related criteria?
4. If the test designer was in-house, what were his or her qualifications?
5. For what settings were the tests first designed? Have the tests been updated? What changes were incorporated?
6. Who administers the tests? The personnel director? An outside consultant?
7. What are the qualifications of that administrator? And who has responsibility for overseeing his or her efforts?
8. Did the population used in validating the tests include a representative sample of minorities?
9. Is there a continuous program of revalidation?
10. Have passing scores been reevaluated and updated? When?
11. Have any applicants who failed a test been hired? Is there information on why and when it happened?
12. Can failed applicants be retested? How and why?
13. Have the tests been applied to current employees as well? What is the standard reaction if they fail?
14. Do all applicants take the same test? If not, why?
15. Are all tests administered uniformly? Are they graded consistently?
16. What are the organization's practices on retaining the results of the tests?

Source: Adapted from Cecelia Dobrish, Rick Wolff, and Brian Zevnik, *Hiring the Right Person for the Right Job.* Copyright © 1984 by the Alexander Hamilton Institute. Used by permission of Franklin Watts, Inc.

The interview offers a chance for the manager to fill in gaps in the information provided by application forms and tests. It may lead to entirely new types of information as well. In particular, interviews are used to assess intangible factors such as motivation and enthusiasm that cannot be shown on an application form.

Interview Scenarios

Interviews can follow several scenarios. In the **group interview** a number of candidates are interviewed at once. Generally they are allowed to discuss job-related matters among themselves while one or more observers rate their performance. This type of interview is usually considered most appropriate in the selection of managers; it can also be used with groups of current employees to evaluate their potential for supervisory roles.

In the **panel interview,** one candidate meets with a panel of two or more representatives of the firm. One of the panelists may act as a chairperson, but each of the firm's representatives takes part in the questioning and discussion. This format allows the interviewers to coordinate their efforts and follow up on each other's questions.

The most common scenario is the **one-on-one interview,** in which the candidate meets privately with a single interviewer. Often a well-qualified candidate will pass through a series of such interviews, first with a member of the human resources department, then with the manager in whose unit there is a job opening, and finally perhaps with the manager's superior. The rest of this section focuses primarily on the one-on-one scenario.

Interview Techniques

The three basic scenarios lend themselves to a variety of specific interviewing techniques. The most common are the structured interview, the nondirective interview, and the situational-problem interview.

In the **structured** or **patterned interview,** the interviewer follows a standard list of questions to be asked of all applicants. This method produces uniformity of data from one interview to the next; it ensures that no important questions will be forgotten; and it helps to guarantee that all the applicants have been treated in the same way. If the interview is too rigidly structured, however, the interviewer may neglect chances for follow-up questions, and the candidate is unlikely to provide any information spontaneously.

The **nondirective interview,** as its name implies, takes the opposite approach. The interviewer's questions are held to a minimum, and they are open-ended. Rather than asking about specific details of the candidate's last job, the interviewer may say, "Tell me about your work in this field." The aim is to follow the applicant's own lead, to let him or her express thoughts and feelings that might be relevant to the job. Instead of filling silences with new questions, the interviewer may simply nod to encourage the applicant to continue.

The nondirective technique can reveal information that would never have come up in a structured interview. It requires substantial time, however, and it may fail to touch on important aspects of the candidate's qualifications. For these reasons, few organizations use it in its pure form. Typically, the interviewer tries to mix the nondirective technique with a structured approach, encouraging the applicant to expand on his or her ideas, but making certain that standard topics are covered.

In the **situational-problem interview,** the candidate is given a specific problem to solve or project to complete. Often this technique is used in the group interview scenario; while the group discusses a problem and works out an answer, the interviewers rate each candidate on, for example, quality of ideas, leadership capacity, and ability to work with others.

Problems in Interviewing

Whatever their format, interviews must overcome a number of typical problems. One is the personal bias of the interviewer. What if the interviewer likes blondes, or dislikes green eyes, or thinks that striped ties look foolish? Those who conduct interviews must learn to ignore their personal preferences. In some cases, however, a belief about a certain category of people may be so deeply ingrained that the interviewer is unaware of its existence. Such stereotypes are a principal factor in discrimination against minorities and women, and they can influence attitudes toward other groups as well. For example, an interviewer may tend to assume, without realizing it, that overweight people are lazy; if so, any candidate who is overweight will suffer from this stereotype.

If an applicant looks very impressive in one particular area, the interviewer may concentrate on that to the exclusion of other matters. Weaknesses in the candidate's background may be overlooked, or their significance may be discounted. This tendency is known as the **halo effect.** The opposite tendency, known as the **horn effect,** is to turn one negative characteristic into a conclusion that the candidate is weak on all fronts.

The proper phrasing and timing of questions is often a difficult problem to solve. In a structured or semistructured interview, questions should be specific enough to draw out the necessary information, but they should not prematurely reveal what answer the interviewer would like to hear. For instance, the question, "Have you had experience running a Model 2000B?" suggests that the operation of a 2000B is a job requirement, and the candidate may be tempted to inflate his or her experience. A better initial question might be, "What kinds of machinery have you handled?" Then a later question could zero in on the 2000B.

Effective Interviewing

Given the importance most organizations attach to interviews, it seems advisable for larger firms, at least, to undertake research and training programs to increase the effectiveness of their interviewing. In many cases these programs may be needed to satisfy antidiscrimination requirements. For example, certain questions should not be asked in an interview because they are potentially discriminatory. (See Table 9.2 for examples of inappropriate interview questions.) Even in smaller firms, interviewers should be selected carefully and trained as much as possible.

Although the needs of different organizations will vary, it is possible to suggest the elements that an effective interview generally includes. The interviewer begins by studying all the materials already available on the candidate. Planning every session in advance, the interviewer knows which topics are critical for each individual applicant.

The candidate is shown to a quiet room, free from distractions. No phones are ringing; no one interrupts with messages for the interviewer. To begin, the interviewer engages in general talk about neutral subjects to put the applicant at ease and establish rapport. Soon, however, the interviewer turns the discussion to the matter at hand.

Whether the format is structured or nondirective, the interviewer listens closely to everything the applicant has to say, avoiding snap judgments and categorizations. One goal is to understand the applicant's own outlook. If the format allows, the interviewer pursues hints and follows up important leads but remains careful not to turn the session into an interrogation. Encouraged to ask questions, the applicant understands that his or her needs are being considered. The interviewer avoids not only verbal threats but also gestures and other nonverbal signals — such as glancing impatiently at the clock — that might increase the applicant's nervousness. If the applicant tends to be aggressive or abrupt, the interviewer remains unruffled.

Throughout the discussion the interviewer focuses on both technical qualifications for the job and the intangible qualifications, such as motivation, energy, and enthusiasm. In evaluating the intangibles, the interviewer considers not just the particular job opening but also the entire staff of that department, the characteristics of the coworkers and superiors, and the organizational climate and culture. The interviewer takes notes on the candidate's answers but does so discreetly, so as not to hinder the discussion.

Before the session ends, the interviewer makes certain that the

TABLE 9.2
Don't ask: A sample of questions forbidden or discouraged by federal antidiscrimination rules

Don't ask if an applicant is single, married, divorced, or separated. Unless this information is job related (and it is very unlikely to be), the firm has no legitimate use for it.

Don't ask the ages of an applicant's children. This question might lead to charges of sex discrimination if the organization declined to hire a woman who had small children at home.

Don't ask about pregnancy or plans for a family. An interviewer may ask how long the applicant plans to stay on the job and whether any absences are anticipated — *if* the same questions are asked of males and females. The firm may also refuse to hire a pregnant woman if the job might endanger her health.

Don't ask someone's age or date of birth. This might lead to age discrimination. The firm may ask if the applicant is between the ages of eighteen and seventy, and if he or she is not, it is permissible to inquire the exact age.

Don't ask an older applicant how much longer he or she plans to work before retiring. Since this question would not be asked of a thirty-year-old, it should not be asked of a sixty-year-old.

Don't ask if the applicant has ever been arrested. The company may ask if the applicant has been convicted of a felony, but only if this is clearly job related.

Don't ask about a person's birthplace, ancestry, citizenship, or "native tongue." The answers might indicate national origin. The firm may inquire whether the applicant is a U.S. citizen and what foreign languages he or she speaks.

Don't ask for a maiden name or the name of the next of kin. Again the matter of national origin is involved. But it is legal to ask for the names of relatives who already work for the organization or for competing firms.

Don't ask if the applicant has a handicap or disability or has ever been treated for certain diseases. The firm may legally ask if the applicant has any health problems that might affect performance on the job.

Source: For more information, see Richard D. Arvey, *Fairness in Selecting Employees* (Reading, Mass.: Addison-Wesley Publishing Company, Inc., 1979), pp. 164–181.

applicant understands the exact nature of the job. It is important for both the company and the candidate that any misconceptions be dispelled. Sometimes an interviewer will need to "sell" the firm — that is, emphasize its attractiveness in order to persuade a good candidate to accept the job — but the persuasion should not encourage unreasonable expectations.

The applicant is given a date by which he or she will learn the firm's decision; or if a next step is already planned, the candidate is told exactly what it will entail. When the interview is over, the interviewer personally conducts the candidate back to the reception area.

Finally, the interviewer writes up the notes from the interview, often on a standardized form. In evaluating the candidate, the interviewer tries to allow for subjective factors that might influence his or her judgment. Was there anything personally objectionable about the applicant? If so, is it related to the job requirements? Do the judgments entered on the interview report have a rational basis?

When the interview follows these guidelines, the firm should have a solid body of information on which to base the last phase of the selection process, the selection decision.

THE SELECTION DECISION

When all of the candidates have been tested and interviewed and their references have been checked, the final decision generally rests with the supervisor or head of the department in which the job opening exists, who will select the one candidate most qualified for the job. The human resources department, however, regularly must approve the salary and benefit package to ensure consistency of pay scales throughout the firm.

The job offer itself can be made by a supervisor, or manager, but in large firms it is frequently handled by the human resources staff. The offer is sometimes extended by phone or in a letter; in other cases, the candidate is called in for a final interview and the offer is made in person. At this time the salary and benefits are stated precisely; the prospective employee is told of any further conditions that must be met, such as passing a physical examination; a starting time is established; and, if the candidate needs time to think the matter over, a date should be set for notifying the firm of acceptance or rejection. Aspects of the position such as salary and benefits should have been discussed earlier in general terms so that the candidate is not surprised by any of the particulars.

In the satisfaction of filling a job opening, the human resources staff should not forget the applicants who failed to get the job. All those who participated in tests or interviews should be quickly notified of the firm's decision, and those who went furthest in the selection process should receive personal letters. Consideration for

for these people is important for the organization's reputation. Moreover, the "near misses" may be candidates for future job openings.

The success of a selection decision depends on all of the previous steps in the staffing process: the initial planning, the recruitment of qualified candidates, and the various selection techniques used to find the best candidate for the job. Only by careful attention to all of these stages can an organization assure itself of hiring capable people.

SUMMARY

Recruitment and selection, the processes by which a firm finds and chooses its employees, are perhaps the most critical tasks any organization faces. Without the right people, no firm can function effectively. For a recruitment program to be successful, managers should cooperate with the human resources staff to define needs and predict vacancies.

Depending on its particular needs, an organization may recruit either from its current staff, from outside the firm, or both. For internal recruiting the principal methods are job posting, the use of computerized skills inventories, and referrals from other departments. For external recruiting, organizations rely on advertisements, public or private placement agencies, and campus and field recruiting. Groups that have experienced discrimination in the past (women, minorities, older workers, and the handicapped) are special targets of contemporary recruiting.

Selection standards should be chosen carefully to predict a candidate's success on the job. For many organizations these standards must also comply with legal requirements. The critical criteria in this regard are job relatedness, reliability, and validity as suggested by the Uniform Guidelines issued by the federal government.

The usual sources of information about applicants include application forms, reference checks, physical examinations, testing, and interviews. Each of these provides important pieces of information. Testing seems perhaps the most objective way of rating candidates on dimensions that may be vital to job performance, but the tests a firm administers should show high levels of validity and job relatedness to avoid charges of discrimination.

Interviewing may be the most subjective phase of the selection process, but many firms consider it the most valuable. In an effective interview, the candidate's own ideas and attitudes will be explored more fully than at any other stage of the selection process. Both the candidate and the firm will then be well prepared for the job offer, the point at which the best applicant is notified of his or her success.

KEY TERMS

recruitment
selection
job posting and bidding
employee referrals
skills inventories
Job Service
executive search firms
campus and field recruiting
reasonable accommodation
screening
reliability

validity
criterion-related validity
content validity
construct validity
job relatedness
Uniform Guidelines on
   Employee Selection
   Procedures
adverse impact
bottom-line principle
weighted application form

group interview
panel interview
one-on-one interview
structured or patterned
   interview
nondirective interview
situational-problem interview
halo effect
horn effect

REVIEW QUESTIONS

1. Describe the recruitment process and discuss the organizational and environmental factors that influence it.
2. What are the basic methods of recruitment? What roles are played by the various managers and professionals, including human resources professionals, in the use of these methods?
3. Discuss how and why organizations attempt to recruit specific groups such as women, minorities, and the handicapped.
4. Describe the selection process and discuss its implications for both the applicant and the organization.
5. What roles do different managers and professionals play in the selection process? Discuss.
6. Explain the concepts of job relatedness, reliability, and validity and their relation to selection standards.
7. Discuss the impact of the legal environment on selection procedures.
8. Discuss the use of application forms, reference checks, and physical examinations in employee selection, including any advantages and difficulties with these procedures.
9. What are some of the advantages and problems associated with testing programs?
10. Describe the different types of interviews, some problems encountered in interviewing, and the characteristics of an effective interview.

OPENING CASE QUESTIONS

Case 9.1   New Components in the Electronics Business

1. What basic projections need to be made before Beth Ann and the company start a major recruiting effort?
2. If you were Beth Ann, what sources would you probably use in your recruiting efforts and what problems would you need to anticipate?
3. Who should do the recruiting and selecting that is facing this company?

CASE 9.2   HIRING THE HANDICAPPED

The text of the chapter notes that discrimination against the handicapped has become an area of growing concern in recent years. This concern has resulted in a good deal of legal activity focusing on the rights of handicapped persons and of employers. Since discrimination against the handicapped is not specifically covered by the Civil Rights Act, most of the laws that bear on this issue have been written at the state level. The courts are continuing to interpret the questions of what constitutes a handicap and, for employers, of what constitutes reasonable accommodation for a handicap. These determinations are obviously important to any human resources department.

However, helping handicapped individuals to overcome discrimination is a question of more than laws and regulations. And many companies are recognizing that active recruitment of handicapped persons can indeed be "good business." Surveys have indicated that the overwhelming majority of handicapped workers rate as good or better than average in several measurable areas, such as absenteeism, turnover, work output, and safety. Because of the hurdles their disabilities create, however, many handicapped people lack the training necessary for employment. As a result, forward-thinking companies are undertaking training programs.

Control Data Corp. recognized the handicapped as an underemployed labor force that could potentially make important contributions in the computer and data processing industry. In 1978, Control Data began Homework, a training system in which handicapped people learn computer programming by working at home on a terminal connected to a Control Data mainframe. Control Data

Case Sources: Donna Raimondi, "Computer Firms Tapping Pool of Programming Talent," *Computerworld*, August 13, 1984, pp. 32–33; "Retraining Plan Grows at CDC," *Computerworld*, August 13, 1984, p. 32; Julie Annette Schapire and Florence Berger, "Responsibilities and Benefits in Hiring the Handicapped," *The Cornell H.R.A. Quarterly* (February 1984): 59–67; and William H. Emer and Catherine B. Frink, "Hiring the Handicapped—What Every Employer Should Know," *Employment Relations Today* (Spring 1984): 69–85.

works with state agencies to find appropriate candidates for the program (acceptance requires high motivation and a demonstrated aptitude for programming) and also to place participants when the program is completed. Graduates bring a special commitment to their work, because getting a job has often had such a positive impact on their lives. One graduate in Minneapolis, for instance, had been bed ridden and destitute before participating in Homework. After completing the program and finding a job, her life turned around; she moved into an apartment of her own and began pursuing a normal career as a programmer. She does some of her work at home, but she also works in her employer's office at times.

Control Data's is a broad service program aimed at helping the handicapped. In other cases, companies may want to hire handicapped individuals because of their suitability for a given job. For example, John Stewart Foote, a hotel executive who has run several large hotels, including one in Hawaii, has found the dependability of handicapped workers to mesh well with several types of jobs in the hotel industry. Dependable provision of services is a critical part of any hotel operation, and Foote has found the handicapped to be exceptionally reliable. He has therefore tried to make accommodations in facilities to allow handicapped employees to work comfortably, and the results have been uniformly positive.

Discussion Question

1. For a company recruiting employees to be trained, what advantages would there be in recruiting the handicapped?

chapter 10

Orientation and Career Transitions

CHAPTER OUTLINE

ORIENTATION
  Characteristics of Orientation Programs /
  Reducing New Employees' Anxiety / **Improving**
  Orientation Programs
INTERNAL STAFFING PROCESS
  Transfer / **Promotion** / **Demotion**
EMPLOYEE SEPARATIONS
  Layoff / **Discharge** / **Resignation** / **Retirement**
MANAGING CAREER CHANGES
  Minimizing Crises / **Career Counseling and**
  Planning

LEARNING OBJECTIVES

- **Explain why the effective management of career transitions is important both to individual employees and to the organization as a whole.**
- **Characterize an effective orientation program.**
- **Describe the procedures commonly used for making promotion decisions.**
- **Give examples of how the labor agreement governs staffing decisions and policies in the organization.**
- **Outline some of the options organizations have for avoiding layoffs.**
- **Identify some actions management can take to ensure that employee terminations are nondiscriminatory.**
- **List the phases of a career crisis and identify ways organizations can minimize crises and offer support.**

CASE 10.1   THE FIRST DAY

Jim Greenlee was embarrassed. This was his first day as production supervisor at Marlin Chemical Company, and he was late for the 8:00 a.m. meeting at which he was supposed to be introduced to the other supervisors. The rain had slowed traffic to a crawl, and the parking lot was jammed. The elevator had taken forever to come, and then it had stopped at every floor.

The meeting was under way when Jim finally arrived, but Jim's new boss, Adele Swanson, sounded warm and pleasant as she introduced him to the group. Jim apologized for being late, and then the meeting turned to other matters. Jim leaned back and tried to look relaxed, but his anxiety was intense. "New job, new people, new surroundings, and I'm off to a bad start," Jim thought. Everyone's name had gone out of his head, and he couldn't concentrate on the meeting. Mostly he watched faces — some of which looked friendlier than others, he decided.

At the end of the meeting, Adele asked for a volunteer to show Jim around the building, escort him to the personnel department, and then bring him back to her office by 10 a.m. Two or three people volunteered, and Murray was given the assignment. Murray seemed friendly enough, and he showed Jim most of the features of the building, including the location of the cafeteria and the washrooms. As they walked, Murray commented on the responsibilities of each of the other supervisors in the department, and Jim detected that Murray had definite likes and dislikes about different members of the group.

Murray also had a comment about Adele: "She's O.K., but she gets so busy she forgets to tell us some important things. Then when you ask for the information you need, she seems irritated about being bothered."

When Jim got back to Adele's office she was on the phone, so Jim sat in slip and other necessary forms. Then he was taken to the employee benefits section, where he was briefed on the retirement plan, various insurance programs, and other company benefits. He understood some of what he was being told, but he left realizing he would have to study the stack of pamphlets he had been given.

When Jim got back to Adele's office she was on the phone, so Jim sat in a comfortable chair outside her office for some fifteen minutes. He tried to concentrate on reading the pamphlets, but his mind was preoccupied with what his group of subordinates would be like and whether there was going to be much resistance to his coming in as the new supervisor. When Adele was free, she escorted Jim to his section and introduced him to the members of his staff. At one point she said, "We're glad to have Jim here. Things are going to be different now." This remark mystified Jim, and he hoped the comment didn't sound as threatening to the others as it did to him. Everyone seemed polite in a guarded sort of way, and Jim tried his best to be friendly.

CASE 10.2   THE PROMOTION DECISION

The position of sales manager in the industrial accounts department of Enterprise Insurance was vacant. The previous department manager, Steve Tanaka, had been very successful and had just been promoted to vice president of sales. He and the company president, Jeffrey Finley, thought Al Thompson might be Steve's logical successor. As a sales representative, Al had shown that he was bright, aggressive, and ambitious.

Jeff and Steve wanted some confirmation that Al was the right candidate for the job, so they hired a psychologist to provide some additional information about Al's qualifications. The psychologist, who had done a good deal of work with the firm over the years, gave Al a battery of tests, interviewed him at length, and wrote a report evaluating his potential as a manager.

Al did well on the tests. He scored very high on the intelligence test, and according to the interest survey, his interests were clearly compatible with the role for which he was being considered. Moreover, his academic credentials were outstanding; they included an advanced degree with honors from the best business school in the region. The psychologist saw no reason not to recommend Al for the managerial position, and she found plenty of evidence for predicting that Al would be successful. She wrote her report accordingly, and Al was offered the job, which he promptly accepted.

Al was very pleased with the job offer, viewing it as a desirable career move as well as an opportunity to earn considerably more money. As a sales representative he had been paid on a salary-plus-commission basis. Now he would receive commissions based on a percentage of all of the insurance sold by his subordinates, as well as a substantial increase in salary.

Shortly after Al accepted the new position, a memo was circulated announcing his promotion to manager, effective the following Monday. Right after lunch on the day this announcement was made, a delegation of Al's new subordinates came to Jeff's office requesting a meeting. To Jeff, it seemed more like a demand than a request. What the delegation wanted to talk about was widespread dissatisfaction with the decision to promote Al to manager.

Jeff immediately called a meeting of all of the industrial salespeople. Steve was included in the meeting, but Al was not invited. It was immediately apparent when the meeting convened that the salespeople were angry about the promotion and that some were ready to leave the company. What bothered them most, they said, was that Al had a reputation for promoting his own interests at the expense of others. He had a long history of taking customers from his peers in ways they perceived as unethical. One sales representative stated it this way: "Al's not a team player; he's out for himself. I don't trust him and I won't work for him." It was clear to Steve and Jeff that they had a serious problem on their hands.

Anyone with working experience can probably identify with Jim Greenlee's experiences in Case 10.1. The first day on a job is an exciting and anxiety-producing transition to a totally new situation. This transition is a significant event not only for new employees but also for their coworkers, supervisors, and managers.

Case 10.2 dramatizes how a promotion, another significant career event, can be perceived positively or negatively by various people close to the situation. In a promotion, an employee leaves one career role and takes on another; what this really means is that an individual is changing his or her relationship with a number of other people. Everyone who has some connection with the promoted employee — both before and after the promotion — will have some perceptions and feelings about the transition and what it means to him or her individually. If there are to be productive outcomes for all concerned and minimal negative effects on job performance and satisfaction, those involved in the promotion decision must be concerned not only with the qualifications of the promotion candidate but also with the consequences of the decision for all affected employees and for the organization itself.

This chapter is about several of the most significant transitions that can occur in people's working lives and that also have major implications for organizations: coming into an organization as a new employee; transferring to another job; being promoted; experiencing a demotion, layoff, or discharge; resigning from an organization; and retiring. Fortunately, many people do not have to face *all* of these career changes, but most will probably experience the first day on a new job, some form of promotion, and eventual retirement. Whether or not one experiences these changes personally, it is important to understand what they mean to people and, better yet, to be able to help manage these transitions as constructively and effectively as possible.

ORIENTATION

On the first day on a new job, an employee is faced with an unfamiliar situation to which he or she must somehow adjust. New surroundings, new coworkers, and new job procedures can make even the calmest and most competent workers feel anxious and insecure. Therefore, most organizations offer some kind of **orientation:** a program designed to help the new employee get acquainted with the company and make a productive beginning on the job.

The orientation procedures vary in their usefulness to the new employee, depending on whether the program is haphazardly or systematically designed. In Case 10.1, most of what happened to Jim Greenlee on his first day on the new job was probably positive. Undoubtedly some things could have been improved, however. Certainly Jim would have felt more at ease if his new boss had communicated more clearly and fully when she introduced him to his new subordinates.

But a poorly planned or nonexistent orientation program can have unfortunate results. Consider the case of a new employee who is assigned to sweeping the warehouse three times a day when once would have sufficed, or the new worker who is sent on foolish errands by other employees. This behavior is known as **hazing,** or harassing with unnecessary tasks or practical jokes. Hazing is damaging to the newcomer's morale and also lengthens the time it takes for the new employee to be productive.

Characteristics of Orientation Programs

Orientation procedures for new employees usually include introductions to coworkers and a tour of the facilities. Comprehensive orientation programs also include information about the daily routine, employee benefits and services, work rules, safety rules and programs, training and promotion practices, company organization and operations, company products or services, and company history.[1] An example of a thorough orientation program is that offered by Corning Glass Works (see Perspective 10.1).

A systematic orientation program may last only a few hours or may extend over several weeks. Information may be given through interviews, group meetings and discussion, handbooks, films, tours, or combinations of these and other methods. Checklists are often used to ensure thoroughness. (An example of an orientation checklist is shown in Figure 10.1.) Many programs include follow-up interviews at the end of three or six months' employment to determine how well the new employee is getting along.

PERSPECTIVE 10.1   Timetable Events in Corning's Orientation System

Material distribution. As soon as possible after a hiring decision is made, orientation material is distributed:

- The new person's supervisor gets a pamphlet titled *A Guide for Supervisors.*
- The new person gets an orientation plan.

The pre-arrival period. During this period the supervisor maintains contact with the new person, helps with housing problems, designs the job and makes a preliminary MBO (management by objectives) list after discussing this with the new person, gets the office ready, notifies the organization that this has been done, and sets the interview schedule.

The first day. On this important day, the new employee has breakfast with his or her supervisor, goes through processing in the personnel department, attends a *Corning and You* seminar, has lunch with the seminar leader, reads the workbook for new employees, is given a tour of the building, and is introduced to co-workers.

The first week. During this week, the new employee (1) has one-to-one interviews with the supervisor, co-workers, and specialists; (2) learns the

how-tos, wheres, and whys connected with the job; (3) answers questions in the workbook; (4) gets settled in the community; and (5) participates with the supervisor in firming up the MBO plan.

The second week. The new person begins regular assignments.

The third and fourth weeks. The new person attends a community seminar and an employee benefits seminar (a spouse or guest may be invited).

The second through the fifth month. During this period, assignments are intensified and the new person has biweekly progress reviews with his or her supervisor, attends six two-hour seminars at intervals (on quality and productivity, technology, performance management and salaried compensation plans, financial and strategic management, employee relations, and EEO and social change), answers workbook questions about each seminar, and reviews answers with the supervisors.

The sixth month. The new employee completes the workbook questions, reviews the MBO list with the supervisor, participates in a performance review with the supervisor, receives a certification of completion for Phase I orientation, and makes plans for Phase II orientation.

The seventh through the 15th months. This period features Phase II orientation: division orientation, function orientation, education programs, MBO reviews, performance reviews, and salary reviews.

Source: Reprinted, by permission of the publisher, from "An Orientation System That Builds Productivity," by Edward J. McGarrell, Jr., *Personnel,* 60 (November-December 1983): 34. © 1983 Periodicals Division, American Management Associations, New York. All rights reserved.

FIGURE 10.1
Orientation checklist

Employee's Name:	Discussion Completed (check *each* item)
I. Word of welcome	
II. Explain overall departmental organization and its relationship to other activities of the company	
III. Explain employee's individual contribution to the objectives of the department and his [or her] starting assignment in broad terms	
IV. Discuss job content with employee and give him [or her] a copy of job description (if available)	
V. Explain departmental training program(s) and salary increase practices and procedures	
VI. Discuss where the employee lives and transportation facilities	
VII. Explain working conditions: a. Hours of work, time sheets b. Use of employee entrance and elevators c. Lunch hours d. Coffee breaks, rest periods e. Personal telephone calls and mail f. Overtime policy and requirements g. Paydays and procedure for being paid h. Lockers i. Other _____	
VIII. Requirements for continuance of employment— explain company standards as to: a. Performance of duties b. Attendance and punctuality c. Handling confidential information d. Behavior e. General appearance f. Wearing of uniforms	
IX. Introduce new staff member to manager(s) and other supervisors. Special attention should be paid to the person to whom the new employee will be assigned.	
X. Release employee to immediate supervisor who will: a. Introduce new staff member to fellow workers b. Familiarize the employee with his [or her] work place c. Begin on-the-job training	

If not applicable, insert N/A in space provided.

_____   _____
Employee's Signature   Supervisor's Signature

_____   _____
Date   Division

Form examined for filing: _____   _____
Date   Personnel Department

Source: Joan Holland and Theodore Curtis. "Orientation of New Employees," in Joseph Famularo ed., *Handbook of Modern Personnel Administration* (New York: McGraw-Hill Book Co., 1972), chap. 23. Reproduced with permission.

A number of potential problems are associated with the orientation procedure for new employees. For example, giving too much information in an orientation session can be as much of a problem as providing too little. If a great deal of information is given to the employee all at once, he or she may feel overwhelmed and is not likely to retain much. Those who design the orientation program should be sensitive to such matters as how much information to provide at a given session, how to sequence the various parts of the program, and how well the new employee is assimilating the information. Providing plenty of opportunity for questions and discussion is an effective way to clarify the presentation.

The new employee's immediate supervisor also plays an important role in the orientation process. First, he or she must cooperate in releasing the new employee from the job to attend orientation sessions. At a minimum, supervisors should also be responsible for introducing the new employee to fellow workers and to his or her assigned tasks. Ideally, supervisors work closely with the human resources department in designing the orientation program, and selected supervisors are invited to give presentations.

Reducing New Employees' Anxiety

An orientation program should have as one of its chief objectives a reduction in the new employee's anxiety. At Texas Instruments, a large electronics manufacturing firm, a research study was undertaken to determine the effectiveness of the standard orientation program. The usual procedure called for a two-hour orientation seminar, after which the employee was sent to the supervisor for job instructions and then on to the work station. Interviews investigating how new assemblers felt about their first day on the job revealed the following:

- The first few days on the job were anxious and disturbing ones for new employees.
- Hazing practices by peers intensified anxiety.
- Anxiety interfered with the training process.
- Turnover of newly hired employees was caused primarily by anxiety.
- New employees were reluctant to discuss problems with their supervisors.

Additional interviews with supervisors and middle managers about their feelings in working with new employees uncovered these insights:

- Supervisors and middle managers experienced as much anxiety as the new employees.
- They felt inadequate with seasoned, competent subordinates.
- They cut off downward communication to conceal ignorance.
- Supervisory defensiveness discouraged upward communication.[2]

The results of these interviews prompted the company to experiment with a different orientation procedure. In this experiment, a group of assemblers who were new to the company first attended the usual two-hour orientation session and then participated in an "anxiety-reduction seminar" for the rest of the day. This seminar focused on presenting new employees with information about the job environment and about the personalities and practices of their new supervisors. The new employees were given statistics indicating the high probability of their success, were told what to expect in the way of hazing and rumors from other employees, and were urged to take the initiative in asking questions of their supervisors. The seminar also allowed considerable opportunity for questions and answers.

The experiment both reduced anxiety and produced other positive results. By the end of four weeks, the experimental group was performing significantly better than a control group in assembling, welding, and inspection. Attendance was also better.[3]

Improving Orientation Programs

Other research suggests ways of increasing the effectiveness of orientation programs. For example, a study in one company found that supervisors frequently lacked the skills to bring new employees aboard (for example, introducing the new employee to fellow workers); there was usually little feedback about early performance; and new employees had many questions and concerns about the reward system, transfer policies, the career development process, and other matters. As a result, a number of corrective measures were taken, including three days of supervisory training in orientation methods and the establishment of procedures to follow the progress of each new employee for six months. In addition, a one-day workshop involving a facilitator's working with supervisors and their new employees was designed to encourage feedback and iron out misunderstandings. The overall results included increased productivity and job satisfaction among new employees, with substantial annual savings stemming from improved performance.[4]

In general, research and experience indicate that orientation procedures should be thoroughly planned and that those conducting the programs should address specific problems faced by new employees. No one orientation system will be best in all circumstances, but it is clear that participative approaches and genuine human warmth and concern for each individual are vital. The human resources department should play a key role in planning and coordinating the orientation program in collaboration with line managers and supervisors.

INTERNAL STAFFING PROCESS

The movement of human resources within an organization is as important as the recruitment and selection of people from outside and calls for the same careful planning and use of fair and systematic procedures. Employees may be reassigned to new positions at the initiative of the organization to fill staff vacancies, to reduce labor costs, or to place workers in jobs that are more appropriate to their interests and abilities. Employees also seek reassignments as their interests and abilities develop through experience. Matching individual needs for growth and development with the needs of the organization is a major goal of the internal staffing process. Inadequate or shortsighted attention to internal staffing changes can have negative effects on morale and productivity, which in turn can seriously impair the organization's ability to attain its objectives.

Most often, supervisors or managers are responsible for initiating employee reassignment. Because the human resources department has an overall view of the organization's staffing needs and goals, that department is typically given the authority to coordinate and review plans for internal staffing changes and to ensure that decisions comply with company policy. In unionized organizations, the labor contract spells out the rules and procedures governing transfer, promotion, and other internal staffing changes.

Transfer

Employees may be reassigned, or asked to **transfer,** from one job to another, one department to another, one shift to another, or one geographic location to another. These reassignments may be initiated by the organization (called **involuntary transfer**) or by the employee with the approval of the organization.

Most organizations have specific transfer policies and procedures that have been developed mainly in response to three problem situations. The first is that of the employee with a history of poor performance or problem behavior whom the department head does not want to keep on staff. Without definite rules about transfers, such employees tend to be reassigned from one department to another in a kind of organizational game of musical chairs. Consequently, many firms put constraints on the transfer of problem employees and require that some other solution be reached. In instances where another supervisor or department head is willing to accept the employee, careful evaluation is necessary to make sure the transfer is fair to everyone involved and that the move is in the interests of the total organization.

The second problem is the need to ensure a close match between an employee's qualifications and the new position. Careful appraisal of an employee's performance and potential should precede any transfer to make certain that his or her qualifications suit the new job. It does not make sense to be careful about initial hiring and then to be casual about a transfer later on. The human resources department can play an important role in this appraisal process by helping to develop thorough procedures and then monitoring transfers to make certain that supervisors are using these procedures appropriately.

The third problem, which can be particularly delicate, is that of relating the employee's present wage or salary to the compensation offered in the new position. It is neither financially sound nor fair to other employees to transfer a worker from a job paying $2,000 per month to one paying $1,000 per month and to continue to pay the higher salary. Ordinarily, such a transfer would be unwise and would suggest that there are issues not being dealt with, such as inadequacies in the employee's performance or in the salary structure.

The transfer or **relocation** of an employee from one location to another presents additional problems. Cost is a major factor. In 1984 it was estimated that it cost, on average, more than $40,000 to relocate a family from one geographic area to another.[5]

Employees transferred at company request are typically reimbursed for moving costs and other expenses. Some examples of relocation costs often absorbed by the organization include assistance in the sale of the present home, a house-hunting trip, subsidized mortgage payments so the employee can afford a new home, travel to the new location, and costs of temporary living arrangements. Obviously, such costs should not be incurred lightly, and organizations must give careful consideration to the merits and drawbacks involved in each transfer decision.

There are human costs as well as financial considerations in-volved in the relocation of human resources, and these are partic-ularly significant in the case of involuntary transfers. According to one source, the relocation of more than half of the 40 million Americans who move each year is due to company transfer. With so many people moving, it is little wonder that greater attention is being paid to the impact of relocation on employees and their families. Research indicates that the impact is greatest on families with school-age children. Spouses, in particular, seem to carry the heaviest burden of the family's adjustment to the new community.[6]

The **dual-career couple** (both spouses are employed) must make difficult choices when one partner faces the possibility of reloca-tion; this also creates a challenge to the organization wishing to transfer one of the partners. This problem is arising more fre-quently as more and more women are moving into professional roles. Sometimes the employee accepts the transfer (or promotion) and the spouse finds employment in the new community; some-times the employee turns down the transfer; and sometimes the employer also hires the spouse. Some of the potential economic advantages and disadvantages of relocating when both spouses are employed are shown in Table 10.1. Housing costs, for example, can vary tremendously from one area to another. To illustrate, in late 1984, the median price of a resale home in Kansas City, Missouri was $57,600, whereas the median price in Orange County, Cali-fornia was $134,900.[7]

TABLE 10.1
Dual-career relocation: Economic considerations

POTENTIAL ADVANTAGES	POTENTIAL DISADVANTAGES
Salary increase for the relocating employee	Salary decrease for the relocating spouse
Salary increase for the relocating spouse	Loss of spouse's salary for x amount of time
Lower cost of living in new area	Higher cost of living in new area
Lower cost of housing in new area	Higher cost of housing in new area
Benefits provided at no or lesser cost by new employer	Benefits provided at increased cost to employee
Additional benefits provided by new employer	Fewer benefits provided by new employer
	Loss of spouse's benefits coverage
	Cost of job-hunting for spouse

Source: Patricia A. Mathews, "The Changing Work Force: Dual Career Couples and Relocation," reprinted from the April, 1984 issue of *Personnel Administrator*, copyright, 1984, The American Society for Personnel Administration, 606 North Washington Street, Alexandria, VA 22314.

More and more common is the commuter marriage, in which each spouse may work three to five days a week in a different location. Even when only one spouse is employed, a commuter marriage can result when a plant or office closes and the employee accepts a position with the company in a different city. Commuter marriages can create stresses and strains in marriage and family relationships.

In the light of these financial and human costs, it is becoming more common for firms to be less insistent that employees accept transfers or promotions to different geographic areas. Further, with rising relocation costs, organizations are more likely to analyze carefully the costs and benefits of shifting human resources from one area to another.

Promotion

A **promotion** is a type of transfer involving the reassignment of an employee to a position that is likely to offer higher pay and greater responsibilities, privileges, and potential opportunities. In general, the purpose of a promotion is to staff a vacant position that is worth more to the organization than the employee's present position. This additional worth is usually reflected in the pay range for the position, although in some instances the organization relies on additional prestige. (An example, in the case of some academic institutions, is the professor who moves into the role of department chair for a term of three or four years. There is prestige attached to the position but frequently no additional pay. This may be why colleagues approach the newly promoted person and cheerfully inquire whether congratulations or condolences are in order!) Sometimes an employee is promoted into a newly created, higher paying position to take advantage of the employee's unique talents.

What constitutes a promotion, as opposed to a transfer or demotion, depends on one's point of view. Sometimes a promotion is offered to a person who considers it a demotion or a step backward in his or her career. An example is the research scientist who is offered the directorship of a research laboratory, but who has no wish to be involved in administration.

In unionized organizations, the labor contract typically requires that **seniority,** or an employee's length of service with the department or organization, be a consideration in promotion decisions. In some contracts, seniority is the only deciding factor; other contracts allow consideration of both seniority and ability. Because management tends to argue for ability and unions tend to emphasize seniority in selecting promotion candidates, labor contracts often reflect a compromise. For example, a contract may call for the use of a formula for making promotion decisions, such as promoting the employee with the greatest seniority if ability and experience are equal. Many contracts permit promotion of any candidate who is "head and shoulders" above others in ability. Practices vary a great deal, however, from firm to firm.

One problem with any promotion decision is that the organization must continue a productive relationship with those employees who are by-passed. Fair and consistent implementation procedures for making promotion decisions will help reduce negative feelings on the part of employees who are not promoted. Some of the procedures or devices used in making promotion decisions are career progression ladders, interviews, testing, peer ratings, the assessment center, and the fallback position.

Career Progression Ladders. **Career progression ladders** (also called job ladders or promotion ladders) are charts that illustrate the horizontal and vertical movement of employees from one job to another within an organization. A sample career ladder is shown in Figure 10.2; a more detailed version might include the salary for each job and the experience and training required.

Career progression ladders are used to help employees visualize potential advancement within the organization and to plan the sequence of training and work experience necessary to reach particular career objectives. The device is also useful in the human resources planning process. For example, charting and examining existing patterns of career progression can be useful in eliminating dead-end paths, in developing training programs, and in advising on staffing decisions. Finally, when available to all employees in the organization, career progression ladders can help create a healthy perspective on the part of supervisors and employees alike: such charts symbolize that there is high mobility in the organization and that change is normal and to be expected. These charts can also enlighten those supervisors and managers who have a tendency to hold on to capable employees long after they have outgrown their jobs and are ready to move on.

Interviewing and Testing. Interviews are widely used to allow potential candidates to express interest in higher-level job opportunities and to evaluate candidates for promotion. As in the selection process, a wide variety of interview approaches is used to make promotion decisions. For example, candidates may each be interviewed by the same interviewer or be involved in a series of one-on-one interviews with several managers. Some interviews may involve one candidate with two or more evaluators present. Usually

FIGURE 10.2 Sample career progression ladder for a food service facility

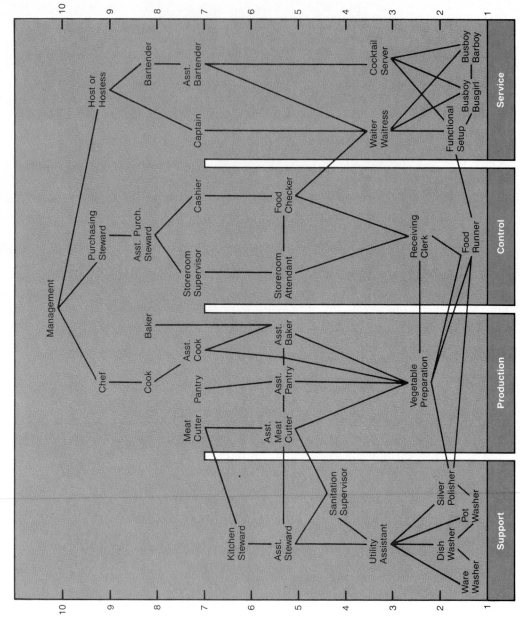

Source: William P. Fisher and Paul Gaurnier, *Career Ladders in the Food Service Industry* (Chicago: National Restaurant Association, 1971), p. 25.

all of the interviewers ask questions; sometimes one evaluator follows a structured interview format while the others observe and take notes.

The extent to which tests are used in the promotion process varies widely by type of job and by industry. For example, one survey found that 17 percent of manufacturing firms use proficiency or aptitude tests in evaluating office-clerical candidates for promotion. In nonmanufacturing the percentage was 28, and in nonbusiness organizations (government, education, hospitals) the percentage was 40. The same study found that tests are used for promotion considerably more often in plant or service jobs than in professional or technical jobs.[8]

Like all selection devices, interview and test results are subject to legal challenge if discrimination or adverse impact is alleged. For example, as a result of an EEOC class-action suit, the CF&I Steel Corp. agreed to pay back awards of $500,000 to 331 Hispanics of both sexes who alleged they had been discriminated against in the selection of supervisors.[9]

Peer Ratings. **Peer ratings** are the evaluation of an employee's performance or potential for advancement by those of equal rank. Research has shown that peer ratings tend to be fairly accurate predictors of supervisory or managerial success.[10] They do not appear to be used very extensively, however, for making promotion decisions. One exception is the promotion procedure at Graphic Controls. In this organization, an open, participatory peer evaluation procedure is commonly used to select executives, including the president. One study found that executives who were involved in this process generally supported the peer-rating procedure.[11]

In Case 10.2 at the beginning of the chapter, the crisis involving the promotion of Al Thompson might have been avoided if information from peers about nominees for sales manager had been solicited. The important information about Al Thompson that the psychologist and top management did not have was that Al was not trusted by his peers. The psychologist could have found this out by interviewing each member of the department or by devising some kind of rating sheet that department members could fill out on a confidential basis.

Assessment Centers. In an **assessment center,** information about an employee's promotability and career development is gathered systematically and analyzed as the candidate participates in a series of tests, interviews, and exercises. The assessment center concept appears to be an effective, although expensive, approach to supervisory and managerial selection. Assessment centers are becoming increasingly popular in a variety of organizations in this country and abroad.

AT&T helped popularize this approach in its Bell System companies before the firm was broken up. Typically, these assessment centers processed about a dozen candidates a week, with each group of candidates spending two and a half to three days in the center. The staff spent the remainder of the week making ratings, discussing results, and writing comprehensive reports. Line managers nominated candidates for the center, or candidates could nominate themselves.

The devices used in assessment centers include extensive interviews; tests of mental ability, skill in reasoning, and knowledge of current affairs; the leaderless group discussion; presentations by each member of the group; and simulation exercises. One popular simulation is the "in-basket" exercise, in which each candidate decides how to handle a series of memos that he or she finds in an in-basket. Other examples are business games in which teams of six candidates manage a toy company; mock interviews; and an exercise called the "Irate Customer Phone Call" (used at J. C. Penney). Staff members observe and score participants' performance on these exercises.[12]

An important component of an effective assessment center program is the feedback session, in which a member of the assessment staff explains the scores and ratings to each participant. These sessions are useful in minimizing participant frustration stemming from lack of information about results, and studies indicate that such feedback contributes to employee learning and development. Studies at Michigan Bell, for example, found that most employees who had participated in the assessment center and feedback process had a good understanding of their ratings and felt that the information given them would be helpful in their careers.[13]

Numerous studies of both men and women managers have found that assessment results are useful predictors of managerial success, which indicates that assessment centers can increase the proportion of successful to unsuccessful managers.[14] In addition, the assessment center is particularly useful in identifying managerial potential among women and minority-group employees. Finally, such centers can help identify lower-level managers who are promotable to higher positions. Here, the center can be a vehicle for upward mobility across department or division lines.

The Fallback Position.   Establishing **fallback positions** is sometimes part of the promotion process. In this procedure, one or more positions that have the same status and pay as the promoted employee's original job are identified ahead of time. Should the promotion prove unsuccessful, the employee is transferred to the fall-back position. This procedure "lets everyone know that (1) there is some risk in the promotion or transfer, (2) the company is willing to accept some of the responsibility for it, and (3) moving into the fallback position does not constitute failure."[15]

Demotion

A **demotion,** sometimes called a "downward transfer," is a type of transfer involving a cut in pay, status, privilege, or opportunity. Demotions may result from organizational staff reductions or disciplinary penalties. With an employee who is unable to perform adequately in a particular job, the purpose of a demotion is to remedy a previous mistake in staffing.

In some instances, demotions are mutually satisfactory arrangements stemming from an employee's health problems or changing interests. A demotion may simply be a return to a fallback position. On the other hand, demotions are frequently a shock to the affected employee and bring about the kinds of reactions associated with a career crisis, which is discussed later in this chapter.

To some extent the impact of a demotion depends on the organization's particular culture. If there is a great deal of movement up, down, and sideways in the organization and general acceptance that most employees have a zigzag pattern of career progression, a downward assignment may be accepted as simply another transfer. Such acceptance probably depends, however, on a high degree of job security and considerable trust in higher management's intentions.

EMPLOYEE SEPARATIONS

Other significant career transitions are those involving the separation of employees from the organization. Employees may leave the organization involuntarily, through layoff or dismissal, or voluntarily, through resignation or retirement. Although the reasons for separation vary, each instance should be analyzed and understood in terms of its impact on the individual employee and on the organization as a whole. Sudden or unexpected removal from the organization can be particularly difficult for the affected employee and can damage the morale of coworkers and the organization's general climate. Even when the employee initiates the separation, the organization must be able to continue functioning until the staff vacancy is filled. Thus, the effective management of employee separations is vital to the healthy and continued functioning of the organization.

Layoff

A **layoff** is the temporary or indefinite removal of employees from the payroll. Generally the purpose of the layoff is to reduce the organization's burden of excess labor costs when human resources cannot be used effectively. Layoffs may affect relatively small groups of employees, but when a large organization runs into serious financial problems, large numbers of workers may be laid off. In some instances, management is too quick to lay off employees because of financial downturn, thus depleting the organization's valuable human resources for the long term and damaging the morale and security of retained employees. In other instances, however, layoffs may be the only option remaining for an organization facing possible bankruptcy.

Although there have been many instances of white-collar and supervisory employee layoffs in recent years, hourly paid production workers are typically the first to be affected by production cutbacks. Some organizations provide accrued vacation pay, supplemental unemployment benefits (SUB), and continued health and life insurance to employees affected by a layoff, especially if the layoff is expected to be temporary. SUB clauses in labor contracts, which provide for company payments to laid-off workers, are designed to extend or enlarge the unemployment benefit payments provided under state law. **Severance pay,** usually a lump-sum payment at the time of permanent separation, is more common for nonunionized salaried workers than for unionized production and maintenance workers.

In a unionized organization, the labor contract governs the order of layoff and method of **recall,** or rehiring of laid-off employees. Seniority is usually the controlling factor: often the most senior employee is laid off last and is the first to be recalled. In such cases the layoff is based on **reverse seniority.** In addition, the contract typically establishes the maximum period during which a laid-off employee has recall and other rights. **Bumping** provisions permit employees with greater seniority to accept a demotion and replace less senior employees who are laid off. Bumping can work effectively only when the more senior employee is qualified and able to perform the work of the less senior employee.

The long-established practice of basing layoff decisions on seniority alone has come squarely into conflict with EEOC requirements that organizations increase the numbers of female and minority employees in their work forces. Court rulings on this issue have been contradictory. For example, in one case involving the Jersey Central Power and Light Co., a court of appeals ruled that a conciliation agreement to establish an affirmative action program to hire more blacks and women could exist side by side with the collective-bargaining agreement that provided for laying off of the least senior people first. Blacks and women would probably be laid off first because they would be apt to have the least seniority. But in *Watkins* v. *United Steelworkers,* a federal district court ordered the employer to apply seniority to white and black workers separately and to allocate future layoffs between black and white workers in proportion to their representation in the work force at the time of the layoffs.[16] Yet in *Firefighters Local 1784* v. *Stotts,* the Supreme Court ruled that a seniority system cannot be overridden to protect an affirmative action program in a layoff situation.[17]

The use of **inverse seniority** in layoff situations is gaining some support as a way out of the dilemma between reverse seniority and affirmative action. Under the concept of inverse seniority, the most senior workers are given the first opportunity to elect layoff. Volunteers may be motivated by such interests as traveling, remodeling the house, or simply desire for a change of pace. Those who volunteer are provided with unemployment compensation plus supplemental unemployment benefits. The success of inverse seniority plans depends on the company's SUB program and the particular state's concurring in the legality of paying unemployment compensation to such workers.

Recent state legislation is also affecting workers who are laid off because of plant closures. For example, in Connecticut, employers of one hundred or more employees who close or relocate their establishments are required to continue to pay existing group health insurance for each affected employee and dependents for up to ninety days.[18]

Discharge

Discharge (also called dismissal, termination, or firing) is management action in which an employee is separated from the organization for violation of company rules or inadequate performance. Because discharge is a traumatic experience for the affected employee, and usually for others as well, most managers are extremely reluctant to dismiss an employee unless there are substantial and well-documented reasons for such action. In many cases, timely warnings and effective supervisory involvement in correcting problems can eliminate the need for employee termination. The policy of many organizations is that each discharge case be reviewed by higher authority before a final decision is reached. Federal civil service regulations, as well as most state and local civil service regulations, require that all dismissals be reviewed.

Termination policies are also affected by laws, EEOC rulings, and court decisions that seek to protect the worker from discrimination and to uphold fair employment practices. While the right to discharge an employee is well established in the United States, management must be careful that discharge practices do not discriminate against female and minority employees. A recent analysis of relevant court cases led to the following conclusions about management's rights to terminate employees:

> First, it is clearly apparent that an employer does have the right to fire or lay off employees for legitimate business reasons, regardless of whether they are members of protected classes. Thus all employees can, justifiably, be fired for the following reasons: unsatisfactory work records (including poor productivity and/or quality of work), poor safety records, refusal of work orders, unexcused absences, inability to perform work, and violation of clearly stated company policies.[19]

To preclude courts from ruling that discharges are a pretext for discrimination, however, management should do the following:

1. Document unsatisfactory performance.
2. Keep all employees informed about the quality of their performance.
3. Give all deficient performers reasonable opportunities to improve.
4. Inform all employees about company policies and rules governing employee behavior and about the contents of their job descriptions.
5. Be consistent in the application of punishment and administer the same punishment to all employees who violate rules.[20]

Resignation

Resignation is the voluntary separation of an employee from the organization. Resignations should be analyzed for their implications for the particular organization. Although some resignations may permit an organization to correct a mistake in staffing or to bring in "new blood," excessive turnover can be very costly: with each departure, the organization loses the investment it has made in recruiting, selecting, and training the departing employee.

Most companies systematically analyze their rate of **turnover,** which is usually calculated as the ratio of separations to total work force for some period, and attempt to maintain it within reasonable proportions. This analysis is sometimes made for particular departments, divisions, or classes of employees to identify areas where turnover is excessive. Obtaining this information is an important first step in understanding and controlling turnover.

Exit interviews are widely used to obtain information about the causes of turnover. Usually the interview is conducted by a representative of the personnel department, who tries to determine why the employee is leaving the organization. These interviews are also used to make certain that company property has been checked in and that the employee understands the disposition of various benefit programs. **Postemployment surveys** that ask separated employees to supply reasons for their resignations are sometimes used in place of exit interviews, on the assumption that data obtained a few weeks later are more valid than those obtained at the time of departure. In either case, supervisors are likely to be defensive about any criticism of their performance, and human resources specialists will need to use the data in a constructive, nonpunitive way if supervisors are to learn from the experience. The resignation of an employee to take a job with greater responsibilities can reflect positively on a supervisor's training and development skills, although it can also be a signal that the organization needs to increase the opportunities for advancement.

Retirement

Retirement is the systematic separation of older workers from the organization, allowing them to pursue interests outside of work while opening up positions and career opportunities for other employees. Under a *flexible* retirement policy, employees are free to choose, within the limits of the company's retirement benefits program, when they will retire; under a *compulsory* retirement policy, the employee must retire by a certain age. With the passage of the Age Discrimination in Employment Act, employers can no longer impose retirement before age seventy in most cases. Most workers, however, choose to retire before that age. A survey of 267 personnel directors in 1980 found that raising the mandatory retirement age had had little or no impact.[21]

The majority of employees in most organizations are retired with a guarantee of a regularly paid retirement income, or **pension,** in addition to their government Social Security payments. One study of 1,454 firms found 83 percent providing some form of pension plan.[22] A study of twenty-six large nonunion firms reported that all had retirement plans.[23]

Retirement can be a difficult transition, since it involves a radical change in lifestyle and can mean the end of a number of meaningful relationships and experiences. Many organizations have responded to this reality by introducing a number of programs to help the older employee prepare for retirement. Activities such as preretirement seminars to discuss retirement problems and opportunities, individual and group counseling, and newsletters or magazines written especially for those of preretirement age are frequently included in such programs. Counseling and information sessions frequently include spouses. In addition, some firms make an effort to continue a relationship with retirees by inviting them to social events, having special days for retirees to visit the company, retaining the names of retired employees on mailing lists for the company's newspaper or magazine, and sponsoring clubs for retired employees. Other organizations, such as churches, universities, unions, and libraries, also sponsor pre- and postretirement programs for their members or the general public. Some companies pay tuition for courses that will be helpful in postretirement careers or hobbies. IBM provides potential retirees and their spouses with up to $2,500 each in tuition aid. Entitlement starts three years before retirement eligibility and continues for two years after retirement.[24]

Phased retirement is becoming increasingly popular in the United States and abroad. Many organizations have developed part-time work or job-sharing approaches that allow employees nearing retirement to reduce gradually the number of hours they work per day, per week, or per year. Among the various versions of phased retirement programs are a gradual reduction of the workweek, progressively longer vacations with pay, or progressively longer leaves without pay. These approaches appear successful when they are voluntary and when the employee's salary, combined with retirement benefits, comes fairly close to the regular salary.[25]

MANAGING CAREER CHANGES

A career change such as demotion, transfer to an undesirable job or location, layoff, discharge, or unemployment for any length of time is typically a traumatic event or **career crisis** for the individual directly involved. The crisis is apt to be particularly severe when the change is sudden and unexpected. Much of the trauma is also experienced by persons close to the situation — coworkers, supervisors, the family, and close friends.

All too often, a financial emergency or some other organizational crisis becomes a career crisis for a number of individuals. For example, a general announcement to a company's employees that 10 percent of the work force will be laid off or that a plant is going to close means negative career changes — and personal crises — for a significant number of workers. Less negative career changes, such as a person's choosing early retirement with substantial financial benefits, may take on crisis proportions if the individual is dissatisfied or unable to cope with the new situation. Any career change becomes particularly difficult if the organization does not provide adequate information and support for the person making the transition.

One theory suggests that people tend to go through a series of predictable phases when faced with a negative career change or crisis. The phases are:

- Shock. The person experiences a threat to preservation, is unable to handle the reality, and experiences helplessness, intense anxiety, confusion, and perhaps panic.
- Defensive retreat. The person clings to the past, reassures self that he or she is still the same person and things have not changed, indulges in wishful thinking, and becomes angry with any threat to this equilibrium. The person's thinking becomes rigid, and he or she refuses to consider any changes in goals, values, or lifestyle.
- Acknowledgement. Defenses break down because others do not support the unrealistic beliefs and because things do not return to their former state. There is a renewed encounter with reality and perhaps renewed stress. There may be depression and bitterness. The person begins to reorganize thinking and attitudes.
- Adaptation and change. The person begins to explore internal resources, thinking and planning are reorganized around new realities and resources, new satisfactions are experienced, anxiety and depression decline, and the person develops a renewed sense of self-worth. The individual is now coping successfully and is no longer in a state of crisis.[26]

This theory has three major implications for human resources management. First, people in a state of shock or defensive retreat because of a career crisis are likely to be substantially less effective in their jobs and in interpersonal and group relationships than formerly. The second implication logically follows: management should do whatever it can to avoid creating unnecessary crises.

Positively handled, a career change can lead to a productive new job.

The costs to the organization and to individuals can be very high. The third implication is that changes and transitions that must occur should be managed as carefully and humanely as possible to prevent or minimize crises.

Minimizing Crises

Numerous companies have responded to an organizational crisis by laying off or terminating employees without looking at other options open to them and without much apparent concern for the individuals affected. On the other hand, many organizations have managed crises in humane and imaginative ways that have minimized the trauma for individuals. For example, when the Brown & Williamson Tobacco Corporation decided it was necessary to close its plant in Kentucky, employees were notified three years in advance. About 350 out of 2,700 hourly workers were assisted in relocating to a new plant in Georgia; the others received at least six months' separation pay and health-care coverage, financial

---

PERSPECTIVE 10.2   How Atlantic Richfield Saves Jobs

When a company decides to cut back staff, too often the only choice is to seek employment elsewhere. Not so at Atlantic Richfield, which since late 1982 has given unassigned employees top priority through its Unassigned Employee Program.

As a result of extensive reorganization at ARCO over the past several years, many employees have found themselves "unassigned." According to personnel staff administration manager Dick Tunison, whose professional and technical resources group coordinates the Unassigned Employee Program, employees "across the board, ranging from entry-level positions to senior management" have been affected. Until late 1982, most of these employees were forced to leave ARCO.

"We recognized that we were losing highly desirable employees," Tunison explains, "and we didn't see any way to close the door on that."

The program's operation is simple. Each of ARCO's operating companies has a director of unassigned employee placement (DUEP), whose main task is to make sure that his or her unassigned employees are given top priority for any ARCO openings for which they qualify. Each DUEP must circulate the names of qualified unassigned employees to other operating companies and to professional placement administrator Ollie Stevenson, who distributes vacancy and unassigned lists among the DUEPs. When an opening appears, each DUEP nominates qualified employees. Only after unassigned candidates have been considered can any position be filled.

Any unassigned employee is automatically placed in the program. Because of the sensitive nature of this issue, the employee's "unassigned" status is held in strict confidence.

ARCO Corporate pays any relocation expenses for unassigned employees — normally the responsibility of the individual operating companies. ARCO is also able to give some unassigned employees "project assignments," jobs of up to six months' duration, which gives them some additional time.

Probably the greatest challenge to the coordinators of the Unassigned Employee Program, says Tunison, is the reaction employees have when they become unassigned. For most, it is an understandably traumatic experience. Many of these people have been doing basically the same thing for years and feel fearful or incapable of doing something different. Others, having been out of the active job market for so long, have virtually forgotten how to seek employment. To help these employees, ARCO Corporate has instituted special seminars entitled "Techniques for a Successful Job Change." Through this two-day program, employees are shown how to assess their skills, how to market themselves effectively (through résumés, letters, and interviews), and how to locate employment opportunities.

Of the 1,200 ARCO employees who have become unassigned since the program went into effect, approximately 30 percent have been internally placed in their own or other ARCO operating companies.

Source: "How Atlantic Richfield Saves Jobs by Reassigning 'Excess' Employees," *Management Review* (September 1984): 39. Reprinted, by permission of the publisher, from *Management Review.* "Management in Practice," September 1984, © 1984 AMA Membership Publications Division, American Management Associations, New York. All rights reserved.

---

counseling, and vocational training for new jobs.[27] When American Oil decided it was necessary to close its refinery in El Dorado, Arkansas, employees were notified nine months in advance and hiring in the company's other facilities was frozen so that every effort could be made to relocate employees at the other sites. All employees were given the option of early retirement, a chance to transfer at company expense, or assistance in locating jobs else-where in the community (called **outplacement**). While there was some initial shock, by and large most employees and the commu-nity were appreciative of the way the company handled the situa-tion.[28]

Outplacement Programs. Outplacement programs, like those con-ducted by American Oil, can assist employees in coping with the personal crisis associated with a layoff or other type of termination. Outplacement programs typically include the following compo-nents:

1. Information to affected employees about the planned action, such as termination payments and extension of benefits and outplace-ment services.
2. Counseling with affected employees concerning job-seeking methods.
3. Announcements to other organizations and to employment agencies about the availability of qualified employees.
4. Newspaper ads urging employers to contact the firm faced with the separations.
5. Development of a résumé for each affected employee to be sent to potential employers.

Figure 10.3 diagrams the components of a thorough outplace-ment and counseling program. Brammer and Humberger identify four phases of counseling that can help a terminated employee develop renewed self-esteem and conduct a successful job search. These are orientation, job evaluation, job targeting, and job campaign.

The first phase, orientation, includes planning and negotiating for services with the outplacement counselors, termination of the employee, immediate counseling with the affected employee, ad-ditional counseling, and life and career planning. In phase 2, the terminated employee is engaged in a process of self-examination through dialogue with the counselor and through a battery of tests. Phase 3 helps the person focus on what types of jobs to pursue and in what arenas — geographic location, industry, and so on — those jobs might be found, and on developing résumés. Phase 4 includes the job campaign and, it is hoped, a new position. The outplacement counselor works with the individual throughout the process.[29]

Retraining Workers. Some organizations that have enjoyed con-tinuous growth have adopted a policy of retraining workers whose present skills are no longer needed rather than laying them off. IBM, for example, avoided layoffs for a thirty-five-year period by

FIGURE 10.3   The outplacement counseling process

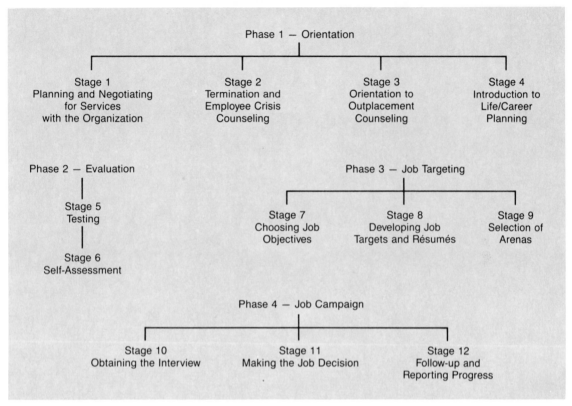

Source: Lawrence M. Brammer and Frank E. Humberger, *Outplacement & Inplacement Counseling*, © 1984, p. 8. Reprinted by permission of Prentice-Hall, Inc., Englewood Cliffs, N.J.

retraining and relocating employees through an extensive corporate education program.[30] Crown Zellerbach paid workers full wages to learn new skills when the company modernized a Louisiana pulp mill. The Boeing Company enrolled laid-off electronic technicians in college, where they learned microprocessing skills.[31]

Contingency Plans.   Should an organizational crisis arise, the very survival of the company may be at stake. Therefore, management is wise to give careful, advance thought to those options or **contingency plans** that can be implemented to minimize negative effects on the company's human resources. A company faced with a severe cash-flow problem, for example, might consider the options shown in Figure 10.4. First, management might impose a hiring

FIGURE 10.4
Options during a cash-flow crisis

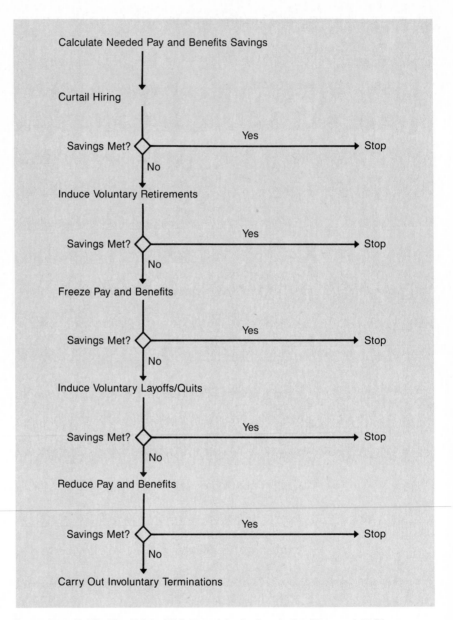

Source: Bruce R. Ellig, "Pay Policies While Downsizing the Organization, "*Personnel*, 60 (May–June 1983):28. Used with permission.

freeze. If this action did not achieve the necessary savings, a voluntary retirement program that might include financial incentives for retiring early could be introduced. If savings targets were still not met, management would have the option of freezing all wages, salaries, and employee benefits for several months.

Next, the organization might move to voluntary layoffs or quits. (Under a voluntary layoff program, employees might be offered a layoff featuring continuation of benefits and a guarantee of a job at the end of a year. The voluntary quit program would include severance pay based on some formula that included length of service.) If labor costs were still too high, the next step would be to reduce the pay of all employees in proportion to salary. An alternative might be to reduce temporarily the hours of employees paid by the hour.

Only after all these procedures had failed to produce the required cost reductions would the organization initiate a program of involuntary terminations or layoffs. These terminations would probably affect the employees with least seniority first and might be made on a departmental, plantwide, or organizationwide basis. Of course, the program would need to comply with antidiscrimination laws and with any union-management contract.[32]

Career Counseling and Planning

Career counseling programs and career planning techniques can help individuals cope with career transitions of various kinds. Career counseling and planning can also be of help to people suddenly confronted by a crisis.

Career counseling is available from personnel department specialists in large organizations or through private agencies or educational institutions. Frequently, line managers do a great deal of informal career counseling. Effective career counseling, according to Edgar Schein, requires "(1) counseling skill; (2) information about the person being counseled — aptitudes, motives, experience, specific strengths and weaknesses; and (3) information about the career options and paths available within and outside the organization." Schein goes on to say that "no one person may be in a position to do the whole job" and that a combination of performance appraisal, personal assessment, and information seeking may be required before an individual is ready to make good judgments about career alternatives.[33]

Life- and career-planning workshops have been used by many individuals to understand more fully their career goals and aspirations and to cope with major changes in their careers such as the loss of a job. (Life or career planning is frequently used in conjunction with outplacement counseling programs; see Figure 10.3.) These workshops, which may be offered within or outside the organization, can last from a few hours to two or three days. Participants are usually strangers or, if from the same organization, are ordinarily assigned to different discussion groups so that openness and confidentiality can be maintained. Under the direction of a qualified trainer, participants become involved in a series of writing and discussion exercises designed to increase an individual's awareness of his or her own needs and feelings. The results of each person's explorations are usually shared and discussed in a small, supportive group under the direction of the trainer. The following assignment is typical:

> Prepare a life inventory of important "happenings" for you, including the following:
>
> a. Any peak experiences you have had.
> b. Things which you do well.
> c. Things which you do poorly.
> d. Things which you would like to stop doing.
> e. Things which you would like to learn to do well.
> f. Peak experiences you would like to have.
> g. Values (e.g., power, money, etc.) you want to achieve.
> h. Things you would like to start doing now.[34]

Herbert Shepard, who is generally credited with developing the life- and career-planning approach, sees life planning as making plans for "life-worth-living" — a process of self-confrontation so that one can make more effective life and career choices.[35]

Much useful career counseling takes place when individuals seek assistance from a counseling psychologist, clinical psychologist, or psychiatrist. Issues about career crises or career directions frequently come up in these sessions. Such counseling can be of great assistance in making career plans, particularly when an individual is experiencing a negative career change.

SUMMARY

Effective management of career transitions is important both to the individuals involved and to the organization. How internal staffing changes and employee separations are planned and managed has significant consequences for organizational effectiveness and employee morale and development. Group orientation methods and attention to individual needs and concerns show promise of reducing turnover and enhancing performance. Transfers are significant matters for both individuals and the organization. The impact of involuntary geographic moves on employees is coming under increased scrutiny by organizations and employees alike.

Assessment centers, although expensive to operate, are being used extensively to identify managerial talent and have proven useful for increasing the movement of women and minorities into management ranks. Career progression ladders and the concept of the fallback position can also be very useful devices.

Traditional seniority rights and affirmative action programs are frequently in direct conflict in many layoff situations, and court decisions are beginning to probe the dilemma. The concept of inverse seniority is being used in some organizations as a partial solution. Outplacement programs have been used successfully by many firms in layoff situations.

The right to discharge nonproductive employees is essential in maintaining standards of performance, but discharge should be for just cause, only after the employee has had a reasonable opportunity to improve, and only after careful review. This approach makes sense as an effective management practice; it is also important in avoiding court rulings that discriminatory practices have occurred.

A variety of practices can assist in managing the transition of employees into retirement, including seminars, counseling, and phased retirement. The exit interview is widely used to obtain data from employees who resign.

Theory and experience suggest that people go through various phases when there is an organizational crisis that creates a personal career crisis, such as being confronted with the possibility of a demotion or being laid off. The more employees and managers alike understand these phases, the more constructive plans can be made to manage crises. Management would be wise to have contingency plans ready for use in a financial crisis, so that a series of steps can be taken that will minimize the impact on the human resources of the organization.

Counseling and life- and career-planning workshops can be very useful in managing the various transitions that individuals face in their work lives. Empathetic and understanding supervisors can be very helpful with these transitions.

The human resources department plays a major role in planning and monitoring orientation programs and procedures and all other career transitions such as transfer, promotion, demotion, and separation. The most effective programs and procedures will recognize that the individuals involved have intense feelings about these matters and that these transitions do not take place in isolation but involve a network of human relationships.

KEY TERMS

orientation	assessment center	resignation
hazing	fallback position	turnover
transfer	demotion	exit interview
involuntary transfer	layoff	postemployment survey
relocation	severance pay	retirement
dual-career couple	recall	pension
promotion	reverse seniority	phased retirement
seniority	bumping	career crisis
career progression ladder	inverse seniority	outplacement
peer rating	discharge	contingency plan

REVIEW QUESTIONS

1. Why is the effective management of career transitions important to individual employees and to the organization?
2. What would be the characteristics of an effective orientation process?
3. Discuss several procedures used in making promotion decisions, including assessment centers, and discuss any problems with each.
4. Describe how the labor agreement governs staffing decisions in the organization.
5. Discuss some procedures that management can use to ensure that employee terminations are nondiscriminatory.
6. Outline some of the options organizations have for avoiding layoffs.
7. What are some of the career crises that employees may face, what happens to people in a crisis situation, and what can the organization do to help alleviate some of the adverse consequences of crisis situations?

OPENING CASE QUESTIONS

Case 10.1   The First Day

1. Was Jim Greenlee's orientation and induction successful? Think about the main purposes for an orientation.
2. If you were the employee benefits person, how would you have improved Jim's orientation process?
3. Adele's remark that "things are going to be different now" really threw Jim. What can he do now to make his staff feel less threatened and to ease his own tension?

Case 10.2 The Promotion Decision

1. Was the psychologist at fault for recommending Al for the promotion, based on the data she had?
2. What other steps could Steve and Jeff have taken to ensure they were doing everything to fill the position with the correct employee?
3. Now what can Steve and Jeff do?

CASE 10.3   OUTPLACEMENT ACTIVITIES

Human resources managers in many organizations are showing an acute awareness of how traumatic job loss can be for the individual. Outplacement activities are a growing specialty, which has engendered a number of professional job counseling services, as well as a host of in-house organizational efforts to help separated employees. Such efforts might range from increased severance payments to lump-sum financial assistance for education or training to just giving laid-off employees a chance to talk to someone about their frustrations. The most comprehensive programs actually put the organization's resources to work to help match each separated employee with the right job.

On January 1, 1983 Interfaith Medical Center in Brooklyn, New York began the first phase of a five-phase, six-month layoff process that would result in the separation of 450 employees. By December 1 of the same year, 250 of the 288 laid-off workers who had taken advantage of Interfaith's outplacement services found new jobs; and these services were continuing. In organizing the outplacement effort, the medical center's human resources department had established the goal of at least one referral to an appropriate job opening for each separated employee seeking help.

There were several aspects to the outplacement program. To begin with, during the process of layoff notification, every attempt was made to make the employees aware of the service, and employees were given a chance to meet with human resources people for orientation. In addition, Interfaith systematically communicated with other potential employers in the area to solicit their cooperation. The human resources department also worked closely with union officials, who were able to contribute placement efforts of their own. This cooperation also helped maintain stable relations during a difficult period.

Case Sources: Nadeem Shahzad, "Outplacement Services at Interfaith Medical Center," *Personnel Administrator* (June 1984): 59–63; "Outplacement Services at Interfaith Medical Center," *Personnel* (March-April 1984): 44–46; John D. Baxter, "How New Jobs Are Found, and New Careers Launched," *Iron Age* (June 21, 1985): 28–29, 33; and a Sue A. Tempero, "A Humane Professional Cost-Effective System for Laid-Off Employees as a Result of the Consolidation of the Des Moines Register and Tribune," *Personnel Administrator* (May 1984): 118–121, 129.

Other features of the program included counseling from outside job placement specialists in job search strategies, career-change options, and possibilities for training, education, and financial aid.

Interfaith's ultimate aim in this effort was to find a job for every laid-off employee who wanted one, but other benefits accrued as well; and the human resources director, Nadeem Shahzad, was aware of them. A medical center, perhaps more than some types of organizations, is influenced by its image in the community it serves. Interfaith's humane policy toward its laid-off workers enhanced that image. In addition, the policy helped bolster morale among retained workers, as well as among those being let go. As an added bonus, it also made the job of the human resources people a little easier to cope with: "Where outplacement services exist, managers and supervisors are not simply the bearers of bad news. They are able to offer something positive to terminated employees, and to express the organization's continuing concern for them in a tangible way."[*]

Discussion Questions

1. At Interfaith, what advantages can you see in extending the layoff process over a six-month period, rather than making all the layoffs at once?
2. Often, the only help laid-off employees receive is a lump-sum severance payment. What flaws do you see in such a policy?

[*]Nadeem Shahzad, "Outplacement Services at Interfaith Medical Center," *Personnel Administrator*, June 1984, p. 60.

part 4

Development and Appraisal

This section focuses on the human resources activities that are intended to improve the performance of individuals and groups in the organization. Chapter 11 discusses skills training programs, which are designed to help employees do their jobs more effectively. Chapter 12 examines management and career development programs, which are aimed at educating employees beyond immediate job requirements to facilitate the attainment of organizational goals. Improving performance is also an important objective of the performance appraisal and review process, discussed in Chapter 13.

Skills Training

CHAPTER OUTLINE

LEARNING OBJECTIVES

- **Define training and distinguish among skills training, skills retraining, and management/career development programs.**
- **Outline the steps involved in determining the organization's need for a skills training program.**
- **Describe the considerations that underlie the selection of individuals for a training program.**
- **List the advantages and disadvantages associated with particular training methods.**
- **Describe the roles of human resources directors and other managers in the development of training programs.**
- **Identify the basic principles of learning underlying an effective training program.**

CASE 11.1   HIGH-TECH TERROR

Penny

Penny was beginning to dread coming to work. Her boss had bought a computer and printer, as well as a word-processing program and several other programs. He claimed the system would cut Penny's typing and calculating workload in half.

But Penny had little hope for that happy prospect, since it was taking her so long to learn how to use the new equipment. The salesperson who had installed the computer had been patient with her but had left after about half an hour with a casual, "The instruction manual is very thorough. Just refer to it if you have any other questions."

Well, she sure had plenty of those! Things were always going wrong, and looking up all the answers in the manual took forever. Often she couldn't find the solution to a particular problem, and one time she had lost almost three hours of work because she hadn't known how to save her work on a storage disk. Twice she had gathered her courage and phoned the salesperson for help, but the second time he had been rather curt, referring her once again to the manual. Clearly, she was on her own in learning this new skill.

Penny couldn't remember when her confidence had been so low. Her work, far from being reduced, was piling up at an alarming rate, and she had the feeling that her boss was beginning to be irritated with her slow progress. She stared wistfully at her old reliable Olivetti typewriter and wished that the world hadn't become so high-tech.

Amy

Amy switched on her computer and inserted the word-processing disk. Within a few seconds, the rough draft she had been working on before lunch was on the screen and ready for further revision. Half an hour later, Amy turned on the printer, which began printing the completed article while she made some telephone calls about her next project.

The new computer and printer had proven to be invaluable in Amy's job as writer and editor for Quality Health Care's monthly newsletter. Amy's assistant, Nick, had previously spent most of his time typing and retyping drafts of Amy's articles. The word processor, however, which enabled Amy to compose and revise right on the computer screen, had eliminated this burden. Nick was now free to do most of the research and legwork connected with the newsletter.

Amy had been a bit apprehensive about the new equipment in the beginning, but before it was installed, her boss had arranged for her and Nick to take a computer and word-processing class at the local community college. That, plus a one-day workshop offered by the computer firm after the equipment was installed, had given Amy and Nick the "hands-on" experience necessary to operate the computer with confidence.

Thanks to the new word processor, much of the time pressure Amy had felt about getting out the newsletter was gone, and she found herself enjoying her job more than ever.

CASE 11.2   SOUTHERN CATERPILLAR SERVICES

George Arnold, supervisor of training for Southern Caterpillar Services, wondered whether the information he had just heard had anything to do with the high dropout rate the company had experienced in its diesel mechanics training program. In an informal discussion, a former trainee had said he was afraid of the training program and had quit to avoid the possibility of failure. More than 70 percent of the trainees in the program were dropping out, which added significantly to the already high cost of the training.

George decided to examine and compare closely the actual work performed by the firm's mechanics with the training program. He eventually discovered that the work pattern consisted of three broad categories of tasks. About 70 percent of the work was basic in-shop mechanics work, 20 percent was out-of-shop work, and about 10 percent was diagnostic work. In the twelve-month training program, by comparison, about 30 percent of the instruction was devoted to supervised diesel mechanics work in the shop, 20 percent to unsupervised out-of-shop work, and about 50 percent to diagnostics.

Southern Caterpillar had operated the training program with the philosophy that every mechanic completing the training should be able to do every job he or she might encounter. Thus the training was long and rigorous. As George reflected on the company's experience, he wondered whether he should make any changes in the training program.

The cases at the beginning of this chapter dramatize the importance of training. Whereas Penny in Case 11.1 was terrified by the prospect of having to use the computer, Amy found her job greatly eased by the word processor. The main element contributing to these different experiences was training. Case 11.2 illustrates the need to examine and compare the relationship between the training program and the actual work performed. Proper training can be as important as the equipment used and other characteristics of the job.

The money annually paid for training by business and industry also demonstrates the importance of training. It has been estimated that American business firms spend $15 to $20 billion per year on training,[1] with some estimates running more than $100 billion.[2] This includes company-owned training centers like Hamburger University, run by McDonald's Corporation in Oak Brook, Illinois, and General Electric's training center in Croton-on-Hudson, New York. Another indication of the importance organizations attach to training is the estimated 45,000 company employees assigned full time to training and development activities.[3]

In the organizational context, **training** can be defined as "the organizationally directed experiences that are designed to further the learning of behaviors that will contribute to organizational goals."[4] In the ideal situation, training helps to further both the goals of the organization and the individual's goals.

This broad definition of training includes both skills training, which is usually of a technical nature, and management and career development programs, which are aimed at educating employees above and beyond the immediate technical requirements of their jobs in order to increase the organization's present and future ability to attain its goals. This chapter focuses on skills training; management and career development are discussed in Chapter 12.

The purpose of skills training is to bring the competencies of individuals up to desired standards for present or future assignments. The purpose of skills **retraining** is to develop new skills and knowledge to replace those that have become obsolete as a result of technological or organizational changes.

This chapter is devoted to developing a skills training program that is useful and rewarding to both the organization and to in-

FIGURE 11.1
Developing a skills training program

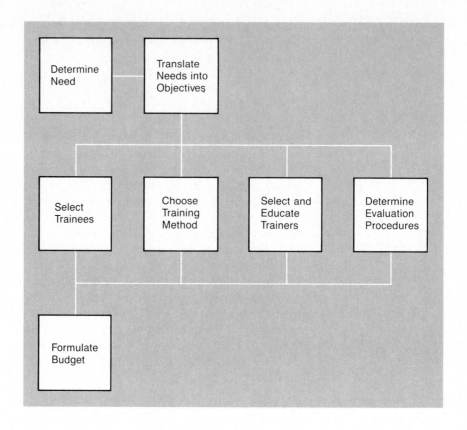

dividual employees. The seven major steps, as shown in Figure 11.1, involve:

1. Determining the need for skills training
2. Translating skills needs into training objectives
3. Selecting trainees
4. Choosing a training method
5. Selecting and educating trainers
6. Determining evaluation procedures
7. Formulating the budget

DETERMINING THE NEED FOR SKILLS TRAINING

The first major step in developing a skills training program is to determine the organization's *need* for such a program. There are several basic reasons for first determining the need for skills training.

First, training can be expensive. Good training, however, justifies its expense, while improper training causes added cost with no corresponding benefits.

Second, training that is not of sufficient quality to meet the needs of the organization and its members can actually be damaging. Workers who go through a skills training program and remain undertrained for the tasks their jobs require can become discouraged, discontented, and perhaps ex-employees.

Third, overtrained workers can become discouraged because of boredom with an unchallenging job or frustration with a lack of appropriate promotion opportunities. Overtrained workers are also apt to leave the firm.

Management and the human resources staff should be alert to any indications that employees need additional training. Excessive customer complaints about service could indicate a need for training. Similarly, excessive waste material could indicate that machine operators need more training. High employee turnover in a department could indicate that supervisors need additional training in human relations.

Although all of these deficiencies might indicate a need for additional training, a more systematic approach is required to assess needs properly. Management should analyze (1) organizational needs, (2) job requirements, and (3) the present skill levels of employees.

Analyzing Organizational Needs

The analysis of organizational needs should revolve around the number of employees with various combinations of skills needed at each level and in every part of the firm for specified periods. One portion of the organizational analysis, for example, might focus on determining which departments need how many qualified welders, and when they will be needed.

The human resources staff should also decide how much about the company's policies employees should learn during skills training. Although not always considered part of skills training, orientation regarding company policy and practices can be particularly important, especially for new employees. For example, some new employees may have acquired their basic skills in a training or vocational program not operated by the hiring organization and may still need instruction in how their new employer does things.

Analyzing Job Specifications

Many organizations have written job specifications that define the skills needed for each job in the firm. By carefully examining these specifications, the human resources staff can obtain a clear idea of the nature of skills needed for each job. A secretarial position, for example, might require skills such as telephone answering, typing, word processing, transcription, and bookkeeping.

The human resources staff must also ensure that the specifications are up-to-date, accurate, and complete. (The written job description for a secretarial position in a firm, for example, may still include skills involving taking dictation and filing, which the firm's secretaries are no longer required to do.) Periodic discussions with supervisors responsible for each job can often be quite helpful in accomplishing this task. The human resources staff can compare the written job specifications with the supervisors' perceptions of the skills they believe workers should have for each job.

The supervisor can also indicate any specific skills that recent employees still lack after completing various training programs. Telephone etiquette and listening skills, for example, may have been omitted. The supervisor's responses can therefore serve as a way to evaluate existing training programs and to improve future ones.

Analyzing Worker Skills and Qualifications

If employee personnel files are up-to-date and accurate, the analysis of worker skills and qualifications can be relatively simple. When conducting this analysis, two steps are key. The first is determining to what extent the organization currently employs individuals with skills needed now and in the future. Second, this analysis should be used to design the specific skills training programs needed to close the gap between the organization's needs and the present qualifications of its employees.

TRANSLATING SKILLS NEEDS INTO TRAINING OBJECTIVES

Once training needs have been determined, the human resources staff is ready to translate the skills needed into specific **training objectives,** or desired outcomes of the program. Training programs should then be designed to meet these objectives.

Training objectives should state the specific number of people to be trained, the specific skills on which the training should focus, and the period within which the training should be completed. For example, part of a firm's training could be based on the following objective:

> To have fourteen employees complete the training program in statistical quality-control techniques by December 1, 1988. The fourteen who complete this program should consist of twelve inspectors and two supervisors, each of whom should be able to provide statistical quality control for any company production line.

Objectives for the training program that do not relate directly to specific job skills should also be considered. Examples of these kinds of objectives include employee health and safety guidelines, promotion opportunities, and self-study opportunities.

SELECTING TRAINEES

Selecting individuals for training is a very important decision for both the organization and the individuals chosen. From the organization's perspective, providing the right training to the right people can help create and maintain a well-trained and stable work force. Conversely, mistakes can be costly. Providing training for individuals with limited performance potential is simply a waste of time, effort, and money. Overlooking individuals with ambition and potential represents a lost opportunity and can contribute to higher employee turnover.

From the individual's perspective, those selected for additional training are likely to receive higher pay, additional prestige, and greater opportunities for promotion. Those not selected can suffer a loss of prestige among fellow workers and effectively can be blocked from promotion.

The overriding considerations are that those individuals who are selected for training programs should be trainable and as likely to stay with the firm, thereby using their new skills to benefit the organization. But three other considerations are also important in selecting trainees: (1) federal regulations and legal guidelines, (2) employee needs and motivation, and (3) employee obsolescence and retraining.

Federal Regulations and Legal Guidelines

Federal regulations and legal guidelines have a significant impact on trainee selection. These guidelines have a twofold purpose. First, some guidelines encourage the selection of economically disadvantaged individuals for training programs as a way of reducing the total number of economically disadvantaged persons in the society. Second, other guidelines focus on preventing discrimination in the selection of trainees because of race, sex, age, and the like.

Ideally, managements of organizations should be interested in getting the best people into their training programs without regard to any factors other than their qualifications. A firm may pursue an affirmative action program, however, either voluntarily or as a legal requirement, by placing a specific number of people from minority backgrounds into certain training programs.

The Equal Employment Opportunity Commission (EEOC) has the authority to investigate complaints and to take legal action to remedy discrimination in training programs. To avoid such legal action, the human resources director must ensure that individuals recommended for training by supervisors are recommended on the basis of their *job-related* abilities and that the selection procedures do not have an adverse impact on any individual because of race, sex, color, religion, or national origin.[5]

Employee Needs and Motivation

Employee needs and motivation for training must also be part of the selection criteria. The human resources staff should try to determine the extent to which the training relates to real job and career needs experienced by the candidate and the extent to which the employee is motivated to work hard in training sessions. Although the determination of need and motivation can be difficult to make accurately, previous performance evaluations, as well as interviews with individual employees and their supervisors, can sometimes be quite helpful. The nature of the employee interview and many of the specific questions asked are similar to the procedures and questions in interviews for hiring purposes. These training interviews are particularly important when the training can significantly upgrade the employee's skill level and job prospects.

Skills Obsolescence and Retraining

Continuous technological progress can cause an employee's skills to become obsolete. Individual firms experience employee skill obsolescence as new processes are adopted and ways of doing things change.

State and federal governments are also becoming more sensitive to retraining issues. California, for example, has created a program that focuses on displaced workers and jobless youngsters. The Employment Training Panel (ETP) is financed by unemployment insurance and can provide organizations with grants for training or retraining current and new employees. The organization chooses the workers to be trained for a specific job and decides whether to conduct the training in-house or at a vocational school or community college. Other states, including New York, have adopted similar programs or are considering them. Organizations with access to these programs can seek their aid in retraining workers whose skills have become obsolete.[6]

Firms can also turn to the federally sponsored Job Training Partnership Act (JTPA) for help in retraining workers. Employers have a greater voice in the JTPA than in previous federal programs, primarily through their involvement and membership in Private Industry Councils (PICs). When PIC members have similar retraining needs, they can influence the type of training provided in their area.[7]

CHOOSING A TRAINING METHOD

Management should now be in a position to make one of the most important training decisions: choosing specific training methods. If the objectives have been stated properly and the trainees selected carefully, selecting the most appropriate training methods should be relatively easy.

On-the-Job Training

Many firms use **on-the-job training (OJT)** as their primary skills training technique. Although OJT can be quite effective, some firms mistakenly view it as putting employees to work and hoping they pick up enough information and experience to survive and perform acceptably. This approach is not true OJT. True OJT includes specific procedures for delivering actual training to the employee. One method for doing this is known as **job instruction training (JIT).**

The JIT system was developed originally by the War Manpower Commission during World War II. The JIT system includes the major characteristics of any effective training program: determination of training needs, recognition of the needs of the trainee, feedback from the trainee, frequent appraisal, and correction.

JIT is the number-one method of training for several reasons. First, it can yield effective training results at a relatively low cost. Second, it is relatively easy to teach to supervisors responsible for providing OJT to their subordinates. Third, different specific train-

PERSPECTIVE 11.1   How Workers Get Their Training

To learn more about occupational training, the Bureau of Labor Statistics, under a contract with the Employment and Training Administration of the U.S. Department of Labor, has analyzed data collected by the Census Bureau in a supplement to the January 1983 Current Population Survey. The supplement was developed around two basic questions: "Did you need specific skills or training to obtain your current job?" and "Since you obtained your present job, did you take any training to improve your skills?" In each case, people who responded "yes" were asked to identify the source or sources of the training and provide additional information. Many workers identified more than one source of training. Individuals did not identify the most important source of training, so the results simply indicate the frequency of a response.

About 55 percent of all workers employed in January 1983 indicated that they needed specific training to qualify for their current job. And about one-third of all workers had taken skill improvement training after obtaining their current job. Many workers had both qualifying training and training to improve their skills; about 72 percent of those who needed training to obtain their jobs subsequently trained to improve their skills.

Source: Excerpted from Max Carey and Alan Eck, "How Workers Get Their Training," *Occupational Outlook Quarterly* (Winter 1984): 3

Among major occupational groups, the proportion of workers who reported needing training to get their jobs varied widely. In professional specialty occupations, 93 percent of the workers needed training, compared to only 8 percent of the workers in private household occupations. With regard to skill improvement, the proportion who took training ranged from 61 percent in professional specialty occupations to 3 percent in private household occupations. The kind of training taken also varied widely, with more than one kind being indicated for each occupation. . . .

Sources of Training

School and informal on-the-job training (OJT) were the most common sources of both qualifying and additional training. About 29 percent of all workers obtained qualifying training in school and 28 percent obtained it on the job. OJT was used to improve skills by 14 percent of all workers; school programs, by 12 percent. Almost the same proportion of workers (10 and 11 percent) used training from formal company programs to qualify for jobs and to improve skills.

Relatively few workers acquired either qualifying or skill improvement training from other sources, such as correspondence courses, the Armed Forces, or friends and relatives.

---

ing techniques can be used in conjunction with JIT, such as classroom training, simulation, and others discussed below. Fourth, since much of the training is provided by an individual's supervisor or coworkers, there is assurance that the training relates directly to the specific work situation.

Apprenticeship Training

Apprenticeship programs, in which employees learn by working with those already skilled in their jobs, are the primary means for entering approximately 400 skilled trades in the United States, such as welding, pipefitting, and other crafts.[8] Most apprenticeship programs begin with classroom training that focuses on theory and on auxiliary skills needed to perform the job. The trainee then goes on the job, where at first he or she is allowed to perform limited tasks only. The performance of more elaborate or sophisticated tasks is allowed and encouraged as the trainee's skill and experience increase. Eventually, the trainee should be able to perform all of the job-related tasks of a skilled craft worker. The typical apprenticeship program lasts approximately four years and is generally conducted under a cooperative relationship among unions, employers, and/or vocational schools.

There is some evidence indicating that apprenticeship programs are the best way to teach craft skills.[9] Some observers, however, believe that many apprenticeship programs have had serious deficiencies in that they have discriminated against minorities and women. In recent years, much progress has been made in allowing minorities and women into apprenticeship programs, particularly in the building trades.

Vestibule Training

Vestibule training is the practice of giving skills training to individuals after they are hired, but before they are assigned to specific jobs. Vestibule training is not widely used because it often focuses on skills that firms expect workers to have when they are hired.

Vestibule training does have certain potential benefits for some organizations, however, such as those that employ a number of disadvantaged individuals (who may not meet minimum job qualifications) and those that need employees with hard-to-find specialized skills (such as firms in various high-technology fields). Organizations such as these may have no alternative but to provide training in basic skills.

Preemployment training programs are a version of vestibule training in which job seekers are tested and instructed in employment fundamentals without pay. Nissan's program in Smyrna, Tennessee lasts up to 360 hours and consists of a battery of manual-dexterity tests and instruction in tool use and manufacturing processes. Trainees are rated on their willingness to work as well as on job aptitude. Nissan hires about 90 percent of its preemployment trainees. The General Motors/Toyota plant in California has also begun preemployment training, and both Mazda and Chrysler are expected to introduce similar programs in the near future. All of these programs operate with some state subsidies.[10]

Off-the-Job Training

All of the training techniques discussed thus far are either OJT approaches or are a major component of an OJT program. A variety of off-the-job training methods can also be effective.

Internal training seminars help employees to perform more effectively in their present jobs, to contribute in future positions, and to work well in teams.

Courtesy of Hewlett-Packard Company

Lectures and Conferences. Many firms use lectures and conferences as vehicles for delivering training in many types of skills. In fact, most training programs, including OJT, use lectures and/or conferences as part of their overall approach. Most training programs, for example, actually begin with a lecture or a conference.

Depending on several factors, lectures and conferences can be held on-site or at facilities away from the firm. Organizations typically conduct these meetings on-site if qualified trainers are available in-house or if trainers can be brought in temporarily and if no special facilities are required. If required training facilities are not available on-site, the training program must be conducted elsewhere. Organizations sometimes hold conferences off-site in order to provide a more relaxed environment and to minimize the usual work-place distractions such as telephone calls.

Programmed, Computer-Assisted Instruction. Programmed, computer-assisted instruction is one of the fastest growing training techniques. Although rudimentary teaching machines were used as early as 1924, the widespread availability of computers has greatly furthered the use of programmed training. Computerized training systems are available for a wide range of jobs, including those of serving person, mechanic, repair person, and jet pilot.[11]

Computer simulation of job situations is of particular importance. Many tasks can be simulated with the aid of a computer to allow the trainee to gain the practical equivalent of on-the-job experience.

The computer also permits training in which the trainee works directly with the computer program.[12] For example, the trainee can read questions directly from the computer screen, supply his or her answer via the keyboard, and immediately receive a grade or a corrected answer. This immediate feedback can be quite beneficial, especially if the trainee must master one unit of material before proceeding to new material.

Audio-Visual Aids. Audio-visual materials, such as films and television, are also used in skills training programs. They can be used with other approaches, such as lectures and conferences, or alone for brush-up training and the like.

The wide availability of videocassette recording (VCR) equipment has encouraged greater use of audio-visual training. A potentially valuable use of VCR materials involves taping training sessions conducted by the best in-house trainers and distributing these tapes throughout the company as instructional cassettes. This approach can yield the benefits of quality training without the expense of sending the best trainers to remote sites. The most serious disad-

---

PERSPECTIVE 11.2 New Ways to Teach Workers What's New

At Ford dealerships, to take a typical use of the new training technology, a mechanic who needs to know more about carburetors can get a closeup of an engine on the screen and then use a light pen to simulate what he would do with a vacuum gauge and screwdriver to get the engine tuned. As he adjusts the carburetor, he hears the engine noise changing. When he thinks he has it right, he touches a certain spot on the screen and the computer either congratulates him or sends him back to where he made a mistake.

Service and sales companies also use the new trainers. At 450 Sizzler restaurants around the U.S., new employees can roll a videodisc system out of a closet when business is slack and take a lesson. The screen will show a customer giving an order, for example, and the employee tries to write it down. Then the screen shows what the order slip should look like.

Both employers and employees like the way high-tech training can brighten up lessons with sound, motion, and color to keep the student involved. J.C. Penney chose interactive training to

teach inventory control partly because classes and books on the subject are so boring. "You can lose half your class," says Ted Boggio, manager of Penney's merchandise systems training. "They doze off. Videodisc is dynamic. We can provide talking heads and interesting visuals. We add life, interest, dialogue, spark, into what is really a deadly dull subject." Penney finds the new course teaches students what they need to know in half the time of the old one.

To employers the cost saving and practicality of high-tech training are at least as appealing as its power to teach. Employers put a lot of resources into training. The American Society for Training and Development estimates the annual costs in the U.S. at $30 billion, not counting the huge training costs of the armed forces. Other estimates go as high as $100 billion if salaries and benefits paid during courses are included. For many companies the biggest cost is the travel and per diem allowances for workers sent off to schools and training centers. Interactive systems can be expensive to set up, but they teach right at or near the workplace. If a company with several plants or branches buys enough copies of the system, travel expenses can be eliminated.

Source: Excerpted from Jeremy Main, "New Ways to Teach Workers What's New," *Fortune,* October 1, 1984, p. 86.

---

vantage of this approach is the lack of interaction between the trainer and the trainee.

Two-way satellite transmission or teleconferencing is another advance in audio-visual technology that can be used in skills training. Although still relatively expensive, this form of transmitting training material may become much more affordable in the future. Its primary advantage is that it allows interaction between trainees and trainers at remote sites.

SELECTING AND EDUCATING TRAINERS

An effective training program cannot be developed if effective trainers are not available. Organizations have the option of using in-house trainers or seeking trainers outside, or doing both.

In-house Trainers

When available, in-house trainers can be less expensive than trainers who are independent contractors, depending on the total training load. Internal training can also be totally designed and executed by the organization. The key to success, however, is selecting the right individuals and providing them with the tools they need to be effective.

Selecting good trainers is often not as easy as it may sound. Many firms, for example, tend to select their best workers as trainers. Although this can work well, two potential problems must be considered. First, the most productive workers are taken away from their production tasks. Second, high productivity does not necessarily mean that a worker will be a good trainer. In addition to possessing expertise, a good trainer must be able to explain and teach.

Once selected, trainers must be educated in the overall process of training and in the specific training program they will be involved with. For example, they must understand the program's objectives so they can develop appropriate presentations. Further, they may need to learn more about how people learn (see the section headed "Principles of Learning" later in this chapter). The human resources manager can be particularly helpful in this area.

Outside Trainers

If in-house trainers are not available because of inadequate qualifications or for reasons such as production pressures, the firm can turn to outside trainers. When outside trainers are sought, both the individual trainers and the training organization must be evaluated carefully to ensure quality training. If external facilities are also to be used, they must naturally be inspected. Before such training begins, at least one conference should be held with members of the outside training organization to discuss issues such as training objectives and to provide any other information the trainers might need.

The use of outside trainers has several advantages. First, productive employees are not taken off the job. Second, firms can be hired that specialize in training and have experienced trainers who understand the process of training and how it should be done. Third, the time, effort, and cost of arranging specialized outside training can sometimes be less than for internal development of a similar training program. Fourth, the organization needing training has a wider choice from which to select training programs, which is particularly important when the training involves skills not currently being used in the firm. Fifth, the firm may have more control because it is generally easier to dismiss an external trainer than to redirect and improve an internal training program.

DETERMINING EVALUATION PROCEDURES

The results of all training programs should be evaluated. The five key purposes of conducting this evaluation are to:

1. Determine whether a program meets its objectives
2. Identify strengths and weaknesses in the training process
3. Calculate the cost/benefit ratio of a program
4. Determine who benefited the most from a program and why
5. Establish a data base for future decisions about the program.[13]

Training programs can be evaluated with a variety of methods. The most popular method involves analyzing questionnaires filled out by the trainees either at the end of the training session or within a few weeks.[14] Although in some situations employees can accurately evaluate the quality of the training program, their subsequent performance or degree of improvement is a more valid measure in other situations.

If specific performance factors can be measured, the trainees' performance after the training can be compared with the objectives for the training program.[15] If the training objectives have been met, then the training has been successful. For example, a training objective could be to train ten people to type a minimum of fifty words per minute with an error rate of less than 1 percent. In this case evaluating the success of the training program would involve testing the typing skills of all trainees both before and after the training. If the objective was found to have been met, the program would be evaluated as having been successful.

FORMULATING THE BUDGET

The human resources director should now be able to determine the cost of the training program and formulate a detailed training budget. Budget constraints may limit the human resources manager's alternatives and must therefore be considered during all phases of the development process.

Costs that must be included in the training budget include staff planning time, trainee wages, trainer wages, and direct expenses such as the cost of training materials, travel, accommodations, and meals. If the desired training program does not fit within budget constraints, the human resources manager must consider modifications, such as fewer trainees, different trainers, different training techniques, and a different training location.

ROLE OF HUMAN RESOURCES DIRECTORS AND OTHER MANAGERS

Both human resources directors and other managers play critical roles in the development of training programs. The human resources director must assume leadership in developing such programs. He or she is responsible for assessing training needs; de-

Career progression at IBM through retraining.

In 1964, Wayne Hazelwood began a new career.

In October 1964, Wayne Hazelwood joined us at IBM.

He was a typewriter assembler at our Lexington, Kentucky, plant.

He was well qualified.

And he was very good at his job.

Then we made changes in the way we manufacture typewriters.

So the job Wayne had been performing so well for us was no longer necessary.

Which raises one of the great questions facing American business today: in a world of rapidly changing technology, how can a company move ahead without leaving good people behind?

In 1975, Wayne Hazelwood began a new career.

At IBM, one solution is retraining.

In November 1975, Wayne was selected to take an intensive IBM training program in typewriter inspection.

He spent over 250 hours learning new skills.

Soon after, he began work with us as a Selectric™ typewriter quality inspector.

He liked his new career.

And he did his job very well.

But in time, as a result of new developments in typewriter technology, he needed to learn new skills.

In 1980, Wayne Hazelwood began a new career.

In October 1980, Wayne was offered the chance to take IBM training in manufacturing instruction.

Within three months, he became an instructor for us.

He was able to use his sixteen years of experience in manufacturing to teach others who were just beginning.

He found his new career to be extremely creative.

And, as always, he did a terrific job.

But because of changes in our product line, well, you know what can happen.

And by now, you know that the ability to change, when changes demand it, is what Wayne's story is all about.

Guess what.

Today, Wayne Hazelwood is a valued member of our electronic card assembly technical staff.

And his twenty-one years and four careers at IBM speak as eloquently about retraining as anything we could say.

Over the years, we've retrained thousands of our employees by offering them the opportunity to learn new skills.

People who worked in supplies manufacturing are now senior assemblers. Customer engineers have been retrained as education coordinators. Machine operators have become senior inspection specialists.

Retraining has shown us how a company and its employees can change together in a changing world. Above all, it has shown us that jobs may come and go.

But people shouldn't.

IBM

Courtesy of International Business Machines Corporation

termining training objectives; selecting trainees; choosing the training method; planning, coordinating, and evaluating the training sessions; selecting and educating trainers; and formulating the training budget. Even when outside trainers are used, the human resources staff is still responsible for all of these tasks, but their direct involvement may be much less than when the training is done in-house. Another major responsibility of the human resources staff is coordinating the training program with managers and supervisors across the organization and getting them involved in the overall effort.

Managers and supervisors throughout the organization play a major role in providing information for the human resources department to use in developing and evaluating training programs. If properly involved, they can supply valuable information regarding training needs, trainee qualifications, training methods, and training evaluation. They can also participate directly in the training program as trainers. In fact, some managers feel that training to increase subordinates' performance capabilities is one of their most productive tasks.[16]

PRINCIPLES OF LEARNING

Several principles of learning are especially relevant to a discussion of skills training. Among these principles are trainee readiness, training significance, and reinforcement.

Trainee Readiness

People who are not ready to learn will not learn. Consequently, an effective training program must comprise individuals who are ready to learn the skills at hand. Determining trainee readiness involves examining two important issues.

First, the trainee must possess the skills and qualifications that are considered prerequisites for the present training. For example, individuals undergoing training to be accounts-receivable or accounts-payable clerks must be fairly adept at arithmetic. Similarly, many trainers are finding that the greatest drawback in teaching people to use personal computers is that many people do not know how to type.

Depending on the situation, when trainees lack the prerequisites, management must either seek other trainee candidates or provide the trainees with the additional background needed to prepare them for the desired training. Such pretraining is often particularly important when the trainees are drawn from affirmative-action-based programs.

Management has a vested interest in trainees' possessing minimum initial qualifications. Trainees who begin a training program without the prerequisites may become frustrated and discouraged. Their confidence in their ability to do the work can be destroyed. When this occurs, trainees are likely to drop out of the training program and, perhaps, leave the organization.

A second aspect of readiness that must be examined is whether the trainee candidates possess the desire to upgrade old skills or gain new skills. Although individuals can sometimes request or otherwise indicate their interest in training, in other situations their interest can sometimes be quite difficult to ascertain. Problems can arise, for example, when training is mandatory, such as when the training is related to a new process or approach the organization is undertaking. Employees often feel threatened by change because they are comfortable with the old ways of doing things. In situations such as these, the training program must be designed so that the trainees learn and understand early the need for the training and why they should participate. Essentially, the trainer must nurture the trainees' desire to be trained.

Training Relevance

Most trainees quickly develop perceptions about whether training is relevant. If trainees perceive that the instruction will actually help them on the job, they are much more likely to be receptive to the training. If they do not perceive relevance, they are more likely to demonstrate active or passive resistance to the training. For example, if automotive mechanics and their supervisors do not perceive the importance of training in customer relations, they certainly won't learn anything. They must first be made aware that their relationship with customers can help minimize customer dissatisfaction and gain repeat business for the firm. (Management may have to stimulate this awareness with positive financial incentives.)

At Southern Caterpillar Services, discussed in Case 11.2, the training was too long and contained material that was not going to be used very often by most of the trainees, particularly during their first few years of employment. Some trainees were frightened by the scope of the training, while others were frustrated by its lack of relevance. If the program had been better designed and the trainees had understood its actual importance, employee turnover might have been less and those remaining with the organization would have been better trained.

Reinforcement

Reinforcement is another critical principle of learning. It involves the process of providing financial rewards or nonfinancial incentives (such as praise or recognition) when the trainee reaches a higher level of skill. Training programs should be divided into segments or phases so the trainees can show improvement and achievement periodically and frequently. The trainer can then provide reinforcement incentives as the trainee reaches each progressive skill level.

Reinforcement can often encourage trainees to become more interested and involved in the training, thereby improving the quality and rate of learning. All training programs should contain a plan for reinforcement.

SUMMARY

Skills training involves experiences directed by the organization to help employees learn information and behavior that contribute to organizational and individual goals. Organizations in the United States spend billions of dollars each year on training programs. Developing a training program consists of seven basic steps.

First, the need for skills training must be determined. To determine the need, management must analyze organizational needs, job specifications, and employees' skill levels.

Second, the skills needs must be translated into specific training objectives. The training objectives should state the specific number of people to be trained, the specific skills on which the training should focus, and the time for completing the training.

Third, the trainees must be selected. When selecting trainees, management must consider relevant federal and legal guidelines, employee needs and motivation for training, and employee obsolescence and retraining needs.

Fourth, a training method(s) must be chosen. On-the-job alternatives include job instruction training, apprenticeship training, and vestibule and preemployment training. Off-the-job training alternatives include lectures and conferences; programmed, computer-assisted instruction; and audio-visual aids.

Fifth, trainers must be selected and educated. Both in-house trainers and outside training specialists can be considered.

Sixth, evaluation procedures for the training program must be determined. The purposes of conducting this evaluation are to determine whether a program meets its objectives, to identify strengths and weaknesses of the program, to calculate the cost/benefit ratio, to determine who benefited the most from a program and why, and to establish a data base for future decisions.

Seventh, the budget for the training program must be formulated. Both the total training budget and the benefits of the specific training program must be considered.

Two other key issues must also be recognized. First, both human resources directors and other managers play critical roles in the development of effective training programs. Second, training programs must be compatible with principles of learning, particularly trainee readiness, training significance, and reinforcement.

KEY TERMS

training   on-the-job training (OJT)   vestibule training
retraining   job instruction training (JIT)
training objectives   apprenticeship programs

REVIEW QUESTIONS

1. Discuss the importance of skills training. List and discuss the major factors that should be analyzed to assess needs properly.
2. Discuss the major issues relating to setting objectives for skills training.
3. Discuss the major factors that should be considered in selecting trainees.
4. List and discuss the major on-the-job and off-the-job training methods.
5. Discuss the major issues regarding using in-house and outside trainers.
6. Why should training programs be evaluated?
7. Discuss the role of human resource managers and line managers in skills training.
8. Discuss the key principles of learning as they pertain to skills training.

OPENING CASE QUESTIONS

Case 11.1   High-Tech Terror

1. Why do Penny and Amy have such different opinions of their word processors. Did Penny get on-the-job training?
2. If you Were Penny's boss, what would you do now? How might you recognize that there is a problem?

Case 11.2   Southern Caterpillar Services

1. What is your opinion of Southern Caterpillar's philosophy that every mechanic be able to do every job that they might encounter?
2. How would you change the training program at Southern Caterpillar?

CASE 11.3   ON-THE-JOB SCHOOLING

Most companies routinely pay for new employees' on-the-job training. Very few people come from school or another job knowing exactly how to operate a company's machines or to manage a company's chain of command. But for more and more companies, on-the-job training has become less important than on-the-job schooling, as companies take over many of the tasks traditionally assigned to high schools and colleges.

Educational programs run in, by, or for businesses are much more extensive than most people would guess. While $60 billion are spent annually on colleges and universities, corporations spend over $40 billion a year to educate close to 8 million employees.

This corporate education takes two different forms: one supplements what employees learned in schools and colleges, while the other tries to make up for what they should have learned, but didn't. The Institute of Textile Technology is an example of the former. Thirty-five textile companies support the Institute, which graduates masters of science who have learned management techniques and the latest high-tech manufacturing skills. The program takes two years, combines work and study, and is as rigorous as many university graduate programs, although it is more directly industry-related.

At the other end of the educational scale are programs like the one at New York Telephone, where 500 to 1,000 employees a year participate in classes focusing on basic math and language skills. The program, which has the seemingly modest goal of raising employees' skills to the ninth or tenth grade level, cost the company about $300,000 in 1985.

Many companies—about three-quarters of those in one survey—sponsor this kind of remedial program because they find that employees often can't handle the simplest kinds of tasks with words or numbers. Such gaps in employees' skills can be costly for a company. Executives tell horror stories of the employee who sent out a check for $2200 rather than $22 because the employee didn't understand the decimal point, or the worker whose inability to use a ruler cost a company $700 worth of material, or the time CBS News correspondent Fred Graham stumbled in his report because the technician turning the teleprompter couldn't read.

Besides providing in-house training, many companies that worry about the state of basic education in the country fund programs like Literacy Volunteers of America, the Coalition for Literacy, and the Business Council for Effective Literacy. Companies also often work in conjunction with schools and colleges, hiring speakers to go to schools to explain the importance of basic skills, or

Case Sources: Ezra Bowen, "Schooling for Survival," *Time,* Vol. 125, No. 6, February 11, 1985, 74; Carey W. English, "As Businesses Turn Offices Into Classrooms," *U.S. News & World Report,* Vol. 98, No. 12, April 1, 1985, 70; "How Business is Joining the Fight Against Functional Illiteracy," *Business Week,* No. 2838, April 16, 1984, 94.

"adopting" a school and providing it with tutors, lecturers, and advice on necessary job skills.

Somewhere between the Institute of Textile Technology and these company remedial programs lie the big corporate educational facilities, among them the widely-respected Wang Institute of Graduate Studies. Started by computer genius An Wang, the institute was the first in the country to offer a full-time master of software engineering degree. Like many company schools, the institute offers modern facilities that any college would envy. Xerox has a 2,265-acre facility near Leesburg, Virginia, that trains 1,200 students a year and provides them with a pool and gyms for their off-hours. IBM spends $700 million on education each year and recently consolidated its four major corporate technical institutes into one.

The DeVry Institutes, a subsidiary of Bell & Howell, take a different approach. A profit-making enterprise with 11 institutes and 30,000 students, DeVry concentrates on "education for the real world," focusing on the technical though requiring students to take some psychology, English, history, and literature courses. DeVry students like the approach and are confident of getting jobs.

Opinions vary about the quality and long-range usefulness of the 12 million courses paid for by businesses. And traditional educators worry that businesses put too much emphasis on specialized knowledge. Still, there is a clear gap in the country's ability to educate itself, and as long as that gap exists, businesses will continue to try to fill it.

Discussion Questions

1. How do you think remedial on-the-job schooling might improve the effectiveness of an organization's job-based skills training?
2. Suppose you are the human resources manager at a printing company that is opening a new manufacturing plant in a small southwestern city. Unemployment in the city is very low, and you are finding it hard to attract applicants for the less-skilled jobs at the new plant; and few of those who do apply meet the basic qualification of functional literacy. You have decided to recommend that the company implement a remedial program at the plant to give applicants the schooling needed to meet the minimum qualification. Will you recommend a vestibule training format, or a preemployment training format open to anyone who wants to attend?

Management and Career Development

LEARNING OBJECTIVES

- Discuss the organizational considerations that underlie the planning of effective development programs.
- Describe the employee needs that must be considered when planning the development program.
- List several factors that influence the success of a management development program.
- Describe on-the-job and off-the-job methods for managerial and supervisory development.
- Indicate specific objectives of career development programs for nonsupervisors, women, and minorities.
- Outline the steps in evaluating management and career development programs.

CASE 12.1   WHERE HAVE ALL THE MANAGERS GONE?

Louise Smith, the human resources manager for Stores, Inc., had a difficult problem. She needed to recommend four store managers for the four new stores the firm was planning to open during the next three months. A close examination of the company's human resources revealed that there were no assistant managers with more than three years' experience, which was far less than the experience necessary for the store manager's position.

Ten years earlier, Stores, Inc. had adopted a fast-growth strategy of opening four to eight new stores each year. At that time, store managers were required to have had at least ten years of experience in positions of increasing responsibility. That requirement had been relaxed considerably to help the organization meet its growing need for managers. The company had also begun to hire experienced managers from competitors at inflated salaries.

Louise did not want to face her boss, the founder of Stores, Inc., with her problem. She was even considering "retiring" herself.

CASE 12.2   HOW MUCH IS ENOUGH?

As Stan Rush, vice president of human resources, read the letter he was both angry and frightened. The Equal Employment Opportunity Commission wanted to know why a firm whose work force was 60 percent female had only 20 percent female managers.

Stan's anger was caused by the fact that he had instituted programs to equalize women's salaries and to hire and promote solely on the basis of qualifications. His fear was that these programs would not matter. Although women employees could seek any managerial position, few had applied. He knew his response to the EEOC would be critical, and that more had to be done to get more women managers on staff.

Management and career development programs represent efforts to increase the organization's present and future ability to meet its goals by providing educational and developmental experiences for managers and all employees above and beyond the immediate technical requirements of their jobs. In today's highly competitive and rapidly changing business world, managerial development is particularly important. In addition to competence in their own areas of specialization, managers must be prepared to handle new assignments and meet the complex demands of modern organizational life.

Formal programs specifically designed to prepare employees for managerial positions are widespread and can be considered part of the overall management and career development effort in organizations. One report states that 30 percent of the people in managerial positions at the beginning of the 1980s will be replaced during the decade.[1] Without managers capable of directing and motivating employees and performing other managerial tasks, high employee skill levels will not be enough to make a firm successful. This chapter focuses on planning and executing effective management and career development programs. Examples of topics covered in such programs are shown in Table 12.1.

PLANNING EFFECTIVE DEVELOPMENT PROGRAMS

The development of appropriate and effective management and career development programs requires consideration of both organizational and employee needs. Five common themes appear to underlie many of the training needs in today's organizations.[2] These themes tend to match prevailing organizational and environmental characteristics:

1. Managerial careers are in a state of flux as new jobs are opening up and traditional, stable jobs are disappearing.

TABLE 12.1
Topics covered in
supervisory training

TOPICS COVERED	PERCENTAGE OF ALL ORGANIZATIONS
Communications	87.6%
Leadership	82.4
Company policies	76.0
Management theory	74.9
Problem solving	72.0
EEO problems	68.8
Goal setting	67.0
Planning	61.3
Counseling	56.6
Training	53.8
Interviewing	53.8
Administration	51.4
Market topics	48.6
Labor relations	47.7
Company history, goals	44.8
Compensation	44.8
Safety	44.2
Technical topics	26.6
Economics	12.7
Other	6.6

Source: Prentice-Hall Inc. and The American Society for Personnel Administration, "Employee Training Survey," in *Personnel Management: Policies and Practices* (Englewood Cliffs, N.J.: Prentice Hall, June 12, 1979), Report No. 2.

2. People want to know more about their immediate jobs, about other jobs in their organization, and about their organization as a whole.
3. Employees need their organization's help to help themselves.
4. Basic skills (for example, mathematics, grammar) are still important and cannot be overlooked.
5. Many career transitions represent ideal training opportunities, such as when employees start a new job, experience technological or other changes on their present jobs, or anticipate organizational changes.

Organizational Considerations

An effective management and career development program must naturally meet the needs of the organization. Management must therefore determine its needs and convert those needs into objectives to guide the formulation of the program. Although each organization may possess a unique combination of needs, it can be helpful to group organizational needs into four basic categories: (1) human resources planning, (2) organization adaptation and improvement, (3) organizational culture and climate, and (4) organizational effectiveness.[3]

Human Resources Planning. Human resources planning is a primary component of the management development program. Since firms that run out of promotable managers face serious consequences, as Louise Smith recognized in Case 12.1, the human resources director must ensure that there are enough managers with appropriate technical and human skills to fill all anticipated positions. Failure to do so typically results in emergency "crash" development programs, the hiring of competent managers away from competitors, or promotion of someone who is simply not ready to handle the job. None of these alternatives is particularly attractive, and all can be more expensive than a well-planned development program.

To ensure continuous availability of managerial talent, the human resources director should carefully analyze the firm's current human resources chart to determine how many managers will be needed in the future and when. This analysis involves two major components. First, management turnover rates must be forecast, such as by tracking managers' ages in relation to retirement and examining normal attrition due to voluntary departures and dismissals. Second, changes in the organization's human resources chart must be analyzed. For example, does the firm anticipate new managerial positions as a result of growth or expansion or fewer managerial positions because of contraction? Stores, Inc. in Case 12.1 had apparently failed to complete this second step adequately, or, if it had, it hadn't followed through on the implications.

The results of this phase of human resources planning should indicate the number of managers needed. Since some individuals may not progress as desired, more prospective candidates should begin the development program than will actually be needed. This means, of course, that candidates should understand that participation in a development program does not guarantee promotion.

Organization Adaptation and Improvement. Another major area of need of management and career development involves organization adaptation and improvement. Successful organizations tend to match or fit the environments in which they operate. Further, they continuously strive to improve their internal processes so that they can more quickly and effectively adapt. Essentially, the management development program should provide the organization with the ability to adapt to changing environmental conditions.

To help ensure environmental fit, the human resources manager must understand the overall goals and strategies of the organization and the character of managerial expertise needed to achieve these goals and strategies. For example, if the organization intends to grow rapidly by developing new products internally, it will need managers able to create and nurture an innovative and entrepreneurial spirit. Conversely, if an organization intends to focus on cost control as the key to success, the management development program should be oriented toward developing managers who are cost conscious and adept at cost control.

Organizational Culture and Climate. The management development program can also focus on maintaining and nurturing the desired organizational culture and climate. When the top management of an organization considers its culture and climate of paramount importance, the management development program, or at least portions of it, must focus on fostering appropriate managerial skills. The top managements of many successful firms, for example, feel that everyone in the organization must be oriented toward delivering customer satisfaction, thereby making high concern for customer needs a key aspect of organizational culture. In these firms, enhancement of customer-oriented attitudes is a priority in all training and development programs.

Organizational Effectiveness. The overriding concern in virtually all management development programs is that they make the organization more effective. Organizational effectiveness is influenced by a variety of factors (see Chapter 4), many of which can be incorporated into management development programs. For example, a clear understanding of available managerial career paths can result in higher job satisfaction, lower management turnover rates, and greater loyalty to the organization. In general, if employees understand the nature of other jobs and managerial positions in the firm, communication throughout the organization can be enhanced, which increases organizational effectiveness.

Employee Considerations

An effective management and career development program can increase employee satisfaction and motivation. If this objective is to be met, employee needs must be considered when the development program is being planned. In addition to employee needs, management must consider union attitudes.

Need Fulfillment.   If designed properly, management development programs can help fulfill higher-order needs of the participants. Many managers, and those who aspire to be managers, have a strong need for achievement. Being selected for a management development program can sometimes be an achievement itself. It can also be a vehicle for subsequent achievement, such as promotion and other career goals. It is therefore important that those responsible for designing management development programs have a clear understanding of participants' needs and provide a clear understanding to the participants of how the program can help them fulfill their needs.

Another need that management development programs can help fulfill is the need to belong. This can be particularly important in supervisory training programs. The program may provide super-

---

PERSPECTIVE 12.1   Culture Club

The company that reads together, succeeds together, Judith Kaplan thought. Which is why she asked her employees to join her for pizza and *Megatrends.*

A minimegatrend statistic herself — Kaplan started a service business and moved it from New York to Florida, two of the directions for the 1980s cited in John Naisbitt's best-selling book — she was obviously a believer. And she wanted no less from her staff. Her theory: "If you understand the big picture, it shouldn't be hard to improve personally."

So last July, Kaplan invited the whole gang from Action Packets, Inc. (a wholesale supplier of gifts, books, and novelty items to public museums and employee gift shops on National Aeronautics and Space Administration bases) over to her Ocala, Fla., house. "I had to do some arm-twisting to get

Source: Excerpted from Ellen Kolton, "Culture Club," reprinted with permission, *Inc.* magazine, February, 1985. Copyright © 1985 by Inc. Publishing Company, 38 Commercial Wharf, Boston, MA 02110.

them to come," she admits. "I told them, 'I really expect you to do this.' "

Initially skeptical, most employees stayed away the first few times. But as word spread, more joined the biweekly discussions until 80% attendance became normal. Each session lasts a couple of hours and focuses on one chapter of the book being studied, with employees taking turns moderating. "There really is no format," Kaplan says. "We relate the book to what's happening in the company." After *Megatrends,* they started on (what else?) *In Search of Excellence.* Next came *A Whack on the Side of the Head,* by Roger von Oech, the self-described creativity guru of Silicon Valley. Kaplan describes *Whack* as "mind expanding."

Besides raising the staff's global consciousness, Kaplan's literary pizza fests also seem to be erasing interdepartmental confusion. Says John Carr, an account executive: "You can't think of these meetings as book-study groups. They are really a springboard for other things.". . .

. . . Judith Kaplan is delighted. "What we're trying to do is make people improve and meet the changes that are going on.". . .

visors with the chance to meet others in similar positions and to discuss problems of mutual interest. Since supervisors are in the awkward position of being directly between management and labor (and often recently part of labor), they may enter the training with feelings of frustration regarding their transition to management. In addition to fulfilling needs to belong, the development program may also show the supervisors that higher-level management does care about them. There is some evidence that these factors may be more important than the actual content of training.[4]

Union Attitudes.   Attitudes held by union leaders can have a tremendous impact on the effectiveness of development programs, particularly those involving members of the labor force who are moving into supervisory management positions. It is important that union leaders approve of the supervisory training programs so that they do not convey negative or cynical opinions to trainees. One way to secure this support is to involve the union leaders in developing the programs.

In actual practice, the degree of the union leaders' involvement in training and development programs varies greatly from organization to organization. Generally, organizations with good labor-management relationships have more union involvement. Union leaders are normally very interested in training and development programs for their members and may, in fact, sponsor their own training programs. By allowing union leaders to participate in the firm's training programs, management puts itself in a better position to become involved in the union's training programs.

Role of the Human Resources Department

Human resources staff members typically assist in determining training and development needs, recommending programs, developing seminars and teaching aids, scheduling classes, obtaining feedback on program effectiveness, and perhaps serving occasionally as trainers or conference leaders. The actual degree of participation in each of these activities often depends on whether the organization is large enough to have a separate training department.

In any organization, the human resources director must involve other managers in the training and development effort. Supervisors must understand and approve of the goals of the development program and help persuade potential participants that the program is relevant and beneficial. Supervisors can also be especially useful in helping to determine who will attend development programs. The enthusiastic support of management often leads to greater interest and enthusiasm among participants.

In less formal training situations, the human resources department may serve as an information source. It can provide information to employees about training opportunities that are not part of the organization's formal training program. It may also provide information about the firm's training policies, such as a college tuition refund program.

Successful Programs and Curricula

Many factors can influence the success of a management development program. Six specific keys to success have been formulated for internal development programs.[5]

1. Assure visible top management support. When top management thinks something is important, so do most other members of the organization. To help build and maintain top management support, efforts must be made by the human resources department to educate senior executives about the program, involve them at every stage, and frequently publicize program successes and positive results.
2. Carefully blend new ways of doing things with organizational norms. Successful programs must sometimes challenge certain organizational norms while respecting others. For example, some firms have found that training programs involving changes tend to be more successful when the traditional chain of command is respected and the program has a look that is polished and professional rather than experimental.
3. Ensure compatibility between individual training and organizational structure and systems. Some programs fail because the individual managers are given training that is wasted in an "overstructured" organizational environment, such as one with too many forms and rigid systems (for example, performance appraisal systems and job-grading schemes). Others fail because of inadequate follow-up. Merrill Lynch, for example, tries to avoid these problems by having top management discuss high-potential management candidates on a quarterly basis, providing mentors and advisory councils, and other activities.
4. Use existing resources, including training programs, information systems, and people. This helps control costs and builds a supportive climate.

FIGURE 12.1 Marion development wheel

MARION DEVELOPMENT WHEEL

FUTURE RESPONSIBILITIES ◆ CURRENT POSITION

INSIDE MARION—ON THE JOB

- On-the-job Coaching by Manager—The most effective means to develop associates. Impart skills and knowledge, answer questions, review work, discuss progress or lack of, and provide direction, work through actual problems as they develop to increase ability to handle future problems.
- Guided Experience—Similar to coaching except that it emphasizes specific development needs. Determine the primary development needs of the associate, build a plan of action, and assign responsibility.
- Job Performance Review and Development Discussion.
- Understudy Training—Prepare an associate to assume the responsibilities of the manager, as a substitute or a replacement.
- Job Enlargement or Enrichment—Expansion of job content to include a wider variety of tasks and greater responsibility.
- Job Rotation—Broaden knowledge and experience, and gain appreciation of viewpoints and inter-relationships of various groups within the organization through job rotation.
- Project, Committee, or Task Force Assignments—Committee or task force assignments to solve particular problems determine how well an individual works with others and demonstrates leadership and organization skills.
- Lateral Transfers or Special Assignments—Provide additional experience and an opportunity to evaluate future potential as shown by adaptation to new situations.
- Vacation or Illness Replacement Assignments—This experience is similar to the three previous items. It is stated separately for emphasis. One of the most underutilized opportunities for development.

OUTSIDE MARION

- Membership in Professional or Technical Societies—Contact with others working in the same field provides opportunities for exchanging information, for keeping up-to-date, and developing new ideas.
- Active Participation in Community and Civic Affairs—A good opportunity to experience leadership, develop communication skills and manage outside the work environment.
- Tuition Reimbursement Program at Local Educational Facilities—Marion provides financial assistance for formal education through colleges and universities.
- Home Study Courses—Another useful form of educational experience.
- Planned Independent Reading in Specialized Fields—Careful selection of management literature, trade journals, and technical books is a valuable development technique.
- Speaking Appearances—Speaking experience and associated preparation can contribute significantly to individual development.
- Attendance at Conferences, Lectures, Workshops, and Seminars—There are a wide variety of external opportunities for development. An action-oriented report to management should be required.

INSIDE MARION—OFF THE JOB

- Participation in Marion Development Programs—Formal development programs provide useful information, practice, and interdivisional discussion in a classroom setting.
- Attendance at Department or Staff Meetings—Another underutilized, yet effective means of broadening the knowledge and perspective of the individual.
- Provide Opportunities to Make Presentations—Develop individual planning and organizing skills and effectiveness in speaking and thinking in front of a group.
- Serving as Instructor, Conference Leader, or Trainer—A valuable way to obtain knowledge, broaden viewpoints, and clarify thinking through teaching others.
- Help From Specialists in the Organization—Encourage cross-functional exposure short of job rotation.
- Studying Manuals, Bulletins, Reports, and Other Printed Material—Excellent source materials are generally available.

Source: Marion Laboratories, Inc.

5. Build multiple feedback loops. Since people learn and gauge the extent of their learning by obtaining feedback from their environment (that is, from friends, supervisors, spouses, technology, meetings, presentations, and the like), training programs should also have built-in feedback. Examples of feedback loops include written evaluations, peer evaluations, discussions with mentors and supervisors, and advisory councils.
6. Promote volunteerism. Since development tends to be a self-initiated activity, firms must provide employees with encouragement and opportunities to volunteer.

A well-planned curriculum is also critical to a successful program. The needs and abilities of program participants and the specific content of the programs will vary widely. Planners should therefore be aware of the basic approaches for planning a specific curriculum.[6]

DEVELOPING MANAGERIAL AND SUPERVISORY ABILITIES

There are many techniques and approaches in use today for furthering managerial and supervisory abilities, and for meeting the developmental needs of employees. Some organizations have a narrow, limited approach. Others, such as Marion Laboratories, have a broad, multiple-faceted approach to management and career development. Figure 12.1, the Marion Development Wheel, shows the many different methods by which employees at Marion can acquire the skills and experiences needed for advancement—and demonstrates a positive, creative approach to career development.

We will turn now to some specific training and development techniques in widespread use today. For convenience, these techniques can be divided into two categories, on-the-job and off-the-job training methods. (As shown in Figure 12.1, note that Marion Laboratories has two off-the-job categories: "inside Marion — off the job" and "outside Marion.")

On-the-Job Training Methods

Although on-the-job training (OJT) methods are considered more useful for skills training, OJT also forms an important part of managerial and supervisory development. Even if an organization has a well-developed off-the-job training program, OJT is still often necessary, particularly to provide an element of practicality to the training. The major OJT methods are coaching, rotation and transfers, understudy assignments, and mentoring.[7]

Coaching.   Coaching can be organized as either an informal or a formal activity. **Informal coaching** typically involves only discussions between a superior and subordinate or between peers. These discussions normally consist simply of question-and-answer sessions that focus on the usefulness and application within the organization of various managerial and supervisory techniques. All training methods should include informal coaching as an important element.

Formal coaching involves periodic scheduled meetings between higher- and lower-level managers to discuss various problems and their potential solutions. Discussions of mutual problems and issues between managers on the same level can also be encouraged. Although this method is called formal coaching, an informal tone can foster greater interaction. Although organizations sometimes overlook formal coaching, it can yield valuable benefits through the sharing of experience.

Rotation and Transfers.   Rotation and transfers are designed to prepare managers to take on additional responsibilities by providing them with experience in different areas of the firm. Rotation and transfers are often based on an analysis of career paths.

Many rotations and transfers are considered lateral promotions. That is, the manager is placed in a position that carries similar authority and responsibility, but in a different part of the firm. The new position can be outside the manager's "specialty." For example, managers hired to work in the human resources or personnel department may have to serve stints as production supervisors or salespeople. Such assignments are not intended to prepare the manager for a career as a supervisor or salesperson. Rather, the varied assignments can help the personnel specialist better understand the unique problems and needs of managers in other operating departments. These experiences should lead to better human resources decisions, such as on the hiring, training, and dismissal of managers.

Understudy Assignments.   **Understudy assignments** involve assigning an inexperienced manager to work for a more experienced manager, often on an "assistant to" basis. The understudy manager normally progresses from performing rather mundane, detailed tasks to more advanced work. Eventually, the understudy should be able to perform at about the same level as the experienced manager. The effectiveness of understudy assignments depends on the willingness and ability of the higher-level manager to share experience and to transfer knowledge to the understudy manager.

A variation of the understudy approach involves placing novice managers on certain committees. The best committees for such assignments include a mixture of experienced and inexperienced managers whose interaction results in a coaching-type situation. Sequencing these assignments so that the inexperienced manager is faced with progressively larger responsibilities can result in effective training. Creating artificial committees or limiting assignments to low-level committees can be counterproductive, however, particularly when the manager perceives the activity as a waste of time and effort.

Mentoring. According to the *American Heritage Dictionary*, a **mentor** is "a wise and trusted counselor or teacher." Using the word *mentor* as a descriptive acronym, it could stand for: Manage, Encourage, Nurture, Teach Organizational Responsibility. Although informal mentoring goes on daily within every type of organization, more and more firms are establishing formal mentoring programs.[8]

Mentors can play several valuable roles:

1. *Sponsor:* to widen opportunities.
2. *Teacher:* to solve real problems, create learning opportunities with hypothetical problems, and impart organizational culture.
3. *Devil's Advocate:* to provide challenges and to give the trainee practice in asserting ideas and influencing the listener.
4. *Coach:* to support trainees in finding out what is important to them, what skills they have, and their interests and deep aspirations.[9]

Several guidelines can help ensure a successful mentoring program:[10]

1. Assure the voluntary participation of mentors.
2. Minimize the "rules" and maximize the mentor's personal freedom.
3. Share and negotiate expectations between mentors and trainees.
4. Reward mentors and increase their visibility.
5. Include the trainees' supervisors in the mentoring program.

These guidelines can help organizations avoid potential problems. Problems can arise because of a lack of chemistry between the mentor and trainee, unrealistic expectations on the part of the trainee (because of a prominent mentor), the myth that a mentor is necessary for success, and too many trainees per mentor.

Off-the-Job Training Methods

The general nature of managerial and supervisory development requires that much of the training be performed off the job. The risk of costly on-the-job errors by novice managers is simply too great for many organizations. Firms unwilling or unable to accept this risk typically prefer that their novice managers gain knowledge and experience off the job before applying their skill on the job.

All the off-the-job training methods discussed in this section can be conducted in-house (but off the job) or by outside firms that specialize in training. In-house training is most often conducted by larger firms that need a large and ongoing supply of managers and supervisors.[11] Smaller firms typically cannot justify the cost of doing much of this kind of training themselves.

Seminars/Lectures. Most management and supervisory training programs include seminars and/or lectures, particularly at the be-

Training and development efforts such as Merck's Middle Management Program address requirements for management and supervisory talent at all levels of the company.

PERSPECTIVE 12.2   Teaching Managers Philosophy

Joseph J. Lavin, vice president of Sandoz Inc., the pharmaceuticals company, and general manager of its Dorsey Laboratories unit, is planning to tackle subjects this summer that he hasn't studied in years. The idea, he says, is to "clear out some of the cobwebs" in his mind.

Sandoz will hand over nearly $10,000 to Dartmouth College to make sure that the process takes place. Mr. Lavin and his wife are joining 100 or so executives from companies across the country for a four-week program in Hanover, N.H., where they will discuss Plato, explore DeTocqueville's observations on American democracy and argue about Horatio Alger's thoughts on the American dream.

"The topics are very pertinent," said Mr. Lavin, 42 years old and a 17-year Sandoz veteran. "They will help me see what we are doing and how it will fit in better to the marketplace."

The directors of programs at Dartmouth, Williams College, and Rhodes College spend a huge portion of their time trying to persuade those who hold the corporate purse strings that teaching philosophy can indeed make good business sense. "This comes under the rubric of mind stretching, of getting out of the tunnel you've been in, getting some distance from yourself and a problem," said Fred Greene, director of Williams College's five-week program.

All three colleges focus on the creative arts and

American civilization and history, subjects usually touched upon only lightly in technical undergraduate programs. Most include at least a smattering of behavioral sciences, philosophy, and scientific research. And most importantly, nearly all try to cast some of the more crucial business issues of the day in a more philosophical light.

For example, students at the liberal arts institutes are discussing the December chemical accident in Bhopal, India, in which more than 2,000 people died, in a different way than their counterparts in business classes. They touch only lightly — if at all — on legal responsibility or potential liability exposure. Instead, they look at what Thea Froling, director of Dartmouth's institute, calls the "larger questions."

"If one country has less stringent safety requirements, are there nonlegal responsibilities a company has?" she asked. "In spite of the laws are there ethical or moral questions an individual has to answer?" . . .

Although it is hard to quantify the value of the programs in terms of immediate bottom-line results, graduates insist that their expanded horizons are of value to their companies. "I became much more of a communicator and more of a participative manager," said Ronald D. Wickens, vice president of engineering and quality assurance at the Federal Express Corporation in Memphis and a recent graduate of the Rhodes College's institute. "The program taught me to listen more and to understand where people are coming from." . . .

Source: Excerpted from "Teaching Arts Instead of Accounting," *New York Times,* March 24, 1985, p. 17. Copyright © 1985 by The New York Times Company. Reprinted by permission.

ginning. Both seminars and lectures involve assembling a group of trainees and a group leader. In seminars, the group leader generally focuses on coordinating and motivating discussion among the group members. Group members obtain benefits by participating in the discussions.

In lectures, the group leader presents material in a classroom-lecture manner. The group members tend to focus on acquisition of knowledge, generally not on application of that knowledge to specific job situations.

Since application of knowledge is not stressed in either seminars or lectures, few firms depend solely on these approaches. Most firms use them early in training programs to help impart basic knowledge and then move on to other methods.

Laboratory Training.   **Laboratory training** can be described as experience-based learning workshops that generally emphasize interaction between trainers and trainees. Their major objective is normally to apply specific managerial and supervisory techniques to actual or simulated work situations. The trainees are required to make various types of decisions and then receive help in attempting to determine the outcome of those decisions. The knowledge applied in laboratory training is often presented through lectures, but laboratory training can incorporate any of the training methods discussed here.

Three approaches can provide the trainees with practice in making managerial decisions. First, **computer simulation models** can be developed to simulate or approximate various business situations. The simulation program generally provides the trainee with information about a specific type of decision, such as forecasting the price of key raw materials. The trainee then analyzes the situation and makes a decision. After receiving the trainee's decision, the simulation program can calculate the outcome and provide feedback to the trainee. Although no computer model can completely simulate an actual business situation, models can provide participants with sufficient realism to allow practice applications without undue risk that the organization's operations will be disrupted or that the firm will lose money.

Second, **case studies** involve providing the trainees with written or videotaped descriptions of decision-making situations. The participants are required to analyze each case and make appropriate decisions. The case is subsequently discussed, with emphasis normally on the trainees' analyses, decisions, implications of those decisions, and probable decision outcomes. Executive MBA programs, for example, are often based on this method.

Third, **role playing** tends to be more appropriate for problems and decisions relating to human relations. Participants are typically provided with a specific situation that they must analyze, and then each assumes and acts out the role of a specific person. Since each role player brings his or her own personality to a given role, all participants experience the realistic variability that managers actually encounter in real job situations.[12]

T-Groups.   T-groups (derived from the term *training groups*) usually involve small groups of approximately ten to twelve participants meeting under the guidance of a trainer. The groups are largely unstructured in the sense that there is a very flexible agenda and a minimum of formal leadership. The discussions are essentially unguided except for a strong focus on learning how to deal with feelings, learning how to communicate feelings and perceptions clearly and in constructive ways, and learning from the perceptions and reactions of others. Frequently, an additional objective is to develop more awareness and understanding of group processes, including the task and emotional aspects of group life. This kind of training is sometimes called "sensitivity training."

Transactional Analysis. **Transactional analysis (TA)** is another training technique requiring a high level of trainee participation.[13] The focus of TA is on viewing the interactions between individuals and groups as transactions. TA is based on the concept that each person has a three-dimensional behavior pattern based on three ego states — parent, child, and adult.

In the parent ego state, an individual feels that what he or she says or does is appropriate simply because he or she said or did it. In the child ego state, the person feels that he or she should do something simply because someone else said to. The individual does

"I've supervised. I've managed. I've directed. I've presided. I've chaired. What else is there?"

not understand the reasons for the order, which often results in a halfhearted effort to perform the task. Transactions between individuals become more difficult when either the parent ego state or the child ego state becomes involved.

The adult ego state involves the feeling that all individuals participating in a transaction are capable of understanding all of its elements and why each occurs. This is the ideal ego state, which makes mature, rational interrelationships possible.

The primary use of TA in business and industrial settings appears to be in helping employees become more sensitive to the nature of their interactions with others. For example, TA can be used to help salespeople improve their relationships with customers. Managers can use TA to help them deal with subordinates by trying to ensure that the adult ego state is used by both parties to a transaction. In general, TA can help improve the quality of communication between individuals and groups.

Behavioral Modeling. **Behavioral modeling** (sometimes called interaction modeling) consists of presenting or showing participants a particular behavior or way of doing something, such as handling employee complaints, and then having the participants practice the behavior through role playing. This approach may consist of six to twelve modules for small groups in a series of two- or three-hour sessions spread over a few weeks or months.

Behavioral modeling emphasizes positive reinforcement for demonstration of appropriate behaviors during the role playing. Whereas other training approaches often address both effective and ineffective management techniques, behavioral modeling usually addresses only useful and effective practices.[14]

In-basket Training. **In-basket training** consists of giving trainees a set of memos, letters, and other items that a manager might find in his or her in-basket upon arriving at work. The trainee is required to respond by: (1) delaying a decision about the issue, (2) referring the issue to someone else in the organization, or (3) making a decision about the issue. The trainer and the group then analyze the responses to see whether any improvements can be made.

The objective of in-basket training is to help trainees determine which decisions can be made quickly, which must or should be delayed, and which should be referred to others. This training emphasizes a critical characteristic of effective management. In-basket training is also useful for teaching good time management, which is important enough in most managerial jobs to justify the cost of the training.

DEVELOPING EMPLOYEE POTENTIAL

Although the development of employee potential is the major objective of all training programs, there are several special cases that should be addressed individually. These special cases include career development for nonsupervisors, women, and minorities, and employee counseling.

Career Development for Professional-Technical Employees

All employees of an organization need some attention to their career development. In addition, there are employees in certain nonsupervisory positions — such as in engineering, accounting, and legal work — that perhaps warrant a wider range of developmental opportunities.

Technological innovation makes special training for engineers and scientists an important part of their career development.

Career development for most nonsupervisory employees may involve only such activities as a standard introduction or orientation, ongoing coaching, and periodic meetings at which executives explain new challenges and opportunities facing the organization. These aspects of career development can be extremely valuable to the organization because of their desirable influence on performance and their potential for creating loyalty and identification with the organization.

Career development for more technical-professional positions such as for engineers, scientists, accountants, and lawyers is typically similar to that for other employees, but additional aspects are needed. These people must keep up with rapid technological, legal, and other changes that are affecting or can affect their jobs and the direction of the organization. Thus, additional development opportunities are required.

Career Development for Women

Although the number of women in the work force continues to increase, the relative proportion of females in managerial positions is much less than for males. This imbalance indicates a need for special career development programs for women. Federal agencies and the court system, for example, have recognized this imbalance and have placed many firms under court order to move more women into managerial positions. Stan Rush, in Case 12.2 at the beginning of the chapter, may be facing a situation of this kind.

One of the primary objectives of career development programs for women is often to convince women that they can and should consider managerial positions and careers. Consequently, part of the training involves changing prevalent attitudes of women.

These training programs should also stress the special problems often faced by women in managerial positions. These problems include lack of acceptance by their male counterparts and by subordinates and lack of support from family for career aspirations. For example, some husbands feel threatened when their wives earn greater incomes, children want their mothers at home more frequently, and wives of other managers resent mixed business trips. Training may need to be focused on each of these and other problems.

Career Development for Minorities

Problems encountered by minorities are often similar to those faced by women managers. One of the greatest problems is likely to be the limited number of role models in higher-level managerial positions. Prejudicial attitudes held by other employees and managers can also be a serious constraint.

Career development for minorities must stress the concept that minorities can in fact achieve managerial positions and careers. Training must also focus on coping with individuals who resist accepting minorities as managers. For example, specific techniques can be provided for dealing with those who think the minority manager was hired as a token rather than for managerial ability and potential. Although one can hope that the need for such programs will diminish in the future, currently there is a need for more rather than fewer of them.

Employee Counseling

Firms should also consider providing individualized counseling beyond formal training programs for all employees, particularly managers.[15] The anxiety and stress associated with family, legal, financial, and other off-the-job problems can prevent managers from performing up to their ability, regardless of their potential and the excellence of the organization's formal training programs. The training programs can and should be used to inform trainees about the availability of individualized counseling and other assistance. Table 12.2 shows the major types of counseling practices by major firms.

TABLE 12.2
Current counseling practices of major U.S. corporations*

Type of counseling provided	Currently in effect	Plan to implement in one year or less	Had in past but discontinued	Not under consideration at this time
Career	73	10	2	12
Dual career	11	2	0	53
Outplacement	60	4	1	20
Retirement	63	12	2	11
Alcoholism/drugs	63	7	1	15
Personal problems	71	6	0	11

N = 97
*Numbers expressed in percentages, which do not necessarily equal 100 percent.

Source: Helen LaVan, Nicholas Mathys, and David Drehmer, "A Look at the Counseling Practices of Major U.S. Corporations," reprinted from the June, 1983 issue of *Personnel Administrator*, copyright, 1983, The American Society for Personnel Administration, 606 North Washington Street, Alexandria, VA 22314.

EVALUATING CAREER DEVELOPMENT PROGRAMS

Career development programs are much more difficult to evaluate than skills training programs. One of the primary difficulties involves establishing specific objectives. General statements, such as to create better managers and improve managers' human relations abilities, provide little guidance for evaluation purposes. Even when good objectives are established, it is difficult to design a single training program that can fulfill all of them. Managerial training tends to be an ongoing process, thereby involving a number of specific training programs over time. These problems compound the difficulties of evaluating career development efforts.

One systematic approach to evaluating programs consists of five steps:

1. Determine the history and rationale of the program.
2. Determine the degree to which the program places primary emphasis on its most important goals.
3. Analyze change occurring in trainees, i.e., program effectiveness, comparing the outcomes of the program with its stated objectives.
4. Examine the general adaptability of the program.
5. Evaluate the program rationale, introducing modifications as required.[16]

Feedback is one of the most critical elements of the evaluation process. The results of the analysis must be presented to the appropriate decision makers in a clear and understandable manner.

SUMMARY

Management and career development programs are aimed at developing managers and educating all employees above and beyond the immediate technical requirements of their jobs. These programs are becoming more popular because organizations are more aware of the need for competent and adaptable employees and managers at all levels. In addition, new jobs are opening up and traditional jobs are disappearing, people want to know more about their jobs, and employees need their organizations' help in order to help themselves. A good management and career development program therefore meets the needs of both the organization and its employees.

A wide variety of training techniques is available. On-the-job training methods include coaching, rotation and transfers, understudy assignments, and mentoring. Off-the-job techniques, which can be conducted by the firm or by external trainers, include seminars and lectures; laboratory training, such as computer simulations, case studies, and role playing; T-groups; transactional analysis; behavioral modeling; and in-basket training.

Several categories of employees often need special attention from the organization to develop their potential. These include nonsupervisors in technical and professional positions, women, and minorities. Employee counseling should be made available for all employees.

Career development programs must be evaluated in order to keep them relevant and serving organizational objectives. Although evaluation is difficult, primarily because management development is a complex and ongoing process, a productive evaluation of the program's contributions to managerial performance can be made through a systematic, step-by-step process.

KEY TERMS

management and career
  development
informal coaching
formal coaching
understudy assignment

mentor
laboratory training
computer simulation model
case study
role playing

T-group
transactional analysis (TA)
behavioral modeling
in-basket training

REVIEW QUESTIONS

1. What is "management and career development"?
2. Discuss the major categories of needs that must be considered in developing management training programs.
3. Discuss the keys to success for internal development programs.
4. What is "mentoring"? Discuss successful mentoring programs.
5. List and discuss *on-the-job* training methods for management training.
6. List and discuss *off-the-job* training methods for management training.
7. How can management development programs be evaluated?

OPENING CASE QUESTIONS

Case 12.1 Where Have All the Managers Gone?

1. What can Mrs. Smith do at this point to overcome the problem?
2. How could the problem have been avoided?

Case 12.2 How Much Is Enough?

1. What would you put in your response to the EEOC?
2. What would you do to get more women into management?

CASE 12.3   WOMEN IN MANAGEMENT: STUCK IN THE MIDDLE

Female executives are encountering an invisible wall when they contemplate moving from middle management to the upper levels. Managers and execu-

Case Sources: "You've Come a Long Way, Baby—but Not as Far as You Thought," *Business Week,* Oct. 1, 1984, pp. 126, 130–131; Susan Fraker, "Why Women Aren't Getting to the Top," *Fortune,* April 16, 1984, pp. 40–45; and Beth McGoldrick and Gregory Miller, "Wall Street Women: You've Come a Short Way, Baby," *Institutional Investor,* June 1985, pp. 85–96.

tives, male and female alike, realize that the wall is there but seem to be at a loss as to what to do about it.

The statistics are clear. Only a small fraction of the nation's upper-level executives are women. As of 1984, only one Fortune 500 company, the Washington Post Co., was headed by a female chief executive officer (and her family holds a controlling interest in the corporation). Perhaps more telling, women at Fortune 500 companies aren't even getting the jobs that might potentially track them toward the top spot in the future.

Stories of overt discrimination are still to be heard. At the Wall Street firm of Goldman Sachs, which by 1985 had no female partners and employed no women expected to become eligible for partnership, a senior executive once began a training session with the observation that women simply aren't ambitious enough to reach the firm's upper tiers. A Chicago account executive was passed over for the position that opened when her boss transferred even though she had the recommendations of her boss and clients and was the applicant most familiar with the markets and accounts she would be overseeing. In her place, the manager involved promoted the one man who had applied for the position—and then spent $20,000 to move him to the area.

Yet, in general, the discrimination that is keeping women concentrated at entry and middle management levels is subtle, often not even conscious. In fact, many senior executives express a desire to have more women at their level. Since the early 1970s, women have made substantial inroads into corporate America. In 1984, about one-quarter of middle managers were women, and about half of entry-level managers were. These figures represent a significant investment in human resources. That investment is clouded by the lack of progress. More damaging, though, is that in increasing numbers, women seem to be leaving corporations to start businesses of their own.

The attitudes that are keeping women off the upper-management track may be deeply cultural, but research suggests that they involve misperceptions. According to one study conducted by Stanford Business School, women, quite simply, manage the same way men do. Many women who have had to confront the wall between females and upper management feel that the problem lies in the subjective nature of upper-management selection. Most top executives are men, frequently older men, and given equal levels of competence, they just feel more comfortable working with another man.

Although such a conclusion makes the situation sound pretty hopeless, there are bright spots on the horizon. Some women and human resources specialists feel that things may improve as the older generation of top executives is replaced by younger managers who have worked closely with women through their careers. In addition, some believe that the sheer numbers of women, as they continue to enter middle management, will force changes. And at least in some companies, awareness of the problem is leading to positive steps to monitor and improve career development paths for female managers. This type of guidance is seen by some as reverse discrimination, but to those involved, it is viewed as a necessary effort to open up the competition for upper-management slots.

Discussion Questions

1. The growth in the number of female middle managers has been spurred, at least partly, by organizations' efforts to create equal employment opportunity through career development. Why do you suppose these efforts have not resulted in a better balance in upper management as well?

2. What types of career development activities do you think a human resources department could use to help ensure that women get on the track to upper management and stay there?

chapter 13

Performance Appraisal and Review

CHAPTER OUTLINE

LEARNING OBJECTIVES

- **Describe the major purposes of performance appraisal.**
- **Explain how the performance appraisal process can affect employee morale either positively or negatively.**
- **Discuss the major considerations involved in developing an appraisal program.**
- **Identify common appraisal errors.**
- **Describe several performance appraisal methods.**
- **Cite the advantages and disadvantages of MBO and team MBO.**
- **Describe several procedures for conducting effective appraisal interviews.**

CASE 13.1   KEEP THEM IN THE DARK

Alex Nord and Mike Greene were having coffee and pie after their victory in the Monday night bowling league. They were good friends and often shared their work experiences even though they worked for different employers. Alex noticed a worried look on Mike's face and commented, "What are you frowning about? We won three straight games tonight."

"Well," said Mike, "tomorrow's my annual performance review and I'm kind of uptight about it. I think I've had a good year, but I'm not sure. Sometimes in the past the boss had really unloaded on me during the appraisal. It's almost like he's saved things up all year long. He's praised me a couple of times this past month, though, so maybe this will be a good session. Anyway, I'll sure be glad when it's over."

"At least you have an appraisal to look forward to," lamented Alex. "I don't think my boss knows what they are. I'm not sure what he expects of me, but I do know that when I goof up, I'll hear about it. Otherwise, he says nothing. We all operate on the principle of 'no news is good news.'"

CASE 13.2   LET'S COMPARE NOTES

It was a dreary, rainy afternoon as Mark's car moved along the freeway toward Leavittville. Mark and his four companions had formed the "Leavittville carpool" about a year before. Tonight's trip home was like most others — the group shared "war stories" about life at the Apex Insurance Company. As driver, Mark got to choose the topic for discussion during the twenty-minute ride. He selected performance appraisal, since he had just had his first annual review that morning.

"I think performance appraisals are a joke," said Bill. "My boss rates us all excellent so he doesn't have to explain poor ratings to anyone. Why should I work harder than others when we are all rated the same?"

"You know," responded Sue, "my boss is just the opposite. He gives us all low ratings. I bet he thinks that motivates us to work harder. Ha!"

"Well," advised Jane, "you just don't know how to use the system. All I do is put on my best behavior for about two to three weeks before my annual review and I always get good marks."

"Yeah, it's even easier for me," said Joe. "My boss and I are fraternity brothers. As long as I cooperate with him during the year, I get excellent ratings."

"Whew," thought Mark, "at least my boss doesn't do those things. He told me this morning that my performance has been average, just like all the rest of the people in the department."

CASE 13.3   THE PAINLESS INTERVIEW

Hal knocked on Joan's office door and entered when she responded, "Come in." "Ah, Hal, you're early, but sit down and let's go over this appraisal material." "Fine," said Hal. "I'm early because I'm concerned about this past year. I don't think my performance has been up to par."

"Well," commented Joan, "let's go over the last year systematically. First, as we look at this appraisal form, where do you think you performed at an above-average or better level?" Hal identified five areas and Joan agreed with him. "Now," she asked, "where was your performance below average, and what factors contributed to that performance?" Again, she and Hal were pretty much in agreement, although Joan indicated that she thought Hal's communication skills also could be improved.

After this discussion, Joan and Hal spent twenty minutes discussing what Hal could do to improve in the areas where he was weak. They concluded by setting some specific performance goals for him during the next year.

"Gee," thought Hal as he walked back to his office, "that Joan is an A-OK boss, and she sure made this interview easy. I'm going to work much harder next year."

Performance appraisal and review is the formal, systematic assessment of how well employees are performing their jobs in relation to established standards and communication of that assessment to employees. As the chapter-opening cases indicate, this process is of great importance to the employees involved. How appraisal systems are used and how appraisal results are communicated affects morale and organizational climate in significant ways. Moreover, the results of performance appraisal also have a significant impact on other human resources processes, such as training and development, compensation, and promotion decisions. This chapter discusses these effects in some detail and provides an overview of commonly used appraisal methods, including the appraisal interview.

Informal appraisals tend to take place on an ongoing basis within the organization as supervisors evaluate their subordinates' work and as subordinates appraise each other and their supervisors on a daily basis. But systematic, formal appraisal of an individual employee is likely to occur at certain intervals throughout that person's history of employment. For example, a person may be appraised when he or she is considered for employment, during the first few days on the job, at the end of six months and each six months thereafter for the purposes of salary review and determining where his or her performance needs improvement, and at the end of a few years to assess suitability for promotion. In a sense, then, the appraisal process as it applies to an individual employee is cyclical, in that it tends to be repeated again and again.

It is important to recognize that performance appraisal, in addition to being periodic, should be an ongoing process. Regularly scheduled formal appraisals should not keep supervisors from appraising or coaching their subordinates whenever necessary. Saving up performance evaluation data — especially negative data — and "dumping" them on the employee once or twice a year is ineffective. Employees desire performance **feedback,** or information on how well they are doing their jobs, and this feedback should be provided to them when it is timely and relevant.

IMPORTANCE OF PERFORMANCE APPRAISAL

Performance appraisal is important in organizations because of its widespread use, the numerous purposes for which it is employed, and its impact on individuals as well as the organization.

Scope of Performance Appraisal

Most industrial organizations use systematic performance appraisal procedures for both nonsupervisory and managerial employees. Nonindustrial organizations — such as the military services, government agencies, hospitals, and universities — also use such procedures extensively. Performance appraisal is now mandatory in most federal agencies under the Civil Service Reform Act of 1978.[1]

One study of 264 firms found that 88 percent had some form of appraisal system for both professional and technical employees, and 63 percent used appraisal systems for production employees. Of those firms having appraisal systems, 67 percent used a rating scale for office employees, and the same percentage used a rating scale for production workers.[2] Another survey of 265 industrial and nonindustrial companies reported that 71 percent of hourly paid workers were evaluated by some type of formal appraisal system.[3]

Purposes of Performance Appraisal

Performance appraisals are used for a variety of purposes. Table 13.1 shows the fourteen most common uses in 256 industrial and nonindustrial organizations.

TABLE 13.1
Rank order of uses of performance appraisal systems (N = 256)

RANK	FUNCTION FOR WHICH APPRAISAL IS USED	PERCENTAGE
1	Merit Increases	91
2	Performance Results/Feedback/Job Counseling	90
3	Promotion	82
4	Termination or Layoff	64
5	Performance Potential	62
6	Succession Planning	57
7	Career Planning	52
8	Transfer	50
9	Manpower Planning	38
10	Bonuses	32
11	Development and Evaluation of Training Programs	29
12	Internal Communication	25
13	Criteria for Selection Procedure Validation	16
14	Expense Control	7

Source: Reprinted, by permission of the publisher, from "Strategic Issues in Performance Appraisal: Theory and Practice," by Charles J. Fombrun and Robert L. Land, *Personnel,* November–December 1983, p. 28, © 1983 Periodicals Division, American Management Associations, New York. All rights reserved.

Generally speaking, the many purposes of performance appraisal can be grouped into two main categories: evaluation goals and coaching and development goals. According to Michael Beer, **evaluation goals** include the following:

1. Giving feedback to employees so they know where they stand.
2. Developing valid data for pay (salary and bonus pay) and promotion decisions and providing a means for communicating these decisions.
3. Helping the manager make retention and discharge decisions and providing a means for warning employees about unsatisfactory performance.

Coaching and development goals include:

1. Counseling and coaching employees in order to improve their performance and develop future potential.
2. Developing commitment to the organization through discussion of career opportunities and career planning.
3. Motivating employees through provision of recognition and support.
4. Strengthening superior-subordinate relations.
5. Diagnosing individual and organizational problems.[4]

Impact on the Individual

Because of the importance of performance appraisals to employees, the appraisal methods used and the manner in which results are communicated can have positive or negative effects on employees' morale. When appraisals are used for discipline, pay increases, promotions, discharges, or layoffs, they are likely to be regarded with apprehension by those employees who tend to underestimate themselves, by the less productive members of the organization, or by those who feel appraisals will be arbitrary or unjust. These feelings can lead to a sense of insecurity.

Similar feelings result when employees don't know or understand the criteria being used to assess them, when they believe they are being compared to others, and when they see the appraisal as overly critical rather than helpful. The more employees understand about the appraisal process, and the more appraisals are used as developmental opportunities rather than occasions for criticism, the more the need for self-actualization will be satisfied.

Impact on the Organization

Performance appraisal can also affect the organization generally. Of particular importance are its effects on other human resources processes. Performance appraisal information can serve as feedback on the success of other personnel functions, as well as on employee performance (see Figure 13.1). Specifically, the results of performance appraisals can provide useful data about the quality of the organization's recruiting, selection, orientation, and training processes. If large numbers of employees are receiving poor appraisals, there may be some deficiencies in these other processes.

Performance appraisal also provides information that can feed into other human resources processes. Appraisal data can serve as

FIGURE 13.1 Performance appraisal system

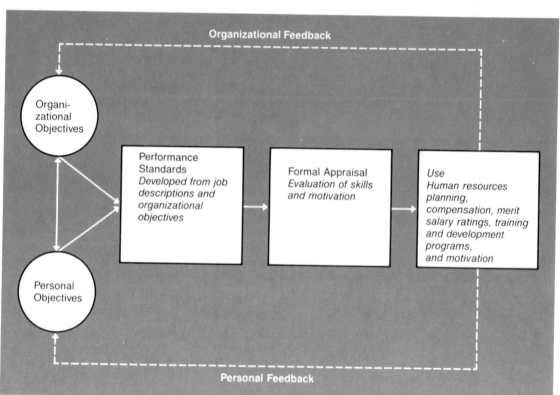

Source: Adapted from Nathan B. Winstanley, "Performance Appraisals and Management Development," *Conference Board Record* (March 1976): 57. Used with permission.

a basis for pay increases. The information helps the training and development process by identifying areas in which employees need additional training or development. This information is also very useful in human resources planning. Appraisal information can indicate employees' suitability for promotion, which is important in assessing the organization's ability to meet its future human resources needs.

DEVELOPING AN APPRAISAL PROGRAM

In designing an appraisal program, attention should be given to relevant laws and court decisions, choice of appraiser, the role of the human resources department, and the validity and reliability of the appraisal methods.

Legal Requirements

Increasingly, courts have applied equal employment opportunity legislation and guidelines to performance appraisals, whether used for test validation, promotion, transfer, layoffs, or other decisions. Three court cases are particularly significant.

In *Rowe* v. *General Motors Corporation,* the Fifth Circuit Court of Appeals found that supervisors' subjective evaluations of the "ability, merit, and capacity" of hourly employees used in promotion decisions had had an adverse impact on black employees. Thus the company had violated Title VII of the Civil Rights Act.[5]

In *Brito* v. *Zia Company,* performance appraisals were used as the basis for deciding whom to lay off. The court determined that a disproportionate number of Spanish-surnamed workers had been laid off, and it ordered the company to suspend performance ratings because the evaluators were not all in a position to observe performance on a daily basis, and the appraisals were not administered and scored under standardized and controlled conditions.[6]

In *Albermarle Paper Company* v. *Moody,* the U.S. Supreme Court confirmed the Equal Employment Opportunity Commission's interpretation that performance ratings were "tests" and criticized the paper company's test-validation procedures in which ratings were used as criteria. The rating procedures were found to be too vague and subject to each supervisor's interpretation.

Overall, these court decisions have carried over into the more recent 1978 Uniform Guidelines on Employee Selection Procedures, which clearly include performance appraisal in their coverage. This means that performance appraisal procedures are subject to the same standards of reliability, validity, and job relatedness as all other selection techniques.

Choosing the Appraiser

Determining who will evaluate employees is critical in designing the appraisal program. It is generally conceded that appraisal by the immediate supervisor is necessary and the most effective. However, other persons are sometimes involved in the appraisal process and in various combinations.

Supervisor Appraisals. Appraisals by the immediate supervisor are the most common. The supervisor has the formal authority to conduct appraisals and usually controls the rewards for performance. In addition, this person is typically in the best position to observe the subordinate's performance and to judge how well that performance serves the goals of the unit and the organization.

Self-appraisals. In some organizations, subordinates appraise their own performance. There are pros (in terms of morale) and cons (ratings tend to be less reliable) to this approach. Self-appraisals can be combined with supervisor appraisals to yield more useful results. Glendale Federal Savings & Loan Association in Glendale, California uses this method. In its system, the supervisor and the employee independently prepare evaluations and then meet to discuss their assessments. They then complete the form's third section, which focuses on future responsibilities, improvement plans, developmental activities, career objectives, and a performance summary.[7] One advantage of the combined approach is that the two independently prepared evaluations provide a formal basis for a discussion to clarify supervisors' and subordinates' expectations and perceptions. (See Figure 13.2 for examples of independently prepared review forms.)

Peer Appraisals. Peer appraisals, while not that common, have the advantage of being relatively reliable. This reliability stems from the fact that peers interact with each other on a daily basis and because the use of peer raters presents a number of independent judgments.[8] Peer ratings can have harmful consequences, however. One study found that negative peer ratings led to significantly lower performance, group cohesion, and satisfaction among those receiving the negative ratings.[9]

Subordinate Appraisals. Appraisals by subordinates, like peer ratings, are not widely used. Some businesses, however, have used

FIGURE 13.2
Example of perform-
ance review forms in-
dependently prepared
by the employee and
supervisor

```
             PERFORMANCE REVIEW:   PRE-DISCUSSION WORKSHEET


    NAME: _____


    Please review/comment on the following areas:

        -Goals set for the Review period, together with your performance
         against these.

        -Ability to meet your position responsibilities, as you understand them.

        -Perceived strengths and areas you need to work on.

        -Training requirements related to your job, and career or job family
         progression if applicable.
```

Source: Courtesy of Analog Devices Human Resources Department.

subordinates' ratings of their supervisors to help managers improve their own performance. In some colleges and universities, students' ratings are used to help professors improve lectures and course content, and in some cases they are used in compensation and promotion decisions as well.

Group or Committee Appraisals.   Although the person who typically performs the appraisal is the immediate supervisor, another approach involves that person plus the next higher level of supervision. This group or committee procedure has been supported on the grounds that several people who know the subject of the rating can provide more data than the supervisor alone.[10] This procedure is used frequently in universities, with higher-ranking professors evaluating those of lower rank.

Role of the Human Resources Department

Basic accountability for scheduling and conducting performance appraisals rests with the immediate supervisor or whoever else is designated to conduct the formal review. The human resources department, however, can play a critical role in the design and implementation of the program. Determining who evaluates and

FIGURE 13.2
(continued)

▶ **ANALOG DEVICES**　　　　　**SALARY EXEMPT**

PERFORMANCE REVIEW　　　　FROM_____ TO_____

NAME_____ JOB TITLE_____

GRADE_____ DEPT_____SUPERVISOR_____DATE DUE_____

INSTRUCTIONS

A.　Please attach a narrative to this form, summarizing the Performance Review in a manner that covers the following areas:

　　1.　Performance related to any expectations set for the Review period, plus the rationale for the chosen Performance Rating.

　　2.　The Employees overall ability to do the job, with particular reference to the levels of competency demonstrated and/or required.

　　3.　Any other Performance factors, such as those related to ADI and Division values.

　　4.　Any job-focused training and development activities that the employee has been involved in, or are planned for in the future.

　　5.　Career development aspects, such as the employees career goals. Your views on these plus any agreed career-focused T&D activities.

B.　Please also attach the Pre-Discussion Worksheet.

C.　Please circle the appropriate Performance Rating description.

　　Marginal　　Needs　　Fully Met　　Commendable　　Distinguished
　　　　　　Improvement　Expectations

D.　Please list any agreed goals for the next Review period on the back of this form and provide the employee with a copy

E.　Comments by Employee on overall Review and discussion.
　　(For optional completion by Employee)

F.　Employee Signature_____　Date _____

　　Supervisor Signature_____　Date _____

　　Approval_____　Date _____

　　H.R. Dept_____　Date _____

what method will be used are design issues that must be handled by the human resources department. In addition, that department can provide organization members with training in how to use the system and how to conduct appraisal interviews. Finally, the hu-

---

PERSPECTIVE 13.1 Appraising the Boss

Most companies use some form of regular performance appraisal to evaluate the work and promotion prospects of managerial employees. Generally, a manager evaluates his [or her] own subordinates. But at Photocircuits, a New York manufacturer of printed circuit boards with 800 employees, managers and supervisors also get a regular performance review by their subordinates.

According to a report in *Management Review* (Vol. 71, No. 8), subordinates at Photocircuits first fill out a questionnaire designed to measure their immediate superiors' attitudes, performance and relationships with colleagues. Some typical questions:

Does your manager show interest in you as an individual?

Is he [or she] a good listener who tries to understand your point of view?

Does he [or she] make sure that you receive the training that you need?

Is he [or she] fair and explicit in his assignments at work?

Does he [or she] provide challenge in your job?

Does he [or she] accept suggestions easily?

Does he [or she] give criticism in a fair and considerate manner?

On a separate sheet, subordinates also summarize their supervisors' strong points and those that need improvement. The subordinate and the manager then meet to discuss the appraisal, after which both must sign it, with one copy going to the manager's superior.

Initially, many employees had difficulty being critical of their bosses, and their first evaluations tended to be uniformly glowing. But the company encouraged honest appraisals of everyone, starting with president John Endee, who was told by one subordinate that he was "too aggressive" and that he "frightened people." "This sort of program doesn't work in a climate of fear," says Endee. "It requires a lot of sensitivity on the part of a manager to encourage a subordinate's honesty."

Source: Berkeley Rice, "Reversing Performance Review," *Psychology Today*, March 1984, p. 80. Reprinted with permission from *Psychology Today* magazine. Copyright © 1984 American Psychological Association.

---

man resources department is the logical group to conduct research on the equity of appraisals throughout departments and on the reliability and validity of whatever systems are established.

Reliability and Validity

The concepts of reliability and validity, discussed in detail in Chapter 9, are also relevant to performance appraisal. In performance appraisal, **reliability** refers to the consistency with which a supervisor rates a subordinate in successive ratings (assuming consistent performance) or the consistency with which two or more supervisors rate performance when they have comparable information. The reliability of appraisal methods can be increased by better training of raters and by using more descriptive standards in appraisal systems.

The **validity** of performance appraisal is the extent to which appraisal procedures measure real differences in performance. Logic suggests that the more the supervisor uses data on actual performance, the more valid the ratings become. Thus, the most valid ratings are those in which actual performance corresponds to rated performance.

Appraisal Errors

The reliability and validity of the appraisal program are especially important in view of equal employment opportunity legislation and guidelines. Unfortunately, supervisors can make several kinds of errors when conducting appraisals that make the process less reliable or less valid than it might otherwise be.

The **halo error** represents the situation in which the rater generalizes from one aspect of a person's job performance to all aspects of performance. For example, the supervisor may rate the "quantity of work" for Bill as "excellent," and then inappropriately rate all other dimensions as "excellent" when they actually are only "average" or "good." The halo error can also work in reverse. (See the discussion of the "horn effect" in Chapter 9.) A form of the halo error is illustrated in Joe's experience in Case 13.2 at the beginning of this chapter.

The **error of central tendency** occurs when the rater tends to rate the performance of all or most of the persons being appraised around the center of the rating scale (perhaps in the "average" category). The central tendency error also occurs on an individual basis if the supervisor is to rate an employee on numerous performance dimensions and rates all of the dimensions in the middle of the scale. Mark's treatment in Case 13.2 represents this error.

The **leniency error** is made by the appraiser who gives employees higher ratings than they deserve. As illustrated by Bill's situation in Case 13.2, this usually results in a distribution of employee ratings that is concentrated toward the high end of the rating scale. Employees expect consistently high ratings to be accompanied by rewards such as merit pay increases and promotion. If such rewards are seldom forthcoming, the entire appraisal system may fail.

PERFORMANCE APPRAISAL METHODS

Many approaches are used in appraising performance. This section examines some of the more commonly used methods.

Graphic Rating Scale

The **graphic rating scale method,** also called the conventional rating method,[11] is used most often. There are many versions of graphic rating scales, but all concentrate on specific employee behaviors or characteristics as they relate to work performance. In early versions of this method, the rater placed a check mark on a form under the word or phrase best describing the degree to which an employee demonstrated each behavior or characteristic.

FIGURE 13.3
Examples of rating scales

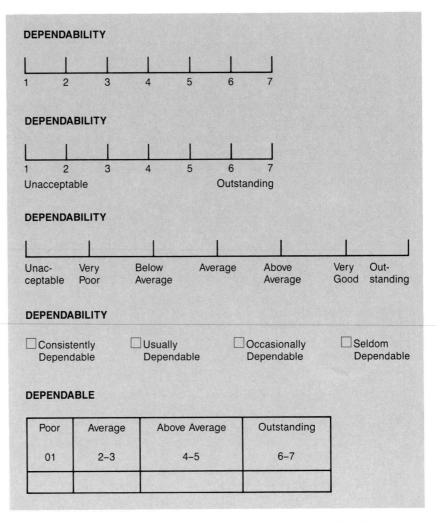

Adapted from: Stephen J. Carroll and Craig E. Schneier, *Performance Appraisal and Review Systems* (Glenview, Ill.: Scott, Foresman & Company, 1982), pp. 104–105.

Among the many types of rating scales in use in organizations, some are numerically based and others present raters with a choice of adjectives with which to describe employee behavior. Figure 13.3 provides some examples of these rating scales.

Contemporary versions of the graphic rating scale are more likely to use only characteristics that are closely related to actual job performance and to exclude such characteristics as "loyalty." In addition, contemporary versions are more likely to use scales that include descriptive statements of different performance levels for each characteristic. Figure 13.4 shows an example of a contemporary graphic rating scale used with some employees at Eastern Airlines.

Checklist Method

Another relatively straightforward appraisal approach uses the **checklist method.** Under this approach, the rater is presented with a list of positive or negative adjectives or descriptive behavioral statements and is asked to check off all those that apply to the person being rated. A score can be developed by tallying the positive checks. The following are illustrative checklist statements:

———— Cooperates with coworkers
———— Keeps work station neat and clean
———— Can be expected to complete work on time
———— Maintains detailed records
———— Reluctant to ever work overtime
———— Cannot accept constructive criticism

In a basic checklist approach, all items are considered to be of equal value. Greater sophistication occurs with the use of a **weighted checklist,** in which each item receives a weighted value based on its perceived importance to successful job performance. Weighted values are determined by those highly familiar with the job.

Checklists are easy to use and are not subject to such rating errors as central tendency or leniency. They are not problem free, however. Because it is important that items in the list be relevant to the job, it may be necessary to develop different lists for different job categories. The process of weighting is difficult and requires professional assistance. Supervisors often complain about "being in the dark" with this approach. They are not sure what the items measure and they have difficulty interpreting the results. This, of course, hinders the developmental counseling aspect of the appraisal process.

FIGURE 13.4 Example of a contemporary graphic rating scale

MANAGEMENT APPRAISAL PROGRAM   🦅 **EASTERN**   *Confidential*
Manager/Director
14-GG-0174C   OPR-988   2 84

NAME (Last Name First)	EMPLOYEE NUMBER	TIME IN POSITION
		YEARS MONTHS
CURRENT JOB TITLE	SALARY GRADE	TIME UNDER APPRAISOR'S SUPERVISION
		YEARS MONTHS
DIVISION/DEPARTMENT	COMAIL ADDRESS	PERFORMANCE PERIOD
		FROM TO

INSTRUCTIONS: In completing this appraisal, remember Eastern's policy is NOT to discriminate on the basis of race, color, sex, religion, national origin, age, disability or veteran status.

NOTE: *Whenever an employee is referred to in the male gender, it should be understood that the statement applies to all employees, male and female alike.*

I. **OVERALL PERFORMANCE RATING**
The primary evaluation of each management employee should be based on his/her **accomplishments** during the rating period. The rating circled below reflects the contribution of the ratee to Eastern's overall performance.

Far Exceeds Requirements	Usually Exceeds Requirements	Fully Meets Requirements	Usually Meets Requirements	Fails To Meet Requirements
10	9 8	7 6 5 4	3 2	1

II. **MAJOR PERFORMANCE FACTORS**
The above performance rating was aided or hindered by the factors noted below. Read each definition carefully and place a check mark in the box which most appropriately indicates his/her performance during this rating period.

TECHNICAL KNOWLEDGE: Job knowledge and skills essential to effective performance of position responsibilities.

☐ **Far Exceeds Requirements**	☐ **Usually Exceeds Requirements**	☐ **Fully Meets Requirements**	☐ **Usually Meets Requirements**	☐ **Fails to Meet Requirements**
Displays broad knowledge and technical background. Sought out for his expertise not only by subordinates but by peers. Uses his knowledge to help develop others rather than to overwhelm them. Applies knowledge in a highly efficient and effective manner.	Uses job knowledge in a helpful manner — work associates look upon him as a resource. Creatively applies his job awareness to achieve desired results.	Utilizes knowledge of the immediate job area to achieve objectives. Exhibits a sound working understanding of those duties required of subordinates as well as his supervisory skills.	Evidences weaknesses in selected areas of the job. Employees are aware of these short-comings and seeks assistance from alternate sources. Fails to keep up to speed on technical aspects of the job.	Lacks basics of the job. Fails to provide requested answers to employees' problems. Overlooks elements of a solution in making recommendations.

PROBLEM ANALYSIS: Ability to recognize problems, secure relevant information, interpret and respond to what others are saying; perceive relationships between things, people, events and time; and identify the probable causes of problems.

☐ **Far Exceeds Requirements**	☐ **Usually Exceeds Requirements**	☐ **Fully Meets Requirements**	☐ **Usually Meets Requirements**	☐ **Fails to Meet Requirements**
Keenly perceives existent or potential problems; maintains open relations with fellow workers so as to monitor deviations from standards as well as to solicit input from others as to how problem might be addressed. Confident in own skills but not unwilling to seek guidance from superior when required.	Responds quickly to problems as they emerge i.e. attendance, attitude. Uses input from other supervisors to monitor trend of operations. Uses logical thought processes in seeking problem solution.	Uses available information to produce solutions. Monitors daily monthly performance for any significant problems. Involves employees in problem-solving process.	Responds to problems when they have been noted by others. Usually able to produce an acceptable solution. At times, fails to involve others critical to the problem-solving process.	Does not detect problems or workable solutions until situation has taken on dramatic proportions. Fails to utilize available resources in seeking solutions.

Source: Courtesy of Eastern Air Lines Incorporated.

FIGURE 13.4 (continued)

JUDGMENT: Skill in evaluating and selecting possible courses of action and reaching logical conclusions.

☐ **Far Exceeds Requirements**	☐ **Usually Exceeds Requirements**	☐ **Fully Meets Requirements**	☐ **Usually Meets Requirements**	☐ **Fails to Meet Requirements**
Provides solutions to identified problems that reflect sensitivity to both financial impact and employee reaction. Recognizes those decisions which require superior review. Good understanding of individuals and their capacity to assume additional responsibilities. Decisions made reflect excellent balance between short-term and long-term needs.	Makes decisions that represent a course of action that is workable and financially feasible. Knows where to more effectively use available resources. Sets sound criteria in evaluating options.	Makes sound decisions. Understands the need to look for alternate methods of dealing with problems. Effectively uses both financial and human resources.	Produces decisions on occasions that lack sensitivity to implementation — good in theory but somewhat unworkable. Expects more from people than they are able to contribute. Makes decisions all too often in a compressed timeframe.	Exhibits extremely narrow range in identifying possible courses of action. Ultimate decisions place Company in poor position, either financially or peoplewise.

ORGANIZING/PLANNING: Ability to systematically structure tasks, set standards, make plans and set objectives; establish priorities and set schedules; allocate resources such as time, people and material; and effectively make use of recordkeeping systems.

☐ **Far Exceeds Requirements**	☐ **Usually Exceeds Requirements**	☐ **Fully Meets Requirements**	☐ **Usually Meets Requirements**	☐ **Fails to Meet Requirements**
Displays uncanny ability to combine resources (people and things) in order to achieve established objectives. Outstanding capability displayed in sorting out demands on a priority basis. Plans always include a method to monitor individual organization performance.	Effectively uses available systems and modifies as appropriate. Keeps self and others for which he is responsible on target with established due dates.	Functions comfortably within established manpower financial constraints. Establishes and communicates schedules so as to keep goals in focus. Aware of and attuned to established priorities.	Periodically fails to assign people equipment in the most efficient manner. Details seem to get away. Employees not always certain of job expectations.	Shows questionable skill in overall planning process. Priorities inappropriately set, causing people to be wrongly assigned and targets to be missed. Employees lack direction.

ORAL COMMUNICATION: Ability to express thoughts, ideas or facts in individual or group situation in a clear, persuasive and/or convincing manner.

☐ **Far Exceeds Requirements**	☐ **Usually Exceeds Requirements**	☐ **Fully Meets Requirements**	☐ **Usually Meets Requirements**	☐ **Fails to Meet Requirements**
Effectively utilizes the flow of information — down, up, and across. Knows how to separate out the extraneous — focuses on crisp concise review of the facts. Able to clearly share his feelings in a group or one-on-one situation. As a result of oral communication, one clearly understands what is expected and why.	Speaks clearly, uses vocabulary that is appropriate for the audience to whom he is communicating. No distracting gestures are used. Does not avoid providing negative feedback but handles it in an effective manner.	Uses skill well. Lets employees know what he wants in a way that they clearly understand. Chooses words that fit the situation when dealing with persons outside his department.	Uses mannerisms occasionally that distract from message. Word choices not totally appropriate for situation or audience. Verbose on occasion.	Loses message all too often in improper speech habits — annoying gestures while talking. When asked to present ideas to peers, becomes somewhat rattled. Word choices/vocabulary ineffective in conveying a crisp, clear message.

WRITTEN COMMUNICATION: Effectiveness in expressing ideas in written format. Ability to write clear and concise memos/reports.

☐ **Far Exceeds Requirements**	☐ **Usually Exceeds Requirements**	☐ **Fully Meets Requirements**	☐ **Usually Meets Requirements**	☐ **Fails to Meet Requirements**
Displays unusual ability to relate even very complex thoughts or instructions clearly, logically and in a convincing manner.	Writes in a very effective manner. Produces a quality letter report in a minimum period of time. Has developed a unique capability to separate the "wheat from the chaff" in distilling down a complex topic.	Produces fully acceptable written work. Final product is understandable and suitable for the intended reader. Only occasional rewrite is required.	Tends to be redundant and excessive in preparing written communications. Syntax and grammatical structure are occasionally inappropriate.	Unable to express thoughts well in writing. Work frequently requires rewrite because it is incomplete, contains faulty grammar or unacceptable tone.

SENSITIVITY: Skill in responding to the needs and feelings of others.

☐ **Far Exceeds Requirements**	☐ **Usually Exceeds Requirements**	☐ **Fully Meets Requirements**	☐ **Usually Meets Requirements**	☐ **Fails to Meet Requirements**
Excellent skill displayed in seeking balance between concern for people and concern for production. Totally aware of short- and long-term impacts of his management style, both on an individual basis as well as impact on the Company. Quick to commend, slow to condemn.	Seen by peers and subordinates as being genuinely interested in their welfare. Understands the impact of performance when people issues are overlooked and/or wrongly applied.	Able to coordinate production/people factors. Rarely seen as insensitive to employees' needs or feelings.	Exhibits momentary lapses in proper employee handling . . . more often when under pressure. Says or does things without recognizing the potential impact. On occasion takes a position which is clearly in opposition to a stated Company position.	Abrasive in relations with others. Overemphasizes need to get things done, resulting in bruised feelings. Imposes unrealistic goals on others which too often results in a sense of failure.

Essay Method

In the **essay method,** the appraiser writes a free-form essay describing the subordinate's performance in a number of broad categories. Some categories that can be included in these forms are (1) overall appraisal of the employee's performance, (2) the employee's promotability, (3) jobs the employee can currently perform, (4) the employee's strengths and limitations, and (5) additional training needs.[12] Sometimes, essay appraisals supplement other appraisal methods rather than substituting for them.

This approach gives the appraiser flexibility by not requiring attention to a specific set of factors. On the other hand, because of the method's open-endedness, it is difficult to compare essay appraisals made by different supervisors. The method is also dependent on the writing skills of the supervisor and is a time-consuming procedure.

Critical-Incidents Method

The **critical-incidents technique** requires the appraiser to keep a record of unusually favorable or unfavorable occurrences in an employee's work. An example of a positive critical incident would be the following:

> 3/15   Employee stayed late to correct machine malfunctions that were causing high number of product rejects for poor quality. Correction of problem enabled completion of special project on time.

An example of a negative critical incident would be:

> 9/12   After repeated warnings to follow all safety procedures, employee failed to close shut-off valve, thereby flooding entire work area.

The positive aspects of this approach are that it provides a factual record for subsequent discussions and decision making and that it provides data that are directly related to job performance.[13] On the negative side, the approach requires close and continuous observation by the appraiser. This is time-consuming and costly, and workers may become very apprehensive when they know their supervisor is keeping a "log" on them.

Behaviorally Anchored Rating Scales

An outgrowth of the critical-incidents technique is the development of **behaviorally anchored rating scales (BARS),** which focus on specific job behaviors rather than traits or characteristics. These scales reduce the amount of judgment or subjectivity required of the rater and rely mostly on the rater's powers of observation.[14] The job relatedness of BARS can also be more readily demonstrated, which makes them less vulnerable to charges of contributing to discriminatory practices.

Figure 13.5 shows an example of a BARS for one performance

FIGURE 13.5 **Appraising checkstand work using a Behaviorally Anchored Rating Scale**

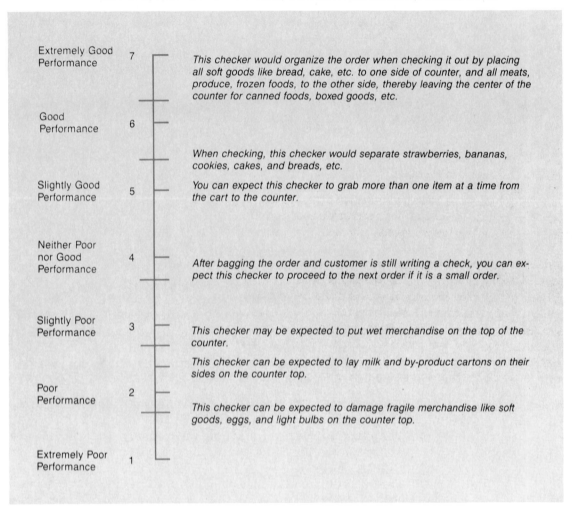

Extremely Good Performance — 7

This checker would organize the order when checking it out by placing all soft goods like bread, cake, etc. to one side of counter, and all meats, produce, frozen foods, to the other side, thereby leaving the center of the counter for canned foods, boxed goods, etc.

Good Performance — 6

When checking, this checker would separate strawberries, bananas, cookies, cakes, and breads, etc.

Slightly Good Performance — 5

You can expect this checker to grab more than one item at a time from the cart to the counter.

Neither Poor nor Good Performance — 4

After bagging the order and customer is still writing a check, you can expect this checker to proceed to the next order if it is a small order.

Slightly Poor Performance — 3

This checker may be expected to put wet merchandise on the top of the counter.

This checker can be expected to lay milk and by-product cartons on their sides on the counter top.

Poor Performance — 2

This checker can be expected to damage fragile merchandise like soft goods, eggs, and light bulbs on the counter top.

Extremely Poor Performance — 1

*Dimension: organizational ability of checkstand work

Source: Lawrence Fogli, Charles Hulin, and Milton R. Blood, "Development of First-Level Behavioral Job Criteria," *Journal of Applied Psychology,* 55 (February 1971): 7. Copyright 1971 by the American Psychological Association. Reprinted by permission of the author.

dimension ("organizational ability") for checkstand work in a grocery store. Similar scales would be developed for other relevant behaviors in this job. The main advantage of this method over less rigorously developed graphic rating scales appears to be that the scales and terminology are clear and demonstrably job related, thus presumably increasing both reliability and validity.[15]

Behavioral Observation Scales

Behavioral observation scales (BOS) are developed through a process similar to that used for BARS. The major difference is that several behaviors are listed individually for each performance dimension, and the rater is required to assess the individual on each behavior. Figure 13.6 illustrates a BOS for a cook.

Behaviorally anchored rating scales and behavioral observation scales are costly to develop. They take considerable time to formulate and scales must be developed for each individual job or for clusters of similar jobs. Because BARS and BOS are based on careful job analysis, however, they are likely to be acceptable to government enforcement agencies and courts.

Management by Objectives (MBO)

Management by objectives (MBO) is a system that features an assessment by a superior and a subordinate on the subordinate's objectives for a particular period and a periodic review of how well the subordinate achieved those objectives. An attempt is usually made to write objectives in quantitative terms, although some experts believe that certain objectives or targets can and should be stated in qualitative terms.

The MBO system generally includes the following steps (see Figure 13.7 on p. 382):

1. The supervisor and the subordinate mutually agree on the primary elements of the subordinate's job.
2. The supervisor and the subordinate mutually agree on the subordinate's specific objectives for the specified period (usually six months or a year).
3. The subordinate establishes a plan of action necessary to meet each objective.
4. During the specified period, the subordinate periodically reviews progress toward objectives. Progress checks may indicate the need to change action plans or modify objectives.

**FIGURE 13.6
Behavior observa-
tions scale — cook**

In completing this form, circle a 1 if the employee has exhibited this behavior 0–49 percent of the time, a 2 if 50–64
percent of the time, a 3 if 65–74 percent of the time, a 4 if
75–89 percent of the time, and a 5 if 90–100 percent of
the time.

1. Is careful not to waste food

   Almost never   1   2   3   4   5   Almost always

2. Uses tongs or spatula rather than hands to handle food

   Almost never   1   2   3   4   5   Almost always

3. Cooks meat that looks and/or smells bad

   Almost always   1   2   3   4   5   Almost never

4. Prepares for the next shift so that the next cook has
   minimum rather than maximum work to do

   Almost never   1   2   3   4   5   Almost always

5. Keeps sink clean

   Almost never   1   2   3   4   5   Almost always

6. Customers complain about the quality of the food

   Almost always   1   2   3   4   5   Almost never

Source: Adapted from Gary P. Latham and Kenneth N. Wexley, *Increasing Productivity Through Performance Appraisal* (Reading, Mass.: Addison-Wesley Publishing Company, 1981), pp. 214–215.

5. At the end of the specified period, the supervisor and subordinate meet to evaluate jointly the subordinate's performance on
objectives.

Advantages of MBO.   Perhaps the greatest benefit of MBO is that
it provides an objective, performance-based method of appraisal.
At the individual level, MBO can give individual employees greater
direction and self-control, build their self-confidence, motivate them,
improve their performance, further their growth and development,

FIGURE 13.7
The MBO process

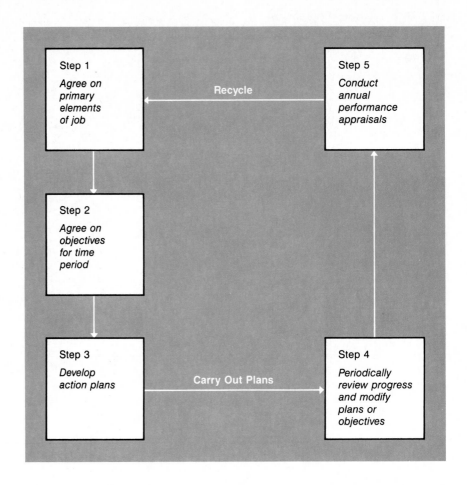

and provide them with full knowledge of the criteria on which they will be evaluated. In an interpersonal sense, MBO can enhance superior-subordinate relationships, improve communications, and provide a better coaching framework. Possible organizational benefits include better overall performance, identification of management advancement potential and developmental needs, better coordination of objectives, and less duplication and overlap of duties and activities.

Disadvantages of MBO. The MBO approach should not be viewed as a perfect system. When effectively used, MBO programs are systems of joint target setting and performance review. When a superior's directives are unreasonable, however, the MBO program can become a one-sided, autocratic, and time-consuming mechanism. Other potential problems include the following:

1. Too much emphasis on measurable quantitative objectives can lead to neglect of other important responsibilities.
2. Emphasis on measurement and quantification may result in sacrifice of quality.
3. If evaluation is based on goal attainment, subordinates may be inclined to set low goals so as to ensure their attainment.
4. There may be a tendency to set and enthusiastically adopt only those objectives that are important to one's superior.
5. Superiors using MBO can falsely assume there is no need for periodic coaching and counseling of subordinates.[16]

Team MBO. Most MBO programs are conducted on a one-on-one superior-subordinate basis. In many instances, one-on-one MBO does not account adequately for the interdependent nature of most jobs, particularly at the managerial and supervisory levels, nor does it ensure optimal coordination of objectives between various organizational groups. Accordingly, it may be useful to take a team approach to reviewing targets and achievements.

Essentially, team MBO involves the application of the basic MBO process to work groups. First, overlapping work units work with "higher" and "lower" units on overall organizational objectives, as well as set unit objectives. Then individuals work with their peers and superiors to define roles and develop individual objectives.[17] This approach can lead to greater participation by subordinates in setting objectives and improve relationships within teams and between superiors and subordinates.

CHOOSING THE BEST APPRAISAL METHOD

With the wide range of appraisal methods currently available, an organization is faced with a difficult task in selecting what it believes will be the best approach for its needs. In making this decision, human resources professionals should carefully examine two areas in particular: (1) the appropriateness of the appraisal method to the jobs being evaluated and (2) various organizational factors that can help or hinder implementation of the appraisal program.

Appropriateness to the Job

In many respects, the choice of an appraisal method boils down to a selection between one that is trait based or one that is behavior based. Appraisal methods that focus on employee traits or characteristics have been used for years. These methods can be developed quickly and easily, and they can be used for many jobs. Their advantages are offset by major shortcomings, however. The primary limitation of trait-based appraisal, especially when applied across jobs, is that it is unlikely to be highly job related. Personal traits or characteristics (such as a sense of humor, neatness, or shyness) may or may not have a bearing on job performance. The issue is basically one of validity, and as pointed out earlier, validity of an appraisal method is critical in today's legal environment.

Partly because the courts have generally favored behavior-based methods,[18] organizations are moving toward increased use of behavior-based performance appraisals developed through job analysis, which contributes to the validity of the process. Behavior-based methods include behaviorally anchored rating scales, behavioral observation scales, and management-by-objectives approaches. More traditional rating methods can still be used, however, as long as organizations take the time and care to develop them around performance-based dimensions that are clearly job related.

Organizational Considerations

Many organizational factors can have an impact on the appraisal system. Two factors that are especially important are organizational climate and training in appraisal procedures.

For example, General Electric Corporation recently found that organizational climate had a significant impact on its appraisal program. Subordinates and appraisers alike felt that appraisals went better when the climate was perceived as promoting trust, support, and openness. In this type of climate the appraisals placed greater emphasis on subordinate development. In addition, subordinates participated more in the appraisals; and appraisal interviews, conducted in an atmosphere of trust, were more open and instructive.[19]

Training in appraisal is also important to the success of any appraisal system. Regardless of which appraisal method is used, appraisers must be coached in how to use it properly. There is no substitute for this training, which can minimize the occurrence of rating errors and improve reliability and validity. One study of training in the use of behavioral-observation and trait-based scales found that when individuals received four hours of training in their use, there was a significant reduction in rating errors in each method.[20]

THE APPRAISAL INTERVIEW

Most performance appraisal systems include an **appraisal interview.** Traditionally, the interview has been a verbal communication of the results of the appraisal to the employee concerned. These interviews are conducted with varying degrees of participation on the part of the person being appraised.

Purposes of the Interview

The overall purpose of the appraisal interview is to let employees know where they stand or how they are doing. Other purposes include, but are not limited to, the following:

1. Encouraging present behavior.
2. Explaining what is expected of employees.
3. Communicating results of salary or promotion decisions.
4. Planning for future performance improvement.
5. Improving supervisor-subordinate relationships.

Interview Procedures

Because appraisal interviews often have the conflicting purposes of evaluating the employee's past performance and helping develop future performance, it is often recommended that the interview have two distinct parts. H. Kent Baker and Philip Morgan suggest the interview be conducted in two stages, each consisting of specific steps. The first is the *evaluation stage,* which provides information for administrative uses, such as pay-increase decisions, and presents base-line data for establishing future goals. There are six steps in this stage:

1. Schedule the interview in advance and prepare for it. Both the supervisor and the subordinate should review the subordinate's performance ahead of time.
2. Create an atmosphere that facilitates two-way communication. Put the subordinate at ease and minimize interruptions.
3. Begin with a statement of the purpose of the interview.
4. Encourage the employee to participate. One way is to ask the employee to appraise his or her own performance verbally.
5. Discuss total performance. Do not focus just on weaknesses; cover strengths as well.

PERSPECTIVE 13.2 Computer Monitoring

Business is finding a new — and controversial — use for the computer: Checking up on the work of employees second by second throughout the business day.

Termed computer monitoring, the process connects work stations in offices, factories and other settings to computers that keep a close watch on the individual worker's production by counting such functions as keystrokes per hour in the case of clerical personnel or the amount of time telephone operators take with callers.

Used by many employers to quicken the work pace and even determine compensation and promotion, the technique is spreading fast.

At least one third of the more than 7 million workers now linked to computers through video display terminals, or VDT's, are thought to be subject to some form of monitoring. Experts think that share will grow to more than half of the 40 million workers expected to be using VDT's by 1990.

Unlike traditional supervisory techniques that measure the final production result, such monitoring goes a step further and measures how em-

Source: Carey W. English, "Is Your Friendly Computer Rating You on the Job?" Excerpted from *U.S. News & World Report* issue of February 18, 1985. Copyright, 1985, U.S. News & World Report, Inc.

ployees achieve their output. Work time can be tracked down to fractions of a second and production goals raised.

"What's profoundly different about computer monitoring is its ability to monitor work as it takes place," says Harley Shaiken, a labor analyst at the Massachusetts Institute of Technology and a leading authority on computer monitoring. "It's a little like knowing your telephone is tapped. You tend to act differently, which is exactly what computer monitoring is supposed to make you do."

From the employer's point of view, the advantages are often substantial. At the Maryland-based Giant Food store chain, optical scanners at checkout counters eliminate pricing guesses by employees, improve inventory control, aid in work scheduling and track the workers' speed — all of which produce savings in excess of 15 million dollars annually. Productivity rating sheets allow employees to personally check how they are doing.

Despite enthusiasm for the system among employers, critics contend that such constant surveillance is counterproductive, leading to increased stress, fatigue and turnover among workers. They also say that the system is easily abused, pointing to instances where employees are reprimanded and even fired for falling below time standards that accompany computer monitoring.

6. Summarize and document the interview. Ask the employee to summarize the key aspects of the session, record the primary conclusions, and have both parties sign the document.

The second stage is the *development stage,* and here the supervisor's role shifts to that of a counselor. The supervisor and the subordinate work together toward performance improvement. There are seven steps in this stage:

1. Repeat steps 1–4 in the evaluation stage.
5. Set future performance goals. This involves establishing specific goals and plans for achieving them.
6. Formulate a development plan. Here the focus is on specific personal growth and development goals, such as acquiring new skills.

FIGURE 13.8 **Factors contributing to the effectiveness of performance appraisal review sessions**

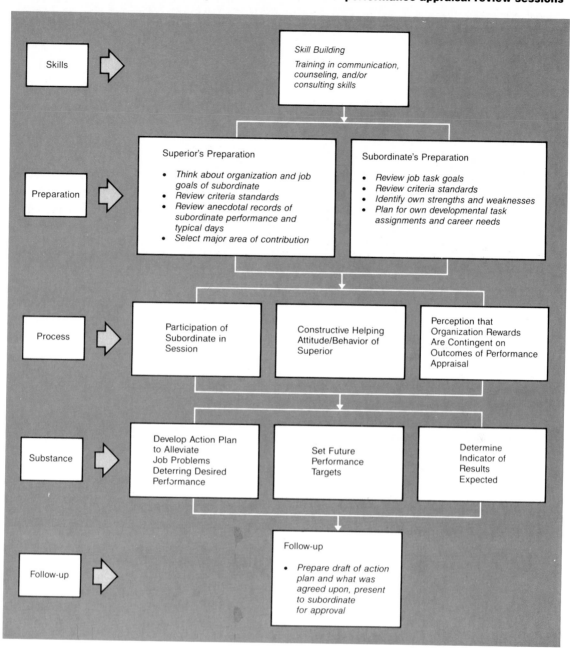

Source: Craig Eric Schneier and Richard W. Beatty, "Combining BARS and MBO: Using an Appraisal System to Diagnose Performance Problems," *Personnel Administrator*, 24 (September 1979): 57.

7. Prepare a working document. Goals and development plans are put in writing.[21]

The conduct of effective performance appraisal interviews requires careful attention to numerous dimensions of the process, which are summarized in Figure 13.8 (on p. 387).

SUMMARY

Performance appraisal is the formal, systematic assessment of how well employees are performing their jobs in relation to established standards and communication of that assessment to employees. How performance appraisal is conducted can have an impact on employees' needs for security, belonging, esteem, and self-actualization.

Appraisals can be conducted by the immediate supervisor(s), the employee, the employee's peers, or the employee's subordinates. The most common approach is to have the immediate supervisor conduct the appraisal on a semiannual or annual basis.

Laws and court cases affect the appraisal process. Performance appraisals are treated like employment tests under the EEOC guidelines and must therefore be reliable and valid. Reliability and validity can be reduced by appraisal errors such as the halo effect, central tendency, or leniency.

Numerous approaches are used in appraising performance, including the graphic rating scale, the checklist, the essay, the critical incidents method, behaviorally anchored rating scales, and behavioral observation scales.

In addition, management by objectives (MBO) is a widely used performance-based approach that focuses on the results achieved by the subordinate. In this method, the superior and subordinate agree on the subordinate's objectives for a specified period, and the subordinate is responsible for monitoring progress toward objectives. Performance reviews are then based on the extent to which objectives have been attained. A team approach to MBO can be used to account for high interdependence between jobs and work units.

Most performance appraisal systems include an appraisal interview. Appraisal interviews meet a variety of employee needs. Some experts feel, however, that the two main purposes of appraisal — evaluation and development — are incompatible and cannot be achieved simultaneously. These individuals recommend a two-stage interview, with the first stage focusing on evaluation and the second on employee development.

KEY TERMS

performance appraisal
feedback
evaluation goals
coaching and development
  goals
reliability
validity
halo error

error of central tendency
leniency error
graphic rating scale method
checklist method
weighted checklist
essay method
critical-incidents technique

behaviorally anchored rating
  scales (BARS)
behavioral observation
  scales (BOS)
management by objectives
  (MBO)
appraisal interview

REVIEW QUESTIONS

1. What are the two major purposes of performance appraisals? Describe each.
2. Discuss the circumstances in which appraisals can have negative affects on employee morale, and circumstances in which appraisals can have positive affects on morale.
3. In what ways are appraisals affected by the Civil Rights Act?
4. Describe halo and horn erros, error of central tendency, and leniency error in the use of appraisals.
5. What is the difference between graphic rating scales, the critical incident method, and behaviorally anchored rating scales?
6. What are the main features of MBO?
7. List and describe the steps that would be taken in a sound appraisal interview process.

OPENING CASE QUESTIONS

Case 13.1   Keep Them in the Dark

1. What mistakes are being made by Mike's and Alex's supervisors relative to performance appraisal?
2. What would be better managerial practice on the part of Mike's and Alex's supervisors?

Case 13.2   Let's Compare Notes

1. What mistakes are being made by the supervisors of the people in the carpool; and what are the consequences?

Case 13.3   The Painless Interview

1. Why, in your opinion, did the interview seem easy to Hal?

CASE 13.4   MBO: A FEW CASE HISTORIES
_____

At Highland Park Hospital outside of Chicago, the purchase and control of equipment and apparatus was fragmented and unstructured. So in December 1980 the top brass decided to use the management-by-objectives approach to put its house in order. After meeting with all department heads, the administrators set up an objective-setting and reporting system that reached from top management down to every last employee. Included in the unbroken chain were the board of trustees, CEO, vice presidents, department directors, unit managers, and all staff personnel. Through a process of negotiation at every level, a list of objectives and target completion dates was mutually defined and accepted; every department agreed to continually document its progress and distribute its record sheets to all employees.

According to the director of materials management, the reaction of unit managers and staff personnel was positive and enthusiastic. Within a year their commitment to the MBO process had clearly paid off: a formal material management department had been created that had achieved a $120,000 cost savings in purchasing, switched from a manual to a computerized requisition/purchase order system, and reduced its warehoused inventory by $50,000.

Another company where MBO has had overwhelmingly concrete results is Advanced Technology Inc. in McLean, Virginia. In six years this professional services firm grew from a start-up to a $42-million-a-year business—largely because of its MBO discipline, says one of its vice presidents and division general managers. Two key policies in the MBO plan are to allow every employee to build and manage a part of the business and to create managerial positions that allow an increasing number of employees to manage profit centers and be directly accountable for their profitability. To guarantee identifiable performance, each employee and manager is expected to set clear-cut annual objectives.

While this MBO strategy is a major reason behind Advanced Technology's success, it has not been revamped to keep pace with the firm's rapid growth and decentralization. For example, the informal channels of communication that sufficed when the company was smaller now cannot handle the needs of new employees (as many as 480 a year). As a result, they have little sense of direction and involvement in the company's objectives. Other factors are contributing to this breakdown in the MBO process. Like the people who moved into top-level positions, the employees who are becoming lower-level managers have come to the company with little or no managerial experience. They don't know how to share credit with or listen to their subordinates. And top-

Case Sources: Drew F. Burton, "Achieving Personnel Goals," *Mortgage Banking* (December 1982): 26–29; Martin Lasden, "Fad In, Fad Out," *Computer Decisions* (May 21, 1985): 74–88; Kenneth E. Vargo, "The MBO Process Applied to Material Management," *Hospital Material Management Quarterly* (May 1982): 50–53; Robert C. Wood, "Every Employee an Entrepreneur," *Inc.*, March 1983, pp. 107–109.

level managers, time-pressured to meet performance goals, are letting financial objectives outweigh their other MBO goals, such as motivating staff and helping them to develop into managers. In 1980 and 1981 professional staff turnover mounted to 35 percent.

Like Advanced Technology, and company with an MBO plan that is not dynamic enough to accommodate changes in the process itself or in the work environment will falter. For one east-coast manufacturer, that environmental change was the recession of the early eighties. When the recession hit, the team spirit of the managers and their mutual sharing of objectives gave way to an attitude of "every group for itself." Since then the annual stating of objectives has become a meaningless formality—one that represents an obstacle to circumvent, says the company's data processing manager.

For another data processing manager, however, flexibility within the MBO system to handle changes that were not predictable at the time of objective setting is one reason for his firm's success. American Automated is an Atlanta-based firm that provides computer services to the mortgage banking industry. One of its MBO objectives is to teach its program developers how to produce highly accurate plans and not to commit to unrealistic schedules. But if unexpected delays do creep into the schedules, managers and subordinates sit down and modify the original objectives as necessary. Effective goal setting, says its president, is a collective effort in the organization.

Discussion Questions

1. These case histories highlight both the strengths and drawbacks of management-by-objectives programs. Using the histories as a starting point, list some of the essential ingredients of an effective MBO program.
2. List some of the pitfalls that MBO programs must avoid.

part 5

Compensation and Reward

This section takes a close look at the compensation and reward process and its effects on the recruitment, retention, satisfaction, and motivation of employees. The design and management of the wage and salary structure are discussed in Chapter 14. Chapter 15 describes a variety of incentive plans that tie rewards to performance for the purpose of increasing motivation. Chapter 16 focuses on employee benefits — the rewards intended to supplement the employee's wage or salary.

Wage and Salary Administration

CONTEMPORARY ISSUES IN WAGE AND SALARY ADMINISTRATION
Comparable Worth / Wage Versus Salaried
Status / The Secrecy Issue
ROLE OF THE HUMAN RESOURCES DEPARTMENT

LEARNING OBJECTIVES

- Identify the goals of an equitable wage and salary program.
- Outline four methods of job evaluation.
- Describe how wage and salary surveys are used to make pay decisions.
- Describe a procedure for developing a pay structure using a graph.
- Explain why specific rules and policies are needed to administer the wage and salary program and to handle pay adjustments.
- Explain how government regulation affects wage and salary administration.
- Define comparable worth and explain its impact on wage and salary administration.

CASE 14.1   CIRCLE O HAMBURGERS

Bill Stevens had just been promoted to personnel director of Circle O, a small fast-food chain specializing in hamburgers and French fries. Circle O now employed about 120 full-time people, mostly supervisors, cooks, and maintenance people, and another 340 or so part-time workers. Most of the part-timers were high school or college students working at or near the minimum wage, but some were in supervisory or craft jobs. The best electrician in the company, for example, was a college senior majoring in physics. Some of the sharpest supervisors were also college students working part time. They came from all kinds of majors — liberal arts, business administration, health sciences, engineering, and others.

Bill was pleased and excited about his new position. He had started working at the counter in one of the restaurants while in college and had quickly worked up to a part-time supervisory job. When he graduated he was immediately promoted into a full-time supervisory job, and within two years he was managing one of the restaurants. He was soon making useful suggestions to top management about management practices, including personnel matters. Early on he had caught the eye of the president and founder of Circle O, and before another two years went by he was promoted into the newly created personnel director's job.

That evening, while having dinner with his fiancée, Peg, Bill mused aloud about his new position. "One of the advantages of my having so much experience with Circle O is that I can see a lot of problems that need working on. The trouble is, I'm not too sure I'll be able to solve some of them. There's going to be a lot more to this job than being concerned about making and selling good hamburgers."

"Say more," Peg responded.

"Well, for one thing," Bill replied, "I've got to get a handle on why there is so much turnover among our full-time supervisors. I suspect it's partly because the pay structure doesn't make any sense. I'm not even sure there is a pay structure. A really good supervisor with a year's full-time experience will get 30 percent more pay in one of our suburban restaurants than if he or she is working downtown. Some of our best full-time supervisors make less on an hourly basis than some of our part-time supervisors. I wonder if that makes sense. Some managers give pay increases twice a year, others only once. Some seem to give pay increases for length of service, some for having a congenial personality, and some for real performance. Some new supervisors are making less than their more experienced subordinates. Some of these things didn't seem fair to me when I was a supervisor. I wonder, too, whether Circle O is really competitive with other growing chains. I know of several of our people who recently went with competitors. You know Karlyn and Jeff — they've both gone with competitors. Maybe I should call them up and ask them why.

"What do you think, Peg? Any reactions to what I'm saying? Sounds like a mess, doesn't it? You've taken a course in personnel management. Maybe you could give me some advice."

"Wow," said Peg. "That sounds like chaos. You're going to earn your pay. I have several reactions — let's start with the frequency of salary review. . . ."

CASE 14.2   PAY SCALES IN THE LABORATORY

Dr. Beverly Scott was the head of a large applied research organization staffed mostly with engineers and scientists, many with advanced degrees. For two years in a row, she had been faced with very unpleasant dilemmas regarding pay increases for employees. Two years ago profits had been down and she could afford to give increases averaging only 3 percent. But inflation was at about 8 percent that year, so there seemed to be no way to make anyone happy. A year ago the company had been losing money, and Beverly had

had to tell her employees that their salaries were going to be reduced 5 percent. That certainly had not been pleasant news, but people had accepted it.

This year the dilemma was a happier one. Profits were up, so Beverly could afford increases averaging 9 percent. At the same time, inflation was down, to only about 5 percent. The dilemma was whether to help everyone regain lost ground in a substantial way or whether to give very large increases to a few of the "superstars" and only modest increases to the other employees. Beverly wanted to ensure that none of the best performers left. On the other hand, everyone in the organization was performing well in spite of what had happened to salaries two years in a row, and there was a real sense of team spirit. She did not want to erode this.

"I'd better do two things first," she thought. "First, I ought to analyze what we have given each person over the last three years. Second, I should think through what our philosophy about rewards really is — or ought to be. Come to think of it, I'd better ask for opinions from the entire top management group to be sure we are all in agreement."

These cases involve a critical aspect of human resources management: the compensation of employees through wages and salaries. An adequate and fair pay system is important in satisfying workers, retaining valuable employees, and remaining competitive with other organizations that provide similar goods and services.

At Circle O Company, Bill Stevens, the new personnel director, senses that a haphazardly designed and inconsistent pay system is at least partly responsible for the high turnover among supervisory employees. He also senses that there may be morale problems in this group. He is also aware of some of the complexities in the situation, such as part-time supervisors working along with full-time supervisors, and downtown versus suburban locations. Bill is aware that high turnover and low morale are costly to Circle O and are harming overall performance. One can infer that a more carefully designed and consistently applied pay system might alleviate some of the turnover, thereby improving the overall effectiveness of the organization.

Case 14.2 suggests the complexity involved in making pay-increase decisions. These decisions must take into account external realities (such as rates of inflation) and internal realities (such as the organization's ability to pay). As Beverly Scott realized, there must also be agreement about the basis for making increases. Pay increases can reward **merit** (quality performance), length of service, or both. But to be fair, the basis for increases should be standardized for all employees doing similar jobs throughout the organization.

The issues Bill Stevens and Beverly Scott face are only some of the typical problems in wage and salary administration. Among the considerations involved in designing an adequate pay system are the following:

- Equity or fairness of pay in comparison with the pay of others in the organization
- Competitiveness of the wages or salaries with those paid by other organizations in the same industry or locality
- The organization's ability to pay
- Whether to give pay increases on the basis of performance, service, or both
- What kind of wage or salary differentials there should be between satisfactory and outstanding performers, and between supervisors and their subordinates
- Rules of administration — for example, how frequently the pay structure and the pay of individuals should be reviewed, and how fast someone can move through a rate range (a range of possible pay amounts)
- What time perspective to have in mind — for example, whether pay decisions should be based strictly on performance over the last year, or whether performance and the organization's ability to pay over the past several years should be taken into account

This chapter addresses these considerations by outlining procedures and methods for determining fair and adequate compensation, describing rules for administering the pay system, and exploring current issues surrounding pay decisions. Government regulation of wage and salary programs is also discussed.

THE WAGE AND SALARY PROGRAM

Wages and salaries — the payment received for performing work — are a major component of the compensation and reward process, which is aimed at reimbursing employees for their work and motivating them to perform to the best of their abilities. In addition to pay, most employees receive benefits such as insurance and retirement pay and nonfinancial rewards, such as security, recognition, and privileges. Although individual employees vary in the extent to which they value pay in relation to other work rewards, for most people the pay received for work is a necessity. Thus, the wage and salary program of any organization is a vital concern to the employees within it.

Definition of Terms

In popular usage, the words *wage* and *salary* are sometimes considered synonymous; strictly speaking, however, they have slightly different meanings. **Wage** refers to an hourly rate of pay and is the pay basis used most frequently for production and maintenance employees (blue-collar workers). **Salary** refers to a weekly, monthly, or yearly rate of pay. Clerical, professional, sales, and management employees (white-collar workers) are usually salaried.

Generally, wage-earning employees are paid only for the actual hours they work, while salaried employees are paid the same amount for each pay period even when they work more or fewer than the regular number of hours in that period. Often, salaried workers also receive certain benefits that wage earners may not, such as time off with pay for personal business, although this practice is changing as more and more organizations place all employees on salaried status. In this chapter, the procedures described for determining pay and for administering the pay system apply to both wage-earning and salaried employees.

Exempt employees are workers not covered by the overtime provisions of the Fair Labor Standards Act (FLSA) and the Walsh-Healey Act. Exempt employees are those in executive, administrative, professional, or outside sales jobs as defined by the Wage and Hour Division of the U.S. Department of Labor. Management is not required by federal law to pay overtime to these employees. **Nonexempt** employees are those workers covered by these two laws and to whom overtime must be paid. Under the FLSA, which applies to most interstate companies, overtime must be paid to nonexempt employees beyond forty hours in one week; under the Walsh-Healey Act, which applies to federal contractors, overtime must be paid beyond eight hours in one day.

Goals of the Wage and Salary Program

Determining wage and salary payments is one of the most critical aspects of human resources management because (1) the organization's reward system has such a profound effect on the recruitment, satisfaction, and motivation of employees and (2) wages and salaries represent a considerable cost to the employer. A carefully designed wage and salary program that is administered according to sound policies and consistently applied rules is essential if human resources are to be used effectively to achieve organizational objectives. In essence, a wage and salary program should be designed with the following goals in mind:

- To meet the needs of employees, including desires for security and self-esteem.
- To motivate workers to achieve desired levels of performance.
- To be cost effective or based on what an organization can afford to pay.
- To be competitive with other organizations providing similar goods or services in order to attract and retain human resources.
- To comply with wage and salary provisions in the labor contract and with federal and state laws and regulations.
- To be fair and consistently applied throughout the organization.
- To be understood and accepted by employees, who must perceive the program as fair in order for them to feel satisfied with their pay.

A wage and salary program should be perceived as fair by employees and should be applied consistently throughout the organization, motivating employees to achieve desired levels of performance.

Courtesy of Hewlett-Packard Company

Factors Affecting the Pay Structure and Pay Decisions

The goals of the wage and salary program suggest that intricate and interrelated factors affect the pay structure of an organization and the pay scale for given jobs. Each employer has the difficult task of weighing these factors and making numerous decisions that ultimately determine how much a specific employee will be paid. Some of these are the relative worth of different jobs, the relative contributions of different employees, the prevailing wages and salaries in the community and industry, collective bargaining, economic considerations, and employees' and managers' perceptions of equity.

Worth of the Job and the Employee. Most people would probably agree that some jobs are worth more to an employer than others. For example, negotiating multimillion-dollar contracts with the government is considered to be worth more than emptying wastepaper baskets. One employee may be worth more than another in the same job. Sales Manager A consistently sells twice as much as Sales Manager B and is considered of more worth than B to the firm.

Prevailing Wages and Salaries. It is important that the organization know the typical wages or salaries being paid in the labor market for the various jobs represented in the organization. If a company pays its computer programmers only half as much as other companies in the community or region, for example, it is likely to lose most of its programmers and find it impossible to recruit competent replacements. If programmers are in very short supply, competition will probably drive up the salaries paid to these specialists. The decision to pay average, below-average, or above-average wages in relation to the external labor market is a major strategic decision in human resources management.

Collective Bargaining. Collective bargaining has a major impact on the pay system within given firms and within industries. In a unionized organization, collective bargaining determines the wages for jobs covered by the contract, rules of wage administration for these jobs, and methods for determining the relative worth of jobs. Nonunionized firms are ultimately affected by collective-bargaining agreements made elsewhere, since those firms compete with unionized firms for the services and loyalties of human resources. In addition, there are strong pressures within a unionized organization to pass along any wage or benefit gains made through contract negotiations to the nonunion segment of the work force.

Economic Realities.   The wage and salary structure and pay decisions affecting individual employees will also be directly influenced by economic realities. Two of these realities are the organization's ability to pay and inflation. If a firm has been highly profitable for several years in a row, it is much more likely to pay significantly above-average wages and to grant liberal pay increases than if it is losing money. If an organization is losing money, there is a strong possibility that a reduction in wages and salaries will be one of the options examined.

If inflation is driving up wages and salaries in the external labor market, many organizations may find it difficult to maintain appropriate balances within their wage and salary structures, particularly if beginning wages and salaries are going up faster than a company can adjust its wage and salary structure. This creates **salary compression** — a narrowing of the differentials between job levels — and reduces the organization's ability to grant merit increases because so much money is required to adjust the overall structure. In 1981, during a period of high inflation, a survey of personnel executives found that inflation and related problems ranked first among the problems facing wage and salary programs.[1]

Perceptions of Equity.   As has been discussed, perceptions of equity are important to job satisfaction and performance. To feel fairly treated, a person must feel that personal contributions (such as education and training, skill, seniority, effort, and job performance) correspond to personal outcomes (such as pay, recognition, privileges, and job satisfaction). In addition, these personal contributions and outcomes must be in line with those of other people, particularly coworkers and employees in the same organization. If they are out of line, job performance and satisfaction will suffer.

JOB EVALUATION

Job evaluation is the systematic determination of the relative worth of jobs in a particular organization. This procedure is used to answer such questions as: will technicians be paid more than researchers? If so, how much more? Will word processors be paid more than secretaries, or should both groups receive the same pay? On what basis can these decisions be justified?

Basically, job evaluation involves gathering information about jobs and then comparing them, using specially constructed scales. The result of this comparison is a hierarchy of jobs based on the extent to which each job presumably contributes to organizational

PERSPECTIVE 14.1   Peak-Time Pay

Almost two years ago, Stuart Mahlin came up with an idea to improve customer service at the Ohio bank where he is vice-president. Why not pay tellers more money the fewer days and hours they worked, he suggested. Ever since, Mahlin has been deluged with inquiries from other banks wanting to do the same.

No, bankers haven't lost their minds — it's just that they're caught in a bind. Customers now want to bank at all hours, and they continue to demand fast service. But getting the tellers to serve them is becoming harder. So Mahlin's employer, Provident Bank of Cincinnati, pays tellers who agree to work at the bank's busiest times $6.60 to $11 an hour, compared to the $5.50 plus earned by full-time tellers. The peak-timers put in an average five-hour day, three days a week. The catch: Unlike full-time tellers, they get no benefits.

Why didn't Provident add more full-time workers? Mahlin explains that the "pronounced peaks and valleys in customer traffic" mean that extra full-time tellers would be idle in non-peak hours. Adding part-time tellers (whom banks traditionally have paid at a lower rate) wouldn't help because turnover is prohibitively high as they leave for higher pay or full-time jobs. But the premium Mahlin offers

his peak-time tellers convinces them to stay put. At five of his 31 branches, he says, there has been no turnover in the past year among the peak-timers.

The peak-time idea is spreading. For example, Western Savings & Loan Association, with 70 branches around Arizona, some in the retirement community of Sun City, has a few unusual scheduling problems. Unlike downtown Phoenix branches, which have a lunch-hour crush, Sun City branches face a morning crowd as retired residents do their banking early so they can have their afternoons free. Flexible peak-time scheduling lets Western Savings meet its needs, says Sheila Black, personnel manager.

The final advantage of a peak-time program, explains Mahlin, is that "we're able to attract people who otherwise wouldn't think of working in a bank. Twenty or thirty years ago, the teller job in banks had status and stability." Today's tellers tend to be young and move on quickly to other jobs. The high peak-time pay, though, attracts well-educated, middle- to upper-income people who wouldn't give up volunteer work or their families for $4.00-an-hour teller jobs, but will work for the high peak-time wages. Into this category fall people who want to spend time at home with young children and entrepreneurs who need money while they start their businesses.

Source: Julie M. Gray, "Banks Pay Peak-Time Premium in Bid for Better Service," *Working Woman*, December 1984, p. 24.

effectiveness. The hierarchy is used to establish and justify different levels of pay for the various positions within the organization.

There is no easy, precise way to determine the exact contribution each job makes to overall effectiveness. A key concern in job evaluation, then, is to identify **job factors** that are considered to be of value and to determine systematically the degree to which each is present in each job. Responsibility, skill, effort, and working conditions are examples of factors that are commonly considered appropriate dimensions for determining relative **job worth,** or value to the organization. The choice of job factors — and the use of job evaluation itself — reflects basic assumptions consistent with equity theory: (1) it is logical to pay more for jobs requiring greater

FIGURE 14.1
Relationship of job analysis, job descriptions, and job evaluation

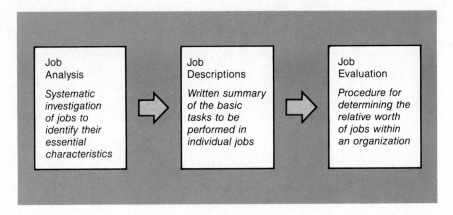

skill and training and demanding more from employees in effort, responsibility, and training and (2) people feel more fairly treated if pay differentials reflect a hierarchy of jobs based on relative worth. Job factors and their relative weights are typically identified by a close study of job descriptions, which are based on job analysis. (Figure 14.1 shows how job analysis is related to job evaluation.)

Job Evaluation Methods

Most organizations that pay wages use job evaluation. For example, if the owner of an insurance brokerage simply decides that the receptionist should be paid more than a typist, an informal job evaluation procedure has been used. Although this procedure may have been too subjective and too quickly applied, nevertheless a rudimentary form of job evaluation has occurred. Unless the decision has been made to pay the same wage to everyone in the organization, the question becomes what job evaluation procedure should be used and how systematically it should be applied. At the Circle O Company in Case 14.1, it appears that the job evaluation procedures are subjective and vary a great deal from restaurant to restaurant.

Formal job evaluation procedures are used in a high proportion of all but the smallest organizations. One study found 74 percent of the firms surveyed using one or more formal job evaluation plans. More than half of the firms using formal plans used two or more plans covering different categories of employees.[2] This practice reflects the common assumption that factors and scales that are adequate for production and maintenance jobs may not be appropriate for clerical, professional-technical, or executive positions. The use of different job evaluation methods for different groups is currently being challenged, however; see the discussion of comparable worth later in this chapter.

Four types of formal job evaluation methods have been particularly conspicuous in the last twenty or thirty years. In order of popularity they are (1) the point method — by far the most widely used; (2) the factor-comparison method, which is much more complicated than the point method; (3) the classification method; and (4) the ranking method.[3] This order of popularity holds for both office and manufacturing jobs.

The Point Method.   The point method of job evaluation uses several factors common to the jobs being evaluated. Scales divided into point distances are used to determine the degree to which these factors are present in a given job. Once all the scales have been applied to each job being studied, the points chosen for each scale are added to provide a total for each job. The point total designates the relative worth of the job. It is important to recognize that these scales are used to measure the job — not the job incumbent.

Figure 14.2 shows the scale used for the factor called "latitude of responsibility" in a point system of job evaluation that encompasses three major categories or areas. These areas are further divided into six job factors. As shown in Figure 14.3, the three areas are "responsibility," "know-how," and "relationships." "Responsibility" is divided into the factors of "latitude" and "authority." "Know-how" is divided into the factors of "diversity," "degree," and "application." "Relationships" is not divided into factors and is simply called "human-relations skill" in the pie chart. This particular system provides a maximum total of 2,000 points, of which 800 are allocated to "responsibility," 800 to "know-how," and 400 to "relationships." For an illustration of how points were allocated for the job of accounting clerk in one organization, see Figure 14.4.

Many versions of the point method of job evaluation are in use today. Although most include responsibility, skill, effort, and working conditions, any one version may have its own unique set of factors. As few as three or as many as twenty-five or more factors may be used, with the average probably about ten. Other factors might be "job complexity," "education and experience required," "mental requirements," "supervisory responsibility," "responsibility for equipment," "outside contacts," and so forth. "Job complexity" is often associated with jobs involving some hazard, such as dealing with toxic substances or radioactive materials. This factor can be used to acknowledge the required safety practices and equipment that increase the complexity and relative worth of the job.

FIGURE 14.2 "Lattitude of responsibility" scale of a point method of job evaluation

A. *Latitude:* Freedom to act as measured by the existence or absence of personal or procedural control over position.

20	65	115	120	305	400
Prescribed	Controlled	Standardized	Generally regulated	Directed	Broad guidance
Directed & detailed instructions; close supervision.	Established work routines; close supervision.	Basic practices & procedures are regulated; general work instructions; supervision of progress & results.	Practices & procedures covered by precendents or well-defined policy; supervisory review.	Broad practice & procedures covered by functional precedents & policies; managerial direction.	Subject only to broad policy and general management guidance.

Used with permission.

FIGURE 14.3
System total—2,000 points

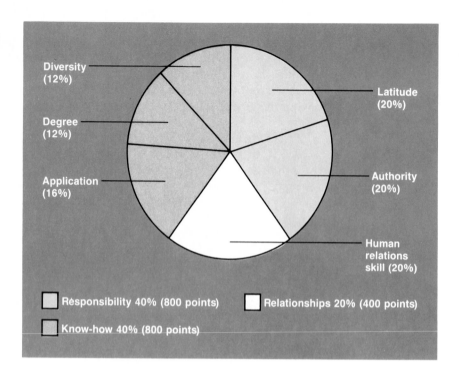

Diversity (12%)

Degree (12%)

Application (16%)

Latitude (20%)

Authority (20%)

Human relations skill (20%)

Responsibility 40% (800 points)   Relationships 20% (400 points)
Know-how 40% (800 points)

FIGURE 14.4
Points allocated to an accounting clerk position

Responsibility	
Latitude	120
Authority	83
Know-how	
Diversity	97
Degree	126
Application	120
Relationship	
Human relations skill	100
TOTAL SCORE	646
SALARY GRADE	7
DATE SCORED _____	BY: _____
	CHECKED: _____

Used with permission.

The widely used Hay Guide Chart-Profile Method of job evaluation includes three major factors: "know-how," "problem solving," and "accountability." Each major factor is further divided into subfactors.[4] A system used in the federal government in recent years, called the Factor Evaluation System (FES), is essentially a point system with nine factors. The factors are: "knowledge required," "supervisory controls," "guidelines," "complexity," "scope and effect," "personal contacts," "purpose of contacts," "physical demands," and "work environment."[5]

Another version of the point method is called the *job component method* of job evaluation. This method uses a questionnaire such as the Position Analysis Questionnaire (PAQ), described briefly in Chapter 7. The PAQ uses 194 items to measure job behaviors required on forty-five job dimensions. These scores are then combined to yield a "job value." Although the procedure appears complicated, it has been used by some organizations to develop wage structures considered equitable by the courts.[6]

The Factor-Comparison Method.   The factor-comparison method is more complicated than the point method, and it will be described only briefly here. Essentially, this method involves ranking *key jobs* in relation to other key jobs on each of several factors. For example, the jobs of executive secretary and administrative assistant may be compared in terms of responsibility, skill, effort, and working conditions. Key jobs are jobs that are found in many organizations and that have a relatively stable content.[7]

The next step is to determine for each key job what part of the present rate of pay is allocated to each of the factors. The remainder of the jobs are then ranked in their proper places in the framework thus established. In this method the points used to determine relative worth are tallied as cents per hour.

The chief problems with the factor-comparison method stem from its complexity. This method is time consuming, and raters need considerable training to implement it accurately. Its complexity may also create suspicion and resentment among employees.

The Classification Method.   The classification method of job evaluation starts with one-paragraph descriptions of a predetermined number of levels, grades, or "classes" of jobs, each of which corresponds to a **pay grade** or range of pay grades. These descriptions feature gradations of job responsibility, skill and education required, and the like. Job descriptions for other jobs in the organization are then examined, and these jobs are classified into grades or levels that seem most appropriate. In contrast to the point and factor-comparison methods, the classification method requires a decision at the outset on the number of pay grades to be included in the wage and salary plan. Actual amounts to be assigned to pay grades, of course, may be made after the job evaluation is completed. Called the General Schedule (GS) classification system in the federal government, this method has been used for years by the U.S. Civil Service Commission. In the GS system, federal jobs are assigned to one of eighteen pay grades.

The Ranking Method. In the ranking method of job evaluation, the raters simply rank order the various jobs examined. No attempt is made to determine the critical factors in each job. Instead, an overall judgment is made of the relative worth of each job and the job is ranked accordingly. Because of the difficulties in ranking a large number of jobs at one time, the paired comparison technique of ranking is sometimes used. With this technique, decisions are made about the relative worth of only two jobs at a time. Since each job is compared with every other job, however, the number of comparisons to be made increases rapidly with the addition of each job to the list.

The chief disadvantage of the ranking method is that there are usually no agreed-upon guidelines to what elements or factors the organization considers valuable. Thus, there are no "yardsticks" for measuring job value, and the underlying assumptions of those doing the ranking may never be brought into the open. There is the obvious danger that the rankings will be done in very subjective fashion and will be based on impressions rather than objective information. This method, then, contrasts with the other three methods, in which job factors can be examined, discussed, and modified as part of the evaluation process.

Problems in Job Evaluation

A number of potential problems can arise no matter which job evaluation method is used. Among these are inaccurate or incomplete job data; negative reactions from unions; and the need for employee understanding, acceptance, and support of the evaluation procedure.

Inaccurate Job Descriptions. If the information recorded in the job description is inaccurate or incomplete, the job evaluation will be inaccurate. For example, a job description may present an inflated picture of the actual job or, conversely, may not do justice to some of the important activities performed. In addition, if employees or supervisors do not believe that job descriptions reflect accurately the jobs actually performed, they will perceive the job evaluation procedures and the resulting wage and salary structure as unfair.

Careful and systematic job-data collection that attempts to secure agreement among employees and supervisors about the accuracy of descriptions can minimize these problems. In addition, job analysis should be repeated when there is reason to believe that the job has changed significantly. Then the job evaluation procedure can be applied to the revised job description to determine whether the job should be paid at a different rate.

Union Reactions.   The attitudes of union leaders toward job evaluation have been mixed over the years but have usually not been supportive. Two officers of the Communications Workers of America say this:

> Unions have traditionally approached job evaluation with apprehension and skepticism, if not open condemnation. The Communications Workers of America . . . has been no exception. Until just a few years ago, our union rejected job evaluation on the grounds that it was a management tool to manipulate wages outside of the collective bargaining process.[8]

An example of long-standing support, however, is the industry-wide job evaluation plan adopted by the United Steelworkers and the steel companies that covers all production and maintenance jobs.[9]

In the context of a joint agreement with AT&T to explore new participative approaches to solving problems, prior to the divestiture of the seven regional companies, the Communications Workers and the company established a joint national Occupational Job Evaluation Committee. The committee then started work to develop a job evaluation plan that would include the following objectives and principles (whether these will carry over into CWA relationships with the divested companies remains to be seen):

- All employees would have the right to appeal the job description, scoring, and relative worth of their jobs.
- Information about the job evaluation plan would be made available to all employees and union representatives.
- No wages would be reduced as a result of the plan.
- The plan would consider the changing technological nature of work as well as the accompanying emotional and psychological effects of technological change.
- Employees would be provided with opportunities to maintain and improve their skills through training, job design, and transfer.[10]

Supervisory and Employee Participation and Acceptance. Supervisors and higher management, as well as other employees, will need to understand, accept, and support the job evaluation system if it is to work. The challenge lies in selecting supervisors and other managers to participate on job evaluation committees and obtaining their commitment of time and attention to the process. Broad participation is necessary for informed decisions and acceptance in the organization; on the other hand, large committees are expensive and sometimes unwieldy.

WAGE AND SALARY SURVEYS

Because the wage and salary program affects the recruitment and retention of qualified employees, whether the organization should pay wages and salaries above, below, or equal to the averages for similar jobs in the community or industry deserves serious consideration. To establish a competitive wage and salary structure, an organization typically relies on data obtained from **wage and salary surveys,** which collect information on wages and salaries paid in other organizations. Wages paid in the surrounding metropolitan area or region tend to be the most important factor in determining general wage levels for most nonmanagement and first-line supervisory jobs. In establishing salary rates for professional and managerial employees, most medium-sized and large organizations examine national and industrywide patterns as well.

Most firms either conduct their own wage and salary surveys or participate in surveys conducted by other organizations, including consulting firms. These surveys may be carried out by mail, telephone, or interview. In addition, surveys are published periodically by the American Management Association, the American Society for Personnel Administration, the U.S. Bureau of Labor Statistics, the Administrative Management Society, the Federal Reserve system, and various employer and professional associations.

A major problem in using data from wage and salary surveys is the need to make accurate comparisons between companies. Careful inquiry needs to be made about the actual scope and responsibilities of the jobs surveyed, since job titles alone or even brief descriptions can be misleading. Appropriate statistical methods need to be used, too, in collecting and analyzing the survey data. A simple average of the wages paid by firms for a certain job does not take into account the numbers of employees involved or the size of the firms. For example, the average salary paid to computer programmers who are long-time employees of a small company may not be typical of the industry as a whole. On the other hand, averages weighted with the numbers of employees may be distorted by inclusion of large, well-paying firms in the sample along with a few small firms that have recently entered the industry. There may also be significant differences between urban and suburban rates of pay, which will affect survey data.

Another important consideration is whether benefits are included in the wage and salary survey. Some firms pay only average wages but offer unusually expensive benefits. Other organizations pay high wages, but are very conservative with employee benefits such as pensions, holidays, and sick leave.

An area of uncertainty about wage and salary surveys is the extent to which there will be future court challenges. Antitrust laws have been used to attack salary survey practices in at least two cases; in these instances, the matter was settled out of court. In one of these cases, salary survey practices of the Boston Survey Group, comprising 34 employer members, were challenged by a women's political action group, "9 to 5." The women's group asserted that the annual survey of this association was used to hold down salaries in various clerical jobs filled primarily by women. The Boston Survey Group entered into a consent decree with the state attorney general and agreed to alter its survey practices. One change agreed upon was that no individuals would be identified and that only aggregate data would be used.[11]

DETERMINING PAY RATES

Once the relative worth of jobs has been established by job evaluation, the actual rates to be paid for particular jobs need to be determined. Although no precise science governs this determination, one procedure commonly used is the two-dimensional graph. In this procedure, job evaluation points for key jobs are plotted against actual amounts paid or against desired pay rates as suggested by wage and salary surveys. A line drawn through the key jobs plotted on the graph suggests the approximate contour the other jobs should follow. Plotting the remaining jobs then reveals which jobs seem to be improperly paid with respect to the key jobs and to each other. Any clustering of jobs can also be observed, and this clustering will suggest which jobs may be grouped in different pay grades.

Figure 14.5 shows the pay grades of a hypothetical pay plan for the administrative-clerical employees of a small organization. The figure also shows how all of the jobs under this pay plan may be plotted on a graph. The horizontal axis represents the points ob-

FIGURE 14.5
Job evaluation points plotted against pay, showing "overpaid" and "underpaid" jobs

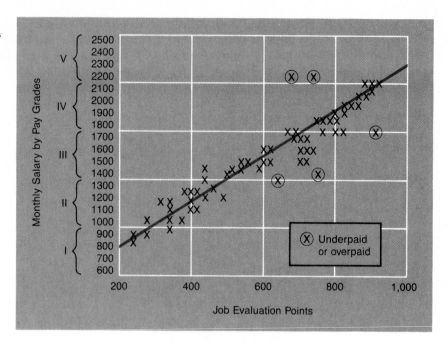

tained through a point system of job evaluation; the vertical axis represents salary levels. Tentative pay grades, or ranges I–V, have been identified on the vertical axis to suggest the structure of this particular plan. The line drawn through the jobs, which leaves approximately the same number of jobs above and below the line, indicates the relationship of pay rates to points. (In this figure, the line has been drawn simply by inspection. A "least squares" or regression line is sometimes computed to establish a more accurate relationship between points and pay.) In this example, two jobs above the line have been tentatively identified as overpaid, while three jobs below the line may be underpaid.

Most organizations probably use a single pay rate (such as $5.00 per hour) for all hourly production and maintenance workers in the same pay grade. Others, however, use **rate ranges** (for example, $5.00 to $6.25 per hour) for these employees. Rate ranges are much more common for nonexempt salaried employees and are almost always used in pay plans for exempt employees. A rate-range plan allows the employee to receive pay increases for the same job on the basis of individual merit, seniority, or both. Typically, the rate range is defined in terms of a minimum, average (or midpoint), or maximum amount.

The number of pay grades assigned to a pay plan is not at all standardized across companies; it may vary from as few as five to as many as thirty. Similarly, there is no typical dollar spread associated with rate ranges or grades. For hourly jobs, the top of a pay grade may range from 10 to 20 percent above the minimum for that grade. For salaried employees, the top of a pay grade may range from 15 to 75 percent above the minimum of a grade.[12] In addition, rate ranges may or may not overlap, although typical practice is to have some overlap to allow a very experienced employee to earn as much as another employee with less experience in the next higher pay grade.

ADJUSTING THE PAY STRUCTURE

As the widespread use of wage and salary surveys indicates, prevailing patterns in wages and salaries have an important impact on pay. Even firms that do not consider wage and salary survey data when designing a pay structure are bound to be affected sooner or later by outside pressures. For example, it would be impossible to staff an organization in a period of high inflation unless wages and salaries were adjusted to accommodate the upward movement of wages and costs of living in the area. In other instances, the need to reduce costs may mean that wages and salaries must be revised downward.

Wage and salary adjustments — whether upward or downward — must be made with great care so that unwanted distortions do not occur within the pay structure. Of chief concern is maintaining adequate pay differentials between jobs at different levels in the organizational hierarchy. Supervisors will understandably feel unfairly treated if there is little or no differential between their pay and that of their subordinates. Studies report that differentials between rank-and-file jobs and supervisory jobs typically range from 15 to 25 percent.[13]

Appropriate differentials must also be maintained between exempt and nonexempt groups to reflect differences in skills and training and to prevent perceptions of unfairness. And, since nonexempt groups are eligible for overtime payments, whereas exempt employees may or may not be paid for overtime, management must be sensitive to any problems created by overtime payments to the former group. Almost half of nearly 1,000 firms surveyed paid overtime to exempt employees, but typical practice is to pay only straight time, rather than time-and-one-half, for overtime hours worked.[14] (Figure 14.6 outlines the steps that are usually taken in developing or revising a wage and salary plan.)

FIGURE 14.6
Steps in developing or revising a wage and salary plan

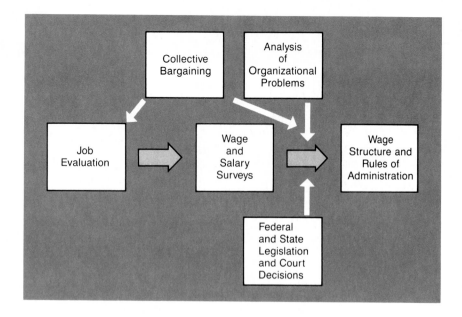

Competition and Inflation

Wages and salaries may need to be adjusted if competition in the labor market causes starting salaries to rise rapidly. If an organization's pay structure is not adjusted to accommodate this upward rise, salary compression will occur, with new people being paid almost as much as those who have been with the organization for years. Concerns about equity will obviously then occur.

The general upward rise in wage and salary levels in this country has meant that all organizations have needed to consider how to handle upward changes in their pay structures. Some firms give general percentage or **across-the-board pay increases** to accommodate pressures from inflation or competition. Across-the-board increases are also frequently used to adjust the wages of the non-unionized part of the work force to reflect increases granted to unionized employees. Other organizations include a general adjustment factor in merit or length-of-service raises, although the organization may not label that portion of the increase as such.

Wage Cuts

The necessity for wage cuts can also be a serious problem. A variety of forces, including government deregulation and a general economic downturn in a number of industries, has forced a significant number of organizations to lower wage and salary levels in recent years. Such pay reductions had to be negotiated when there was a contract with unionized employees, of course. In some instances, certain benefits such as profit sharing were extracted by the union as the price of making wage concessions. In instances where top management took significant cuts in pay, rank-and-file employees accepted pay reductions with less resentment than when management did not bear a comparable burden. For example, after Delta Air Lines' executives took pay cuts in the summer of 1983, a pay freeze for nonunion employees later in the year was more palatable than it might have been otherwise.[15]

In some cases management has successfully pressed unions for wage reductions, only to raise its own salaries or the salaries of nonunion employees subsequently. For example, early in 1981, union employees at Braniff Airways agreed to a 10 percent pay cut. A few weeks later, management approved a pay increase of 11.4 percent for lower and middle managers and secretaries.[16] As one might expect, such actions were promptly branded as unfair by the union. The other side of this coin is that management may have been trying to prevent serious turnover, particularly in the managerial ranks. A company in economic difficulty is subject to talent raids by other organizations.[17]

RULES OF ADMINISTRATION

In addition to guidelines about handling such matters as general adjustments, overpaid or underpaid jobs, and differentials between supervisors and their subordinates, various other rules need to be developed to administer the wage and salary program effectively. For example, it must be determined to what extent salary advancement will be based on length of service and to what extent on merit, how often salaries will be reviewed and adjusted, what controls over total wage and salary costs will be used, and what rules will govern reclassification of a job into a higher grade.

Length of Service Versus Merit

Deciding on the general philosophy and rules about rewarding length of service versus merit and measuring merit are particularly complex matters. Some organizations reward both length of service and quality of performance. That is, employees who are performing satisfactorily receive pay increases on the basis of length of service.

Outstanding performers are moved through the range faster, while below-standard performers receive no pay increases. Instead, they are given warnings and some coaching about their performance.

Skills-Based Pay

Other organizations have moved in the direction of skills-based pay. Workers at TRW Inc., for example, are paid in accordance with the number of skills they have mastered.[18] This concept has been successfully applied in a number of organizations, particularly those using self-managed teams.

Controlling Wage and Salary Expenditures

Rules are needed to maintain some control over wage and salary expenditures by the various units within the organization and by the organization as a whole. One mechanism used successfully is the **compa ratio,** a calculation that tells to what degree the jobs within a pay grade will average out near the midpoint of the range. If the midpoint value were 100, a compa ratio of 105 would mean that the average salary for the jobs in that pay grade was 5 percent above the midpoint. Organizations use compa ratios as controls by requiring managers to stay within certain percentage limits for each job grade or for all job grades combined.[19] Other indices that can be used in wage and salary control are budgets, comparisons among departments or divisions, total payroll, and unit labor costs.

Pay Increases

Additional rules are needed to handle promotions from one pay grade to another or from one pay plan to another. Since managers will be inclined to try to obtain more money for people who have reached the top of a range — particularly long-service employees or outstanding employees for whom no genuine promotion is available — control must be maintained to resist such pressures. Otherwise, people will be moved into higher pay brackets when there has been no genuine promotion. Another pressure that is sometimes exerted is a request that the job be reevaluated, with the idea of using an inflated job description to justify reclassification into a higher pay grade. Such practices tend to subvert the meaning and usefulness of job evaluation and introduce inequities in compensation administration.

There are usually more variables operating in pay-increase decisions than most employees — and even many employers — realize. Figure 14.7 shows many of them. Some variables that affect merit ratings, such as the superior's perception of the quantity and quality of the work performed, are related directly to individual performance. But other variables may be much more subjective. For example, the supervisor making a decision about a subordinate's pay increase may be influenced by his or her superior's impressions of that subordinate. Or, the supervisor may give a larger increase than is warranted just to avoid unpleasantness. Other subjective factors may be biases about personality, age, sex, or race.

As shown in Figure 14.7, some of the variables that affect pay-increase decisions have little or nothing to do with individual performance or the supervisor's perception of performance. Some of these variables have to do with the organization's ability to pay, the need to maintain pay differentials between supervisors and nonsupervisors, the current level of morale among certain groups of employees, the extent to which top management wants employee compensation to keep up with inflation or the cost of living, labor-market competition, and affirmative action requirements. For example, the organization may be under a court order to raise the salary levels of women and minorities. Levels of education, training, and seniority can also be factors if the organization has a policy of moving employees to higher pay brackets based on these factors.

GOVERNMENT REGULATION

Federal and state legislation has an impact on basic wage payments, particularly through minimum-wage laws and overtime regulations. The Equal Pay Act of 1963, aimed at correcting imbalances between the pay of men and women for equal work, is having far-reaching consequences.

Minimum and Overtime Wage Laws

Under the Fair Labor Standards Act (FLSA), as amended, employees "engaged in commerce or in the production of goods for commerce" must be paid wages of at least $3.35 per hour. The law provides for even higher minimum wages in certain industries, as prescribed by the administrator of the Wage and Hour Division of the U.S. Department of Labor. Most states also have minimum wage laws.

FIGURE 14.7   Probable variables affecting pay increase decisions

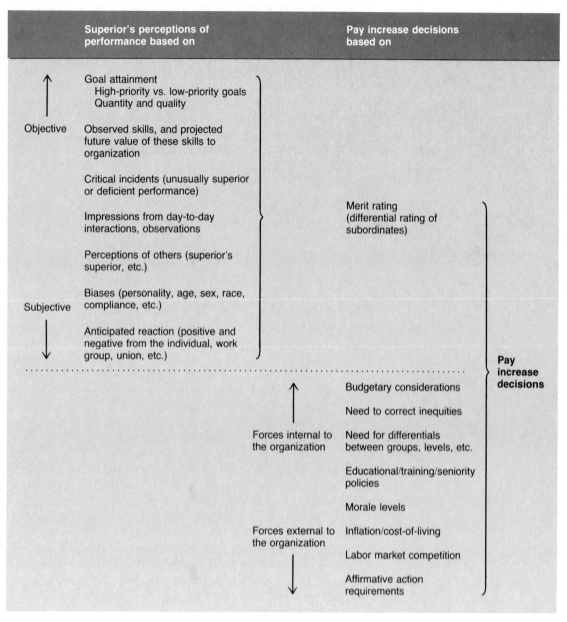

Further, as we indicated earlier, overtime payments must be paid to nonexempt employees but are not required for exempt employees.[20] Thus, it is important for organizations to be aware of the current criteria used by the Labor Department to determine which employees fit the exempt and nonexempt categories.

A case involving Howard Johnson's restaurant and motel chain illustrates the significance of these laws. To settle proceedings brought by the U.S. Department of Labor, the company agreed to pay some $5 million in overtime wages to 5,000 current and former employees whom top management had treated as exempt. Among these employees were salaried manager trainees and assistant managers earning less than $250 per week, as well as hourly managers and manager trainees. Howard Johnson's contended that these employees were exempt from overtime pay because they were part of "management." The Department of Labor insisted this was not correct because investigation showed that the employees were spending more than 40 percent of their time in "routine, non-management" work and that they earned less than $250 per week.[21]

Equal Pay Act

The Equal Pay Act of 1963, which amends the Fair Labor Standards Act, prohibits discrimination in wage payments for equal work on the basis of sex. According to this law, male and female employees are to receive the same pay "for equal work on jobs the performance of which requires equal skill, effort, and responsibility, and which are performed under similar working conditions. . . ."[22] (Note the four major job evaluation factors explicit in the law.)

As a consequence of the Equal Pay Act, many corporations have been faced with lawsuits on behalf of female employees. In a large number of instances, companies have been required to pay sizable sums in back pay and to increase wage scales for female employees. In the Corning Glass case, the first to reach the Supreme Court, the Court held that the Corning Glass Works had discriminated against women by paying a higher base wage rate to male night-shift operators than to female operators on the day shift.[23] In *Schultz* v. *Wheaton Glass Company,* a U.S. circuit court ruled against the employer, who was charged with discrimination against female inspector-packers. These employees were awarded nearly $1 million in back pay. The Supreme Court refused to hear the case on appeal, thus confirming the decision. The case is significant because the decision supports the notion that the jobs must be "substantially equal" and not "identical" to warrant equal pay.[24]

In another case, Northwest Airlines was ordered to pay nearly $60 million in back pay to female flight attendants. In this suit, the female attendants charged that male attendants doing similar work were paid more, that women were required to share double rooms on layovers while men were given single rooms, that the company paid cleaning allowances for uniforms only to the men, and that only women were required to meet weight restrictions. A federal district court ruled in favor of the female flight attendants, and the decision was upheld by a federal appeals court. The airline said it would appeal the decision to the Supreme Court.[25]

CONTEMPORARY ISSUES IN WAGE AND SALARY ADMINISTRATION

A number of contemporary issues surrounding pay decisions affect wage and salary practices in organizations today. Chief among them is the issue of comparable worth, a highly sensitive, complicated, and still unresolved question that continues to stimulate much debate and legal action. Other important issues concern the desirability of placing all workers on salaried status and the need for secrecy about pay decisions. (Another issue, to be discussed in Chapter 18, is whether the long-term effects of "two-tier" wage scales will be beneficial or detrimental in employee relations.)

Comparable Worth

In essence, **comparable worth** is the notion that women should receive the same compensation as men for work of comparable worth as well as for equal work. The fact that jobs held predominantly by women generally pay less than those held predominantly by men has focused attention on the question of whether pay differences among occupations are based on real job worth, or whether they simply reflect a long tradition of sex discrimination. Debate on this question is far from over. The former chair of the Equal Employment Opportunity Commission, Eleanor Holmes, has referred to comparable worth as the "discrimination issue of the 1980s." It appears that court cases and legislation on this issue are likely to extend the debate well into the 1990s. Comparable worth has also become an issue in collective bargaining. For example, in 1981, 1,500 city workers in San Jose, California walked off their jobs over the issue.[26] It also motivated a walkout by 1,600 technical and clerical employees at Yale University, led by the newly organized local 34 of the Federation of University Employees.[27]

The comparable worth issue stems in part from the fact that, on average, women are paid less than men. Estimates of women's pay vary from 60 to 65 percent of men's earnings. Differences in years of labor-force experience and vocational and occupational training can explain close to half the disparity, but a sizable proportion appears to stem from other factors.[28]

Many explanations for the persistent earnings gap have been put forward. One study found that men and women view the reasons for the disparity very differently. Women are much more likely to attribute the earnings gap to organizational practices, whereas men are much more likely to place the responsibility for the gap on the women themselves.[29] Geraldine Ferraro's explanation is as follows: "Women's earnings hover at just 60% of men's despite decades of social, legislative, and demographic change. . . . Women are first channeled into certain sectors of the economy, then they are clustered into the lowest paying occupations within those sectors, and finally they are confined to jobs that, by virtue of being female-dominated, are undervalued and underpaid."[30] Comparable worth is seen by some as a way of overcoming this gap in earnings. Those who support the concept assert that (1) women have historically been "crowded" into certain occupations through discriminatory practices in society; (2) the labor market reflects this crowding and thus the employment discrimination that caused the crowding; and (3) if the labor market is discriminatory, so too are the pay systems based on it.[31]

Bringing the argument closer to the organization, Helen Remick states: "The practice of setting wages according to job families (occupation) is a sure way of producing sex-biased results. It is clear that the market place is biased against women; therefore to use the market place as a basis for paying clerical workers less than maintenance workers, for example, is to perpetuate discrimination."[32]

Remick would minimize market effects by relying largely on a single job evaluation system within a given organization. In fact, she defines comparable worth in this way: "*the application of a single bias-free point factor evaluation system within a given establishment, across job families, both to rank-order jobs and to set salaries.*"[33] Fairness, according to Remick, would be enhanced by looking for bias in the following areas:

1. *Factors chosen for analysis.* Does the job evaluation system include factors usually associated with women's work (e.g., responsibility for people rather than things, literacy, the noise of office machines, or the poor working conditions created by many word processors)?

2. *Factor weights.* Are factors usually associated with women's work always given less weight? Can such differences be justified on bases other than sex?

3. *Application.* The best system in the world can be undone with a biased application. Are your job descriptions bias free, or do men manage and women supervise, men interpret and women use? Are the evaluators sensitive to the full scope of women's jobs?

4. *Salary setting.* Is a single salary scale used? If not, do the

scales for women's jobs give consistently less return (lower salary) for worth (points)?[34]

Those who oppose the comparable-worth concept argue that job evaluation does provide a procedure for determining relative job worth, but that there are circumstances in which jobs and their contexts are too dissimilar to use one job evaluation scheme to cover all jobs. In addition, relating labor-market rates to key jobs is a fundamental aspect of using job evaluation to determine wages.[35] According to George Hildebrand:

> Certain jobs are standardized, usually due to technology across many firms in a given local labor market; in fact, they reach across several industries as well. For example, on the blue collar side, there are machinists and millwrights, or computer programmers, secretaries, and accountants on the clerical side. These jobs provide the basis upon which the wage curve can be built, precisely because they tie the external and internal markets together. For these reasons, they are called key jobs.[36]

Donald Treiman emphasizes that the recruitment and retention of employees with different technical or professional skills requires attention to quite different labor markets, some local and some national.[37] Further, the argument continues, the way to reduce differences in the pay of men and women is to increase the upward mobility of women into the professional and managerial ranks.

It is uncertain where the arguments will lead; but as of late 1985, federal government action and court decisions had tipped in the direction of rejecting the concept of comparable worth. During that year, the EEOC rejected the concept and ruled it would not litigate comparable worth claims,[38] and the U.S. Civil Service Commission voted five-to-two to reject the concept as a remedy for pay differentials between men and women.[39] In September of 1985, the U.S. Circuit Court of Appeals overturned a district court decision that had previously found the state of Washington discriminating against women by paying them less than men performing comparable work. The state employees union said it would appeal the case to the U.S. Supreme Court.[40] The debate appears to be far from over.

Wage Versus Salaried Status

In recent years, some firms have placed all employees on salaried status. The change has usually been made because differences between the salaried and wage payroll in such benefit areas as sick-pay eligibility and time off with pay for personal reasons were not great, were irritating to wage employees, and were difficult to jus-

PERSPECTIVE 14.2 Sifting the Traits of Comparable Worth

The janitor's job is repetitious, needs only basic skills, rarely requires contact with other employees and has limited impact on the company. Give the janitor 75 points.

The president's job is wide-ranging, calls for fairly specialized skills and requires supervision of 4000 employees and accountability for the entire $500 million manufacturing concern. Give the president 4456 points.

The points translate into dollars in this hypothetical case study created by a Philadelphia-based consulting firm called the Hay Group. The points are awarded for know-how, problem-solving ability and accountability. Sex, race and even impressive job titles count for nothing. Stress also isn't considered because what causes one person to panic can cause another to thrive. All jobs that add up to the same point totals net the same paycheck.

"We do not look at the person, their background or their performance," said Thomas B. Wilson, general manager of Hay's Boston office. "We want to find out what a company needs to be paying to be fair internally and to be competitive externally."

Hay's evaluation system, known as the Hay Guide Chart Profile Method, has gained popularity as the notion of comparable worth — equal pay for work of equal value — has gained wider acceptance. Mutual Bank of Boston, Choate-Symmes Health Services in Woburn, Prime Computer Inc. in Natick and the state government of Massachusetts are just a few institutions Hay has worked

with on the concept, considered one way to close the wage gap that historically has existed between female-dominated and male-dominated jobs.

The debate over comparable worth has been going on for years, but it clearly gained momentum when women attained the majority position in the nation's work force. Women's groups and unions claim that jobs held by women traditionally have been underrated in importance. In Massachusetts, for example, starting salaries for state cleaning-service matrons are $1000 a year less than male janitors. . . .

Hay begins with detailed documentation of all jobs at a particular company, sometimes relying on questionnaires and other times using one-on-one interviews. Next is an evaluation that helps Hay determine the basis for comparing salaries. Each of the three categories — know-how, problem solving and accountability — is broken down into several subgroups. For example, necessary skills can be defined as anything from "basic" to "professional mastery." Breadth of know-how can run from "none" to "total." Thinking challenges run from "repetitive" to "uncharted."

Every extra requirement, down to the equipment workers must operate or the thought processes necessary to do a job, are accounted for in the chart. A janitor who uses electrical equipment, for instance, would win a few more points than one who uses only a broom. A research job requiring specific knowledge of chemistry would win more points than one requiring only a broad knowledge of economics. All of the decisions are made in committee and checked against an extensive data base.

Source: Excerpted from Lynda Gorov, "Sifting the Traits of Comparable Worth," *Boston Sunday Globe*, May 26, 1985, pp. 59, 64.

tify. Other reasons include the perception by many employees that salaried status carries more prestige and may provide more job security. In many instances management has concluded that the costs of placing workers on salaried status would not be large and that there might be gains in good will and employee relations.

Salaried status does not guarantee job security, however. And while salaried status may carry more prestige, it does not necessarily mean more pay, because many blue-collar workers are paid higher hourly rates than many white-collar workers.

The major problems involved in shifting large groups of employees from wage to salaried status usually relate to changes in employee benefits. Generally, the shift to salaried status means an increase in benefits such as sick leave, major medical insurance, severance pay, group life insurance, time off for personal business, and so forth. Therefore, management must agree on the purposes of such a move and examine the true cost implications carefully. The reaction of those employees already on the salaried payroll must also be considered. If part of their "income" has been higher status and more liberal privileges and benefits than those of the

*"Oh, I've made money in my time, but, frankly,
I'd have settled for a lot more."*

hourly employees, they may react by pressing for higher wages, either individually or through unionization.

The Secrecy Issue

The extent to which employees are informed of the details of wage and salary programs varies widely. Most unionized workers are informed through the wage contract about details of their respective wage programs, particularly if single rates are paid for given categories of jobs. In other words, they know exactly how much each fellow employee is being paid. Probably a small percentage of nonunion employees has very accurate knowledge of the specific salaries being paid individuals. About one-third of the companies surveyed, however, provide copies of wage schedules and progression plans pertaining to employees' own job categories, and the other two-thirds make this information available. More than half of the firms provide access to information about wage schedules for job categories other than the employees' own.[41]

Whether or not to make the actual salaries paid individuals common knowledge is a controversial matter. An argument against making salary information available is that such information tends to create considerable friction in the organization. Although management may be prepared to defend the overall program, supervisors often have great difficulty justifying the legitimacy of minor differentials between people. Since people are likely to compare their own performance with that of their peers and these judgments can easily differ from those made by supervisors and higher managers, disagreements over relative ranking are bound to occur. Most managers try to minimize this problem — and the time and effort spent dealing with complaints — by maintaining secrecy about salary data. A policy of secrecy also may assume that employees are thus spared unnecessary stress and the behind-the-scenes commiseration that would otherwise occur.

Some research suggests that secrecy about average salaries and salary ranges (not necessarily salaries of individuals) may create dissatisfaction rather than prevent it. One researcher surveyed 563 middle and lower managers in seven organizations and found that they tended (1) to underestimate the salaries of their superiors, (2) to overestimate the salaries of subordinates, and (3) to overestimate the salaries of their peers. Associated with these inaccuracies in perception was dissatisfaction with the differentials among themselves and between themselves and both superiors and subordinates.[42] Other researchers, however, queried 575 professional employees in an organization and found that only about half were willing to have their salaries known to others. This held true by occupational group, by self-assessed performance level, and by age. There was also some tendency for the more highly paid persons to prefer to have salaries kept confidential.[43]

ROLE OF THE HUMAN RESOURCES DEPARTMENT

In most organizations, the human resources department plays a major role in wage and salary administration. One survey of 630 organizations — three-fourths of them business and industrial firms — found that the human resources department in 77 percent of the organizations had "all" of the responsibility for the wage and salary administration program and in another 20 percent had "some" responsibility.[44]

The human resources department is likely to develop the job evaluation system, perhaps with the help of an outside consultant, and will coordinate and manage the system. This includes making certain that accurate job descriptions are written and having one or more representatives on a job evaluation committee.

As a rule, the human resources department conducts surveys of wages and salaries or participates in surveys the department uses in revising the pay structure. Once top management has approved modification of the overall pay structure, the human resources department typically monitors compliance with that structure and with the rules that have been established. Generally, individual managers make decisions about the pay of subordinates within the framework of wage and salary plans, and the human resources department ensures that the limits are not exceeded and that the spirit and intent of the plans are adhered to.

SUMMARY

Determining wages and salaries is one of the most critical aspects of human resources management, since it has such a profound effect on the recruitment, retention, satisfaction, and motivation of employees. Careful job analysis, job evaluation, and design of the wage and salary structure and rules of administration are crucial to effective management of organizations.

Job evaluation is the process of determining the relative worth of jobs to the organization. Basically, job evaluation includes gathering information about jobs and then using some kind of scale or scales to develop a hierarchy based on value to the organization. The point method of job evaluation is the most widely used.

Wage and salary surveys are used to establish pay grades, and job evaluation is used to allocate jobs to the different grades. In conducting surveys, care must be taken to assess accurately the scope and responsibilities of the jobs surveyed, since job titles or brief descriptions can be misleading.

Many questions need to be answered in determining the wage structure. Judgments and perceptions about equity, competition in the region or industry, and ability to pay provide partial answers to these questions.

To carry out the philosophy of the compensation system, maintain the integrity of the pay plans, and control costs, it is necessary to develop rules about progression within salary ranges and the movement of jobs into higher pay grades. One useful cost-control tool is the compa ratio. Developing a philosophy about how merit and length of service relate to salary progression and developing procedures for determining relative merit are particularly important matters. Some organizations, particularly those that have developed and encouraged self-managed teams, have used the concept of skills-based pay.

Collective bargaining has a major impact on wage structures within organizations and industries. Union leaders have generally been resistant to job evaluation, but there have been notable instances of cooperation in the establishment of job evaluation systems.

At any one time, many variables affect pay-increase decisions. Even if measures of performance are entirely objective, numerous additional forces, both inside and outside the organization, affect these decisions.

Minimum wage legislation and laws that control overtime payments — the Fair Labor Standards Act and the Walsh-Healey Act in particular — need to be adhered to if an organization is to avoid serious penalties. The Equal Pay Act prohibits discrimination in pay for equal work based on sex and is having far-reaching effects. The concept of comparable worth goes beyond the concept of equal pay for equal work and extends to equal pay for work of comparable worth. How widely this controversial concept should be applied is likely to be a subject of debate, lawsuits and court decisions, and proposed legislation well into the 1990s.

Other contemporary issues include whether to place all employees on salaried status and the extent to which wage and salary information should be open or secret.

The human resources department plays a major role in wage and salary administration in most organizations. That department is heavily involved in the job evaluation program, in salary and benefits surveys, in recommending changes in the structure and rules of the compensation program, and in coordinating and monitoring the overall program.

KEY TERMS

merit
wage
salary
exempt
nonexempt
salary compression

job evaluation
job factor
job worth
pay grade
wage and salary survey

rate range
across-the-board pay
 increase
compa ratio
comparable worth

REVIEW QUESTIONS

1. What are the goals of an equitable wage and salary program?
2. Discuss the forces influencing the pay structure and pay decisions.
3. Briefly describe four methods of job evaluation.
4. Describe how wage and salary surveys are used to affect the compensation structure and pay decisions.
5. Discuss the kinds of rules and procedures that are needed to administer a wage and salary program and the reasons for these procedures.
6. Explain how governmental regulation affects wage and salary administration.
7. Define comparable worth and discuss its impact on wage and salary administration.
8. Discuss the pros and cons of secrecy in wage and salary matters.
9. Discuss the role of the human resources department in wage and salary administration.

OPENING CASE QUESTIONS

Case 14.1   Circle O Hamburgers

1. What are some of the questions Bill should ask in determining the extent to which the wage structure is equitable and serving the needs of the organization?
2. What can Bill do about different managers giving widely different pay increases?
3. What can Bill do about the turnover rate?

Case 14.2   Pay Scales in the Laboratory

1. What additional factors besides inflation and performance should Beverly Scott consider in determining pay increases?
2. Should Beverly Scott reward a few "superstars" with large increases and give only modest increases to others?

CASE 14.3   COMPARABLE WORTH: THE WAGE DEBATE WAGES ON

Although comparable worth is the subject of heated political debate, no one is disputing the facts: clearly, men and women do not receive the same pay for jobs that demand similar education and skills. Nor is anyone disputing the principle: wage discrimination against women is unfair.

The crux of the comparable-worth argument is this: How do you determine the value, and thus the comparable worth, of jobs? This question was the key issue in the most recent and well-known comparable-worth case to date. In 1983, a federal district court ruled that the state of Washington had practiced illegal discrimination in employment and compensation after a consulting firm (hired to evaluate state-government jobs) concluded that job classifications that were 70-percent filled by women were paid 20-percent less than those 70-percent filled by men. The court ordered the state to compensate 15,500 workers more than $500 million in retroactive pay.

The state appealed the decision, and in September 1985 the appeals court upheld that appeal and overturned the 1983 decision (which is now being appealed to the U.S. Supreme Court), saying: "Economic reality is that the value of a particular job to an employer is but one factor influencing the rate of compensation for that job. Other considerations may include the availability of workers willing to do the job. . . ."

Thus the already murky and subjective area of job evaluation—the determination of relative worth of a job—became the obstacle to the implementation of the comparable-worth concept.

How *do* you determine the worth of a job? In several important cases, the Supreme Court has ruled that Title VII of the Civil Rights Act of 1964 (equal pay for similar work) can be used to correct wage discrimination not covered by the Equal Pay Act of 1963 (equal pay for equal work). But no legislation states how the value of jobs can be determined.

Those who support comparable worth suggest that an organization use a single job evaluation system that is based on real, measurable criteria and is applicable to a wide array of jobs. (Currently, many companies use one system for clerical and secretarial positions and a different system for other positions.) They claim that developing a means of equalizing wage structures between men and women would pump more money into the economy, attract men to previously all-female jobs, and reduce the number of working poor families, especially those headed by women.

Case Sources: Carole Bodger, "Sixth Annual Salary Survey," *Working Woman,* January 1985, pp. 65–67; Carrie Dolan and Leonard M. Apcar, "Washington State Union to Fight Ruling That Hurts Equal Pay–Equal Jobs Drive," *Wall Street Journal,* September 6, 1985, p. 5; Linda Chavez, "Pay Equity Is Unfair to Woman," *Fortune,* March 4, 1985, pp. 163–164; The Equal Employment Advisory Council, "Twenty Questions on Comparable Worth," *Personnel Administrator* (April 1985): 64–68; and Chris Lee, "Comparable Worth (The Saga Continues)," *Training,* (June 1985): 28–33, 37.

In contrast, opponents of comparable worth say that a single job evaluation system would create a total imbalance in the economic marketplace system. It would remove the marketplace from the picture and instead substitute an artificially contrived economic model that does not reflect the real world. The skills involved in a job and the internal importance of a job to a company must be balanced against its relative worth in the marketplace (that is, vis-à-vis supply and demand). Otherwise, say comparable-worth adversaries, employers will be forced to overpay for jobs that would command low pay in the marketplace. With no analogous rise in productivity or increase in services, and without decreasing wages for others, employers will have to raise consumer prices or else reduce the number of available jobs.

Opponents of comparable worth also feel that the marketplace should have input into the determination of wages because most people think they're worth more than the marketplace is likely to pay. Moreover, they claim, the marketplace represents another reality: even though equal opportunity is guaranteed by law, many women continue to seek employment in female-dominated, low-paying jobs—such as nursing, secretarial, and teaching jobs.

Everyone agrees that discriminatory practices and social conditions that foster pay inequity between men and women should be eliminated. Organizations should pay equitably. But though there is agreement in theory on the concept of comparable worth, implementation remains a Pandora's box. And as both sides fight it out, other societal and cultural biases creep into the debate over whether an imposed system can attempt to place a market value on positions and correct what has historically been an inequitable situation.

Discussion Questions

1. As the manager of a firm, what factors would you want to be aware of in order to make your job evaluations more objective?
2. What are the two main factors in determination of job worth that are at the heart of the debate between proponents and opponents of comparable worth? Why?

Incentive Plans

CHAPTER OUTLINE

LEARNING OBJECTIVES

- **Outline various incentive plans used to motivate production workers, sales personnel, and professional and managerial employees on an individual basis.**
- **Discuss the problems associated with individual incentive plans.**
- **Describe the conditions under which group incentive plans are particularly effective.**
- **List the objectives of productivity gainsharing and profit-sharing plans.**
- **Describe the suggestion plan system and indicate some of the problems involved in implementing such plans.**
- **Identify the incentives that may be used in a positive reinforcement program.**

CASE 15.1   DO WE NEED INCENTIVES?

George Sims, production manager at HiQuality Furniture Manufacturing, had just come back from his quarterly meeting with the production department employees. There had been seventy-two people there, including George's assistant, the six supervisors, and the three clerical assistants. At the meeting, George had given his usual pep talk about the importance of maintaining quality, decreasing the number of rejected parts, and working more efficiently to raise production. He had also told the group that the company wasn't in bad shape, but profits and HiQuality's share of the market were slipping some. His remarks had prompted a few questions, but no one had offered any concrete suggestions for improving the department's performance. By and large, apathy had characterized the meeting, and that apathy was disturbing.

George believed that the employees generally liked and trusted him, but he could also sense their lack of enthusiasm for really getting down to work and improving things. "I wonder whether we need an incentive system of some kind," he thought. "Maybe we should give people a bonus for turning out components at a rate above some standard. As it is, everyone in the same job classification gets the same pay, and there's no real incentive to do an outstanding job. I think I'll get the supervisors in here and toss around the idea of an incentive plan with them."

When George met with the supervisors, he found general agreement that people were not working up to capacity but no suspicions that they were deliberately goldbricking. A lively discussion followed his proposal to introduce an incentive plan that would reward highly productive workers with extra pay. Several supervisors felt an incentive plan would be a good idea, but one commented, "We'll have nothing but bickering with the union if we go that route. They'll argue about every standard, and getting them ever to raise a standard will be like pulling teeth." Another supervisor remarked, "When I worked for Mountain View Furniture, workers played incredible games to beat the system. They even constructed a bin under the floor where they hid finished pieces to pull out when someone got behind. No one ever figured out how they built that bin and the trap door without being seen."

But another supervisor said, "Yes, but at FurnitureTech they've got a plant-wide incentive system, and everyone is making at least 50 percent more than we're making here, including the supervisors. I understand they spend a lot of their time in meetings, though."

Those remarks prompted discussion and joking about whether supervisors should be included in the incentive system and comments like, "Who needs more meetings?" One of the young, new supervisors then said, "Yeah, but if people go to meetings to figure out how to work smarter, maybe that's not so dumb. . . ."

The meeting concluded with George's saying, "Thanks for your ideas. We'd better get more information on incentive plans and then talk some more. I can see this is a more complicated issue than I thought."

CASE 15.2   THE BONUS IS COMING OUT OF OUR HIDES

The hospital administrator of Vistaview Hospital had recently started a bonus system for department heads, providing them with quarterly bonuses based on cost savings within individual departments. The administrator was thinking of extending the system to all employees if it worked well with department heads, but he had kept the idea to himself, not wanting to raise expectations and then disappoint people if the system didn't work out.

Sue and Al, members of the surgical nursing staff, were eating lunch in the hospital cafeteria with three other members of the surgical unit. Sue was usually cheerful and positive, but today it was clear that she was unhappy. Considerable resentment showed in her tone.

"What do you think of the department-head bonus system, Al?" she inquired. She didn't wait for an answer but went on to say, with some heat, "I think the department-head bonuses are coming out of our hides. We work harder and save money for the hospital, and then the department head gets a bonus. To top it all off, now they're going to lay off one of the new nurses in a cost-cutting move. It'll be whoever has the least seniority."

Al sighed, "It doesn't sit very well with me, either. I can see why we have to get costs down. But it seems to me we're all in the same boat. I felt better about cooperating in cost reduction before the administrator started the bonus system. Now it seems as if it's the department heads' cost-reduction program, not ours. Makes me feel like a lackey. My wife says I should bring it up at the next department meeting. But that puts me in the position of appearing greedy."

"So it's okay for the department heads to be greedy, but not us, eh?" Sue responded. "I'll tell you what it makes me feel like doing — I just won't mention some ideas I have for reducing costs. It looks as if all we'll get for our efforts is more work and some folks losing their jobs."

"I agree," said Al. "Maybe we should check around, and if others feel the same way, we should bring the matter up when the administrator meets with the staff next week. She's a good sort, and probably we should give her a chance to extend the program to everyone before we try to kill it. How do the rest of you see it?"

Incentive plans provide financial or nonfinancial rewards to employees who make substantial contributions to organizational effectiveness. There are many kinds of incentive plans, offering various rewards on different bases. Some plans tie rewards to the output of individual employees; others reward the productivity of groups; still others are based on the overall profitability of the organization. But the common purpose of all incentive plans is to encourage employees to achieve specific organizational goals, such as increasing profits, lowering costs, raising productivity, improving product quality, and so on.

The opening cases illustrate some of the challenges and problems associated with the use of incentive plans. On the one hand, it seems reasonable to try to motivate workers by offering rewards for exceptional performance, as George Sims suggested in Case 15.1 and the hospital administrator attempted in Case 15.2. On the other hand, there are real difficulties in implementing this idea in an equitable and manageable fashion. Among the considerations involved are these:

- What incentives should be offered to encourage higher productivity and performance? That is, to what extent does higher pay guarantee greater output?
- Can nonfinancial rewards encourage desired performance? If leadership style shifts toward praise and recognition for superior performance, will the rewards be adequate in the long run if profits increase?
- How will productivity and quality be measured?
- Will cooperation and productive relationships among workers and groups be threatened by the reward system? (In Case 15.2, the bonus system for department heads was beginning to lessen cooperation between the nursing staff and the department head.)

- How will traditional pay differentials between supervisors and employees be affected if employees can earn extra pay for producing more? (In Case 15.1, there was some joking among the supervisors about what would happen to their compensation; that joking was probably masking a real issue.)
- Is there sufficient trust between management and workers to implement an incentive system? That is, will the plan be viewed positively by employees, or will they perceive it as pressure to work harder without a corresponding increase in compensation?

These and other issues will be explored in this chapter, which focuses on the purposes, limitations, and benefits of a variety of incentive plans found in organizations today. The chapter begins by describing the relationship of incentives to motivation, performance, and satisfaction. Next, an overview of commonly used incentive systems concludes with a look at suggestion plans and positive reinforcement programs. Finally, the chapter discusses external influences on incentive plans, various factors that affect the choice of an incentive system for a particular organization, and the role of the human resources department in managing the system selected.

INCENTIVES, MOTIVATION, PERFORMANCE, AND SATISFACTION

The motivation-performance-satisfaction relationship shown in Figure 5.3 (Chapter 5) provides a convenient way of thinking about the potential value of incentive systems as well as some potential drawbacks. If, under an incentive plan, more pay is desired (positive valence) and there is a high expectancy that extra effort will lead to higher performance and, in turn, to higher reward, motivation is likely to be high. Satisfaction is a likely outcome.

If, on the other hand, employees mistrust management and fear a work speedup, in which there is pressure to work harder to meet ever-rising standards without a corresponding increase in compensation, motivation under an incentive plan and employee satisfaction are likely to be low. Similarly, if employees fear that increased productivity will reduce the number of employees needed and thus result in layoffs (an outcome with a negative valence) or that management will reap most of the benefits (lack of perceived equity), motivation and satisfaction will be low. Under these circumstances, incentive plans do not meet individual needs and goals, and group norms will develop in opposition to such plans. Resistance may be overt, as through a union, or it may take covert and subtle forms, such as the withholding of cooperation.

FIGURE 15.1
Four major types of incentive plans tie financial rewards directly to performance

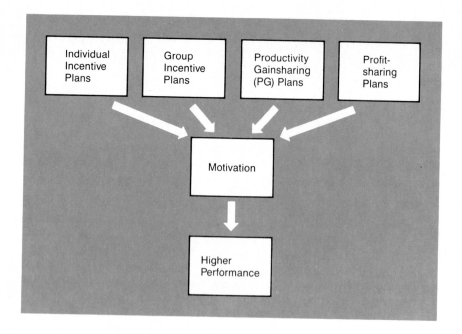

The four major types of incentive plans to be discussed in this chapter are individual incentive plans, group incentive plans, productivity gainsharing plans, and profit-sharing plans (see Figure 15.1). In addition, we will discuss suggestion plans and positive reinforcement programs, both of which can be considered incentive plans.

INDIVIDUAL INCENTIVE PLANS

Reward systems tied to the performance of individual employees are known as **individual incentive plans.** These plans take several forms, depending on the category of workers for which they are designed. In most cases, a certain pay rate is guaranteed, and the rewards represent additional compensation. An exception is the merit-pay plan, in which the incentive payment is represented by an increase in the base salary itself.

Merit-Pay Plans

Under a merit-pay plan, pay raises known as merit increases are determined by job performance. That is, employees who achieve a certain level of performance "earn" an increase in their regular

PERSPECTIVE 15.1 "Pay for Performance" — Good News or Bad?

The old idea that employees should be paid according to how well they do their jobs is making a comeback.

After years of neglecting the concept entirely or paying it little more than lip service, many companies are adopting tough, new "pay for performance" systems that either replace or greatly expand existing merit and incentive-pay policies.

"Pay for performance has been around for years, but it was more of a philosophical statement and less of a practical reality," observes Walton Winder, vice president of Towers, Perrin, Forster & Crosby, a New York-based management consulting firm. "Companies always had the ability to reward better-performing people, but they rarely exercised it. What we're seeing now is genuine interest in putting teeth behind the concept."

Companies that once granted annual, across-the-board increases to all white-collar workers and linked only a nominal portion of their salaries to performance now are serving notice that automatic pay raises are a thing of the past.

Year-Long Scrutiny

To make the plans work, companies are substituting formal employee-evaluation procedures for makeshift systems that lacked carefully defined goals. Under the new systems, greater effort is made at the beginning of each year to outline precise job expectations to the employee and areas of performance that need improvement. The employee's work is monitored through the year, and a formal appraisal made at year's end.

Experts say the pay-for-performance drive grew out of the recession, as employers who were forced to trim bloated payrolls looked for new ways to hold down recurring expenses and increase efficiency after the recovery took hold.

"Many companies view this business expansion as a new opportunity to relate pay directly to performance, both of the individual and the company," says Fred Crandall, a salary specialist in the Chicago office of Sibson & Company, a compensation consulting firm.

Analysts say that low inflation and moderate pay hikes forecast for this year are also spurring the trend. Average 1985 salary increases are expected to range from 6 percent for middle management to 6.5 percent for top management, according to a national survey covering more than 600,000 employees by the Wyatt Company, an actuarial, compensation and employee-benefits consulting firm.

"Companies are saying that with more-limited resources for pay increases, with, in effect, a 'smaller pool to play in,' they are going to be more discriminating and make distinctions among employees in a more meaningful way," notes Winder. "They're saying, 'Some people are going to get nothing or only very modest increases of 2 to 3 percent so that we have enough left to pay better performers the 9 to 10 percent they deserve.' "

Already, companies as large as General Motors, Ford and Bell Atlantic have taken the plunge, and more are on the way.

rate of pay. Typically, merit-pay decisions are based on a performance appraisal system that translates performance ratings into pay increases.

On the whole, merit increases represent the most commonly used incentive plan. The use of merit-pay plans is largely restricted, however, to management and other exempt and office and clerical employees. A recent survey of nearly 200 organizations revealed that more than half of the respondents offer merit increases, but only 8 percent of this group includes production and service employees in the merit-pay plan. (See Tables 15.1 and 15.2 for complete results of this survey.)

Despite their relative popularity, merit-pay plans sometimes prove to be ineffective motivators of performance. If, for example, the organization's performance appraisal system does not adequately distinguish superior levels of performance, pay-increase decisions are likely to be influenced by non-performance-related variables. (These variables are identified in Figure 14.6 in the preceding chapter.) Or, if the merit system is not carefully controlled, increases tend to be granted automatically at regular intervals, and employees may perceive that increases are based on length of service as much as on actual performance. Under these circumstances, the merit-pay plan may have no impact on performance or satisfaction.

TABLE 15.1 Financial incentive plans most likely to be offered by employers*

	PERCENT OF COMPANIES					
	All Companies	By Industry			By Size	
		Mfg.	Nonmfg.	Nonbus.	Large	Small
	(195)	(87)	(53)	(55)	(92)	(103)
HAVE GROUP INCENTIVE PLANS	32%	45%	42%	4%	38%	27%
Type of group plan:						
• Profit-sharing	19	22	34	2	20	19
• Employee stock ownership	18	29	17	2	25	12
• Scanlon	1	1	2	—	2	—
• Improshare	1	—	2	—	1	—
HAVE INDIVIDUAL INCENTIVE PLANS	63	63	75	51	67	59
Type of individual plan:						
• Merit increases	53	52	62	45	59	48
• Performance bonuses	40	44	57	18	42	38
• Piecework	10	17	8	—	14	6
NO FINANCIAL INCENTIVE PROGRAMS	31	24	20	48	28	33

Note: Percentages may add to more than 100 because of multiple responses.

Source: The Bureau of National Affairs, Inc., "Productivity Improvement Programs," *Personnel Policies Forum,* Survey No. 138, September 1984, p. 7. Reprinted by permission.

*Author's Note: The categories in this table are different from those used in this textbook. For example, we include the Scanlon plan and Improshare under the broader heading of productivity gainsharing (PG) plans and we treat employee stock ownership plans (ESOPs) under the category of employee benefits in the next chapter.

TABLE 15.2   **Financial incentive plans by type of employee group covered**

| | PERCENT OF COMPANIES | | | | |
| | Group Incentive Plans | | Individual Incentive Plans | | |
	Profit Sharing Plan	Employee Stock Ownership Plan	Merit Increases	Performance Bonuses	Piecework
	(38)	(35)	(103)	(78)	(19)
PLAN COVERS ALL EMPLOYEES	63%	57%	59%	14%	—%
PLAN COVERS SOME EMPLOYEE GROUPS	37	43	41	86	100
Groups covered—					
• Management/Exempt	37	43	33	79	—
• Office/Clerical	13	26	33	8	5
• Production/Service	—	6	8	9	100

Note: Percentages are based on the number of companies that have each type of financial incentive plan, as shown in parentheses.

Source: The Bureau of National Affairs, Inc., "Productivity Improvement Programs," *Personnel Policies Forum,* Survey No. 138, September 1984, p. 8. Reprinted by permission.

What the organization communicates about pay increases may also diminish the motivating effects of merit-pay plans. For example, in some organizations merit increases are not clearly distinguished from across-the-board increases made to adjust the entire pay structure in response to inflation or labor-market competition. And even when merit pay is clearly labeled as such, the rising cost of living often minimizes the incentive power of the pay increase.

Incentives for Production Workers

Individual incentive plans for production workers typically offer additional financial compensation to those employees who produce work over and above a specified quantity and/or quality. When properly designed, these plans can contribute to organizational efficiency by raising worker productivity and lowering the production cost of each unit. Such plans are intended to *assist* in increasing efficiency, however, not to accomplish it alone. In manufacturing, for example, incentive plans are often designed in conjunction with acceptable changes in work methods to sustain efficiencies gained through time-and-motion studies or through work simplification. In other words, some job-design strategies can be used to organize tasks more efficiently or to simplify them, while the incentive system is designed to motivate the worker to use the more efficient methods. (Some job design strategies, as we discussed in Chapter 7, are aimed at creating more meaningful and challenging jobs and to be intrinsically more motivating.)

One incentive system traditionally used with production workers is the **piece-rate plan** (or piecework plan), in which compensation is based on the number of units produced. In most piece-rate plans, the worker is guaranteed a *base rate,* or minimum hourly wage that assumes a certain rate of production, and is paid extra for production above that rate. Under straight piece-rate plans, the worker is paid an additional set amount of each unit produced above the standard. Under **differential piece-rate plans,** the worker who exceeds standard production is compensated at a higher rate for all work than workers who satisfy only the minimum standard. For either type of plan, base rates are often determined through job evaluation and wage surveys, whereas production standards are frequently established by time-and-motion studies.

Under **production-bonus** incentive systems, workers who surpass minimum production standards are given a bonus payment based on cost savings associated with higher productivity. An example is the **standard-hour plan,** under which "standard time" for completing a particular job or task is established. The worker is paid the standard rate even when he or she completes the job in less than standard time. For example, if the standard time for a particular job is nine hours, and an employee completes it in six hours, the employee's earnings are still nine times the hourly rate.[1]

Another type of individual incentive plan is the **measured-day-rate plan.** Under this plan, employees are rated every two or three months on several factors, such as productivity, quality of work, dependability, and versatility. If rated high, they may make as much as 20 percent above the current pay rate. This merit rating fixes the wage until the next merit rating, when the individual's pay may be raised or lowered. This plan differs from typical merit-rating plans in that it gives significantly greater weight to productivity, and wages can be reduced if the rating falls.[2]

Incentives for Sales Personnel

Sales-pay plans featuring **commissions,** or bonuses based on the number of items or dollar volume sold, can also be considered individual incentive plans. One study of nearly 200 firms found that 83 percent paid sales personnel some combination of salary and commission.[3] Most stockbrokers and many real estate agents, on the other hand, are paid solely on a commission basis.[4]

One of the advantages to the organization of commission payments is that they tend to be tied to revenues and profits. Presumably they stimulate both, but when a firm is faced with a recession, a commission system automatically allows it to lower its costs. The main disadvantage to the employee on a straight commission, of course, is that his or her standard of living is less secure than if he or she were paid a base salary.

Incentives for Managerial and Professional Employees

As shown in Table 15.2, performance bonuses of some kind are the most frequently used incentive plans for management and exempt employees. The details vary greatly from company to company. For example, bonuses may be allocated on the basis of an overall judgment about a manager's or a professional's contribution, or end-of-year bonuses may be allocated on the basis of the extent to which the person attains the objectives agreed on at the beginning of the year under an MBO plan.

Another form of incentive is the **stock option.** Under such a plan, the executive, manager, or professional is granted the right to buy a certain number of shares of the company's stock at a given price and by a specified date. The number of shares allocated is determined by an appraisal of the person's performance. If the value of the stock goes up substantially over the predetermined price, the person can make a significant profit when the option is exercised. If the stock price goes down, the option is not exercised.

One version of the stock option takes the form of **stock appreciation rights (SARs).** Under an SAR plan, an executive can relinquish the right to purchase the stock and receive an amount equal to the increased value of the stock from the date the stock option was granted.[5]

In recent years, there has been substantial criticism of executive incentive plans on the grounds that most focus on short-term rather than long-term results. For example, one study found 85 percent of the responding firms rewarding executives on the basis of growth in earnings per share of the company's stock. Earnings-per-share growth, however, does not necessarily correlate with stock-price growth.[6] Earnings per share can easily be manipulated in the short term — for example, by cutting back on research and development or by selling assets — in ways that do not contribute to the long-term success of the organization.[7] As a result, many corporations have established incentive systems that reward executives on the basis of return on equity and growth.

Hazel Hankin/Stock, Boston

Performance bonuses of some kind are frequently used incentive plans for management and exempt employees.

An unusual incentive for professionals is the IBM Fellows program. Under this program, scientists and engineers at IBM who have contributed fifteen to twenty years of highly creative work are given five years to do research on any problem of their choosing. During the five years they are paid at executive salary levels and receive necessary resources to support their research. The program is not aimed at developing new, breakthrough products; the purpose is "primarily for recognition of outstanding work."[8]

Problems with Individual Incentive Plans

Problems in the use of individual incentive plans are numerous. Several have already been mentioned: the financial insecurity associated with straight commissions; the fact that executive bonuses frequently reward short-term rather than long-term performance; and employee resistance based on fear of a work speed-up or of layoffs stemming from higher productivity. (In Case 15.2, nursing-staff members were concerned about layoffs being an outcome of the department-head bonus plan.) Employees will resist the incentive plan unless they are convinced that the system works for them and not against them. This means the system must be explained as carefully as it is designed.

Dissension can occur if workers' take-home pay under an incentive plan exceeds that of their supervisors. This can happen if the supervisors are not included in the incentive plan, or if an adequate differential is not provided between the employee incentive plan and the supervisory pay plan.

Establishing Reward Standards. One of the most difficult problems is establishing standards to determine what amount of productivity or what level of performance should be rewarded. No matter how skilled and fair the person or committee establishing the standards may be, standards always involve value judgments. In setting standards for production jobs, for instance, opinions will differ on what rate of output should be considered average or normal, and results of time-and-motion studies cannot be considered 100 percent reliable. The problem of establishing standards is even more complex for professional and managerial jobs, in which output is less easily measured and evaluations of individual performance tend to be more subjective.[9]

A growing number of firms are measuring productivity with computer work monitoring, which is much faster and more accurate than time-and-motion studies using a stopwatch. One such firm is Equitable Life Assurance Society, where the standard for processing a simple claim is 6.5 minutes.[10] To date, computer monitoring is not commonly used in connection with most incentive systems, but some organizations use it to provide objective measures for merit-pay decisions. The danger is that computer monitoring may be perceived as a repressive and overly controlling system; in turn, this can damage morale and lower performance, especially if production standards are unreasonable. But if tied to a reward system that has gained employee acceptance, computer monitoring can be a constructive tool that provides an accurate measure of productivity.

Nonperformance Variables. Other problems may arise when forces over which the employee has no control affect productivity or performance. For example, production workers will resent pay reductions for lower output caused by machine breakdown, defective raw materials, and so forth. Salespeople will resent low commissions when sales decline because of ineffective advertising, inferior manufacturing, or a downturn in the economy. Productivity on some jobs is so much a function of variables other than individual performance that individual incentive systems may not be applicable at all.

Beating the System.   Other problems arise from the understandable tendency of the worker to try to "beat the system" — that is, to get the system to pay off in the rewards the worker wants. For example, unless standards of cooperation and quality are built into the system, some employees may attempt to maximize earnings at the expense of quality or of other workers' production. A salesclerk may "push" easy-to-sell items that may not be the most profitable ones. Moreover, incentives tied directly to output do not guarantee consistently high production rates. Workers may, for instance, perform rapidly at times and then hide surplus production to cover periods when they wish to slow down or when machines are being set up or repaired. (See the example in Chapter 5 of work banking in which workers buried thirty-foot propeller shafts behind the factory.) Or, while engineers are studying the job, a worker may deliberately slow down in order to obtain a low standard that will later yield a large bonus when it is exceeded. Reducing output because of group pressures and fears that standards will be raised has been extensively documented over the years.[11]

Managerial and professional employees have devised their own ways of "beating the system." For example, when bonuses are tied to the achievement of specific objectives like those in an MBO system, there may be a tendency to set one's objective fairly low in order to obtain a large bonus rather easily. The type of bonus system can also affect the accounting procedures executives use. If the bonus plan is related to profits and has an upper limit, executives are inclined to choose accounting procedures that carry over profits until the executive needs them to sustain his or her income.[12]

Another example of an incentive bonus system for professionals that produced unintended results comes from a large bank. To maximize their bonuses, employees in the loan department at Chase Manhattan Bank built up a huge portfolio with a high-risk borrower that subsequently defaulted on interest payments.[13] This problem could have been avoided if the incentive system had been designed to reward employees for the *quality* of the loans they made, not just their dollar value.

It is natural for workers at all levels to want to maximize personal outcomes under an incentive system — in a sense, that is why incentives are offered in the first place. But an effectively designed incentive system will protect organizational interests by providing safeguards against potential abuse by individual employees.

GROUP INCENTIVE PLANS

Most **group incentive plans** are individual plans applied to small groups of workers. Piece-rate compensation is the most prevalent group incentive, but commissions and production bonuses can also be applied to groups. In general, the purpose of group incentive plans is to encourage the teamwork and cooperation needed to attain high productivity or performance. Group plans are particularly appropriate where several employees must work together to perform a single task and where the contributions of particular individuals are difficult to measure.

An example of a successful group incentive plan is that agreed on by Crown Zellerbach Corp. and the International Woodworkers of America to compensate loggers in Washington and Oregon. Under the plan, logging crews are compensated as a group on a piece-

---

PERSPECTIVE 15.2   Jayco's Travel Incentive Program

When its dealers do a better job, Jayco Inc. sends them packing. Jayco, a $40-million maker of recreation vehicles in Middlebury, Ind., runs a travel incentive program every year from September to February, the period when demand for RVs usually cools off. This year, the reward for high-performing dealers is a one-week trip for two to Austria, including stopovers in Vienna and Salzburg and a scenic cruise down the Danube River.

Jayco separated its 270 dealers nationwide into five categories according to sales volume, with trips to Austria promised to the top-selling dealers in each group. The categories were established to give smaller dealerships a better chance to win than they would otherwise have had. Every winner had to reach at least a minimum sales performance established by the company. The trip to Austria was planned and run by AHI Inc., in Des Plaines, Ill., a group-travel operator that specializes in incentive trips. Jayco, which usually contracts its travel contests to third-party administrators like AHI, is

paying AHI about $500,000, which will cover all expenses.

"The prospect of winning a trip pushes everyone to a greater effort, but it particularly improves the morale of smaller dealers in far-flung areas," says Al Yoder, Jayco's executive vice-president. "It gives them a chance to win something, too."

Yoder says the yearly travel contests usually prevent sales from sinking too far into the fall-to-winter doldrums. This year about 90 dealerships won, and around 280 people representing those dealerships will be leaving for Austria this October.

"The trip itself acts as an incentive, but people also strive to be part of an elite group," says Richard Douglas, vice-president of marketing for AHI. "Unlike prizes like cash or a toaster, a trip is highly visible and makes a dealer feel special." Douglas says this year's travel agenda for Jayco's winning dealers will include a grand ball in the Hofburg Palace in Vienna, where the president of Austria still lives, and performances by the Mozart Boys Choir and the Austrian Ballet. At the palace, dealers will be heralded by royal trumpeters, served by waiters dressed in livery, and provided with formal suits and gowns in the style of the royal empire.

Source: "Selling Themselves Down the River," *INC*, May 1984, p. 206.

rate basis. Pay is based on how much wood the crew cuts and hauls to the mill each day, measured in cubic feet. The new incentive system was accompanied by certain changes in work methods and greater worker participation in decision making and problem solving. Each crew was given the freedom to set its own hours and allocate tasks to maximize productivity. (For example, older workers could be assigned to less strenuous tasks.) Moreover, workers now participate in local labor-management committees that tackle issues of safety and quality. A strong emphasis on safety is particularly important for both the company and the union when an incentive system is used in a hazardous industry. A few months after the incentive system was implemented, management reported that many employees were making more money and that some fifty jobs had been saved as a result of increased productivity.[14]

Group incentive plans — and individual incentive plans, too — tend to be practical when some or all of the following conditions are present:

1. Units of production are readily measured.
2. Handling or processing by workers is a major determinant of productivity.
3. Time-and-motion study or work simplification can increase job efficiency, and the company employs experts in these specialties.
4. Technological changes affecting jobs are relatively infrequent.
5. Competition requires better predictability of unit labor costs.
6. Close supervision is impractical.
7. Employees trust management not to change standards arbitrarily.

Many individual plans have recently been converted to group plans to encourage cooperation. For example, in 1983, the International Harvester Company and the United Auto Workers agreed to change from an individual incentive system to a group incentive plan to help improve productivity at the Melrose, Illinois plant.[15]

PRODUCTIVITY GAINSHARING PLANS

More and more companies are offering incentives based on the productivity of the organization or a plant as a whole. These incentives, frequently called **productivity gainsharing (PG) plans,** attempt to stimulate production efficiency by allowing employees to share in overall labor- and production-cost savings through periodic bonus payments. Broad employee participation is a feature of many PG plans. Typically, workers participate in committees that develop and process suggestions about various production matters such as work methods, equipment and materials, scrap reduction, plant layout, and so on.

The Scanlon Plan

The Scanlon-plan is a well-known gainsharing plan that not only allows but requires extensive participation. The plan is based on a ratio of labor costs to productivity. When labor costs decline in relation to productivity, the employees are entitled to a share of the savings through bonus payments. When labor costs do not go down, of course, there are no savings to share. Ordinarily, all employees benefit from cost savings, including production, clerical, sales, and supervisory personnel.

The Scanlon plan is distinguished by its emphasis on union-management cooperation and committee participation by employees at all levels. (In fact, the originator of the plan, Joseph Scanlon, would not institute the plan without union consent and participation.) A production committee in each department, whose members include union-elected or appointed representatives and supervisors, meets regularly to discuss ways of increasing production and to evaluate suggestions from employees for improving efficiency. These suggestions are referred for further consideration to a company-wide screening committee consisting of union officials and top management.[16]

Other PG Plans

Other group incentive and participation systems paying bonuses for cost savings are the Rucker Share-of-Production Plan and the Kaiser-Steel Union Sharing Plan. The Rucker plan is similar to the Scanlon plan, but its bonus payments are based on a more complex analysis, including an "economic engineering audit" of operations for several preceding years. Under the Kaiser plan, savings in labor, supplies, or materials stemming from increased efficiency are shared with employees. The company receives 67.5 percent of the savings, and the other 32.5 percent is distributed to employees in the form of monthly bonuses.[17]

The Lincoln Incentive Compensation Plan of the Lincoln Electric Company combines the features of plantwide productivity plans, group incentive plans, and individual piece-rate plans. At Lincoln Electric, individual workers are compensated on a piece-rate basis, but employees work together on productivity committees to explore ways to lower costs and increase profitability. Each employee is rated by superiors on quality and quantity of production, and a bonus is calculated accordingly. The typical worker's take-home pay is about double that for similar jobs in competitive firms. This plan is coupled with other benefits, including guaranteed lifetime employment and an employee stock ownership program.[18]

One of the newest PG plans is Improshare, which depends less on participation than the other plans mentioned. Improshare was developed by Mitchell Fein, who incorporated into the plan certain refinements of more traditional individual and plant-wide incentive systems. The plan has been adopted by such firms as Firestone, Rockwell International, Stanley Home Products, and McGraw-Edison.[19] Improshare focuses on the number of hours saved for a given number of units produced by subtracting from the hours allotted for those units the hours it actually took to produce them. The savings realized by producing the units in a shorter than expected time are then shared by the firm and the worker.[20]

Improshare is distinguished by the fact that participative procedures such as production committees and consideration of employee suggestions for improving efficiency are optional. For this reason, executives and union officials who place less value on employee participation but are nevertheless interested in increasing efficiency may find Improshare an appropriate incentive system. For the plan to succeed in a unionized firm, however, some minimum level of trust and cooperation must exist between management and labor.

Problems with PG Plans

Workers' lack of understanding or willingness to focus on production problems can cause serious difficulties under participative PG plans. Effective communications by both management and the union and the involvement of middle management in participative procedures are also essential to the success of these plans. A particularly sensitive problem with the administration of these plans is the opportunity given workers or union officials to criticize management in any area. Unless criticism is given and accepted in a constructive manner, relationships between workers and management may deteriorate seriously.[21]

In general, the success of most PG plans seems to depend on the following factors:

1. Top management and top union-leadership support.
2. Mutual trust among management, union, and employees.
3. Careful planning and installation to ensure both understanding and acceptance.

4. Sincere and diligent efforts by all parties to make the plan work.
5. Extensive and real participation by employees, union officials, supervisors, and other managers at all levels, and assumption by all parties of the responsibilities that accompany constructive and cooperative problem solving.
6. An emphasis on teamwork and sharing of information at all levels.
7. Workers who try to work smarter, not faster, and who press for better planning and more efficient management.[22]

PROFIT-SHARING PLANS

A **profit-sharing plan** is an incentive system in which some portion of the organization's earnings is distributed to employees to supplement their usual wages or salaries. Generally, the purpose of

Profit-sharing plans may be used to encourage cooperation, boost morale, and increase employees' financial security.

Courtesy of Pitney-Bowes

these plans is to motivate employees to contribute to organizational profitability. Profit-sharing plans may also be used to encourage cooperation, boost morale, and increase employees' financial security. The profit-sharing plans of a particular organization may include all employees or may cover only a selected group of top executives and managerial personnel.

There are three types of profit-sharing plans: (1) current-distribution or cash plans, (2) deferred-distribution plans, and (3) combined plans that involve both current and deferred distribution. Under current-distribution plans, some percentage of profits — for example, 25 percent of net profits — is distributed in cash at intervals of one year or less. Under deferred-distribution plans, some percentage of profits is deposited in an irrevocable trust and credited to the accounts of individual employees, with the money made available at retirement or termination. Some plans permit employees to contribute additional amounts to their accounts. Various methods are used to allocate the pool of profit-sharing money to individual employees. For example, the amount an employee receives may be based on the individual's base salary, on seniority, on merit rating, or on some combination of these factors.

The Profit Sharing Research Foundation, based in Chicago, estimates that there are some 430,000 profit-sharing plans in existence in the United States. Of these about 70 percent are deferred-distribution plans, about 15 percent are cash plans, and the remainder are combination plans.[23] More and more companies, however, are adopting current-distribution plans tied to employee productivity. For example, some automobile manufacturing companies, faced with intense foreign competition and declining profits, have negotiated cash profit-sharing plans with the United Auto Workers. In 1984, payments averaging about $1,000 were made to General Motors employees covered by profit sharing; payments to Ford employees averaged about $1,600. Some airlines, including American, TWA, and Western, have offered cash profit-sharing plans as a way of motivating employees to focus on productivity and efficiency.[24] About 17 percent of the banks surveyed in one study were using incentive systems, and these were predominantly cash profit-sharing plans for managers and professionals, such as mortgage loan officers.[25]

Problems with Profit-Sharing Plans

The most difficult problem in profit-sharing plans is determining the formula for distributing profits to employees. Such critical matters as payments to stockholders, taxes, and investment capital must be taken into account.[26] Whether to allocate profit shares on the basis of rank, length of service, merit, or plant or departmental performance must be dealt with.

Under deferred-distribution plans, a problem can be the lack of an immediate relationship between the employer's efforts and rewards. Rewards that are payable upon retirement may seem a long way off and may prove to be ineffective motivators of present performance. Another problem with any profit-sharing plan is the effect on employee morale when profits are down or nonexistent, and there are no profit distributions to share. When profit-sharing funds are invested in stocks, employees can become very unhappy when the stock market declines. In fact, some lawsuits have been brought when stock-market declines have sharply reduced the value of employee profit-sharing accounts.[27]

SUGGESTION PLANS

A **suggestion plan** is an incentive system under which employees are rewarded if they offer useful ideas for improving organizational effectiveness. The usual reward is a cash payment, although a number of firms offer merchandise or travel. (Both cash and merchandise awards are considered taxable income to the employee.) Suggestion plans are commonly used to obtain employees' ideas on reducing costs, increasing safety, or improving product quality. Some companies, however, promote suggestion plans to give employees more opportunity to participate in company matters. In other words, suggestion plans can be useful devices for improving communications with management. Supervisory and professional employees are often excluded from these plans, however, on the assumption that cost control is a regular part of their jobs.

The typical suggestion plan features boxes placed at convenient locations throughout the workplace, with appropriate forms available. Employees use the forms to write out their suggestions and deposit them in the box for subsequent evaluation, usually by a special committee. If a suggestion is accepted, a cash award is usually paid, based on some percentage of the first year's savings resulting from the suggestion. A flat fee or standard amount is paid when cost savings are difficult to measure or for nonrevenue-producing suggestions such as safety improvements. If a suggestion is rejected, the contributor is usually given an explanation of why.

Plans soliciting suggestions from individuals have been around for a long time. For example, in 1954 Congress approved the Government Employees' Incentive Awards Act, which provided not only for cash awards for accepted suggestions but also for substantial cash awards for "superior accomplishments" or "special acts or services."

Team approaches to suggestion plans, however, are of more recent origin. For example, the Ford Motor Company now permits groups of hourly workers to win its top suggestion award of $6,000.[28] The National Association of Suggestion Systems (NASS) sponsors a Team Idea Plan through which small groups of employees are encouraged to develop and submit ideas and are rewarded as teams.

Reports on cost savings resulting from suggestion systems have generally been favorable. According to the NASS, in 1983 such plans saved 700 companies about $800 million.[29] A survey by the same organization found that, on the average, for each dollar spent on a suggestion system an organization would realize $5.70 in tangible net-cost savings.[30] In many instances, a suggestion can result in huge cost savings for the employer, yielding a substantial reward to the contributor. Here are some examples:

- An airline flight officer suggested that air cargo be shifted slightly to the rear of the aircraft, thereby altering the center of gravity and reducing the fuel required for takeoff. The suggestion saved the airline $458,500 the first year and earned the employee $45,850.[31]
- At a General Tire & Rubber Company plant, a master mechanic made a suggestion to modify equipment used in the manufacture of latex and earned a $25,000 award.[32]
- A General Motors worker, William Harbaugh, collected $135,000 through the GM system over a twenty-year period.[33]
- Rhonda Pease, an inspector for Pratt & Whitney's Aircraft Group, suggested a procedure that allowed inspectors to avoid writing identical headings on each page of the multipage forms they used daily. Her suggestion saved the company 12,500 hours per year, and Pease won the company's maximum award of $7,500, plus a $1,000 bonus.[34]

Problems with Suggestion Plans

In spite of many successes, suggestion plans have a number of inherent problems. Evaluating suggestions is a challenging task that requires an analysis of the possible ramifications of implementing a particular idea. Cost-saving suggestions that involve the elimination of jobs must be carefully weighed in terms of their effects on other workers and on the overall climate of the organization. Another problem relates to the origin of the idea. Since many ideas originate as fragments of ideas supplied by others, a claim for an award by one worker may be resented by others who believe they had a hand in formulating the suggestion. Conversely, many ideas probably do not mature because of fears that someone will steal them. Team approaches to suggestion systems may have an advantage in enhancing cooperation and avoiding disputes over the origin of ideas.

Another problem is making the rejection of an idea acceptable to the contributor. In particular, it can be difficult to convince the suggester that the idea had already been put forward by someone else or that it is already being worked on. Lawsuits can and do occur because of these problems. For example, two United Airlines employees sued the company on the grounds that it had rejected their idea and later adopted it independently. In court, the company argued that it had been studying the idea long before the employees made their suggestion. Subsequently, the company made $1,000 "incentive awards" to the two employees. United then dropped its suggestion plan, indicating there had been a large number of disagreements about the size of awards. IBM, on the other hand, describes its plan as "extremely worthwhile," and suggests that, with 250,000 suggestions each year and recent yearly awards totaling $12 million, "a lawsuit now and again is not surprising."[35]

A particularly serious issue is that many suggestion systems bypass the supervisor. Supervisors may interpret suggestions as a reflection on their competence and may retaliate in some way, or else workers may simply fear such retaliation. Some of these problems are minimized or avoided under participative gainsharing plans such as the Scanlon plan. Although this plan gives recognition to individuals for suggestions, all employees, including supervisors, stand to gain from accepted suggestions because bonuses are distributed to all.

The high mortality rate of suggestion systems suggests that these plans need to be managed carefully. The National Association of Suggestion Systems offers several guidelines for administering suggestion plans, recommending that

- what is a suggestion be defined carefully.
- strict eligibility standards be developed.
- the system be explained clearly to all employees and the most important points of the policy be printed on the suggestion form.
- suggestions be acted on quickly.
- a "fair and reasonable" award be made for every adopted suggestion.
- an employee be told in writing why a suggestion is rejected.

- there be an appeals procedure available to employees who want a suggestion reconsidered.[36]

As with any incentive program, full and continuing support by top management is essential. Timely response to constructive suggestions and tactful explanations for rejected ideas are ways of demonstrating such support and can help ensure broad participation in the plan. A suggestion system that is installed and then ignored will very quickly be viewed as useless.

POSITIVE REINFORCEMENT PROGRAMS

Positive reinforcement programs, in which the principles of behavior modification and operant conditioning are used to influence worker behavior, are found in a number of companies today. (See Chapter 5 for a review of reinforcement theory.) Unlike incentive plans that rely on financial rewards to reinforce desired behaviors (productivity, cooperation, and so on), many positive reinforcement programs rely primarily on nonfinancial incentives. These incentives or reinforcers include praise, recognition, and avoidance of punishment.

One of the first companies to use a positive reinforcement program was Emery Air Freight. Emery's program involved four key steps: (1) defining the behavioral aspects of performance and conducting a performance audit; (2) establishing specific goals for each worker, ideally through participative approaches; (3) allowing employees to keep records of their own work; and (4) praising the positive aspects of employees' performance and withholding praise for substandard work.[37] These steps are summarized in Figure 15.2. Other organizations that have used this approach are Mich-

FIGURE 15.2 Steps in establishing a positive reinforcement program

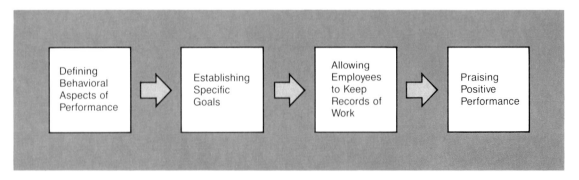

igan Bell (to improve operator and maintenance services), General Electric (in training programs for supervisors of minority female employees), and the B. F. Goodrich Chemical Group. Programs established by the Weyerhaeuser Company (to improve productivity of clerical workers, tree planters, middle-level managers, and scientists) and the city of Detroit (to improve its garbage collection service) include financial rewards among other positive reinforcers.[38]

The results of these programs as reported by Hamner and Hamner include cost savings at Emery Air Freight; improved cost efficiency, safety, and service at Michigan Bell; cost savings and increased productivity at GE; and substantially increased productivity at B. F. Goodrich Chemical. At Weyerhaeuser, productivity increased in two groups of workers but decreased in a third. The city of Detroit experienced substantial savings and a decrease in citizen complaints and paid an average annual bonus of $350 to each collector.

Positive reinforcement programs, like other incentive programs, typically involve attention to many variables in the work situation. For example, increased attention is usually paid to training, to communications, and to union-management relations under these programs. Therefore, reported gains and improvements may not always be the direct result of nonfinancial incentives.

Problems with Positive Reinforcement Programs

In many instances, employee compensation is not changed when an organization institutes a positive reinforcement program. There are indications, however, that money ultimately becomes a consideration for those involved in the program, especially if increased productivity leads to higher profits. It is not stretching equity theory too far to speculate that increased profitability stemming from employee performance will create considerable tension among workers if they do not share in the organization's financial gains. In other words, while the avoidance of layoffs or bankruptcy may be perceived by employees as a fair exchange for improved productivity, higher and higher profits without a return to employees will ultimately be perceived as inequitable. Indeed, in the Michigan Bell positive reinforcement program, it was found that satisfaction with pay decreased; as equity theory would explain it, the employees began to perceive their outcomes as inadequate relative to their contributions.

EXTERNAL INFLUENCES ON INCENTIVE PLANS

Federal and state laws have some impact on incentive systems in that they put a floor under such plans through minimum-wage provisions. Further, laws set forth rules for computing base and overtime pay and specify the records that must be kept.

In addition, profit-sharing plans must be approved by the U.S. Treasury Department to comply with federal income tax laws. Also, reports to the government on deferred-distribution profit-sharing plans are required under the Employee Retirement Income Security Act (ERISA).

Labor leaders share no universal policy on incentive systems; in fact, union attitudes vary from opposition to enthusiasm. Some incentive plans have been established at the insistence of unions; others have been discontinued at their insistence. Historically, union attitudes have shifted from unqualified opposition to a desire to bargain over the details of such plans and to monitor their administration. Notably, the United Auto Workers have been pressing for profit sharing for almost a quarter of a century, but it was not until 1982 that profit-sharing plans were successfully negotiated with Ford and General Motors.[39] The UAW's position on profit sharing is not unqualified, however; the union believes profit sharing and productivity sharing should be supplemental to a base wage structure that protects workers' purchasing power.[40]

CHOOSING AN INCENTIVE PLAN

Several important variables affect the selection and administration of incentive plans in a particular setting. A major consideration is the *technology* being used by the organization. For example, piece-rate systems are seldom used where the pace of work is governed largely by machines, such as on an automobile assembly line.[41] Another important variable is the *size of the unit for which performance gains are measured;* that is, whether the incentive plan focuses on individuals, groups, a total plant or organization, or a combination of these. Another variable is *participation:* how much those affected are involved in the selection, design, and administration of the plan itself; and to what extent employees are encouraged to cooperate with peers and supervisors in improving unitwide and plantwide productivity.

Other important variables include management philosophy and organizational culture and climate. If it is management's stated philosophy, for example, that all employees should benefit directly from significant organizational gains, the organization might well move toward a plantwide or organizationwide incentive plan that will allow employees to "share the wealth." If the culture of the organization includes the notions that top management is omniscient, that the employee's role is to do as he or she is told, and that people who ask questions or make suggestions are troublemakers, a participative incentive system can never work and will probably not be attempted. If the organizational climate includes a great deal of mistrust, an incentive system, to succeed, would need to be very simply designed, with little chance for either management or employees to distort the results.

Contemporary thought about incentive systems suggests that variables such as these are important in determining the "fit" between a given incentive system and a particular organization. Further, as organizational culture and climate change, incentive systems can be modified accordingly. For example, as trust levels and skills in cooperation increase in the organization, a firm might move from an individual incentive plan to a highly participative plantwide plan that includes extensive committee work.[42]

The number of firms using individual incentive plans appears to be declining. It is unclear whether the use of group incentives is increasing, but some firms have switched from individual to group plans in recent years. It appears that plantwide productivity plans (or productivity gainsharing plans) are on the increase. Merit-rating plans are more widely used than other incentive systems.

ROLE OF THE HUMAN RESOURCES DEPARTMENT

A survey of 630 organizations found the human resources department had all or some responsibility for the following activities in 75 percent or more of those organizations in which the activity was found:

- Pension/profit-sharing plan administration (89%)
- Suggestion systems (82%)
- Executive compensation administration (80%)
- Stock plan administration (75%)[43]

Thus in organizations having incentive systems, the human resources department is likely to be heavily involved in their management. Further, the human resources department is extensively involved in wage and salary administration matters, including job evaluation, that serve as the foundation for most incentive plans. In addition, that department will be actively involved in negotiating any incentive plans pertaining to unionized employees.

Like most other human resources activities, incentive systems require the active collaboration of the entire management team. The controller or chief financial officer, in particular, must be extensively involved because of his or her expertise in accounting and financial matters. Individual and group piece-rate systems need the expertise of industrial engineers, and gainsharing plans require the assistance of both accountants and industrial engineers. Production managers, of course, are key people in the management of any incentive systems that have to do with quantity and quality of production.

An area of human resources department responsibility that should be emphasized in the management of incentive plans is training. Ongoing training of various kinds is important to the success of almost any incentive plan: skills training so that employees can successfully earn bonuses; supervisory training so that supervisors will have the technical and leadership skills to assist their subordinates (this is particularly important for group incentive or gain-sharing plans that have a strong participative component); training in work simplification and work methods; and so on.

The human resources department also has a major role in communicating with employees about the purposes and philosophy underlying any incentive programs. A description of the role of the personnel director with respect to the Scanlon plan at the De Soto paint company illustrates this role:

> Another role in the maintenance of the plan is the company personnel manager. His overall goal consists of communicating what Scanlon is and what it is not to all levels of personnel. Bob Highland, personnel manager, has successfully achieved this goal. He provides orientation to all new personnel regarding the plan and notes plan activity that could be useful for future training and promotion decisions. More importantly, Bob Highland often serves as a reinforcer of the policy that affects the other roles previously discussed. In other words, he not only provides training and discussion for where De Soto is but also for where De Soto wants to be in the future.[44]

SUMMARY

Properly planned, installed, and administered incentive plans can increase efficiency and productivity, decrease costs, and increase the pay of employees, supervisors, and managers. Effective incentive plans, however, require attention to a wide range of organizational variables.

Four major categories of incentive plans are tied directly to performance. These are individual plans, group plans, plantwide productivity plans (or productivity gainsharing [PG] plans), and profit-sharing plans.

Individual and group plans tend to be practical when worker handling or processing is a major determinant of productivity, units of production are readily measured, and employees can trust management not to change standards arbitrarily. Piece-rate plans tend not to be used when the pace of work is governed largely by machines. Group plans are particularly appropriate when workers' jobs are highly interdependent and cooperation is essential. Productivity gainsharing plans appear to have the most promise for promoting collaboration between employees, supervisors, and management to achieve organizationwide or plantwide cost savings and productivity improvements. Important variables in the applicability and long-term success of various kinds of incentive plans are management philosophy and organizational culture and climate. Scanlon plans, for example, require a commitment to extensive participation and considerable mutual support and trust.

Extensive use of suggestion systems and widespread reports of significant cost savings attest to the value of these programs. To be successful, however, these plans need such features as clear rules, fair and reasonable awards, prompt administration, and appeal procedures. Team approaches to suggestion plans, a recent innovation, would appear to have promise in enhancing cooperation and in avoiding disputes about the origin of ideas.

Positive reinforcement programs, based on operant conditioning and behavior modification principles, have met with some success. Employee compensation is ordinarily not changed when these plans are instituted, but there are indications that money ultimately becomes a concern if increased productivity leads to higher profits.

Environmental influences on incentive systems include collective bargaining and the impact of federal and state laws. Laws establish minimum wages and rules for the calculation of basic rates and overtime. They also stipulate what records must be kept. Profit-sharing plans must be approved by the U.S. Treasury Department, and reports must be made to the federal government on deferred-distribution plans. Recently, unions have won profit-sharing plans from management in return for wage concessions, particularly in the automobile industry.

The human resources department is likely to be extensively involved in the management of incentive systems. Such management will be collaborative, involving production managers, industrial engineers, accounting and finance professionals, and supervisors. In particular, the human resources department plays key roles in the compensation aspects of incentive programs and in the training and the communications necessary for the long-term success of these plans.

KEY TERMS

incentive plan
individual incentive plan
piece-rate plan
differential piece-rate plan
production bonus
standard-hour plan

measured day-rate plan
commission
stock option
stock appreciation rights
   (SARs)
group incentive plan

productivity gainsharing (PG)
   plan
profit-sharing plan
suggestion plan
positive reinforcement
   program

REVIEW QUESTIONS

1. Briefly describe various individual incentive plans used for production workers, sales personnel, and professional/managerial employees. What are some of the problems associated with using these plans?
2. Under what conditions are group incentive plans particularly effective?
3. Discuss some of the features of productivity gainsharing plans and some of the problems associated with these plans.
4. What are profit-sharing plans and what are some of the problems with them?
5. Discuss the advantages and disadvantages of suggestion plans.
6. What are the basic features of positive reinforcement programs, and what are some ptoential problems with these programs?

OPENING CASE QUESTIONS

Case 15.1   Do We Need Incentives?

1. What is the purpose for an incentive plan and does it address HiQuality Furniture Manufacturing's immediate problem and needs?
2. What kinds of questions regarding an incentive plan should George and the supervisors ask?

Case 15.2   The Bonus Is Coming out of Our Hides

1. What could the hospital administrator have done to prevent unhappy employees?
2. What does this situation say about the secrecy factor in wage, salary, and bonus systems?

CASE 15.3   GOLDEN PARACHUTES: INCENTIVE OR RIPOFF?

In 1982, William Agee, then chief executive officer of Bendix Corporation, accepted a forty-nine-percent reduction in compensation because he had been running the company with decidedly lackluster results. The next year, Agee left Bendix, and he received $4.1 million in compensation to take with him. During the recent failure of Continental Illinois Corporation, four of the banking firm's leading executives received $3.1 million when they resigned.

Are these executives being rewarded for doing a poor job? Some experts see it that way; and in fact, the Federal Deposit Insurance Corporation, which rescued Continental Illinois, is trying to recover the $3.1 million through court action. However, golden parachutes—huge severance awards that are written into top executives' contracts—are widespread in U.S. business. It has been estimated that up to fifty percent of the companies on *Fortune's* list of 1,000 make use of them.

The practice of offering golden parachutes was a response to increases in take-over activity. In theory, the aim of the parachutes is to protect top executives financially should they be forced out because of a change in corporate control. The reasoning behind the practice is that an executive who doesn't have to worry about financial security will act more objectively and better represent stockholders during takeover negotiations. However, parachutes have also been put in place to make a company less attractive as a target for hostile take-over bids. And many of them take effect simply in the event that the makeup of the board of directors changes to the disadvantage of the chief executive officer.

Severance payments like those to Agee and the Continental Illinois executives seem to be clear abuses of the golden parachute principle. But there is considerable controversy as well about whether parachutes are proper and whether they effectively act as incentives, even in take-over situations. The comments of some analysts and the recent public outcry and shareholder rebellion against parachutes suggest that the awards aren't perceived as justifiable. However, at least one research effort has concluded that they do indeed positively influence top executives, especially in situations where the potential for a take-over attempt is high.

There is also disagreement about whether golden parachutes are going to last as a practice. Some feel that they are on the wane because of shareholder and government scrutiny. In recent years, mass-media coverage of some parachutes (Agee's is an example) has led to criticism from the public at large.

However, one expert feels that the corporate popularity of parachutes persists, with troublesome implications for the perception of American manage-

Case Sources: Jeffrey A. Trachtenberg, "Parachute Punishment," *Forbes*, June 3, 1985; Richard A. Lambert and David F. Larcker, "Golden Parachutes, Executive Decision-Making, and Shareholder Wealth," *Journal of Accounting and Economics*, 7 (1985): 179–203; and Peter G. Scotese, "Fold up Those Golden Parachutes," *Harvard Business Review* (March-April 1985): 168–171.

ment. According to Peter G. Scotese, "Arguments on behalf of golden parachutes attempt to legitimize giving million-dollar bribes to executives for doing what they were paid to do anyway."* In the end, says Scotese, one must "remember that integrity cannot be bought. The best defense against excesses such as golden parachutes is a company's culture and the quality of the people it employs."†

Discussion Questions

1. If restricted to a situation in which an executive is forced out because of a take over, do you think a golden parachute is a valid form of incentive compensation? Why or why not?
2. What makes a golden parachute so different from other forms of executive compensation? Isn't it just another way to attract and reward top-notch executives?

---

*Peter G. Scotese, "Fold up Those Golden Parachutes," *Harvard Business Review*, (March-April 1985): 170.

†Ibid., p. 171.

Employee Benefits

CHAPTER OUTLINE

LEARNING OBJECTIVES

- **Identify the factors involved in the determination of benefits for a particular organization.**
- **Describe the major types of benefits that require significant financial contributions from employers.**
- **Explain the impact of ERISA on private pension plans.**
- **List the advantages of flexible benefit plans.**
- **Explain the importance of controlling benefits expenditures and identify some cost-control measures.**
- **Outline the role of the human resources department in benefits administration.**

CASE 16.1   THE BOTTOM LINE

Phil Chase, owner and president of Phil's Bakery, was worried and upset. Tom Williams, personnel director, had just handed him the report he had requested on the costs of employee benefits. Phil had flipped to the summary on the last page, where the last two lines read, "Average hourly earnings are $9.20. Benefits are an additional $3.87 per hour. Employee benefits are now 42 percent of payroll."

Phil exploded, "Holy cow! For every buck we're spending for wages, we're paying another 42 cents for benefits. We can't afford that. That's above average for food manufacturing companies, and I'll bet it's way above average for bakeries. We may be a good-sized bakery, but we're not that big. And we're sure not rich. What are we going to do, Tom?"

"Well," Tom said, "I guess we'd better go over this report item by item and see whether there's anything we have any control over. It's going to be hard to take back any paid holidays, and we're required by law to pay some things like social security and unemployment insurance. I wish we hadn't started giving away free coffee in the cafeteria a couple of years ago, and I'm regretting that we liberalized our policy on time off for personal business."

"You're probably right," Phil responded. "On the other hand, some of those things buy us a lot of good will. I sure don't want to look like Scrooge, but I don't want to be Santa Claus, either. One place where we probably should have been tougher was in the negotiations with the union on pensions. That's a big chunk of dough, if you'll pardon the pun."

CASE 16.2　　　**THE HOLIDAY TURKEY CAPER**

"And a happy New Year to you, too," muttered Len Colfax, human resources director for Nutritional Foods, as John Andrews stalked from Len's office. John was the best supervisor of shipping the company had ever had. But he was almost belligerent in his insistence on equitable treatment for the people in his department.

This morning, John had blustered in to complain about the turkeys the company had given each employee the day before the holidays. "The idea of giving holiday turkeys is fine," John had grumbled. "But they all ought to weigh the same. Several people in my group weighed their birds and found discrepancies of as much as two pounds. They joked about it, but I could see that a couple of people were irritated. Someone said they suspected that the sales department people got turkeys as much as five pounds larger. I don't know about that, but the company ought to do a better job of being fair about these things." With that, John stalked out.

Len groaned. Talk about looking a gift horse in the mouth! Still, one lesson he'd learned in his years as human resources director was that employees can be very sensitive to what they perceive as unfair treatment. There was no reason why the supplier couldn't have provided turkeys closer to the same weight. Next year Len would insist on that. Also, next year it might be a good idea to explain that, even though the company had done everything possible to provide turkeys of equal size, there might be differences of a few ounces but that it would probably even out over the years.

Len made some notes for his file and smiled ruefully. "Live and learn," he thought.

In addition to compensation in the form of wages and salaries, organizations provide workers with various services and programs known as **employee benefits.** In the past, these programs and services were often called fringe benefits, but now they make up such a large part of the total compensation package that the term *fringe* is no longer appropriate. The term *supplementary benefits*, however, is still commonly used to refer to this aspect of employee compensation.

The chapter-opening cases give only a few examples of the many kinds of benefits a particular organization may offer. These range from legally required benefits (such as social security payments) to time off with pay (for holidays, personal business, vacation, and so on) and optional "give-away" items such as free coffee or gifts at certain holidays. While these benefits may be offered at no expense to the employee, they certainly are not "free." Benefits represent a significant cost to the organization, as the owner of Phil's

Bakery came to appreciate in Case 16.1. And, as Case 16.2 suggests, the allocation of benefits is as sensitive a matter as wage and salary administration in that perceived fairness and determining what is equitable treatment are crucial considerations in designing a successful benefits program.

CURRENT PRACTICES AND PROBLEMS

Although equity considerations affect the design of a benefits program just as they affect the organization's wage and salary program, the process of determining benefit payments is somewhat less complicated than establishing pay rates. Figure 16.1 shows the factors involved in determining benefits for a particular organization. Job analysis, job evaluation, and merit ratings are not directly involved in this process. But because many benefit payments (sick leave, vacations, and holiday pay) stem from the actual wages and salaries paid to employees, determining base pay is the first step in establishing the benefits program. Probably the most critical and time-consuming step is the analysis of relevant data, including benefit surveys (to ascertain benefit practices in com-

FIGURE 16.1 Process of determining employee benefits

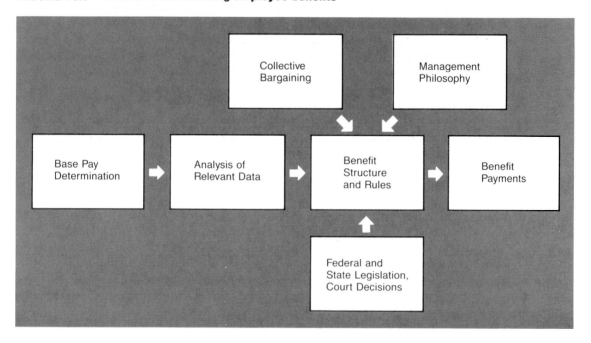

peting firms); cost analysis of various benefits and the organization's ability to finance them; and identification of employee preferences for particular programs and services. Federal and state legislation will have a bearing on benefits decisions, as will collective bargaining in the unionized organization. In fact, many benefits are required by law or are specified by the labor agreement. And in any organization, management philosophy will have some impact on benefit decisions. Many employee benefits are initiated by management's desire to enhance morale, to avoid unionization, or to compete with other organizations in recruiting and retaining qualified workers.

The Importance of Employee Benefits

In addition to basic wages and salaries, the benefits supplied by the organization are very important to the well-being and security of its employees. Consider the tragic situation of an employee who declines to participate in a permanent disability program and who later suffers an injury and becomes permanently disabled. Benefit programs can be crucial to maintaining an employee's standard of living when health problems occur.

Employee benefits are also important to the organization in some positive ways. If carefully selected and properly managed, they can be helpful in recruiting and retaining qualified employees. For example, the generous benefits provided by the Marion Laboratories (see Figure 16.2) undoubtedly are a factor in the company's success in attracting applicants and in retaining talented people. In addition, some benefits can reduce costs in other areas. For example, Bechtel Group, Inc., found that its commuter vans and other ride-sharing programs at its southern California facility made it unnecessary to build a previously planned $3.5 million parking garage.[1]

As another example, some organizations have found that the costs of exercise and fitness programs have been partly offset by reduced health-care claims from those employees who work out regularly.[2]

Employee benefits are significant in a negative sense because they have grown increasingly expensive, and if a company is not careful, it may "give away the store." Case 16.1 illustrates how benefit costs can be a major concern to top management. In fact, as a percentage of pay, employee benefits have increased faster than basic wages and salaries in most years for several decades. Figure 16.3 shows the growth of employee benefits as a percentage of wages and salaries since 1929. Between 1963 and 1983, employee

FIGURE 16.2 Comprehensive benefit plans available from Marion Laboratories

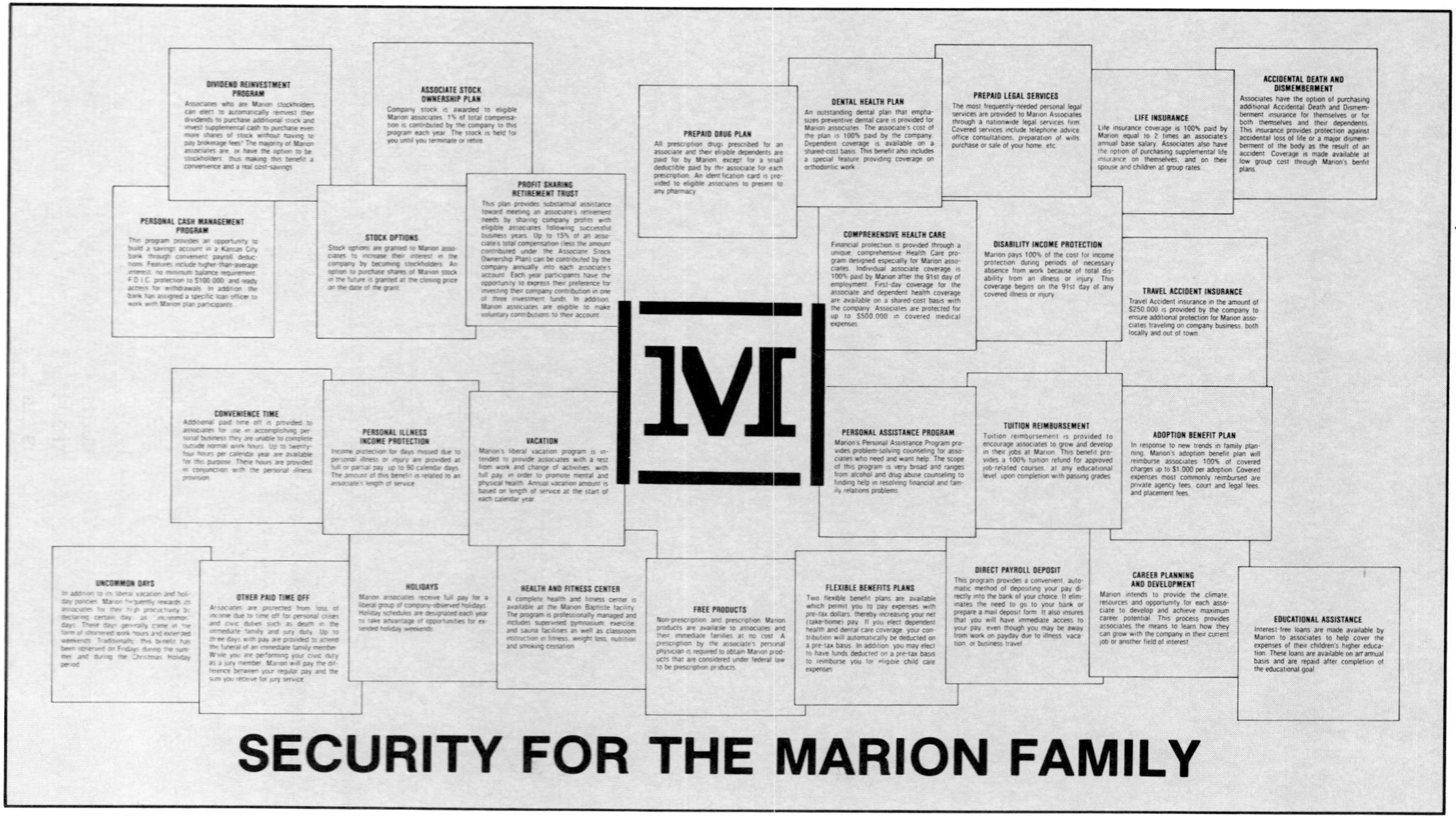

SECURITY FOR THE MARION FAMILY

Source: Courtesy of Marion Laboratories, Inc.

FIGURE 16.3
Growth of employee benefits,* 1929–1982

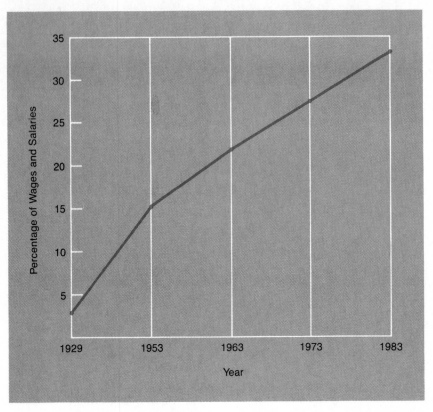

* Total benefits include those legally required under Social Security and other governmental provisions, agreed upon benefits such as pensions and insurance, rest periods, payment for time not worked, and benefits such as bonuses and profit-sharing.

Source: Employee Benefits 1983 (Washington, D.C.: Chamber of Commerce of the United States, 1984), p. 30. Used with permission.

benefits grew from 22 to 33.2 percent of direct pay.[3] In recent recession years, the managements of some organizations have literally "taken back" some employee benefits to prevent losses or serious cash-flow problems. As a result, benefits as a percentage of wages and salaries dropped slightly in 1982 and 1983.[4]

Types of Employee Benefits

There are many employee benefits from which to choose. Some, such as social security, are **mandatory benefits;** that is, organizations are required by law to provide them. Many organizations offer other, nonmandatory benefits that are attractive to both the employer and the employee. Among these are insurance plans; pensions; payment for time not worked; and any number of optional payments and services such as tuition refunds, van pools, and a variety of discount programs. It would be impossible to describe *all* the benefits found in contemporary organizations, but it is useful to be familiar with the major types to which organizations make substantial financial contributions.

Mandatory Benefits. Federal and state laws require most organizations to provide certain benefits that essentially protect workers in the event of illness or accidents and during periods of unemployment and retirement. These benefits are provided through the Old-Age, Survivors, Disability, and Health Insurance program, more commonly known as **social security.** The Social Security Act of 1935 as amended makes mandatory the provision of pension payments, unemployment compensation, and workers' compensation. The pension benefits are paid for through the Federal Insurance

---

PERSPECTIVE 16.1 Social Security's Vital Statistics

Who's Covered

People in practically all lines of work, including members of Congress, the President, newly hired federal workers and the self-employed are covered.

Some 116 million contribute to Social Security through payroll taxes on wages, salaries, commissions and tips. Contributions will total an estimated 215 billion dollars in the 1984 fiscal year ending September 30.

Who Pays

Employees — They currently pay 6.7 percent of their first $37,800 of annual wages or salary — a maximum tax of $2,532.60.

Employers — They more than match their workers' share, paying 7 percent on the same wage base.

Self-employed persons, including farmers, owners of small businesses, some members of the clergy — they pay 11.3 percent of their first $37,800 of pay this year.

Tax rates and wage bases are scheduled to rise in years ahead.

"Social Security's Vital Statistics," excerpted from *U.S. News & World Report* issue of September 17, 1984. Copyright, 1984, U.S. News & World Report, Inc.

Who Gets Checks

Approximately 1 of every 6 persons in the U.S. now gets a monthly Social Security check.

These 36 million beneficiaries include retired and disabled workers, their dependents and survivors.

Total benefits paid out: 174 billion dollars in fiscal 1984.

For retirees, full benefits begin at age 65. Workers can retire as early as 62 with reduced benefits.

Size of Benefits

Benefits are based on the size of a retiree's pay while working. Adjustments are made to keep pace with inflation.

Spouses at age 65 can receive half of a retired worker's benefit.

Maximum benefit for persons retiring in 1984 at age 65 — $703 per month for a single worker, $1,054 for a couple.

Some people who retired in earlier years receive more than that because of recent changes in the benefit formula plus cost-of-living adjustments.

Benefits are partially taxable this year for the first time.

Contributions Act (FICA) deductions from employee paychecks, matched by employers' contributions. The employer is responsible for withholding social security taxes and for making contributions to the federal government on a quarterly basis.

As the number of people eligible to receive social security benefits grows, social security taxes are rising dramatically. Starting in 1984, employees were required to contribute 6.7 percent of the first $37,800 earned and employers had to match that amount. By 1988 the percentage is projected to be 7.15 on a wage base of $50,100.

Unemployment compensation is administered under a dual system of state and federal laws. The purpose of these laws is to provide emergency income to people when they are unemployed and to encourage employers to provide stable employment. The Federal Unemployment Tax Act of 1935 as amended requires employers of four or more employees performing types of work covered by the act to pay an unemployment insurance tax to the federal government. The federal government then makes refunds to the various states. Typically, unemployment compensation benefits are available from state governments for a period of up to twenty-six weeks. Individual states are free to authorize or prohibit the payment of unemployment compensation to workers who are on strike.[5]

Workers' compensation provides payments to workers or dependents in the event of job-incurred injuries, illnesses, or death. Medical and rehabilitation services are also provided. These benefit programs are administered by the state. The total cost is borne by employers, although the method of insuring may vary from state to state and may involve a state fund, approved insurance companies, or special funds set up by employers. In 1980, total workers' compensation payments made in the United States totaled $13.4 billion.[6]

Pensions.　　In many cases, social security payments provide only a minimum income for retirement and must be supplemented with other funds. Therefore, many organizations offer pension benefits beyond those required by the Social Security Act, representing a significant cost in the typical benefit program. It is estimated that more than 80 percent of all employees participate in an employer-sponsored pension plan.[7]

There are many kinds of pension plans. Under *contributory plans*, both employees and employers are required to contribute to the pension fund. Under *noncontributory plans*, pension funding is the sole responsibility of the employer. The actual payments received during retirement may be specified on the basis of an employee's salary level and length of service; in noncontributory plans where contributions are based on company profits (*deferred profit-*

sharing plans), accumulated funds are usually allocated on the basis of salary (and the size of the pension fund depends on profit size).

All private pensions are now regulated under the Employee Retirement Income Security Act (ERISA) of 1974, which was passed to help ensure that pension plans are adequately funded and protected against failure. Although the act does not *require* a company to establish a pension plan, it does benefit workers in a number of significant ways. First, the law creates a tax incentive for employers to set aside certain funds for pension plans and establishes an insurance program to protect those funds. Second, the law broadens employee participation in pension plans by prohibiting overly strict eligibility rules. A pension plan must now include all employees who are at least twenty-five years of age and who have worked in the organization for at least one year. Third, the law establishes minimum **vesting** standards, under which an employee who has worked a certain length of time or reached a certain age is entitled to receive the employer's contributions to the pension fund even if the employee leaves the job before retirement. **Portability,** however, or an employee's ability to transfer vested benefits to another employer (to maintain all retirement moneys in one account) or to an individual retirement account, requires the agreement of the employer.[8]

A new pension benefit program adopted by many organizations in recent years is the **salary reduction plan,** also known as the "401(k) plan." Under Section 401 (k) of the Internal Revenue Code, an employer may establish a retirement savings plan to which employees can contribute through payroll deductions. The employee's contributions reduce the employee's taxable income, and no income taxes are paid until the employee starts drawing from the fund after retirement. Frequently, companies match employees' contributions, and employees can choose which of several investments they wish to participate in, such as money market funds or company stock purchase plans. Under the Internal Revenue Code, such plans are required to have broad employee participation, including significant participation by lower paid employees.[9]

Employees can also save for retirement and pay reduced taxes by participating in an **employee stock ownership plan (ESOP).** Under these plans, employees may purchase company stock through payroll-deduction or installment plans, usually below market price. Generally, the employee is eligible to sell the stock or withdraw dividends only on retirement or termination of employment, when he or she must pay taxes on those assets. Advocates of ESOPs point out the potential morale and incentive value of employees' owning stock; conversely, however, the effect on morale if the value of the stock declines needs to be considered. ESOPs were given a boost by favorable clauses in ERISA.[10] It was estimated that 7,000 companies had enrolled 10 million workers in ESOPs by early 1985.[11]

There appear to be some potential abuses of ESOPs. Critics point out, for example, that employees are often represented only by an ESOP trustee, and frequently that person is a company official. This gives workers little say in major decisions, such as what course of action to take in the event of a hostile take-over attempt by another company. Advocates point out that companies sharing ownership with most or all employees have been growing two to four times as fast as companies in which employees do not own stock.[12]

Insurance.   Companies typically provide health, life, and disability insurance and frequently dental and accident insurance. Such insurance contributes to the financial security of employees or their families in the event of illness, death, or accident. A U.S. Chamber of Commerce study indicates that 85 percent of 1,454 responding firms made payments to life insurance plans for employees; 92 percent made payments to employee health insurance plans.[13] These benefits may be based partly on employee contributions (contributory) or may be furnished entirely by the employer (noncontributory).

Company-sponsored insurance plans are typically group plans that provide benefits at lower cost than if coverage were purchased for individuals. Because all or most employees are included, the employer can negotiate favorable rates with the insurance company or health-care provider.

One of the fastest-growing forms of medical insurance is health-care coverage through a health maintenance organization (HMO). For a monthly fee, these organizations essentially provide total health care, including physical examinations, laboratory tests, surgical and hospital services, consulting-nurse and emergency-room services, and prescriptions filled at the HMO pharmacy. Small charges may be made for prescriptions, and limits may be set on some kinds of services — for example, the number of consultations at a mental health clinic. Examples of such organizations are the Kaiser-Permanente Medical Program (California), Group Health Cooperative of Puget Sound (Washington), Community Health Care Center Plan (Connecticut), and Harvard Community Health Plan (Massachusetts; not connected with Harvard University).[14]

Some insurance plans offered build on a basic foundation of other plans. For example, a company might pay for a basic hospital and surgical plan but provide a major medical plan and a salary-continuation plan on a contributory basis. The major medical plan

Tufts Associated Health Plan/Photo by Gustav Freedman

For a monthly fee, an HMO provides total health care.

picks up coverage where the basic plan leaves off and helps employees meet hospital and medical expenses associated with catastrophic situations such as long-term illnesses. Salary-continuation insurance provides a designated level of income for a stated period after an employee's sick-leave eligibility runs out.

Payment for Time Not Worked. Payments for time not worked averaged 9.4 percent of payroll in 1983. Included were paid vacations and holidays, paid sick leave, and time off with pay for such reasons as National Guard or jury duty. Payments for such matters as paid rest periods, wash-up time, and clothes-change time averaged another 2.3 percent of payroll, for a total of 11.7 percent.[15]

These benefits are obviously important to employees but are a significant cost to employers. Unless there are adequate controls, the firm can easily subsidize a great deal of employee time that is not devoted to organizational purposes. In addition, managers and supervisors must spend considerable time making certain that time-off benefits are administered equitably. On the other hand, time-off-with-pay benefits are important in keeping the organization competitive in recruiting and retaining employees. Further, it is clearly in the interests of the organization to have employees who remain healthy and who have opportunities to renew both energy and perspective.

Other Benefits and Services. Many other benefits are found in American organizations. Some are common; others are unusual. Here are some examples of these benefits (with, in some cases, names of some organizations that offer them):

- Prepaid legal services.[16]
- Physical fitness programs (PepsiCo, Xerox, and Fluor Corporation).[17]
- College tuition loans to employees' children.[18]
- Van-pool programs. (A common practice with commuter van pools is to assign a ten-passenger van to one employee who drives nine other employees, all of whom pay a fee that is less than the actual costs of commuting; in 1983 it was estimated that there were 24,000 company-subsidized commuter vans operating in the U.S.)[19]
- Free bus passes to employees.[20]
- Paid sabbaticals of several weeks to several months (Tandem Computers, Rolm Corp., McDonald's, and Intel).[21]
- Free turkeys to all employees at Christmas (Russell Stover Candies).[22]
- Sick-leave "banks" (pooling of compensated-leave days in a common fund to cover extensive illness).[23]
- Movies in factory cafeteria during lunch.[24]
- Payments of up to $2,500 to assist employees in adopting children.[25]
- Special medical plans for handicapped children of employees.[26]
- Tuition reimbursement prior to and after retirement.[27]
- Mental health insurance for services of psychologists and psychiatrists.[28]
- Child development center on company premises (PCA International, Inc. in North Carolina runs such a center for employees with small children and pays half the costs).[29]
- Discount programs for employee travel and entertainment (see Table 16.1).[30]
- Financial counseling for executives.[31]

Some of these benefits, such as movies during lunch in the company cafeteria, are relatively inexpensive. Others, such as paid leaves of absence, are very expensive and ordinarily are feasible only in very large organizations or in circumstances where on-

TABLE 16.1
Types of travel and entertainment discount programs offered by organizations (N = 248)

PROGRAM TYPE	NUMBER OFFERING	PERCENT OF TOTAL
Amusement parks	158	63.7
Hotels and motels	124	50.0
Car and truck rentals	96	38.7
Professional sports	74	29.8
Airlines	70	28.2
Restaurants	60	24.2
Auto repair and emergency service	36	14.5
Bus	23	9.3
Campgrounds	21	8.5
Ship lines	17	6.9
Train	11	4.4

Source: Reprinted, by permission of the publisher, from "A Survey of Travel and Entertainment Programs," by Kenneth R. Evans et al., *Personnel*, March 1985, p. 65. © Periodicals Division, American Management Associations, New York. All rights reserved.

going professional development is critical in meeting organizational goals.

Costs of Benefits

Employee benefits are now receiving more attention than in the past because they have become a major part of the cost of being in business and because, with the exception of two recent years, they have been increasing more rapidly than wages and salaries. The costs of health care, in particular, have escalated dramatically in recent years. Health-care premiums increased 15 percent or more in 1984 over the previous year.[32]

Relative costs of various employee benefits across business and industry in 1983 are shown in Table 16.2, which is based on a survey of 1,454 companies of all sizes. According to this survey, employee benefit payments for all companies averaged 36.6 percent of payroll. The biggest costs in the typical benefit program are social security taxes, pension plans, and insurance premiums, including medical insurance premiums. Payment for time not worked represents another substantial cost. As indicated above, if costs of rest periods, lunch periods, and so on are added, compensation for nonwork time totals 11.7 percent of payroll.

It should be noted, however, that there are wide variations in the mix and level of employee benefits among companies and industries. For example, the level of benefits in chemicals and allied

TABLE 16.2 Cost of employee benefits, by type of benefit, 1983

TYPE OF BENEFIT	TOTAL, ALL COMPANIES	TOTAL, ALL MANUFAC-TURING	TOTAL, ALL NONMANU-FACTURING
Total employee benefits as percent of payroll	36.6	38.7	34.9
1. Legally required payments (employer's share only)	9.0	10.1	8.1
a. Old-Age, Survivors, Disability, and Health Insurance (FICA taxes)	6.3	6.4	6.2
b. Unemployment Compensation	1.4	1.8	1.0
c. Workers' compensation (including estimated cost of self-insured)	1.2	1.8	0.8
d. Railroad Retirement Tax, Railroad Unemployment and Cash Sickness Insurance, state sickness benefits insurance, etc.**	0.1	0.1	0.1
2. Pension, insurance, and other agreed-upon payments (employer's share only)	13.6	14.2	13.0
a. Pension plan premiums and pension payments not covered by insurance-type plan (net)	5.0	4.4	5.4
b. Life insurance premiums; death benefits; hospital, surgical, medical, and major medical insurance premiums, etc. (net)	7.0	8.4	6.0
c. Short-term disability	0.3	0.5	0.2
d. Salary continuation or long-term disability	0.3	0.2	0.3
e. Dental insurance premiums	0.5	0.5	0.4
f. Discounts on goods and services purchased from company by employees	0.1	*	0.2
g. Employee meals furnished by company	0.1	*	0.2
h. Miscellaneous payments (vision care, prescription drugs, separation or termination pay, moving expenses, etc.)	0.3	0.2	0.3
3. Paid rest periods, lunch periods, wash-up time, travel time, clothes-change time, get-ready time, etc.	2.3	2.4	2.1

products industries (40 percent of payroll) is much higher than in department stores (31.8 percent).[33]

Flexible Benefit Plans

Flexible benefit plans (or "cafeteria benefit plans") are gradually being adopted by more and more organizations. Under these plans,

TABLE 16.2 *(Continued)*

TYPE OF BENEFIT	TOTAL, ALL COMPANIES	TOTAL, ALL MANUFAC- TURING	TOTAL, ALL NONMANU- FACTURING
4. Payments for time not worked	9.4	9.6	9.6
a. Paid vacations and payments in lieu of vacation	4.8	5.1	4.7
b. Payments for holidays not worked	2.9	3.2	2.7
c. Paid sick leave	1.3	0.9	1.7
d. Payments for State or National Guard duty; jury, witness, and voting pay allowances; payments for time lost due to death in family or other personal reasons, etc.	0.4	0.4	0.5
5. Other items	2.3	2.4	2.1
a. Profit-sharing payments	1.0	1.2	0.9
b. Contributions to employee thrift plans	0.5	0.4	0.5
c. Christmas or other special bonuses, service awards, suggestion awards, etc.	0.3	0.5	0.2
d. Employee education expenditures (tuition refunds, etc.)	0.3	0.1	0.3
e. Special wage payments ordered by courts, payments to union stewards, etc.	0.2	0.2	0.2
Total employee benefits as cents per payroll hour ...	369.1	393.2	349.9
Total employee benefits as dollars per year per employee	7,582	8,110	7,163

*Less than 0.05%

**Figure shown is considerably less than legal rate, because most reporting companies had only a small proportion of employees covered by tax.

Source: Employee Benefits 1983 (Washington, D.C.: Chamber of Commerce of the United States, 1984), p. 8. Reprinted with the permission of the U.S. Chamber of Commerce.

employees can choose a particular mix of benefits adding up to a certain dollar amount. Some of the first organizations to offer these plans were TRW, Educational Testing Service, American Can, Northern States Power Company, and PepsiCo.[34]

There are four basic approaches to flexible benefit plans: core, module, flexible spending account, and combined.[35] The *core* approach provides a basic "core" of benefits that the company considers important. This core represents a reduction in total benefits from previous levels, and employees can then use the dollar difference to select from a "menu" those benefits that fit their particular circumstances. The *module* approach provides several packages of equivalent value from which the employee can select his or her benefits program. For example, an employee burdened with poor health might choose a package that provides a large amount of disability insurance and extensive medical coverage with low deductibles. The *flexible spending account* approach provides each employee with a certain dollar total from which to select benefits. *Combined* approaches feature various mixtures of the other three approaches.[36]

Flexible benefit plans are likely to be adopted by more and more organizations in the future. One factor supporting this trend is the availability of the microcomputer, which makes it easier to develop and administer such programs and to provide information to employees. In addition, the flexible benefit approach gives some organizations a better way to control benefit costs. A particularly

---

PERSPECTIVE 16.2   Being Flexible

While flexible benefits, or cafeteria plans, have been around since the early 1970s, they have been available almost exclusively at companies with thousands of employees. But in the past year or so, the plans have been installed more frequently at smaller companies, thanks in part to software packages that cut the ongoing expense of maintaining the benefits programs and to more interest in working with growing businesses on the part of consulting firms and insurance companies.

BGS Systems Inc., in Waltham, Mass., will be paying a total of $240,000 per year for the cafeteria plan it adopted last January, says Edward Hellenbeck III, second vice-president at Unionmutual of Portland, Maine, which drew up BGS's program. That fee covers a variety of insurance options now available to employees, including medical and dental coverage, disability insurance, and life insurance. For Ted Kelley, the $9.1-million specialty software company's human resources director, the cafeteria

Source: Tom Watterson, "Being Flexible," *INC.*, June 1985, p. 120. Reprinted with permission. Copyright © 1985 by INC. Publishing Company, 38 Commercial Wharf, Boston, MA 02110.

plan is clearly a strong recruitment tool for BGS: "We're trying to compete against the Wangs, the DECs, and the Primes — companies that want the same kind of worker *we* have," he says.

Given the likelihood of major changes in the tax laws this year, the future of these benefit plans is uncertain. Yet one proposal, backed by the Reagan Administration, might actually *increase* interest in flexible benefits. Under this scenario, all fringe benefits would be taxable to the employee, whether or not they are in a flexible program. As a result, employees would tend to choose only those items they needed most. A single person with no children, for instance, might take little or no life insurance.

If the "major driving force" behind flexible benefits is to give employees tax-free fringe benefits, says Mike Davis, a vice-president in the Boston office of The Wyatt Co., then perhaps companies should wait and see how the tax-law debate turns out. But most companies, he adds, are instituting flexible benefits to stay competitive. For them, he says, there is no reason to wait.

important factor, of course, is employee acceptance, and employees have generally been enthusiastic about such plans.[37] Unions, too, are gradually endorsing flexible benefit plans. For example, a recent contract between Alcoa and the Aluminum, Brick and Glass Workers included such a plan.[38]

IMPACT OF ENVIRONMENT

Numerous forces in the environment influence the level and type of benefits paid for or provided by employers. Among these are laws, court decisions, collective bargaining, economic conditions, and changes in the work force.

Laws and Court Decisions

Federal and state laws and some recent court decisions have had significant effects on benefit policies and practices in modern organizations. The mandatory benefits prescribed by the Social Security Act and the impact of ERISA on pension benefits have already been discussed. But other important laws regulating benefits also influence the design and administration of benefit programs directly.

The Welfare and Pension Plans Disclosure Act of 1958, with subsequent amendments, placed a record-keeping and report-submitting burden on employers and unions that administer pension and welfare plans. Under this law, organizations administering welfare and pension funds are required to submit reports to the secretary of labor, must have bonded officials to handle such funds, and are subject to legal action if they misuse such funds.[39]

The Retirement Equity Act of 1984 amended ERISA in a number of significant ways, particularly with respect to the rights of spouses. For example, pension and profit-sharing plans must now pay survivor's benefits to the spouse if the employee dies before retirement. After retirement, if the participant in the pension plan dies first, the spouse must continue to receive a monthly benefit of at least 50 percent of what was being paid the retiree, unless the spouse has cosigned a benefit election form choosing some other option. Further, the law prevents workers from losing their vested benefits when they stop working temporarily, a provision that will benefit women who wish to stay home with their children for a few years.[40]

The 1978 amendments to the Age Discrimination in Employment Act (ADEA) raised the permissible upper limit on private-sector employees' retirement age from sixty-five to seventy. A survey of

267 firms conducted in 1980 found 86 percent of the firms had experienced little or no impact on benefit plans. The most frequent changes were the improvement of medical insurance benefits for early retirees and the initiation of preretirement counseling or planning programs.[41]

The Equal Pay Act of 1963 has also had a major influence on benefits. Under this law, it is "an unlawful employment practice for an employer to discriminate between men and women with regard to fringes." In particular, benefits designed to assist the "head of the household" or "principal wage earner" are considered discriminatory when the effect is to favor male employees. Similarly, it is unlawful to have pension or retirement plans that provide for different benefits or that set different compulsory or optional retirement ages based on sex.[42]

In the landmark *Arizona* v. *Norris* decision, the Supreme Court ruled in 1983 that women and men must be paid equal pension benefits for equal contributions. The case was brought by Nathalie Norris, an employee of the state of Arizona, who had joined an annuity plan offered by the state through a commercial insurance company. Her contribution per month was $199, the same as for male employees, but her monthly benefit beginning at age sixty-five was scheduled to be $33.96 less than for male employees. Norris claimed that this was sex discrimination under Title VII of the Civil Rights Act. The Supreme Court agreed with her, thus overturning the traditional practice of insurance companies and pension plans of paying women smaller benefits because women generally live longer than men and draw benefits longer.[43]

Under the Pregnancy Discrimination Act of 1978, an amendment of Title VII, employers must give pregnant workers the same group health insurance or disability benefits they give other workers suffering medical problems or disabilities. EEOC guidelines on this law included a controversial provision that wives of employees were also entitled to insurance coverage for pregnancy when the employer's insurance program covered spouses for other disabilities.[44] In a related case but with implications beyond pregnancy care, the Supreme Court, in *Newport News Shipbuilding and Dry Dock* v. *EEOC* (1983), ruled that employers must treat female and male employees equally in providing health insurance for their spouses.[45]

A federal law pertaining to holidays for government employees is having a major effect on holiday practices throughout the country. Under this law, federal employees observe the following holidays on Monday: George Washington's birthday, Memorial Day, Columbus Day, and Veterans Day. As a result, most states adopted similar laws pertaining to state employees, and a large proportion of private employers subsequently moved the observance of these holidays to Mondays.[46]

The Revenue Act of 1978 gives organizations more latitude in designing supplementary compensation plans. For example, flexible benefits plans receive favorable tax treatment providing they meet certain terms. As another example, almost all educational assistance for employees provided by employers is exempt from income and employment taxes. Previously, company expenses or reimbursements for educational courses were taxable income to employees unless the courses were directly job related.[47]

Collective Bargaining and Economic Conditions

Over the years, collective bargaining has had a major impact on the benefits provided unionized employees. Furthermore, when benefits are negotiated between management and unions, similar benefits are often extended to nonunionized employees in the same organization. In addition, unions typically call attention to benefits negotiated elsewhere to support arguments for increasing benefits in a particular firm.

Union efforts to increase benefits are sometimes motivated by factors other than the enhancement of benefits for workers. For example, assuming that premium pay on Sundays or holidays is a supplementary benefit, double or triple time for work on those days may be sought by the union to discourage supervisors from scheduling such work. Additional holidays or vacation time may be sought to reduce unemployment, since more time off with pay requires additional workers to operate plants.

Labor-market conditions also affect the benefits paid by organizations. Shortages of certain skills and competition for those skills tend to be factors in increasing benefits. For example, if competition for engineers is keen, a company may endeavor to attract employees by initiating a tuition-payment and time-off program that permits engineers to work on advanced degrees at nearby universities.

The organization's ability to finance supplementary programs and services will directly affect the size and scope of its benefits package. A young, struggling firm will not be able to afford an extensive benefit program, nor will a firm in a profit slump want to expand its employee benefits. On the other hand, if a company is experiencing high profits and rapid growth, management may be inclined to be generous in expanding the employee benefit package.

Canceling benefits when times are less favorable is difficult because employees have come to expect them. Nevertheless, during recent recessions, many companies have been forced to reduce benefits. For example, in 1982, International Harvester and the United Auto Workers agreed to subtract a week of paid vacation and three paid personal holidays. This concession by the union saved the company $200 million over two years. (The benefits were restored in 1985.)[48] In some instances, unions have traded wage cuts for benefits such as stock-ownership plans. For example, Republic Airlines, facing heavy losses, reached an agreement with the Airline Employees Association to extend a 15 percent pay cut for a year and a half in exchange for an employee stock-ownership plan and profit sharing.[49]

Work Force Changes

Changes in the composition of the work force also have an effect on employee benefits. For example, the growing number of single-parent families and of employed women with children has increased the pressure for day-care centers as well as more flexible work schedules. These factors probably account for heightened employee interest in flexible benefit packages.

If an organization's work force consists of a high percentage of young people just out of school who remain with the firm an average of two years, there may be little demand for a pension plan and little interest on the part of top management in establishing one. On the other hand, there may be need for careful attention to good cafeteria services, carefully managed rest periods, and liberal vacation and unpaid leave policies. If the work force includes a high percentage of employees with families, both employees and management may be greatly interested in group medical and life insurance programs and other benefits designed to increase family security.

MANAGING EMPLOYEE BENEFITS

The management of employee benefits is a critical concern in any organization. In the first place, benefits are expensive. At the same time, an organization is likely to be at a severe disadvantage in recruiting and keeping qualified employees if management does not try to maintain a reasonably attractive benefit package. Moreover, employee benefits cannot be managed capriciously without adverse consequences. In Case 16.2 at the beginning of the chapter, Len Colfax, the human resources director, was reminded that even small, unexplained differences in employee benefits can lead to perceptions of unfair treatment and, in turn, irritation or anger. For these reasons, careful attention must be paid to the design and administration of the benefit program.

Benefit Surveys

Because of rapidly rising costs, managers have been paying more attention to **benefit surveys,** surveys of the benefits offered by other firms. Benefits for unionized firms are usually surveyed by both management and the union prior to contract negotiations.

Because employee benefits are part of the total compensation package, benefit surveys should be made simultaneously with wage and salary surveys to obtain the most complete and useful data. To establish or revise either aspect of the total package without giving attention to the other is to ignore a significant component of the overall compensation strategy.

Employee Preferences

Management can obtain important guidance in modifying benefit programs by periodically identifying employee preferences. Some of the methods used to identify these preferences are personal interviews with a cross section of employees, meetings with small groups of employees, and questionnaires accompanied by computer printouts of current benefits so that employees can readily visualize the present package.[50]

More sophisticated methods of measuring employee preferences are also available. For example, an organization might ask a random sample of employees to rank various combinations of benefits and services. Various pairs of benefits at different levels of cost and coverage are printed on separate cards so that employees can make a series of choices between various pairings. A statistical analysis of the rankings and of the costs of each pair can help management make decisions among various options.[51]

Benefit Structure and Rules

Detailed administration rules are usually developed before benefit programs are implemented. For example, for sick-leave benefits, rules must be established on the length of time salaries or wages will be continued, when benefits will start, the relationship between benefits and length of service, the maximum sick leave that will be

*"I see you have a nice tan, Parker. I suppose that's one way
to spend one's vacation, isn't it?"*

Drawing by Weber; © 1983 The New Yorker Magazine, Inc.

granted in any one year, and whether a physician's statement will
be required as proof of illness.

If careful attention is not given to the development of benefit
rules, policy must be decided quickly the first time the occasion
arises, which means making a hasty decision that may later be
regretted. Such spur-of-the-moment decision making can result in
inconsistent or costly practices. Suppose a company has not considered what sick-leave benefits are to be given to newly hired employees. A new person joins the firm, calls in sick on the third day
of employment, reporting that he has mononucleosis, and, on the
basis of a supervisor's "top-of-the-head" decision, draws full pay
for six months. From the organization's point of view, this is a
costly decision offering little or no return. Thus, without detailed
rules of administration there will be no controls on benefit costs.
In addition, there can be no realistic cost forecasts because there
will be too many unanticipated variables affecting expenditures.

Equitable, explainable rules are also necessary to ensure that
benefit policies are fair and applied consistently to all employees.
For example, using the above illustration of the six-month paid
leave for the new employee, assume that an employee with three
years' service in a different department becomes ill and is told that,
under company policy, the maximum sick leave that can be drawn

is two months' pay. Almost certainly, the employee will perceive this treatment as inequitable and react angrily. According to equity theory, contributions (hard work, three years' service) and outcomes (two months' sick leave) will be perceived as grossly out of line as compared with the new employee's contributions (two days of getting oriented to the job) and outcomes (six months' leave with pay). Typically, the longer a person has been an employee, the longer the allowable sick leave.

In the interest of fairness and to safeguard morale, management must examine benefits and privileges within and across major categories of employees carefully and develop policies and practices that are perceived as equitable by everyone in the organization. No one is immune to negative feelings that stem from perceptions of inequitable treatment. For example, federal bankruptcy judges are excluded from many of the privileges enjoyed by U.S. district court and appeals judges, including use of the judges' dining room, use of a special elevator, and use of the judges' parking lot. One former federal bankruptcy judge reported that the system made him feel "like a second-class citizen."[52]

Managing Costs

Carefully developed rules are important in managing the costs of employee benefits. It is also important that organizations periodically conduct detailed cost analyses of expenditures in each benefit area. These analyses can provide guidance for cost-containment.

General Motors, for example, found that less than 2 percent of its workers accounted for 20 percent of the absenteeism. In other words, a high percentage of the costs associated with absenteeism (sick pay, training time, inefficiencies, and so on) were generated by just a very few people. Working with the United Auto Workers, the company and union agreed to trim the vacation, sickness, and accident pay of workers who are chronically absent during a six-month period. Benefits are cut by the percentage of absent days. Thus, a worker who is absent for 20 percent of the working days in the first half of the year loses 20 percent of the usual holiday pay during the second half of the year. In addition, the company and union have agreed to pay workers bonuses of up to $500 for perfect attendance during the year.[53]

Health-care costs have risen so rapidly that many organizations are working hard to control and reduce them. According to one survey, some of the most popular cost-containment techniques are:

- Careful internal administration of claims submitted by employees.

- Creating "fitness" or "wellness" programs. (Tenneco Corporation's main reason for building an exercise facility for its employee fitness program was to gain an advantage in recruiting high-talent employees, but the company found that about 40 percent of the cost was returned through reduced medical claims.)[54]
- Increasing or introducing deductibles (for example, employees might be required to pay the first $250 of medical care during a one-year period instead of the first $100).
- Joining with other companies to form a coalition to work with local health-service providers to keep costs down.
- Conducting an analysis of the extent to which various benefits are used. (General Motors' analysis of the proportion of workers using sick leave is an example.)
- Offering health-care coverage through a health maintenance organization.[55]

Other methods of reducing benefit costs include paying bonuses to employees who have no absences for a certain number of weeks.[56] Some organizations offer end-of-the year bonuses to employees who have not used up money set aside for health coverage,[57] and bonuses may also be paid to employees who quit smoking for a full year. (Smokers are reported to cost more in terms of fire insurance, workers' compensation, and life and health insurance premiums).[58] In addition, flexible benefit plans can be used to control costs of employee benefits.

ROLE OF THE HUMAN RESOURCES DEPARTMENT

Human resources departments typically have a major role in the development and management of employee benefit programs. A survey of 636 organizations of all kinds reported the proportion of organizations in which human resources departments have total or some responsibility for the following programs:

- Insurance benefits, 94%
- Unemployment compensation, 94%
- Workers' compensation, 93%
- Vacation/leave processing, 89%
- Recreation/social/recognition, 86%
- Tuition aid/scholarships, 74%
- Health/medical services, 74%
- Relocation services, 64%
- Thrift/savings plans, 52%
- Food services, 37%[59]

A number of these benefit programs are based on accounting, financial, and statistical information. Therefore, the organization's interests are best served if the human resources department works closely with other professionals in accounting, finance, and insurance, as well as legal counsel, in administering these programs. In addition, the expertise of these departments will be invaluable in analyzing costs and cost trends. Finally, changes in employee benefit programs should be based on broad consultation with managers across the organization, and new programs will require top management approval before implementation.

Assessing Alternatives and Employee Reactions

A major contribution the human resources department can make to organizational efficiency is to examine various benefit alternatives carefully. The first steps are to establish specific objectives for the entire benefit program and to determine the purpose of offering benefits in particular areas. The human resources department is often responsible for exploring various benefit options and for determining which options are the most cost effective. For example, faced with a higher proportion of women employees, including women managers, and a higher proportion of single parents, many companies are looking at ways to provide day-care service to families with young children. A company-run day-care facility is only one possible solution, and the human resources department might explore the advantages and disadvantages of a number of other options. The alternatives include establishing a service that refers employees to day-care centers already available in the community, contracting with quality day-care centers for a certain number of spaces and then providing these spaces for employees' children at a discount to the employees, or establishing a voucher system through which the organization pays some fraction of day-care services selected by the employee.[60]

Periodically assessing employee and supervisory reaction to the usefulness of various benefit programs will assist the human resources department in planning revisions in those programs. Questionnaires and interviews are probably the most useful devices for making this assessment. When extensive modifications in benefits are being considered, and when choices must be made about where benefit dollars are to be spent, inquiry into employee preferences can provide the organization with important guidance. The opinions and feedback of employees are important to the success of a benefit program, and the human resources department can help ensure that employee opinions are solicited and responded to in a conscientious and ongoing fashion.

Communicating Benefit Information

The human resources department plays a major role in how effectively information about benefit programs is provided to employees. Studies over the years have shown that many employees are unaware of some of the benefits that are provided, and many tend to underestimate substantially the costs of those benefits of which they are aware. Lack of awareness, of course, reduces the motivational value employee benefits may have and may lead to lack of uniformity in employee use. Lack of awareness can also contribute to inadequate planning by the employee. For example, not understanding the savings and tax advantages of a salary reduction plan can lead to an employee's not taking advantage of the plan, thus reducing his or her eventual retirement income. The human resources department, therefore, has a major challenge to provide information and counseling about employee benefits.

The human resources department also has some information obligations under the law. Under ERISA, an employee participating in a retirement plan must be furnished information such as an understandable summary of the plan and an annual report on its financial status. The employee is entitled to certain information upon request, including his or her total accrued benefits.[61]

Sensitivity to Equity Issues

Finally, human resources specialists can make a major contribution to the management of benefit programs by being sensitive to issues of equity. As benefit programs are developed and proposed, it is particularly important that differences in benefits among groups of employees be justifiable and readily explained. For example, production and maintenance employees may accept the notion of special parking privileges for top management if executives must leave the plant with some frequency during workdays, but it is more difficult to accept special parking privileges for supervisors who are on the same work schedule as other employees. A decreasing scale of benefits and privileges down through the managerial and supervisory ranks is usually more defensible than a system in which only a few top managers have extraordinary benefits and department heads just below them have very few.

Because it is difficult to anticipate every circumstance that might arise in the administration of a given benefit program, human resources specialists are wise to keep a log of decisions made in order to treat people consistently and to clarify policies when necessary. Such recording can help the human resources department identify practices that need to be curtailed.

SUMMARY

Employee benefits are important to the well-being and security of employees and important to organizations for the purpose of attracting and retaining qualified personnel.

Employee benefits have grown increasingly costly to employers. Payments required by law accounted for more than one-fourth of this amount.

The level and type of benefit programs available to employees vary widely among firms and industries. Flexible benefit plans (or "cafeteria compensation plans") are gradually being adopted by organizations across the country. Many federal and state laws and court decisions influence the type and level of employee benefits provided by employers. By law, most employers are required to pay into social security, unemployment compensation, and workers' compensation funds. Other laws regulate voluntary benefits, ensure nondiscriminatory benefit practices, or establish taxable status.

Collective bargaining that increases the benefits of unionized employees tends to result in increased benefits for nonunionized employees. Competition in recruiting qualified talent tends to increase employee benefits, while lack of financial resources will obviously restrict an organization's ability to offer generous programs. The changing nature of the work force has also influenced employee benefits. Management philosophy is also a major factor in the type and level of employee benefits.

Benefits must be managed carefully to enhance recruitment and retention efforts and morale, to avoid excessive costs, and to avoid problems of perceived inequity. Tools in the management of benefit programs are benefit surveys, other assessments of employee preferences, carefully planned rules of administration, and careful cost analysis. Many techniques can be used for controlling costs, including establishing deductibles and ceilings on benefits, and even providing rewards for not using the benefit.

The human resources department has a major role in the development and management of benefit programs. It is in everyone's interests for that department to draw on the expertise of specialists in accounting, finance, and insurance in administering these programs and in analyzing costs and cost trends. Changes in benefit programs should be based on consultation with managers across the organization and will require top management approval before implementation. Ideally, employees' ideas and support will be solicited in making changes in benefit programs.

KEY TERMS

employee benefits	workers' compensation	employee stock ownership
mandatory benefits	vesting	plan
social security	portability	flexible benefit plans
unemployment compensation	salary reduction plan	benefit surveys

REVIEW QUESTIONS

1. Discuss the significance of employee benefits to the employee and to the organization.
2. What are the major factors in the determination of employee benefits in a particular organization?
3. Explain the impact of ERISA on private pension plans.
4. Discuss the advantages of flexible benefit plans and some of the problems associated with such plans.
5. Explain the importance of controlling the costs of benefits and identify some cost-control measures.
6. Outline the role of the human resources department in benefits administration.

OPENING CASE QUESTIONS

Case 16.1   The Bottom Line

1. Are the policies of free coffee in the cafeteria and liberalized time off for personal business hurting Phil's Bakery?
2. What must Phil and Tom look at in deciding if they can change any of their current benefits?
3. What other organizational processes must be considered in benefit decisions?

Case 16.2   The Holiday Turkey Caper

1. What does this case demonstrate about employee attitudes regarding benefits?
2. Why do you think there is so much concern in the work force regarding equitable treatment?

CASE 16.3   EX-CELL-O COMMUNICATES FLEXIBILITY

In 1984, Ex-Cell-O Corp. conducted a highly ambitious communication campaign in an effort to get employees to think about and choose their own benefits. The campaign won at least one trade publication award, but more importantly, it enabled Ex-Cell-O to smoothly implement a flexible benefits plan for 4,100 salaried members of its work force of 15,000. By 1985, the plan was being expanded to cover other employees at the company's forty-one locations around the country.

Ex-Cell-O's flexible package allows employees to choose their benefits from a variety of options in four areas—medical, dental, vacation, and life insurance. In addition, employees may choose to contribute to a fund to hold money for health care costs not covered and to a 401(k) tax-deferred savings plan that includes corporate matching of up to two-and-one-half percent of employee contributions.

To determine payment for the new benefits, employees are given credits approximating the worth of their benefits under the old plan. An employee who chooses benefits that cost more than his or her credits pays the difference through pay-check deductions; if an employee chooses less costly options, the difference is added to each pay check.

Ex-Cell-O felt the switch to flexible benefits was wise for several reasons. For one thing, the company's human resources department recognized that changing demographics was creating a work force with varied needs. A married man with four children whose wife isn't employed, for instance, clearly has different requirements than a partner in a working couple with no children. In addition, the geographic diversity of Ex-Cell-O's locations added further variety to employees' situations.

However, one of Ex-Cell-O's primary aims in implementing flexible benefits was to make employees aware of what they are getting in the form of benefits, and that's where the massive communication effort came in. Before embarking on the program, Ex-Cell-O's management felt employees didn't understand how much their benefits were worth. Getting employees to appreciate benefits and to participate in choosing them, it was hoped, would help show the value of benefits and would contribute to employee satisfaction.

To help ensure an effective and comprehensive communication campaign, Ex-Cell-O hired a consulting firm, the Wyatt Co. of Washington, to participate in the plan's design. Wyatt's specialists communicated with employees all over the country to get a sense of what kind of format for publicizing the new plan would appeal to Ex-Cell-O's broad spectrum of people. To begin the campaign, a letter was sent to each employee explaining that benefits were to be changed.

Case Sources: Diane Lynn Kastiel, "Ex-Cell-O's Package Is a 'Total' Winner," *Business Insurance*, (July 30, 1984): 19–20; "Ex-Cell-O's Flexible Plan Begins Second Year," *Employee Benefit Plan Review* (April 1985): 18–20; and Kenneth H. Loeffler, "Flexible Benefits at Ex-Cell-O: A Case Study," *Personnel Journal* (June 1985): 106.

Then, for six weeks, newsletters went out that described each new option under the flexible plan. Soon after that, orientation meetings were held, led by trained Ex-Cell-O people who could answer questions and guide employees through the plan's many possibilities. These sessions included an appealing videotape that dramatized, with some humor, decision making about the plan by employees in different personal situations.

Finally, employees were given personalized workbooks that they could use to calculate how their benefit credits meshed with the choices they were considering under the new plan. At that point, they were ready to put together their benefits package and submit it. The company then sent confirmation of each employee's choices to make sure there had been no oversights.

This initial communication effort was an unqualified success. All but three of the employees involved submitted their benefit-election forms as instructed, and 98 percent chose one or more of the options that increased or altered the coverage of the standard package. Ex-Cell-O has, in fact, not gotten any negative feedback about the flexible plan. And the aim of increasing awareness of benefits has been served well. Says Ex-Cell-O vice president and treasurer Thomas J. Stuart, "There's been more discussion of benefits in this company in the past four months than there probably has been in the past forty years."*

Discussion Questions

1. What are some of the positive aspects of a flexible benefits plan like that at Ex-Cell-O?
2. Would you prefer to have your employer provide you with a set package of benefits that are excellent compared to those of other employers, or would you rather choose your own benefits under a flexible plan with benefit credits, possibly paying for some of them? Why?

*Quoted in Diane Lynn Kastiel, "Ex-Cell-O's Package Is a Total Winner," *Business Insurance* (July 30, 1984): 20.

Employee Protection and Representation

This section focuses on the ways in which personnel policies, organized labor, and governmental regulations protect the rights and well-being of employees. Chapter 17 deals with the role of labor organizations and the current status of the labor movement. Labor-management negotiations and the collective bargaining process are discussed in Chapter 18. Chapter 19 is devoted to employee rights and organizational due process, a rapidly evolving area in human resources management. Finally, Chapter 20 focuses on health and safety management, including governmental regulations intended to promote the safety and well-being of employees.

Labor Organizations

CHAPTER OUTLINE

LEARNING OBJECTIVES

- **Explain why workers join unions.**
- **Describe the major types of labor organizations.**
- **Identify the legal constraints on management and on labor during the unionization process.**
- **Outline the steps in the unionization process.**
- **Discuss current issues in the labor movement, including changing trends in union membership and relevant economic and social issues.**

CASE 17.1   TO ORGANIZE OR NOT TO ORGANIZE

Candice Larscheid and her good friend and coworker Mary Butler had just finished their shift at the Millersburg textile mill where they had been employed for more than fifteen years. Candice and Mary were both hourly employees and earned $4.25 per hour. The mill had never been organized but the union had finally obtained enough support to force an election to decide whether the employees would have representation for the purposes of collective bargaining. The election was to be held the next day and neither Candice nor Mary had quite made up their minds whether to vote for or against the union. As they walked toward the parking lot Candice said to Mary:

"Well, tomorrow is the day. I still don't know what I'm going to do. I went to the meeting last night and I listened to what the union guy had to say. He says we don't make enough money and that the places they've organized all make more than we do. I could use more money."

"Look Candice, I didn't go to that meeting but I know what management thinks about all this. They are really upset and some of them are talking like they might just shut the mill down if we go ahead and vote for a union. I know we don't make much money but it is better than nothing."

"It isn't just the money. I get hassled all the time in there. Some jerk is always trying to get me to have a beer with him after work and the foreman keeps suggesting we get together. I don't think I would have so much trouble if we had a union and I could complain about things to someone we select instead of someone the company tells us we have to deal with."

"Well you know, Candice, it might not be so great with the union either. Everything around here will end up being based on seniority. Now we can talk with management and not have to go through some union officer who could care less whether you or I are better qualified than some guy who has been here longer." . . .

CASE 17.2   PUBLIC EMPLOYMENT AND THE RIGHT TO STRIKE

Under increasing pressure from several public employee unions, the state legislature began consideration of a bill that would give all public employees the right to organize into trade unions and to engage in work stoppages. The bill contained a clause that read: "There shall be no difference in the treatment accorded public employees and employees in the private sector." State Senator Claridge, who was the principal sponsor of the bill, argued for passage and in the course of his speech observed:

"There is no basis in principle for different treatment of public employees. They work as hard and they work as long. They are paid for what they do and there is no reason to deny them the same rights as are enjoyed by other employees. It is a fundamental violation of their rights to exercise their own judgement about their own interests. Let them form unions and let them bargain with their employers. Let them, finally, strike, if they believe that is the only way to get the other side to come to an agreement. If the police go on strike it won't last very long or be very dangerous. The police are responsible citizens who will not let criminals simply roam the streets."

State Senator Monroe, who opposed the bill and had been opposed in his election campaign by the public employee unions, disagreed: "Public employees are different from employees in the private sector. Public employees are hired to serve the public. There is no right to work for the public. Public employment is a privilege and may be subject to conditions that would not be proper in the private sector. If we let public employees strike we are giving them a gun to put to the head of the public. The public must have protection and must have public services. If a company shuts down production, production can be made up later, after an agreement has been reached with the union. If the police, or the fire department shuts down, who is going to bring back to life the victim of the killer; who is going to bring back the house that has been destroyed by the arsonist?"

The right of workers to organize and bargain collectively with employers has been well established in the United States since the passage of the Wagner Act (or National Labor Relations Act) in 1935. National and local unions, as well as professional associations and associations of government employees that have become bargaining agents, are major participants in the determination of wages, hours, and conditions of work.

Through union membership, employees play a part in creating rules governing the work place, in contrast to one-sided decision making by the employer. To deal effectively with organized labor and even to manage relations with nonunionized employees, all managers and human resources professionals need to understand how unions operate, why they are formed, and the laws and regulations that govern them. This chapter addresses these issues; Chapter 18 is devoted to the topic of labor contract negotiations.

WHY WORKERS JOIN UNIONS

Much has been written about why workers join unions. It is generally agreed that not only economic but also sociological and psychological factors are involved. Thus unionization has been described as the result of workers' belief that union membership will help them to achieve the following conditions or goals:

1. Companionship and respect of others
2. Degree of economic comfort and security enjoyed by those with whom they associate
3. Control over their own affairs
4. Understanding of the forces and factors at work in the world around them
5. Fair treatment for themselves and others and respect for personal integrity[1]

This list suggests that while the desire to improve wages and benefits is important, it is only one of the reasons workers join unions. Indeed, one study of white-collar employees found that dissatisfaction with leadership and supervision actually provided a stronger push toward unionization than that supplied by dissatisfaction with financial rewards.[2]

Forming a union or joining one may be an attempt to increase personal job satisfaction, but it is more often a reaction against what is seen to be unfair treatment. Unionization, in other words, is frequently the result of workers' efforts to bring about justice and order in the workplace. This was indeed one of the main intents of Congress when it passed the Wagner Act. (In Case 17.1, the reasons Candace wanted a union were several, including the expectation that the union would assist employees with their grievances.)

Unionization, therefore, is an attempt to fulfill a variety of human needs, including those for security, community, and esteem, that have not been otherwise satisfied in the workplace. At least in part, membership in a union has met these needs for the great majority of union members. If this were not true, unions would never have been able to organize successfully even with the protections provided by the Wagner Act; and the incidence of decertification of bargaining units, the procedure by which workers renounce a union, would be much higher than it is.

For some workers, however, union membership may not be a matter of choice. Under the union-shop provisions of some labor contracts, employees are required to join the union as a condition of employment. But once a union has been certified as the bargaining agent, the majority of union members tend to favor retention of the union to other alternatives.

TYPES OF LABOR ORGANIZATIONS

The union is the most prevalent type of labor organization through which employees bargain collectively. But unions are not the only agents representing organized labor. A number of professional associations (such as the National Education Association [NEA], which were originally created to advance the professional interests of their members, now engage in collective bargaining with employers. In this chapter, the term **employee association** includes these organizations as well as associations of state and local government employees that bargain with employers but do not refer to themselves as unions.

Although labor organizations have come to include a growing number of white-collar workers, unionization began with blue-collar workers, who still supply by far the largest proportion of trade union members in the United States. Nearly all blue-collar workers are organized into either craft or industrial unions.

Craft Unions

Craft unions are composed of workers who possess the same skill or perform essentially the same task or function. Among the earliest craft unions were shoemakers, cigar wrappers, and printers. Among present craft unions, the carpenters and machinists are two of the largest. A craft union attempts to organize all the practitioners of that craft who are employed by the same employer or located within a particular area. If it is successful in this endeavor, employers that need workers skilled in that craft will have no choice but to deal with the union.

Craft unions seek not only to represent all those who engage in the craft but also to restrict the number who can enter the craft. Apprentice programs requiring as much as several years of instruction as well as state licensing requirements limit the supply of craft workers and enhance the union's ability to demand higher wages.

Because the members of craft unions may work for more than one employer during any given year, contracts frequently cover an entire geographic region rather than a single employer. The building trades union, in particular, tries to negotiate an agreement with all the construction companies within a given area. Members such as plumbers and electricians can then move among construction sites without having to enter into a separate round of bargaining with each company.

A craft union often employs a **business agent** to negotiate and administer the labor contract and to handle the union's day-to-day business affairs. The **steward** is a major source of the information from which the business agent determines whether the employer is in compliance with all the terms of the labor agreement. The steward represents the workers only for the duration of a particular job at the site where the craft union is providing workers. When the job is finished, the steward is once again simply another member of the union.

Industrial Unions

While the members of craft unions tend to be skilled trades workers, **industrial unions** are composed mainly of unskilled workers. Craft unions, as we have seen, organize all the practitioners of a particular craft such as, for example, electricians; industrial unions attempt to organize all the workers in a given industry, no matter what jobs these workers perform. Thus all the workers engaged in the production of automobiles in unionized plants are members of the United Auto Workers of America, and all the workers employed in the different stages of steel production in unionized steel plants are members of the United Steelworkers. Besides autoworkers and steelworkers, industrial unions include organizations of rubber workers, miners, textile workers, truck drivers, and others.

Local industrial unions are usually administered by union officers, who are not only elected from among but very often continue to be full-time workers. In addition to its local officers, the membership elects **shop stewards.** Operating at the department or line level, the stewards serve as a connecting link between the union members and the officers. They forward the complaints and the desires of the membership to union officials and pass information back to the members. They participate in the adjustment of **grievances** (formal complaints by union workers) and are active in the negotiation of the collective bargaining agreement.

White-Collar Organizations

The reluctance of white-collar employees to organize has diminished considerably as the nature of white-collar work has changed. An increasing movement toward large organizations and the requirements of technical efficiency in the computer age have dramatically reduced the differences between assembly-line workers and many clerks and technicians.

As white-collar work has become more routine and bureaucratized, and white-collar workers have become easier to replace, they have also become more willing to consider a union to protect their jobs and advance their interests. Thus while there were only 4.9 million white-collar union members in 1970, a figure that represented 21.8 percent of total union or association membership, there were 6.3 million in 1978, or 25.8 percent.[3] By 1985, the AFL-CIO claimed that fully 41 percent of union members held white-collar jobs.[4]

In addition to the sheer increase in membership, unions were established in white-collar occupations that had not previously been organized. Insurance workers, government inspectors, school administrators, and even professionals at the National Labor Relations Board were for the first time organized into unions.

The Wagner Act, which granted employees the right to organize and to engage in collective bargaining, specifically excluded public employees. Eventually, however, changes in federal and state law permitted and thereby encouraged the transformation of public-employee associations from organizations that could only engage in informal negotiations with government employers to ones that could bargain collectively.

Though many public employees can now bargain collectively, the process is not the same as that available to organized employees in the private sector. Government employees generally, and federal employees in particular, do not have the right to strike. (Whether or not public employees should have the right to strike is a controversial matter, as illustrated in case 17.2.) In addition, federal employees are permitted to bargain only on working conditions and on grievance procedures; they may not bargain over wages, hours, or any other matter excluded by law.

Teachers in the public schools constitute nearly one-third of all the public employees in the United States, and they have organized themselves in numbers and at a rate that the most powerful industrial unions can only envy. In 1985 the NEA represented 1.7 million teachers; only the Teamsters, with a membership of slightly more than 1.8 million, was larger. Moreover, unlike federal employees, public-school teachers have been quite willing to strike,

Carolyn Salisbury/National Education Association

Teachers are the second largest single group of organized employees in the United States.

even though it is against the law in nearly every state. Nor is this simply the result of local organizations deciding the matter for themselves. At its 1967 convention the NEA reversed its long-standing opposition to strikes and declared its readiness to supply its affiliated state and local associations with legal services and financial support when they struck school systems.[5]

STRUCTURE OF UNION ORGANIZATIONS

Most unions in the United States are organized on four levels: local, intermediate, national or, in the case of those with members in both the United States and Canada, international, and a federation of unions. The United Auto Workers (UAW), for example, is an international union with headquarters in Detroit, Michigan and is headed by an elected president. The UAW is divided, however, into ten intermediate bodies or regions, each of which has an elected regional director. Each region, in turn, is made up of dozens of local unions, the members of which elect their own local officers.

Finally, the UAW is a member of the American Federation of Labor-Congress of Industrial Organizations (AFL-CIO). To put this in perspective, a worker at the Ford Motor Company's River Rouge plant, just outside Dearborn, Michigan, the company's world headquarters, would be a member of Ford Local 600, of UAW Region 1-A, of the UAW, and of the AFL-CIO.

Local Union

The local is the basic unit of union organization. In a craft union the local may include all the unionized practitioners of that craft in a city. In an industrial union the local is ordinarily made up of all the union members in a single plant or mill. The local union negotiates at least part of the collective bargaining agreement with the company, manages the routine operations of the agreement, handles most of the grievances brought by workers, supervises the conduct of strikes, and, when necessary, disciplines union members.

Most local unions are run according to democratic principles. Officers are elected by the dues-paying members, usually for a one-year term. Under the election rules of most unions, advance notice must be given that an election is to be held, nominations must be open to any member, and the election itself must be by secret ballot. When the officers — typically a president, a secretary-treasurer, and an executive board — have been elected, they run the affairs of the local and preside over its monthly meetings.

National Union

Although the local union elects its own officers and plays an important role in representing its members' interests, it is not necessarily autonomous. Most local unions are chartered by a national union and must comply with the provisions of the national organization's constitution. Moreover, the national union often has the ultimate authority to approve settlements negotiated at the local level, to decide whether a strike is legitimate, to supervise local elections, and to determine financial procedures and practices. It also has the authority to decide whether national rules have been ignored, and if it finds that they have, to determine whether to remove the local officers and administer the affairs of the local directly through the imposition of a trusteeship.

The national union is governed by periodic conventions of local-union representatives. National conventions are held by most unions either every year or every other year. The convention may amend the constitution, establish union policy, and elect the officers who will lead the union. Between conventions the national union is governed by the elected officers, usually a president and an executive board.

The national union provides a wide range of services to its locals. In many cases the national union attempts to organize the unorganized workers within the jurisdiction of a local and provides assistance with grievance and arbitration administration and with strike activities. It also may represent the interest of locals and their membership in political activities at both the state and national levels. Some national unions, of which the UAW is one of the best examples, have even become heavily involved in the internal affairs of political parties.[6]

Intermediate Bodies

Between the local union and the national are frequently found organizational bodies designed to coordinate the activities of a number of locals and to provide an intermediate unit of union governance. Intermediate bodies are often established on a geographic basis. In craft unions they provide greater bargaining power with local employers. In industrial unions they make it possible for the services provided by the national to be more closely tailored to the needs of the locals.

The intermediate body is designated by a number of different terms. The United Auto Workers, as previously noted, is divided into regions. The United Steelworkers is divided into districts. Within the railroad industry, on the other hand, all the locals of each company are organized into a railroad federation.

AFL-CIO

The majority of national and international unions belong to the AFL-CIO. In fact, the AFL-CIO is perhaps better known to the American public than any of the ninety five national and international unions that make it up. With more than 55,000 local unions and 13.8 million union members, the AFL-CIO is the largest and most powerful labor organization in the United States.[7] (Figure 17.1 is an organizational chart of the AFL-CIO.)

The basic policies of the AFL-CIO are determined by a convention that meets every two years. The convention is composed of delegates sent by each affiliated national and international union in

FIGURE 17.1   **AFL-CIO organization chart**

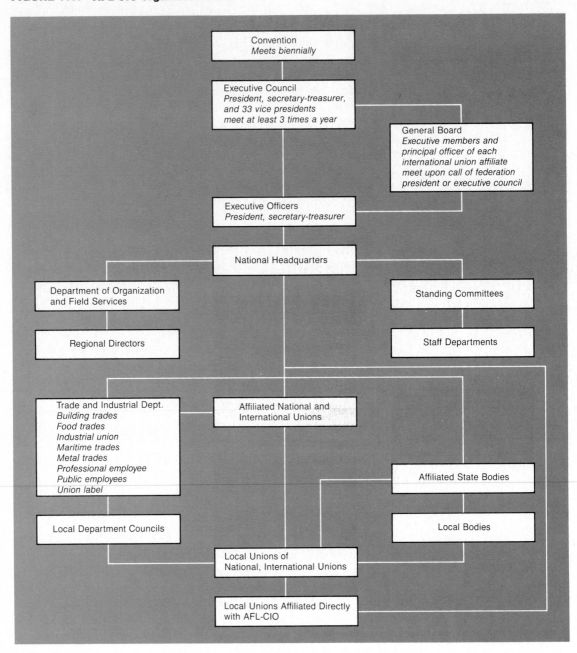

Source: Courtney D. Gifford, ed., *Directory of U.S. Labor Organizations*, 1982–83 Edition, p. 7. Copyright © by the Bureau of National Affairs, Inc., Washington, D.C.

proportion to the size of its membership. Between conventions the AFL-CIO is governed by an executive council made up of the federation's president, secretary-treasurer, and thirty-three vice-presidents, all of whom are elected by majority vote of the convention.

LEGAL IMPACT ON THE LABOR MOVEMENT

Under Section 7 of the Wagner Act, employees were guaranteed the right to form and organize their own labor organizations and to become members of labor unions or refuse to join. The act allowed union employees to choose representatives who exercise exclusive bargaining rights for all employees in that union.

The process of organizing a union and inducing workers to join it is subject to numerous provisions of both the Taft-Hartley Act, passed in 1947, and the Landrum-Griffin Act of 1959. Some of the regulations pertaining to organizing campaigns apply to the union and some apply to management. All these regulations are enforced by the National Labor Relations Board (NLRB).

The NLRB

The NLRB was created, as we saw in Chapter 2, under the Wagner Act. The board has five members, each of them nominated by the president of the United States and confirmed by the Senate to serve a six-year term. The board determines policy and also serves as the judge in appeals to the NLRB.

The NLRB may enforce its decisions through court order and injunctions or, in some cases, by fine or even imprisonment when a court order has been disobeyed. More specifically, Section 10 of the Taft-Hartley Act empowers the NLRB to require persons to "cease and desist" from unfair labor practices, to reinstate employees with or without back pay, to require reports showing the extent to which parties have complied with orders, and to petition federal courts to enforce its orders. NLRB orders, however, like the orders of any federal administrative agency, are subject to review by the courts. Decisions of the NLRB may be appealed to the United States Circuit Court of Appeals and, ultimately, to the Supreme Court of the United States.

Legal Constraints on Management

During an organizing drive, management is not free to do whatever it wishes to oppose the formation of a union. Most of the following restrictions were written into the Wagner Act and subsequently became part of the Taft-Hartley Act:

- Employers may not "interfere with, restrain, or coerce employees in the exercise of [their] rights" to organize a union and bargain collectively or to refrain from union activity. This prohibits direct or implied threats to fire workers if they join a union or to close the plant if a union is organized. (In Case 17.1, if management threats to shut down the mill actually occurred, this would be an illegal act.)
- Employers may not "dominate or interfere with the formation or administration of any labor organization. . . ." Thus a union that receives financial assistance from the company is illegal. The union is supposed to be, and is required by law to be, the sole creation and agent of the workers.
- Employers may not discriminate against any employee in hiring, tenure of employment, or terms and conditions of employment either to encourage or discourage union membership. This does not apply, however, to the situation in which a labor agreement requires union membership as a condition of employment. In that case, if the employee does not pay the required initiation fee and membership dues, he or she may be discharged.
- Employers may not discriminate against workers for filing charges or giving testimony in an NLRB proceeding.
- Payments of money or the provision of other things of value by management or its representatives to an official of a union that is attempting to organize a company's employees is illegal, as is the acceptance of such payments or demands for them.

Legal Constraints on Labor

Just as there are major prohibitions on the conduct of management, labor must operate in the face of several important constraints imposed by the Taft-Hartley Act:

- Unions may not restrain or coerce workers in their right to refrain from union activity. Mass picketing, for example, that prevents entrance into a plant by nonstriking employees, or the refusal to process a grievance because the employee has been critical of the union, are violations of the prohibition.
- A union may not cause an employer to discriminate against an employee with regard to wages, hours, and conditions of employment or for the purpose of influencing the decision whether or not to join a union. Under this prohibition it would be illegal to compel the employer to discharge employees who criticize a union practice or speak out against a contract proposal.

- A union may not strike against an employer to compel the employer to recognize or bargain with that union when another union has already been certified as the representative of the employees of that employer.

The Landrum-Griffin Act placed several major limitations on the use of picketing by unions. Within one month of beginning to picket a firm for organization purposes, the union must file for an election. If the election goes against the union, picketing must stop for at least twelve months. Picketing to inform the public that a company is nonunion is legal unless the picketing stops deliveries to and from the company or causes other employees to withhold their services.

THE NATURE OF THE CAMPAIGN

The sequence of events in unionization is described in Figure 17.2. The first phase begins with an organizing effort of some kind. The initiative for organizing workers may come from the employees

FIGURE 17.2   Unionization process

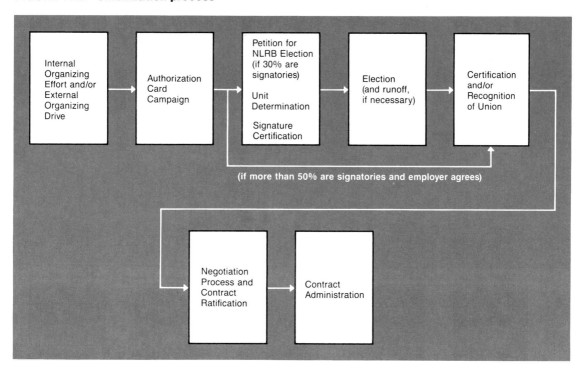

themselves, from a union that already represents some of the employees of the firm, or from a union that represents workers elsewhere. Typically, an organizing drive starts with an aggressive campaign by a union that already represents part of a company's work force or with a campaign conducted by an outside union.

The first phases of a drive for organization are likely to be quiet. Workers may be contacted at their homes or in restaurants or other places near work, and a good deal of soliciting and compaigning may take place between fellow workers on the job. Sometimes an outside union will contact workers on the job, as is often the case, for example, in retail stores. Management's first indication that a unionization drive is under way may be nothing more tangible than rumor or nothing more threatening than a simple handbill. (See Figure 17.3 for an example of an actual handbill used in an organizing drive. Names and location only have been changed.)

Role of the Human Resources Department

Once management realizes that an organizing drive has begun, it must itself become organized. The emotional, legal, and power aspects of the unionization drive require that management responses

FIGURE 17.3   Handbill used in unionization drive

ATTENTION! ALL OFFICE AND LABORATORY PERSONNEL OF THE XYZ COMPANY

Recently a large number of non-union employees in the labs and offices have contacted the Local 1 of the Plant Workers in regard to representation for wages, hours and working conditions. They are interested in representation which provides the know-how in dealing with the Company for working conditions and other Contract provisions as they affect monthly salaried office and laboratory employees.

This Union has been the bargaining agent for the wage personnel at XYZ Company for almost 20 years, and has been very successful in meeting all the situations peculiar to the XYZ Company, and has obtained for its members a broader range of benefits than has been obtained by other unions in this area.

Why stake YOUR job-security, YOUR opportunity for advancement, on the whims of your boss or supervisor? Make him follow the rules for advancement, wage progression, and job-security as set forth by a Labor Organization of your own choosing.

Why should your rates, rate ranges, and wage progressions be controlled solely by the vagaries of a capricious boss? Why not have a definitie rate range, with automatic progression, as set forth in a bona-fide Union Contract? It is a protection you do not have now, but which you *will* have if you fill in and sign the attached card and drop it in the mail TODAY! Signing this card does not obligate you in any way. It merely indicates your desire to be represented by a progressive Union of your own choosing — Local 1 of the Plant Workers.

All Names Will Be Held In the Strictest Confidence! Sign it — and mail it — Today!

NOTICE .... NOTICE

In order to acquaint you more fully with the benefits obtainable with your organization, there will be a MASS MEETING of all eligible personnel, to be held in the ballroom of the Johnson Hotel, Monday evening, March 3rd, at 8:00 P.M.

be coordinated by one individual and one department within the company. If there is a centralized human resources or industrial relations department, this assignment will ordinarily be given to the human resources or labor relations director.

The human resources department helps protect the interests of the company by watching for unfair labor practices by union organizers and for unlawful infringements on the company's property rights. That department also advises first-line supervisors and other managers about what they can and cannot do during the unionization campaign.

The drive for unionization is almost always filled with emotion, and, for this reason, efforts by the human resources department to minimize the defensive behavior of both supervisors and employees may, if the union is recognized, be especially beneficial during the early stages of the collective bargaining relationship. The sooner hostile feelings diminish, the sooner both parties can move to establish a constructive working relationship.

Petition for NLRB Election

Before the Wagner Act, a union could usually obtain recognition only by demonstrating employee support through the use of the strike. Labor relations were often conducted as though there were a quasi-war. The Wagner Act and the NLRB have changed what was once an all too frequently violent confrontation between management and labor into a peaceful and closely regulated process in which the employees are left to choose for themselves whether or not to become members of a union for the purpose of collective bargaining.

This process usually begins when an organization wishing to become the bargaining representative for employees files a petition with the appropriate regional office of the NLRB. The petition will ask that the NLRB supervise an election of the employees to determine whether a majority of them favor this organization as their bargaining representative. The petition, in most cases, is filed only after the union has asked for recognition from management and the request has been refused. The petition must be supported by evidence that a substantial interest in union representation exists among the employees. This evidence is usually supplied through authorization cards signed by more than 30 percent of the employees in the bargaining unit.

Once a petition has been filed, and the NLRB has determined it has jurisdiction, the board will hold a conference with both the union and the company to see whether there is agreement on the appropriate bargaining unit, voter eligibility, and the form of ballot, as well as the date, time, and place for the election. If the parties agree on all these items, a **consent election** will be held. If there is disagreement on even one of these items, the NLRB has authority to determine the employees' choice of a bargaining representative and the appropriateness of a bargaining unit in industries engaged in interstate commerce (with the exception of railroads, airlines, agriculture, and government agencies).

Determining the Bargaining Unit

An **appropriate bargaining unit** is a group of employees who share common employment conditions and interests and who may reasonably act together for purposes of collective bargaining. The NLRB is empowered to decide the appropriate bargaining unit subject to certain provisions of the Taft-Hartley Act.

The board will consider, for example, the extent to which the proposed unit reflects a distinct community of interest among the employees to be represented with respect to wages, working conditions, skill, and the like. It will examine the history of collective bargaining at that location or at other facilities owned and operated by the organization. It will seek to discover whether distinct crafts are involved. It will analyze the relationship of the proposed unit to the organizational structure of the company, the scope of the required unit, and the scope of the employer's bargaining practices (that is, whether the employer bargains as part of an employers' association). If this examination leads to no clear conclusion on the appropriateness of the bargaining unit, the NLRB may hold an election to determine the interests of the employees.

Representation Election

Once the bargaining unit has been determined, the level of interest in representation has been deemed substantial, and no barrier has been found to exist, the representation election is conducted by officials of the NLRB. The election is conducted at the employer's location during working hours. A secret ballot is used that carries the appropriate company and union designations. The NLRB, however, may choose to conduct the election by mail ballot if it believes that a regular election would not be fair because, for example, adverse weather is expected or excessive travel is required to get to a central voting location.

The purpose of the election is to determine whether a majority of the employees in the bargaining unit wish to have representation. The NLRB defines a majority as a simple majority of those who actually participate in the election. If there are more than two choices on the ballot — if, for example, employees are asked whether they favor unionization and, if so, which of several competing labor organizations they wish to join — a **run-off election** will be held if no single choice receives a majority on the first ballot. Once the employees have voted to be represented by a union, the NLRB formally certifies that union as the recognized bargaining agent for those workers.

Decertification

Just as employees in a bargaining unit have the right to decide whether they wish to form or join a union, they have the right to decide whether to end their affiliation with the union. To petition for what is called a **decertification election,** an employee or employee representative files a petition supported by at least 30 percent of the employees in the bargaining unit. The petition may be filed, however, only at least twelve months after the union has been certified as the recognized bargaining agent of the employees or when the labor contract that has been negotiated between the union and management expires.

Although only the employees can petition for a decertification election, the employer may achieve the same effect by raising a question about whether the union continues to enjoy the support of a majority of the employees and petitioning the NLRB for a representation election. It is not enough simply to file a petition; the petition must be accompanied by evidence demonstrating that a majority of the employees in the bargaining unit no longer want to be represented by the union. Even when a petition is filed, the employer remains obligated to bargain with the union until the representation issue has been resolved.[8] Whether the employee files a petition for a decertification election, or the employer files a petition for a representation election, if the employees vote to decertify their union, twelve months must pass before another representation election can be held.

CURRENT ISSUES IN THE LABOR MOVEMENT

Labor unions have become an established part of American life, and the great majority of their members continue to believe that unions make a difference in their lives. Unions, however, like other institutions, have undergone some substantial changes and face some significant challenges. Organized labor must deal with several very difficult economic and social issues. Inflation, deflation, and foreign competition threaten the whole American economy and the ability of organized labor to retain and attract members by providing increased economic benefits. Moreover, the changing characteristics of union members will affect greatly the way in which unions seek to deal with the substantive problems they face.

Changing Trends in Union Membership

Membership in unions and employee associations dropped from 20.1 million in 1980 to 17.4 million in 1984. This was a loss of 2.7 million members. During the same four-year period, the total number of employed wage and salary workers increased by nearly 4 million, from 87.5 million to 91.3 million. Thus, as a proportion of all employees, union membership declined from 23 percent in 1980 to 19.1 percent in 1984. This continued a trend that began at the end of World War II.[9] (See Table 17.1 and Figure 17.4 for changes in union and employee membership from 1980 to 1984.)

In response to this declining rate of union membership, unions in the future are likely to recruit new members from those segments of the work force that are growing most rapidly. Efforts to unionize professional and white-collar employees and to increase the levels of female and minority membership are also likely to continue. (For example, only 14 percent to female employees belong to unions compared to 23.3 percent of male employees.[10])

Economic and Social Issues

Technological Change and Competition.   Perhaps the most serious problems faced by the American labor movement are the result of rapid technological change. These problems are only intensified by a decline in the rate of productivity increases in the United States in comparison with other major industrial nations. Management, confronted with high labor costs, high taxes, and the high cost of energy, and facing competition from abroad that sometimes has at least the advantage of significantly lower labor costs, is constantly seeking new machinery and new methods to increase efficiency. The requirements for both the number of workers and their specific skills are changing almost continually, and temporary layoffs are becoming inevitable.

When businesses fail or find it necessary to engage in massive

TABLE 17.1 Employed wage and salary workers and numbers and proportions of union members, by industry, May 1980 and the average for the year ended in September 1984

[Workers in thousands]

Industry	Number of employed wage and salary workers — Total			Union members			Percent of employed wage and salary workers who were union members		
	May 1980	Year ended Sept. 1984	1980–84 change	May 1980	Year ended Sept. 1984	1980–84 change	May 1980	Year ended Sept. 1984	1980–84 percentage-point change
All industries[1]	87,480	91,331	+3,851	20,095	17,417	−2,678	23.0	19.1	−3.9
Private sector[1]	71,424	75,582	+4,158	14,332	11,756	−2,567	20.1	15.6	−4.5
Goods-producing[1]	27,590	26,787	−803	8,428	6,569	−1,859	30.5	24.5	−6.0
Mining	891	903	(²)	285	162	−123	32.0	17.9	−14.1
Construction	4,437	4,413	(²)	1,371	1,072	−299	30.9	24.3	−6.6
Manufacturing	20,824	20,038	−786	6,726	5,302	−1,424	32.3	26.5	−5.8
Durable goods	12,419	11,980	−479	4,328	3,339	−989	34.8	28.0	−6.8
Nondurable goods	8,405	8,098	−307	2,398	1,963	−435	28.5	24.2	−4.3
Service-producing	43,834	48,795	+4,961	5,904	5,188	−716	13.5	10.6	−2.9
Transportation, communications, and public utilities	5,277	5,414	+137	2,554	2,146	−408	48.4	39.6	−8.8
Wholesale and retail trade	17,287	18,680	+1,393	1,746	1,525	−221	10.1	8.2	−1.9
Finance, insurance, and real estate	5,062	5,753	+691	162	156	(²)	3.2	2.7	(²)
Service	16,168	18,948	+2,780	1,439	1,361	(²)	8.9	7.2	−1.7
Government	16,056	15,748	−308	5,764	5,661	(²)	35.9	35.9	—

[1]Includes agriculture, forestry, and fisheries not shown separately.
[2]Change not statistically significant.
NOTE: Due to rounding, sums of individual items may not equal totals.

Source: Larry T. Adams, "Changing Employment Patterns of Organized Workers," *Monthly Labor Review*, 108 (February 1985): 26.

FIGURE 17.4
**Distribution of em-
ployed wage and sal-
ary workers, by union
membership status,
in May 1980 and in
the year ended in
September 1984**

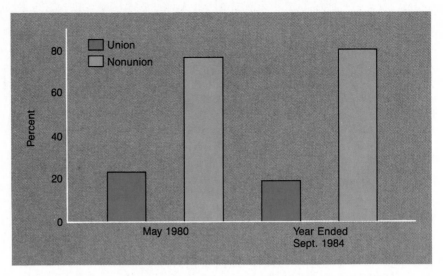

Larry T. Adams, "Changing Employment Patterns of Organized Workers," *Monthly Labor Review*,
108 (February 1985): 27.

reorganizations to avoid financial losses, as has happened in automobiles, steel, coal, and other basic industries, plants are closed
and layoff situations become much more serious. The response of
a union may vary from (1) resistance to all changes, to (2) support
for changes combined with efforts to minimize layoffs and other
adverse effects on employees, to (3) cooperation with management
in the solution of cost, production, and quality-of-work-life
problems.

The reactions of unions to technological change and the introduction of new work methods have been anything but uniform. In
general, craft unions tend to resist change more than industrial
unions because, with membership based on a particular craft, efficiencies that result in layoffs are likely to reduce the number of
dues-paying members. On the other hand, competition may also
stimulate change in situations where it is obvious that without new
equipment and methods a particular craft may be unable to survive.

For industrial unions, the situation is somewhat different. Technological changes often create new occupations that may remain
in the bargaining unit and, for that reason, resistance to change
is likely to be lower.

From the standpoints of its power to affect the nation's standard
of living, its ability to meet foreign competition, and its capacity
to assist underdeveloped countries, the labor movement needs to
adopt a policy of support for technological change while working

---

PERSPECTIVE 17.1 Women Flex Muscles in Union Movement

·For most of her life, Kathy Kerr rarely paid any attention to labor unions. "I thought they were some kind of social club for truckdrivers, steelworkers and construction people," says the 21-year-old resident of Boulder, Colo.

In the last year, all that has changed. Not only has the manufacturing plant where Kerr works as an assembler been unionized, but she and the rest of the mostly female work force have their first union contract. Today, Kerr is a departmental steward in her union local.

Like Kerr, an increasing number of women workers are for the first time coming into contact with organized labor. At the same time that women are showing new concern over improving their pay and working conditions, unions are pushing organizing campaigns to expand membership.

As a result —

■ The ranks of women within organized labor have swelled. One out of every 3 union members is a woman, according to the AFL-CIO, and women account for half of the total increase in union membership in the past 20 years. More than 7 million women belong to unions — up from approximately 4 million a decade ago.

Source: Excerpted from Carey W. English, "Women Flex Muscles in Union Movement," excerpted from *U.S. News & World Report* issue of October 24, 1984. Copyright, 1984, U.S. News & World Reports, Inc.

■ Ten years after its founding by 3,000 union women, the Coalition of Labor Union Women has grown from 10 chapters to 75 chapters around the country and has 18,000 dues-paying members — from the rank-and-file up to international vice presidents.

■ Women have risen to the position of secretary-treasurer in four major state labor bodies, served as either president or secretary-treasurer of more than 100 regional union councils and held the presidencies of hundreds of local unions.

■ A year ago, Teamsters President Jackie Presser named Vicki Saporta, a graduate of Cornell University's School of Industrial and Labor Relations, head organizer of the 1.9-million-member union — the first woman ever to hold the post. About 350,000 women, among them truckdrivers, clerical personnel, healthcare workers and airline flight attendants, now belong to the union.

■ Before 1980, no woman had ever sat on the AFL-CIO's executive council, the key policymaking group for the federation. Today, two women — Joyce Miller of the Clothing and Textile Workers and Barbara Hutchinson of the American Federation of Government Employees — are members.

"With women constituting well over half of the nation's labor force, you're seeing more and more unions getting involved in organizing drives in predominantly female industries," says Miller.

---

with management and government to minimize the adverse effects of change on individual workers. Training programs, moving allowances, severance pay, supplemental unemployment benefits, extended unemployment compensation, and aggressive counseling and placement are only some of the methods that require the cooperation of labor, business, and government.

Right-to-Work Laws and Union Security. Right-to-work laws have now been passed in more than twenty states. These laws prohibit both (1) the **closed shop,** in which the employer may hire only union members, a practice declared illegal under the Taft-Hartley Act (although the Landrum-Griffin Act modified the Taft-Hartley Act to permit what is almost a closed shop in the building and construction industry), and (2) **union-shop** provisions in contracts, which make union membership a necessary condition for continued employment. Right-to-work laws also outlaw **maintenance of membership requirements** — clauses that require workers who belong to a union at the beginning of a contract's term to remain members throughout the period covered by the contract (except for a specified interval near the contract's expiration date when withdrawal is permitted).

Not surprisingly, unions object to right-to-work laws, in part for economic reasons. In general, unions feel that those who are represented should be required to assume the financial and other responsibilities of membership; they feel that allowing anyone to enjoy the benefits without paying the costs of collective bargaining will ultimately destroy labor organizations. The financial problems occasioned by right-to-work laws may be minimized by **agency-shop** provisions, by which nonunion members of the bargaining unit must contribute to the union an amount usually equivalent to the regular dues. Agency-shop provisions, however, are seldom found in union contracts and have even been declared illegal in some right-to-work states.

Though state right-to-work laws are a threat to union security and a constant irritant to organized labor, nearly 89 percent of all union contracts contain union security provisions, with 82 percent providing for one or more of the principal forms of union security: the union shop, modified union shop, maintenance of membership, or agency shop.[11]

Changing Public Image of Labor. The public's impression of organized labor has changed over the years, and government policy has frequently been altered in accordance with those changes. In

---

PERSPECTIVE 17.2 Controversy over Idaho's Right-to-Work Law

Idaho became the 21st State to enact a "right-to-work" law, but union leaders won a court order temporarily blocking implementation of the law. The labor leaders contended that the law was illegal because it was to become effective immediately, thwarting the citizens' right to a referendum on all laws passed by the legislature.

Under the Idaho law, employers would be prohibited from entering into agreements with unions under which only union members or dues-paying workers could be employed.

The last State to enact a right-to-work law was Louisiana, in 1976.

Source: "Idaho's 'Right-to-Work' Law Temporarily Blocked," *Monthly Labor Review,* 108 (April 1985): 61.

general, public opinion has tended to favor the regulation of union-management relations by government. Moreover, by 1981 only 55 percent of the American public approved of unions generally. Four years later, this percentage had fallen to the point that less than half of the public approved of unions.[12]

Although unions have been seen by the public as too powerful, there has, ironically, been considerable ambivalence in recent years on the part of workers themselves about the effect of unionization on economic benefits. In 1985, the AFL-CIO reported:

> Over 75 percent of all workers — and over 75 percent of non-union workers — state that they agree that unions in general improve the wages and working conditions of workers. Over 80 percent of all workers agree that unions are needed so that the legitimate complaints of workers can be heard. Yet when asked to assess the effect of organization on their present employer, 53 percent of non-union workers state that wages and fringe benefits would not improve and 74 percent state that job security would not improve.[13]

Perhaps most disconcerting of all from the point of view of organized labor was the discovery that:

> [N]on-union workers do not perceive unions as pursuing an institutional agenda drawn from the needs and desires of their members. Sixty-five percent of such workers express agreement with the statement that "unions force members to go along with decisions they don't like." Sixty-three percent state that they believe that union leaders — as distinguished from union members — decide whether to go on strike. . . . And, among the population as a whole . . . 50 percent state that they believe that most union leaders no longer represent the workers in their unions.[14]

Overcoming this negative image is essential if the labor movement is to reverse its declining rate of growth.

SUMMARY

Employees join unions for a number of reasons. Because unionization appears to conflict with the authority and power exercised by managers within the organization, many managers view collective bargaining as an infringement of established organizational processes. They therefore tend to resist attempts at unionization.

The process of unionization is regulated by federal law, and unions and employers are both restricted in what they can do during an organizational campaign. Most of these restrictions are imposed by the two major statutes which, along with the Wagner Act of 1935, constitute the foundation of labor law in the United States

— the Taft-Hartley Act of 1947 and the Landrum-Griffin Act of 1959.

The employer's response to the drive for unionization is usually coordinated by the human resources department. That department is in a position to minimize conflict and tension that if not kept in control could seriously interfere with the early stages of collective bargaining following union recognition.

The American trade union movement is still strong in numbers and well established in law and public policy. It is, however, faced with growing difficulties. The membership is declining in proportion to the total work force as larger percentages of that work force are employed in service, trade, and professional occupations. Unions are attempting to deal with this problem by redoubling their efforts to organize white-collar workers. The greatest success so far has been among state and federal employees. Unionization among public employees has been given substantial assistance by executive orders encouraging it and the passage of state laws permitting the organization of government employees.

Managerial pressure for rapid technological change and improved productivity has also presented a major challenge. Unions have had to choose between resisting change to protect the immediate interests of some workers and encouraging change while minimizing the effects of worker displacement to acquire long-term advantages for the majority of American workers. This course is rapidly becoming the policy of the trade union movement as a whole.

KEY TERMS

employee association	grievance	closed shop
craft union	consent election	union shop
business agent	appropriate bargaining unit	maintenance of membership
steward	run-off election	requirements
industrial union	decertification election	agency shop
shop steward	right-to-work laws	

REVIEW QUESTIONS

1. Why do workers join unions?
2. Describe the difference between craft unions and industrial unions.
3. Discuss the role of the shop steward.
4. List at least three constraints on management and two on the unions relative to a unionization drive.
5. Describe the steps that usually occur in the formation and recognition of a union as bargaining agent for employees.
6. What steps occur in the decertification of a union?
7. Discuss several issues facing the labor union movement.

OPENING CASE QUESTIONS

Case 17.1   To Organize or Not to Organize?

1. Why is Candice leaning toward voting for the union?
2. Why is Mary resisting the notion of a union?

Case 17.2   Public Employment and the Right to Strike

1. What are the pros and cons of giving public employees the right to strike, based on the conversation between the two state senators?

CASE 17.3   THE SATURN AGREEMENT

In 1984, U.S. auto workers were receiving about $11.80 more per hour in pay and fringe benefits than their Japanese counterparts. That works out to a cost disadvantage of roughly $2,000 per car. By now, it is no secret, either, that Japanese cars have a reputation for high quality that works against American models. The implications are clear. It has been estimated that by 1988, foreign companies could control 44 percent of the U.S. automobile market. That figure takes in foreign cars that are, increasingly, being put together in this country.

In an effort to adapt to this state of affairs, at least in a partial way, General Motors has set out on a revolutionary new venture. GM is creating a new, wholly owned subsidiary company, called Saturn Corp., that is to build a new kind of American car—a subcompact that is supposed to compete successfully with Japanese entries. The company will be located entirely in Spring Hill, Tennessee. It will create 6,000 jobs of its own and should account for up to 20,000 related jobs. The centerpiece of the new corporation is an unprecedented labor agreement with the United Auto Workers.

Under the agreement, Saturn will be run by consensus, and *all* employees will participate. The union and workers will be involved at all levels of the organization and will have a role in decision making from the plant floor to the upper management level. In fact, the union will be able to veto any decision management makes. If the planned system works, however, cooperation should be more common than vetoes.

Another feature of the agreement is that eighty percent of the company's workers, who will be chosen from GM's current labor force and laid-off GM employees, will have their jobs guaranteed for life. And all workers will be paid a salary, rather than an hourly wage.

Of course, the union, too, has made concessions in the agreement. The workers' salaries will be only 80 percent of the average wages in the industry. However, workers will be able to earn incentive pay based on the plant's profit and the quality of its cars.

The union's main concession is in the area of work rules. The usual elaborate U.A.W. structure of multiple job classifications will be absent at Saturn—there will be only six. Workers will perform multiple tasks. They will work in teams, each responsible for a major section of the car, and they will decide themselves how to allocate tasks among team members. Job rotation will undoubtedly be a feature. In addition, the union's complicated and adversarial grievance procedures will be streamlined, and the union steward's role will be reduced.

Case Sources: Charles P. Alexander, "GM Picks the Winner," *Time*, Aug. 5, 1985, pp. 42–43; David Pauly, et al., "2001: A Union Odyssey," *Newsweek*, August 5, 1985, pp. 40–42; Micheline Maynard, "A Labor Deal that Clears the Way for GM's Saturn," *U.S. News and World Report*, August 5, 1985, p. 22; and Sharon Cohen, " 'Milsetone' Accord for GM, Union," *Boston Globe*, July 27, 1985, pp. 1, 4.

Underpinning this system will be an environment in which communications flow freely and workers and managers work together as equals. At Saturn, labor and management will use the same entrances (they don't at other U.A.W. plants), and there will be one cafeteria for everyone, rather than the usual two. No one will have a special parking place or similar privileges, and all will be referred to as Saturn "members."

Some U.A.W. leaders decry the new pact, fearing that it will undermine the union's power. But the U.A.W.'s national leaders approved it because they believed that it would help the union survive. (The union is in as much trouble as the industry, having lost a third of its membership in recent years.) Although union leaders vigorously deny that they will let Saturn set a precedent for any other labor agreement, they apparently agree with GM that both management and labor must try something new to increase productivity and cut costs. According to experts, the individual components of the venture aren't revolutionary in themselves; but taken together as a whole, they constitute an arrangement that hasn't been seen before in American industry.

Discussion Questions

1. Do you think the Saturn agreement will better fulfill workers' needs in joining a union than the traditional, more rigid union arrangement can? Why?
2. Spring Hill, Tennessee, is 536 miles from Detroit. Why do you suppose GM decided to locate the plant so far from the company's center of activity?
3. Why do you think it has taken so long for some large U.S. manufacturer to try an agreement like the Saturn one?

18

Negotiating the Labor Agreement

CHAPTER OUTLINE

LEARNING OBJECTIVES

- **Define collective bargaining and identify its major purposes.**
- **Identify activities and tactics that are signs of good-faith bargaining.**
- **Describe the major types of bargaining relationships.**
- **Indicate what is involved in preparing, analyzing, and resolving bargaining proposals from the points of view of both labor and management.**
- **Explain how negotiating impasses may be resolved.**
- **Describe the role of strikes and lockouts in the collective bargaining process.**

CASE 18.1   THE MANAGEMENT NEGOTIATING TEAM

Jack Warren and Peter Jacobs were both members of the negotiating team for the Jupiter Automobile Company and had been in intensive negotiations with the union for over a week. The strike deadline was only forty-eight hours away. Utterly exhausted, Warren remarked: "I'm fed up. Let them strike. We can take a strike and probably ride it out. At least if it doesn't go more than sixty days. I don't think the union can go that long. We might even break the union if we take them on. They have been completely unreasonable and have made the most outrageous demands I have ever heard. Don't they know we barely made a profit last year?"

Jacobs looked across the table where they had just finished lunch and said to Warren. "You must be out of your mind. The union wants you to think like that. They would love to have you decide that a strike is all right. Then they can throw the whole blame for it on us. They want a strike. Their new president wants to show he is tougher than the guy he beat in the last election. If they want to have a strike let's make sure it is because they want it and not because we appeared to force them to do it. Forget what they have put out on the table. All we do is react to what they demand. Why don't we put together a complete proposal of our own and tell them, and the public, that we are ready to negotiate around the clock to avoid a strike?"

CASE 18.2   THE LABOR NEGOTIATING TEAM

Art Baroni and Mike Walsh, the two top labor negotiators, were having lunch at a coffee shop just down the block from the headquarters of Jupiter Automobile Company. With only forty-eight hours to go before the strike deadline they were both irritable. Walsh, who had been through every contract negotiation with Jupiter for the last thirty years, had a look of complete disgust. "This guy Warren is the worst ever. Where do they get these guys? He has about as much idea of what it takes to feed a family or what it is like to work on the line as you could expect from someone who was born rich, lived rich, and if we are lucky, will die rich real soon. I asked him why he thought a ten percent wage increase was too much and he said any wage increase was too much. I asked him whether he thought we were entitled to at least recover the wage concessions we made during the last three years and he said we were lucky to have jobs. God, I wanted to shoot him. What are we going to do? Charlie got elected president of the union because all the guys believed he could get a good contract and avoid a strike."

Baroni, who seldom said anything, had listened patiently while Walsh complained about everything the management team had done or said. But now, as Walsh seemed on the verge of beating his head against the table, he smiled slightly and said: "It doesn't matter. Jacobs isn't terribly bright, and the other guy, Warren, is nothing. They don't decide anything. Jupiter isn't going to permit a strike and we don't want one. Charlie has a private meeting with Jupiter's president late tonight. This thing will be over tomorrow and those two guys in there will never have any idea what happened."

Once a union has been certified as the exclusive bargaining agent for a group of employees, management and the union are both required by the Taft-Hartley Act to bargain collectively with each other over wages, hours, and conditions of employment. **Collective bargaining,** the process by which a formal agreement is established between workers and management regarding wages, hours, working conditions, and similar matters, is a key aspect of labor-management relations. This bargaining normally proceeds through discussion and debate over proposed provisions in the contract. The provisions proposed may be based on contracts already in existence in similar plants or industries or on alterations one side or the other would like to have made in the practice followed in the past. After the initial labor contract has been agreed upon, signed, and implemented, subsequent negotiations will be concerned with how the existing contract is to be changed.

The end of the collective bargaining process is signified by the signing of the labor-management contract. A contract is a means by which the parties establish the rules that will govern their relationship, and, as former Solicitor General Archibald Cox once described it, the labor contract is "the basic legislation governing the lives of workers in the plant."[1] In other words, the purpose of collective bargaining is to reach agreement on the specific ways labor and management will conduct themselves until the expiration of the contract.

Collective bargaining, which may on the surface appear to resemble the give-and-take that goes on between a buyer and a seller in an open-air market or on a used-car lot, is in reality much more complex. Labor and management conduct their negotiations within a web of government regulations that both limits their strength and protects their rights. Both sides also come to the bargaining table with considerably more power than any two individuals are ever likely to have. The union may elect to strike rather than agree to less than what labor demands, while management may decide to lock out the employees (or close down operations) rather than continue to operate without a contract it finds satisfactory. The process becomes even more complicated when the government or a neutral third party intervenes to resolve bargaining disputes.

GOVERNMENT RULES AND REGULATIONS

Federal labor law imposes a wide range of legal constraints on both labor and management during the negotiating process. In particular, there are legal guidelines pertaining to good-faith bargaining, issues that are negotiable, and the power that can be exercised by both labor and management.

Obligation to Bargain in Good Faith

The Taft-Hartley Act requires that labor and management "meet at reasonable times and confer in good faith with respect to wages, hours, and other terms and conditions of employment . . . but such obligation does not compel either party to agree to a proposal or require the making of a concession."[2]

Precisely what constitutes bargaining in good faith is a problem with which both the National Labor Relations Board (NLRB) and the courts have struggled for years. The NLRB and the courts have, however, developed general guidelines under which certain activities or tactics are taken as indicative of either an intent to bargain in good faith or a refusal to do so. Thus, an intent to reach an agreement, active participation, and the making of counterproposals are all signs of good-faith bargaining. Stalling tactics, sudden shifts in position when agreement seems close, rejection of provisions that are a routine part of almost any labor contract, and refusal to sign the contract after agreement has apparently been reached are clear indications of bargaining in bad faith.[3]

Moreover, the refusal to furnish data necessary for bargaining is an unfair labor practice. This means that the company is legally required to supply information about individual earnings, job rates and classifications, pensions, operations and earnings of the incentive system if there is one, merit increases, time-study data, and piece rates. Furthermore, when a company attempts to justify a refusal to grant a wage increase on economic grounds, the obligation to bargain in good faith requires the company to furnish enough data to the union to permit it to bargain in an informed fashion.

Even where no single action constitutes a failure to bargain in good faith, a combination of actions, sometimes referred to as **totality of conduct,** may violate the duty to bargain in good faith. Perhaps the most famous example of this is a tactic employed by General Electric, which came to be called *Boulwarism,* after company vice president Lemuel Boulware.

GE formulated a contract proposal based on management interpretation of a survey it had conducted of employee attitudes and wants. This proposal was then offered to the union as the company's final position. While some, including GE, considered this a realistic approach that eliminated the exchange of initial offers that are unlikely to be acceptable, the NLRB concluded that the company's totality of conduct did not meet the standards of good-faith bargaining.

The obligation to bargain in good faith, although something each side has a right to expect of the other, may nonetheless be violated without serious legal consequences. Other than issuing an order directing the violator to stop bargaining in bad faith, there is very little the NLRB can do. In addition, the Supreme Court upheld the Taft-Hartley provision that the obligation to bargain in good faith "does not compel either party to agree to a proposal or require the making of a concession."[4]

In other words, a contract cannot be imposed on the parties; both labor and management must agree to it. And if for any reason, including an unwillingness to bargain in good faith, one side or the other refuses to agree, there is nothing anyone can do about it. Fortunately for the sake of labor-management relations, this kind of determined bad-faith bargaining is seldom seen.

What Is Negotiable

Determining the subjects that can be negotiated through collective bargaining is an extension of the good-faith problem. The NLRB has established three categories of bargaining issues: illegal, mandatory, and voluntary. **Illegal bargaining issues** are those that would conflict with the law and may therefore not be made a part of the labor contract even if both sides agree to do so. For example, an agreement not to pay employees overtime for time worked beyond forty hours in a week would be illegal because it violates the Fair Labor Standards Act, which requires overtime pay. A refusal to bargain over demands that are contrary to the law, the NLRB has ruled, is not an unfair labor practice.

Mandatory bargaining issues include wages, hours, and conditions of work, while **voluntary bargaining issues** include all those that are lawful but not mandatory. Table 18.1 lists examples of typical items in union-management agreements, most or all of which are probably mandatory items. Refusal to bargain to a genuine **impasse** (or deadlock in negotiations) over mandatory issues is an unfair labor practice, and so is insistence on negotiating to an impasse over voluntary issues.[5] On the other hand, insistence on negotiating to an impasse over voluntary issues is also an unfair labor practice.

It has sometimes been difficult to determine precisely the distinction between mandatory and voluntary issues. But it is rea-

TABLE 18.1 **Examples of typical items in union-management agreements**

Absenteeism	Leave of absence	Strikes, lockouts
Apprenticeship and training	Management rights	Subcontracting
Arbitration	Meal periods	Supplemental unemployment compensation
Call-in pay	Merit rating	Supplementary benefits
Contract length	Overtime pay	
Discipline, discharge	Overtime rules	Tardiness
Discrimination		Tests
Dues checkoff	Pensions	Time off for union business
	Premium pay (Saturday)	Tools
Grievances	Premium pay (Sunday)	Transfers
Holidays	Premium pay (holidays)	Travel allowances
Hours (daily)	Promotions	
Hours (weekly)		Union literature, distribution of
	Recall	Union security
Incentive rates or standards	Rest periods	
Insurance, health	Retirement	Vacations
Insurance, life		
	Safety	Wages
Job posting and bidding	Seniority	Work clothes
	Severance pay	Workload
Labor-management committees	Shift differentials	Work rules
Layoffs	Sick leave	

sonably certain that the NLRB and the courts consider at least the following matters to be mandatory subjects of collective bargaining: subcontracting, profit-sharing plans, stock-purchase plans, pension and employee welfare plans, Christmas bonuses, workloads, production standards, plant rules, and successorship clauses requiring a new owner to assume the contractual obligation of the employer.[6]

Legal Constraints on Labor and Management

When negotiations are not successful and the union decides to strike or the company decides to lock out the employees, federal law imposes several major obligations on both management and labor. The party that desires to terminate or modify a contract must give written notice at least sixty days before the effective date of the termination or modification. A strike or lockout during this period constitutes an unfair labor practice.

Once a strike actually takes place, management may not refuse

The American Federation of Labor emphasized the use of strong bargaining tactics in the 1930s, such as this sit-down strike at the Fisher Body Plant in Flint, Michigan

to deal with the union but must instead continue to bargain in good faith. Moreover, management can replace strikers with new employees only during an **economic strike,** or a strike over wages, hours, or conditions of work. If the strike is in response to an unfair labor practice by management, the company may be required to release the replacements and reinstate and provide back pay to the workers. Even when an economic strike is over, management must rehire the strikers, providing there are openings for which they qualify are open. As a practical matter, the union will frequently insist on reinstatement of all striking employees as a condition of bringing the strike to an end.

The union is also limited by the law in what it can do during a strike. Unions or their agents may not threaten employees with loss of their jobs or with bodily injury for failing to support the union's activities. Unions may not engage in what are called **secondary boycotts.** For example, if a union picketed a retail store that handled the products of a manufacturer with which the union had a dispute, that would be a secondary boycott and therefore illegal. It is also illegal to engage in **jurisdictional strikes,** or strikes to force an employer to assign work to one union, trade, or craft instead of some other, unless the employer is refusing to comply with an NLRB order regarding such work.

National Emergency Disputes

When a strike occurs that could threaten the economic well-being of the nation or imperil the national defense, called a **national emergency dispute,** the president of the United States is empowered by the Taft-Hartley Act to take steps to avoid it. The president may direct the attorney general to petition the appropriate federal district court to forbid a strike or lockout for a period of eighty days. If the dispute has not been settled after sixty days, the NLRB will conduct an election to determine whether the employees will accept management's last offer. If the employees vote to turn this offer down, the union may legally strike at the end of the eighty-day period. As a last resort, the president is authorized to report on the situation to the Congress, with a recommendation for action appropriate to protect the national interest.

TYPES OF BARGAINING RELATIONSHIPS

Collective bargaining is often regarded as a struggle between management and labor in which management attempts to give as little as possible while labor seeks to get everything it can. From this perspective, collective bargaining is mainly a battle over the division of wealth and power. This type of bargaining is called **distributive bargaining** because it involves the distribution of things that exist in limited quantity. The gain that one side makes is necessarily at the expense of the other.

Distributive bargaining is of course not the only form of collective bargaining. The second major type, called **integrative bargaining,** describes the situation in which both sides, not just one, benefit from an agreement because both labor and management share common goals and concerns. There are several forms of integrative bargaining, and these are discussed after a more detailed look at the distributive bargaining approach.[7] (Cases 18.1 and 18.2 provide examples of distributive bargaining.)

Distributive Bargaining Approach

Distributive bargaining is the most common strategy used in the United States. Before negotiations begin, the union presents in writing its initial demands for changes in the contract. At least some of these demands are beyond what the union reasonably expects to obtain and may form part of the agenda the union will pursue in years to come. By mentioning them at the outset the union provides itself with something it can afford to give up as part of the bargaining that will take place and, in addition, begins the process of making the proposals credible by bringing them before both management and the public.

Management may or may not present a list of its own demands, but if it does, the list will typically be shorter than the union's. Management may also have in mind some contractual changes but, in the belief that the union will also be in favor of them, will let them be suggested by the other side.

In the initial bargaining sessions the union explains and defends its demands for nonwage and nonfringe benefits, while management explains its position. Many of these early sessions may be slow moving and frustrating to the participants, and much haggling may occur over procedural matters.

Eventually, the parties proceed to earnest bargaining over noneconomic issues with the understanding that any agreement reached will remain tentative until the entire contract has been negotiated. Management will concede certain items, but only if the union drops some other demands or agrees to several of the contract changes management has proposed.

Once items that carry no economic cost have been agreed on, negotiations become considerably more tedious and intense as the

FIGURE 18.1
Distributive bargaining approach

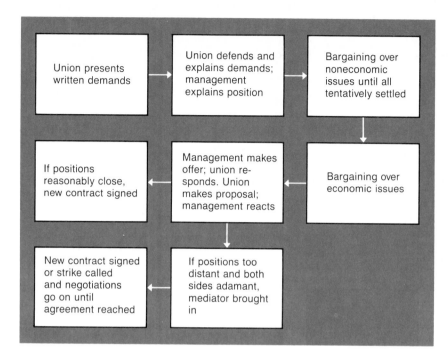

bargaining shifts to wages and employee benefits. Each side attempts to get the other to move toward its position, and each seeks to discover the other's final position without disclosing its own. Gradually the union's wage demands begin to be lowered and the company's wage offer begins to rise. (See Figure 18.1.)

If the positions are reasonably close, the parties will more than likely split the difference and sign a new contract. If the positions are too far apart, each side will try to convince the other that it views the prospect of a work stoppage with perfect equanimity. Management or labor or both may even seek to widen the arena within which the conflict takes place by publicizing their positions through the print and electronic media.

When agreement is finally reached on a new contract, the mood almost always shifts from the somber and sometimes belligerent tone taken during collective bargaining to a festive atmosphere. The labor and management representatives joke, shake hands, and make statements to the press that the settlement is fair and just to employees, management, and shareholders alike. This ritual relaxes the tensions that have built up and eases the way for the mutual cooperation that will be necessary for proper administration of the contract during the period it is in force.

Integrative Bargaining Approach

Though far less prevalent than distributive bargaining, examples of integrative bargaining have been appearing with increasing frequency. The integrative strategies require that both management and the union drop combative attitudes and adopt a genuine interest in the joint exploration of solutions to common problems. To work effectively, integrative bargaining must become a way of life for the two parties that includes continual efforts to improve relationships through regular discussions of problems at all levels and a willingness to attempt to settle these problems without third-party intervention. Solutions to the most difficult problems can be approached by establishing special committees, whose members are drawn from both management and labor, to study the issues and determine the facts.

There are three major forms of integrative bargaining: **concessionary bargaining,** in which labor actually gives up something it had earlier won; **productivity bargaining,** in which wage increases are tied to the union's acceptance of work practices that will increase efficiency; and **quality-of-work-life projects,** which, as the phrase suggests, are collaborative attempts by labor and management to improve the working lives of employees to enhance their ability to produce.

Concessionary Bargaining.   In recent years the serious economic difficulties faced by many American organizations have led a number of them to seek concessions from the unions that represent their employees. One of the most interesting examples of this took place in the automobile industry in 1981, when General Motors negotiated a contract with the United Auto Workers (UAW) in which the union agreed to several major concessions.

The UAW, which for more than a generation had extracted significant wage increases for its members in every new contract, agreed to a wage freeze. It also agreed to give back nine paid holidays it had won in previous negotiations and to defer three cost-of-living adjustments for a year and a half. In exchange for these and other concessions, General Motors promised to keep open four of seven plants that had been scheduled for closing, began a profit-sharing plan for employees, guaranteed that workers with ten years or more of seniority would have an income should they be laid off, and stipulated that in the future supervisory personnel would be laid off in proportion to hourly workers.[8]

As this example demonstrates, concessionary bargaining presupposes a willingness by both sides to seek a solution to a common problem in a spirit of tolerance and trust. Had the UAW sought to hold on to everything it could, or had General Motors demanded

---

PERSPECTIVE 18.1 Concessionary Bargaining Saves Jobs

What would Frederick Winslow Taylor have made of it all? He pioneered time-and-motion management at Bethlehem Steel in the early part of this century. By getting workers to do single, specific tasks, he helped the company move four times as much pig iron as before, and for only two thirds more pay. In March this year, the steelmaker agreed with the United Steelworkers of America (USW) to a pay-cut deal for a loss-making bar-rod-and-wire plant; in return for the pay cut the workers got job flexibility and an equity stake in the company. . . .

The Bethlehem Steel plant . . . was losing at least $5m a month and its managers say that it would have closed if the USW had not reached the deal that it did. As it is, a quarter of the 2,100 workers will lose their jobs. By way of "equality of sacrifice," half the 800 salaried staff will go, too. Those who survive have agreed to reduced benefits and to defer a chunk of their wages until retirement. In return, workers get preference shares in the company that will pay dividends only when profits return.

Workers have also agreed to rub out job demarcation lines. Bethlehem is converting the plant into a mini-mill with costs sufficiently slimmed, it hopes, to compete with steel from foreign and non-

Source: Excerpted from "Managing to Save Jobs," *The Economist* (June 14, 1985): 72. Reprinted by permission of the New York Times Syndicate.

union American mills. The switch followed joint visits to such competitors by Bethlehem's managers and union men to see just how uncompetitive their own operation had become. LTV Corporation and Kaiser Aluminum have negotiated similar deals.

The USW is not, though, the only American union to be won over to the idea of workers giving up wages, rights and benefits in return for a financial stake in their company. At Eastern Airlines and at Chrysler, union leaders have joined the board of directors; at the People Express airline, every full-time employee is a shareholder.

. . . General Motors' workers helped design a warehousing system at a Buick division in Michigan; General Electric's helped with an aero-engine plant in Massachusetts. At Chrysler, GM and Ford, union leaders and managers discuss their firm's investment plans, labour needs, administration and marketing.

The co-operation in Detroit arises from the job-security provisions agreed last year between the carmakers and the United Automobile Workers (UAW) that bring labour and management closer together. Ford is spending $15m a year on a new retraining centre for workers whose old skills are redundant. General Motors, in the past a stickler for keeping labour out of management, opened a $5.5m training centre in May that it will run jointly with the UAW. . . .

---

sacrifices from the union without making any of its own, the ultimate result might very well have been disastrous for the automobile industry as a whole.

One of the most significant kinds of adjustments that have been negotiated in concessionary bargaining is the two-tier or "B" wage scale. A **two-tier wage scale** features a wage scale for new hires that is significantly lower than that for employees already on the payroll. Contracts with such provisions have been particularly prevalent in the airline and grocery industries in recent years. Although two-tier wage scales have aided companies in remaining competitive, such systems have led to dissention and conflict within unions and between companies and unions, including a strike by the pilots of United Airlines.[9]

Productivity Bargaining.   Under the productivity bargaining approach, management offers wage increases on the condition that the union agree to changes in work rules and practices that will increase productivity. In the United States, one of the most interesting examples of productivity bargaining again involved the United Auto Workers. The UAW and the Harmon International Company, which manufactures automobile mirrors, agreed to what they called a Work Improvement Program. After an attitude survey was conducted to identify major problems, a labor-management committee was set up to review the results and, on the basis of its findings, to design experiments to improve the ways in which the work was done.

Small groups of workers and supervisors were given the authority to change their methods of work with the aim of improving both productivity and their own satisfaction with their jobs. One project used a system of rewards in which workers who exceeded the production standard for eight hours in less time could choose either to take the balance of the time off or to earn more money by working the full eight-hour shift. Productivity increased, and the workers requested more in-plant training with which to take advantage of the new opportunity for more free time or more money.[10]

Quality-of-Work-Life Projects.   Many collaborative efforts to improve both productivity and the working life of employees — frequently called quality-of-work-life (QWL) projects — are both a result and an illustration of integrative bargaining. Although QWL projects are not limited to unionized settings, most of them have in fact involved union-management cooperation.[11] (Quality-of-work-life projects are discussed in some detail in Chapter 21.)

CONDUCTING NEGOTIATIONS

Negotiators of the labor agreement are chosen representatives of labor and management. Generally both sides develop a plan to carry out their bargaining strategies. Figure 18.2 shows the usual composition of both the management and union negotiating teams. This section describes how these negotiators are selected and their responsibilities in the negotiation process.

The Management Team

Management is usually represented in collective bargaining by the top-ranking human resources professional who calls on operating managers for advice and assistance during the negotiations and

FIGURE 18.2
Membership of bargaining teams

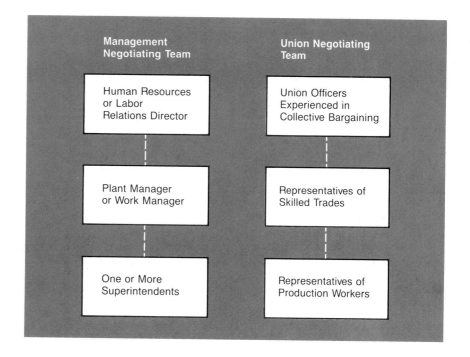

who may team up with one or more operating managers to form a bargaining team. In some large corporations, each plant manager is expected to take charge of labor relations and to either conduct negotiations personally or delegate that responsibility to a staff specialist. The negotiations may be followed closely by corporate headquarters, or they may be evaluated only in the context of the overall performance of the plant.

Most corporations, however, do not withdraw so completely from the conduct of negotiations. If each plant is left on its own, the union that represents the employees in all of the company's plants will be able to insist that an advantage gained at one plant should be applied to all the others, a tactic known as **whipsawing.** To prevent the union from exploiting this possibility, nearly all large corporations have a centralized labor relations department to monitor negotiations at each of their operating facilities.[12]

The management team that is assembled to conduct negotiations normally ranges in size from two to six, with an average of three or four. In addition to the human resources or labor relations director, who is almost always a member and usually the chief spokesperson, the management team usually includes the plant manager or works manager and superintendents. Many firms use lawyers for legal advice during negotiations, but few have included them as active members of the negotiating team.

The authority of management's negotiating team is usually limited by guidelines established by the top management of the company. The negotiating team is expected to keep the president of the company informed of the progress of negotiations. If the union demands anything that requires either a major financial commitment or major changes in plant operations, no decision can be made and no concessions granted without the president's prior approval.

The imposition of these limitations is quite logical, since contract negotiations affect the entire enterprise, sometimes decisively. They are also necessary to protect the negotiators from the consequences of their own impulsive behavior. But because the president of the company has the power to change the guidelines at any time, the president could, if he or she were a member of the negotiating team, ignore them at will. For this reason, company presidents seldom participate directly in negotiations as members of negotiating teams. (In Cases 18.1 and 18.2, if Art Berroni is right, Jupiter's president and the union president are about to reach an agreement outside of the formal bargaining session in order to avert a strike. It appears fortunate that the company president has not been caught up in the rancor of the bargaining session.)

The Labor Team

Just as the composition of management's negotiating team may depend on the degree to which the plant manager is permitted to operate independently of corporate headquarters, membership on labor's team will be influenced by the relationship between the local and the national union. Four basic union structures that determine the role of the local union in collective bargaining negotiations are:

1. National negotiations: The national union negotiates wages and employee benefits with the employer as, for example, takes place in the steel and automobile industries.
2. Pattern bargaining: The local unions in a single company or industry negotiate and sign individual collective bargaining agreements but as part of an effort coordinated or controlled by the national union.
3. Council bargaining: Several local unions negotiate through a council structure in which the officers of each local select a bargaining team to represent them all.
4. Independent bargaining by locals: A local union negotiates all the terms of the agreement directly with the employer.

No matter which of the four structures a local union finds itself operating under, it must select a committee to represent it in negotiations. The local usually selects the bargaining committee at a meeting of its membership. Although the committee is occasionally composed of the local's officers, it is more frequently made up of a combination of officers and ordinary members selected by the membership for the express purpose of serving on the union's negotiating team. (See Figure 18.2.)

The selection of bargaining representatives in the local union often involves political considerations as well as the issue of competence. For example, a union member elected to the bargaining committee can use the position to enhance his or her popularity. Selection of the bargaining committee, then, is a part of the political process that is a constant characteristic of life in a local union.[13]

Preparing, Analyzing, and Resolving Proposals

Although management tries to anticipate what labor will propose in order to formulate an appropriate response, most employers do not develop bargaining proposals of their own. They prefer to react to the demands put forward by the union rather than risk revealing too much of what they are actually prepared to concede by making an initial offer of their own. Those that do make proposals, moreover, tend to do so only after analyzing the existing labor contract carefully to see how changes can be made to reduce the cost of labor and increase the control and discretion of management.[14]

Management's major concern, and the principal question it must ask about every proposal put forward by the union, is what it will cost the company. Negotiators for management will attempt to calculate costs on the basis of prior experience. For example, statistical summaries of employees broken down by age, sex, seniority, and job classification supply information from which it is possible to establish the cost of union proposals that would change such things as vacation time, pensions, and health insurance. Management can also quickly determine the total cost of a wage increase by using a formula that multiplies the increase by the number of affected employees and adds the consequent increases in premiums paid for holidays and overtime and in outlays for such benefits as social security.

The proposals that are made by the union and analyzed by management may be divided into five major categories.

1. Wages and benefits: Among the most important issues to be resolved during negotiations are increases in the base wage rate, changes in incentive-rate formulas, differences in wages

between shifts, compensation for overtime, and the cost-of-living allowance (COLA). These proposals have an obvious effect on the direct cost of labor, as do employee benefits.

2. Working conditions: Health and safety standards, work schedules, shift assignments, and work rules are the principal issues in this category.

3. Job security: Proposals regarding promotions, transfers, layoffs, unemployment compensation, and severance pay policies fall into this category.

4. Management rights: Management almost always reserves the right to control the type and pace of production and to discipline employees within the limits established by the contract. Moreover, management frequently insists on a provision that clearly states that anything not mentioned in the contract continues to be within the range of management's authority.

5. Individual rights: Labor contracts usually establish a procedure under which employees can obtain a remedy for grievances or alleged violations of the contract by management. (The grievance-arbitration procedure is discussed in detail in Chapter 19.)

RESOLVING NEGOTIATING IMPASSES

When negotiations reach an impasse, several options are available. A third party may be called upon to help resolve the dispute, or the government may intervene and try to pressure both sides to do what is necessary to reach an agreement. In some cases, the union and management will exercise their considerable power by engaging in pressure tactics such as a strike or lockout.

Mediation and Conciliation

Mediation and conciliation is a system under which a third party helps labor and management to come to an agreement. **Conciliation** means to help the parties develop and adhere to an agenda, as well as give them encouragement to address as objectively as possible the issues on which they are divided. **Mediation,** on the other hand, suggests a rather more active role in which the third party suggests specific alternatives for the consideration of the two sides. Unlike arbitration, neither mediation nor conciliation empowers the third party to make decisions that labor and management must then accept; mediation and conciliation depend entirely on the ability of the third party to assist the parties to reach an agreement voluntarily. Obviously, the mediator must win the trust of both parties.

The great majority of mediators are supplied by the state and federal governments. Because mediators must be trusted by both labor and management to be effective, the Federal Mediation and Conciliation Service (FMCS), which was created by the Taft-Hartley Act in 1947, is an independent agency. The FMCS is notified automatically of a potential dispute because the Taft-Hartley Act requires that a party that wants to terminate or modify a labor contract must notify the other party sixty days, and the agency at least thirty days, before the date on which the contract expires.

Med-arb

Med-arb is a combination of mediation and arbitration in which the union and management agree that those issues that cannot be settled by mediation will be decided by the third party. As in normal arbitration, what the third party decides becomes final and binding.[15] (Arbitration is discussed in Chapter 19.)

Government Intervention and Fact-Finding

In **fact-finding,** a neutral party, either an individual or a panel, is appointed to determine the facts in a dispute. The fact-finder then makes a report that, it is hoped, will provide the parties with a more accurate understanding of the situation and thus increase the likelihood that an agreement can be reached. Even if the parties themselves are not persuaded by the facts to alter their bargaining positions, the public, when fully informed of the real basis of the disagreement, often brings pressure to bear on the parties to end the conflict. Fact-finders, however, have even less power than mediators; they may not even make recommendations to the parties unless this authority has been expressly given.

Pressure Tactics: Strikes and Lockouts

Strikes and lockouts, or the threat of them, are an integral part of the collective bargaining process. Both the **strike** (a work stoppage by employees) and the **lockout** (in which management prevents employees from working) are methods by which one side attempts to obtain concessions from the other through the application of economic pressure. In the lockout, management literally locks out the employees in the hope that they, or the union that represents them, will be more eager to reach agreement when they no longer have an income.

PERSPECTIVE 18.2 Work-to-Rule Struck Down

The Massachusetts Supreme Judicial Court has struck a fatal blow (so far, fatal only in that state) to that labor tactic known as work-to-rule — a collective bargaining strategy used in jurisdictions where teachers (or other employees) are prohibited by law from going on strike. In schools, the work-to-rule action usually means teachers refuse to perform any duties not carried out during the regular school day: They show up and teach their classes, but they refuse to correct homework at home, meet with parents after school, or work on other after-hours tasks that are not spelled out (literally) in the union contract.

In a decision that puts a judicial endorsement

Source: David A. Splitt, "Work-to-Rule Struck Down," excerpted with permission from *The Executive Educator*, Copyright March 1985 by *The Executive Educator*. All rights reserved.

on the notion that teaching entails far different responsibilities than, say, working in a factory, the Massachusetts court ruled that work-to-rule tactics are, in fact, illegal strikes. Teachers who refuse to perform traditional after-school duties — including paperwork and conferences — are subject to reprimands or other disciplinary action, said the court.

The ruling followed a finding by the state's Labor Relations Commission that teachers in Lenox, Mass., broke the law when they failed to perform work customarily done in connection with classroom duties, even though the after-school tasks were not listed specifically in the current labor contract. The court agreed: Under a collective bargaining agreement, the court said, all past practices of the employee group are duties by implication — "unless they are expressly *excluded.*"

Though the lockout puts pressure on the employees, it also puts a stop to production. Workers lose wages, but management loses profits. The lockout is usually used only when a union strikes against one member of an employers' association and all the members of the association retaliate by locking out their employees.

The strike is labor's ultimate weapon. Through the strike economic pressure is brought to bear on the employer. Workers withhold their services and, unless management is both willing and able to replace the strikers with other, nonunion workers, the company's operations are interrupted. The strike, however, is a two-edged sword; it hurts the business by stopping work, but when work stops so do wages.

But the union does not always need to put all its members on strike to cause the company economic hardship. **Selective strikes,** or strikes against only some of a large employer's plants, are sometimes used to reduce the number of employees taken off the organization's payroll. This in turn decreases the burden placed on the fund the union has created to provide financial assistance to union members on strike.

Strikes involve considerable preparation by both labor and management. They also involve, paradoxically, a certain amount of cooperation between them. Unions, for example, have usually cooperated with management to minimize damage to equipment dur-

AP/Wide World Photos

The strike is labor's ultimate weapon.

ing a shutdown and have almost always allowed maintenance crews to maintain and repair equipment during a strike. The union fully expects the strike to end eventually and wants to protect the company's capacity to employ its members.

Confronted with the possibility of a strike, management needs to make plans in a number of areas. Relations with customers and suppliers, protection of the plant, whether to operate with non-striking or new employees, and the continuation or suspension of employee benefits are all matters that have to be considered before the strike actually takes place. To ensure that the proper plans are made, strike committees are usually established in organizations that have had experience with strikes. Among the executives of a company, the human resources director is almost always on the strike committee. The other members typically include vice presidents in charge of such functions as sales, manufacturing, purchasing, and engineering.

Among the most important and difficult questions the strike committee must address are how to treat any nonunionized segment of the work force during a strike and whether to replace the striking employees with other workers. If the strike is not likely to last very long, most companies keep white-collar workers on the job. These employees have a legal right to ignore the strike by union members and to cross any picket line that may be put up. While occasional outbreaks of violence still occur, most strikes and picket lines are relatively free from physical danger.

The second issue, whether to replace strikers, is more difficult to deal with. Although it is legal to replace strikers in a strike over wages and benefits, it is not legal to do so when the strike concerns an alleged unfair labor practice by management. But replacing strikers with other workers can transform a work stoppage into a bitter struggle for the survival of the union and may create problems once the strike is over. What, for example, is to be the status of replacements in relation to returning strikers? Moreover, employee morale may be seriously harmed, perhaps permanently, and harmony in the workplace may become an impossibility.

IMPLICATIONS FOR HUMAN RESOURCES MANAGERS

With unionization, and the collective bargaining that goes with it, decisions about the organization of work and about staffing, appraisal, and compensation are no longer made by management alone. A labor contract now governs much of the work situation, and management faces serious limitations even in the areas where it can still make decisions about human resources independently of the union. Provisions of the union contract are usually quite extensive in their reach.

One of the most stringent limitations on management discretion and power results from the insistence by unions that seniority alone determine most staffing and pay decisions. There is little point in continuing to collect performance information with which to make personnel decisions when those decisions will be made under the contract on seniority alone, unless the data are used for other purposes, such as coaching and training.

The coming of the union also alters the structure of authority within the organization. Typically there is a tendency to centralize direct contact with the union in a single official, usually the human resources director or industrial relations manager. Moreover, management can no longer deal unilaterally with employees with respect to wages, hours, and working conditions, and this loss of flexibility is often seen as a major disadvantage.

One consequence may be to place greater emphasis on both human resources planning and external staffing. Human resources planning becomes more important because, for example, a contract that provides for supplementary unemployment benefits (as do the contracts negotiated in the auto industry by the UAW) dramatically increases the cost attached to laying off employees. The importance of external staffing increases because this is almost the only decision at the bargaining-unit level the employer can make independently of the union.

SUMMARY

Collective bargaining is the process by which a formal agreement is established between workers and management regarding wages, hours, working conditions, and grievance procedures. Collective bargaining presents opportunities for enhancing cooperative and productive relations between labor and management. It also permits the possibility of conflict and the pursuit of narrow and immediate economic self-interest. Strikes and lockouts, powerful bargaining tools of labor and management respectively, are subject to various laws and regulations that limit the exercise of power by either side.

Both unions and management have much to gain by sending to the bargaining table negotiators who are mature, intelligent, well trained, and well prepared and much to lose if they do not. Precisely these same qualities of maturity, intelligence, and diligent application to the task at hand are required of government officials or other third parties who become involved in the collective bargaining process as fact-finders, mediators, or arbitrators.

Although distributive bargaining continues to be the most frequently used method of collective bargaining, the integrative approach offers the possibility of solving problems to the mutual benefit of the parties, especially with respect to the issues of productivity, job interest, and employee participation in workplace decisions. Cooperation, not confrontation, increasingly characterizes labor-management relations in the United States.

KEY TERMS

collective bargaining	jurisdictional strikes	whipsawing
totality of conduct	national emergency dispute	conciliation
illegal bargaining issues	distributive bargaining	mediation
mandatory bargaining issues	integrative bargaining	fact-finding
voluntary bargaining issues	concessionary bargaining	strike
impasse	productivity bargaining	lockout
economic strike	quality-of-work-life projects	selective strikes
secondary boycott	two-tier wage scale	

REVIEW QUESTIONS

1. What is collective bargaining, and what are its purposes?
2. What is good-faith bargaining?
3. Describe the differences between distributive and integrative bargaining.
4. What is meant by "concessionary bargaining"? Give examples.
5. What is meant by "productivity bargaining"? Give examples.
6. What are some typical steps involved in both the management and the union preparing for and conducting negotiations?
7. What is the role of the mediator?
8. What is "fact-finding" in labor relations?
9. What are some of the problems a company strike committee needs to address in the event of a strike? Discuss.

OPENING CASE QUESTIONS

Case 18.1   The Management Negotiating Team

1. What are some of the factors that are behind the perceptions of the company negotiators?

Case 18.2   The Labor Negotiating Team

1. What are some of the factors that are behind the perceptions of the union negotiators?
2. What type of relationship exists between the union and the Jupiter Automobile Company? (This answer will be partly based on information in Case 18.1.)

CASE 18.3 BASEBALL'S TROUBLED RELATIONS

Unions have for decades been part of the nation's fabric, and there are probably few Americans who don't have opinions about them. To the average citizen, though, the employee associations in professional sports form a rather bizarre subset of the labor movement and its social and economic tradition. Perhaps nowhere are the goings on in labor-management relations stranger than in baseball.

In 1983 and 1984, even with the fifty-day 1981 baseball strike fresh in their memories, baseball fans were flocking to games in record numbers. The average major league player salary in 1984 was $330,000. In 1983, baseball owners negotiated a six-year $1.1 billion television contract to supplement revenues from gate receipts and concessions. Yet in the summer of 1985, both players and owners were dissatisfied with their pieces of the baseball pie—so much so that after months of acrimonious negotiations failed to bring a new basic agreement between the players' association and the owners, the players threatened and then called a strike—*again*.

To the relief of outraged fans, the strike was settled almost immediately this time, and only a few games were missed (it's possible that fan outrage—somewhat more pronounced than in 1981—had something to do with the quick settlement). Still, it remains difficult for the average fan to understand how well-heeled players and owners can so regularly drive each other toward mutual disaster. And it isn't just the periodic squabbles over the basic agreement that expose the combative relationship. Every year, dozens of players file for salary arbitration. Under baseball's arbitration system, players with less than six years in the big leagues can go to arbitration if they're unable to reach a contract agreement with the team owners. An independent arbitrator studies each side's case and decides either that the player's demand must be met or that he must sign the contract offered by management. There is no compromise. Thus, an award can be far out of line with a player's performance if management's offer is seen as even a little more unfair than the player's demand, and vice versa. In the first major award under arbitration, Chicago pitcher Bruce Sutter was awarded a $700,000 salary—twice what he had been offered.

Although owners have won the majority of arbitration decisions, the system has worked to the players' advantage, because few filers actually reach the final hearing. Owners, when faced with the prospect of a hearing, usually increase their contract offer to avoid it. The whole process further escalates the game's spiraling salary structure. For their part, the owners belligerently attack the salary structure, although they created it themselves in the view of

Case Sources: Charles P. Alexander, "A Called Strike Looms," *Time,* July 29, 1985, pp. 60–61; Tim Kurkjian, "Arbitration's Clout," *Dallas Morning News*, January 16, 1984, pp. 1B, 6B; and "Labor Dispute Threatens Baseball," *U.S. News and World Report,* July 29, 1985, p. 8.

many fans and players. They agreed to the arbitration system to prevent younger players from being able to go to free agency, where several clubs could bid for their services, and part of the dispute over the 1985 agreement centered on the owner's demand for a salary cap on teams.

The owners claim that baseball is in trouble, and they seem to blame what they call ruinous losses primarily on high players' salaries. A few teams clearly are financially strapped. But when all the owners as a group opened their books during the recent negotiations, the figures suggested that management might be crying wolf. The players and the owners each hired an expert to review the records; both said the owners were using circuitous accounting methods to create paper losses. The owners' own expert put actual losses at about two-thirds of what the owners claimed. The players' analyst insisted that baseball was actually profitable. There's a great deal of money in the sport, he said, "plenty for everybody."

Players and owners alike might do well to remember where that money comes from. Another strike might kill the appeal of a product—major league baseball—that is currently enjoying its greatest success ever.

Discussion Questions

1. Clearly the owners and players take a distributive bargaining approach. Why might a different approach be more productive? What kind would you recommend?
2. "Baseball players receive six- and seven-digit salaries, so they have little to fear from management. They shouldn't be allowed to have a union." Discuss.

chapter 19

Employee Rights, Responsibilities and Justice

LEARNING OBJECTIVES

- **List some rights of employees protected by law.**
- **Outline the employer's legal obligations in relation to sexual harassment.**
- **Cite instances in which the employment-at-will doctrine is legally invalid.**
- **Define organizational due process and describe formal and informal procedures for handling grievances in the nonunionized organization.**
- **Describe the grievance-arbitration procedure and its purposes.**
- **Explain the role of the human resources department in protecting employee rights.**

CASE 19.1   THE OPEN-DOOR POLICY

Plastic Products, Inc. was proud of its "open-door" policy, which encouraged employees to communicate their problems and concerns to management. When Al Tompkins, a student at Western University, was hired on a part-time basis, he was informed that this policy was the organization's way of responding to employees' suggestions and complaints and maintaining good relations throughout the firm. Al's supervisor, Stuart Lopez, explained it this way: "We have an open-door policy around here. That means if you have a complaint or a disagreement with me we can't settle, you're free to go to my boss with the problem. And you won't suffer any repercussions, either." Al was also told by both the personnel recruiter and his supervisor that he could approach the personnel department for advice about any matter pertaining to his employment at Plastic Products. Al's private opinion was that the open-door policy was probably fluff, and that anybody who took a complaint beyond his or her immediate supervisor would probably be in deep trouble as a result.

Al had no occasion to test the policy until his second year with the company. He had been working four days a week from 5:00 until 9:00 p.m., but during spring quarter of his senior year the university offered a management seminar that met twice a week from 3:30 until 7:00 p.m. Al very much wanted to enroll in the seminar, so he talked with Stuart about the possibility of changing his work schedule. Stuart listened to everything Al had to say and then said, "Well, let me think about it. I've got to consider the reaction of other people in the department, how we would cover your work, and so on. But frankly, I'm doubtful at this point — I'm just not sure the department can accommodate a change like that."

The next day, Stuart walked over to Al's work station and said, "I'm afraid

I've got bad news. I don't see how we can arrange a different schedule for you. We're too short on people, and we don't have much flexibility. I'm sorry. Is there some other class you could take instead?"

Al was disappointed and irritated. He saw himself as a hard worker and a valuable employee, and it seemed to him that the company should be able to handle this request. "Well," Al said, "that's a real disappointment. But thanks for considering the matter."

But the matter didn't go away for Al. He worried about it for a couple of days, and then he went to Stuart's office. "Stuart, about my wanting to change my working hours around for a few months — if you don't mind, let me take the case to Gary Schuler. When I was hired, you told me it was O.K. to appeal things beyond you to your boss."

"That's perfectly all right," Stuart responded. "I'm truly sorry my decision was so unsatisfactory to you, but you know I had to think of the department as a whole. Maybe Gary can figure out a way to cover your job that I haven't considered. I have a suggestion. Let's the two of us meet with him and lay out both sides of the matter, and we'll see where it goes from there."

The meeting with Gary Schuler was very cordial. Al was struck by how carefully Gary listened to both sides of the problem. At no time did Al feel he was doing something that was inappropriate or unappreciated. It was also clear that Gary had great respect for Stuart and the job he was doing for the company. The best part was that, in the end, Gary and Stuart figured out a way to accommodate Al's request, and everyone was satisfied with the arrangements that were made.

A few weeks later, the subject of open-door policies was discussed in the senior seminar. Al was eager to speak up. "Let me tell you about an experience I had that proves some companies are serious about responding to what their employees have to say," he said. "I was skeptical, but now I'm convinced that an open-door policy is one way an employee can be heard and understood. Believe me, Plastic Products is a great place to work. Here's what happened."

CASE 19.2   THE ENGINE THAT COULDN'T*

Art Jones was an abrasive, technically effective employee who tended to taunt his supervisors. He was a mechanic in a small company that sold and repaired marine engines for both fishing vessels and pleasure craft. He had been with the firm for more than twenty years. The shop supervisor, Dan Gulbrandson, did not like him, but his fellow workers were generally tolerant and took some pleasure in Art's baiting the supervisory staff.

*From Wendell L. French, Fremont E. Kast, and James E. Rosenzweig, *Understanding Human Behavior in Organizations* (New York: Harper & Row, 1985), pp. 484–485. Used with permission of Harper & Row.

One day, Dan received a call from the general manager saying there had been a complaint that a part had been installed incorrectly in the engine of a large sailboat: the engine was cutting out, and the owner was furious. Art Jones was the mechanic who had been assigned to repair the engine.

Dan summoned Art to his office and used some strong language in accusing Art of installing the part upside down. Art vehemently denied that he had installed the part incorrectly and used some strong language of his own. He went on to indicate that the management staff was too busy drinking coffee and talking about their social lives to know what was going on. Dan ended the interview by saying, "Get the hell out of here. We'll see . . ." Art went back to his work station. Dan went down to the general manager's office.

The next day, Art was handed a discharge slip by his foreman, who said, "I'm sorry about this, but that's the way it's got to be." Art locked up his tools, went home, telephoned the representative of the international union, and filed a grievance.

Over the next few days a good deal of time was spent by the mechanics in the shop discussing Art's discharge and commiserating with each other about a wide range of things they didn't like about their working conditions. By the end of the week, Art's grievance had become a cause célèbre.

As the grievance went through several steps, the company insisted that Jones had been properly discharged for unsatisfactory work and a bad attitude and, furthermore, that he probably should have been discharged long before. The union was equally insistent that the discharge was improper. The case went to arbitration.

The arbitrator held that there had been no progressive discipline, such as warnings in the file, that Art was not aware that the meeting in Dan's office could lead to discharge, and that discharge was too severe a penalty under the circumstances. The arbitrator ordered Art reinstated, but without back pay and with an implied admonition to him to shape up.

A rapidly evolving area in human resources management is employee rights and organizational justice. Outside the work situation, the United States Constitution guarantees many rights, such as freedom of speech, freedom of the press, freedom of assembly, and the right to due process of law. (**Due process** refers to legal proceedings carried out in accordance with established rules and principles that acknowledge the rights of individual citizens.) But what rights, if any, does an employee have on the job?

The chapter-opening cases give a partial answer to this question. In Case 19.1, Al Tompkins had the right of appeal beyond his immediate supervisor, a right granted through company policy and supported by the behavior of Al's superiors. (Had management not supported the open-door policy, Al would undoubtedly have received clear signals that going over the boss's head was not a wise thing to do.) In Case 19.2, unionized employees of the marine engine shop had the right to appeal management's decisions through the grievance-arbitration procedure. This right was guaranteed by the labor contract negotiated through collective bargaining. Both cases are examples of how organizations may follow specific procedures to respond to employees' complaints or remedy injustice out of respect for the rights of workers.

Fair treatment of employees and a concern for individual rights represent a challenge to every organization because the possibility of injustice exists over a wide range of managerial decision areas. Compounding this challenge is the tendency of employees to evaluate the fairness or equity of decisions and actions that affect them either directly or indirectly. Minimizing perceptions of inequity and determining what is just treatment are major concerns in hu-

"You can be glad you're having problems, Harkness. A man without problems is usually dead."

man resources management, and they are problems every manager confronts daily.

This chapter discusses the rights of employees, the responsibilities these rights imply for both employers and employees, and the problem of justice in the workplace. In particular, the chapter explores the various ways organizations accommodate the wants, needs, and rights of individuals in an effort to ensure just and fair treatment of all employees. There is a growing body of law and an emerging pattern of personnel practice pertaining to organizational justice. Because of these laws and practices, many organizations conscientiously follow fair and orderly procedures in making decisions that affect employees' lives. The extent to which a particular organization actually "tunes in" to employee perceptions of equity and adheres to a concern for employee rights is affected by many variables, such as management philosophy, organizational culture, and prevailing leadership style. But in the ideal situation, organizational justice remains an overriding goal of all management decision making, and procedures are adopted to guarantee substantial responsiveness to the rights of individual workers.

EMPLOYEE RIGHTS

Historically, there has been little constitutional or legal protection of the rights of workers on the job. William Kaplin states the matter directly: "Because the Constitution was designed to limit only the exercise of government power, it does not prohibit private individuals or corporations from impinging on such freedoms as free speech, equal protection, and due process."[1]

This condition is gradually changing, however. Some rights of employees are now specifically identified and protected through government policy, federal and state laws, and various court decisions. At the same time, rising levels of education and other social changes have affected the attitudes and expectations of many workers, who are now more likely to expect fair treatment in the workplace. The employee rights protected by law, the responsibilities and obligations these rights imply, and the impact of rights protection on management and human resources practices is the focus of this section.

Prohibitions Against Discrimination

As discussed in several preceding chapters, laws, court decisions, and administrative rulings have created major protections for job

PERSPECTIVE 19.1   Racial Remarks in the Work Place: Humor or Harassment?

A black man employed by a Minnesota trucking company had racial slurs directed at him and was the target of graffiti written by fellow workers. A U.S. district court held that the trucking company violated Title VII of the Civil Rights Act of 1964 and ordered it to take affirmative action and disciplinary measures against offending employees. Furthermore, the court ordered the company to educate and sensitize its supervisors and managers in order to eliminate racial and national-origin hostility from the work environment.

The U.S. Court of Appeals (Fifth Circuit) reached a different decision in a case involving an offshore oil rig worker. Employee behavior that included "raw pranks, crude practical jokes," and oral racial abuse did not amount to harassment sufficient to support a black employee's claim that fellow workers forced him to quit his job on the rig. Few, if any, workers on the rig were spared; white as well as black employees were the target of obscene and racially derogatory remarks. The court ruled that in this instance the employer was not responsible for the actions of its employees.

Source: Reprinted by permission of the Harvard Business Review. Excerpt from "Racial Remarks in the Workplace: Humor or Harrassment?" by Terry L. Leap and Larry R. Smeltzer (November/December 1984). Copyright © 1984 by the President and Fellows of Harvard College; all rights reserved.

These two cases exemplify situations faced with increasing frequency — and "solved" with some inconsistency — by the Equal Employment Opportunity Commission (EEOC) and the courts. Even so, this form of harassment is little understood, perhaps because it, unlike sexual harassment in organizations, has received scant attention in the legal arena and academic literature. But harassment along racial and ethnic lines has the potential to create disrupting tensions in the workplace.

What constitutes harassment is hard to say. The telling and sharing of crude jokes is commonplace in many organizational settings. Employees banter in racially derogatory terms during the normal course of their work. While such "humor" is perceived by some as being crude, vulgar, degrading, or inappropriate, to others it is just a form of hazing and perfectly harmless.

It is often difficult to determine whether an employer or supervisor who tolerates or condones such behavior is legally liable under civil rights legislation governing employment conditions. The courts, in trying to decide whether the conduct was appropriate, have often tried to evaluate the work environment and context in which slurs, epithets, and jokes were uttered. The appropriateness often depends on the legal and social distinction between harassment and hazing.

applicants and employees against discrimination based on race, color, religion, national origin, sex, age, or handicapped status. Veterans have certain protections under government contracts, in federal employment, and in some state employment situations. Nondiscriminatory treatment in the workplace is a basic employee right, and laws prohibiting discrimination affect all areas of human resources management.

An aspect of discrimination that has not yet been discussed is **sexual harassment,** which is now illegal under federal law. Sexual harassment was defined by the Third Circuit Court of Appeals in *Tompkins* v. *Public Service Electric & Gas Company:*

> Title VII of the Civil Rights Act is violated when a supervisor, with the actual or constructive knowledge of the employer, makes sexual

advances or demands toward a subordinate employee and conditions that employee's job status — evaluation, continued employment, promotion, or other aspects of career development — on a favorable response to those advances or demands, and the employer does not take prompt action and appropriate remedial action after acquiring such knowledge.[2]

Under the law, an employer may be held liable for not investigating and taking appropriate action should a problem of sexual harassment develop between two employees. Although employees of either sex may be subject to sexual harassment, probably most of the victims are women; certainly the plaintiffs in most of the suits filed under Title VII are women.

One of the earliest suits that brought an employer to court involved a male vice president of Johns-Manville Corporation, who discharged a woman project coordinator who refused to have an affair with him. Subsequently, a district court in Denver found the corporation guilty of sexual discrimination under the Civil Rights Act and liable for damages. An out-of-court settlement was made for a reported $100,000.[3]

In 1980 the Equal Employment Opportunity Commission issued guidelines clarifying the illegal aspects of sexual harassment. One provision states that an employer may be held liable for unlawful sexual discrimination against employees who were qualified for, but denied, employment opportunities and benefits secured by a fellow employee who submitted to the employer's sexual advances.[4]

The liability of employers in instances of sexual harassment means that organizations are legally responsible for safeguarding their employees from such treatment. To protect the rights of individual employees and the interests of the organization, top management should issue a strong policy statement prohibiting sexual harassment and stating the disciplinary steps that will be taken if this policy is violated. In addition, management must make certain that there will be no retaliation against an employee for bringing complaints of policy violation and that all complaints will receive a fair hearing.[5]

Freedom to Organize and Contract Rights

The right of nonsupervisory employees in business and industry to organize and bargain collectively with an employer has long been recognized in the United States. This right is not absolute because many procedural rules must be followed, but it is extensive and includes the right to engage in union-organizing activities without reprisal from the employer. Moreover, the right to organize and bargain collectively is gradually being extended into new domains through state and federal laws and rulings. For example, union organizing and collective bargaining are now protected in not-for-profit hospitals, nursing homes, and federal and state government agencies.

Under collective bargaining agreements, the right to organize and bargain collectively is reinforced by **contract rights.** That is, employees are guaranteed the rights for which they have contracted with management for the duration of the agreement. These rights are enforceable through arbitration procedures and the courts. Rights negotiated into the agreement typically include the right to file grievances and to take individual cases to arbitration, and employees are usually protected against dismissal without **just cause.** In essence, dismissal for just cause means that employment can be terminated only for valid, job-related reasons, such as poor performance and violation of company rules. Employees' rights to procedural or legal due process are implied or specified in most collective bargaining agreements and underlie employment conditions in state agencies and other institutions in which personnel decisions are considered state actions.

Individual employees in nonunionized organizations can also enter into contracts with their employers. An example is a salary and benefits contract between a company and an executive or between a professional football player and a club owner. Contracts like these provide rights for the duration of the agreement and are enforceable through the court system.[6]

Speech Rights and Obligations

Freedom of speech is a right many American citizens take for granted. But under prevailing court decisions and currently accepted standards, an employee does not have complete freedom in what he or she can say about superiors and the employing organization. David Ewing explains the limitations of free speech in the workplace this way:

> First, no employee should have a right to divulge information about legal and ethical plans, practices, operations, inventions, and other matters that the organization must keep confidential in order to do its job in an efficient manner.
>
> Second, no employee should have a right to make personal accusations or slurs which are irrelevant to questions about policies and actions that seem illegal or irresponsible.
>
> Third, no employee should be entitled to disrupt an organization or hurt its morale by making speeches and accusations that do not reflect a conviction that wrong is being done.

Fourth, no employee should be entitled to rail against the competence of a supervisor or senior manager to make everyday work decisions that have nothing to do with the legality, morality, or responsibility of management actions.

In addition, no employee is entitled to object to discharge, transfer, or demotion if management can demonstrate that unsatisfactory performance or violation of a code of conduct was the reason for its action.[7]

These statements imply that employees must act in a responsible manner but that they also have the right to speak out or "blow the whistle" if the organization is engaging in illegal, immoral, or irresponsible practices. The courts have tended to support these limited speech rights. The Supreme Court has ruled that the constitutional guarantees of free speech do not extend to complaining about working conditions and supervisors, and that employees who do so can be fired.[8]

But in addition, numerous court decisions and some state laws are enforcing the right of employees to "blow the whistle," particularly in public employment. Here are some examples:

- In *Pickering* v. *Board of Education* (1968), the Supreme Court reinstated an Illinois high school teacher, Pickering, who had been fired for criticizing the local school board for improperly using funds from a bond issue to build an athletic field. The Court, ruling under the First Amendment to the Constitution, which says, "Congress shall make no law abridging the freedom of speech, or of the press," found that Pickering's "right to speak on issues of public importance may not furnish the basis for his dismissal from public employment."[9]
- In 1973, in *Rafferty* v. *Philadelphia Psychiatric Center,* the Court reinstated a psychiatric nurse who had been fired for being critical of patient care and staff behavior at the hospital where she worked.[10]
- In a 1979 Supreme Court case, *Girhan* v. *Western Line Consolidated School District,* a schoolteacher was reinstated after her contract had not been renewed because of "insulting," "hostile," "arrogant," and "loud" comments made to her principal during a private conversation. The Court ruled that the First Amendment protected public employees' conversations with a superior.[11]

Whether these protections will be extended very far into the private sector remains to be seen. Some court cases and legislation suggest a gradual extension of protection, however, particularly where an incident internal to the organization overlaps with the activities of a public agency or is contrary to public policy. For example:

- In 1959, in *Petermann* v. *International Brotherhood of Teamsters,* a California Appeals Court reinstated a union business agent who had been fired for refusing to commit perjury on the orders of his boss.[12]
- In 1980 the Connecticut Supreme Court ruled that an employee of a frozen foods plant could not be fired for protesting to his superiors that the company was putting less meat into the entrees than the label indicated.[13]
- The Occupational Safety and Health Act (OSHA), the Coal Mine Safety Act, and the Water Pollution Control Act protect employees who report violations of these laws.[14]
- In 1984 a New Jersey jury found that the Mobil Corporation had unfairly fired a research biologist who had tried to get the company to report two toxic chemical accidents that she believed should have been reported under the law. The company claimed the employee was fired for being incompetent but settled by paying $425,000 in compensatory and punitive damages.[15]

By the end of 1984, five states had passed "whistle-blower" protection laws. These states were Connecticut (the first to pass such a law), Michigan, Maine, New York, and California.[16]

Privacy Protection

Under the Privacy Act of 1974, federal employees have considerable protection against misuse of personnel records. This law establishes strict requirements for the collection and distribution of personnel data. In most employment situations, however, employee privacy is not guaranteed by law. That is, establishing a policy of confidentiality and controlled access to personnel records is the option of the employer, and there have been many instances in which personnel information has been managed irresponsibly.

Some organizations routinely divulge medical, salary, appraisal, and disciplinary information without employee permission to outside sources such as government agencies, credit bureaus, insurance companies, law firms, or unions.[17] This problem is made more acute by the computerization of personnel records, which makes access to data that much easier. In other cases, access to information is so restricted that employees themselves are not allowed to inspect their own files and correct inaccurate data.

Current debate centers on whether privacy safeguards should be legislated by the government or established voluntarily by organizational policy. On the one hand, several states have passed laws requiring that employees be granted access to their personnel files. (In 1984, these states included California, Connecticut, North

Carolina, Wisconsin, Oregon, Maine, Michigan, and Pennsylvania.)[18] On the other hand, the Federal Privacy Protection Study Commission has urged that organizations voluntarily adopt practices that ensure confidentiality and responsible control of personnel records. The commission's recommendations are as follows:

1. Limit the collection of information on employees and applicants to what is relevant to specific personnel decisions.
2. Give employees access to, and the right to copy, their personnel records upon request.
3. Inform employees and applicants about the uses to which their records are (or will be) put.
4. Designate and separate those records not available to an employee (the commission expressed a strong preference for few such records). The commission specifically suggested that individual employment performance, medical, and insurance records be available to employees.
5. Correct records the employee identifies as inaccurate or explain why corrections were not made.
6. Curb the release of information to third parties without the employee's consent, except for routine directory information concerning position held, employment dates, and salary.
7. Limit the internal use of records maintained on employees and applicants.[19]

Presumably, salary information would be released only to confirm the salary already reported by an employee to an outside party.

Protection Against Arbitrary Dismissal

The extent to which employers are free to dismiss workers and the rights of workers facing dismissal have not been established in any final or absolute sense by the legal system. Traditionally, federal and state courts have supported an **employment-at-will rule** (sometimes called a *termination-at-will* rule or the *absolute right to discharge*), which specifies that an employer in a private institution may dismiss an employee, with or without specific cause, in the absence of a written employment agreement. The rule is based on the assumption that the employee may also quit at any time, without notice, and for any reason. This rule is gradually being modified, however, by Congress and by state and federal courts.[20]

There are now specific situations in which at-will dismissal is illegal, and various court decisions have upheld the rights of workers who have been dismissed unfairly. For example, the employment-at-will rule does not apply when dismissal of an employee constitutes discrimination or any violation of civil rights laws. Moreover, the concept of "just cause" overrides the at-will doctrine under many collective bargaining agreements; it is, in other words, a breach of contract to dismiss an employee for anything but legitimate business reasons. As discussed, dismissal that violates a significant public policy is also forbidden by law — largely through the weight of court decisions.

Several other exceptions to employment at will should be mentioned. The first pertains mostly to public employment; the others apply more generally.

The Job as a Property Right.   Through a series of decisions, the Supreme Court has established that employees of state and public institutions have a right to a fair hearing whenever personnel decisions deprive them of a "property interest" or "liberty interest" under the Fourteenth Amendment to the Constitution. This clause reads, "Nor shall any state deprive any person of life, liberty, or property, without due process of law." In general, the principle is not that state and public employees have an absolute right to their jobs, but that dismissal cannot occur without procedural due process.

For example, in *Board of Regents* v. *Roth* (1972), the Court maintained that faculty members of a state university have property rights to their jobs and are therefore safeguarded by due process. The due-process principle means that the employee is to be given fair notice of charges as well as an opportunity to speak in his or her own defense.

Even in the private sector, legislation and court actions have sometimes indicated that employees have a property interest in their jobs. In one case, for example, employees of a bankrupt company were allowed to file claims against the employer for accrued vacation benefits.[21] In the event of bankruptcy or liquidation of a company, employee pension claims take legal precedence over all other claims (except taxes) up to 30 percent of the net worth of the firm.[22]

Good Faith and Fair Dealing.   Court decisions in at least three states indicate that employers must deal fairly and in good faith with employees, even in organizations operating under the employment-at-will rule. The Massachusetts Appellate Court held that a jury could decide whether an employer had discharged a long-term employee in order to avoid paying him large sales commissions. The court ignored a written contract reserving the employer's right to discharge an employee for any reason and ruled that if the jury found the employer's motives suspect, the discharge was improper because the law imposes a covenant of good faith and fair dealing on all contracts.

The Montana Supreme Court upheld a $50,000 award to a cashier who claimed she was discharged without warning and had been forced to sign a resignation letter. The court found that the jury had sufficient evidence to find fraud, oppression, or malice on the part of the employer. In California, a court found that an employee could sue for wrongful discharge when the company violated its own procedures for handling employee disputes.[23]

The Implied Contract. Finally, the employment-at-will rule may be deemed invalid in situations governed by an **implied contract,** or an inferred understanding of the conditions of continued employment. Court decisions in thirteen states have ruled against companies that violate promises of job tenure implied in employee handbooks, personnel policy manuals, or in statements made in employment interviews.[24]

GRIEVANCE PROCEDURES AND DUE PROCESS IN NONUNIONIZED ORGANIZATIONS

Most of the employee rights described in the previous section are protected by legislation and court decisions. In unionized firms, the collective bargaining agreement specifies the contract rights of workers, which are also enforceable through the courts. But management can also take steps to protect the rights of employees by adhering to what is called **organizational due process.** Organizational due process consists of established procedures for handling employee complaints and grievances, protection against punitive action for using these procedures, and systematic and thorough review of complaints and grievances by unbiased or neutral parties. In employment situations governed by a sincere commitment to organizational due process, employees have the right to object to management action and to be heard without fear of management retaliation.

The systems and procedures for carrying out organizational due process vary from informal methods (such as the open-door policy described in Case 19.1) to formal systems (such as the grievance-arbitration procedure specified in most labor contracts). Appeal procedures in military, civil service, and some business and industrial organizations reflect a commitment to organizational due process, as do tenure policies and procedures in colleges and universities. In general, all these methods share one major purpose: to provide a means for reviewing (and possibly modifying) management actions in cases where employees believe they have been treated unfairly.

Informal Procedures

One way of handling grievances is through an **open-door policy,** in which employees are given access to their superiors so that problems can be brought into the open and resolved in a mutually satisfying way. Many complaints of unjust treatment can be handled through informal discussion of the problem by the employee and his or her supervisor. If the supervisor is an effective listener and genuinely interested in seeing that justice is done, problems can often be solved and inequities minimized with little time and cost.

If this discussion does not resolve the issue, employees in some organizations are encouraged to take the problem to the human resources department or to higher management so that the merit of the grievance can be evaluated objectively. An effective resolution of the grievance at this level requires a fair assessment of all sides of the case. That is, the human resources or management representative may need to confer with the supervisor, consider the needs of other employees, and take into account perceptions of equity in order to determine the validity of the complaint and to decide what further action should be taken.

PERSPECTIVE 19.2 BankAmerica's "Let's Talk" Program

BankAmerica is committed to providing a positive work environment that fosters job satisfaction and support for employee concerns.

As much as we try, things don't always go right at work. Problems and conflicts sometimes arise concerning your work or the people you work with.

Many work-related problems can be magnified by poor communications or misunderstandings of

Source: Courtesy of BankAmerica Corporation.

intent. This can create frustration as well as an unpleasant work environment.

BankAmerica wants to address such situations, quickly, openly and candidly. For this reason, BankAmerica has a program to help you solve work-related problems that you haven't been able to resolve with your manager. The program is called "Let's Talk." It is based on the idea that many on-the-job problems can be cleared up by frank and prompt discussion.

Formal Grievance and Appeal Procedures

Employee complaints of unjust treatment can also be handled through formal grievance procedures that allow employees to present their complaints to designated parties and that generally specify who is ultimately responsible for settling the issue. The most common formal system for handling grievances is the grievance-arbitration procedure found under collective-bargaining agreements. Most American workers, however, are not covered by collective-bargaining agreements. Of these nonunion employees, the majority work in organizations that do not include formal grievance procedures in their personnel policies. A survey of organizations with nonunion employees found that only 44 percent of the respondents had established formal grievance procedures and only three of these organizations specified **arbitration,** or outside appeal to a neutral party, as the final step in the procedure. (All three were government agencies or government-regulated.) Nonbusiness organizations, such as government agencies, were more likely to have a formal grievance procedure than business organizations.[25]

The grievance procedure is generally available to those employees who feel that company policy or a management decision has been improperly or unfairly applied to them. A substantial number of nonunion organizations, however, place limits on the kinds of management actions that can be appealed. One study of 218 nonunion organizations found that 71 percent provided formal appeal procedures only for disciplinary action (such as discharge, suspension, or demotion). This study also found that in more than half of these organizations, the president or CEO makes the final decision on the appeal. Only 2 percent use outside arbitration to settle appeals, while 16 percent delegate this authority to the personnel or employee relations manager. In this sample, only nonbusiness organizations used arbitrators.[26]

Disciplinary Review Boards

Disciplinary review boards are sometimes used in business and industrial firms to review instances of disciplinary action and to correct or amend a penalty that an employee considers unfair or too harsh. These boards usually consist of a committee of three or more managers and, in a small number of companies, a psychiatrist or psychologist. By emphasizing a corrective, problem-solving approach, disciplinary review boards can successfully counteract any punitive tendencies in supervisors' dealings with subordinates.

The Corporate Ombudsman

A unique institution in the administration of organizational justice, the **ombudsman,** has appeared on the American scene in recent years. *Ombudsman* is a Swedish word meaning representative or attorney.[27] Originally, the ombudsman was typically an eminent attorney appointed by a legislative body to investigate citizens' complaints against administrative officials and to report on the findings. More recently, some corporations and other types of institutions have begun to use this role for internal investigation and resolution of employees' complaints. A complaint is brought by the employee, the ombudsman investigates, and then uses his or her influence to resolve the matter.

Though a few American organizations such as Xerox Corporation, General Electric, Boeing Vertol Company, Massachusetts Institute of Technology, and the University of Washington have had some experience with a corporate or institutional ombudsman, little of this experience has been reported in the literature.[28] What reports have emerged have suggested that an ombudsman can be very effective in combating subtle abuses of subordinates.[29] In some organizations, an executive with other responsibilities is assigned the ombudsman role. For example, one company uses the director of communications to handle complaints, and another designates a "Where-to-Turn" person who reports directly to the president of the company.[30]

There is a risk that an ombudsman will be more loyal to management than to employees. This will depend in large part, however, on how the ombudsman is chosen and the degree to which management truly wishes to be responsive to complaints and grievances. One author recommends that ombudsmen be picked from lists of state-licensed specialists and that they be chosen jointly by management and employee representatives.[31]

Access to the Courts and Government Agencies

Although all citizens have access to the courts, judges will usually not become involved in an alleged injustice in the employment relationship unless laws have been violated. An exception is the increasing involvement of the courts in reviewing whether due process has occurred, usually in cases of state employment (or state-related employment) and under the Fourteenth Amendment.

The government involves itself in organizational justice through the action of administrative agencies responsible for enforcing laws pertaining to minimum wages, child labor, overtime, fair employment, and unfair labor practices. Decisions handed down by these agencies are usually enforced by court action upon proper judicial review. Appeals of such decisions are also normally handled by the courts. For the most part, however, courts have held that the aggrieved employee must exhaust all of the organization's internal procedures before seeking a judicial remedy.

GRIEVANCE-ARBITRATION PROCEDURES IN UNIONIZED ORGANIZATIONS

In unionized organizations, employee grievances are usually handled through **grievance-arbitration** procedures specified by the labor contract. These procedures involve systematic, union-management deliberation of a complaint at successively higher organizational levels. If the problem is not settled at any of these internal levels, the complaint is submitted to an outside, impartial party, or *arbitrator*, whose decision is final and binding. Most grievances are brought by employees, although management may use this procedure to process a complaint about the union. Almost all labor contracts contain grievance procedures, and about 96 percent contain provisions for arbitration as a final step.[32]

The grievance-arbitration procedure is shown in Figure 19.1. Typically the grievance procedure is set in motion when an employee, or a union officer on behalf of the employee, brings a verbal or written complaint to the employee's immediate supervisor. About 55 percent of labor contracts require that the grievance be presented in writing at the first step.[33]

If the problem is not handled to the satisfaction of the employee at this first step, he or she may then take the grievance to the next higher managerial level designated in the contract, through a total of three, four, or five steps. The most common practice is for the contract to provide for three steps, exclusive of arbitration.[34]

At these later stages, the grievance is always presented in writing, and the employee is almost always represented by a union official or committee who meets with management representatives. (Figure 19.2 is an example of a form used for making a grievance statement.) Management is often represented by a grievance committee that includes a member of the personnel or industrial relations department. In fact, the human resources department is usually involved in all internal deliberations on the grievance. Sometimes a contract specifies that the general manager or company president will participate in the last stage of internal deliberations.

Finally, a grievance that cannot be settled between the union and management is submitted to an arbitrator. The arbitrator conducts

FIGURE 19.1
Typical grievance procedure under a union contract

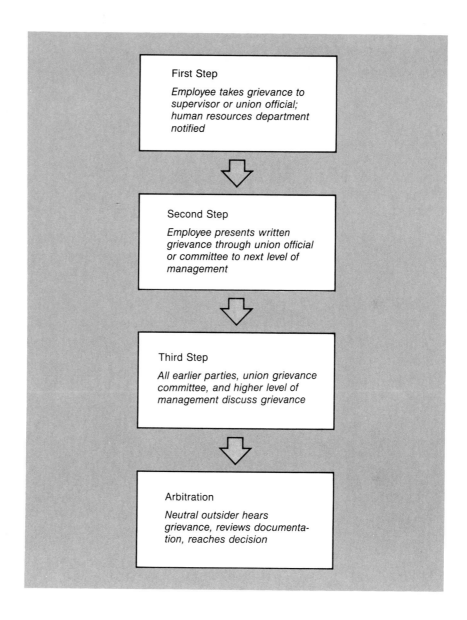

First Step

Employee takes grievance to supervisor or union official; human resources department notified

Second Step

Employee presents written grievance through union official or committee to next level of management

Third Step

All earlier parties, union grievance committee, and higher level of management discuss grievance

Arbitration

Neutral outsider hears grievance, reviews documentation, reaches decision

a hearing and hands down a decision that both parties have agreed in advance to accept as final and binding. (Figure 19.3 shows the types of issues and number of cases brought to arbitration in 1980.)

Selection of Arbitrators

The procedure for selecting arbitrators (who are sometimes called *umpires*) is spelled out in the labor contract. In most cases, deci-

FIGURE 19.2
**Example of a form
used for submitting a
grievance**

GRIEVANCE STATEMENT

EMPLOYEE: _____ CLOCK NO.: _____ SHIFT: _____

JOB CLASSIFICATION: _____ PLANT: _____ DEPT.: _____

DEPT. FOREMAN: _____

STATEMENT OF GRIEVANCE: _____

_____

_____

_____

_____

_____

_____

_____

_____

_____

_____

EMPLOYEE: _____ DEPT. STEWARD: _____
           Signature   Signature

RECEIVED BY: _____ TIME: _____ DATE: _____
           Supervisor or Foreman

Prepare in quadruplicate for distribution

1. Original and one copy (Labor Relations) UNION FILE NO. _____
2. Department
3. Chief Steward   LABOR RELATIONS NO. _____

sions are made by a single arbitrator. Some contracts, however, call for three-member arbitration boards that consist of union and company representatives plus an impartial chairperson. (This practice has been criticized, however, because of the natural tendency for union and management to sympathize with their respective board members, which means that only the chairperson is truly a neutral decision maker.) The majority of contracts state that the parties will try to agree on an arbitrator; if they cannot agree, they must turn to an impartial agency for the selection.[35]

The agencies used most widely in selecting arbitrators are the Federal Mediation and Conciliation Service and the American Arbitration Association. Both maintain up-to-date rosters of qualified arbitrators and will supply lists from which an arbitrator can be chosen. If desired, these agencies will select the arbitrator. Many arbitrators, however, are selected directly by the parties without going through an intermediary.

FIGURE 19.3
Number of cases, by type of issue, reported in FMCS Closed Arbitration Cases, 1980

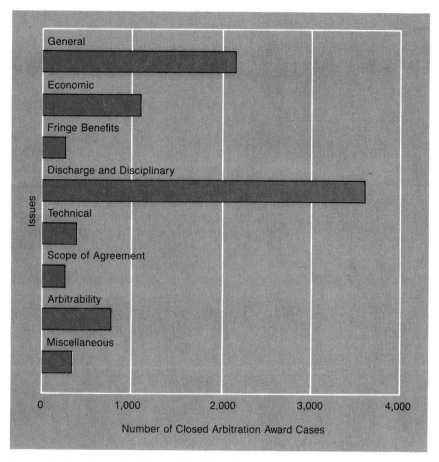

Source: Based on Federal Mediation and Conciliation Service, 34th Annual Report, Fiscal Year 1981, pp. 40–41.

Under **ad hoc arbitration,** an arbitrator is appointed for each case. Less common is the permanent umpire system, under which the parties agree to use a particular arbitrator, or several arbitrators in rotation, for the life of the contract. The advantage of permanent arbitration is that the arbitrator can develop an understanding of the particular characteristics and unique problems of the parties involved.

Labor arbitrators come from many walks of life, but generally they are highly knowledgeable and experienced in labor-management relations. According to a survey of the National Academy of Arbitrators, professors and lawyers constitute the majority of members. About 36 percent were found to have degrees in law, and 29 percent had doctorates. The average age was fifty-seven.[36]

Role of the Arbitrator

The arbitrator's role is generally considered **quasi-judicial,** that is, analogous to or approaching the role of a judge. The arbitrator is expected to listen to evidence, weigh it impartially and objectively, and make a decision based on the labor contract.

There are some important differences between the role of an arbitrator and that of a judge, however. First, arbitration hearings tend to be much more informal than courtroom proceedings. The parties may or may not have legal counsel present at the hearings, and the proceedings are not bound by the rules of evidence, as they are in a court of law. Nevertheless, the proceedings are expected to be conducted with dignity and fairness, and they are likely to include cross-examination and the submission of documents as evidence.[37]

In addition, arbitrators are not bound by precedent to the extent that judges are expected to adhere to legal precedents in the judicial process.[38] Although an arbitrator may study other arbitrators' decisions to sharpen his or her understanding of the issues and although both parties may cite arbitration decisions in support of their positions, the arbitrator's decision is not limited or constrained by the decisions of arbitrators in other cases.

While both labor and management ordinarily expect the arbitrator to assume a quasi-judicial role, other expectations and the arbitrator's own convictions about his or her role do come into play, which can create dilemmas for the arbitrator in the decision-making process. According to Harold Davey, the arbitrator may be expected to play the role of "mutual friend," a "father confessor," or a "labor-relations psychiatrist" and is sometimes expected to use a "split-the-difference" approach.[39] In general, however, the decision-making authority of the arbitrator is limited by the **submission agreement,** which is signed by both labor and management representatives. This agreement, sometimes called a "stipulation" or "an agreement to arbitrate," describes the dispute and the authority the arbitrator can exercise.

Legal Support for Arbitration Decisions

In general, federal and state courts have tended to uphold decisions reached through arbitration. This is not surprising given the fact that, under the labor contract, union and management have agreed in writing to abide by the decision of an impartial third party; in effect, both parties have agreed in advance not to appeal the decision. Ordinarily, arbitration decisions are subject to legal challenge only when the courts find evidence of fraud, corruption, incorrect calculations, or misconduct on the part of the arbitrator (such as refusal to hear evidence or lack of impartiality in relation to one of the parties).[40] In the *Trilogy* cases, as they have come to be called, the Court held that an award must be enforced if the arbitrator based the decision on an interpretation of the labor contract.

More recently, however, two Supreme Court cases have slightly modified legal support for the arbitration process. In the 1974 *Alexander* v. *Gardner-Denver* case, the Court held that an arbitrator's decision is not final and binding if the decision violates Title VII of the Civil Rights Act. In this case, an arbitrator upheld a company's discharge of a black employee, but the employee took the matter to court. The lower courts upheld the arbitrator's decision, but the Supreme Court sent the case back to the federal district court to determine whether the employee's civil rights had been violated in the discharge.[41]

In *Hines* v. *Anchor Motor Freight* (1976), the Court established the principle that courts can negate arbitration awards when the union has not adequately represented employees. In the *Hines* case, three truck drivers were discharged for allegedly falsifying expense sheets pertaining to a certain motel. They insisted to the union that they were innocent, but the union representatives ignored their assertions and simply pled for mercy at the subsequent arbitration hearing. The arbitrator upheld the discharges. Several months later, the motel clerk admitted that he had embezzled the money, and the truck drivers sued both the union and the company. The Supreme Court maintained that the union's misconduct had "seriously undermined" the arbitration process and that the employees were entitled to relief from both the union and the employer.[42]

Other Kinds of Arbitration

Arbitration is most often used during contract administration. That is, once the labor contract has been successfully negotiated and put into effect, arbitration is used to resolve differing interpretations of the agreement that arise during day-to-day operations of the organization. Occasionally, however, arbitration is used to resolve impasses in the negotiation of the contract itself.

Interest arbitration involves submitting to an arbitrator any point the parties cannot agree on in negotiating a contract. For example, under the Experimental Negotiation Agreement between the United Steelworkers and ten steel companies, points of dispute in bargaining are submitted to an arbitrator, and both sides agree not to resort to a strike or lockout.[43] Interest arbitration is mandatory under some state laws, particularly in collective-bargaining situations involving police and firefighters.[44]

In interest arbitration, the arbitrator is no longer in a quasi-judicial role. His or her role is now legislative, meaning that the arbitrator is "expected to fashion a wage and benefit package for the parties based on his [or her] judgment of what is fair, reasonable and appropriate."[45] This procedure has been argued against because of this dilemma: if the arbitrator is wise, skillful, and imaginative in making decisions, the parties will tend to rely too heavily on arbitration, thus undermining the system of free collective bargaining. On the other hand, if the arbitrator is unwise, blundering, and unimaginative, the parties will try to avoid "the scourge of compulsory arbitration."[46] In either case, the legislative role can be an extremely uncomfortable one for the arbitrator.

Final-offer arbitration, sometimes called "last-offer ballot" or "forced-choice arbitration," may also be used to resolve bargaining impasses. Under this procedure, each party submits a package of contract provisions to an arbitrator, who must make a choice. The usual procedure is for the arbitrator to choose one complete package or the other, but some contracts permit the arbitrator to make choices, item by item.[47] An advantage of final-offer arbitration is that both sides must bargain reasonably to obtain the arbitrator's approval of the package; a disadvantage is that the final award may be very one-sided.

One other type of arbitration procedure should be mentioned. In an effort to minimize the financial costs and time delays associated with grievance arbitration, the American Arbitration Association has initiated an accelerated procedure known as **expedited arbitration.** The rules for this procedure are that the two parties in the dispute do not file prehearing or posthearing briefs, no stenographic record is taken, awards are made within five days of the end of the hearing, and the arbitrator's opinions, when required, are kept very short. Since this alternative approach was introduced in 1972, experience has shown that expedited arbitration can increase the efficiency and cost-effectiveness of the grievance procedure.

IMPLICATIONS FOR THE HUMAN RESOURCES DEPARTMENT

The human resources department plays a major role in protecting employee rights and developing procedures for carrying out organizational due process. The importance of this role continues to grow as laws, practice, and theory pertaining to organizational justice evolve. Human resources specialists, as well as all managers, face a special challenge in determining what is fair and equitable treatment and in following procedures for correcting unfair decisions and remedying injustice. Moreover, the human resources department is in a unique position to influence organizational climate and culture so that management and employees are sensitive to their respective rights and responsibilities. At the same time, the human resources department can monitor organizational policy and management practices to ensure consistency, fairness, and cost-effectiveness in resolving grievances and handling disciplinary problems.

Protecting Employee Rights

As one of its most important responsibilities, the human resources department can play an active role in helping the organization avoid discrimination and unjust practices at the policy level. The department can take the lead in developing strong policy statements against all forms of discrimination and can secure top management support in monitoring and enforcing these policies. Providing information on and training in nondiscriminatory decision making and the legal rights of employees is another way the human resources department can promote organizational justice. Moreover, the human resources staff needs to be knowledgeable about what the organization legally may or may not do should employees attempt to unionize and be prepared to advise supervisors and managers accordingly.

One of the main things the human resources department can do in the area of speech rights and obligations is to help the organization develop multiple avenues for employees to be heard and understood. This may mean providing training programs for supervisors that include sessions on active listening and participative approaches to running meetings. The department may also recommend that small-group discussion sessions be held to allow employees to communicate with members of top management on a regular basis. In addition, a human resources specialist can act as a mediator between an employee and supervisor in cases of misunderstanding or disagreement so that a constructive relationship can be restored and maintained. And because rights imply responsibilities, the human resources staff can play a major role in counseling employees about the limits of free speech in the workplace.

To protect employee privacy, the human resources director is wise to promote the adoption of safeguards to ensure confidentiality of personnel data as recommended by the Federal Privacy

Study Commission. In addition, the human resources staff should protect privacy on a day-to-day basis by ensuring confidentiality of staffing decisions, compensation and benefits administration, grievance resolutions, and so on. Privacy protection by the human resources department "establishes the basic pattern for handling employee privacy within the organization, since managers will likely follow the tone of the 'examples' on this issue set by their personnel administrators."[48]

Avoiding Legal Action

To avoid possible litigation as well as to enhance employees' motivation and commitment, the human resources department should be an advocate of organizational due process. In particular, the department should insist on progressive discipline procedures (see Chapter 8) and thorough review procedures in potential discharge cases.

Company handbooks and personnel policy manuals present a special dilemma for human resources departments. On the one hand, it is reasonable to acknowledge that due process, reasonable job security, and discharge for just cause are basic components of the organization's personnel policy. On the other hand, if handbooks and manuals state or imply that the employee's job is guaranteed in the absence of just and sufficient cause for discharge, dismissed employees may be able to sue the employer on the basis of implied contract violation. Legal action seems particularly likely when employment procedures and policy statements have helped create expectations of job permanence in the mind of the employee and when his or her record of pay increases and promotions suggests a pattern of satisfactory performance. Statements of policy and conditions of employment, then, must be carefully worded and qualified so that management is not unnecessarily restricted in the dismissal actions it can take. A team of lawyers makes the following suggestions:

> Although many employers may not yet have adopted detailed "just cause" disciplinary procedures in their employee manuals, thereby avoiding difficulties confronted by employers who fail to follow their own procedures, it is a good idea in any event to state in writing the fact that discharge is solely at the employer's discretion. If grounds for dismissal are stated in a manual, the employer should also state that the list is not exhaustive and is subject to unilateral change. In addition, an employer may want to state that progressive disciplinary measures or grievance steps may be dispensed with at the employer's discretion, depending upon the nature of the discharge.[49]

A survey of 222 firms of all types found that 78 percent had taken specific measures to avoid legal problems in the event of employee dismissals. Of those that had taken measures, more than six out of ten changed or removed wording in company manuals or handbooks to avoid any suggestion of an employment contract. About half of these firms added wording to handbooks and application forms specifying that employment could be terminated for any reason. An example is the following statement found in the employee handbook of a small manufacturing company: "Neither this handbook nor any other communication by employer representatives, written or oral, is intended in any way to create an employment contract binding on either party."[50] Typically, the human resources department plays a major role in the development of such statements, which attempt to keep the organization out of legal entanglements but at the same time try to enhance the motivation and commitment of the work force.

Handling Grievances

Normally, the human resources department is heavily involved in the handling of complaints through formal grievance procedures. Ordinarily, that department (or the industrial relations section) will be consulted at various steps of the grievance procedure. (Figure 19.4 is an example of a check list the human resources department might use or hand out to supervisors to ensure the constructive handling of grievances.) Depending on the particular organization, top operating officials or the human resources director, or both, will decide the organization's position on whether a case will go to arbitration. Usually, the human resources department is at least consulted in this decision.

When a case goes to arbitration, the immediate supervisor involved in the case and other members of management are likely to participate in planning the arbitration presentation, and they may be used as witnesses. The human resources or personnel director, however, is likely to be the chief strategist for the organization unless it is represented by an attorney.

SUMMARY

Employees in the United States have a significant number of rights based on law, court decisions, and administrative rulings. Among these rights are prohibitions against discrimination based on race, color, religion, national origin, sex, age, or handicapped status. Sexual harassment is now illegal under federal law.

FIGURE 19.4 Check list for constructive grievance handling

	Yes	No
I. Background Preparation		

A. Do you have a current copy of the labor contract? ___ ___
B. Have you carefully read the contract? ___ ___
C. Have you attended supervisory training sessions on contract administration? ___ ___
D. Have you clarified ambiguous clauses with upper management? ___ ___
E. Do you know the steps in the grievance procedure and your responsibilities under each step? ___ ___
F. Are you aware of the interpersonal relations in your area and sensitive to potential grievance issues? ___ ___
G. Are you familiar with job responsibilities and job descriptions in your area? ___ ___
H. Have you reviewed past grievance decisions and all relevant company policies? ___ ___
I. Do you know the union representative in your area? ___ ___

II. Initial Interaction with Employees

A. Do you take time to deal with an employee's problem immediately or within a reasonable time? ___ ___
B. Are you an active listener? ___ ___
C. Do you let employees express their points of view without interrupting? ___ ___
D. Do you remain objective during the dialogue with an employee? ___ ___
E. Are you sensitive to the needs of employees as well as the strict rules of the organization? ___ ___
F. Do you deal with employees as individuals? ___ ___
G. Do you initiate immediate action relative to the issue? ___ ___
H. Do you follow through with your decision? ___ ___

III. First Step in Grievance Procedure (Investigation)

A. Do you take complete and accurate notes during discussions with the employee? ___ ___
B. Do you ask questions and seek clarification on certain issues to improve your understanding of the issues? ___ ___
C. Do you remain objective and not give the appearance of having prejudged the outcome? ___ ___
D. Have you attempted to determine the causes of the grievance as well as the grievance itself? ___ ___
E. Are specific answers given to questions involving the who, what, where, when, and why of the grievance? ___ ___

(Evaluation)

A. Have you discussed the issue with other supervisors or members of upper management? ___ ___
B. If the problem involves a major issue, have you consulted with the industrial relations department or appropriate legal counsel? ___ ___
C. Are you aware of the intent of the contract as well as the literal interpretation? ___ ___
D. Is the incident a clear violation of contract, law, or precedent? ___ ___
E. Have you analyzed the grievance with respect to its effect on subsequent management decisions and its effect on the employee? ___ ___

(Implementation)

A. Are you sensitive in communicating decisions to employees? ___ ___
B. Do you use the grievance procedure as an opportunity to improve your own effectiveness as a supervisor? ___ ___
C. Do you explain the reasoning behind your decisions and encourage employees to discuss issues with you? ___ ___
D. Do you follow through with your decisions and attempt to prevent subsequent grievances? ___ ___
E. Do you create an environment of active communications? ___ ___

The above items are designed to direct the supervisor in constructive grievance handling. If you answer no to any of the questions, you may be losing the opportunity to improve your effectiveness in handling employee grievances.

Source: Reprinted by permission from *Supervisory Management: Tools and Techniques,* edited by M. Gene Newport; copyright © 1976 by West Publishing Company. All rights reserved.

Nonsupervisory workers have the right to organize and bargain collectively. This right is reinforced by contract rights stemming from labor-management agreements. Individual employees can also enter into contracts with the employer in nonunionized situations.

Employees do not have complete freedom in what they can say about their supervisors and the employing organization. In a number of states, however, public employees appear to have the right to "blow the whistle" on illegal, immoral, or irresponsible acts.

Employees are thus far not protected legally from invasions of privacy stemming from misuse of personnel records. A federal commission, however, has urged business firms to adopt safeguards voluntarily.

The "employment-at-will" doctrine is gradually being modified by courts. Some court decisions indicate that employers must deal fairly and in good faith with an employee in the case of a dismissal.

Organizations vary in the degree to which organizational due process is followed for complaints or grievances. Informal processes, such as effective listening and problem solving by supervisors, often solve many problems. Aggrieved employees also have access to government agencies and the courts, although courts have traditionally avoided getting involved in alleged injustices unless laws have been violated.

Almost all labor contracts provide for grievance-arbitration procedures. The typical procedure involves joint union-management deliberation of the problem, starting at the supervisory level and then moving to successively higher managerial levels.

Discipline and discharge cases are the most likely to be heard by an arbitrator. Labor contracts typically call for a single ad hoc arbitrator who is selected jointly by the union and management.

The arbitrator's role is quasi-judicial. Arbitration hearings are more informal than courtroom proceedings and are not bound by the rules of evidence, nor is the arbitrator bound by precedent.

The human resources department plays a major role in ensuring that employees at all levels are heard and understood and that they are treated equitably. That department should ensure that there are adequate safeguards against misuse of the information in personnel records, that progressive discipline procedures are followed, and that any potential discharge cases are reviewed thoroughly. The human resources department usually also is involved in monitoring grievance procedures, advising supervisors and managers at the various stages of grievance hearings, setting strategy, and making the decision about whether a case will go to arbitration.

KEY TERMS

due process	organizational due process	ad hoc arbitration
sexual harassment	open-door policy	quasi-judicial
contract rights	arbitration	submission agreement
just cause	disciplinary review board	interest arbitration
employment-at-will rule	ombudsman	final-offer arbitration
implied contract	grievance arbitration	expedited arbitration

REVIEW QUESTIONS

1. List some employee rights protected by law.
2. Discuss the extent to which employees in private enterprise have the right of free speech.
3. Outline the employer's legal obligations in relation to sexual harassment.
4. What is the employment-at-will doctrine? Cite instances in which the doctrine is invalid.
5. Define organizational due process and describe formal and informal procedures for carrying out justice in the nonunion organization.
6. Describe the grievance-arbitration process and the role of the arbitrator.
7. What is the role of the human resources department in protecting employee rights?

OPENING CASE QUESTIONS

Case 19.1 The Open Door Policy

1. Discuss work situations you have encountered that are similar to Al's. In what ways could your experience have been improved?
2. If you worked with Al, how would you feel about taking on an increased workload so Al could attend his class?

Case 19.2 The Engine That Couldn't

1. What should Dan have done regarding Art's past behavior?
2. How could Dan have handled the situation with Art regarding the upset customer?
3. If you were Art, what would be your reasons for filing the grievance?

CASE 19.3 QUOTAS MAY STAY, DESPITE THE JUSTICE DEPARTMENT

Many people thought the Reagan administration in general, and the Justice Department's civil rights chief, William Bradford Reynolds, in particular, would bring an end to affirmative action and other programs aimed at giving women and minorities equal rights in the workplace and business world. But when, in early 1985, Reynolds asked cities and states to abandon the quotas and goals that the Justice Department had previously supported, many ignored him.

An aide to Denver's mayor Federico Pena expressed a widespread reaction to the Reagan administration's move to dismantle quota plans: "We're not dismantling anything—we're forging ahead." Many cities—and businesses— have come to accept affirmative action goals and to appreciate the benefits of hiring more women and non-whites. Eleanor Holmes Norton, former chief of the federal Equal Employment Opportunity Commission, warned that morale problems would occur if companies began to adopt the Reagan view. The National Association of Manufacturers endorsed affirmative action in a May, 1985 vote; a personnel director at Ford said, "Businesses decided that affirmative action is the right thing to do"; and, in an ironic reversal, the city of Indianapolis is fighting the government in court in order to keep its affirmative-action quotas.

Of course, the battle is far from over. The number of race and sex bias complaints rises every year, and the Reagan administration's support of reverse-bias cases has already led to changes in hiring and firing rules. The Justice Department's new attitude seems to separate those people and businesses who really believed in affirmative action from those who merely went along with hiring rules out of fear. Many of the latter are now slipping back into their old practices.

One area in which women, especially, still find themselves frustrated is business lending. Under the ten-year-old Equal Credit Opportunity Act, banks aren't allowed to ask women applying for personal loans if they're married. Yet they can ask that question of women applying for business loans; and they often do, sometimes requiring women to get their husband's signature on a loan agreement. Time after time, businesswomen complain, banks turn down female borrowers because their husbands' credit is shaky, or because they aren't married and the banks worry that they will go out of business if they do marry. Such marital-status bias is being fought in courts around the country, and many businesswomen see it as just another form of sex discrim-

Case Sources: "Battle Heats Up Over Sex, Race Bias in Jobs," *U.S. News & World Report*, May 27, 1985, p. 49; Daniel B. Moskowitz, "Battling Another Bias in Business Lending," *Business Week*, May 27, 1985, p. 68; Ted Gest, "Why Drive on Job Bias Is Still Going Strong," *U.S. News & World Report*, June 17, 1985, p. 67.

or single, it's used against you." Those on both sides of the civil rights debate saw 1985 as a mixed year.

Discussion Questions

1. To what extent would human resources management activities influence an organization's decision to continue to vigorously pursue affirmative action?
2. When does affirmative action become reverse bias? What factors should be considered?

20

Health and Safety Management

MANAGING HEALTH AND SAFETY PROGRAMS
Elements of Sound Safety and Health Programs /
Top Management Commitment / Role of
Supervisors / Specialists / Role of the Human
Resources Department

LEARNING OBJECTIVES

· **Give several reasons why organizations are actively involved in health and safety management.**
· **Explain the major provisions of the Occupational Safety and Health Act (OSHA) and describe the impact this law has had.**
· **Describe some common accident-prevention methods.**
· **List some physical and environmental hazards commonly associated with occupational disease.**
· **Describe the purpose of an employee-assistance program.**
· **Characterize an effectively managed health and safety program.**

CASE 20.1   IN THE AFTERMATH OF BHOPAL

Jack Pyron, safety director for High Quality Chemicals, Inc., walked into his boss's office with a copy of the morning's *Wall Street Journal.* His boss, Maurice Kreifels, was vice president for human resources.

"Maury, did you see the new article on the Bhopal disaster in this morning's *Journal?*" Jack inquired. "Nope. Haven't had time yet," Maurice replied. "What's up?"

"Well, nothing new, except the figures are even worse. It says that the gas leak at the Union Carbide plant in India killed about 1,700 people and injured another 200,000 more.[1] Obviously, it's a tragedy of monumental proportions, and industry all over the world has got to learn from this." Jack went on: "What worries me is that the federal government is going to be all over us like a tent and nitpick us to death about safety standards. The feds and the public are going to forget that we've had several stretches of three or four years without a single day lost as a result of job-related illness or injuries, and that it's safer working here than staying at home."

"Yep, I know," Maurice responded. "The whole industry is going to be suspect for a while. But we know we've been a leader in health and safety standards, and we have a super record. We'll just have to keep reminding our employees and the public of our record and keep plugging away to make it even better. What are our employees thinking and saying these days?"

Jack thought for a moment. "Well, basically they're saying it couldn't happen here. They're saying that everybody — top management, the union, supervisors, employees — is committed to safety. I think everybody is proud of our record. Somehow, I think that people are more shocked, embarrassed, and angry that a company in the industry let them down. They've always suspected that there are fly-by-night outfits out there contaminating their employees and the environment, but when a big, well-known company does it — well, that's a different matter."

"Interesting, interesting," Maurice replied. "I'm sure you've already thought of this, but now would be a good time to ask the safety and health committees to take a fresh look at how we're doing things. There's always the danger of getting complacent. I see some opportunities for increasing the safety program budget, too. You've been hammering at me for that new monitoring equipment, and I'll just bet the finance committee will go for it now."

"Good," said Jack. "and you're right — this would be a good time to get people discussing the Bhopal disaster's implications for us."

CASE 20.2   JUST WHO AM I PROTECTING?

Jill Meyer, head of the data processing department, was troubled. One of her long-term employees, Jerry Hawkins, had come to work late, and he appeared to be slightly tipsy. His speech was a little slurred, and he was bubbling over with friendliness. Ordinarily Jill didn't have close contact with Jerry, because Jerry reported to one of the supervisors, Bob Scott. But today Jill had been in Bob's area when Jerry arrived, and both had seen Jerry's condition.

Jill went back to her office and within a minute Bob joined her. Bob was obviously upset. "We've got to do something about Jerry," Bob blurted out. "We've talked about him before — he's come in half drunk or hung over from time to time for years — but now it's happening more frequently. I've confronted Jerry several times and he always denies he's had anything to drink, or he claims he's been to a wedding breakfast, or something. Trouble is, he's such a nice guy and does such a good job when he's sober that it's hard to confront him. I'm not sleeping well at night these days, worrying about what to do."

"You're absolutely right," Jill responded. "We've got to do something. What do the other members of your group say about it?"

Bob's reply was immediate. "They're demoralized. They're tired of covering for Jerry and tired of correcting his mistakes. I think one of my best people is going to quit if we don't take action. The trouble is, I'm not sure what to do."

"Have you documented any of this — his condition, his mistakes, or any other ways his performance is affected?" Jill asked.

"Unfortunately, no," Bob replied.

"Here's a suggestion, then," said Jill. "Go right back to your unit and give Jerry some short work assignment that ordinarily he could do accurately — like making some computer entries and doing a printout — and see what you get. I think you're going to find that he makes a lot of mistakes. If so, sit down with him in the conference room, confront him with the data, and give him an ultimatum. And let's put it in writing."

"I'll do it," said Bob. "But I may want to come back and check signals with you before I have my session with him. We need to decide whether our ultimatum means a warning, a layoff, or a discharge."

"Yes, we should," Jill replied. "I'll call up the personnel department to see what advice they have for us. I should have faced up to this a long time ago."

Before Jill placed her call, she sat thinking for a minute. "Wow," she thought, "I wonder if Bob and I have been protecting Jerry because he's such a nice guy and usually such a good worker, or whether we've been protecting ourselves from the pain of facing up to something very unpleasant. When I hear Bob say he can't sleep at night and that his people are demoralized, it's easy to see that protecting one person is making life miserable for a bunch of other folks."

Jill picked up the telephone and dialed Personnel.

Case 20.1 is a reminder of how vital it is that organizations have effective health and safety practices, not only for the welfare of employees but also because of consequences to families and the broader community. High Quality Chemicals has a long and successful record in health and safety, and clearly top management wants to keep it that way. But the case also shows that the historical evolution of excellent practices in one organization may not necessarily be duplicated in another plant, or in a different industry, or in a different country. Unsafe practices and the potential for death, disease, and disability are still with us. Clearly, those American organizations with the best safety records should not become complacent, and those with substandard records must improve. And it may be that developing countries have a lot of catching up to do. This also suggests that government may play an important role in effective health and safety management. Government may undercontrol and thus allow serious conditions to exist. Or, as illustrated by Jack Pyron's concern, government can overcontrol and get in the way of the effective management of the health and safety program of a plant.

Case 20.2 is about alcohol abuse and the difficult problems it creates for the person, fellow workers, and management. A serious and costly problem, substance abuse is often met with a kind of conspiracy of silence, but it must be confronted for the good of the person and the organization. In this case, the department head, Jill Meyer, has begun to realize that protecting one person from a confrontation may be doing great harm to others and to the organization.

This chapter is about the important matter of health and safety in the workplace. It discusses why managers and employees alike must be concerned about this issue and describes federal regulations pertaining to health and safety, variables related to accidents, and problems associated with the prevention of occupational disease. Also discussed are alcohol and drug abuse, excessive stress, and emotional illness — all health problems that can be very costly to organizations and to the individuals involved as well as to families and communities. The chapter ends with some principles about how to manage health and safety programs.

THE CONCERN FOR EMPLOYEE SAFETY AND HEALTH

Ensuring the physical well-being of employees in the workplace is the primary goal of the health and safety management process. In recent years, the human resources department has taken on greater and greater responsibility in this area, but in fact, organizations began shouldering some of this responsibility even before the modern personnel department came into existence. Once the Supreme Court upheld the constitutionality of state workers' compensation laws in 1911, safety specialists were commonly employed in industrial firms. Naturally these organizations wanted to hold down the costs of insurance and reduce the number of claims filed by their employees, so they depended on safety specialists to help establish and maintain safer working conditions in their plants.

Today, health and safety management is a complex activity requiring the expertise of specialists from many disciplines, such as industrial hygiene, occupational medicine, ecology, psychology, and safety engineering, to name only a few. Moreover, concerns in health and safety management now reach beyond physical conditions in the workplace to embrace a regard for workers' mental and emotional well-being and a commitment to protecting the surrounding community from pollution and exposure to toxic substances.

Involvement in health and safety management represents an organization's response to a number of compelling influences, the most basic of which is a sense of social and humanitarian responsibility. Government intervention, pressure from labor unions, and the general public consciousness account for much of the progress

---

PERSPECTIVE 20.1   State Helps Businesses to Curb Smoking

[Associated Press]

State health officials, who have banned smoking in their own offices and conference rooms, say they plan to continue efforts to help Massachusetts private businesses create a smoke-free environment for employees.

"We get calls every day from companies that want advice on how to go about doing this," Petra Langer, a spokeswoman for the state Department of Public Health, said after her agency cosponsored a forum on smoking in the workplace. "More and more employees are concerned about exposure to other people's tobacco smoke and the possible health effects of that — especially at the workplace where people spend so many hours of their life."

More than 200 company chief executive officers and personnel directors last week attended the Natick forum, cosponsored by the American Cancer Society and health and industry groups. State officials plan to survey the participants again in six months.

Source: "State Helps Businesses to Curb Smoking," *The Boston Globe,* Monday, April 1, 1985, p. 18. Associated Press article.

At the conference, Robert Shillman, president of Cognex Corp., a Needham computer firm of 100 employees, said he hires only nonsmokers. Flexcon, a laminating firm in Spencer, last April started a certificate program in which workers receive bonuses up to $30 for not smoking at work. Flexcon's JoAnne Quinn said more than 40 percent of the workforce has quit,

All cigarette machines in New England Life Insurance Co.'s Boston building were removed 10 years ago; smoking is restricted to certain rooms, and group health insurance premium discounts are under consideration for nonsmokers, a spokesman said.

A recent American Cancer Society survey of 2200 Masachusetts companies with 100 or more employees in January showed 205 had no written policy on smoking. Eighty-eight have measures ranging from posted smoking areas to requirements that employees punch off the clock when they want to smoke.

About two-thirds of Massachusetts adults don't smoke and are getting more vocal against inhaling second-hand smoke, Langer said.

---

in this area. Finally, experience and knowledge of issues in worker protection have led to a greater appreciation of how health and safety management is directly related to organizational effectiveness. To protect the well-being of employees is to protect the organization's most valuable resource and to avoid the staggering costs and negative public image associated with safety neglect.

Social and Humanitarian Responsibility

A sense of social responsibility grows out of the recognition that organizations do more than make profits. Organizational activities affect workers as people and society as a whole, and these effects should be considered in the planning and management of all day-to-day operations. The establishment of safe, healthful, and environmentally sound working conditions is a priority in any socially responsible organization.

Health and safety practices in a number of firms go far beyond the standards required by law, which suggests that many organizations do consider health and safety management a prime social responsibility (see Figure 20.1). Exceptional safety records stand

FIGURE 20.1
Safety procedures established and followed by the Phillips Petroleum Company

INTRODUCTION: SAFETY PROGRAM OPERATING INSTRUCTIONS

SECTION I: ADMINISTRATION

SAFETY/TRAINING PROGRAMS

Rig Orientation and Indoctrination Program
Rig Safety Training Video Tape Programs
Safety and Training Bulletins
Safety Training Requirements
Rig Incentive Bonus Program - Safety
Crew Safety Award Card Program
Annual Safety Award Program

RIG SAFETY MEETINGS, INSPECTIONS, DRILLS/PERMITS

Work Group Safety Meetings/Inspection/Drills
General Crew Safety Meetings/Drills
Zone Inspection
Rig Safety Audit
Safety Program Audit
Work Permits

SECTION II: CRITICAL SAFETY OPERATING PROCEDURES

Person-In-Charge and Emergency Response Procedures
Drills and Emergency Signals - Safety Meeting Topic
Man Overboard - Safety Meeting Topic
Man Overboard - Emergency Procedures and Drill
Personal Injury - Safety Meeting Topic
Personal Injury - Emergency Procedures and Drill
Fire - Safety Meeting Topic
Fire - Emergency Procedures and Drill

Source: Courtesy Phillips Petroleum Company

as proof of this commitment. For example, between March 1974 and April 1980, Du Pont's Chattanooga plant accumulated 48 million continuous working hours in which not a single employee was absent from work because of occupational illness or injury.[2]

The extent to which an organization demonstrates social responsibility is part of the firm's public image, and a positive safety record can contribute to positive public relations. But genuine humanitarian concerns are reflected in a commitment to employee health and safety as well. These concerns are expressed in the feelings people have for each other when an illness or accident causes serious injury or death, and in the sense of purpose displayed by those responsible for safety and health programs. Certainly the effects of a job-related illness or injury go far beyond the economic loss to the organization and extend to long-term consequences to workers and their families.

Influence of Labor Unions

Historically, labor unions have generally been active in matters of health and safety and have pressed management to improve working conditions. An example of current union concern is expressed in the increasing number of industrial hygienists employed by labor unions to monitor the working conditions of their members, particularly in the chemical, rubber, oil, auto, and primary-metals industries. This development is due to pressure from rank-and-file members, as well as from union leadership, and is aimed at identifying health hazards and securing corrective action.

Unions also tend to bargain strenuously for health and safety provisions in labor contracts. For example, a recent study of labor-management agreements found that 87 percent of the contracts in manufacturing firms contain safety and health clauses. Safety equipment was mentioned in 100 percent of the contracts in the mining and rubber industries.[3]

Moreover, unions are increasingly requesting membership on plant safety and health committees and asking that workers be paid by the company for time devoted to meetings. Provisions for joint management-union committees are found in 45 percent of labor contracts; pay for time spent on committee activities is specified in about one-third of the clauses providing for joint committees.[4] In addition, many unions are asking for company contributions of several cents per hour for safety and health research and for compensation for time spent accompanying government occupational safety and health officers on plant-site inspections. In support of these efforts, the AFL-CIO established a Department of Occupational Safety and Health to work with industry in identifying problem areas and reducing industrial accidents and personal injuries.[5]

Costs

The costs to an organization of accidents, injuries, and occupational diseases are both tangible and intangible. The tangible costs are the measurable financial expenses. The intangible costs include lowered employee morale, less favorable public relations, and weakened ability to recruit and retain employees.

Frequently, organizations ignore or are not aware of the tangible but "hidden" costs of occupational illness or injury. The following list gives some idea of the costs associated with a single accident in the workplace:

- The cost of wages paid to workers who are attracted to the accident site and therefore not working.
- Equipment or work in process that is interrupted, spoiled, or damaged. Interruptions in the work of the injured person as well as the work of those who came to the scene lead to slowdowns at later production stations.
- The repair of damaged equipment or work in process.
- Cleanup costs.
- Payments to the injured employee in excess of workers' compensation.
- Dispensary services provided by the plant nurse, company infirmary, and so on.
- The diminished productivity of the injured person after his or her return to the job but before full work output can be sustained.
- Cost of supervisory time (incurred because accidents must be investigated, and reports must be made and processed).
- Extra overtime costs occasioned by the initial interruption of work.
- Costs associated with the recruitment, selection or transfer, and training of a replacement for the recuperating worker.
- Costs associated with the higher scrap, spoilage, or generally lower efficiency of the replacement.
- Legal costs for advice with respect to any potential claim.
- Costs of rental equipment placed temporarily in service while unsafe equipment is repaired or replaced.[6]

The National Safety Council estimated that in 1982 80 million days were lost as a result of new and previous accidents in the workplace in the United States. The council also estimated that another 110 million days would be lost in future years because of the accidents that occurred in that year. The costs were estimated at $31.4 billion.[7]

Public Awareness

Extensive media attention, widespread concern about environmental pollution, pressure from advocacy groups, rising levels of education, and the availability of information have heightened public awareness of health and safety issues in the workplace. For example, the media have reported that Ralph Nader's Health Research Group found through a review of recently released government documents that some 250,000 employees run higher-than-normal risks of developing various diseases, including cancer, from exposure to toxic substances at work. The group reported that some 59,000 foundry workers risk cancer and respiratory diseases because of exposure to such substances as metal fumes and coal tar. Some 50,000 miners exposed to silica and uranium dust have increased risks of silicosis and lung and respiratory cancer.[8] As another example, the government has reported that among certain asbestos-factory workers, cancer death rates of 40 to 45 percent have occurred, and lung abnormalities have been found in 38 percent of some asbestos workers' family members.[9]

Such reports tend to heighten public awareness. In turn, public awareness tends to result in pressure on organizations to develop more effective health and safety programs. Public pressure has also prompted some organizations to provide more health and safety information to employees and to the public. After the disaster at the Union Carbide plant in Bhopal, India, for example, Monsanto announced it would immediately start publicizing information about the toxic products the company makes within the communities where these products are made. In announcing this policy, Richard Mahoney, Monsanto's CEO, said, "People are tremendously more interested than they were before [Bhopal], and to tell them, 'We're doing everything, don't worry' just isn't enough. I'd like to explain what we do and what our safeguards are. I think they're entitled to know."[10]

Legal Obligations

Organizations have extensive legal obligations with regard to health and safety. One major obligation is paying workers' compensation insurance premiums under state workers' compensation laws. This

Courtesy GE Plastics Group

Safety glasses, hard hats, and other protective equipment have become requirements for production workers in many industries.

insurance provides benefits to workers who suffer occupational injuries regardless of fault. In many states organizations have an incentive to improve safety conditions, since their insurance premiums are affected by the number of claims made by their employees.

For many years, workers' compensation benefits were paid only in cases in which a worker suffered physical impairment as a result of a work accident. In recent years, however, state laws and court decisions have increasingly brought emotional and physical impairment due to job stress within the arena of compensable claims. For example, the California labor code allows compensation for injuries caused by "repetitive mentally or physically traumatic activities extending over a period of time, the combined effect of which causes any disability or need for medical treatment."[11] Thus, employers' legal liability is being extended into the emotional and mental health area.

Various labor laws also refer to worker health and safety. For example, the Walsh-Healey Act states that no part of a government contract shall be performed "under working conditions which are unsanitary or hazardous or dangerous to the health of employees engaged in the performance of said contract. Compliance with the safety, sanitary, and factory inspection laws of the State in which the work or part thereof is to be performed shall be prima-facie evidence of compliance with this subsection."[12] The Federal Mine Safety and Health Act of 1977 (previously called the Coal Mine Health and Safety Act) goes into considerable detail about such matters as dust concentration, ventilation, roof supports, the use of explosives, emergency procedures, and inspections.[13]

In addition, various laws provide for civil and/or criminal penalties for violations. For example, under the Federal Mine Safety and Health Act, a mine operator can be fined $25,000 or imprisoned for a year, or both, for a willful violation of a health or safety standard.[14] In 1984, prosecutors of the state of Illinois obtained a grand jury indictment charging five top officers of a company with the murder of an employee, Stefan Golab, who died from cyanide poisoning. Golab was employed by Film Recovery Systems, a company that specialized in extracting silver from used film. The prosecutors alleged that the company officials were fully aware of the dangers of cyanide and failed to ensure the protection of workers by providing the proper equipment. In June of 1985, a Cook County judge found three of the corporate officials guilty of murder in Golab's death — the former president, plant manager, and plant foreman of the now defunct company. Such prosecution is part of a growing trend of criminal prosecutions for workplace safety violations.[15]

Probably the most far-reaching legal obligations of employers in health and safety matters have been established by the Occupational Safety and Health Act. This important law and its implications for human resources management are described in the next section.

THE OCCUPATIONAL SAFETY AND HEALTH ACT

In 1969, in the aftermath of a tragic explosion that claimed the lives of seventy-eight coal miners and amid reports of a high incidence of black-lung disease among miners, Congress passed the Coal Mine Health and Safety Act. The following year, continuing public and government concern about health and safety in the workplace was reflected in passage of the Occupational Safety and Health Act (OSHA). The law's purpose was to establish and enforce health and safety standards to reduce the incidence of occupational injury, illness, and death.

The act covers nearly all employees; exempted are miners, who are covered by the Federal Mine Safety and Health Act, and government agencies that are covered by other laws. (If, however, those agencies do not regulate health and safety in specific areas, OSHA standards apply.) Gradually, OSHA standards are superseding those established under various laws such as the Walsh-Healey Act and the Construction Safety Act.[16]

Administration

Administration of OSHA is through the Occupational Safety and Health Administration in the U.S. Department of Labor (DOL), an agency that establishes and enforces occupational safety and health standards through inspections, citations, and fines; it also provides consultation services. State OSHA programs (State Occupational Safety and Health Administration programs) are found in those states that have assumed responsibility for administration of the act. Under special plans negotiated with the DOL, states agree to establish programs of inspection, citation, and training that meet or exceed the minimum standards enforced on the federal level.[17]

Rights of Employees and Employers

Both employees and employers have certain rights under the act. The rights provided to the employee or the employee's representative include the following:

- Any employee or employee representative who believes a violation of a safety or a health standard exists that threatens physical harm may, in writing, request the Department of Labor to make an inspection. (The complainant may remain anonymous, and an employee may not be discriminated against or discharged for filing a complaint.)
- In the unionized setting, an employee representative has the right to accompany the OSHA representative on his or her inspection. (This has been called the **walk-around right.**)
- If the employer is given an abatement period and/or fine and then protests the decision, the employee may participate in the subsequent hearing.
- The employee is entitled to his or her exposure record in the case of toxic materials or other harmful agents, may observe any monitoring or measuring of hazardous materials, and has the right to see these records.
- The employee's authorized representative may ask the government to determine whether substances in the work environment have potentially toxic effects and to set standards for safe exposure levels.

- The employee is entitled to be paid for any time spent on OSHA inspection activities.[18]

Employers also have certain rights, which include:

- Requesting and receiving proper identification from OSHA representatives.
- Being advised of the reasons for the inspection.
- Participating in the walk-around inspection and in the opening and closing conferences with the OSHA representative.
- Contesting a citation.
- Applying for a temporary or permanent variance of a standard.[19]

Inspections

OSHA inspections are conducted by **compliance officers.** These inspectors are men and women from the safety and health field who have attended at least four weeks of specialized training at OSHA's Training Institute near Chicago. They also take additional specialized training once each year in areas such as industrial hygiene, construction, or maritime safety and health.[20]

OSHA's blanket authority to enter and inspect a workplace was tempered by a Supreme Court decision in 1978. In the case of *Marshall, Secretary of Labor, et al.* v. *Barlow's Inc.,* the Court ruled that an employer could require OSHA to obtain a search warrant before entering for inspection.[21]

The inspection process starts with the compliance officer's presenting his or her credentials and asking to see the appropriate employer representative. If the inspection has resulted from an employee complaint, the compliance officer should give to the employer a copy of the complaint with the complainant's name withheld, as well as copies of any applicable laws and safety and health standards. The inspector may also want to see the organization's safety and health records.[22]

Before a **walk-through inspection,** the compliance officer will want to meet with a representative of the employees if the company is unionized. If it is not, an employee selected by the members of the plant safety committee might be appropriate, or the employees may be asked to select a representative. Both an employee representative and an employer representative typically accompany the compliance officer during the inspection. The compliance officer may also want to interview various employees at his or her discretion about safety and health conditions. The act gives the compliance officer the right to take photographs, make instrument readings, and examine records. Trade secrets observed by the compliance officer are kept confidential, however. Violation of this principle could result in the inspector's being subject to a $1,000 fine and/or one year in jail.[23]

After the inspection, procedures call for the officer to discuss his or her observations with the employer and review possible violations. The employer should indicate the time needed to correct any hazardous conditions noted by the officer. Citations and penalties are not issued at this time, nor can the officer order that an establishment or part of it be closed down immediately. If an imminent danger exists, OSHA administrators can go to the Federal District Court for prompt legal action.[24]

Violations and Citations

If after the walk-through inspection an OSHA standard is found to have been violated, the area director determines what citations and penalties, if any, will be issued, as well as a proposed time period for abatement.[25] If an employer believes the citation is unreasonable or the abatement period is insufficient, he or she may contest it. The act provides an appeal procedure and a review agency, the Occupational Safety and Health Review Commission, which is independent of the Department of Labor.

Civil penalties from $60 to $10,000 may be imposed for each violation. Criminal penalties are levied in the most serious cases. For example, a willful violation that results in the death of an employee can bring a court-imposed fine of up to $10,000, or imprisonment for up to six months, or both. A second conviction can result in these penalties being doubled. Falsifying records can result in a fine of up to $10,000 and six months in jail.[26]

OCCUPATIONAL ACCIDENTS

Accident prevention is a major goal of health and safety management. OSHA requires employers to keep a log of on-the-job accidents, and accident investigation and measurement can supply useful data for developing effective safety programs and improving working conditions. These data can be useful to safety specialists as well as to worker-management safety committees.

Variables Related to Accident Rates

To develop strategies for reducing accidents, it is important to understand the conditions associated with high accident rates. A good deal is known about those conditions. For example, size of organization, work schedules, type of industry and occupation, and worker behavior have been shown to be related to accident rates.

Size of Organization.   Research has shown that the highest accident rates occur in firms with at least fifty but fewer than one hundred employees. In such businesses the operations are large enough so that the owner or manager may not personally appear in the production areas very often and may not have first-hand knowledge of dangerous conditions. Further, such businesses are ordinarily too small to warrant the employment of a full-time and experienced safety officer, and safety management tends to be the responsibility of a manager who has a wide variety of other duties. In contrast, the small-business operator may also be a producing craftsperson who is frequently on the shop floor and keeping an eye on safety conditions.[27]

Work Schedules.   Studies show that accidents occur more frequently on night shifts. This may be because night workers are more likely than day workers to have been active for extended amounts of time before reporting to work, and thus become fatigued more quickly. Moreover, a high proportion of night-shift workers sleep less than day workers and their sleep is of a less restful quality.[28]

Research has also found that workers on rotating shifts have more accidents and generally experience more problems than employees who work on regular schedules. Although the number of sick days taken is not significantly different from the number taken by nonrotated employees, the problems tend to be more serious and chronic.[29] (See the discussion in Chapter 8 on shift work.)

Type of Occupation.   Some occupations are inherently more dangerous than others. Deep-shaft mining and urban law enforcement, for example, all too often provide settings for tragedy. But there are also high risks associated with certain industrial processes and areas like stairways that employees use only infrequently. Falls in such areas are the third most common cause of accidents in industrial settings, even though relatively few workers must stand on ladders or scaffolding.

Table 20.1 shows the relative dangers of different industries in 1982. The "fatality incidence rate" represents the number of fatalities per 100,000 full-time workers. Mining is clearly the most dangerous industry, with the construction industry and agriculture, forestry, and fishing also having very high fatality incidence rates.

TABLE 20.1
Fatality incidence rate by industry, 1982

	FATALITY INCIDENCE RATE 1982
Private Sector (average)	**7.4**
Agriculture, forestry, and fishing	28.4
Mining	44.3
Construction	28.7
Manufacturing	4.5
Transportation and public utilities	21.9
Wholesale and retail trade	3.8
Finance, insurance, and real estate	2.5
Services	3.5

Source: U. S. Department of Labor, *Monthly Labor Review,* 107 (March 1984): 44.

Figure 20.2 shows accident incidence rates for 1982 compiled by the National Safety Council. This reporting shows a more detailed breakdown of industry groups. The left-hand column shows the number of cases involving deaths and lost workdays per 100 full-time employees. The figures in parentheses show the number of cases that were recordable — more serious than first-aid cases, but not necessarily requiring days away from work. The right-hand column shows the number of days away from work per 100 full-time employees. The figures in parentheses show the total lost workdays plus restricted-activity days per 100 employees due to accidents. (The injured worker may be at the work site but performing only limited activity.)[30] A quick inspection of this figure indicates that aircraft, chemical, textile manufacturing, pipeline transportation, and communications are fairly safe industries in the United States. On the other hand, the chances of an accident are much higher in the transit, trucking, ship and boat building, meat products, and lumber and wood products industries. Surprisingly, there is a relatively high incidence of accidents in general government.

Table 20.2 shows the most common types of fatalities across industries with the exception of coal, metal and nonmetal mining, and railroads. (Data were not available for those industries.) Accidents involving over-the-road vehicles accounted for the highest proportion of fatalities in the industries surveyed, with falls accounting for the second highest proportion.

"Accident Proneness" and Worker Behavior. It would be a mistake to attribute very many accidents to "accident proneness" on the part of employees. After a review of the research, Willard Kerr

FIGURE 20.2
**1982 incidence rates
of principal industries**

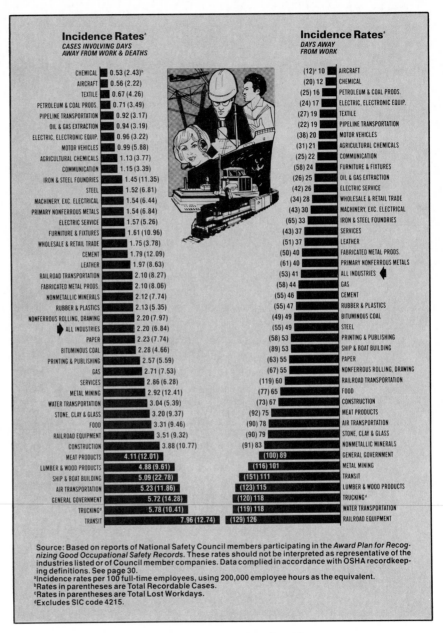

Incidence Rates[a] CASES INVOLVING DAYS AWAY FROM WORK & DEATHS	
CHEMICAL	0.53 (2.43)[b]
AIRCRAFT	0.56 (2.22)
TEXTILE	0.67 (4.26)
PETROLEUM & COAL PRODS.	0.71 (3.49)
PIPELINE TRANSPORTATION	0.92 (3.17)
OIL & GAS EXTRACTION	0.94 (3.19)
ELECTRIC, ELECTRONIC EQUIP.	0.96 (3.22)
MOTOR VEHICLES	0.99 (5.88)
AGRICULTURAL CHEMICALS	1.13 (3.77)
COMMUNICATION	1.15 (3.39)
IRON & STEEL FOUNDRIES	1.45 (11.35)
STEEL	1.52 (6.81)
MACHINERY, EXC. ELECTRICAL	1.54 (6.44)
PRIMARY NONFERROUS METALS	1.54 (6.84)
ELECTRIC SERVICE	1.57 (5.26)
FURNITURE & FIXTURES	1.61 (10.96)
WHOLESALE & RETAIL TRADE	1.75 (3.78)
CEMENT	1.79 (12.09)
LEATHER	1.97 (8.63)
RAILROAD TRANSPORTATION	2.10 (8.27)
FABRICATED METAL PRODS.	2.10 (8.06)
NONMETALLIC MINERALS	2.12 (7.74)
RUBBER & PLASTICS	2.13 (5.35)
NONFERROUS ROLLING, DRAWING	2.20 (7.97)
ALL INDUSTRIES	2.20 (6.84)
PAPER	2.23 (7.74)
BITUMINOUS COAL	2.28 (4.66)
PRINTING & PUBLISHING	2.57 (5.59)
GAS	2.71 (7.53)
SERVICES	2.86 (6.28)
METAL MINING	2.92 (12.41)
WATER TRANSPORTATION	3.04 (5.39)
STONE, CLAY & GLASS	3.20 (9.37)
FOOD	3.31 (9.46)
RAILROAD EQUIPMENT	3.51 (9.32)
CONSTRUCTION	3.88 (10.77)
MEAT PRODUCTS	4.11 (12.01)
LUMBER & WOOD PRODUCTS	4.88 (9.61)
SHIP & BOAT BUILDING	5.09 (22.78)
AIR TRANSPORTATION	5.23 (11.86)
GENERAL GOVERNMENT	5.72 (14.28)
TRUCKING[d]	5.78 (10.41)
TRANSIT	7.96 (12.74)

Incidence Rates[a] DAYS AWAY FROM WORK	
(12)[c] 10	AIRCRAFT
(20) 12	CHEMICAL
(25) 16	PETROLEUM & COAL PRODS.
(24) 17	ELECTRIC, ELECTRONIC EQUIP.
(27) 19	TEXTILE
(22) 19	PIPELINE TRANSPORTATION
(38) 20	MOTOR VEHICLES
(31) 21	AGRICULTURAL CHEMICALS
(25) 22	COMMUNICATION
(58) 24	FURNITURE & FIXTURES
(26) 25	OIL & GAS EXTRACTION
(42) 26	ELECTRIC SERVICE
(34) 28	WHOLESALE & RETAIL TRADE
(43) 30	MACHINERY, EXC. ELECTRICAL
(65) 33	IRON & STEEL FOUNDRIES
(43) 37	SERVICES
(51) 37	LEATHER
(50) 40	FABRICATED METAL PRODS.
(61) 40	PRIMARY NONFERROUS METALS
(53) 41	ALL INDUSTRIES
(58) 44	GAS
(55) 46	CEMENT
(55) 47	RUBBER & PLASTICS
(49) 49	BITUMINOUS COAL
(55) 49	STEEL
(58) 53	PRINTING & PUBLISHING
(89) 53	SHIP & BOAT BUILDING
(63) 55	PAPER
(67) 55	NONFERROUS ROLLING, DRAWING
(119) 60	RAILROAD TRANSPORTATION
(77) 65	FOOD
(73) 67	CONSTRUCTION
(92) 75	MEAT PRODUCTS
(90) 78	AIR TRANSPORTATION
(90) 79	STONE, CLAY & GLASS
(91) 83	NONMETALLIC MINERALS
(100) 89	GENERAL GOVERNMENT
(116) 101	METAL MINING
(151) 111	TRANSIT
(123) 115	LUMBER & WOOD PRODUCTS
(120) 118	TRUCKING[d]
(119) 118	WATER TRANSPORTATION
(129) 126	RAILROAD EQUIPMENT

Source: Based on reports of National Safety Council members participating in the *Award Plan for Recognizing Good Occupational Safety Records.* These rates should not be interpreted as representative of the industries listed or of Council member companies. Data complied in accordance with OSHA recordkeeping definitions. See page 30.
[a]Incidence rates per 100 full-time employees, using 200,000 employee hours as the equivalent.
[b]Rates in parentheses are Total Recordable Cases.
[c]Rates in parentheses are Total Lost Workdays.
[d]Excludes SIC code 4215.

Source: Accident Facts, 1983 (Chicago: National Safety Council), p. 32.

concludes that only 1 to 15 percent of the variance in accident rates could be accounted for by any "accident proneness," leaving 85 percent or more of the variance unaccounted for. Further, he concludes that most of the 15 percent of the potential variance was

TABLE 20.2
Occupational fatalities by cause, 1981–1982 average

	ALL INDUSTRY
Total, all causes	**100[1]**
Over-the-road motor vehicles	27
Falls	12
Heart attacks	10
Industrial vehicles or equipment	10
Nonaccidental injuries	7
Struck by objects other than vehicles or equipment	6
Electrocutions	6
Caught in, under, or between objects other than vehicles or equipment	6
Aircraft crashes	4
Fires	3
Plant machinery operations	3
Explosions	2
Gas inhalations	2
All other	3

[1]*Excludes coal, metal and nonmetal mining, and railroads.*

Source: U.S. Department of Labor, *Monthly Labor Review,* 107 (March 1984): 44.

really due to environmental factors such as temperature, fumes, or space congestion.[31] Norman Maier and Gertrude Verser conclude that "accident proneness as a permanent trait may be relatively rare."[32]

The individual worker does have a good deal of control, however, over his/her own safety. Workers do injure themselves through carelessness, use of improper techniques, unwise decisions in situations with obvious risk, and use of inappropriate tools or inadequately maintained equipment. If records show that a given worker is committing unsafe acts or reporting injuries frequently, the most common approach to the problem is counseling. Increased supervision, transfer to a less hazardous job, and special training are other common approaches.[33]

Accident Prevention

Accident prevention is a complicated matter, requiring control of all the variables described in the previous section. Experience has shown that safety training, protective equipment, and emergency plans are particularly important in accident-prevention efforts.

Safety Training and Communications. In an accident-prevention program, safety training must be an ongoing concern, starting with orientation to the job and continuing over the course of a worker's employment, particularly in the more hazardous industries. In addition, the importance of accident prevention should be reinforced through various communications with employees. Most organizations have ongoing programs to promote safety awareness. Some of the communications methods they use to promote this awareness are posters, meetings, fire drills, articles in employee publications, booklets and handbooks, slogans, safety awards, and guest speakers.[34]

Most organizations provide safety training to both supervisors and employees, and, when provided, this training is usually mandatory. Further, a high proportion of organizations requires that employees pass proficiency tests before they are allowed to use hazardous equipment.[35]

According to a survey by the Bureau of National Affairs, company safety specialists are responsible for safety training in three-fifths of organizations with safety programs, but supervisors are also used in two-fifths of the programs. Outside trainers, community fire department officials, Red Cross representatives, and medical professionals are also used in about two-fifths of the safety programs.[36] Good safety performance is recognized through formal safety award programs in more than a third of the organizations surveyed.

Protective Equipment. Some of the most frequently used personal safety devices are earplugs, hard hats, safety goggles or glasses, safety boots, gloves, face shields, hairnets, safety belts, respiratory equipment, and protective clothing. Devices commonly used to make the job environment safer are machine guards, emergency first-aid equipment, heat and fire detectors, shower facilities, and the marking of exits and aisles. Motivating employees to use safety equipment properly, of course, is more complicated than just providing the equipment. The worker and the group have a great deal of control over the extent to which protective equipment is used properly.

Emergency Plans. Some risks to employee safety, plant security, and community safety are posed by chance occurrences. Geological catastrophes, such as earthquakes and volcanic eruptions, vandalism and arson, equipment failure, and such medical emergencies as heart attacks are unpredictable. The intensity of hurricanes, typhoons, and river flooding may be slightly more predictable. Yet organizations must be prepared to attend to the needs of employees and citizens in the surrounding community if catastrophes occur. The Bhopal disaster in India in 1984 pointed up inadequacies both in plant safety procedures and in the plant's ability to protect the lives and health of the people in the surrounding area. The nuclear plant accident at Three Mile Island in 1979 clearly demonstrated the wisdom of having carefully developed emergency plans and may have pointed up the need for even more reliable equipment and procedures. Managers of chemical plants in tornado-prone areas have long known the importance of disaster plans.

Organizations must be prepared to provide competent first aid at a moment's notice or even to evacuate employees and nearby residents from the site. Such contingency preparation necessitates training, and emergency procedures must also be coordinated with the outside community through the police, firefighters, and hospitals.

OCCUPATIONAL DISEASE

Occupational disease can be defined as a job-induced disturbance of the normal functioning of the body or a person's mental and emotional capacities. Examples of common occupational diseases are silicosis from breathing silica dust, rashes from handling insecticides, impaired hearing from exposure to noisy machines, and lead poisoning from exposure to lead in paint. Excessive and prolonged job stress, which is beginning to be recognized as a serious problem in many contemporary organizations, can also be considered an occupational disease.

Potential lawsuits and criminal charges are reason enough for organizations to be very interested in the prevention of occupational disease. The economics of occupational disease are also of major concern. It has been estimated that American business and industry pays half of the nation's health-care bills, and any reasonable preventive measures organizations can take would seem to make economic sense.[37]

Common Health Hazards

Health hazards on some kinds of jobs have been mentioned throughout this chapter. In general, some of the common causes of occupational illness are exposure to toxic substances and dangerous chemicals, radiation, cigarette smoke, harmful fumes and vapors aggravated by poor ventilation, excessive noise, and inadequate lighting. Although there is no known serious health hazard from video display terminals (VDTs), there can be problems with visual and muscular fatigue.[38]

In some ways, avoiding occupational disease is more difficult for organizations than avoiding accidents. In the first place, occupational diseases are frequently diagnosed only in their advanced stages. Workers may not notice the small, incremental changes in their physical condition that may occur from week to week or even year to year. Second, there is no opportunity to identify with certainty the precise moment the problem began and what the precise circumstances were. A third problem is whether an occupational disease is attributable to repeated exposure and progressive debilitation over time, or whether one exposure produced the disease. Thus the strategy for minimizing health risks may need to be very complex and may be very expensive.

Minimizing Health Risks

When the nature of a health hazard is understood, a hierarchy of approaches, in order of preference, has been suggested:

1. Substitution of materials that are less toxic.
2. Enclosure of the process, with automatic or remote operation as far away as possible.
3. Isolation of the harmful process from the rest of the facility, while also providing special protection for all who must work in that operation.
4. Exhaust ventilation (local).
5. Ventilation (general).
6. Wet methods (to keep dust down).
7. The use of personal protective devices, with special emphasis on personal respiratory protective gear.
8. Decreased daily exposure through shorter work periods or rotating job assignments.
9. Personal hygiene including the use of protective creams.
10. High standards of housekeeping and general maintenance.
11. Warnings and publicity.[39]

Obviously, several approaches might be used at one time.

As more is learned about the connections between industrial environments and medical consequences, employers will undoubtedly be required to shoulder more of the responsibility for both initial and cumulative exposure prevention, as well as for compensation of victims. It is also likely that health and safety departments will need to devote more time and expense to (1) maintaining records of industrial exposures faced by employees, (2) monitoring cumulative exposure effects on a routine basis, and (3) checking the degree to which safety measures are routinely applied.

OTHER HEALTH PROBLEMS AND THEIR MANAGEMENT

Alcohol and drug abuse, prolonged job stress, and emotional illness are enormously costly problems that need to be addressed through programs within organizations as well as through broader community programs. Drug abuse, in particular, appears to be a growing problem. In economic terms alone, drug use in the civilian work force was estimated to have cost employers some $16.4 billion in 1981.[40] Excessive job stress is estimated to cost American business and industry some $75-to-$100 billion each year.[41] Mental health problems have been estimated to cost employers $17 billion annually.[42] These costs are of various kinds, and they include losses stemming from absenteeism, lowered productivity, and treatment expenses. What cost figures do not show, of course, is the mental and emotional anguish these problems cause fellow workers, family members, and others. Obviously, drug, alcohol, and emotional problems off the job carry over into the job setting, and vice versa.

Substance Abuse

Estimates of the percentage of workers abusing alcohol run from 5 to 10 percent.[43] Drug abuse appears to be growing at an alarming rate. One indication of an escalating problem is that industry referrals to federal drug programs doubled between 1977 and 1979.[44] A labor lawyer in Los Angeles reports that his work for employers who have drug problems with their employees has "tripled or quadrupled in the last few years."[45] Any level or section of the organization can be affected. Clearly, alcohol and drug abuse are so extensive as to constitute a potential major health problem for any organization.

Increasingly, alcohol abuse is seen as a disease. Arbitrators, for example, in discharge cases involving alcoholism, tend to disapprove of the imposition of severe penalties unless counseling and treatment have been tried first. On the other hand, arbitrators tend to support discipline in cases involving drugs.[46]

Most major employers offer counseling and treatment for alcohol or drug abuse as part of their employee benefit packages. Most medium-sized and large organizations also work with government and community agencies such as Alcoholics Anonymous, and some are establishing their own employee assistance programs (see Fig-

FIGURE 20.3
Employee assistance program: The supervisor's role

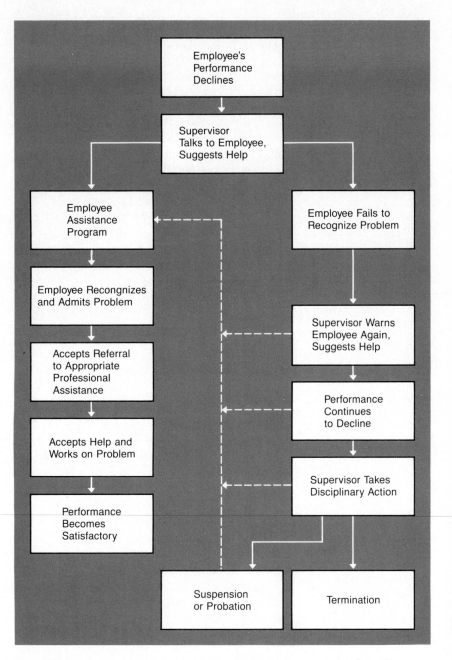

ure 20.3). Often various kinds of family support are part of the total program, because it has been recognized that the affected person's total environment must be supportive if change is to occur. The union and management must also work together to make sure the employee is not ostracized by the work group. It is essential, however, that appropriate performance standards be maintained.

Table 20.3 outlines some suggested steps in dealing with an employee whose performance is below standard and when alcohol or drug abuse is suspected. Notice that there is an emphasis on job performance throughout the process.

Denial is a typical response of the alcoholic or addicted person. But the problem must be confronted before treatment can be effective. According to one expert:

> As job performance is adversely affected, the person is confronted, and offered the program to help with problems that may be causing the performance deterioration. Increasing pressure is applied as performance continues to deteriorate, and the final step

TABLE 20.3
Guidelines for supervisors in approaching the troubled employee

HOW TO APPROACH A TROUBLED EMPLOYEE

1. Establish levels of work performances you expect.
2. Be specific about supportive behavioral criteria, i.e., absenteeism, poor job performance and others.
3. Be consistent.
4. Try not to diagnose the problem.
5. Restrict criticism to job performance.
6. Be firm.
7. Be prepared to cope with the employee's resistance, defensiveness or hostility.
8. Try to get the employee to acknowledge the problem.
9. Show him [or her] he [or she] cannot play you against higher management and/or union.
10. Point out the availability of counseling services.
11. Discuss drinking only if it occurs on the job or the employee is obviously intoxicated.
12. Get a commitment from the employee to meet specific work criteria and monitor this with a plan for improvement based on work performance.
13. Explain that the employee must decide for himself [or herself] whether or not to seek assistance.
14. Emphasize confidentiality of the program.

Source: Christine A. Filipowicz, "The Troubled Employee: Whose Responsibility?" Reprinted from the June 1979 issue of *Personnel Administrator*, copyright, 1979, The American Society for Personnel Administration, 606 North Washington Street, Alexandria, VA 22314.

is "either-or" which is crucial to any program. The alcoholic is given a choice — either to go to the program and cooperate fully with it, or be terminated.

This crisis is the reason for the success of occupational alcoholism programs. It forces the alcoholic, often for the first time, to be open to the program and to treatment. The recovery rates in occupational programs are higher than any other approach.[47]

According to William Mayer, psychiatrist and member of the Alcohol, Drug Abuse and Mental Health Administration, the employee's supervisor "plays an important role in bringing the troubled employee into treatment."[48]

Stress

Concern about stress and how to manage it have recently become major issues in safety and health. Hans Selye, one of the foremost authorities on this subject, defines **stress** as follows:

> . . . by stress the physician means the common results of exposure to any stimulus. For example, the bodily changes produced whether a person is exposed to nervous tension, physical injury, infection, cold, heat, X-rays, or anything else are what we call stress.[49]

The problem is not stress itself but prolonged and unchecked stress. When the body remains in an excited state after a crisis has passed, harmful effects begin to set in.

Studies indicate that prolonged stress is linked to subsequent physical injury, debilitation, and disease, including heart disease. Cardiovascular diseases are responsible for more than half of all deaths in the United States, and heart attacks are the leading cause of death among males over the age of thirty-five. Further, there are links between stress and gastrointestinal diseases, arthritis, and rheumatism, which are major sources of employee disability.[50]

Some of the causes of excessive stress in organizations are unresolved conflict, overdemanding superiors, harassment of various kinds, and intense and prolonged competition. In particular, according to one researcher, excessive stress tends to occur in jobs in which there are heavy psychological demands but the worker has little control over how to get the job done. Examples are machine-paced jobs such as garment stitcher, assembly-line worker, and freight handler. Other examples are service jobs in which the employee has little control over how to relate to the client, such as telephone operator, nurse's aid, and cashier.[51] Air traffic control appears to be another high-stress job, particularly when there is heavy traffic and bad weather. In these circumstances, the controller may be juggling the positions and flight paths of twenty or more aircraft, all of which may be navigating entirely by instruments.[52]

Numerous stress-reduction techniques are available, including individual, group, and organizational approaches. Some of the individual approaches are exercise and physical activity, diet and nutrition, and meditation and relaxation techniques. Support groups of various kinds probably have valuable stress-reduction benefits. Organizational approaches include more openness in communications so that discussion can occur about things that are causing distress, clarification of job duties, restructuring of jobs to provide more autonomy, shifts in organization climate toward more support and the working through of conflict, provision of exercise facilities, and health profiling (through means such as questionnaires and physical examinations).[53] Other approaches include life and career planning and counseling (see Chapter 10).

PERSPECTIVE 20.2 How Business Beats Stress

American business has had to take stress seriously. Stress-related illnesses among executives alone cost it an estimated $20 billion a year. Some 80% goes on replacing executives when they die, and meeting insurance bills; 14% on lost workdays; 3% on hospital treatment and 1% on outpatient costs. Control Data, a computer firm, says spending on employee health in the United States rose from $24.6 billion in 1975 to more than $60 billion in 1981.

Some hapless employers have faced rather different costs. Several employees have successfully sued on the grounds that they have suffered undue stress at work. A policeman in the state of Maine received compensation after complaining that work-related stress had damaged his sex life. An as-sembly-line worker was also awarded compensation after coming down with the "blues."

Many companies (about one in five of the Fortune 500 companies) have responded by establishing stress-management programmes, backed up by general employment assistance programmes which concentrate on health education, advising on risks such as smoking, drinking and eating fatty foods. Several companies, including Tenneco and Control Data, also employ teams of doctors and psychologists to help staff members who cannot cope with the pressures of the job or home-life. Other firms buy in their medical assistance from the burgeoning number of specialised private agencies.

Does any of this help? Canada Life and North American Life, two Canadian insurance companies, put 1,125 employees through an intensive fitness course at the companies' expense. Absenteeism declined by 22% among the participants and productivity also increased. . .

Source: Excerpted from "How Business Beats Stress," *The Economist* (April 13, 1985): 83. Reprinted by permission of the New York Times Syndicate

Employee-Assistance Programs

A random sample of American Society for Personnel Administration members found that 49 percent of sixty-five firms offered in-house counseling when an employee problem involved a personal or family crisis, 46 percent offered counseling when alcoholism was involved, and 34 percent offered counseling in cases of emotional illness. The personnel department was usually responsible for such counseling.[54]

Counseling programs in organizations are sometimes called **employee-assistance programs** or *EAPs*. These programs have been defined as "more or less structured programs that utilize technical, administrative, and professional human services and personnel people, on either a contractual or employment basis, to meet the needs of troubled employees."[55] The counseling conducted usually focuses on such problems as mental health, stress, alcohol and drug use, compulsive gambling, family and marital matters, legal or personal financial difficulties, and job adjustment.[56]

Employee-assistance programs for larger firms are typically offered within the organization. For cost reasons, however, many small and medium-sized firms have formed consortia to offer such services. In a consortium arrangement, EAP services are available to the employees of all the cooperating organizations.[57] Still another alternative is for organizations to refer employees to outside agencies and to pay all or some fraction of the costs.

Most organizations may not be able to afford full-time counselors, clinical psychologists, or psychiatrists, but some can. Certainly a significant proportion of firms could afford the part-time services of such specialists. In any event, it would seem that every enterprise should be prepared to refer seriously troubled employees to outside specialized agencies. In organizations large enough to have a human resources department, members of that department, in particular, should have knowledge about such services and be skilled in making referrals.

Ideally, every supervisor should have skills in effective listening and enough knowledge of nondirective counseling to give "emotional first aid." Such interviewing can not only help the employee's general mental health and reduce stress in the organization; it can also enhance communications between superior and subordinate.

MANAGING HEALTH AND SAFETY PROGRAMS

Managing safety and health is one of the more difficult areas of management. One reason for this difficulty is that influencing the attitudes and behaviors that contribute to accidents is an extremely complex matter. Most harmful events result from failure to apply known principles to control these events. The challenge of safety management is to influence people to apply these principles.[58] Experience seems to show that this challenge can be met most effectively if there is extensive employee participation in establishing safety and health goals and in recommending changes in procedures to minimize risks. Another reason health and safety management is a difficult area is that there is insufficient knowledge about the long-term effects of exposure to materials such as metals, solvents and fuels, pesticides, and a variety of air pollutants.[59]

Elements of Sound Safety and Health Programs

According to the Occupational Safety and Health Administration, an effective accident-prevention program includes the following characteristics:

1. Top management assumes the leadership role.
2. Responsibility for safety and health activities is clearly assigned.
3. Possible accident causes are properly identified and either eliminated or controlled.
4. Appropriate safety and health-related training is instituted.
5. An accident record system is maintained.
6. A medical and first-aid system is ready for possible use.
7. There is continued activity designed to foster an on-the-job awareness and acceptance of safety and health responsibility by every employee.[60]

Top Management Commitment

One of the most important factors influencing safety and health management is commitment from the top. This level of support is necessary so that those directly responsible can effectively carry out their mission. This philosophy is pervasive at Du Pont:

> At Du Pont, safety is a responsibility of line management. Each supervisor is responsible for the safety of his employees, and each employee knows that he is responsible for his own safety and that of his fellow workers. But perhaps the essential element of the company's program is the commitment by top management to employee safety.[61]

Top management commitment is demonstrated through the provision of employee and supervisory training programs, taking safety and health management into account in evaluating the performance of supervisors, the establishment of safety committees, and allocation of sufficient financial resources to the health and safety program. In addition, top management commitment is demonstrated through a strong policy statement about safety and health.[62]

Role of Supervisors

The supervisor plays a central role in health and safety management. In fact, as three experts state it, "Everything that everybody else does is worthless if the supervisor does not do his [or her] job."[63] Four key tasks are seen as making up the supervisor's role in the safety program:

1. *Investigating* all accidents to determine underlying causes
2. *Inspecting* his or her area routinely and regularly to uncover hazards
3. *Coaching* (training) his or her people so they know how to work safely.
4. *Motivating* his or her people so they want to work safely[64]

Specialists

The safety and health department usually consists of a manager and various specialists, inspectors, and technicians. The most common location for this unit is in the human resources or personnel department, with the safety and health manager reporting to its director.

Frequently there are three levels of safety practitioners in large organizations. First is the **safety director** or safety manager, who is responsible for organizing, stimulating, and guiding the safety program and for serving as a spokesperson to management and the union.

A second category of practitioner is the **safety engineer.** This person is the "one who analyzes exposures to physical injury or illness hazards, analyzes the capabilities and limitations of the human organism as related to the operation of equipment and processes, and tries to design the job and work place to fit the real people who must work there."[65]

A third category of practitioner is the **safety inspector.** This job is usually an entry-level position and involves auditing compliance with policies and procedures.[66]

Other practitioners are health and industrial hygienists. The job of these specialists is to maintain the health of the work force by preventing or controlling occupational and nonoccupational diseases and disabilities. Industrial-hygiene specialists deal with the identification, evaluation, and control of chemical, biological, and physical agents and psychological stresses in the workplace that may affect employees' health.[67]

Role of the Human Resources Department

A survey of 631 organizations of all types, found 98 percent with formal safety programs. In 83 percent of those organizations with such programs, personnel departments were partly or fully responsible for them. Health and medical services were offered in 85 percent of the organizations, with personnel departments having some or total responsibility for these services in 87 percent of the organizations offering them. Employee-assistance or counseling programs were offered by 79 percent of the organizations, and the personnel department had total or some responsibility for 95 percent of these.[68] Clearly, the human resources department has a major role in the management of health, safety, and employee-assistance programs.

In addition to directing and coordinating the activities of the various health, safety, and employee-assistance specialists, the human resources director has a major role in linking these activities to other human resources processes. For example, information about these activities needs to be incorporated in employee orientation and training programs. Supervisors and higher managers need training in effective listening and in making referrals to employee-assistance specialists. Effective health and safety practices need to be considered in performance appraisal systems and in making reward decisions. In the unionized setting, health and safety matters are areas for collective bargaining and, ideally, should become areas for collaborative problem solving. Safety and health need to be considerations in job design, work rules, and schedules. Disciplinary procedures need to be developed for serious infractions of safety rules.

The human resources director also has a major role in interpreting the needs of the health, safety, and employee-assistance programs to the top management group. This includes the ability to convince top management of the value of long-range preventive programs as well as to secure immediate support and cooperation in taking corrective action when necessary.

Finally, the human resources department has a broad communications responsibility in the areas of health, safety, and employee assistance. It is important that employees, supervisors, and all other members of management be kept informed of the status of ongoing programs and of changes in programs. Ideally, there is a great deal of interactive communication so that the expertise of the whole work force is tapped in diagnosing and remedying problems and in maintaining and improving ongoing programs.

SUMMARY

There are numerous compelling reasons for being concerned about health and safety practices in organizations. These involve humanitarian considerations, labor relations, legal and contractual compliance, and cost.

The Occupational Health and Safety Act establishes safety and health standards affecting most organizations and provides for inspections that can lead to citations and penalties. Both employers and employees have certain rights under the act.

Some of the variables affecting accident rates are organization size, type of industry, and work schedules. Training and increasing awareness are important partial remedies.

Occupational disease is a particularly difficult problem for many reasons, including the fact that the onset of some diseases is very gradual and very hard to detect. It is likely that organizations will be required to shoulder more responsibility for prevention of both initial and cumulative exposure in the future.

Substance abuse is a significant problem in many organizations. Increasingly, alcoholism is seen as a disease. In handing down awards under labor-management contracts, arbitrators typically insist that companies offer counseling and treatment before workers are discharged for poor performance stemming from alcohol abuse. Arbitrators are less sympathetic with respect to drug use.

Prolonged stress is associated with enough health and accident problems for stress to be an important area of concern for organizations. A wide variety of programs is currently being used to help organizations and employees manage or reduce stress.

Employee-assistance programs offer help to the troubled employee. Human resources department members and all supervisors and managers need to be skilled in referring people suffering from emotional illness or from family or other crises to employee-assistance specialists.

In organizations large enough to employ specialists, the health and safety department typically reports to the human resources department. The human resources director has significant responsibilities in coordinating health, safety, and employee-assistance activities with the management of other human resources processes. Ideally, this coordination is highly interactive and draws on the expertise and involvement of organization members at all levels. Excellence in health and safety matters requires high-quality teamwork.

KEY TERMS

walk-around right	stress	safety director
compliance officer	employee-assistance	safety engineer
walk-through inspection	program	safety inspector
occupational disease		

REVIEW QUESTIONS

1. Provide several reasons why organizations must be concerned about health and safety management.
2. Discuss some of the hidden costs of job accidents.
3. Explain the major features of the Occupational Safety and Health Act and discuss the impact of the law.
4. Discuss some of the rights that both employees and employers have under the Occupational Safety and Health Act.
5. Describe some common accident-prevention methods.
6. List some approaches to minimizing health risks from toxic or dangerous chemicals.
7. What are employee-assistance programs, and what are their purposes?
8. Describe an effectively managed health and safety program.

OPENING CASE QUESTIONS

Case 20.1   In the Aftermath of Bhopal

1. What are some of OSHA's recommendations for a good accident-prevention program?
2. What role does training play in a good health and safety program?

Case 20.2   Just Who Am I Protecting?

1. Is it possible that Jill and Bob's experiment to catch Jerry "in the act" will be unsuccessful? Why or why not?
2. What can Jill and Bob do now?

CASE 20.3   BHOPAL: IS SAFETY POSSIBLE?

Several months after the unimaginable catastrophe at Bhopal, Union Carbide's own technical report on the accident made one fact clear: the plant should not have been operating. The facility was unsafe, not because it lacked requisite safety features, although there are some questions about the safety of its manufacturing procedures; it was unsafe because many of its built-in safety mechanisms weren't functioning at the time of the accident.

The root cause of the disaster was the introduction of water into the tank of methyl isocyanate (MIC) that eventually leaked. Water and MIC react together very quickly, producing heat and, when confined in a tank, pressure. It isn't known how the water got into the tank; it may have happened when someone hooked up the wrong tube and pumped water in thinking it was nitrogen, which is used to pressurize the tanks. However, what happened after the water/MIC reaction began appears to be fairly clear.

As the reaction proceeded and pressure rose, climbing temperature should have triggered an alarm and the gas should have been fed through a refrigeration unit that would have slowed down the reaction. The refrigeration unit had been out of service for five months, and the alarm with it.

With nothing to check the reaction, pressure rose beyond the tank's tolerance, and a relief valve opened. A vent gas scrubber should then have neutralized the escaping gas, but it wasn't turned on until the situation had gotten out of hand and there was too much gas for it to handle. (Why it wasn't turned on isn't clear, but it may have been because control-panel and alarm malfunctions left operators unaware of how grave matters had become.) Still, there was a final safety mechanism that could have averted tragedy. But the flare tower that should have burned the gas away was not operating because it was undergoing maintenance repairs. Thus the gas spread from the plant area and descended on Bhopal.

There was, of course, a human side to what went on in the plant, too. According to one report, a control panel was missing that could have helped operators realize sooner what was happening. As the situation became clear and worsened, the plant workers apparently panicked. While some tried heroically to cool the leaking tank by spraying it with water, others ran away. In the end, only one supervisor remained in the plant. He was overcome by the gas while still trying to stop the leak. By the time outside engineers arrived to seal the tank, it was empty.

Sources: Kenneth Brooks, "Carbide's Report: How Bhopal Happened," *Chemical Week* (March 27, 1985): 8–10; "Union Carbide Fights for Its Life," *Business Week*, December 24, 1984, pp. 52–56; Pico Iyer, "India's Night of Death," *Time*, December 17, 1984, pp. 22–31; "How Will Carbide's Misfortune Shape Chemicals' Future?" *Chemical Week* (December 12, 1984): 8–10; and "What Happened at Bhopal?" *Occupational Hazards* (May 1985): 71–72.

There are other factors that helped create the potential for catastrophe at the Bhopal plant. Union Carbide's similar plant in Institute, West Virginia, for instance, has a computerized warning system that Bhopal did not. Some in the industry feel that Union Carbide's methods of handling the gas are less safe than they could be. Mitsubishi Chemicals of Japan, for example, doesn't even store MIC but processes it immediately into pesticides.

Yet in the circumstance at Bhopal, evidence strongly suggests that the disaster could have been averted if only the plant's basic safety equipment were functioning as it should have been. Union Carbide chairman Warren M. Anderson acknowledges that the plant was not adhering to "standard operating procedures." But he claims that responsibility for safety procedures must rest with plant personnel in all Union Carbide facilities. The Bhopal plant, of which Union Carbide owns 51 percent, is Indian run, and Anderson asserts that culpability for the condition of the plant cannot be shifted to corporate head-quarters. However, Union Carbide is extremely attentive to safety management and obviously feels some responsibility for the safety of its subsidiary oper-ations. In 1982, UC safety inspectors from this country traveled to Bhopal and cited the plant for ten serious flaws. Managers in Bhopal told corporate head-quarters that most of the problems had been corrected by June 1984, but no corporate inspectors had returned to the plant by the time of the disaster in December of 1984.

Discussion Questions

1. Despite the Bhopal tragedy, the U.S. chemical industry has an excellent industrial safety record, and the industry's largest members generally as-sume a cooperative attitude toward safety-advocate and environmental groups. With this in mind, discuss the implications of Bhopal.
2. Do you agree with Chairman Anderson that Carbide's corporate head-quarters cannot be held responsible for what happened at Bhopal?

part 7

The Future of Human Resources Management

This section discusses significant changes and current directions in the field of human resources management. Chapter 21 focuses on techniques for increasing employee participation to enhance morale and increase the organization's overall effectiveness. Chapter 22 outlines career opportunities in the field and emerging roles of human resources professionals. The chapter also presents some ideas about how human resources management will evolve to meet changing environmental conditions and the challenges of greater productivity and improved quality of work life.

chapter 21

Participative Strategies for Organization Improvement

CHAPTER OUTLINE

LEARNING OBJECTIVES

- **Describe the goals and objectives of participative strategies for organization improvement.**
- **Characterize the conditions under which an organization improvement strategy is likely to succeed.**
- **Explain the role of a qualified facilitator in resolving conflicts between individuals and groups.**
- **Describe several techniques for improving teamwork in a group setting.**
- **Identify major features of each of the comprehensive improvement strategies described in this chapter.**

CASE 21.1   WHAT CAUSED THAT FIASCO?

Emily Page, human resources director at Bayshore Technical Products Corporation, was annoyed and disappointed. In an effort to involve employees more directly in improving quality and productivity, she had encouraged the company to initiate a program called "Employee Participation in Quality and Productivity Improvement" (or the "EP program" for short). Things had not gone well, and Emily was discussing the results with Sterling Jones, a consultant who had been hired by the company president, Mark Andrews. The hope was that Sterling would be able to help get the EP program back on track. Mark had given him only a short briefing and then referred him to Emily. As Mark put it, "It's really Emily's program. She got us going in this direction, and we're behind her, but I want her to be the company expert as well as the coordinator of the EP effort."

"We started with groups of about twelve employees in each of three departments," Emily explained to Sterling. "One group is coming up with good recommendations, but the other two have really bombed out. In fact, one group doesn't meet anymore. Apparently a couple of outspoken people started dominating that group and nobody else could get a word in edgewise. People lost interest, and almost everyone dropped out. With only two or three people showing up and the rest making excuses, there didn't seem to be any point in continuing."

"What about the other two groups?" Sterling asked.

"Well, take the group that's limping along," Emily began. "They've been meeting for an hour each week for two months now, but I can't say that they're really accomplishing anything. They seem to be floundering, and I think they're pretty discouraged. At the supervisor's suggestion, the members elected one of the hourly workers as the chairperson, but I don't think she knows much about running meetings. The group that is beginning to generate really good ideas seems to be working well together. My hunch is that it's because they like the supervisor, who also seems to know how to run meetings."

"Well, it seems to me that maybe you've made a better start than you realize," said Sterling. "One group seems successful, and one group can probably be salvaged. I'd have to do some informal chatting with the supervisor and the employees in the disbanded group to see if anything can be done to resurrect it. But before I go poking around in the organization, I've got quite a few questions for you. For example, who's behind this program so far? What's the prevailing leadership style in the organization? Is the union involved? How much training have group leaders had? Who reviews recommendations? What do employees see as the end product of the program?"

"I guess you're covering all the angles," Emily responded. "Let's start with who's behind the program. But before we finish talking today, I hope you can give me some ideas on how we could have avoided that one fiasco."

CASE 21.2   APPRECIATIONS AND CONCERNS

Linda Carr, an experienced management consultant and group dynamics trainer, had been hired by Paul Silverstein to conduct some "team building" sessions with the top management group of his division. Paul's division manufactured motorcycles, and his was the largest, most profitable division of Transport Systems, Inc. The other divisions manufactured snow vehicles, all-terrain vehicles, and special vehicles for the military.

Paul had been feeling for some time that teamwork and cooperation weren't as high in his management group as they had once been. He also sensed that his group wasn't as innovative as the management groups in some of the other divisions. Although the group had been together for several years — the newest member, the division controller, had come aboard three years ago — they really didn't know each other very well. At least, that's the way it seemed to Paul.

When Paul had discussed some of these concerns with the division managers at a recent staff meeting, one manager had suggested holding a retreat so the group could get together in a comfortable environment and discuss where things stood, suggest improvements, and make plans for the future. Paul said he felt the group should hire a specialist in team building to run the workshop if such a retreat were to take place, and he was pleased with the generally enthusiastic response to this idea. A committee was appointed to interview consultants with expertise in group work, and Linda Carr was unanimously recommended. When Paul met with Linda, he too was favorably impressed. He arranged for her to start interviewing each of the seven managers in the group on an individual basis, a procedure she had recommended.

Several things were evident to Linda when she reviewed her notes from the interviews. One clear theme was that each member of the group had some concerns about the way two or three other members were going about their jobs but that these concerns were not particularly serious. Linda sensed that the problems could probably be worked through fairly easily, but for some reason or other, people were keeping their concerns to themselves. Another clear theme was that people were feeling tired, unappreciated, and taken for granted. Still another theme was that Paul's subordinates liked him and basically supported his managerial approach, but a number of them wished he would be more direct with them about how he saw their performance.

When the group met with Linda at the two-day retreat, held at a resort in a rustic setting, the first thing she did was tell the members about the themes she had identified from the interviews. She also elaborated a little on each theme and showed how they tended to be interrelated. She then proposed a sequence of issues for the group to work on based on the themes, starting with interpersonal and group issues and ending with long-range planning items. The group seemed satisfied with the design, and Linda gave them their first assignment.

"What I would like you to do," Linda said, "is to take a pencil and paper and jot down one to three concerns that you have about how each person in the group is handling his or her job. The concerns can be little ones or major ones. Be as descriptive as possible about what the person is doing, and comment on how it affects you or your work. Then, after you have done that, jot down one to three things you appreciate about each member of the group."

After about fifteen minutes, when it appeared that each person had finished making notes, Linda said, "We'll deal with concerns first. The rule will be that you can ask for clarification, but you can't argue with what someone says until after you have heard from everyone. Who wants to go first?" "I'll go first," Paul volunteered. "I probably make the most mistakes." One member of the group immediately shot back, "That's right, boss. None of the rest of us ever make mistakes. I figure I'm more or less perfect." Everybody laughed.

One of the concerns expressed to Paul was echoed by several members of the group. It went something like this: "When you review my work, your criticisms are all so vague that I don't know which areas really concern you. In addition, I don't get a clear sense of which aspects of my work you think are outstanding. I'd like to hear specific feedback more often." One person said, "I know you're awfully busy, but when you flip through your appointment book or look at your watch when we're meeting together, I get anxious and start hurrying through things — and then I get even more anxious when I sense I'm not presenting things well."

Paul and the others found the morning intense and engrossing. The time seemed to go by quickly. Six people had received feedback by lunchtime. Linda noticed that each had taken notes on the comments, and all had asked some questions to clarify what was said about them.

During lunch the conversation focused on politics and sports. Nothing was said about the exercise, although as people were getting up from the table everyone laughed when someone asked, "O.K., which of the last two people is going to be in the barrel next?"

After each person had been the focal point of the discussion, Linda said, "Now let's do some contracting before we move into the appreciation part of the exercise. Jot down what you are willing to do differently, and indicate what help you need from specific individuals and the group if you are to do these things successfully." After several minutes of making notes, each person, in turn, asked for various kinds of assistance from different individuals. Linda made notes on flip-chart paper about each agreement that was made. "I'm going to ask you to review these agreements and how things are going about three months from now," she said.

The appreciation exercise seemed to be unusually rewarding for some members of the group. For example, the manufacturing manager was visibly moved when several colleagues commented on how much they appreciated his willingness to listen and help. "Thanks a lot," he said, "that's better than a pay increase. Well, maybe not better, but just as good." Everyone laughed and the moment was gone. But the sense of being appreciated stayed with the manager for a long time.

Although the first day's session had been intense, people seemed to be lively and full of energy during the second day of the retreat. They tackled some major issues in a constructive way — including how to improve their relationships with the other divisions — and moved on to do some long-range planning before they adjourned. Paul was very pleased with the results, as were other members of the group. They agreed to hold a one-day follow-up session with the consultant in three months and monitor ongoing progress during regular staff meetings as well.

These cases describe efforts to increase overall organizational effectiveness through employee participation. These efforts can be labeled **participative improvement strategies** because they aim to increase active and constructive involvement by employees in the achievement of organizational goals. Underlying these strategies is the belief that employees can and want to make contributions to organizational effectiveness beyond what is required of them in a job description. The assumption is that employees can help increase the effectiveness of their own work groups in solving problems and can help build teamwork and cooperation that facilitate the attainment of shared goals.

As Case 21.1 illustrates, effective employee participation in organizational improvement is not easily achieved. Participative strategies cannot work unless employees are equipped with participative skills, and the greater the level of participation, the greater the need for interpersonal, group, intergroup, and leadership skills. It is likely that the limited success of the EP program at Bayshore Corporation can be attributed to a shortage of participative skills. The consultant may suggest that the best way to revive the program is to develop these skills systematically so that individual members remain interested and involved in the program and work together more effectively when they meet as a group. The consultant might want to work with each group *as a group* in teaching new skills.

Case 21.2 illustrates how an experienced consultant goes about diagnosing problems in a particular work group and encouraging those involved to confront these problems in a direct, constructive fashion. Through interviews with individual staff members, Linda Carr was able to identify issues that affected the functioning of the group. For example, one problem was an avoidance of dealing with interpersonal concerns; another was a withholding of appreciation when someone did something well. Linda then conducted a concerns-and-appreciation exercise designed to improve interpersonal relationships as a first step in improving the overall effectiveness of the group. By the end of the retreat, the group had made substantial progress in identifying ways of increasing their contributions to organization improvement.

When employees do participate effectively in organization improvement efforts, the payoff in enhanced morale and performance can be substantial. That is why many organizations today seek to give employees more opportunities for participation and to help develop the skills with which to participate effectively. This chapter discusses various kinds of improvement strategies that build on the relationship between participative skills and overall effectiveness. The role of the human resources department in implementing these strategies is also described.

ORGANIZATION IMPROVEMENT AND EMPLOYEE PARTICIPATION

Improvement strategies represent organizational responses to challenges posed by the rapidly changing world in which we live. From the organization's perspective, the challenge is to achieve more effective and efficient production of goods and services. From the employee's perspective, the challenge is to enhance the quality of work life so that the organization is an attractive and satisfying place to work. Providing opportunities for meaningful participation is a way of meeting both challenges at once.

PERSPECTIVE 21.1 Participative Management at Nissan, U.S.A.

Managers of the best plants have convinced workers that their enemy is not management but the competition, and that they must pull together to survive. In fact, managers and workers at the best plants have merged into a single team. No, these shops aren't holding worker-management love-ins, nor have workers' complaints stopped, although they have been substantially reduced. But it isn't too much to say that, in general, trust has replaced strife, and communication has been substituted for confrontation. In most well-managed plants, workers now get frequent reports on plant profits, product quality and cost, the competitive situation, and other subjects — information that wasn't normally released to them before.

Marvin T. Runyon, 59, president of Nissan Motor Manufacturing Corp. USA, doesn't exaggerate too much when he says: "Our people are our management." This former Ford vice president walks the floor of the 78-acre Smyrna plant like an industrial Pied Piper. Everyone wants to talk to him about his or her work in this friendly plant. Runyon now finds that he has to stay off the floor so as not to interfere. "Decisions," adds Runyon, "should be made at the lowest possible level." Workers get so caught up in the effort to do a good job that at the best plants — Lincoln Electric, for example —

machinists have been known to make their own tools to do their work better.

The Smyrna plant isn't unionized, but well-managed plants that are demonstrate the same kind of worker enthusiasm. For example, at AT&T Technologies' circuit board plant in Richmond, workers in one department felt that the machines were being underused. On their own initiative they pinpointed the cause: long waits for maintenance men who replaced worn-out parts. The workers' solution: they would do it themselves from now on. Maintenance men didn't mind giving up a job they didn't particularly care for.

In case anyone doubted it, the experience at the best plants shows that American workers and managers can turn out world-class quality products at the lowest possible cost. Until recently one set of doubting Thomases — or doubting Hiros — were the top executives at Nissan in Japan. They questioned whether Americans, especially those who had never worked in the industry before, could turn out trucks approaching the quality of trucks made in Japan.

Nissan's Smyrna plant has surprised — and somewhat humiliated — the Japanese. Although many managers there are refugees from Detroit — the plant is managed entirely by Americans — 80% of the work force had no experience building automobiles. Yet only a year after the plant opened, pickup trucks built in Smyrna are measurably better than their Japanese counterparts, according to customer surveys. . . .

Source: Excerpted from Gene Bylinsky, "America's Best-Managed Factories," *Fortune*, (May 28, 1984), pp. 22, 24. Copyright

Current Attitudes Toward Participation

A national study recently commissioned by IBM reached some interesting conclusions about employee participation. In the summer of 1983, 785 "opinion leaders" were interviewed at length by telephone and asked, among other questions, what innovations in human resources management they saw as promising and what ones they saw as fads. The one clear trend that was seen as promising was employee participation and participative management. When the respondents were asked to look to the future and suggest what changes they felt were needed in the management of human resources, one of the strongest themes that emerged was more employee participation and greater employee involvement in planning and in work decisions.[1]

Today's work force also demonstrates a growing interest in participation, as John Naisbitt suggests in his book *Megatrends*.

> The ethic of participation is spreading bottom up across America and radically altering the way we think people in institutions should be governed. Citizens, workers, and consumers are demanding and getting a greater voice in government, business, and the marketplace.

Naisbitt also describes how American companies are taking a hard look at the value of worker participation at a time when there is a "confluence of both changing values and economic necessity." The economic necessity he is referring to stems from lagging productivity and quality and increased competition.[2]

Different Kinds of Participation

The degree to which employees participate in problem solving and decision making is a function of many variables and will vary with the type of problem or decision that must be dealt with, the extent to which a work group is experienced in participative skills, and the willingness of management to delegate authority to employees. Degree of participation also varies from one organizational setting to another, depending on organizational culture, management philosophy, and prevailing leadership style.

There are also different kinds of participation. Participation can vary in the extent of employee authority, the number of people interacting, whether participation is direct or representative, and whether it is voluntary or mandatory.

Extent of Authority.   Supervisors and managers are usually selective about what decisions will involve employee participation. In some instances, employees may have an equal say in a decision; at other times, their involvement may be limited to providing information and ideas so that the manager can make an informed decision. As participative skills are developed, employees may gradually be given more and more authority in decision making. In time, some decisions may be made completely by employees.

Figure 4.3 in Chapter 4, which illustrates the continuum of manager-nonmanager behavior, shows the various ways authority can be shared between subordinates and managers. At one extreme, there is no employee participation in the decision-making process; at the other extreme, managers and employees engage in joint decision making, which implies genuine participation and considerable authority on the part of employees.

Number of People Interacting.   Participation can involve an entire work group meeting to address particular problems, or it can take place in a one-on-one situation, such as a performance review discussion between a supervisor and subordinate. The interpersonal dynamics are quite different under each of these circumstances (see Figure 21.1) and will tend to evoke different participative skills from those involved. When an **intact work group** (group members plus the supervisor) meets, more information can be shared and ideas can be discussed more thoroughly than if just two people are meeting. But because of the number of people involved, there are more complexities to manage than when a supervisor and subordinate meet together.

When several groups are brought together to address shared concerns or when employees participate in a large conference, the

FIGURE 21.1
Dynamics of an intact work group contrasted with discussion between supervisor and employee

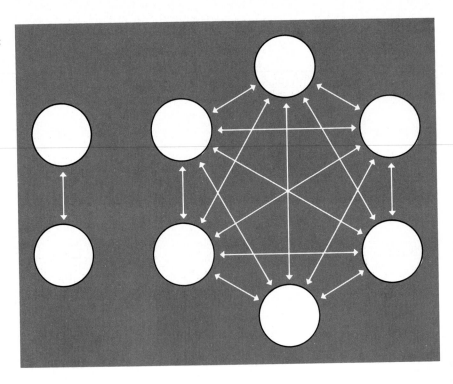

complexities multiply. Conducting a meeting of several intact groups or running a large conference requires much more preplanning of both the agenda and the physical arrangements than does a small-group meeting or a one-on-one discussion.

Direct or Representative Participation.

In **direct participation,** employees interact directly with those in authority; in **representative participation,** employees elect representatives to take part in decision making with higher levels of management. An example of the indirect, representative kind of participation popular in Europe is **co-determination,** in which union representatives sit on boards of directors. Another example of representative participation is the union bargaining committee that meets with management to negotiate a labor contract.

Voluntary or Obligatory Participation.

A meeting of a supervisor with his or her subordinates to solve a production problem is ordinarily a voluntary matter on the part of the supervisor and the organization. (The subordinates, however, may be required to attend the meeting!) In contrast, the mechanisms for worker participation under co-determination in West Germany are established by law.[3]

The participative improvement strategies described in this chapter do not involve representative or obligatory kinds of participation. The strategies we will describe focus on one-to-one interactions and some on relationships between groups. All the improvement strategies discussed involve firsthand rather than representative participation and participation that is usually undertaken on a voluntary basis.

Conditions for Success

Effective participation is not easy to achieve, and many consultants and researchers are still trying to improve the way participation is fostered in the organizational setting. But experience with participative improvement strategies suggests a number of conditions that need to be present for these strategies to succeed.

Lack of Coercion.

Organizational improvement strategies work best when employees choose to participate instead of being coerced. Forcing people to exercise more initiative is a contradiction in terms, and it tends not to work. Occasionally, managers will try to require employee involvement in various programs, but when people feel coerced or manipulated, their participation tends to be lackluster or ineffective. Therefore, it is important that management be sensitive to how much people want to be involved. Usually, employees feel they do not have enough involvement, and they are willing and frequently eager to participate in matters affecting their jobs, their work groups, and the organization.

Qualified Facilitators.   Another condition that needs to be present for many participative improvement efforts to be successful is a qualified facilitator. A **facilitator** (or *consultant-facilitator*) is a professional who has been specially trained in participative skill development. Although their backgrounds vary, most facilitators have extensive training in group dynamics, social psychology, counseling or clinical psychology, and consultation skills.[4] Linda Carr, in Case 21.2 at the beginning of the chapter, is employed in the facilitator role.

Facilitators may come from outside or within the organization. For example, TRW Electronic Systems Group in California and Polaroid have trained a number of their own human resources professionals for the facilitator role, who are called upon from time to time to act as consultants to various departments and divisions. It is important, however, that facilitators come from outside the units they are trying to help. Experience suggests it is impossible for a facilitator to be sufficiently objective if he or she is part of the ongoing dynamics of the unit. This not to say that a well-trained person cannot be helpful to his or her own group, but optimal effectiveness in the facilitator role requires enough detachment so that, for example, the facilitator can confront a group (including the boss) with whatever issues the group may be avoiding.

A Sense of Need for Improvement.   In general, organization improvement efforts are undertaken when top management or heads of major units within the organization feel that major aspects of organizational performance (such as productivity, product quality, internal cooperation, or employee satisfaction) are not as high as they could be. Accompanying this feeling is a sense of urgency — a sense that addressing organizational problems in a direct and constructive fashion is the only way to eliminate their negative effects on performance.

Commitment and Follow-up.   It is important that people be persevering enough to work through problems. Changing human relationships in an organization is a complicated process, and those involved need to exercise patience in working things through. Sometimes managers and subordinates want a "quick fix" to a problem; most organization improvement efforts cannot be quick fixes and require a serious commitment of time and effort to succeed.[5]

Organization improvement efforts also require systematic follow-up to ensure lasting gains. In many instances, participative techniques yield immediate, positive results. But these improvements tend to "disappear into the woodwork" if the change effort is not viewed as an ongoing process.

A Systems View. Organization improvement efforts generally embrace a systems view of the organization and its problems. According to this perspective, changes in one organizational relationship or process need to be sustained and reinforced by changes in other areas.[6] Suppose, for example, that an intact work team agrees that holding weekly meetings will be important for smooth operation of the unit and for effective problem solving. The supervisor's boss, however, believes that meetings are "silly and a waste of time" and communicates this to the supervisor. The outcome is predictable. The supervisor is going to be very reluctant to hold the meetings and probably won't schedule them. If, on the other hand, the supervisor has kept the boss informed of the group's ideas and recommendations for improving effectiveness and has solicited his or her cooperation, the improvement effort is much more likely to be sustained. If the supervisor's boss compliments the supervisor on the group's efforts and offers to provide whatever support is needed, the effort is even more likely to be successful.

BUILDING INTERPERSONAL SKILLS AND TEAMWORK

A common goal of many organization improvement strategies is to elicit greater cooperation and teamwork among employees. To achieve this goal, certain techniques can be used to improve the way individual workers relate to other people in one-on-one situations. Other useful techniques focus on the individual's ability to function effectively as part of a team, while still others emphasize how an entire group relates to another group. This section provides an overview of some specific techniques with which to build a comprehensive strategy for organization improvement.

Two-Person Techniques

Techniques that involve two people attempt to develop fundamental interpersonal skills that employees need to participate effectively.

The purpose of these techniques is to improve communication and understanding between two people so they can interact more effectively and manage their differences constructively.

Active Listening.   One of the most fundamental communication skills is **active listening,** which involves listening carefully to the words and feelings being expressed and feeding these back in such a way that the speaker knows he or she has been understood. An important part of this skill is checking on meaning, or paraphrasing, in which the listener says back to the speaker what he or she senses the speaker is trying to communicate. To paraphrase accurately, the listener must suspend judgment and prejudice and focus on the feelings underlying the message. As Edgar Schein puts it, the listener must concentrate on "relaxing the critical mind."[7]

Active listening is critical in any participative effort because misunderstanding and inability to communicate will damage or destroy any human relationship or cooperative undertaking. Therefore, training in active listening and exercises that develop paraphrasing skills are an important part of many organization improvement strategies.

Two-Person Conflict Resolution.   When serious disagreement arises between two people about how work should be done, conflict that interferes with organizational performance can result. A facilitator is often effective in helping to resolve these conflicts and in restoring more constructive relationships. As a neutral third party, the facilitator can help both parties listen to each other and work through whatever problems exist. A technique like the following might be used:

Step 1.   The facilitator asks each person to develop two lists:
        a. Things appreciated or liked about the relationship and the way the other person carries out his or her responsibilities.
        b. Things that annoy the person about the relationship and the way the other person carries out his or her responsibilities.

Step 2.   Each person shares with the other what he or she has listed. The facilitator discourages any arguing and helps the two people focus on listening and understanding. The facilitator might, from time to time, ask each person to paraphrase what the other is saying.

Step 3.   Each person offers information that might help to clarify matters.

Step 4. The parties negotiate changes with each other. The facilitator lists the agreements and notes unresolved issues.

Step 5. The parties and the facilitator plan how to work on the unresolved issues and arrange a follow-up session.[8]

The success of this conflict-resolution technique depends on the desire of the two parties to improve the relationship and their willingness to work hard at it. Obviously, success also depends on the skill of the facilitator and the extent to which he or she earns the two parties' trust.

Group Techniques

Experience and research in organizational improvement indicate that when all members of a work group, including the supervisor, work together on common problems, the overall functioning and morale of the group improves dramatically. More effective teamwork can be fostered through such approaches as participative staff meetings, team-building techniques, sensing, team MBO, and quality circles.

Staff Meetings. Supervisors and managers can build teamwork by encouraging greater employee participation in regular staff meetings. A staff meeting is a logical setting in which to build participative skills in group problem solving and decision making. But there are other ways to improve participation even before the meeting is held. For example, the supervisor can solicit agenda items from group members beforehand and give priority to those items during the meeting. If the group is large — say, beyond eight members or so — the supervisor can ask members to meet in smaller groups to discuss certain problem areas and to develop recommendations that can be reported back to the entire group during the staff meeting. In this way, more people are likely to have a chance to participate, and the total group can make use of the resources of all of its members.

Team Building. **Team building** is the name commonly given to a one- to three-day diagnostic, problem-solving meeting involving an intact work group and a facilitator. The facilitator works collaboratively with the members of the group and the formal leader to identify both strengths and problem areas and to assist in making plans for improvement. The group could include all of the members of management in a small company, or even all of the employees in a very small organization. Linda Carr's work with the management group in Case 21.2 is an example of team building.

Typically, the facilitator interviews each member of the group, including the supervisor, asking questions like, "What things are going well in this group?" and "What things are getting in the way of the group's effectiveness?" The facilitator takes notes during the interviews and later extracts themes that are fed back anonymously to the group at the beginning of the workshop or retreat. These themes form the agenda around which the workshop is designed. Table 21.1 lists some themes from interviews with a fictional group — themes that are not at all unusual in consulting experience.

Many techniques can be used in team building. For example, suppose that "Our staff meetings aren't as effective as we'd like" is a high-priority problem. If the group consists of eight to twelve people, the facilitator may ask them to break into two or three smaller groups to tackle this assignment: "Describe what is wrong with staff meetings." After the responses have been shared and major similarities have been noted on flip-chart paper, the facilitator might ask small groups (with the same or different members) to develop recommendations for changing the meetings. These recommendations are then reported back and, through discussion, consensus is reached on what actions to take to achieve needed changes.

As another example, suppose a high-priority problem is lack of clarity about various roles, such as the role of the purchasing manager and the role of administrative assistant. The facilitator might sound out the purchasing manager and the administrative assistant about their willingness to participate in a **role analysis process (RAP).** If they appear to be fairly comfortable with the

---

TABLE 21.1

Sample themes from team-building workshops

Our goals are unclear.

We are unclear about the roles of the purchasing manager and the administrative assistant.

Our staff meetings aren't as effective as we'd like.

There is a conflict between _____ and _____ that is getting in the way.

We don't do a good job of listening to each other.

Trust and mutual support are too low.

We don't follow up on decisions we make.

How are we going to organize for project X?

First-line supervisors have difficulty communicating with us.

idea, the facilitator would then ask for one of the two to volunteer to be first. The process, which involves discussion of various aspects of a particular job as seen by members of a group, would then be explained to the group, and, ideally, several other members would volunteer to have their roles discussed.

Assuming the purchasing manager volunteered to go first, the group would be asked to respond to the question, "If the purchasing manager were operating in an optimally effective way, what would he or she be doing?" The purchasing manager would listen while answers were recorded on flip-chart paper. The purchasing manager could ask questions for clarification but could not debate any item until the listing was completed. Following this step, the purchasing manager would then be given the opportunity to respond, followed by discussion and any agreements about changes.

Typically what happens through the role analysis process is a renegotiation of several aspects of the role to the satisfaction of all concerned, including the incumbent, his or her peers, and the supervisor. The flip-chart material becomes a kind of dynamic job description that role incumbents frequently tape on the walls of their offices or have typed for convenient reference. (See Table 21.2 for the steps of this process.)

Sensing. Another technique that involves groups — but in this case not intact work groups — is **sensing.** Jack Fordyce and Raymond Weil provide a clear illustration of this technique in which groups of workers interact with members of top management. The general manager of an organization employing 2,000 people wants to find out what matters are of the most concern to employees so

TABLE 21.2
Procedure for using role analysis process (RAP)

ROLE ANALYSIS PROCESS

1. Role incumbent listens while members of the group answer this question:

   If the (Job Title) were operating in an optimally effective way, what would he or she be doing?

2. All responses are listed on flip-chart paper.
3. Role incumbent may ask questions for clarification but may not argue until Step 2 is complete.
4. Role incumbent responds.
5. Discussion takes place and any changes are agreed upon.

Source: Based on Wendell L. French and Cecil H. Bell, Jr., *Organization Development: Behavioral Science Interventions for Organization Improvement,* 3d ed. (Englewood Cliffs, N. J.: Prentice-Hall, 1984), pp. 146–148; and I. Dayal and J. M. Thomas, "Operation KPE: Developing a New Organization," *Journal of Applied Behavioral Science,* 4 (No. 4, 1968): 473–506.

he or she can address these concerns, and how they might be alleviated, in the annual report to employees. He or she asks the personnel director to schedule a series of meetings with a cross section of employees so that he or she can find out what is on people's minds.

The personnel director selects four groups of twelve employees each. One group is drawn from nonsupervisory shop, technical, and office employees. A second group is drawn from among professional employees and staff specialists. A third group is selected from among the supervisors. A fourth group is made up of a cross section of employees from various departments and levels.

Before selecting the participants and scheduling the meetings, the personnel director talks with the supervisors of prospective participants to explain the process, to assure them that no direct actions affecting their units will be taken as a result of the meetings, and to secure their cooperation. Before each meeting, the personnel director meets for half an hour with the participants to brief them on the general manager's purpose and to help them begin to talk about some of their concerns as a way of warming up to the task. During the meeting the general manager mostly listens but occasionally asks questions for clarification. Occasionally, he or she expresses thoughts or plans already made about some of the topics raised.[9]

The sensing process is valuable because it can open up direct communication across the organizational hierarchy. There is some risk, however, that the role of the supervisor will be undermined, especially if employees by-pass their immediate superiors and reserve their recommendations only for the sensing session. Moreover, management response to significant concerns must be evident to employees in order to maintain their support and participation in the process.

Team MBO. **Team MBO** is similar to traditional management-by-objectives programs except for some additional features (see Chapter 13). One additional feature is that group objectives are developed by the team and progress on them is reviewed by the team. Another feature is that individual objectives are discussed with the team as well as with the supervisor, thus opening up the process to peer interaction and influence. Progress on these objectives is also reported to and discussed with peers.

Team MBO obviously requires a strong commitment on the part of team members to work together and to help each other. The success of this approach also depends on the group's becoming relatively highly skilled in active listening and in group problem solving.[10]

Quality Circles. Invented in the United States, imported and perfected by the Japanese, and recently adopted by American firms, **quality circles** are currently popular nationally and internationally. Basically, a quality circle is a group of employees — usually from seven to ten — from the same unit who voluntarily meet together regularly — usually for one hour a week — to identify, analyze, and make recommendations about quality problems and other production problems in their area. (The quality circle process is shown in Figure 21.2.) The meetings are typically chaired by the supervisor, but sometimes the chairperson is elected, as in one of the groups in Case 21.1. Occasionally, the chair is rotated among members of the group. Recommendations developed by the quality circle are typically reported to a management committee that is part of the regular decision-making structure of the organization.

To ensure full participation, leaders of quality circles are often trained in group dynamics so that they can lead effective group discussions. One technique for ensuring full participation is for

FIGURE 21.2 The quality circle process

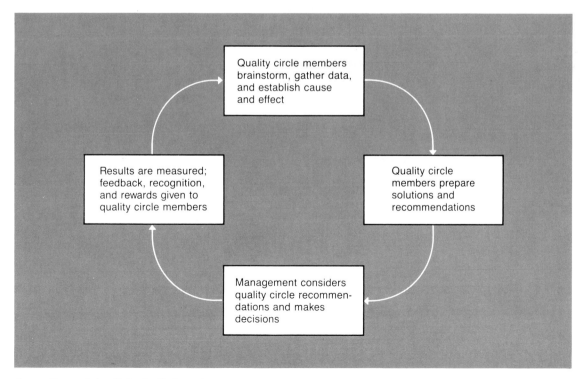

Source: Thomas Baker, Ph.D., Pacific Coast Research Institute, 5516 Waverly Avenue, La Jolla, CA 92037.

the leader to ask each person around the table, in turn, to provide one idea about a matter. Additional comments can be made after each person has had a turn. Group members may also be given a background in group dynamics and are sometimes taught certain analytical techniques (such as statistical quality-control methods) to help them make more informed decisions about quality and production.

Frequently, organizations using quality circles appoint a qualified member of the human resources department as a coordinator or a facilitator for the quality circle groups. This person can provide training in group methods and can sit in on meetings and be of assistance when groups need help.

To be successful, the quality circle approach to organization improvement (like other participative approaches) must be compatible with management's philosophy about how to relate to employees. In addition, success requires management support and involvement. Management must be heavily involved in evaluating recommendations emerging from groups and in providing recognition for workable and useful ideas.

Called Employee Involvement (EI) at the Ford Motor Company, the quality circle program has improved product quality and reduced production costs and absenteeism. With the support of the United Auto Workers, thousands of Ford employees in eighty-six of the company's ninety-one plants and depots meet once a week in small groups to deal with quality, production, and work-environment problems.[11]

Intergroup Problem Solving and Conflict Management

Intergroup relationships are very important to the success of the organization. Groups must be able to cooperate in solving shared problems and to manage differences that arise during day-to-day operations. Thus it is important that the manager and subordinates of each unit pay some attention to the quality of their relationships with other units.

If a relationship between groups has deteriorated because of an unresolved conflict, or if two groups simply wish to improve an already good relationship, a participative technique similar to the third-party peacemaking advocated for two-person conflict resolution can be immensely helpful:

Step 1. The facilitator asks each group to develop three lists about the other group: (1) a positive list — things liked about the other group; (2) a negative list — things the other group is doing that reduce the effectiveness of one's own group or of the organization as a whole; and (3) a list of predictions about what the other group will include on its first two lists. The two groups meet in separate rooms to prepare their lists, which are recorded on flip-chart paper.

Step 2. The two groups return to a common room and present what they have listed. The rules imposed by the facilitator are the same as in two-party conflict resolution: no arguing is allowed during the presentation phase; only questions to gain clarification are permitted.

Step 3. The groups again meet separately to discuss the implications of what they have heard. Frequently, the groups find that their differences are not as great as they had imagined and that a good deal of misunderstanding is based on inadequate information and inaccurate perceptions. Each group develops a list of priority concerns that need to be addressed.

Subgroups are frequently created and assigned tasks in team-building and intergroup sessions.

Merck & Co., Inc.

Step 4. The groups share their new lists and, with the facilitator's help, make a composite list of what both groups agree are priority matters.

Step 5. The procedure may vary, but a likely next step is for the facilitator to appoint subgroups composed of members of both groups. Each subgroup is then asked to meet and further diagnose an assigned problem and to report back to a general session of all the participants with recommendations for action. During this general session, an attempt is made to reach consensus on action steps, and individuals are given specific assignments with agreed-upon completion dates. Action steps and assignments are recorded.

Step 6. A follow-up session is held involving both groups or the leaders of both groups. Progress is reviewed and further action plans are made if necessary.[12]

Ideally, this approach is used only after both groups have had some experience with team building in their own units. Sometimes, however, misunderstandings and conflict become so crippling to organizational effectiveness that it is wise for management to engage a facilitator and move directly into the conflict situation. But this requires at least a modest level of understanding and acceptance of the process. Obviously, the facilitator must earn the trust of both groups if he or she is to be effective.

COMPREHENSIVE IMPROVEMENT STRATEGIES

When viewed individually, the techniques described thus far are somewhat limited in scope. It is true that many of them can be used to solve problems and improve relationships within the organization on an ad hoc basis. But improvement in morale and overall performance can be more extensive and lasting when participative techniques are carefully chosen and implemented in the context of an organization-wide improvement strategy.

Three comprehensive improvement strategies are described in this section: survey feedback, organization development programs, and quality-of-work-life projects. These strategies, which are used extensively both in the United States and abroad, share some common features. Because in actual use these strategies may be given different labels, it is necessary to examine the specific techniques being used in an organization improvement effort to understand exactly what strategy is being used.

Survey Feedback

The dynamics of **survey feedback** are similar to those of team building except that questionnaires rather than interviews are used to gather data from employees. The questionnaire typically surveys employees from several departments or all employees within the organization. Ordinarily, in team building, data are obtained from only one unit at a time.

The survey feedback process typically unfolds this way:

1. The top management of the organization is involved in preliminary planning. The human resources director typically is given responsibility for coordinating the effort with consultant help.
2. It is decided to collect data about organizational climate, perceptions about human resources policies and practices from all organization members.
3. A questionnaire is purchased from a publisher or consulting firm and adapted for the particular organization. (The organization may design the questionnaire completely; this is very time-consuming and should involve pretesting.)
4. The questionnaire is filled out anonymously. Participation is voluntary, but organization members are encouraged to participate.
5. Data are tabulated and results fed back to the top management team and then down through the hierarchy. Floyd Mann calls this an "interlocking chain of conferences."[14] Specific data obtained from each unit are fed back to the particular unit, usually along with more general data about the whole organization or division. (Specific data from other, comparable units are usually not provided to prevent one unit from blaming or embarrassing another.)
6. Each manager presides at a meeting or workshop with his or her subordinates during which (a) subordinates are asked to participate in interpreting the data, (b) problems are identified and further diagnosed, (c) action plans are made for remedying deficiencies and making constructive changes, (d) plans are made for interacting with other groups to solve problems that involve more than one unit, and (e) plans are made for discussing the data at the next lower level.
7. Most feedback sessions involve a consultant-facilitator who helps prepare the superior for the meeting and who serves as a resource person to the group.[13]

This process is quite different from top management's administering a questionnaire and then trying to interpret the results and take action.

Organization Development Programs

Organization development can be defined as follows:

> Organization development is a top-management-supported, long-range effort to improve an organization's problem-solving and renewal processes, particularly through a more effective and collaborative diagnosis and management of organization culture — with special emphasis on formal work team, temporary team, and intergroup culture — with the assistance of a consultant-facilitator and the use of the theory and technology of applied behavioral science, including action research.[15]

According to this definition, organization development (OD) programs are those improvement strategies focused on shaping a de-

---

PERSPECTIVE 21.2   The Link Between Participative Management and Organizational Success

Despite the diversity, almost every one of the "100 Best" has something distinctive to offer its employees. At some the benefits are very tangible, from the huge fortunes attainable at Trammell Crow to the 25-cent gourmet lunch prepared by a French chef at Merle Norman Cosmetics or the million-dollar employee center with swimming pools, Jacuzzis, and handball courts at ROLM. Other places, like Gore and Kollmorgen, offer unusual management styles. Each company is unique, but there were certain themes we heard over and over again, and the urge to draw a kind of composite picture of the ideal company is irresistible. Beyond good pay and strong benefits, such a company would:

1. Make people feel that they are part of a team or, in some cases, a family.

2. Encourage open communication, informing its people of new development and encouraging them to offer suggestions and complaints.

3. Promote from within; let its own people bid for jobs before hiring outsiders.

4. Stress quality, enabling people to feel pride in the products or services they are providing.

5. Allow its employees to share in the profits, through profit-sharing or stock ownership or both.

6. Reduce the distinctions of rank between the top management and those in entry-level jobs; put everyone on a first-name basis; bar executive dining rooms and exclusive perks for high-level people.

7. Devote attention and resources to creating as pleasant a workplace environment as possible; hire good architects.

8. Encourage its employees to be active in community service by giving money to organizations in which employees participate.

9. Help employees save by matching the funds they save.

10. Try not to lay off people without first making an effort to place them in other jobs either within the company or elsewhere.

11. Care enough about the health of its employees to provide physical fitness centers and regular exercise and medical programs.

12. Expand the skills of its people through training programs and reimbursement of tuition for outside courses.

Source: Excerpted from Robert Levering, Milton Moskowitz, and Michael Katz, *The 100 Best Companies to Work for in America*, © 1984 Addison-Wesley, Reading, Massachusetts. pg. ix. Reprinted with permission

sirable organizational culture with the help of trained consultants and behavioral science techniques. Many of the techniques described earlier in the chapter — team building, third-party conflict resolution, and survey feedback — are based on behavioral science theory and research and are typical components of comprehensive OD efforts.

To a large extent, the focal point of most OD programs is the prevailing culture of various groups and of the organization as a whole. That is, there is a conscious effort to examine widely shared beliefs, values, and norms to see which of these increase organizational effectiveness and which need to be changed.

The definition also refers to **action research,** the process of gathering information, feeding it back, and developing plans for implementing desired changes. In a typical OD program, action research involves gathering information (usually through interviews and questionnaires), making that information visible (for example, reporting interview themes to a group on flip-chart paper), and then facilitating employee participation in a diagnostic and problem-solving effort. Figure 21.3 illustrates action research in the context of team building or survey feedback.

When top management or some key person in the organization senses there are deficiencies in the way the organization is functioning that are due partly to an inappropriate organizational culture, an OD program may be initiated. The process might go something like this:

1. A qualified consultant (or possibly a team of consultants) is selected. The consultant acts as a facilitator to intact work teams and helps manage the entire OD process as it unfolds.
2. Team building (or a combination of survey feedback and team building) starts with the top team and is extended gradually to subordinate teams as it is found helpful and as managers request this assistance.
3. The team building is supported with individual and group training in group process and leadership skills. Some of this training will occur during team-building workshops; some of it may occur in special training sessions.
4. Intergroup problem-solving sessions are held when data gathering reveals conflicts and misunderstanding between groups.
5. Other techniques, such as sensing, are used as relevant.
6. A steering committee, representing a cross section and all levels of the organization, is appointed early in the process. This committee advises top management and the consultant(s) on next steps in the process.
7. There is extensive follow-up of action plans in regular unit or department meetings.

FIGURE 21.3
The action research model

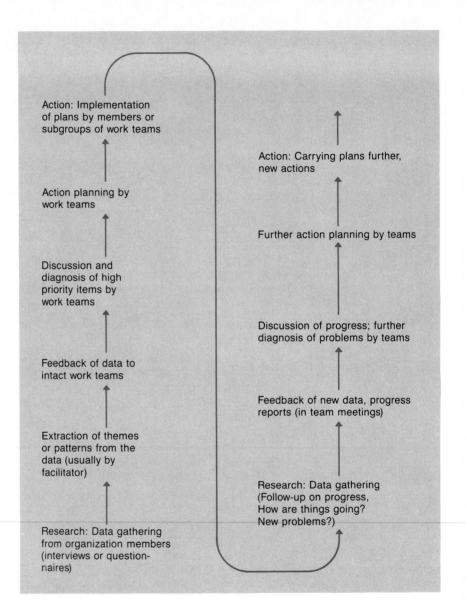

8. As organization members develop their participative skills through the OD process, they begin to display greater effectiveness in their interpersonal and group interactions. They become better equipped to solve problems and cope with issues that affect the entire organization, such as developing new markets, improving products, and so on.

9. As teamwork, support, and openness increase, participative management of the organization's culture becomes the norm. Rather than treating the organizational culture as a given, all members of the organization can play an active role in shaping the desired culture.

10. Human resources policies and management practices are revised as necessary to be congruent with and supportive of the emerging culture. For example, the organization may adjust its compensation policy to reward effective participation by individuals and groups; managers may recognize and reward employees for their skills in cooperation and collaborative problem solving along with their technical skills; and training and management development programs may give a new emphasis to interpersonal and group skills.

11. Organization members apply what they have learned to changing opportunities and challenges in the organization's external environment — to user response to the organization's products, to new technology, to changing economic conditions, and so on.

12. Action research becomes a way of life. When it is relevant to do so, systematic efforts are made to find out what organization members are perceiving, feeling, and thinking in order to maintain increased efficiency and high morale.

Quality-of-Work-Life Projects

Collaborative efforts by management and employees to improve both productivity and the conditions of working life are called **quality-of-work-life (QWL) projects**. Many of these projects are implemented in unionized organizations as a result of integrative bargaining between companies and unions. QWL projects are not limited to the unionized setting, however. Richard Walton estimates that there are at least a thousand plants, both union and nonunion, using QWL programs in the United States, with "many times that number somewhere in the transitional stage," that is, beginning to use some participative programs like quality circles.[16]

Features of QWL Projects. Some of the common features of QWL and OD programs include a focus on intact work teams, problem-solving sessions by work teams ranging over many aspects of work life, the availability of additional training, the availability of facilitators, and increased responsiveness by supervisors and managers to employees (both a feature and an outcome). Overall, there tends to be a heightened level of participation and involvement by employees in matters affecting their work. But in contrast with many OD programs, which tend to start at the managerial and professional levels, QWL efforts tend to be focused on supervisory and production employees. Ideally, an organization improvement strategy will blend features of OD and QWL and encompass the entire organization.

At General Motors, QWL projects have included these characteristics:

- Union agreement with and participation in the process
- Voluntary participation on the part of employees
- Assurance of job security (no loss of jobs as a result of the program)
- Training programs in team problem solving
- The use of quality circles through which employees meet to discuss problems affecting the plant's performance and their work environment
- Encouragement of job rotation and skill development within work teams
- Availability of skills training
- Work-team involvement in forecasting staffing needs, in work planning, and in team-member and team-leader selection
- Periodic plant and team meetings to discuss such matters as quality, schedules, safety, and customer orders
- Responsiveness to employee concerns[17]

Limitations of QWL Projects.   Many QWL projects have had at least modest success, but frequently there have been difficulties in sustaining or expanding the process beyond a few years. Research suggests that there are reasons for the limited success of some QWL projects. First, changes in union (or management) leadership can destroy the continuity of a QWL program. Second, expectations about how fast improvements would occur may have been too high. Third, these efforts are often aimed at the production or clerical work force with little attempt to change the culture at the managerial and professional levels. Finally, there has usually been little attention paid to long-term financial rewards for the participants.[18]

ROLE OF THE HUMAN RESOURCES DEPARTMENT

Some indication of the extensive involvement of human resources professionals in participative strategies for organization improvement can be seen in a recent survey. Among firms with formal productivity improvement programs of some kind, which included "worker participation programs," the personnel director developed the program in 43 percent. In 59 percent of the firms, the program was developed by "top executives."[19] Since these numbers total more than 100%, some programs were undoubtedly a joint effort of the human resources department and other managers in many of the organizations.

Joint Planning and Management of Strategy

Experience indicates that optimal success in organization improvement efforts requires joint planning and development of the process by human resources professionals and managers at all levels of the organization. Top management support and involvement are crucial. The talents and insights of middle managers and first-line supervisors are essential as well. If these people are not extensively involved, not only is a major resource being underused, but they will also tend to thwart or undermine the program because of misinformation or an understandable desire to protect themselves from changes over which they have no control.

The human resources department needs to be extensively involved because that department houses those people who advocate careful and thoughtful attention to the development and use of *all* the human talent in the organization. Further, the human resources department needs to be heavily involved in any major improvement effort so that human resources policies and practices are congruent with the thrust of the effort. The reverse is also important: the human resources department needs to be involved so that improvement efforts are not launched that are inconsistent with the organization's philosophy and policies with respect to human resources.

The human resources department is the logical unit to employ one or more professionals trained in participative approaches to organization improvement. For example, one or two members of that department, depending on its size, might be hired partly because of their team building skills or might be given training to develop those skills. Similarly, the department might develop a staff member to become the coordinator and facilitator for a quality circle program.

Sustaining Employee Participation

In organizations where management wishes the culture and climate to become more participative, it would seem that all human resources professionals could profit from training and experience in action research methods. Skills in interviewing, in designing and administering questionnaires, and in running workshops can be immensely helpful in the context of broad organization improvement strategies.

Members of the human resources department can also profitably use action research methods in reviewing and improving various personnel practices. For example, if the human resources department or top management wishes to investigate the potential usefulness of a plant-wide productivity incentive program of some kind, gathering data through such mechanisms as interviews, questionnaires, and meetings can be very helpful in diagnosing what problems need to be solved and deciding whether such an incentive system might be appropriate for solving them. Members of personnel departments all too frequently sell management on a new program of some kind without careful diagnosis of organization strengths and weaknesses. Top management is prone to do the same thing, and the human resources department can provide a major service by helping managers do a better job of diagnosing problems and soliciting employees' ideas about solutions.

Finally, it is important that the human resources department anticipate, and help other managers be aware of, the various implications and ramifications of changes that are proposed or started. For example, launching a cost-cutting program without thinking through its impact on jobs and people is very short sighted, but it is sometimes done. The human resources director needs to be persuasive in convincing managers that consultation with the human resources department on major changes would be wise. Being helpful when the problem is brought to the human resources department is obviously important if managers, including top management, are to continue to consult with that department.

SUMMARY

This chapter has been about participative strategies and techniques for organization improvement. The trend is toward more opportunities for participation by employees in meaningful aspects of their work. This suggests the need for more effective participation. Participation can vary in the extent of freedom, the number of people interacting, whether the participation is direct or through representatives, and whether it is voluntary or has some legal or contractual basis.

A number of conditions are necessary for optimal success in the use of the various improvement strategies described: voluntary participation, qualified facilitators, key people's sensing a need for organization improvement, a willingness on the part of all participants to work through problems and to follow up on action steps that are taken, and a systems view of the organization and its problems.

Some of the reasons for difficulties in sustaining participative improvement programs have included changes in union and management leadership, expectations that are too high, lack of attention to the culture at the top of the organization, and insufficient attention to long-term financial rewards for the participants. Resistance to these programs by supervisors and middle managers has also been a problem in some instances.

Optimal success in organization improvement efforts requires joint planning and development of the process by human resources professionals and managers at all levels of the organization. Top management support is crucial. The human resources department needs to be heavily involved in any major improvement effort because of its advocacy of careful attention to human resources and so that change efforts are congruent with the organization's philosophy and policies with respect to human resources.

The human resources department is the logical unit to employ one or more professionals trained in participative approaches to organization improvement. Further, if the organization wishes to become more participative, human resources professionals can make extensive use of action research methods. Finally, the human resources department needs to have a systems view of change and improvement in order to help manage improvement efforts effectively.

KEY TERMS

participative improvement strategy	facilitator	quality circle
intact work group	active listening	survey feedback
direct participation	team building	organization development
representative participation	role analysis process (RAP)	action research
co-determination	sensing	quality-of-work-life (QWL)
	team MBO	project

REVIEW QUESTIONS

1. Describe several different forms of participation.
2. What conditions are necessary for the success of a participative improvement effort?
3. Explain the role of a qualified facilitator in change programs and in resolving conflicts.
4. Describe several techniques for improving teamwork using group methods.
5. What is team building?
6. Describe the major features of survey feedback, organization development, and quality-of-work-life projects.
7. What is the role of the human resources department in organization improvement efforts?

OPENING CASE QUESTIONS

Case 21.1   What Caused That Fiasco?

1. How would you respond to Emily's question about how the fiasco could have been avoided?
2. If you were the consultant, what recommendations would you have for Emily at this point?

Case 21.2   Appreciations and Concerns

1. Why was the exercise in concerns and appreciations Linda's first assignment to the group?
2. What seem to be some of the values and assumptions of an organization development program?

CASE 21.3   PARTICIPATION IN A TROUBLED INDUSTRY

The U.S. steel industry is struggling along at perhaps only sixty percent of capacity, and massive layoffs have been common for the last several years. Steel industry executives claim that only capital investment and vigilant control of foreign imports can alleviate the situation. Yet the industry recognizes that quality of work life and cumbersome work rules also need to improve if there is to be any chance for a worthwhile recovery. In 1982 and 1983, seven of the largest steel companies were implementing a program of "labor-management participation teams" that had been agreed to by union and management in a landmark contract settlement in 1980.

The participatory approach has been far from uniformly popular in the industry. In 1983, a union leader estimated that at Jones & Laughlin Steel Corp., which was then further into the program than many companies, from fifty to seventy-five percent of the company's plant workers distrusted the approach and thought it was a management trick designed to squeeze labor. Many supervisors are wary of worker participation because they fear it will reduce their authority and accomplish little. Moreover, many executives, while they generally support the approach, are easily irritated by suggestions that it is a quick fix for all that ails the industry. Some in steel management, in fact, ridicule the notion that low productivity and quality are important contributors to the industry's decline—blaming instead cheap foreign labor.

Nonetheless, where the program has been offered and workers have accepted it (participation is voluntary), successes seem to have outweighed difficulties. The participation teams have introduced valuable efficiencies, and morale has clearly improved among team members. One worker at Jones & Laughlin's Aliquippa, Pennsylvania works publicly claims he has gained insight into the problems the corporation faces and how they threaten job security. This kind of awareness makes union members more amenable to streamlining work rules and making needed sacrifices. Other workers express pride in and commitment to team-created solutions. Supervisors, too, are finding that the workers' input can be valuable and that working in a team can make many supervisory tasks easier on everyone involved. In one case at Aliquippa, a participation team voluntarily took over the foreman's onerous job of taking care of unsafe-practice reports.

Surprisingly, to some doubters in management, participation teams have vigorously grappled with difficult efficiency problems which, in some cases, have befuddled management for years. At the Aliquippa works, a team was able to establish a reliable system for making sure proper tools were available at cast-making sites. In the past, different shifts had even hidden tools to make

Sources: Donald B. Thompson, "LMPTs: New Hope for Steel?" *Industry Week,* February 22, 1982, pp. 72–75,78; "Steel Listens to Workers and Likes What it Hears," *Business Week,* December 19, 1983, p. 92; and "'I've Been Exposed to the Company's Problems,'" *Business Week,* May 16, 1983, p. 102.

sure they'd be able to find them again. The team's seemingly simple solution was to color-code the tools by shift and store them in an orderly way. In addition, the team set up a system for tracking tools undergoing repair. Savings could run to $300,000 a year. At another Jones & Laughlin plant, workers found a way to keep slab making waste hot while it was being moved half a mile back to the blast furnace for reuse, thus avoiding the need reheat the steel before remelting. The resulting annual savings are estimated at $4 million.

The level of worker participation isn't superficial. If a participation team recommends any capital outlay for a change, it must justify the expenditure by calculating both the cost and the expected payback. This procedure has had two important effects: it has opened workers' eyes to the intricate frustrations that managers often face; and it has led management to make workers aware of the facts and figures that reflect the details of company performance—something unheard of in the industry before.

To help workers feel comfortable with the program, management has so far avoided scrutinizing productivity levels under the team approach. The short-term aim of the program, according to executives, is to begin an evolution in steel's traditional corporate culture. If the program survives, the long-term benefits will be inevitable. So far, results, although hampered by the industry's condition, have suggested a hopeful prognosis. In a rather poignant demonstration of how the program can instill commitment, one Jones & Laughlin participation team continued to meet after their plant was shut down. The laid-off team members came up with a plan for cost reduction to make the silent plant competitive if it should reopen—even though they knew that it probably never would.

Discussion Questions

1. How can steel-industry management answer the workers who criticize the participation program and try to win their support? And how does the industry's condition hamper those efforts?
2. Why do you think participation teams can arrive at simple solutions to problems that management could not solve?

chapter 22

Looking Ahead in Human Resources Management

CHAPTER OUTLINE

LEARNING OBJECTIVES

- **Justify the increased status of the modern human resources department.**
- **Identify the means by which human resources professionals can develop their careers.**
- **Describe future roles of the human resources department.**
- **Characterize some of the significant trends and developments within each of the human resources processes.**
- **Give a summary explanation of how human resources management is changing to meet current conditions and future developments successfully.**

CASE 22.1   THE ASSIGNMENT

David O'Neill, vice president of human resources at Superior Mills, was an adjunct professor at City University. Twice each year he taught an introductory course in human resources management in the university's evening program. He liked teaching the course because it helped him keep up to date in his specialty, and it was stimulating to interact with the students.

David was sitting at his desk at home, jotting down ideas. Tomorrow evening he was to meet with his class, and he was busy preparing an assignment that he wanted teams of four or five people to carry out.

He was contemplating a project in which the teams would develop reports on how various processes in human resources management might change in the face of future conditions and events. For example, one team might look at recruitment and selection, a second at appraisal, a third at compensation, and so on. The teams could draw on past and present literature, and they could interview personnel directors and other managers in organizations. On the basis of their research on current trends and developments, they could then speculate about what the future might hold in the particular area assigned to them.

But David had another idea he was mulling over. "I think they would do a good job projecting trends into the future," he thought. "It should be interesting and productive. But there's something missing. What I would really like to know is their vision of the *ideal organization,* based on what they have learned about human resources management to date. They would need to bear in mind that the ideal organization would have to create useful products or services, that it would have to make a profit, and that it would need to comply with laws and high ethical standards. I wonder what they would come up with. And I wonder how similar or dissimilar their reports would be."

After making some notes on his note pad, David finally drafted this assignment:

> You are the top management team in a company of about _____ employees in the _____ industry in the state of _____. You believe that productivity and profitability are much lower than they should be and that product quality and quality of work life should be higher. You have some notions about what an ideal organization would be like from your personal experiences and from your classwork and reading. You have decided to meet as a group to develop a statement of management philosophy and to sketch out the basic personnel policies and procedures you think would help create the kind of organization you envision. You will be making your presentation to the rest of the class, who will represent your company's board of directors. The members of the board are friendly and supportive, but they will expect a clear, thorough report and will ask penetrating questions.

David gave the assignment to the class. Each team was to choose a type of company and industry. Each team member was expected to participate in making the presentation.

CASE 22.2   WE'VE GOT TO LOOK TO THE FUTURE

Martha and Frank King owned a rapidly growing firm that specialized in manufacturing of stylish sports clothes. Between them, they handled all of the responsibilities of president of the company and chairman of the board. Business was good and was getting better. Martha and Frank had assembled a group of highly talented people in design, marketing, and manufacturing, and profits had grown steadily during each year of operation.

Martha and Frank had shared human resources management responsibilities since they started the business five years ago, but the firm was getting too large and growing too fast for them to devote sufficient attention to these matters. In particular, they realized that they were being less thorough in recruiting and checking references for professional and managerial people and that they were spending too little time making compensation and promotion decisions. So far, they had not made any major mistakes, but they were afraid they might. In addition, they realized they had not developed a statement about their management philosophy, nor had they developed a comprehensive set of human resources policies that could be applied uniformly in the organization. They had talked from time to time about hiring a human resources director, but their busy schedules had interfered with making a final decision in the matter.

Today they were having lunch together, and the conversation went like this:

"Frank, we've got to decide on the qualifications and hire a human resources director. We're not keeping up with the recruiting, let alone planning for the future."

"You're right, Martha, things are getting a bit haphazard in the people side of the business. We're doing lots of things without much thought. Mostly what we do seems to turn out all right, but I would have more peace of mind if we had someone to help us really think through a total human resources program."

"To pick up on that idea, Frank, I think it's probably crucial that we develop sound policies and practices that will take us where we think we'd like to be in the next, say, five to ten years. Maybe we should develop some ideas about what high-performing organizations in our business might look like in the future as part of an overall strategic plan and then hire a personnel director with the qualifications to help take us there." Martha then added, "But no matter whom we hire, that person has got to be committed to our philosophy about how people should be managed."

"I agree," said Frank, "but exactly what is our philosophy? I think we generally see eye to eye, but maybe it's time we tried to put our philosophy in writing. We need a draft of a statement that others could react to. Here's a suggestion: let's get our top staff members out of the office for a day some time over the next two weeks and hammer out the first draft of a statement of philosophy and some broad guidelines about personnel policies and practices. Then we'll have some coherent statements about people management that we can use when we advertise and interview for our new human resources director. Once on board, the new person can suggest changes and help us refine our various policy and procedure statements."

Martha's response was immediate. "Let's do it," she said. "Now, on to another important executive decision — what are we going to have for dessert?"

T he chapter-opening cases suggest that people in charge of organizations and of the human resources within those or- ganizations need to give some thought to the future and prepare accordingly. A conscious effort to anticipate change, in- stead of merely reacting to change as it happens, makes manage- ment a far-sighted, goal-oriented process in which careful analysis of significant trends within and outside the organization is a key component.

In Case 22.1, David O'Neill's assignment reflects the conviction that managers throughout the organization have a great deal of responsibility and control over both the quality of working life and the quality of human resources practices in a particular setting. Moreover, his assignment attempts to demonstrate the need for congruence among philosophy, policy, and procedures in order to achieve desired organizational goals.

In Case 22.2, Martha and Frank were beginning to think seri- ously about which human resources policies and practices would help ensure the future success of their company. They realized that they would be the key architects of those policies and practices and that the need to develop a comprehensive human resources program could no longer be ignored. In addition, they recognized that this program must be coordinated with a clear statement of management philosophy and their strategic plans for the entire operation.

Implicit in both cases is the idea that management has a great opportunity and challenge to manage organizations in such a way that economic and productivity objectives are met at the same time that human needs and aspirations are met. In terms of the long-range success of the organization, these objectives are inseparable. And the extent to which all of these objectives are attained is a measure of how well the organization is performing as a whole.

Management — owners, managers, supervisors, boards of directors — must pay careful attention to the effective use of human resources along with financial, technological, and physical resources if organizations are to achieve desired outcomes. At the same time, management must pay careful attention to the outside environment. The talent and motivation represented by the organization's human resources are the keys to how effectively the organization relates to that external environment and to how effectively financial, technological, and physical resources are used in the pursuit of organizational goals.

This chapter presents some ideas about how organizations over the next five or ten to twenty or thirty years will need to manage human resources to create this successful integration. First, the chapter summarizes the current importance and responsibilities of human resources departments and outlines job and career opportunities in the field itself. It then describes possible future roles for the human resources department and suggests the kinds of changes that might be anticipated in each of the major processes in human resources management.

THE MODERN HUMAN RESOURCES DEPARTMENT

As discussed in Chapter 2, the personnel or human resources department emerged around 1912 as several specialists were brought together in one department: the employment agent, the social or welfare secretary, the labor department specialist, the wage or rate clerk, the pension administrator, the safety director, the company physician, and the training specialist. It was an important department then; today it carries even greater stature and importance.

Importance of the Human Resources Department

Until about twenty years ago, human resources departments were perceived by many executives as performing routine support activities; now they are perceived as performing activities central to the ongoing health and vitality of organizations. Symptomatic of that shift in perception are the responses given in a nationwide survey of 785 opinion leaders, including corporate officers and human resources executives in some of the nation's largest firms, faculty and placement directors in major universities, leading consultants in management and human resources management, and editors of major business journals. The respondents were asked, "On the whole, how much importance would you place on human resources policies and practices as a factor in business success?" Of those interviewed, 92 percent answered "utmost importance" or "very important." Only 8 percent said "some importance," and 1 percent said "little or no importance."[1]

In another study, eighteen chief executive officers were asked to rank four management responsibilities — financial, people, marketing, and operations — in order of importance. "People" received eight first choices, "marketing" five first choices, "operations" two, and "financial" one first choice. Two executives made no ranking. One of the CEOs who made no ranking said, "There needs to be a proper balance between all four areas. All four areas are like vital organs of the human body. Who is to say that one is more important than the other to survival and good health?"[2]

While there is no question that all four areas are vital management responsibilities, the overall impression given by these interviews is that top management considers human resources management extremely important. These interview studies are consistent with articles that have appeared in recent years with titles like "The Expanding Role of the Personnel Function,"[3] "Personnel Directors are the New Corporate Heroes,"[4] and "Managers See a Bright Future for the Human Resources Function."[5]

Responsibilities of the Human Resources Department

Table 22.1 (on p. 658) shows the activities for which personnel or human resources departments are typically responsible. This table reports the results of a survey in which personnel and industrial relations executives in 630 organizations of all types were asked to indicate whether their department had sole responsibility, some responsibility, or no responsibility for each of the 49 activities listed. Although a look down the "all" column gives a fairly good idea of the extent of personnel department involvement, a better index may be derived by adding the percentage in the "all" and "some" columns for each item. After all, in actual practice the management of most human resources activities is shared to some extent between the human resources department and other managers, even when the human resources department is formally assigned the prime responsibility. By adding across, one can see that 94 percent or more of the personnel departments had at least some responsibility for these activities:

- Personnel records, reports, and information systems, 99%
- Recruiting, interviewing, and hiring, 98%
- Wage and salary administration, 97%
- EEO compliance and affirmative action, 97%
- Complaint and disciplinary procedures, 97%
- Insurance benefits administration, 97%
- Induction and orientation, 96%
- Promotions, transfers, and separation processing, 96%
- Job evaluation, 95%
- Unemployment compensation administration, 94%

Figure 22.1 (on p. 660) is a position description for the top human resources position at Erie Insurance Group, a position currently having the rank of executive vice-president. This position reflects the wide range of responsibilities typically assigned to the human resources department.

CAREER OPPORTUNITIES AND PROFESSIONAL DEVELOPMENT

The importance accorded human resources management and the lengthy list of activities in which most human resources departments are involved suggest that there are extensive career opportunities in the human resources field. The following sections describe employment opportunities and professional development opportunities available to those who wish to enter the field or add to their training.

Employment Opportunities

Some idea of the employment opportunities in human resources management can be obtained by looking at government projections of employment in this field and by examining the various specialties and typical entry jobs. Salary data may also be of interest.

TABLE 22.1 Activities handled by the personnel department

ACTIVITY	PERCENT OF COMPANIES (630)†			
	Extent of Personnel Department's Responsibility			No Such Activity at Company/Facility
	All	Some	None	
Personnel records/reports/information systems	88	11	1	*
EEO compliance/affirmative action	84	13	2	1
Insurance benefits administration	83	14	3	—
Unemployment compensation administration	82	12	5	1
Personnel research	78	7	1	14
Wage/salary administration	77	20	2	1
Workers' compensation administration	75	17	8	*
Job evaluation	68	27	3	2
Pre-employment testing	67	10	3	21
Promotion/transfer/separation processing	64	32	4	*
Induction/orientation	62	34	3	1
Retirement preparation programs	61	11	5	24
Health/medical services	60	14	10	16
Recruiting/interviewing/hiring	58	40	1	*
Vacation/leave processing	57	32	11	*
Pension/profit-sharing plan administration	57	28	10	5
Tuition aid/scholarships	56	18	15	11
Recreation/social/recognition programs	56	30	9	5
Complaint/disciplinary procedures	54	43	2	1
Employee assistance plan/counseling program	53	19	5	23
Human resource planning	51	37	4	8
Attitude surveys	50	11	4	35
College recruiting	47	18	3	32
Executive compensation administration	47	27	18	8
Union/labor relations	47	13	3	37
Outplacement services	45	7	4	44
Relocation services administration	45	19	8	28

Employment Profile. Figure 22.2 (on p. 661) shows the total employment of personnel and labor relations specialists in the United States in 1982 compared with low, moderate, and high projections for 1995. Using a moderate projection, employment in the human resources field is expected to grow 23.2 percent by that year. In 1982 employment in human resources management was almost

TABLE 22.1 *(Continued)*

	PERCENT OF COMPANIES (631)†			
	Extent of Personnel Department's Responsibility			No Such Activity at
ACTIVITY	All	Some	None	Company/Facility
Employee communications/publications	44	30	21	5
Safety programs/OSHA compliance	44	37	17	3
Performance evaluation, nonmanagement	41	44	12	3
Supervisory training	41	40	13	5
Thrift/savings plan administration	38	14	6	41
Management development	37	40	15	9
Career planning/development	32	36	7	25
Suggestion systems	32	18	11	40
Community relations/fund drives	31	34	30	5
Food services	31	6	32	31
Management appraisal/MBO	30	39	14	18
Organization development	26	40	15	19
Security measures/property protection	25	16	56	4
Stock plan administration	20	10	10	60
Skill training, nonmanagement	18	44	32	6
Productivity/motivation programs	18	50	15	17
Public relations	16	25	52	7
Payroll processing	16	24	58	3
Administrative services (mail, phone, messengers, etc.)	13	14	71	2
Library	12	4	40	44
Travel/transportation services administration	9	20	51	20
Maintenance/janitorial services	6	7	82	5

†Six of the 630 total survey participants did not provide usable data on personnel activities.
*Less than 0.45 percent.

Source: The Bureau of National Affairs, Inc. "Personnel Activities, Budgets, and Staffs: 1984–1985," *Bulletin to Management,* ASPA-BNA Survey No. 48, No. 1832, May 23, 1985.

evenly divided between men and women. The largest area of employment for these specialists was durable goods manufacturing. The greatest growth in employment, however, is expected in the service-producing industries, because these industries are expected to account for about 75 percent of all new jobs between 1982 and 1995.[6] (See Figure 22.3 on p. 662.)

FIGURE 22.1
**Position description
for a senior personnel
administrator**

ERIE
INSURANCE
GROUP

	EXEMPT POSITION DESCRIPTION		

<table>
<tr><td rowspan="7">POSITION INFO</td><td>COMPANY TITLE
Division Officer – Human Resources</td><td colspan="2">DATE
2-1-84 R</td></tr>
<tr><td>FUNCTIONAL (GENERIC) TITLE
Division Officer</td><td colspan="2"></td></tr>
<tr><td>INCUMBENT</td><td colspan="2"></td></tr>
<tr><td>REPORTS TO (NAME/POSITION)
Chairman of the Board/President</td><td colspan="2">E/P/A ☒
O/T ☐
S/P/M ☐</td></tr>
<tr><td>DIVISION
Human Resources</td><td>DEPARTMENT ☐
SECTION ☐
UNIT ☐</td><td>GRADE</td></tr>
</table>

BASIC FUNCTION

Responsible for developing, implementing, coordinating, and reviewing the ERIE's personnel policies, practices, procedures, and programs and the like. Specific personnel practices under the general direction of the incumbent are: recruitment, selection, orientation and placement of employees; compensation administration, employee relations, health and welfare, training and development, safety, security, communications, employee services, and all other related personnel functions.

PRINCIPAL FUNCTIONAL RESPONSIBILITIES

1. Directs and coordinates the implementation of all new and revised personnel policies, practices, procedures, programs and the like in conformance with the ERIE's personnel philosophy and compliance with the letter and spirit of federal, state, and local law.

2. Monitors the day-to-day application of all personnel policies, practices, procedures, programs, and the like to assure uniformity and conformity to the ERIE's philosophy and compliance with the letter and spirit of federal, state, and local law.

3. Plays a key role in developing new or revising the ERIE's personnel philosophy.

4. Develops or directs the development of progressive personnel policies, practices, procedures, and programs consistent with the ERIE's and employee needs.

5. Implements or directs the implementation of all new and revised personnel practices to meet the needs of the ERIE and employees.

6. Keeps the Office of the Chairman and other executives informed of the effectiveness of present personnel policies and practices. Recommends changes as required. Keeps others informed as to the possible effects on the ERIE of developments and changes taking place in the nation, government, region, and the industry.

7. Supervises and coordinates the activities of personnel directing the functions of communications, employee relations, employment practices, education, compensation, employee welfare and related services.

8. Directs and maintains various managerial activities designed to maintain the division's personnel at a high level of cooperation with resulting operational effectiveness and efficiency.

9. Directs the preparation and maintenance of such reports as are necessary to maintain the activities of the Division. Prepares and presents reports to the Office of the Chairman, or others as requested or required.

10. Represents the ERIE on all employment practices inquiries, investigations, etc., when interacting with people not employed by the ERIE.

11. Directly or indirectly represents the ERIE in any types of negotiations involving or affecting personnel policies and practices.

12. See also "General Responsibilities for Management Positions."

Source: Designed by M.P. Eisert, Erie Insurance Group.

FIGURE 22.2
Projected employ-ment of human re-sources specialists in 1995

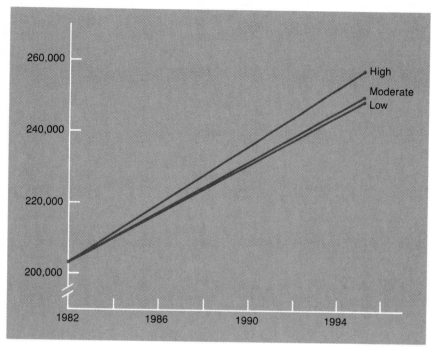

Source: Based on U.S. Department of Labor, *Occupational Projections and Training Data, 1984 Edition,* Bureau of Labor Statistics, Bulletin 2206, May 1984, p. 14

Specialties and Entry Jobs. Table 22.2 shows ten specialty areas within human resources management identified by the American Society for Personnel Administration (ASPA). In small organizations, human resources professionals are likely to be responsible for all or several of these areas. In larger organizations, there may be one or more specialists for each area. For example, in the staffing area, large organizations are likely to employ interviewers, test specialists, college recruiters, and job analysts. In the employment communications area, there might be an editor for the company magazine and one or more people who specialize in writing handbooks and manuals. Specialties may be combined in various ways. For example, trainers employed in the training unit might also write and edit special publications such as employee benefits pamphlets or handbooks on safety.

There is no single entry job in human resources management; the type of entry job depends on the size of the organization. Typical entry-level positions are employment interviewer, personnel assistant, job analyst, and training specialist. If the job of employment interviewer is any indication, there should be substantial opportunity for securing entry-level positions over the next decade.

FIGURE 22.3
Employment projections for service-producing industries compared with goods-producing industries

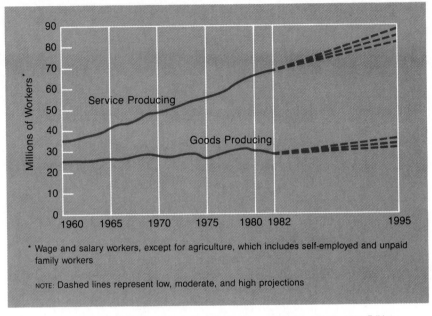

* Wage and salary workers, except for agriculture, which includes self-employed and unpaid family workers

NOTE: Dashed lines represent low, moderate, and high projections

Source: U.S. Department of Labor, *Occupational Projections and Training Data, 1984 Edition,* Bureau of Labor Statistics, Bulletin 2206, May 1984, p. 14.

Table 22.3 shows that the job of employment interviewer is expected to be one of the twenty fastest-growing occupations during the period 1982–1995.

Organizations show no definite pattern of recruiting from within or from outside in filling entry-level personnel jobs. It is clear, however, that additional work experience and education can give an applicant an edge over those with less experience and/or education.

Salaries. Salaries for human resources management jobs vary greatly, depending on such factors as number of employees in the organization, level of responsibility, the specialist's level of education and amount of experience, whether the person has international responsibilities as well as national, type of industry, and geographic location. For example, a 1984 study found that the median total compensation for top personnel and industrial relations executives ranged from $38,425 to $107,446 per year based on the total number of employees per firm — from fewer than 500 to 10,000 or more. (The highest paid executives in the survey made substantially more than $235,000 per year.) Recruitment managers with a graduate degree made 42 percent more than recruit-

TABLE 22.2
Specialties of the personnel and industrial relations field as defined by ASPA

1. **Staffing.** Screening; interviewing; recruitment; testing; personnel records; job analysis; job description; staffing tables; promotion; transfer; job enlargement.
2. **Personnel Maintenance.** Counseling; personnel appraisal inventories; turnover; health services and accident prevention; employee benefits and services.
3. **Labor Relations.** Group relationships with organized or unorganized employees; negotiations; contract administration; grievances; arbitration; third-party involvement; mutual aid pacts.
4. **Training/Development.** Job training; supervisor and foreman training; managerial and executive development; pre-employment and special purpose training; retraining.
5. **Compensation.** Wage and salary surveys; incentive pay plans; profit-sharing; stock ownership; financial and non-financial rewards; job enrichment; wage and salary controls.
6. **Employee Communications.** House organ [company newsletter]; employment handbook; rumor control; listening; attitude; morale and expectation surveys; feedback analysis.
7. **Organization.** Structural design, planning, and evaluation; innovation; utilization of formal and informal; reducing conflict; overcoming resistance to organizational change.
8. **Administration.** Explanation and interpretation of options — authoritative, consultative, participative self-management styles; assistance in change.
9. **Personnel Policy and Planning.** Defining organizational goals; policy guidelines and strategies; identifying, translating, and complying with public manager policy; forecasting manpower needs; selecting optional courses.
10. **Review Audit Research.** Program reporting/recording; evaluation of policies and programs; theory testing; innovation; experimentation; cost/benefit studies.

Source: Gary B. Hansen, "Professional Education for Careers in Human Resource Administration," reprinted from the January 1984 issue of *Personnel Administrator*, copyright, 1984, The American Society for Personnel Administration, 606 North Washington Street, Alexandria, VA 22314.

ment managers without a college degree.[7] Tables 22.4 and 22.5 show how the salaries of human resources professionals vary by degree of responsibility, by industry, and by geographical region.

Development of Human Resources Professionals

There are many avenues by which one can further his or her career or professional standing in the human resources management profession. Career-development opportunities are available through academic training, attendance at professional association meetings

TABLE 22.3
Twenty fastest growing occupations, 1982–1995

OCCUPATION	PERCENT GROWTH IN EMPLOYMENT
Computer service technicians	96.8
Legal assistants	94.3
Computer systems analysts	85.3
Computer programmers	76.9
Computer operators	75.8
Office machine repairers	71.7
Physical therapy assistants	67.8
Electrical engineers	65.3
Civil engineering technicians	63.9
Peripheral EDP equipment operators	63.5
Insurance clerks, medical	62.2
Electrical and electronic technicians	60.7
Occupational therapists	59.8
Surveyor helpers	58.6
Credit clerks, banking and insurance	54.1
Physical therapists	53.6
Employment interviewers	52.5
Mechanical engineers	52.1
Mechanical engineering technicians	51.6
Compression and injection mold machine operators, plastics	50.3

Note: Includes only detailed occupations with 1982 employment of 25,000 or more. Data for 1995 are based on moderate-trend projections.

Source: U.S. Department of Labor, *Occupational Projections and Training Data, 1984 Edition,* Bureau of Labor Statistics, Bulletin 2206, May 1984, p. 7.

and seminars, accreditation by a professional agency, and reading professional journals and books.

College and University Courses.   A high proportion of colleges and universities offer courses in human resources management, and many schools offer majors or fields of concentration in this area at the undergraduate or graduate level. A survey of 130 members of the Personnel/Human Resources Division of the Academy of Management, whose members are mostly professors in business schools, found that 77 percent of the schools responding offered one or more personnel and industrial relations courses at the undergraduate level, and 65 percent offered one or more courses at the graduate level.[8] The human resources or personnel management major typically includes additional specialized courses such · as wage and salary administration, recruitment and selection, and

TABLE 22.4 **Salaries of human resources professionals (by job and by industry)**

INDUSTRY	EMPLOYMENT INTERVIEWER	SENIOR COMPEN-SATION ANALYST	HEAD OF EMPLOYEE RELATIONS	HEAD OF HUMAN RESOURCES II	HEAD OF HUMAN RESOURCES III
(Survey average)	$28,900	$38,600	$51,200	$76,300	$158,100
Natural resources, chemicals, and pharmaceuticals	29,000	41,400	56,900	86,800	182,500
High technology	26,600	33,500	46,200	78,200	188,900
Other manufacturing	27,300	37,300	49,600	77,000	146,700
Utilities	31,600	43,100	54,600	71,500	148,400
Transportation and communications	36,800	47,400	52,300	80,200	175,100
Banks and diversified financials	22,400	34,200	—	71,800	189,600
Insurance	23,500	31,000	43,300	70,300	123,100

Note: Figures include base salaries and bonuses; exclude benefits, services, and deferred forms of compensation.

Source: Hay Access, 1985, The Hay Group, Inc.

training and development. Courses in such disciplines as psychology, sociology, statistics, and labor law are frequently recommended as electives.

Professional Associations and Seminars. Professional associations allow persons who are active in the human resources field to keep up with current trends and developments through conferences, publications, seminars, workshops, and research projects. The American Society for Personnel Administration (ASPA) is the largest professional association to which human resources professionals may belong. This organization has chapters in all fifty states and the District of Columbia, Guam, and Puerto Rico, as well as in Bermuda, British Columbia, Korea, and Mexico. There are chapters in most metropolitan areas throughout the United States, as well as student chapters at nearly 200 colleges and universities in most of the states and in the District of Columbia and Puerto Rico.[9] Another example is the International Personnel Management Association (IPMA), which draws its membership largely from human resources professionals in municipal, county, state, and federal government employment. IPMA has both individual memberships

TABLE 22.5 **Salaries of human resources professionals (averages by region)**

REGION	EMPLOYMENT INTERVIEWER	SENIOR COMPEN-SATION ANALYST	HEAD OF EMPLOYEE RELATIONS	HEAD OF HUMAN RESOURCES II	HEAD OF HUMAN RESOURCES III
(Survey average)	$28,900	$38,600	$51,200	$76,300	$158,100
Northeast (excluding Connecticut and NYC)	23,600	36,100	48,500	75,500	136,300
NYC area and Connecticut	35,300	43,600	55,100	84,200	182,100
Southeast	28,200	35,600	49,200	73,200	187,900
Midwest (excluding Chicago and Milwaukee)	28,400	35,200	48,800	75,900	160,500
Texas and Oklahoma	27,400	41,900	51,700	78,700	154,000
West (excluding Hawaii)	30,700	36,400	53,300	66,300	—
California	34,500	32,500	45,800	82,600	—
Chicago/Milwaukee area	25,200	35,700	50,600	73,100	150,400

Note: Figures include base salaries and bonuses; exclude benefits, services, and deferred forms of compensation.

Source: Hay Access, 1985, The Hay Group, Inc.

(some 4,500 in 1985) and agency memberships. Personnel professionals in some 1,100 government agencies are members by virtue of agency membership. IPMA has about fifty chapters nationwide. Other professional associations, such as the American Society for Training and Development and the American Compensation Association, tend to draw their memberships from particular specialties within the field.

Most of these associations hold national or regional conferences annually; their local chapters may meet more often. Most of them also offer specialized one- to three-day seminars. The American Management Association, various private consulting firms, and many colleges and universities also offer seminars on both general and specialized aspects of human resources management.

Accreditation. **Accreditation** is a way of recognizing a specified level of competence within a particular field. The Personnel Ac-

Courtesy of Hewlett-Packard Company

Professional seminars are one means of keeping up with developments in human resources management.

creditation Institute (PAI) was incorporated in 1975, following three years of research and development by a task force established by the American Society for Personnel Administration. The purposes of the accreditation, as described in the PAI handbook, are as follows:

- To recognize individuals who have demonstrated expertise in particular fields.
- To raise and maintain professional standards in the field.
- To identify the body of knowledge as a guide to practitioners, consultants, educators, and researchers.
- To aid employers in identifying qualified practitioners.
- To provide an overview of the field as a guide to self-development.[10]

The PAI has two levels of accreditation: *basic,* which requires an examination and some experience and covers the general body of knowledge; and *senior,* which requires an examination, senior experience, and policy-developing responsibilities. Within the senior category, a person can become accredited either as a **specialist** (a practitioner, consultant, educator, or researcher who has in-depth expertise in one area of the field) or as a **generalist** (a practitioner who has broad responsibilities and knowledge).[11]

Journals.   There are many respected journals that allow both human resources professionals and other managers to add to their store of knowledge about human resources management. These journals are an important source of timely information about changes and developments in the field, and men and women making career decisions may find it useful to browse through some of them.

Here is a sample of some well-known journals that specialize in human resources management:

- *Arbitration Journal*
- *Compensation & Benefits Management*
- *Compensation Review*
- *Employee Benefit Plan Review*
- *Employee Relations Law Journal*
- *Human Resource Management*
- *Human Resource Planning*
- *Industrial and Labor Relations Review*
- *Industrial Relations*
- *Industrial Relations Journal*
- *Industrial Relations Law Journal*
- *Labor History*
- *Labor Law Journal*
- *Monthly Labor Review*
- *Occupational Health & Safety*
- *Occupational Outlook Quarterly*
- *Personnel*
- *Personnel Administrator*
- *Personnel Journal*
- *Personnel Management Abstracts*
- *Public Personnel Management*
- *Personnel Psychology*
- *Training: The Magazine of Human Resources Development*
- *Training and Development Journal*

There are also numerous business and management publications that periodically include articles on human resources management or articles that are highly relevant to the field. Some of these are:

- *Academy of Management Journal*
- *Academy of Management Review*
- *Across the Board*
- *American Journal of Sociology*
- *American Psychologist*

- *Business Horizons*
- *Business Week*
- *California Management Review*
- *Fortune*
- *Group & Organization Studies*
- *Harvard Business Review*
- *Human Relations*
- *Journal of Applied Behavioral Science*
- *Journal of Applied Psychology*
- *Leadership & Organization Development Journal*
- *Long-Range Planning*
- *Management Review*
- *New Management*
- *OD Practitioner*
- *Organization Development Journal*
- *Organizational Behavior and Human Decision Processes*
- *Organizational Dynamics*
- *Sloan Management Review*
- *Supervision*
- *Supervisory Management*
- *Wall Street Journal*

FUTURE ROLES OF HUMAN RESOURCES PROFESSIONALS

Recent surveys of CEOs and human resources directors help indicate the kinds of roles human resources professionals and departments are likely to adopt so that organizations can meet future challenges and changes successfully. Table 22.6 (on p. 672) shows how 93 CEOs answered the question, "Which human resources areas should receive increased attention?" (Twenty-seven choices were listed, and the executives were asked to select the three most deserving items.) Productivity improvement, employee communications, management succession planning, management education and development, performance appraisal, career planning and development, performance incentives, job design, and controlling benefit costs were ranked highest.[12]

In another survey, human resources executives were asked to identify those areas of human resources management that were expected to be critical issues over the next year. The seven areas considered the most critical were:

- Productivity improvement programs
- Controlling employee benefit costs
- Compensation planning and administration
- Employee communications
- Improving management development programs

PERSPECTIVE 22.1   Tomorrow's Work Force: Considerations for Human Resources Managers

Tomorrow's work force will probably be older, more diverse in terms of gender and race, marked by intense competition for jobs and promotions, less unionized, and better educated.

The realignment of values and aspirations resulting from these changes is likely to exert considerable influence on the nature of work in coming years.

As the large post-World War II "baby boom" generation matures, the average age of American workers will increase steadily through the end of this century.

Just as this generation's entrance into the labor force lowered the average age of workers, the aging of the same generation will raise the average age from 34.8 years in 1982 to 37.3 years by 1995.

As this generation reaches and passes middle age, the shortage of advancement opportunities may result in significant job discontent and eventually a demand for young workers to fill vacancies at entry level positions.

Even without promotion, the demand for increased earnings resulting from seniority, experi-

ence and the economic needs of mid-life will push wage levels up despite competition for employment opportunities.

The growing participation of women in the labor force will also have significant effect. As the percentage of women in the labor force climbed from 31.8% in 1947 to 52.6% in 1982, the female proportion of the total labor force has increased from 27.4% to 43.3% during the same period.

By 1995, the labor force participation of women is projected to reach 60.3%, as compared to 76.1% for men. The average woman of the future is likely to work during all stages of the life and family cycle.

The dual-income household is well on its way to becoming the norm of the future, creating a need for new relations between home and work and demanding changes in both areas.

Minorities as a proportion of the American labor force increased from 10.7% to 12.8% between 1954 and 1982, and a combination of demographic and immigration trends are expected to increase this proportion to 14.5% by 1995.

Unemployment for minorities has been almost twice that of non-minorities. Therefore, pressures for equal opportunity from groups that have historically been disenfranchised will persist.

- Organization development programs
- Management succession planning[13]

There is a good deal of similarity in these two studies. It is significant that productivity improvement is first on both lists, reflecting the intensity of national and international competition. Clearly, both chief executive officers and human resources executives recognize that the human resources department plays a central part in the future survival and success of the organization.

Finally, in the survey of 785 opinion leaders cited earlier, respondents were asked in an open-ended question to name the characteristics of organizations that manage people well. (No example items were provided by the interviewers.) Several characteristics emerged consistently. In descending order of frequency of mention these included:

Other longstanding characteristics of the work force are also likely to change. Current trends suggest that the extent of union affiliation may decline. . . .

Finally, the educational background of the American labor force has been rising steadily. High school graduation has now become the norm for most entry level jobs, and the proportion of the U.S. labor force that has completed four years of college or more grew from 14.7% to 24.2% between 1970 and 1983.

During the past two decades, assumed conditions of economic affluence and security, coupled with political pressures for social equality, fostered values that were commonly perceived to change the traditional American "work ethic."

Key trends in this shift seemed to include the de-emphasized importance of material wealth as a motivator of work activity, pressures for equality and resistance to authority, desire to realign the balance between work and other aspects of life, and increased concern with finding intrinsically interesting and personally rewarding work.

Most studies indicate that these trends have not reduced the motivation to work, but instead increased expectations concerning the conditions and rewards of work.

Although many of these "new" values are not likely to disappear, turbulent economic conditions, changes in the work force, and progression of the baby boom generation through the life cycle are likely to force a compromise between aspirations and reality during the next few decades.

Unstable economic conditions and the demands of mid-life expenditures will reassert the importance of income as a motivator for work.

At the same time, social values developed during the 1960s and 1970s will create a high priority for work environment reforms, such as participative decision making, pleasant work conditions, considerate management, and such supportive facilities as day care centers.

Factors such as these will be critical variables in determining which technologies are developed and how technology is used. Thus, although technology must be given central attention in forecasting the future of work, it is important to recognize that the nature and rate of technological change will evolve within the context of human priorities and prevailing socio-economic conditions.

- Genuine concern for people; a positive view of employees as assets
- Good training, development, and advancement opportunities
- Pay well; good compensation programs
- Able to retain employees; low turnover
- Good internal communication; open communication
- Top management committed to and supportive of HR [human resources]
- Encourage employee participation.[14]

Taken together, the opinions expressed in these surveys may well reflect the essence of sound human resources practices for the future.

To achieve a desirable climate and an enlightened culture within the organization — and to cope with the critical challenges that

TABLE 22.6   **Human resources activities that deserve increased attention, as identified by top managers**

RANKING	SUBJECT	NUMBER	PERCENT*
1	Productivity improvement	29	31.2
2	Employee communications	26	30.0
3/4	Management succession planning	19	20.4
3/4	Management education & development	19	20.4
5	Performance appraisal	15	16.1
6/7	Career planning & development	13	14.0
6/7	Performance incentives (e.g., bonuses)	13	14.0
8	Job design	12	12.9
9	Controlling benefit costs	11	11.8
10	Forecasting staffing needs	9	9.7
11/12	Identification & evaluation of talent	7	7.5
11/12	Technical training & education	7	7.5
13/14	Maintaining a safe work environment	5	5.4
13/14	Determining competitive pay levels	5	5.4
15/16	Merit pay	4	4.3
15/16	Determining competitive benefit levels	4	4.3
17/18/19	Monitoring staff levels	3	3.2
17/18/19	Executive recruiting	3	3.2
17/18/19	Job evaluation & internal equity	3	3.2
20	Union-management relations	2	2.2
21/22/23	Maintaining adequate plant staffing	1	1.1
21/22/23	Outplacement	1	1.1
21/22/23	Flexible working hours	1	1.1

*Based on total number (93) responding.

Source: Roy Foltz, Karn Rosenberg, and Julie Foehrenbach, "Senior Management Views the Human Resource Function," reprinted from the September, 1982 issue of *Personnel Administrator*, copyright, 1982, The American Society for Personnel Administration, 606 North Washington Street, Alexandria, VA 22314.

the future will bring — human resources professionals are likely to assume certain roles with greater frequency. These are the diagnostic role, the catalyst-facilitator role, the consultant role, and the evaluator role.

The Diagnostic Role

Increasingly, human resources professionals are expected to be experts in the **diagnostic role.** That is, they are expected to identify the underlying causes of an organizational problem as distinct from its symptoms and to come up with solutions — or systems for solving the problem — that correspond with the diagnosis. All too often, programs of various kinds, like MBO, job enrichment, incentive systems, and so on, are proposed by managers or human resources people and then "bought" as quick cures without consideration for their effects on existing systems and on other aspects of organizational life. What is usually needed is an accurate and precise description of the problem to be solved, a careful analysis of the dynamics of that problem, and a close look at alternative solutions and their ramifications before a program is implemented. A useful way of making such a diagnosis and looking at options is action research, as described in the previous chapter. All supervisors and managers should be knowledgeable about this process because effective action research is a collaborative undertaking. This diagnostic role and the use of action research can be applied to each of the major processes in human resources management.

The Catalyst-Facilitator Role

The human resources director has a unique opportunity to serve in a **catalyst role** in stimulating a top-management discussion about management philosophy, leadership style, and organizational culture and climate. It is important that management develop a clear view of these interrelated matters and that management be self-conscious about them on an ongoing basis. If these areas are not consciously examined and managed, the organization and the people in it can become victims of dysfunctional values, beliefs, assumptions, myths, norms, and practices rather than being masters of these dimensions. The human resources director is the logical person to make these dimensions priority concerns of top management. In addition, the human resources director can serve as a resource person about these concepts and their links to organizational outcomes such as effectiveness, efficiency, development, and participant satisfaction.

Another emerging role for human resources professionals is that of facilitator. Not only will they become more active in the catalyst role, but they will have more training and expertise in the use of behavioral science methods and techniques for bringing about constructive change. As an example, they will be skilled in working with groups and in helping them to diagnose problems and make action plans. More and more human resources professionals will be used as consultant-facilitators in team building and intergroup problem solving, as discussed in the previous chapter.

The Consultant Role

A role that overlaps the diagnostic, catalyst, and facilitator roles is the **consultant role.** In this role, the human resources department will be called upon more and more to advise management at all levels about the motivational and morale, as well as legal implications of various policies and practices. As another example, human resources professionals will collaborate more extensively in the overall strategic planning of the organization. Finally, as pressures for heightened productivity and product quality intensify, the human resources department can help ensure that management remains aware of the need to protect, develop, and reward human resources adequately.

The Evaluator Role

One of the most difficult roles for human resources professionals is the **evaluator role,** or assessing the effectiveness of various human resources policies and practices. As the human resources department grows in stature, however, it is likely to be held increasingly accountable for its effectiveness. A comprehensive evaluation of the effectiveness of an organization's human resources policies and practices is called a human resources management audit or personnel management audit.

At least three kinds of measurements can be used regularly or as part of a comprehensive human resources management audit. They are (1) informed management judgment, (2) perceptions of employees, and (3) statistical and cost analysis.

One of the most valuable sources of information in the evaluation of human resources programs is the informed reactions and judgment of supervisors and managers. Simply asking supervisors and managers how a particular program or practice is going and what might be done to make it better can be an extraordinarily valuable way of evaluating and improving programs. Such measurement needs to be systematic and thorough enough so that the human resources department does not rely on the impressions of just one or two managers.

A similar kind of measurement is the use of questionnaires, or a series of interviews, to solicit employees' perceptions of the impact of particular practices or programs. If 95 percent of the employees report that the method of allocating merit increases is "unfair" or "very unfair," the human resources department has strong evidence that there is a serious problem requiring prompt attention.

A statistical or cost analysis of other practices can also be very useful. For example, a company might wish to analyze the relative merits of recruiting professionals through campus visits and through newspaper advertisements and interviews in large cities. Some of the dimensions that would need to be included in analyzing the costs of each method would be planning time, travel time and costs, advertising costs, numbers and qualifications of people interviewed, numbers and qualifications of persons hired, and job performance and retention rates. As a result of such an analysis, a company might wish to drop one of the two methods of recruiting or emphasize one approach more than the other.

Only careful analysis will reveal some of the hidden costs of some practices or outcomes. An illustration is Wayne Cascio's analysis of the costs of absenteeism. Hidden costs include substantial losses in supervisory salaries resulting from time spent managing problems of absenteeism, such as in instructing replacement employees and counseling and disciplining absentees.[15]

A comprehensive human resources audit might use all of these methods and analyze a wide array of human resources practices and outcomes. For example, an audit might include an analysis of the costs of and/or trends in absenteeism and turnover; tardiness; accidents and accident prevention; disciplinary cases; complaints, grievances, and arbitration; employee benefits; recruitment; training and development; incentive systems; organizational climate; and supervisory morale.[16]

HUMAN RESOURCES PROCESSES IN THE FUTURE

How will the emerging roles described in the previous section be applied to particular processes in human resources management? To put the question another way, in what directions should human resources management move to help organizations achieve the important outcomes of effectiveness, efficiency, development, and participant satisfaction? In this section, current trends and developments within each of the major human resources processes are described. The discussion is largely based on what some organizations have already accomplished, demonstrating that there are desirable and achievable human resources practices that can help an enterprise confront existing challenges and be adequately prepared for the future.

Human Resources Planning

It is clear that, in the future, human resources staff members will be called upon in more and more organizations to link human resources planning to the strategic planning process. Increasingly, professionals must be knowledgeable about and involved in those deliberations that determine the organization's overall goals and objectives. In addition, it is clear that top management increasingly expects the human resources department to assist in management succession planning at all levels. This will require expertise in the development of effective recruitment, selection, and promotion-assessment methods.

Job and Work Design

One of the most promising trends in job design is the increased use of the self-managed team. This concept may have wide application, but it is important that key managers, with the assistance of human resources professionals, make a careful diagnosis of its usefulness with the particular technology and other circumstances of the organization. To move in the direction of self-managed teams requires a reformulation of the role of first-line supervisors, and perhaps that of middle managers, as well as a participative leadership style from the top to the bottom of the organization.

As described in Chapter 7, the self-managed team concept means that the organization assigns teams to be responsible for the production of an entire item or a "whole" task and gives the team considerable autonomy in managing the work. Because the team is heavily involved in such matters as allocating tasks, making product improvements, and selecting new team members, it is essential that team members be trained in effective team membership and leadership skills. The availability of skill training is also important because the ongoing effectiveness of the team depends on each member's developing a range of skills. These and other ramifications of the self-managed team concept have extensive implications for human resources management, all of which support Harold Leavitt's view that it is important to think of teams "as the basic building blocks for an organization."[17]

As lifestyles and attitudes toward work continue to change, experiments with alternative work schedules will also become more and more common. It is likely that flextime, permanent part-time work, and peak-time employment in particular will be tried by many organizations in the near future. As with other human resources programs, however, careful diagnosis of organizational problems, a review of the associated costs and benefits, and an analysis of the labor market need to occur before these alternatives can be implemented successfully.

Staffing

One of the most promising developments in the staffing area is the increased awareness among human resources directors and other managers of the importance and complexity of the various transitions people face in their working lives. Orientation, transfer, promotion, layoff, discharge, and retirement can be treated casually, but such an approach heightens the possibility of injustice, human pain, and organizational inefficiency. Enlightened managers and human resources professionals will want to manage transitions carefully and with foresight. Viewing these changes as complex human, group, and organizational processes can have positive results in terms of employee morale, loyalty, organizational harmony, and other constructive outcomes. Many human resources departments now use small-group techniques in such processes as orientation and preretirement planning.

In addition, organizations seem to be showing more openness and giving employees greater access to information about the various staffing processes. Job posting is increasingly used, and more and more organizations are developing career ladders to assist employees in visualizing advancement opportunities. The selection procedure in many assessment centers is supplemented by a career counseling component so that candidates can learn from the process.

Finally, because of the legal requirements for fair employment practices, the development of valid selection devices continues to be a necessity. Human resources professionals must stay abreast of new regulations and court decisions as they pay close attention to the job relatedness of employment and promotion criteria.

Training and Development

Changes in technology and work methods mean that the human resources staff must be actively engaged in developing training programs to provide employees with needed skills. Making certain that there is considerable opportunity for long-time employees to take on new and challenging assignments and making specialized training programs and seminars available to all workers can help avoid mid-career obsolescence. As the diagnostic role becomes more prominent, however, human resources departments will tend to make careful analyses of training and development needs before launching programs.

As discussed in the previous chapter, the more the organization moves toward participative approaches, the more supervisors, managers, and employees alike need to develop their participative skills. This means that training and development programs must pay attention to skill building in the areas of listening, group decision methods and processes, running meetings, and leadership

PERSPECTIVE 22.2 Schooling for Survival

Every year Charlottesville's Institute of Textile Technology (I.T.T.) turns out a new crop of masters of science imbued with the latest high-tech manufacturing and management skills. "It's a lot different from other graduate programs," [Don] Alexander [a second-year student] says of I.T.T.'s curriculum. "It's more industry related." Not affiliated with a university, the institute is completely supported by some 35 textile companies that it serves as a supplier of the kinds of cutting-edge team players regular schools of higher education have not been turning out.

As such, according to a report last week by the Carnegie Foundation for the Advancement of Teaching, I.T.T. stands as a prime example of the growing commitment by U.S. corporations to education for the workplace. At a time when galloping technology can render an engineer's training obsolete within five years, the study notes that "America's business has become its own educational provider." Says Del Lippert, vice president for educational services at Digital Equipment Corp.: "It's a matter of survival."

The 224-page study, called *Corporate Classrooms: The Learning Business*, represents more than two years of research by Carnegie Trustee Nell Eurich on what has been a disconnected and poorly observed educational behemoth. U.S. companies, Eurich reports, are training and educating nearly 8 million people, close to the total enrollment in America's four-year colleges and universities. According to Carnegie President Ernest Boyer, the corporate classroom has quietly become "a kind of third leg of the education system in the U.S." And it is one of the strongest forces for continuing adult education. Courses range from remedial English to nuclear engineering. Some subjects, such as language and accounting, overlap those in the nation's traditional schools. Others compensate for gaps in the conventional curriculum. General Electric's manager of management education, James Baughman, for one, says, "There is vast illiteracy on business-school faculties" in both the mechanics of advanced technology and its management implications. Says a Texas Instruments executive: "As technology changes, universities tend to lag one to three years behind what's happening in the workplace."

In their scramble to educate employees, corporations spend upwards of $40 billion a year (*vs.* $60 billion-plus for colleges and universities). That kind of money has bought some magnificent facilities, of which the most awesome is Xerox's 2,265-acre complex outside Leesburg, Va. Here an average of 1,200 students a year take company training programs one to seven weeks long. When not in class, they luxuriate in the outdoor pool; racquetball, squash, tennis, and basketball courts; beauty parlor, bar, and dance floor. Almost as impressive is AT&T's center near Princeton, N.J., with 23 classrooms, seven laboratories, four conference rooms, library, auditorium, and 300-bed residence hall. This fall IBM, whose reported $700 million annual education expenditures probably lead those of all other corporations, plans to consolidate its four corporate technical institutes at a 250-acre supercampus in Thornwood, N.Y.

At such facilities, and humbler ones, corporations educate in ways that "surpass many universities" in the judgment of the Carnegie study. Courses have clear goals centered on getting results. "I'm going to take what I learn here Monday and Tuesday," says a Digital Equipment student, "and apply it Wednesday or Thursday." . . .

and supervision. Good intentions are a step in the right direction, but by themselves they are not enough. Effective participation in organizations requires training, skill, and experience.

Performance Appraisal and Review

Appraising the performance of subordinates and communicating effectively about that performance are difficult areas of management. In the future, maintaining high standards of performance will continue to be important, but there may be less emphasis on forms and procedures. What will receive more attention, it is hoped, will be the interpersonal and group skills and organizational climate and culture that permit the appraisal process to be more effective.

Consistent with this point of view are the results of a long-term study at General Electric that concludes:

> At best, it's [performance appraisal] two people sharing their perceptions of each other, their relationships, their work, and their organization — sharing that results in better performance, better feelings, and a more effective organization. At its worst, it is one person in the name of the organization trying to force his or her will on another with the result of miscommunication, misperception, disappointment, and alienation. The best is achievable, but only with considerable effort, careful design, constant attention to the process, and support by top management.[18]

Compensation and Reward

The comparable worth issue is likely to be a major concern for human resources directors, wage and salary administrators, and top management for the next several years. In general, management would be wise to work hard at developing job evaluation systems that are as free from bias as possible. Organizations that can develop single job evaluation systems covering all jobs in the organization will probably be the least vulnerable to legal challenge.

As the self-managed team concept spreads, so will the concept of skills-based pay. Support for this compensation system is suggested by equity theory and by the logical connection between job-related skill training and job performance. In addition, gainsharing plans are congruent with the thrust toward more teamwork, more collaborative problem solving, and more autonomy for employees; and their popularity will probably continue to grow. In contrast, there is evidence that individual incentive plans are declining in number, although these pay systems are still used in many organizations.

The greatly increased costs of employee benefits in recent years have led to major efforts by top management and human resources directors to contain these costs. (Controlling benefit costs is seen by top management as needing increased attention; see Table 22.6.) Flexible benefits programs will continue to grow as one way of controlling costs, unless changes in IRS rules make these programs less practical. Employer-sponsored physical fitness programs and day-care centers are likely to be seen in more and more organizations, particularly in circumstances where it can be demonstrated that they are cost-effective.

Protection and Representation

In Part 6, it was suggested that labor-management relations are beginning to take on problem-solving characteristics in some settings. In addition, organizations are providing greater protection for employee rights and working harder to ensure health and safety in the workplace. All of these developments represent new directions in the protection and representation process.

Labor Relations.   More and more labor-management relationships will move toward integrative bargaining in the future. Integrative bargaining has been shown to be highly relevant across a wide range of problems, such as health and safety matters, job and work design, the introduction of technological improvements, and associated problems of worker displacement and compensation. Such a shift from distributive bargaining requires an emphasis on participative leadership skills and group problem-solving skills in contrast to an exclusive reliance on bargaining tactics.

That a more open, participative managerial style can be implemented successfully in a unionized organization is evidenced by the experience at the Bolivar plant of Harmon International Industries. At that plant, a participative, cooperative organization improvement effort between the union and management resulted in more job security, less alienation, a sharp reduction in accidents, and more work-improvement ideas provided by employees.[19]

Employee Rights and Justice.   Employee protections against discrimination under the Civil Rights Act will continue to be embodied in company policy and practice. In particular, organizations will be likely to adopt strong policies prohibiting sexual harassment. State legislatures will gradually extend whistle-blowing rights in public employment. It is also safe to assume that more and more organizations will voluntarily adopt rules preventing misuse of employee records.

To minimize perceived inequity and to ensure fairness, organizations will find it useful to adhere to concepts of organizational due process. This means that the human resources department will play a key role in settling disputes and monitoring grievance procedures. It is hoped that an even more fundamental evolution will continue: that supervisors will become better listeners and better joint problem solvers, particularly as top management supports and practices a more collaborative style. The human resources department will be active in this evolution in several ways, particularly through its training and development programs and through extensive use of action research.

Health and Safety. The tragedy at the pesticide plant at Bhopal, India, which *Business Week* has called "history's worst industrial accident,"[20] and accidents like the one at the Three Mile Island nuclear plant have focused the attention of management, unions, employees, the public, and the government on the importance of industrial health and safety. Incidents like these intensify the pressure on top management and health and safety specialists to increase the quality of protection provided the worker and the community against hazards. It has long been recognized that top management support of health and safety programs and their active involvement are essential to the success of these programs.

The health problems of individual employees will also receive greater attention as organizations increase their commitment to protecting human resources. There will be less of a tendency to hide or avoid these problems because of the growing realization of the heavy costs to fellow employees, to the organization, and to the employees directly involved. It is reasonable to expect, therefore, a growth in employee-assistance programs and increased skill in confronting and dealing with personal problems of substance abuse and emotional health. The human resources department will play an increasingly important role in the development of appropriate policies and practices and in training supervisors and managers in effective methods of confrontation.

While stress-management programs may be a fad, they do reflect heightened awareness of the negative consequences of excess on-the-job stress. Human resources professionals can help build organizational cultures and climates in which stress management becomes a collective responsibility. This responsibility might be carried out by establishing group norms that permit open discussion of stress, collaboratively shifting workloads within teams, organizational support of recreation opportunities, and support of employee counseling programs.

Organization Improvement

More successful integration of various kinds of participative improvement programs is likely in the future, possibly along the lines of quality-of-work-life projects that synthesize organization development, self-managed teams, and integrative bargaining approaches. Underlying such improvement efforts are commitments to the importance of each employee in every role and at every level, to employee participation, and to action research methods. In addition, a focus on effective teams, sharing of rewards, and long-term management of the improvement effort will be important in improvement programs of the future.

Experience and research will continue to provide valuable insights into the effective management of participative improvement strategies, including the systems ramifications that must be dealt with. For example, management is beginning to be aware that the compensation system must usually be revised to support and sustain long-term, collaborative, team approaches to organization improvement.

The Employee Involvement program at Ford. More participative improvement programs are likely in the future.

Photo courtesy of Ford Motor Company

Ideally, the human resources director or one or more staff members will have extensive training and skill in the management of organization improvement efforts. They will be skilled facilitators themselves or will work collaboratively and effectively with outside facilitators and managers in change efforts. Moreover, these departments will use participative and action-research approaches to keep their own units at peak effectiveness and to be of greatest service to the total organization.

As discussed earlier, the human resources director in more and more organizations will be the catalyst who will precipitate a top-management dialogue about the desired organizational culture and climate. This will be the starting point for many organization improvement efforts.

SUMMARY

Exciting and significant challenges are ahead in human resources management for all supervisors, managers, and human resources professionals. This chapter has suggested a number of ways in which human resources management will evolve to meet changing conditions in the external environment and internal challenges of increased productivity and improved quality of work life. The following list summarizes current trends and future directions in effective human resources management:

- Human resources professionals with more expertise in diagnosing problems and in the use of action research
- Human resources professionals increasingly linking human resources planning to the strategic planning processes of the organization and being involved in these processes
- Human resources professionals increasingly involved in succession planning
- Growing use of the self-managed team concept, with accompanying shifts toward participative leadership styles
- Increased training in group and leadership skills for supervisors, managers, and team members
- Increased emphasis on effective teams and on effective intergroup cooperation
- Increased application of alternative forms of work scheduling such as flextime, permanent part-time work, and peak-time employment
- More understanding of and attention to career transitions
- More openness and information about the various staffing processes (for example, more use of job posting and career ladders)

- Increased expertise and care in diagnosing training and development needs to meet rapidly changing needs and conditions
- More attention to interpersonal and group skills and to organizational climate and culture that permits the appraisal process to be more effective
- Increased emphasis on developing bias-free job evaluation methods
- Increased use of the concept of skills-based pay
- Spreading adoption of gainsharing plans
- Increased attention to controlling benefit costs and increased use of flexible benefits programs
- More and more labor-management relationships moving toward integrative bargaining
- Continued employee protections under the Civil Rights Act
- More and more organizations developing strong policies on sexual harassment
- More and more organizations voluntarily adopting rules preventing misuse of employee records
- More and more adherence to organizational due process
- Supervisors and managers becoming better listeners and participative problem solvers
- Increased attention to industrial hazards
- Increased skill in confronting alcohol- and drug-abuse problems and a growth in employee-assistance programs
- Increased attention to collaborative approaches to managing stress in the organization
- More successful integration of various kinds of participative improvement strategies, and more understanding of the systems ramifications that must be managed
- More expertise on the part of human resources professionals as facilitators and in the management of organization improvement strategies
- More use by human resources professionals of participative, action research methods in keeping their own departments at peak effectiveness in order to better assist the total organization
- More human resources directors becoming the catalyst to precipitate a top management discussion about desired organizational culture and climate

KEY TERMS

accreditation
specialist
generalist

diagnostic role
catalyst role

consultant role
evaluator role

REVIEW QUESTIONS

1. What are the reasons for the increased status of the human resources department?
2. Identify ways in which human resources professionals may enhance their professional development.
3. Describe several future roles that seem to be emerging for human resources professionals.
4. Characterize one or two significant trends and developments within each of the human resources processes.

OPENING CASE QUESTIONS

Case 22.1   The Assignment

1. With the knowledge you have about intergroup behavior and effective human resources management, how would you go about organizing this assignment for your group?
2. What are some specific areas in human resources that you might focus on in developing your ideal organization? Keep in mind areas that will be crucial to organizations in the future.

Case 22.2   We've Got To Look To the Future

1. Why does Martha bring up the company's philosophy when she talks about hiring a human resources director and implementing a human resources program?
2. What are some of the emerging roles that human resources professionals may face with regard to the organization in the future?

CASE 22.3   HUMAN RESOURCES MANAGEMENT: STILL EVOLVING

As the 1980s unfold, it is clear that the field of human resources management has come of age as a critical component of the organization and as a highly potent career venue. Long gone are the days when the "personnel department" was viewed as a dead-end holding area for the insufficiently ambitious.

As the human resources function becomes more elaborate and essential, companies are beginning to rely more on consultants to supplement in-house staff. This trend is increasing with the continued growth in the number of smaller organizations. The role of the in-house specialist is thus changing. Skill is required in assessing organizational needs and then arranging to contract for services that will satisfy those needs.

Yet it is still the in-house manager's job to enforce effectiveness in human resources programs. He or she must make sure that such programs constitute a cooperative effort on the part of human resources specialists and operational employees. Strategically, as the human resources function takes on greater significance in the life of the organization, it must reflect and support overall organizational goals and objectives; and it must diligently predict and prepare for impacts from the organization's environment. The position of the organization and of the human resources activities within it must be subjects of constant evaluation.

At the consulting level, career opportunities may begin to multiply, bringing a new entrepreneurial potential to the human resources career picture. In addition, specialization is likely to be in demand, for both consulting firms and in-house staffs, as such new programs as computer-aided training, fitness training, and human resources research and strategy grow in importance.

As a result of all these developments, there is another new trend in the human resources field. Many entrants are now seeking advanced degrees before starting their careers. During the early maturation of the human resources function, many professionals happened into the field by accident and acquired additional education and training as their careers progressed. Those days, too, seem to be coming to an end as more and more entrants, recognizing the potential of upper-level human resources management as a career, seek to prepare themselves for rapid advancement in a competitive and lucrative field.

Sources: Mark L. Pabst, "Search for Excellence Makes Its Way into Human Resources," *ABA Banking Journal* (February 1985): p. 12; and Neal Chalofsky, "HRD Careers Update," *Training and Development Journal* (May 1985): 64–65.

Discussion Questions

1. Why are there more opportunities for consultants in the human resources management field?
2. For those persons planning a career in human resources management, what are the pros and cons of working on an advanced degree?
3. For those persons planning to hold supervisory or management positions, in what aspects of human resources management will considerable skill and/or knowledge be useful?

Notes

CHAPTER 1

1. Roy Foltz, Karen Rosenberg, and Julie Foehrenbach, "Senior Management Views the Human Resource Function," *Personnel Administrator,* 27 (September 1982): 38.
2. Foltz, Rosenberg, and Foehrenbach, "Senior Management Views the Human Resource Function," 37–50; and American Society for Personnel Administration, "The Changing Role of the Human Resource Professional, *1984 ASPA Annual Report,* p. 7.

CHAPTER 2

1. Frederick Winslow Taylor, *The Principles of Scientific Management* (New York: Harper & Brothers, 1919), Copyright © 1911, pp. 21–37, 130.
2. Frank B. Gilbreth, *Motion Study* (New York: Van Nostrand, 1911).
3. Lillian M. Gilbreth, *The Psychology of Management* (New York: Macmillan, 1914).
4. E. Dorothea Pround, *Welfare Work* (London: G. Bell and Sons, 1916), p. 5.
5. Henry Eilbirt, "The Development of Personnel Management in the United States," *Business History Review* 30 (Autumn 1959): 349.
6. Ibid., pp. 348–349.
7. Hugo Münsterberg, *Psychology and Industrial Efficiency* (Boston: Houghton Mifflin Company, 1913), pp. 63–75.
8. Ibid., Chapter 10. For further discussion of Münsterberg, see "Famous Firsts: Measuring Minds for Jobs," *Business Week*, January 29, 1966, p. 60; and Merle J. Moskowitz, "Hugo Münsterberg: A Study in the History of Applied Psychology," *American Psychologist* 32 (October 1977): 824–842.
9. B. Von Haller Gilmer, *Industrial Psychology* (New York: McGraw-Hill, 1961), pp. 21–22.
10. Howard W. Johnson, "The Hawthorne Studies: The Legend and the Legacy," in Eugene L. Cass and Frederick G. Zimmer, eds., *Man and Work in Society* (New York: Van Nostrand Reinhold Company, 1975), pp. 273–275.
11. F. J. Roethlisberger and W. J. Dickson, *Management and the Worker* (Cambridge, Mass.: Harvard University Press, 1939); T. North Whitehead, *The Industrial Worker* I–II (Cambridge, Mass.: Harvard University Press, 1938); and G. A. Pennock, "Industrial Research at Hawthorne and Experimental Investigation of Rest Periods, Working Conditions, and Other Influences," *Personnel Journal* 8 (February 1930): 296–309.
12. Sanford Cohen, *Labor in the United States* (Columbus, Ohio: Charles E. Merrill, 1960), p. 70.
13. Ibid., p. 449.
14. Foster Rhea Dulles, *Labor in America*, 2nd rev. ed. (New York: Thomas Y. Crowell, 1960), pp. 126–149.
15. Ibid., pp. 150–165.
16. Arthur A. Sloane and Fred Whitney, *Labor Relations*, 4th ed. (Englewood Cliffs, N.J.: Prentice-Hall, 1981), p. 91. See also *Business Week*, May 6, 1961, pp. 90–91.

17. Dulles, *Labor in America*, pp. 195–196; and George S. Gibb and Evelyn H. Knowlton, *The Resurgent Years, 1911–1927: History of Standard Oil Company (New Jersey)* (New York: Harper & Brothers, 1956), p. 136.
18. *Business Week*, September 3, 1979, pp. 26–28.
19. Paul P. Van Riper, *History of the United States Civil Service* (Evanston, Ill.: Row, Peterson, 1958), pp. 96–112.
20. Ordway Tead and Henry C. Metcalf, *Personnel Administration* (New York: McGraw-Hill, 1920).
21. Eilbirt, "The Development of Personnel Management in the United States," p. 352.
22. C. V. Carpenter, "The Working of a Labor Department in Industrial Establishments," *Engineering Magazine* 25 (April 1903): 1–9.
23. F. W. Taylor, "Shop Management," *Transactions*, American Society of Mechanical Engineers, 24 (1903): 1399–1404.
24. William F. Willoughby, *Workingman's Insurance* (New York: Thomas Y. Crowell, 1898), p. 282.
25. Thomas G. Spates, *Human Values Where People Work* (New York: Harper & Brothers, 1960), p. 73.
26. Louis A. Boettiger, *Employee Welfare Work: A Critical and Historical Study* (New York: Ronald Press, 1923), pp. 127–133.
27. Gibb and Knowlton, *The Resurgent Years*, pp. 572–577.

CHAPTER 3

1. *Monthly Labor Review*, 108 (February 1985): 43.
2. William F. Rothenbach and Alan G. Rash, "Difference in Work Force Expectations," *Personnel Administrator*, 29 (May 1984): 122–128.
3. Howard Hayghe, "Working Mothers Reach Record Numbers in 1984," *Monthly Labor Review*, 107 (December 1984): 31.
4. *Business Week* (January 28, 1985): 80.
5. Richard E. Walton, "Criteria for Quality of Working Life," in *The Quality of Working Life*, vol. 1, ed. Louis E. Davis and Albert B. Cherns (New York: The Free Press, 1975), pp. 91–104.
6. Ibid., p. 93.
7. Ibid., pp. 94–95.
8. *The Wall Street Journal*, February 6, 1985.
9. *The Wall Street Journal*, February 7, 1985.
10. *The Wall Street Journal*, December 31, 1984.
11. "The Death of Mining," *Business Week*, December 17, 1984, pp. 64–67.
12. "Deregulating America," *Business Week*, November 28, 1983, pp. 80–96.
13. *Business Week*, July 1, 1985, p. 16: 92; and Sylvia Nasar, "Good News Ahead for Productivity," *Fortune* (December 10, 1984): 40–50.
14. Douglas L. Fleuter, *The Workweek Revolution* (Reading, Mass.: Addison-Wesley, 1975), pp. 73–75.
15. *Fortune*, February 4, 1985, p. 8.
16. *Monthly Labor Review*, 107 (April 1984): 48.
17. *Monthly Labor Review*, 107 (August 1984): 39.

CHAPTER 4

1. Fremont E. Kast and James E. Rosenzweig, *Organization and Management: A Systems and Contingency Approach*, 3rd ed. (New York: McGraw-Hill Book Company, 1979), p. 21.
2. "The Toughest Job in Business: How They're Remaking U.S. Steel," *Business Week* (February 25, 1982): 53.
3. Douglas McGregor, *The Human Side of Enterprise* (New York: McGraw-Hill Book Company, 1960), pp. 33–34, 47–48.
4. Ibid., pp. 35, 43–49; see also Warren Bennis, "Douglas McGregor's *The* Human Side of Enterprise," *New Management,* 3 (Summer 1985): 60–61.
5. William G. Ouichi, *Theory Z: How American Business Can Meet the Japanese Challenge* (Reading, Mass.: Addison-Wesley Publishing Company, 1981), p. 230.
6. Thomas H. Melohn, "How to Build Employee Trust and Productivity," *Harvard Business Review,* 83(1) (January-February, 1983): 56–57.
7. Ibid., pp. 56–57, 60–61.
8. Ibid., pp. 56–57.
9. Ricky Griffin, *Management* (Boston: Houghton Mifflin, 1984), p. 421.
10. Edwin A. Fleishman and Edwin F. Harris, "Patterns of Leadership Behavior Related to Employee Grievances and Turnover," *Personnel Psychology,* 15 (Spring 1962): 43–44; Robert L. Kahn, "Productivity and Job Satisfaction," *Personnel Psychology,* 13 (Autumn 1960): 275–287; and Robert R. Blake and Jane S. Mouton, *The Managerial Grid* (Houston: Gulf Publishing, 1964).
11. Jay W. Lorsch and John J. Morse, *Organizations and Their Members* (New York: Harper & Row, 1974); and Fred E. Fiedler and Martin M. Chemers, *Leadership and Effective Management* (Glenview, Ill.: Scott, Foresman and Company, 1974).
12. Robert Tannenbaum and Warren H. Schmidt, "How to Choose a Leadership Pattern," *Harvard Business Review,* 36(2) (March-April 1958): 95–101.
13. Ibid.
14. Marshall Sashkin, *A Manager's Guide to Participative Management* (New York: American Management Associations, 1982), pp. 60–61.
15. See Edwin A. Locke and David M. Schweiger, "Participation in Decision-Making: One More Look," in *Research in Organizational Behavior,* Vol. 1, ed. Barry M. Staw (Greenwich, Conn.: JAI Press, 1979), pp. 265–339.
16. See Robert R. Blake and Jane Srygley Mouton, "Theory and Research for Developing a Science of Leadership," *The Journal of Applied Behavioral Science,* 18 (1982): 290.

17. Sashkin, *A Manager's Guide to Participative Management,* pp. 60–61.
18. Richard T. Pascale, "The Paradox of 'Corporate Culture': Reconciling Ourselves to Socialization," *California Management Review* 27 (Winter 1985):31.
19. *The Arizona Republic,* January 28, 1985 p. c–1.
20. Homer J. Hagedorn, "Everybody Into the Pool," *Across the Board* 21 (October 1984): 26.
21. Pascale, "The Paradox of 'Corporate Culture,'" p. 26.
22. Based on George H. Litwin, John W. Humphrey, and Thomas B. Wilson, "Organizational Climate: A Proven Tool for Improving Performance," in *The Cutting Edge: Current Theory and Practice in Organization Development,* ed. W. Warner Burke (La Jolla, Calif.: University Associates, 1978), pp. 187–205.
23. George H. Litwin and Robert A. Stringer, *Motivation and Organization Climate* (Boston: Graduate School of Business Administration, Harvard University, 1968), pp. 81–82.
24. William F. Dowling, "At General Motors: System 4 Builds Performance and Profits," *Organizational Dynamics* 4 (Winter 1975): 23–38; and Rensis Likert and Jane Gibson Likert, *New Ways of Managing Conflict* (New York: McGraw-Hill Book Company, 1976), pp. 71–86.

CHAPTER 5

1. A.H. Maslow, *Motivation and Personality,* 2nd ed. (New York: Harper & Brothers, 1970), Chapters 3–7.
2. Clayton P. Alderfer, *Existence, Relatedness, and Growth: Human Needs in Organizational Settings* (New York: The Free Press, 1972) pp. 6–13, 133.
3. D. C. McClelland, *The Achieving Society* (Princeton, N.J.: Van Nostrand, 1961); and D. C. McClelland, *Assessing Human Motivation* (New York: General Learning Press, 1971).
4. David C. McClelland and David H. Burnham, "Power Is the Great Motivator," *Harvard Business Review,* 54 (March-April 1976):100–110.
5. Frederick Herzberg, Bernard Mausner, and Barbara Snyderman, *The Motivation to Work,* 2nd ed. (New York: John Wiley & Sons, 1959), pp. 59–62, 60–74; and Frederick Herzberg, *Work and the Nature of Man* (Cleveland: The World Publishing Company, 1966).
6. D. P. Schwab, W. H. DeVitt, and L. L. Cummings, "A Test of the Adequacy of the Two-factor Theory as a Predictor of Self-report Performance Effects," *Personnel Psychology,* 24 (Summer 1971): 293–304.
7. Based on Walter R. Nord, "Beyond the Teaching Machine," in Walter R. Nord, ed., *Concepts and Controversy in Organizational Behavior,* 2nd ed. (Pacific Palisades, Calif.: Goodyear Publishing Company, Inc., 1972), pp. 151–174.
8. George C. Homans, *Social Behavior: Its Elementary Forms* (New York: Harcourt, Brace & World, 1961), Chapter 12; and J. Stacy Adams, "Toward an Understanding of Inequity," *Journal of Abnormal and Social Psychology,* 67 (1963): 422–424.
9. William M. Evan, and Roberta G. Simmons, "Organizational Effects of Inequitable Rewards: Two Experiments in Status Inconsistency," *Administrative Science Quarterly,* 14 (June 1969): 224–237; Paul S. Goodman, "Effect of Perceived Inequity on Salary Allocation Decisions," *Journal of Applied Psychology,* 60 (June 1975): 372–375; Adams, "Toward an Understanding of Inequity," p. 434; and Paul R. Timm, "Worker Responses to Supervisory Communication Inequity: An Exploratory Study," *The Journal of Business Communication,* 16 (Fall 1978):11–24.
10. David A. Nadler and Edward E. Lawler III, "Motivation: A Diagnostic Approach," pp. 27–29 in J. Richard Hackman, Edward E. Lawler III, and Lyman W. Porter, eds., *Perspectives on Behavior in Organizations* (New York: McGraw-Hill Book Company, 1977).
11. For a study on predispositions toward job satisfaction, see Elaine D. Pulakos and Neal Schmitt, "A Longitudinal Study of a Valence Model Approach for the Prediction of Job Satisfaction of New Employees," *Journal of Applied Psychology,* 68 (May 1983):307–312.
12. See Nadler and Lawler, "Motivation: A Diagnostic Approach," p. 36; and Edward E. Lawler III and Lyman W. Porter, "The Effect of Performance on Job Satisfaction," *Industrial Relations,* 7 (October 1967):20–28.
13. Nadler and Lawler, "Motivation: A Diagnostic Approach," p. 29.
14. Paul Spector, "Relationships of Organizational Frustration with Reported Behavioral Reactions of Employees," *Journal of Applied Psychology,* 60 (October 1975): 635–637.
15. "Navy Identifies Plane Saboteurs," *The Seattle Times,* September 23, 1980, p. A4.
16. Richard M. Steers and Susan R. Rhodes, "Major Influences on Employee Attendance: A Process Model," *Journal of Applied Psychology,* 63 (August 1978):391–407.
17. M. C. Knowles, "Labour Turnover: Aspects of Its Significance," *Industrial Relations* (Australia), 18 (March 1976):67–75.
18. See Graham L. Staines and Robert P. Quinn, "American Workers Evaluate the Quality of Their Jobs," *Monthly Labor Review,* 102 (January 1979):5–6; Charles N. Weaver, "Job Satisfaction in the United States in the 1970s," *Journal of Applied Psychology,* 65 (June 1980):364–367.
19. Richard T. Pascale, "The Paradox of 'Corporate Culture,'" *California Management Review,* 27 (Winter 1985):31.
20. See Wendell L. French, Fremont E. Kast, and James

E. Rosenzweig, *Understanding Human Behavior in Organizations* (New York: Harper & Row, 1985), p. 228.

21. See F. J. Roethlisberger and William J. Dickson, *Management and the Worker* (Cambridge, Mass.: Harvard University Press, 1939; reprinted 1956), pp. 417–423.

22. Martin Patchen, "Supervisory Methods and Group Performance Norms," *Administrative Science Quarterly*, 7 (December 1962):275–294.

23. Robert L. Kahn, "Productivity and Job Satisfaction," *Personnel Psychology*, 13 (Autumn 1960):285.

24. Robert Schrank, *Ten Thousand Working Days* (Cambridge, Mass.: The MIT Press, 1978), p. 82.

25. This discussion is drawn partly from Rensis Likert, *New Patterns of Management* (New York: McGraw-Hill Book Company, 1961), pp. 166–167; and Kenneth D. Benne and Paul Sheats, "Functional Roles of Group Members," *The Journal of Social Issues*, 4 (Spring 1948):41–49.

26. Thomas J. Peters and Robert H. Waterman, Jr., *In Search of Excellence* (New York: Harper & Row, 1982), p. 217.

27. Based on Robert R. Blake, Herbert A. Shepard, and Jane S. Mouton, *Managing Intergroup Conflict in Industry* (Houston: Gulf Publishing Company, 1964), pp. 19–41; Muzafer Sherif, *Group Conflict and Cooperation* (London: Routledge and Kegan Paul, 1966); and Robert R. Blake and Jane S. Mouton, "Reactions to Intergroup Competition Under Win-Lose Conditions," *Management Science* 4 (July 1961):420–435.

CHAPTER 6

1. James W. Walker, *Human Resource Planning* (New York: McGraw-Hill Book Company, 1980), pp. 11–22.

2. Ibid.

3. Ibid., p. 10.

4. *Business Week*, September 17, 1984, p. 66.

5. For information on relevant computer software, see George E. Biles and Richard A. Bassler, "Low-Priced Automation for Personnel Management Functions," *Personnel Administrator*, 29 (August 1984): 53–58; and Barbara E. Heiken and James W. Randell, Jr., "Customizing Software for Human Resources," *Personnel Administrator*, 29 (August 1984): 43–48.

6. U.S. Department of Labor, *Occupational Outlook Handbook, 1982–83 Edition*, Bureau of Labor Statistics, Bulletin 2200, April 1982, p. 18.

7. Ibid.

8. Mack A. Player, *Federal Law of Employment Discrimination* (St. Paul, Minn.: West Publishing, 1976), p. 116.

9. Bureau of National Affairs, *Labor Relations Reporter, Fair Employment Practices Manual*, 451 (January 1980): 1–5.

10. Title VII, Civil Rights Act of 1964, Sections 706–707.

11. Ruth G. Shaeffer, *Nondiscrimination in Employment, 1973–1975* (New York: The Conference Board, 1975), p. 6.

12. *Business Week*, June 21, 1976, p. 38.

13. *Resource* (February 1984): 12.

14. *Impact* (Prentice-Hall), 7, no. 8, January 19, 1983, p. 8.

15. *Monthly Labor Review*, 107 (February 1984): 66.

16. U.S. Department of Labor, *Dictionary of Occupational Titles*, 4th ed., Employment and Training Administration, 1977.

17. American Society for Personnel Administration, *Fair Employment Digest* (December 1971): p. 3.

18. *U.S. News and World Report*, December 1, 1980, p. 79.

19. *Wall Street Journal*, June 6, 1972, p. 1.

20. U.S. Department of Labor, *Perspectives on Working Women*, Bureau of Labor Statistics, October 1980, pp. 10–11.

21. "Women in Work—Facts and Fictions," *Newsletter*, Institute for Social Research, University of Michigan, Autumn 1972, pp. 4–5.

22. Donald P. Schwab and Herbert G. Heneman III, "Effects of Age and Experience on Productivity," in Robert L. Taylor, Michael J. O'Connell, Robert A. Zawacki, and D. D. Warrick, eds., *Academy of Management Proceedings*, Proceedings of the 36th Annual Meeting of the Academy of Management, Kansas City, Missouri, August 11–14, 1976, pp. 281–283.

23. Howard J. Anderson, *Primer of Equal Employment Opportunity* (Washington, D.C.: Bureau of National Affairs, 1978), p. 55.

24. George S. Roukis, "Protecting Workers' Civil Rights: Equality in the Workplace," *Labor Law Journal*, 26 (January 1975): 11.

25. *Wall Street Journal*, November 21, 1983, p. 2.

26. *Wall Street Journal*, January 9, 1985, p. 5.

27. *Monthly Labor Review*, 108 (March 1985): 49.

28. "Wounded Executives Fight Back on Age Bias," *Business Week*, July 21, 1980, p. 109.

29. Peter M. Jamero, "Handicapped Individuals in the Changing Workforce," *Journal of Contemporary Business*, 8 (November 4, 1979): 33–42.

30. Julie Wysock and Paul Wysock, "An Employer's Guide to Employment and Disability," *Journal of Contemporary Business*, 8 (November 4, 1979): 59–66.

31. Jamero, "Handicapped Individuals in the Changing Workforce," p. 36.

32. *Affirmative Action for Disabled People: A Pocket Guide*, The President's Committee on Employment of the Handicapped (pamphlet, no date).

33. For other examples, see Cyril M. Rappaport, "Hiring the Handicapped," *Personnel Administrator*, 25 (November 1980): 81–88.

34. Kenneth L. Sovereign, *Personnel Law* (Reston, Virginia: Reston Publishing Company, 1984), p. 81.

35. U.S. Department of Labor, Office of Federal Contract Compliance Programs, "Compliance Responsibility for Equal Employment Opportunity," *Federal Register*, Friday, October 20, 1978, pp. 49240–49283.

36. Equal Employment Opportunity Commission, "Affirmative Action Guidelines," *Federal Register*, Friday, January 19, 1979, p. 4425. See also U.S. Department of Labor, "Compliance Responsibility for Equal Employment Opportunity," pp. 49240–49283; and U.S. Department of Labor, *OFCCP: Making EEO and Affirmative Action Work*, Office of Federal Contract Compliance Programs, October 1979 (pamphlet).

37. *Wall Street Journal*, April 15, 1980, p. 6.

38. *Wall Street Journal*, July 16, 1980, p. 13.

39. William L. Kandel, "Current Developments in EEO," *Employee Relations Law Journal*, 5 (Winter 1979–1980):416–429; and Gregory J. Mounts, "Labor and the Supreme Court: Significant Decisions of 1978–79," *Monthly Labor Review*, 103 (January 1980): 14–21.

40. *Monthly Labor Review*, 107 (August 1984): 39.

41. Bureau of National Affairs, "Personnel Activities, Budgets, and Staffs: 1983–1984," *Bulletin to Management*, No. 1785—Part II, June 21, 1984, p. 2.

42. Allan R. Janger, *Personnel Function: Changing Objectives and Organization* (New York: The Conference Board, 1977), p. 38.

43. Kenneth F. Misa and Timothy Stein, "Strategic HRM and the Bottom Line," *Personnel Administrator*, 28 (October 1983): 27–30.

CHAPTER 7

1. J. Richard Hackman and Greg R. Oldham, *Work Redesign* (Reading, Mass.: Addison-Wesley Publishing Company, Inc., 1980), pp. 77–80.

2. Ibid., pp. 3–21.

3. Ibid., p. 20.

4. Ibid., pp. 82–88.

5. Ibid., pp. 103–129. See pp. 275–315 of Hackman and Oldham for a copy of the JDS scoring key and guidelines for use.

6. Robert N. Ford, "Job Enrichment Lessons from AT&T," *Harvard Business Review*, 51 (January–February 1973): 96–106.

7. Ibid., pp. 96–106.

8. William J. Paul, Keith B. Robertson, and Frederick Herzberg, "Job Enrichment Pays Off," *Harvard Business Review*, 47 (March–April 1969): 61–78.

9. M. Scott Myers, "Every Employee a Manager," *California Management Review*, 10 (Spring 1968): 9–20.

10. M. Scott Myers, *Every Employee a Manager* (New York: McGraw-Hill Book Company, 1970), pp. 74–87.

11. Peter G. Gyllenhammar, *People at Work* (Reading, Mass.: Addison-Wesley Publishing Company, Inc., 1977); and A. Mikalachki, "The Effects of Job Design in Turnover, Absenteeism and Health," *Industrial Relations*, 30 (August 1975): 377–388.

12. E. L. Trist, G. W. Higgin, H. Murray, and A. B. Pollock, *Organizational Choice* (London: Tavistock Publications, 1965).

13. A. K. Rice, "Productivity and Social Organization in an Indian Weaving Shed," *Human Relations*, 6 (1953): 297–329.

14. Richard E. Walton, "From Hawthorne to Topeka and Kalmar," in Eugene L. Cass and Frederick G. Zimmer, eds., *Man and Work in Society* (New York: Van Nostrand Reinhold, 1975), p. 119.

15. Paul, Robertson, and Herzberg, "Job Enrichment Pays Off," pp. 61–78.

16. Ford, "Job Enrichment Lessons from AT&T," pp. 96–106.

17. Myers, *Every Employee a Manager*, pp. 74–87; and *Business Week*, April 27, 1968, p. 60.

18. Mikalachki, "The Effects of Job Design," pp. 377–388.

19. Trist, et al., *Organizational Choice*, p. 294; and Rice, "Productivity and Social Organization," pp. 297–329.

20. See David A. Whitsett and Lyle Yorks, "Looking Back at Topeka: General Foods and the Quality-of-Work-Life Experiment," *California Management Review*, 25 (Summer 1983): 93–109; Richard E. Walton, "Innovative Restructuring of Work," in Jerome E. Rosow, ed., *The Worker and the Job* (Englewood Cliffs, N.J.: Prentice-Hall, 1974), p. 162; and Richard E. Walton, "Work Innovations at Topeka: After Six Years," *The Journal of Applied Behavioral Science*, 13 (July–August–September 1977): 422–433.

21. U.S. Department of Labor, "Job Redesign: Some Case Histories," *Manpower* (May 1973): 18–19.

22. Seminar with Ake Magnusson of Stockholm School of Economics, November 14, 1975, Graduate School of Business Administration, University of Washington.

23. Ernesto J. Poza and M. Lynne Markus, "Success Story: The Team Approach to Work Restructuring," *Organizational Dynamics*, 8 (Winter 1980): 3–21.

24. See Ernest J. McCormick, "Job and Task Analysis," in Marvin D. Dunnette, ed., *Handbook of Industrial and Organizational Psychology* (Chicago: Rand McNally, 1976), pp. 652–654.

25. Ernest J. McCormick, Paul R. Jeanneret, and Robert C. Mecham, "A Study of Job Characteristics and Job Dimensions as Based on the Position Analysis Questionnaire (PAQ)," *Journal of Applied Psychology Monograph*, 56 (August 1972): 347–368.

26. Ibid., pp. 363–366.

27. Wayne F. Cascio, *Applied Psychology in Personnel*

Management (Reston, Virginia: Reston Publishing, 1978), pp. 141–142.

28. U.S. Supreme Court, *Willis S. Griggs et al.* v. *Duke Power Company,* March 8, 1971.

29. *Wall Street Journal,* May 6, 1983, p. 1.

30. *Ideas & Trends in Personnel,* Commerce Clearing House, No. 69, July 13, 1984, p. 108.

CHAPTER 8

1. Perry Garfinkel, "Smoker Seg," *Across the Board,* 21 (July/August 1984): 29.

2. Douglas Massengill and Donald J. Petersen, "Smokers vs. Nonsmokers in the Work Place: Clearing the Air," *Employee Relations Law Journal,* 10 (Winter 1984–85): 510.

3. *Wall Street Journal,* January 25, 1983, p. 25.

4. "Absenteeism and Lateness," *Personnel Policies and Practices* (Prentice-Hall, 1981), p. 16.

5. Bureau of National Affairs, "Employee Conduct and Discipline," *Personnel Policies Forum,* 102 (August 1972): 6.

6. *Wall Street Journal,* March 30, 1982, p. 1.

7. Robert W. Fisher, "When Workers Are Discharged — An Overview," *Monthly Labor Review,* 96 (June 1973): 8.

8. Bureau of National Affairs, *Bulletin to Management,* June 19, 1975.

9. O. L. Harvey, "The 10-Hour Day in the Philadelphia Navy Yard, 1835–36," *Monthly Labor Review,* 85 (March 1962): 258–260.

10. Douglas L. Fleuter, *The Workweek Revolution: A Guide to the Changing Workweek* (Reading, Mass.: Addison-Wesley Publishing Company, Inc., 1975), p. iv.

11. *Monthly Labor Review,* 108 (January 1985): 76.

12. U.S. Department of Labor, "Hours of Work: A Brief History," *Employment and Training Report of the President* (Washington, D.C.: Government Printing Office, 1979), pp. 77–79.

13. See U.S. Department of Labor, Wage and Hour Division, *Reference Guide to the Fair Labor Standards Act,* WH Publication 1282, revised January 1981.

14. W. P. Colquhoun and J. Rutenfranz, *Studies of Shiftwork* (London: Taylor & Francis, Ltd., 1980), p. ix.

15. Peter Finn, "The Effects of Shift Work on the Lives of Employees," *Monthly Labor Review,* 104 (October 1981): 31.

16. Colquhoun and Rutenfranz, *Studies of Shiftwork,* p. 5.

17. Finn, "The Effects of Shift Work on the Lives of Employees," p. 32.

18. Ibid., p. 32.

19. Graham L. Staines and Joseph H. Pleck, "Nonstandard Work Schedules and Family Life," *Journal of Applied Psychology,* 69 (August 1984): 515–523.

20. Finn, "The Effects of Shift Work on the Lives of Employees," p. 34.

21. U.S. Department of Labor, "Hours of Work: A Brief History," pp. 77–79.

22. *Monthly Labor Review,* 98 (January 1975): 85.

23. U.S. Department of Labor, *Employment and Training Report of the President,* 1979, p. 84.

24. Kenneth E. Wheeler, Richard Gurman, and Dale Tarnowieski, *The Four-Day Week* (New York: American Management Association, 1972), pp. 1–3.

25. Douglas L. Fleuter, *The Workweek Revolution: A Guide to the Changing Workweek* (Reading, Mass.: Addison-Wesley Publishing Company, Inc., 1975), pp. 12–15; and Allan R. Cohen and Herman Gadon, *Alternative Work Schedules: Integrating Individual and Organizational Needs* (Reading, Mass.: Addison-Wesley Publishing Company, Inc., 1978), pp. 49–64.

26. Stanley D. Nollen, *New Work Schedules in Practice* (New York: Van Nostrand Reinhold, 1982), p. 6.

27. "Flexible Work Hours Gather Momentum," *U.S. News & World Report,* September 28, 1981; and "Flexitime Flexibility," *Wall Street Journal,* December 2, 1980, p. 1.

28. Fleuter, *The Workweek Revolution,* pp. 73–102.

29. Based on Fleuter, *The Workweek Revolution,* pp. 77–84; R. T. Golembiewski, R. Hilles, and M. S. Kagno, "A Longitudinal Study of Flex-Time Effects," *Journal of Applied Behavioral Science,* 10 (October 1974): 503–532; and Simcha Ronen and Sophia B. Primps, "The Compressed Work Week as Organizational Change: Behavioral and Attitudinal Outcomes," *Academy of Management Review,* 6 (January 1981): 61–74.

30. *U.S. News & World Report,* October 4, 1982, p. 74.

31. For example, see R. A. Winett and M. S. Neale, "Results of Experimental Study on Flexitime and Family Life," *Monthly Labor Review,* 103 (November 1980): 29–32.

32. *Resource* (August 1984): 2; and *Seattle Business Journal,* August 20, 1984, p. 11.

33. *Wall Street Journal,* February 8, 1983, p. 1.

34. *Wall Street Journal,* February 12, 1985, p. 1.

35. Stanley Nollen, *New Patterns of Work* (Scarsdale, N.Y.: Work in America Institute, 1979), pp. 5–6.

36. *Wall Street Journal,* June 2, 1982, p. 48.

37. Nollen, *New Patterns of Work,* p. 6.

38. Howard E. Miller and James R. Terborg, "Job Attitudes of Part-Time and Full-Time Employees," *Journal of Applied Psychology,* 64 (August 1979): 380–386.

39. See Michael Frease and Robert A. Zawacki, "Job Sharing: An Answer to Productivity Problems," *The Personnel Administrator,* 24 (October 1979): 35–38.

40. David Clutterbuck, "Why a Job Shared Is Not a Job Halved," *International Management,* 34 (October 1979): 45–47.

41. Nollen, *New Work Schedules in Practice,* pp. 141–147.

42. Frease and Zawacki, "Job Sharing," pp. 35–37, 56; and Clutterbuck, "Why a Job Shared Is Not a Job Halved," pp. 45–47.
43. *Business Week,* May 3, 1982, p. 66.
44. *Wall Street Journal,* August 4, 1981, p. 46.
45. *Wall Street Journal,* February 13, 1985, p. 31.
46. See *Business Week,* May 3, 1982, p. 66; *Business Week,* January 23, 1984, p. 99; and *Wall Street Journal,* February 13, 1985, p. 31.
47. *Wall Street Journal,* February 13, 1985, p. 31; *Business Week,* May 3, 1982, p. 66; and *Business Week,* January 23, 1984, p. 99.
48. *Wall Street Journal,* February 13, 1985, p. 31.

CHAPTER 9

1. U.S. Department of Labor, *Job Seeking Methods Used by American Workers,* Bulletin No. 1886 (Washington, D.C., 1975), p. 4.
2. Ellen Sehgal and Joyce Violet, "Documenting the Undocumented," *Monthly Labor Review,* 103 (October 1980): 18–21.
3. See Mary T. Matthies, "The Developing Law of Equal Opportunity," *Journal of Contemporary Business,* 5 (Winter 1976): 37; and Ruth Gilbert Schaeffer and Edith F. Lynton, *Corporate Experiences in Improving Women's Job Opportunities* (New York: The Conference Board, 1979), pp. 36–39.
4. Bureau of National Affairs, *Recruiting Policies and Practices,* Personnel Policies Forum, Survey No. 126 (Washington, D.C., July 1979), p. 2.
5. See Richard T. Cronin, "Executive Recruiters: Are They Necessary?" *Personnel Administrator,* 26 (February 1981): 31–32.
6. U.S. Department of Labor, *Job Seeking Methods,* pp. 1–10.
7. James A. Breaugh, "Relationships Between Recruiting Sources and Employee Performance, Absenteeism, and Work Attitudes," *Academy of Management Journal,* 24 (March 1981): 145.
8. See the March 1984 figures displayed in Chapter 6, Table 6.2, which indicate that more than 43 percent of employed civilians are female. See also Office of the Secretary of the Women's Bureau, *Facts on Women Workers* (Washington, D.C.: Department of Labor, 1980).
9. Schaeffer and Lynton, *Corporate Experiences,* p. 42.
10. Bureau of National Affairs, *Recruiting Policies and Practices,* p. 5.
11. See Patricia C. Smith, "Behavior, Results, and Organizational Effectiveness: The Problem of Criteria," in Marvin D. Dunnette, ed., *Handbook of Industrial and Organizational Psychology* (Chicago: Rand McNally, 1976), pp. 745–775.
12. Frank L. Schmidt, John E. Hunter, Robert C. McKenzie, and Tressie W. Muldrow, "Impact of Valid Selection Procedures on Work-Force Productivity," *Journal of Applied Psychology,* 64 (December 1979): pp. 609–626.
13. "Uniform Guidelines on Employee Selection Procedures," Section 3, D, *Federal Register,* Vol. 43, No. 166 (Friday, August 25, 1978), p. 38297.
14. On weighted data, see William A. Owens, "Background Data," in Dunnette, ed., *Handbook,* p. 617. For a sample of studies in particular job categories, see Stanley R. Novack, "Developing an Effective Application Blank," *Personnel Journal,* 49 (May 1970): 419–423; W. K. Kirchner and M. D. Dunnette, "Applying the Weighted Application Blank in a Variety of Office Jobs," *Journal of Applied Psychology,* 41 (August 1957): 206–208; Richard D. Scott and Richard W. Johnson, "Use of the Weighted Application Blank in Selecting Unskilled Employees," *Journal of Applied Psychology,* 51 (October 1967): 393–395.
15. Equal Employment Opportunity Commission, *Employment Application Form Questions Which May Lead to Discrimination* (Washington, D.C., August 14, 1972; mimeographed).
16. See Commerce Clearing House, *Employment Practices Guide,* 1193, August 3, 1972; and M. L. Howell, "Complying with the Fair Credit Reporting Act," *Personnel Administrator,* 17 (January–February 1972): 10–12.
17. For further discussion of this subject, see John D. Rice, "Privacy Legislation: Its Effect on Pre-Employment Reference Checking," *Personnel Administrator,* 23 (February 1978): 46–51.
18. See National Commission on State Workmen's Compensation Laws, *Report of the National Commission on State Workmen's Compensation Laws* (Washington, D.C., 1972).
19. Bureau of National Affairs, *Selection Procedures and Personnel Records,* Personnel Policies Forum, Survey No. 114 (September 1976), p. 7, compares studies on the use of psychological tests in 1963 and 1976.
20. The U.S. Employment Service has reported increased use of its test battery: Employment and Training Administration, *Employment and Training Report of the President* (Washington, D.C.: Department of Labor, 1980), pp. 64–65.
21. FEP Commission, State of Illinois, *Myart* v. *Motorola* (1964). See the discussion in Howard C. Lockwood, "Testing Minority Applicants for Employment," *Personnel Journal,* 44 (July–August 1965): 356–360ff.
22. U.S. Supreme Court, *Griggs* v. *Duke Power Company.*
23. See American Society for Personnel Administration, *Fair Employment Digest,* (March 1978): 2.
24. See John H. Kirkwood, "Selection Techniques and the Law: To Test or Not to Test," *Personnel,* 44 (November–December 1967): 18–26.
25. "Employee Testing and Selection Procedures — Where

Are They Headed?" (P-H/ASPA Survey), *Personnel Management: Policies and Practices* (Englewood Cliffs, N.J.: Prentice-Hall, 1975), pp. 651–653.

CHAPTER 10

1. Based on Bureau of National Affairs, *Bulletin to Management,* No. 1436, August 25, 1977, p. 7.
2. Earl R. Gomersall and M. Scott Myers, "Breakthrough in On-the-Job Training," *Harvard Business Review,* 44 (July–August 1966): 62–72.
3. Ibid., pp. 66–68.
4. John P. Cotter, "Managing the Joining-Up Process," *Personnel,* 49 (July–August 1972): 46–56. See also Daniel C. Feldman, "A Socialization Process That Helps New Recruits Succeed," *Personnel,* 57 (March–April 1980): 11–23.
5. Arlene A. Johnson, "Relocation: Getting More for the Dollars You Spend," *Personnel Administrator,* 29 (April 1984): 29.
6. Lionel Tiger, "Is This Trip Necessary? The Heavy Human Costs of Moving Executives Around," *Fortune,* September, 1974, pp. 139–141ff.
7. *Wall Street Journal,* January 28, 1985, p. 33.
8. Bureau of National Affairs, Employee Promotion & Transfer Policies, *Personnel Policies Forum,* No. 120, January 1978, pp. 12–13.
9. American Society for Personnel Administration, *Fair Employment Digest* (December 1980): 2.
10. See, for example, Allen I. Kraut, "Prediction of Managerial Success by Peer and Training-Staff Ratings," *Journal of Applied Psychology,* 60 (February 1975):14–19.
11. Ernest C. Miller, "Hire in Haste, Repent at Leisure — The Team Selection Procedure at Graphic Controls," *Organizational Dynamics,* 8 (Spring 1980): 3–26.
12. Ann Howard, "An Assessment of Assessment Centers," *Academy of Management Journal,* 17 (March 1974): 115–134.
13. William E. Dodd, "Attitudes Toward Assessment Center Programs," in Joseph L. Moses and William C. Byham, eds., *Applying the Assessment Center Method* (New York: Pergamon, 1977), pp. 169–170.
14. See, for example, Richard J. Ritchie and Joseph L. Moses, "Assessment Center Correlates of Women's Advancement into Middle Management: A 7-Year Longitudinal Analysis," *Journal of Applied Psychology,* 68 (May 1983): 227–231; Neal Schmitt, Raymond Noe, Ronni Meritt, and Michael Fitzgerald, "Validity of Assessment Center Ratings for the Prediction of Performance Ratings and School Climate of School Administrators," *Journal of Applied Psychology,* 69 (May 1984): 207–213; and Aharon Tziner and Shimon Dolan, "Validity of an Assessment Center for Identifying Future Female Officers in the Military," *Journal of Applied Psychology,* 67 (December 1982): 728–736.

15. Douglas T. Hall and Francine S. Hall, "What's New in Career Management," *Organizational Dynamics,* 5 (Summer 1976): 23–24.
16. William R. Walter and Anthony J. Obadal, "Layoffs: The Judicial View," *The Personnel Administrator,* 20 (May 1975): 13–16.
17. Douglas F. Seaver, "The *Stotts* Decision: Is It the Death Knell for Seniority Systems?" *Employee Relations Law Journal,* 10 (Winter 1984–1985): 497–504.
18. Richard R. Nelson, "State Labor Legislation Enacted in 1983," *Monthly Labor Review,* 107 (January 1983): 63.
19. Janisse Klotchman and Linda L. Neider, "EEO Alert: Watch Out for Discrimination in Discharge Cases," *Personnel,* 60 (January–February 1983): 64.
20. Ibid., p. 65.
21. Bureau of National Affairs, "Retirement Policies and Programs," *Bulletin to Management,* ASPA-BNA Survey No. 39, January 24, 1980, pp. 10–11.
22. Chamber of Commerce of the United States, *Employee Benefits 1983* (1984), p. 5.
23. Fred K. Foulkes, *Personnel Policies in Large Nonunion Companies* (Englewood Cliffs, N.J.: Prentice-Hall, 1980), p. 229.
24. Beverly Jacobson, *Young Programs for Older Workers: Case Studies in Progressive Personnel Policies* (New York: Van Nostrand, 1980), p. 17.
25. Jeffrey M. Miller, *Innovations in Working Patterns: Report of the U.S. Trade Union Seminar on Alternative Work Patterns in Europe* (Washington, D.C.: The Communications Workers of America and the George Marshall Fund of the United States, 1978), p. 17.
26. Stephen L. Fink, Joel Beak, and Kenneth Taddeo, "Organizational Crisis and Change," *The Journal of Applied Behavioral Science,* 7 (November 1, 1971): 15–37.
27. *Wall Street Journal,* April 12, 1983, p. 1.
28. *Wall Street Journal,* February 28, 1972, p. 1.
29. Lawrence M. Brammer and Frank E. Humberger, *Outplacement & Inplacement Counseling* (Englewood Cliffs, N.J.: Prentice-Hall, 1984).
30. *Business Week,* November 10, 1975, p. 110.
31. *Wall Street Journal,* May 29, 1984, p. 1.
32. Bruce R. Ellig, "Pay Policies While Downsizing the Organization: A Systematic Approach," *Personnel,* 60 (May–June 1983): 26–35.
33. Edgar H. Schein, *Career Dynamics: Matching Individual and Organizational Needs* (Reading, Massachusetts: Addison-Wesley Publishing Company, Inc., 1978), p. 211.
34. From Wendell L. French and Cecil H. Bell, Jr., *Organization Development,* 3d ed. (Englewood Cliffs, N.J.: Prentice-Hall, 1984), p. 172.
35. See Herbert Shepard, "Life Planning," in Kenneth D. Benne, Leland P. Bradford, Jack R. Gibb, and Ronald Lippitt, eds., *The Laboratory Method of Changing and Learning: Theory and Application* (Palo Alto, Calif.: Sci-

ence and Behavior Books, 1975), pp. 240–251. See also Richard N. Bolles, *The Three Boxes of Life* (Berkeley, Calif.: Ten Speed Press, 1981).

CHAPTER 11

1. *Wall Street Journal*, August 16, 1984, p. 25.
2. S. Norman Feingold, "Tracking New Career Categories Will Become a Pre-Occupation for Job Seekers and Managers," *Personnel Administrator*, 28 (December 1983):, 86–91.
3. H. G. Flinn, Jr., "The Emerging Role of the Professional Educator in Business," *Harvard Graduate School of Education Bulletin*, 23 (Spring 1979):31.
4. John R. Hinrichs, "Personnel Training," in Marvin D. Dunnette, ed., *Handbook of Industrial and Organizational Psychology* (Chicago: Rand McNally, 1976), p. 832.
5. Mark Giorgini, "Training and the Law: What You Don't Know Might Hurt," *Training/HRD* (November 1981): 34.
6. Joan M. O'Connell and John Hoerr, "There Really Are Jobs After Retraining," *Business Week*, January 28, 1985, p. 76.
7. "Business Takes Lead with New Jobs Training Act," *Resource* (February 1983): 7.
8. U.S. Department of Labor, *Employment and Training Report of the President* (1976), p. 129.
9. Robert W. Glover, "Breadth of Training in Apprenticeship," *Monthly Labor Review*, 98 (May 1975): 46–47.
10. "Pre-Employment Training Catches on in U.S.," *Resource* (March 1985): 3.
11. Jeremy Main, "New Ways to Teach Workers What's New," *Fortune*, October 1, 1984, p. 85.
12. Stephen Schwade, "Is It Time To Consider Computer-Based Training?" *Personnel Administrator*, 30 (February 1985): 25–35.
13. "How to Measure Return on Training," *Impact* (June 22, 1983): 4.
14. Bureau of National Affairs, "Training Programs and Tuition Aid Plans," *Personnel Policies Forum,* Survey No. 123, 1978, p. 7.
15. Donald L. Kirkpatrick, "Four Steps to Measuring Training Effectiveness," *Personnel Administrator*, 28 (November 1983): 19–25.
16. Andrew S. Grove, "Why Training Is the Boss's Job," *Fortune*, January 1984, p. 94.

CHAPTER 12

1. George S. Odiorne, "Management Development," in Stephen R. Michael, Fred Luthans, George S. Odiorne, W. Warner Burke, Spencer Hayden, *Techniques of Organizational Change* (New York: McGraw-Hill, 1981), p. 141.
2. Vicki S. Kaman and John P. Mohr, "Training Needs

Assessment in the Eighties: Five Guideposts," *Personnel Administrator*, 29 (October 1984): 47–53.
3. See also Donald L. Kirkpatrick, "Effective Supervisory Training and Development, Part 1: Responsibility, Needs, and Objectives," *Personnel* (November–December 1984): 25–30; and Karen L. Vinton, Arben O. Clark, and John W. Seybolt, "Assessment of Training Needs for Supervisors," *Personnel Administrator*, 28 (November 1983): 45–51.
4. James A. Belasco and Harrison M. Trice, *The Assessment of Change in Training and Therapy* (New York: McGraw-Hill, 1969), pp. 147–148.
5. Drawn from Caela Farren and Beverly Kaye, "The Principles of Program Design: A Successful Career Development Model," *Personnel Administrator*, 29 (June 1984): 109–118.
6. William J. Rothwell, "Curriculum Design in Training: An Overview," *Personnel Administrator*, 28 (November 1983): 53–57.
7. Donald L. Kirkpatrick, "Effective Supervisory Training and Development, Part 2: In-House Approaches and Techniques," *Personnel* (January 1985): 52–56.
8. Caela Farren, Janet Dreyfus Gray, and Beverly Kaye, "Mentoring: A Boon to Career Development," *Personnel* (November–December 1984): 20–24.
9. Ibid.
10. Ibid.
11. "Company-Built Retreats Reflect Firms' Cultures and Personalities," *Wall Street Journal,* August 16, 1984, p. 25.
12. See for example, Peter Petre, "Games That Teach You to Manage," *Fortune,* October 29, 1984, pp. 65–72.
13. See Eric Berne, *Games People Play: The Psychology of Human Relationships* (New York: Grove Press, 1964), Chapters 1–2; and T. Harris, *I'm OK — You're OK* (New York: Avon Books, 1969).
14. For more behavioral modeling, see William Byham and James Robinson, "Interaction Modeling: A New Concept in Supervisory Training," *Training and Development Journal*, 30 (February 1976): 20–30.
15. Helen LaVan, Nicholas Mathys, and David Drehmer, "A Look At the Counseling Practices of Major U.S. Corporations," *Personnel Administrator,* 28 (June 1983): 76+.
16. H. Wayne Smith and Clay E. George, "Evaluating Internal Advanced Management Programs," *Personnel Administrator,* 29 (August 1984): 118+.

CHAPTER 13

1. *Code of Federal Regulations,* 5, Administrative Personnel, rev., January 1, 1980.
2. Bureau of National Affairs, "Performance Appraisal Programs," *Personnel Policies Forum Survey,* Survey No. 135, February, 1983, pp. 3–6.

3. Charles J. Fombrun and Robert L. Laud, "Strategic Issues in Performance Appraisal: Theory and Practice," *Personnel,* 60 (November–December, 1983): 23–31.

4. Michael Beer, "Note on Performance Appraisal," in Michael Beer and Bert Spector, *Readings in Human Resource Management* (New York: The Free Press, 1985), p. 315.

5. Richard D. Arvey, *Fairness in Selecting Employees* (Reading, Mass.: Addison-Wesley Publishing Company, 1979), p. 113.

6. William H. Holley and Hubert S. Field, "Performance Appraisal and the Law," *Labor Law Journal,* 26 (July 1975): 423–430.

7. William J. Birch, "Performance Appraisal: One Company's Experience," *Personnel Journal,* 60 (June 1981): 456–460.

8. Gary P. Latham and Kenneth N. Wexley, *Increasing Productivity Through Performance Appraisal* (Reading, Mass.: Addison-Wesley Publishing Company, 1981), pp. 84–85.

9. Angelo S. DeNisi, W. Alan Randolph, and Allyn G. Blencoe, "Potential Problems with Peer Ratings," *Academy of Management Journal,* 26 (September 1983): 457–463.

10. See Richard S. Elster, Gerald L. Musgrave, and William H. Githens, "Employee Development Using Group Appraisal," *The Journal of Navy Civilian Manpower Management,* 9 (Fall 1975): 1–5ff.

11. L. L. Cummings and Donald P. Schwab, *Performance in Organizations: Determinants & Appraisal* (Glenview, Ill.: Scott, Foresman & Company, 1973), p. 90.

12. Richard Henderson, *Performance Appraisal: Theory to Practice* (Reston, Va.: Reston Publishing Company, 1980), pp. 137–138.

13. See John C. Flanagan and Robert K. Burns, "The Employee Performance Record: A New Appraisal and Development Tool," *Harvard Business Review,* 33 (September–October 1955): 95–102. A later version that has been suggested provides the rater with a specimen checklist that assists the rater in recalling incidents. See Barry M. Cohen, "A New Look at Performance Appraisal: The Specimen Checklist," *Human Resource Management,* 11 (Spring 1972): 18–22.

14. Donald P. Schwab, Herbert G. Heneman III, and Thomas A. DeCotiis, "Behaviorally Anchored Rating Scales: A Review of the Literature," *Personnel Psychology,* 28 (Winter 1975): 550.

15. Ibid., pp. 551–552, 560.

16. See Harry Levinson, "Management by Whose Objectives?" *Harvard Business Review,* 48 (July–August 1970): 125–134; and George Strauss, "Management by Objectives: A Critical View," *Training and Development Journal,* 26 (April 1972): 10–15.

17. Wendell L. French and Robert W. Hollmann, "Management by Objectives: The Team Approach," *California Management Review,* 13 (Spring 1975): 13–22; and Rensis Likert and M. Scott Fisher, "MBGO: Putting Some Team Spirit into MBO," *Personnel,* 54 (January–February 1977): 40–47. See also Wendell L. French and John A. Drexler, Jr., "A Team Approach to MBO: History and Conditions for Success," *Leadership and Organization Development Journal,* 5 (1984): 22–26.

18. Hubert S. Field and William H. Holley, "The Relationship of Performance Appraisal System Characteristic to Verdicts in Selected Employment Discrimination Cases," *Academy of Management Journal,* 25 (June 1982): 392–406.

19. Edward E. Lawler III, Alan M. Mohrman, Jr., and Susan M. Resnick, "Performance Appraisal Revisited," *Organizational Dynamics,* 13 (Summer 1984): 20–35.

20. Charles H. Fay and Gary P. Latham, "Effects of Training and Rating Scales on Rating Errors," *Personnel Psychology,* 35 (Spring 1982): 105–116.

21. H. Kent Baker and Philip I. Morgan, "Two Goals in Every Performance Appraisal," *Personnel Journal,* 63 (September 1984): 74–78.

CHAPTER 14

1. Bureau of National Affairs, "Wage and Salary Administration," *Personnel Policies Forum,* Survey no. 131, July 1981, p. 1.

2. Bureau of National Affairs, "Job Evaluation Policies and Procedures," *Personnel Policies Forum,* Survey no. 113, June 1976, pp. 1–3.

3. Ibid., p. 4.

4. Donald J. Treiman, *Job Evaluation: An Analytic Review,* Interim Report to the Equal Employment Opportunity Commission (Washington, D.C.: National Academy of Sciences, 1979), p. 22.

5. J. D. Williams, *Public Administration* (Boston: Little, Brown and Company, 1980), pp. 436–438.

6. P. R. Jeanneret, "Equitable Job Evaluation and Classification with the Position Analysis Questionnaire," *Compensation Review,* 12 (First Quarter 1980): 32–42; Robert C. Mecham, "Quantitative Job Evaluation Using the Position Analysis Questionnaire," *Personnel Administrator,* 28 (June 1983): 82–88, 124; and Donald J. Treiman and Heidi I. Hartmann, eds., *Women, Work, and Wages: Equal Pay for Equal Value* (Washington, D.C.: National Academy Press, 1981), pp. 125–126.

7. Donald P. Schwab, "Job Evaluation and Pay Setting: Concepts and Practices," in E. Robert Livernash, ed., *Comparable Worth: Issues and Alternatives* (Washington, D.C.: Equal Employment Advisory Council, 1980), p. 55.

8. Ronnie J. Straw and Lorel E. Foged, "Job Evaluation: One Union's Experience," *ILR Report,* 19 (Spring 1982): 24.

9. Treiman, *Job Evaluation,* p. 11.

10. Straw and Foged, "Job Evaluation," pp. 24–26.
11. Garry D. Fisher, "Salary Surveys — An Antitrust Perspective," *Personnel Administrator,* 30 (April 1985): 87–97, 154.
12. David W. Belcher, *Compensation Administration* (Englewood Cliffs, N.J.: Prentice-Hall, 1974), p. 345. See also George T. Milkovich and Jerry M. Newman, *Compensation* (Plano, Texas: Business Publications, 1984), p. 256.
13. See for example, Bureau of National Affairs, "Wage and Salary Administration," p. 17.
14. Burton W. Teague, *Overtime Pay Practices for Exempt Employees* (New York: The Conference Board, 1981), p. vi.
15. *Wall Street Journal,* November 11, 1983, p. 5.
16. *Wall Street Journal,* April 13, 1981, p. 33.
17. Graef S. Crystal, "The Re-emergence of Industry Pay Differentials," *Compensation Review,* 15 (Third Quarter 1983): 29–32.
18. *Wall Street Journal,* May 22, 1984, p. 1.
19. See William W. Seithel and Jeff S. Emans, "Calculating Merit Increases: A Structured Approach," *Personnel,* 60 (September–October 1983): 56–68.
20. U.S. Department of Labor, *The Fair Labor Standards Act of 1938, As Amended,* Employment Standards Administration, Wage and Hour Division, WH Publication 1318, rev. February 1980, Section 7, p. 9.
21. *Monthly Labor Review,* 105 (December 1982): 50.
22. U.S. Department of Labor, "Equal Pay for Equal Work Under the Fair Labor Standards Act, Interpretative Bulletin," WH Publication 1209, p. 6.
23. George S. Roukis, "Protecting Workers' Civil Rights: Equality in the Workplace," *Labor Law Journal,* 26 (January 1975): 3–16.
24. *Business Week,* November 25, 1972, p. 44.
25. *Wall Street Journal,* July 23, 1984, p. 9.
26. *Business Week,* July 20, 1981.
27. *Business Week,* November 26, 1984, p. 92.
28. Janice Shack-Marquez, "Earnings Differences Between Men and Women: An Introductory Note," *Monthly Labor Review,* 107 (June 1984): 15.
29. Benson Rosen, Sara Rynes, and Thomas A. Mahoney, "Compensation, Jobs, and Gender," *Harvard Business Review,* 83 (July–August 1983): 174.
30. Geraldine A. Ferraro, "Bridging the Wage Gap: Pay Equity and Job Evaluations," *American Psychologist,* 39 (October 1984): 1166–1167.
31. George T. Milkovich, "The Emerging Debate," in Livernash, ed., *Comparable Worth,* p. 36.
32. Helen Remick, "Strategies for Creating Sound, Bias Free Job Evaluation Plans," *Job Evaluation and EEO: The Emerging Issues* (New York: Industrial Relations Counselors, 1978), p. 91.
33. Helen Remick, "The Comparable Worth Controversy,"

Public Personnel Management Journal, 10 (Winter 1981): 377.
34. Ibid., p. 376.
35. Schwab, "Job Evaluation and Pay Setting: Concepts and Practices," in Livernash, ed., *Comparable Worth,* p. 68.
36. George H. Hildebrand, "The Market System," in Livernash, ed., *Comparable Worth,* p. 91.
37. Treiman, *Job Evaluation,* p. 46.
38. *Resource,* July 1985, p. 1.
39. *Wall Street Journal,* April 12, 1985, p. 52.
40. *Wall Street Journal,* September 6, 1985, p. 5.
41. Bureau of National Affairs, "Wage and Salary Administration," p. 23.
42. Edward E. Lawler III, "The Mythology of Management Compensation," *California Management Review,* 9 (Fall 1966): 11–12.
43. Jay Schuster and Jerome Colletti, "Pay Secrecy: Who is For and Against It?" *Academy of Management Journal,* 16 (March 1973): 35–40.
44. Bureau of National Affairs, "Personnel Activities, Budgets, and Staffs: 1984–1985," *Bulletin to Management,* ASPA-BNA Survey No. 48, No. 1832 May 23, 1985, p. 2.

CHAPTER 15

1. David W. Belcher, *Compensation Administration* (Englewood Cliffs, N.J.: Prentice-Hall, 1974), p. 317.
2. See Mary Cook, "Piecework vs. Daywork: The Big Dilemma," *Personnel Administrator,* 18 (November–December 1973): 2–4.
3. David A. Weeks, "Incentive Plans for Salesmen," National Industrial Conference Board, *Studies in Personnel Policy,* No. 217, 1970, p. 3.
4. *Wall Street Journal,* June 19, 1984, p. 33.
5. Harlan Fox, *Top Executive Compensation, 1980 Edition* (New York: The Conference Board, 1980), p. 6.
6. Jude T. Rich and John A. Larson, "Why Some Long-Term Incentives Fail," *Compensation Review,* 16 (First Quarter 1984): 26–37.
7. *Business Week,* May 9, 1983, p. 80; and *Business Week,* April 2, 1984, pp. 99–100.
8. Walter Kiechel III, "Managing Innovators," *Fortune,* March 4, 1985, p. 182.
9. For some of the complexities in establishing incentive systems for managers, see Bruce R. Ellig, "Incentive Plans: Over the Long Term," *Compensation Review,* 16 (Second Quarter 1984): 39–54.
10. Bureau of National Affairs, *Bulletin to Management,* No. 1798, September 20, 1984, p. 8.
11. See F. J. Roethlisberger and William J. Dickson, *Management and the Worker* (Cambridge, Mass.: Harvard University Press, 1956), Chapter 18.

12. Ford S. Worthy, "Manipulating Profits: How It's Done," *Fortune*, June 25, 1984, pp. 50–54.

13. *Wall Street Journal,* July 15, 1982, p. 27.

14. *Wall Street Journal,* June 14, 1983, p. 1; and *Business Week,* November 29, 1982, p. 35.

15. *Monthly Labor Review,* 106 (November 1983): 74.

16. James W. Driscoll, "Working Creatively with a Union: Lessons from the Scanlon Plan," *Organizational Dynamics,* 8 (Summer 1979): 61–80.

17. David W. Belcher, *Compensation Administration* (Englewood Cliffs, N.J.: Prentice-Hall, 1974), pp. 331–335.

18. A. D. Sharplin, "Lincoln Electric's Unique Policies," *Personnel Administrator,* 28 (June 1983): 8–10; and David Jenkins, *Job Power* (London: William Heinemann, 1974), pp. 216–219.

19. Brian E. Graham-Moore and Timothy L. Ross, *Productivity Gainsharing: How Employee Incentive Programs Can Improve Business Performance* (Englewood Cliffs, N.J.: Prentice-Hall, 1983), pp. 23–24.

20. Ibid., p. 24.

21. For a description of challenges and problems in the administration of a successful Scanlon plan, see Robert J. Schulhof, "Five Years with the Scanlon Plan," *Personnel Administrator,* 24 (June 1979): 55–62.

22. For an analysis of research studies that support these statements, see Edward E. Lawler III, *Pay and Organization Development* (Reading, Mass.: Addison-Wesley Publishing Company, Inc., 1981), pp. 146–152; and J. Kenneth White, "The Scanlon Plan: Causes and Correlates of Success," *Academy of Management Journal,* 22 (June 1979): 292–312.

23. *Wall Street Journal,* November 5, 1984, p. 27.

24. Ibid.

25. Bureau of National Affairs, *Bulletin to Management,* No. 1797, September 13, 1984, p. 1.

26. National Industrial Conference Board, "Sharing Profits with Employees," *Studies in Personnel Policy,* No. 162, 1956, pp. 16–21.

27. "Employee Wrath Hits Profit-Sharing Plans," *Business Week,* July 18, 1977, p. 25.

28. *Wall Street Journal,* May 15, 1984, p. 1.

29. *Wall Street Journal,* July 23, 1984, p. 15.

30. Milton A. Tatter, "Turning Ideas into Gold," *Management Review,* 64 (March 1975): 5.

31. Ibid., pp. 5–6.

32. Ibid.

33. *Wall Street Journal,* September 23, 1980, p. 1.

34. Gail Gregg, "The Power of Suggestion," *Across the Board,* 20 (December 1983): 30.

35. Ibid., pp. 29–31.

36. Ibid., p. 31.

37. W. Clay Hamner and Ellen P. Hamner, "Behavior Modification on the Bottom Line," *Organizational Dynamics,* 4 (Spring 1976): 8–9.

38. Ibid.

39. *Wall Street Journal,* November 23, 1983, p. 6.

40. Raymond E. Maejerus, "Workers Have a Right to a Share of Profits," *Harvard Business Review,* 62 (September–October 1984): 42, 43, 50.

41. Richard I. Henderson, *Compensation Management: Rewarding Performance,* 3d ed. (Reston, Virginia: Reston Publishing Company, 1982), p. 351.

42. See Graham-Moore and Ross, *Productivity Gainsharing,* pp. 1–15.

43. Bureau of National Affairs, "Personnel Activities, Budgets, and Staffs: 1984–1985," *Bulletin to Management,* ASPA-BNA Survey No. 48, No. 1832, May 23, 1985, p. 2.

44. Graham-Moore and Ross, *Productivity Gainsharing,* p. 79.

CHAPTER 16

1. *Wall Street Journal*, April 29, 1983, p. 27.

2. Bureau of National Affairs, *Bulletin to Management*, No. 1811, December 20, 1984, p. 1.

3. *Employee Benefits 1983* (Washington, D.C.: Chamber of Commerce of the United States, 1984), p. 30.

4. Ibid., p. 28.

5. Bureau of National Affairs, "Unemployment Compensation," *Labor Relations Expediter*, July 13, 1981, pp. LRX 795–796.

6. National Safety Council, *Accident Facts, 1983 Edition* (Chicago, 1983), p. 39.

7. Judy D. Olian, Stephen J. Carroll, Jr., and Craig Eric Schneier, "It's Time to Start Using Your Pension System to Improve the Bottom Line," *Personnel Administrator*, 30 (April 1985): 77.

8. This discussion is based on Donald G. Carlson, "Responding to the Pension Reform Law," *Harvard Business Review*, 52 (November–December 1974): 133–144; and Robert Frumkin and Donald Schmitt, "Pension Improvements Since 1976 Reflect Inflation, U.S. Law," *Monthly Labor Review*, 102 (April 1979): 32–37.

9. Hiram F. Moody, Jr. and Edward D. Higgins, "Selling the 401 (k) Plan to Employees," *Harvard Business Review*, 84 (November–December 1984): 68–73.

10. Charles G. Burck, "There's More to ESOP Than Meets the Eye," *Fortune*, March 1976, pp. 128–132 ff.

11. *Business Week*, April 15, 1985, p. 94.

12. Ibid.

13. *Employee Benefits 1983*, p. 18.

14. David A. Weeks, *Rethinking Employee Benefits Assumptions* (New York: The Conference Board, 1978), p. 63; and *Wall Street Journal*, March 26, 1985, p. 4.

15. *Employee Benefits 1983*, p. 8.

16. Stephen F. Gordon, "The Case for Company Sponsored Prepaid Legal Services," *Personnel Administrator*, 25 (July 1980): 79–82; and Roger M. Williams, "Perks," *Across the Board*, 20 (October 1983): 17–24.

17. *Wall Street Journal*, August 31, 1982, p. 1; and Jack N. Kondrasuk, "Corporate Physical Fitness Programs: The Role of the Personnel Department," *Personnel Administrator*, 29 (December 1984): 75–80.
18. *Wall Street Journal*, July 15, 1980, p. 1.
19. *Wall Street Journal*, April 29, 1983, p. 27.
20. Mary Zippo, "Subsidized Employee Transportation," *Personnel*, 57 (May–June 1980): 40–42.
21. *Wall Street Journal*, March 26, 1985, p. 39.
22. *Wall Street Journal*, December 19, 1984, p. 31
23. *Business Week*, March 13, 1978, p. 79.
24. *Wall Street Journal*, April 15, 1980, p. 1.
25. *Business Week*, November 2, 1981, p. 56.
26. Weeks, *Rethinking Employee Benefits Assumptions*, p. 87.
27. Ibid., p. 88.
28. *Wall Street Journal*, June 21, 1983, p. 1.
29. Barbara Anne Solomon, "A Company That Benefits from Child-Care Benefits," *Personnel*, 62 (February 1985): 4–6.
30. Kenneth R. Evans, Richard F. Beltramini, and George W. Bohlander, "A Survey of Travel and Entertainment Discount Programs," *Personnel*, 62 (March 1985): 64–66.
31. *Wall Street Journal*, February 1, 1983, p. 1.
32. Bureau of National Affairs, *Bulletin to Management*, No. 1809, December 6, 1984, p. 2.
33. *Employee Benefits 1983*, p. 14.
34. Dale Gifford, "The Status of Flexible Compensation," *Personnel Administrator*, 20 (May 1984): 19.
35. Robert C. Wender and Ronald L. Sladky, "Flexible Benefit Opportunities for the Small Employer," *Personnel Administrator*, 29 (December 1984): 111–118.
36. Ibid., pp. 112–113.
37. Susan J. Velleman, "Flexible Benefits Packages That Satisfy Employees and the IRS," *Personnel*, 62 (March 1985): 33–41.
38. *Fortune*, August 8, 1983, p. 105.
39. Bureau of National Affairs, *Bulletin to Management*, March 22, 1962, p. 8.
40. Judith F. Mazo, "Another Compliance Challenge for Employers: The Retirement Equity Act," *Personnel*, 62 (February 1985): 43–49.
41. Bureau of National Affairs, *Bulletin to Management*, ASPA-BNA Survey No. 39, January 24, 1980, pp. 1–12.
42. "Equal Employment Opportunity Commission Guidelines on Discrimination Based on Sex," amended April 4, 1972, Section 1604.9, Fringe Benefits.
43. *Monthly Labor Review*, 106 (September 1983): 36.
44. American Society for Personnel Administration, *Washington Vantage Point*, May 1979, p. 1.
45. *Monthly Labor Review*, 106 (August 1983): 40.
46. Bureau of National Affairs, *Personnel Management*, BNA Policy and Practice Series, 223: 351.
47. Frederick W. Cook, "The Revenue Act of 1978," *Compensation Review*, 11 (First Quarter 1979): 22–30.
48. *Wall Street Journal*, January 25, 1985, p. 37.
49. *Wall Street Journal*, July 3, 1984, p. 7.
50. J. Brad Chapman and Robert Otteman, "Employee Preference for Various Compensation and Fringe Benefit Options," *Personnel Administrator*, 20 (November 1975), special insert, 6 pp.
51. Philip Kienast, Douglas MacLachlan, Leigh McAlister, and David Sampson, "The Modern Way to Redesign Compensation Packages," *Personnel Administrator*, 28 (June 1983): 127–133.
52. *Wall Street Journal*, September 25, 1984, p. 1.
53. *Wall Street Journal*, March 19, 1985, p. 1.
54. Bureau of National Affairs, *Bulletin to Management*, No. 1811, December 20, 1984, p. 1.
55. The entire list is based largely on Bureau of National Affairs, "Controlling Health Care Costs: Crisis in Employee Benefits," *Bulletin to Management*, PPP BM No. 1759-Part II, December 15, 1983, p. 6.
56. Barron H. Harvey, Judy A. Schultze, and Jerome F. Rogers, "Rewarding Employees for Not Using Sick Leave," *Personnel Administrator*, 28 (May 1983): 55–59.
57. *Business Week*, March 21, 1983, p. 146.
58. Bureau of National Affairs, *Bulletin to Management*, No. 1794, August 23, 1984, p. 1.
59. Based on Bureau of National Affairs, "Personnel Activities, Budgets, and Staffs: 1984–1985," *Bulletin to Management*, ASPA-BNA Survey No. 48, No. 1832, May 23, 1985, p. 2.
60. See Karen Greenberg and Mary Zippo, "The Next Wave: Company-Supported Day Care?" *Personnel*, 60 (January–February 1983): 58–59.
61. James Ledvinka, *Federal Regulation of Personnel and Human Resource Management* (Boston: Kent Publishing Company, 1982), pp. 235–238.

CHAPTER 17

1. E. Wight Bakke, "To Join or Not to Join," in E. Wight Bakke, Clark Kerr, and Charles W. Anrod, eds., *Unions, Management and the Public*, 3rd ed. (New York: Harcourt, Brace, 1967), pp. 85–92. See also Jeanne M. Brett, "Why Employees Want Unions," *Organizational Dynamics*, 8 (Spring 1980): 47–59.
2. W. Clay Hamner and Frank J. Smith, "Work Attitudes as Predictors of Unionization Activity," *Journal of Applied Psychology*, 63 (August 1978): 415–421.
3. U.S. Department of Labor, *Directory of National Unions and Employee Associations 1979*, Bureau of Labor Statistics, 1980, p. 64.
4. AFL-CIO, *The Changing Situation of Workers and Their Unions: A Report by the AFL-CIO Committee on the Evolution of Work* (Washington, D.C., AFL-CIO), February 1985, p. 15.
5. Advisory Commission on Inter-governmental Relations,

Labor-Management Policies of State and Local Government (Washington, D.C.), September 1969, pp. 8–9.

6. See Dudley W. Buffa, *Union Power and American Democracy: The UAW and the Democratic Party, 1935–72* (Ann Arbor: The University of Michigan Press, 1984), and *Union Power and American Democracy: The UAW and the Democratic Party, 1972–83* (Ann Arbor: The University of Michigan Press, 1984).

7. AFL-CIO, *This Is the AFL-CIO,* pub. 20 (Washington, D.C.: AFL-CIO, 1984).

8. I. Chafetz and C. R. P. Fraser, "Union Decertification: An Elementary Analysis," *Industrial Relations,* 18 (Winter 1979): 68.

9. Larry T. Adams, "Changing Employment Patterns of Organized Workers," *Monthly Labor Review,* 108 (February 1985): 25–26.

10. Ibid., p. 30.

11. Bureau of National Affairs, *Basic Patterns in Union Contracts,* 87 (May 26, 1983): 1.

12. James J. Kilpatrick, "Labor Unions Lose Public Support," nationally syndicated column, May 18, 1985.

13. AFL-CIO, *The Changing Situation of Workers,* pp. 12–13.

14. Ibid., p. 13.

CHAPTER 18

1. Archibald Cox, "Rights Under a Labor Agreement," *Harvard Law Review,* 69 (February 1956): 606.

2. Labor Management Relations Act, 1947 (as amended, 1959), Section 8(d).

3. Robben W. Fleming, "The Obligation to Bargain in Good Faith," in Joseph Shister, Benjamin Aaron, and Clyde W. Summers, *Public Policy and Collective Bargaining* (New York: Harper and Row, 1962), p. 63.

4. *H. K. Porter Co.* v. *NLRB*, 397 U.S. 99 (1970).

5. Fleming, "Good Faith," pp. 63, 64.

6. Benjamin J. Taylor and Fred Whitney, *Labor Relations Law,* 4th ed. (Englewood Cliffs, N.J.: Prentice-Hall, 1983), p. 408.

7. For a discussion of distributive and integrative bargaining, see Richard E. Walton and Robert B. McKersie, *A Behavioral Theory of Labor Negotiations* (New York: McGraw-Hill, 1965), pp. 4–6.

8. The UAW has traditionally taken a much broader approach than the business unionism practiced by many other labor organizations. This is reflected in, among other things, the union's attitude toward political participation. On this point see Dudley W. Buffa, *Union Power and American Democracy: The UAW and the Democratic Party, 1935–1972,* and *Union Power and American Democracy: The UAW and the Democratic Party, 1972–1983* (Ann Arbor, University of Michigan Press, 1984).

9. *Monthly Labor Review,* 108 (September 1985): 52; *Business Week,* June 3, 1985, pp. 42–43; and *Wall Street Journal*, October 14, 1985, pp. 1, 10.

10. Edgar Weinberg, "Labor-Management Cooperation: A Report on Recent Initiatives," *Monthly Labor Review,* 99 (April 1976): 17–18.

11. See John A. Drexler, Jr., and Edward E. Lawler III, "A Union-Management Cooperative Project to Improve the Quality of Work Life," *Journal of Applied Behavioral Science,* 13 (1977): 373–374.

12. Daniel Quinn Mills, *Labor-Management Relations,* 2nd ed. (New York: McGraw-Hill, 1982), p. 264.

13. Mills, *Labor-Management Relations,* p. 246.

14. William H. Holley and Kenneth M. Jennings, *The Labor Relations Process,* 2nd ed. (Chicago: The Dryden Press, 1984), p. 175.

15. See Sam Kagel, "Combining Mediation and Arbitration," *Monthly Labor Review,* 96 (September 1973): 62.

CHAPTER 19

1. William A. Kaplin, *The Law of Higher Education* (San Francisco: Jossey-Bass, Inc., 1979), p. 20.

2. Patricia A. Somers and Judith Clementson-Mohr, "Sexual Extortion in the Workplace," *Personnel Administrator,* 24 (April 1979): 27.

3. "Sexual Harassment Lands Companies in Court," *Business Week,* October 1, 1979, pp. 120–122.

4. Equal Employment Opportunity Commission, "Final Amendments to Guidelines to Discrimination Because of Sex," *Federal Register,* November 10, 1980, p. 74677.

5. See Patricia Linenberger and Timothy J. Keaveny, "Sexual Harassment: The Employer's Legal Obligations," *Personnel,* 58 (November-December 1981): 66–68; and U.S. Department of Labor, *A Working Woman's Guide to Her Job Rights,* Women's Bureau, January 1985, leaflet 55, pp. 21–23.

6. See Kenneth Sovereign, *Personnel Law* (Reston, Va.: Reston Publishing Company, 1984), p. 269.

7. David W. Ewing, *Freedom Inside the Organization* (New York: E. P. Dutton, 1977), pp. 108–110.

8. *Monthly Labor Review,* 106 (June 1983): 48.

9. Kenneth D. Walters, "Your Employees' Right to Blow the Whistle," *Harvard Business Review,* 53 (July–August 1975): 26–34ff.

10. Ibid.

11. Gregory J. Mounts, "Significant Decisions in Labor Cases," *Monthly Labor Review,* 102 (April 1979): 61.

12. Ewing, *Freedom Inside the Organization,* p. 233.

13. "Fight for Rights," *Wall Street Journal,* July 24, 1980, p. 38.

14. Ewing, *Freedom Inside the Organization,* pp. 101–102.

15. *Wall Street Journal,* December 31, 1984, p.11.

16. Ibid.

17. Ewing, *Freedom Inside the Organization,* p. 129.

18. Philip Adler, Jr., Charles K. Parsons, and Scott B. Zolke, "Employee Privacy: Legal and Research Developments and Implications for Personnel Administration," *Sloan Management Review,* 26 (Winter 1985): 14. For more on privacy, see Wayne N. Outten and Noah A. Kinigstein, *The Rights of Employees: The Basic ACLU Guide to an Employee's Rights* (New York: Bantam Books, 1983), Chapter 4.

19. John G. Fox and Paul J. Ostling, "Employee and Government Access to Personnel Files: Rights and Requirements," *Employee Relations Law Journal,* 5 (Summer 1979): 70.

20. Vernon and Gray, "Termination at Will," pp. 25–27.

21. Commerce Clearing House, *Pension Plan Guide,* 1979, par. 9207.

22. Peter F. Drucker, "The Job as Property Right," *Wall Street Journal,* March 4, 1980, p. 22. See also Commerce Clearing House, "Plan Terminations under ERISA," *Pension Plan Guide,* pp. 7–29.

23. Jack Stieber, "Most U.S. Workers Still May Be Fired Under the Employment-at-Will Doctrine," *Monthly Labor Review,* 107 (May 1984): 34–35.

24. Ibid., p. 35.

25. Bureau of National Affairs, "Policies for Unorganized Employees," *Personnel Policies Forum,* Survey No. 125, April 1979, pp. 5–6, 11.

26. Bureau of National Affairs, "Employee Discipline and Discharge," *Personnel Policies Forum,* Survey No. 139, January 1985, p. 10.

27. In 1809 Sweden instituted an ombudsman who was appointed to report directly to Parliament. See Ewing, *Freedom Inside the Organization,* p. 167. The term *ombudsperson* is frequently used in the United States.

28. Xerox Corporation appointed an ombudsman for managers and salaried employees in 1972. See *Business Week,* May 3, 1976, pp. 114–116.

29. Ewing, *Freedom Inside the Organization,* pp. 166–170.

30. Bureau of National Affairs, "Policies for Unorganized Employees," p. 6.

31. Daryl G. Hatano, "Employee Rights and Corporate Restrictions," *California Management Review,* 24 (Winter 1981): 11.

32. Bureau of National Affairs, *Personnel Management,* Sec. 263 (1983):105.

33. Ibid.

34. Ibid.

35. Bureau of National Affairs, *Collective Bargaining, Vol. 2,* 263: 503.

36. Maurice S. Trotta, *Arbitration of Labor-Management Disputes* (New York: Amacom, 1974), p. 65.

37. For more details on the expected conduct of the arbitrator, see "Code of Professional Responsibility for Arbitrators of Labor-Management Disputes," approved by the National Academy of Arbitrators, the American Arbitration Association, and the Federal Mediation and Conciliation Service, April 1975. Reprinted in Bureau of National Affairs, *Collective Bargaining, Vol. 1,* 17 (May 22, 1975): 51–59.

38. The entire maxim is *stare decisis et non quieta movere:* "to adhere to precedents and not unsettle things which are established." See Henry Campbell Black, *Black's Law Dictionary,* rev. 4th ed. (St. Paul, Minn.: West Publishing Company, 1968), pp. 1577–1578.

39. Harold W. Davey, *Contemporary Collective Bargaining,* 3rd ed. (Englewood Cliffs, N.J.: Prentice-Hall, 1972), p. 38.

40. George H. Friedman, "Correcting Arbitrator Error: The Limited Scope of Judicial Review," *Arbitration Journal,* 33 (December 1978): 9–16.

41. Arthur A. Sloane and Fred Whitney, *Labor Relations,* 4th ed. (Englewood Cliffs, N.J.: Prentice-Hall, 1981), p. 225.

42. Based on Thomas W. Jennings, "The Crossroads of the Future," *Labor Law Journal,* 31 (August 1980): 498–502.

43. Betty Southard Murphy, "The Chairman Looks at the NLRB," *Personnel Administrator,* 21 (May 1976): 26.

44. See John A. Fossum, *Labor Relations: Development, Structure, Process* (Dallas: Business Publications, 1979), p. 405.

45. Tim Bornstein, "Interest Arbitration in Public Employment: An Arbitrator Views the Process," *Labor Law Journal,* 29 (February 1978): 79.

46. Ibid., pp. 77–86.

47. Paul D. Staudohar, "Results of Final-Offer Arbitration of Bargaining Disputes," *California Management Review,* 18 (Fall 1975): 57–61.

48. Adler, Parsons, and Zolke, "Employee Privacy," p. 20.

49. Lorber et al., *Fear of Firing,* p. 22.

50. Bureau of National Affairs, "Employee Discipline and Discharge," pp. 26–27.

CHAPTER 20

1. *Wall Street Journal,* May 16, 1985, p. 30.

2. *Accident Facts, 1983 Edition* (Chicago: National Safety Council), p. 38.

3. Bureau of National Affairs, *Collective Bargaining: Negotiations and Contracts,* 95 (May 26, 1983): 1.

4. Ibid., p. 4.

5. John E. Aberton, "Labor Unions and Accident Prevention: Champion or Adversary?" *Professional Safety,* 25 (November 1980): 19–20.

6. Dan Petersen, *Safety Supervision* (New York: Amacom, 1976), pp. 50–53.

7. *Accident Facts, 1983 Edition* (Chicago: National Safety Council), pp. 24–25.

8. *Wall Street Journal,* January 25, 1985, p. 10.

9. U.S. Department of Labor, "Health Hazards of Asbestos," Occupational Safety and Health Administration pamphlet 3040, 1979, p.1.

10. *Resource,* March 1985, p. 6.

11. John M. Ivancevich, Michael T. Matteson, and Edward P. Richards III, "Who's Liable for Stress on the Job?" *Harvard Business Review,* 64 (March–April 1985): 60.

12. Section 1 (e), The Walsh-Healey Public Contracts Act, as amended.

13. *U.S. Code, 1982 Edition*, (Washington, D.C.: U.S. Government Printing Office, 1983), p. 120 ff.

14. *U.S. Code, 1982 Edition*, (Washington, D.C.: U.S. Government Printing Office, 1983), p. 143.

15. *Wall Street Journal,* June 17, 1985, p. 2.

16. U.S. Department of Labor, *All About OSHA,* Occupational Safety and Health Administration pamphlet 2056 (rev.) 1980, p. 3; and Occupational Safety and Health Act of 1970, Public Law 91–596, 91st Cong., S. 2193, December 29, 1970.

17. U.S. Department of Health, Education, and Welfare, National Institute for Occupational Safety and Health, DHEW (NIOSH), Loren L. Hatch, et al., *Self Evaluation of Occupational Safety and Health Programs,* Publication No. 78–187, October 1978, p. 1.

18. Based on U.S. Department of Labor, "OSHA: Your Workplace Rights in Action, Worker's Rights Under OSHA," Occupational Safety and Health Administration pamphlet 3021, 1979; *All About OSHA,* p. 44; and Fred K. Foulkes, "Learning to live with OSHA," *Harvard Business Review,* 51 (November–December 1973): 58.

19. *All About OSHA,* pp. 40–41.

20. U.S. Department of Labor, *OSHA Inspections, Programs and Policies Series,* Occupational Safety and Health Administration pamphlet 2098, June 1975, p. 2.

21. *Marshall, Secretary of Labor, et al.* v. *Barlow's Inc.,* May 23, 1978. Docket No. 76-1143.

22. *OSHA Inspections,* pp. 4–7; and Foulkes, "Learning to Live with OSHA," pp. 57–67.

23. *OSHA Inspections,* pp. 4–7, and *All About OSHA,* p. 24.

24. *All About OSHA,* p. 21; and *OSHA Inspections,* p. 6.

25. *All About OSHA,* p. 27; and *OSHA Inspections,* p. 6.

26. *All About OSHA,* p. 30.

27. Robin L. Ballau and Roy M. Buchan, "Study Shows That Gender Is Not a Major Factor in Accident Etiology," *Occupational Health and Safety,* 47 (September–October 1978): 54–58.

28. David Margolick, "The Lonely World of Night Work," *Fortune,* December 15, 1980, pp. 108–114.

29. "Rotating Shift Work Causes Many Problems," *Occupational Safety and Health,* 47 (September–October 1978): 21.

30. *Accident Facts, 1983 Edition,* pp. 30–33.

31. Willard Kerr, "Complementary Theories of Safety Psychology," *Journal of Social Psychology,* 45 (No. 1, 1957): 3–9.

32. Norman R. F. Maier and Gertrude Casselman Verser, *Psychology in Industrial Relations,* 5th ed. (Boston: Houghton Mifflin Company, 1982), p. 447.

33. "Safety Policies & the Impact of OSHA," p. 12.

34. Ibid., p. 7.

35. Ibid., p. 6.

36. Ibid., p. 8.

37. William S. Cohen, "Health Promotion in the Workplace," *American Psychologist,* 40 (February 1985): 213–216.

38. *Wall Street Journal,* May 21, 1985, p. 1; and Vico Henriques and Charlotte LeGates, "A Look at VDTs and Their Impact on the Workplace and an Overview of a New Science Called Ergonomics," *Personnel Administrator,* 29 (September 1984): 64–68.

39. Ward Gardner and Peter Taylor, *Health at Work* (New York: John Wiley & Sons, 1975), pp. 72–73.

40. Peter B. Bensinger, "Drugs in the Workplace," *Harvard Business Review,* 60 (November–December 1982): 48.

41. Cohen, "Health Promotion in the Workplace," p. 215.

42. Donald W. Myers, *Establishing and Building Employee Assistance Programs* (Westport, Conn.: Quorum Books, 1984), p. 11.

43. Edward L. Johnson, "Ways Employers Can Help Drinkers, Drug Addicts," *U.S. News & World Report,* August 29, 1979, pp. 61–62; and Robert D. Dugan, "Affirmative Action for Alcoholics and Addicts?" *Employee Relations Law Journal,* 5 (Autumn 1979): 236.

44. Bensinger, "Drugs in the Workplace," p. 49.

45. *Business Week,* February 18, 1985, p. 37.

46. G. J. Provost, et al., "Alcohol or Drug Abuse on the Job: A Study of Arbitration Cases," *Employee Relations Law Journal,* 5 (Autumn 1979): 245–253.

47. Paul Sherman as quoted in Dugan, "Affirmative Action for Alcoholics and Addicts?" pp. 240–241.

48. William Mayer, "Alcohol Abuse and Alcoholism: The Psychologist's Role in Prevention, Research, and Treatment," *American Psychologist,* 38 (October 1983): 1119.

49. Hans Selye, *Stress Without Distress* (New York: The New American Library, 1974), p. 151.

50. James House, "Occupational Stress and Physical Health," *Manpower,* 5 (October 1973): 3.

51. *U.S. News and World Report,* September 5, 1983, p. 45.

52. *Business Week,* May 27, 1985, pp. 124, 126.

53. John M. Ivancevich and Michael T. Matteson, "Optimizing Human Resources: A Case for Preventive Health and Stress Management," *Organizational Dynamics,* 9 (Autumn 1980): 5–25.

54. Bureau of National Affairs, *Bulletin to Management,* ASPA-BNA Survey No. 34, March 23, 1978, pp. 1–10.

55. Myers, *Establishing and Building Employee Assistance Programs,* p. 4.

56. Ibid., p. 16.

57. Harvey Shore, "SRM Forum: Employee Assistance Programs — Reaping the Benefits," *Sloan Management Review,* 25(Spring 1984):70.

58. Grimaldi and Simonds, *Safety Management,* p. 5.

59. See Bernard Weiss, "Behavioral Toxicology and Envi-

ronmental Health Science," *American Psychologist,* 38 (November 1983): 1174–1187.

60. U.S. Department of Labor, *OSHA Handbook for Small Businesses,* Occupational Safety and Health Administration, Safety Management Series, OSHA 2209, rev. 1979, p. 2.

61. "OSHA: Minimizing Health Risks at Du Pont," *Personnel,* 54 (November–December 1977): 48.

62. Ibid., p. 64; and Grimaldi and Simonds, *Safety Management,* p. 107.

63. F. W. Heinrich, Dan Petersen, and Nestor Roos, *Indusrial Accident Prevention,* 5th ed. (New York: McGraw-Hill Book Company, 1980), p. 300.

64. Ibid., p. 300.

65. William English, "What Is Safety Management?" *Professional Safety,* 25(September 1980): 27.

66. Ibid., p. 27.

67. L.L. Hatch, et al., *Self-Evaluation of Occupational Safety and Health Programs,* U.S. Department of Health, Education, and Welfare, National Institute for Occupational Safety and Health, DHEW (NIOSH) Publication No. 78–187, October 1978, pp. 5–6.

68. Bureau of National Affairs, "Personnel Activities, Budgets, and Staffs: 1984–1985," *Bulletin to Management,* ASPA-BNA Survey No. 48, No. 1832, May 23, 1985, p. 2.

CHAPTER 21

1. Sirota and Alper Associates, Inc., *Survey of Views Toward Human Resources Policies and Practices,* unpublished report to respondents, November 1983, pp. 1, 13–14; and S. William Alper and Russell E. Mandel, "What Policies and Practices Characterize the Most Effective HR Departments?" *Personnel Administrator,* 29 (November 1984): 120–124.

2. John Naisbitt, *Megatrends: Ten New Directions Transforming Our Lives* (New York: Warner Books, 1982), pp. 159, 182–183.

3. See Sar A. Levitan and Diane Werneke, "Worker Participation and Productivity Change," *Monthly Labor Review,* 107 (September 1984): 28–33; and Friederich Furstenberg, "Co-Determination and Its Contribution to Industrial Democracy: A Critical Evaluation," *Proceedings of the Thirty-Third Annual Meeting,* Industrial Relations Research Association, 1981, pp. 185–190.

4. Many professionally trained facilitators have chosen to participate in an accreditation process through Certified Consultants International, Box 573, Brentwood, Tennessee 37027.

5. For more on this, see Ralph H. Kilmann, *Beyond the Quick Fix: Managing Five Tracks to Organizational Success* (San Francisco: Jossey-Bass, 1984).

6. For some of the theory see Kurt Lewin, *Field Theory in Social Science* (New York: Harper & Bros., 1951); and

Ludwig von Bertalanffy, *General Systems Theory* (New York: George Braziller, 1968).

7. Edgar H. Schein, "Improving Face-to-Face Relationships," *SMR Portfolio: The Art of Managing Change and Uncertainty,* a collection of reprints from the *Sloan Management Review,* 1983, p. 34.

8. Based on Jack K. Fordyce and Raymond Weil, *Managing With People* (Reading, Mass.: Addison-Wesley Publishing Company, 1971), pp. 114–116.

9. Ibid., pp. 143–146.

10. For further elaboration, see Wendell L. French and Robert Hollmann, "Management by Objectives: The Team Approach," *California Management Review,* 17 (Spring 1975): 13–22; and Rensis Likert and M. Scott Fisher, "MBGO: Putting Some Team Spirit into MBO," *Personnel,* 54 (January–February 1977): 40–47.

11. *Business Week,* July 30, 1984, p. 80.

12. Based on Robert Blake, H. A. Shepard, and Jane S. Mouton, *Managing Intergroup Conflict in Industry* (Houston: Gulf Publishing Company, 1964); and Fordyce and Weil, *Managing With People,* pp. 124–130.

13. Based on Floyd C. Mann, "Studying and Creating Change," in W. G. Bennis, K. D. Benne, and R. Chin, eds., *The Planning of Change* (New York: Rinehart and Winston, 1961), pp. 605–613; and Wendell L. French and Cecil H. Bell, Jr., *Organization Development: Behavioral Science Interventions for Organization Improvement,* 3d ed. (Englewood Cliffs, N.J.: Prentice-Hall, 1984), pp. 181–185.

14. Mann, "Studying and Creating Change," p. 609.

15. Wendell L. French and Cecil H. Bell, Jr., *Organization Development,* p. 17.

16. Richard E. Walton, "From Control to Commitment in the Workplace," *Harvard Business Review,* 64 (March–April 1985): 84.

17. Stephen H. Fuller, "How Quality-of-Worklife Projects Work for General Motors," *Monthly Labor Review,* 103 (July 1980): 37–39; and Irving Bluestone, "How Quality-of-Worklife Projects Work for the United Auto Workers," *Monthly Labor Review* 103 (July 1980): 39–41.

18. Paul S. Goodman, "Quality of Work Life Projects in the 1980s," *Labor Law Journal,* 31 (August 1980): 487–494.

19. Bureau of National Affairs, "Productivity Improvement Programs," *Personnel Policies Forum,* Survey No. 138, September 1984, p. 3.

CHAPTER 22

1. S. William Alper and Russell E. Mandel, "What Policies and Practices Characterize the Most Effective HR Departments?" *Personnel Administrator,* 29 (November 1984): 120–124.

2. Roy Foltz, Karn Rosenberg, and Julie Foehrenbach, "Senior Management Views the Human Resources Function," *Personnel Administrator,* 27 (September 1982): 37.

3. Fred K. Foulkes, *Harvard Business Review*, 53 (March–April 1975): 71–84.

4. Herbert E. Meyer, *Fortune*, February 1976, pp. 84–88ff.

5. Mary Zippo, *Personnel*, 58 (March–April 1981): 36.

6. U.S. Department of Labor, *Occupational Projections and Training Data, 1984 Edition*, Bulletin 2206, Bureau of Labor Statistics, May 1984, p. 4.

7. Steven Langer, "Personnel Salaries: Who Makes What — and Why," *Personnel Journal*, 64 (January 1985): 69–71.

8. Donald P. Rogers, "The Basic Course in Personnel Administration/Industrial Relations," *Collegiate News and Views*, 38 (Fall–Winter, 1984): 5–7.

9. See *Who's Who in ASPA 1984* (Alexandria, Va.: American Society for Personnel Administration, 1984), pp. 16–27.

10. Personnel Accreditation Institute, *Accreditation for Personnel and Human Resource Professionals*, p. 1 (pamphlet). (P.O. Box 19648, Alexandria, Va. 22320.)

11. Ibid., p. 3.

12. Foltz, Rosenberg, and Foehrenbach, "Senior Management Views the Human Resource Function," pp. 37–50.

13. Jack Herring, "Human Resource Managers Rank Their Pressure Points," *Personnel Administrator* 28 (June 1983): 113–116 ff.

14. Alper and Mandel, "What Policies and Practices Characterize the Most Effective HR Departments?" p. 121; and Sirota and Alper Associates, Inc., *Survey of Views Toward Human Resources Policies and Practices*, unpublished report to respondents, November 1983, p. 4.

15. Wayne F. Cascio, *Costing Human Resources: The Financial Impact of Behavior in Organizations* (Boston: Kent Publishing Company, 1982), pp. 45–55.

16. For more on the human resources audit, see John A. Hooper, "A Strategy for Increasing the Human Resource Department's Effectiveness," *Personnel Administrator*, 29 (June 1984): 141–148; Frederick E. Schuster, "A Tool for Evaluating and Controlling the Management of Human Resources," *Personnel Administrator*, 27 (October 1982): 63–69; and Mary Anne Devanna, Charles Fombrun, and Noel Tichy, "Human Resources Management: A Strategic Perspective," *Organizational Dynamics*, 9 (Winter 1981): 51–67.

17. Harold J. Leavitt, "Suppose We Took Groups Seriously . . ." in Eugene L. Cass and Frederick G. Zimmer, eds., *Man and Work in Society* (New York: Van Nostrand Reinhold Company, 1975), p. 67.

18. Edward E. Lawler III, Allan M. Mohrman, Jr., and Susan M. Resnick, "Performance Appraisal Revisited," *Organizational Dynamics*, 13 (Summer 1984): 35.

19. Barry A. Macy, "The Quality-of-Worklife Project at Bolivar: An Assessment," *Monthly Labor Review*, 103 (July 1980): 41–43.

20. *Business Week*, December 17, 1984, p. 32.

Index